ALSO BY RONALD HAYMAN

Proust: A Biography
Sartre
Kafka: A Biography
Brecht: A Biography
Nietzsche: A Critical Life
Secrets: Boyhood in a Jewish Hotel
Techniques of Acting
How to Read a Play
Artaud and After
De Sade: A Critical Biography
Samuel Beckett
Harold Pinter
Tom Stoppard
British Theatre Since 1955
Tennessee Williams: Everyone Else Is an Audience

Thomas Mann

A Biography

Ronald Hayman

SCRIBNER

NEW YORK LONDON TORONTO
SYDNEY TOKYO SINGAPORE

SCRIBNER
1230 Avenue of the Americas
New York, NY 10020

Designed by Ellen R. Sasahara

Manufactured in the United States of America

10 9 8 7 6 5 4 3 2 1

Library of Congress Cataloging-in-Publication Data
Hayman, Ronald, 1932–
Thomas Mann: a biography/by Ronald Hayman.
p.   cm.
Includes bibliographical references and index.
1. Mann, Thomas, 1875–1955–Biography. 2. Novelists, German–20th
century–Biography.   I. Title.
PT2625.A44Z6113   1994
833′.912–dc20
[B]
94-32467
CIP
ISBN 0-684-19319-1

For Jan

EX · LIBRIS

de Wildt

Contents

	Acknowledgments	9
	Chronology	11
Prologue	Sidestepping Happiness	63

PART ONE

1	Like a Prince	81
2	Decaying Family	93
3	Stormy Spring	105
4	Nothing but Rice	114
5	Rounding Up the Dogs	124
6	Establishing Himself	137
7	Lust for Fame	150
8	Fair Hair and Blue Eyes	162
9	Writing My Life	178

PART TWO

10	Like a Princess	193
11	Giving Myself a Constitution	206
12	Representing Other People	218
13	Marxist Fairy Story	232
14	Leading Man	243
15	Mountain Air	255
16	A New Home	269

PART THREE

17	World War	279
18	I Hate Democracy	292
19	Sons of Defeat	306
20	Unchartered Love	320
21	Fraternal Armistice	334

22	Jewish Jesuit	342
23	Years of Plenty	352
24	Myth and Madam World	364
25	Nobel Prize	373
26	My Task Is to Liquidate	387

PART FOUR

27	The Rule of Silence	403
28	Speaking Out	418
29	Hitler Is My Brother	431
30	Heil Chamberlain!	443
31	In Goethe's Footsteps	449
32	Edge of Los Angeles	460
33	Citadels of Stupidity	474

PART FIVE

34	Twelve-Tone Syphilis	487
35	Incurable Fatherland	500
36	Come Like a Good Doctor	516
37	Staring into Grayness	531
38	Suicidal Son	546
39	Both Germanies	560
40	Winsome Waiter	573
41	Ridiculous Satisfaction	587
42	Love and Mischief	600

| Epilogue | Tasks | 616 |

Notes	621
Selected Bibliography	652
Index	656

Acknowledgments

I'VE BECOME INDEBTED in a variety of ways to many friends, acquaintances, and people who started out as strangers. Any attempt to thank everyone is likely to fail.

The first words of encouragement were spoken by Linden Lawson when she was a senior editor at Weidenfeld. She made me believe I ought to write a biography of Thomas Mann. I hope she won't come to regret what she said.

Mann's only surviving child, Elisabeth Mann Borgese, was hospitable and extremely generous with her time when I went to see her in Nova Scotia. What she said about her father and the family was memorable. So was the experience of seeing her play a duet with one of her dogs on a specially made piano with wide keys. The dog hit them with his nose.

Jeffrey Meyers was extremely generous in another way. When I'd written the first hundred pages of this book, he read through them, making a lot of useful pencil annotations in tiny handwriting. When the book was finished, he read through it, again annotating minutely and helpfully.

When I was researching in Zurich, the staff of the Thomas Mann Archive was patient and helpful, as was the staff of the Buddenbrookshaus when I was in Lübeck. I must also thank Thomas Mann's publishers, Fischer Verlag, for lending me proofs of the still unpublished final volume of his diaries. I've also been given a lot of help by librarians in the New York Public Library and the Goethe Institut Library, London.

Dr. Wolfgang Fischer was kind enough to give me a photocopy of the Thomas Mann letter he owns, and Paul Griffiths helped by sending a photocopy of Janet Flanner's two-part profile of Thomas Mann in *The New Yorker*.

At Scribner, Bill Goldstein, Erika Goldman, Ted Lee, Carole McCurdy, and Brian Desmond, and freelancers Jane Herman, Fred Sawyer, and Pauline Piekarz, have all made valuable contributions to this book.

All the translations from Thomas Mann are my own, unless the work first appeared in English.

Chronology

CHAPTER ONE

1644	Johann Mann born at Parchim
1728	Joachim Siegmund Mann, TM's great-great-grandfather, born
1790	
May 23	Johann Siegmund Mann, TM's great-grandfather, establishes his own business in Lübeck and
1794	becomes a citizen of the town
1797	his son, also named Johann Siegmund Mann, born
1810	Lübeck is annexed by Napoleon
1811	Elisabeth Marty born
1815	Lübeck becomes a free city again when Napoleon is defeated
1821	birth of Johann Ludwig Hermann Bruhns, TM's maternal grandfather
1837	Elisabeth Marty marries Johann Siegmund Mann
1840	
Aug. 22	Thomas Johann Heinrich Mann, Thomas's father, born
1851	
Aug. 14	Julia da Silva Bruhns, Thomas's mother, born in Angra dos Reis, Brazil
1863	Thomas's father takes over the firm, Johann Siegmund Mann Corn Merchants, Commission and Transport Agents
1869	
June 4	Thomas Johann Heinrich Mann marries Julia da Silva Bruhns
1870	They move into a rented house at 54 Breite Strasse
1871	
March 27	Luiz Heinrich Mann born
1872	Consul Mann buys a house at 36 Breite Strasse
1875	
June 6	Paul Thomas Mann born
1877	
Feb. 19	Consul Mann elected to the Lübeck senate

Aug. 23	Julia Elisabeth Therese Mann born

1881

Sept. 23	Carla Augusta Olga Maria Mann born

CHAPTER TWO

1882

spring	Thomas starts going to a private preparatory school
summer	first in a series of holidays at Travemünde

1883

spring	the family moves into the new house at 52 Beckergrube
July 24	Katia Pringsheim born in Munich

1889

spring	Thomas starts going to the Katharineum
summer	Heinrich passes the *Abitur* and two of his stories are published in the *Lübecker Zeitung*. He leaves school and starts work in a Dresden bookshop
winter	with his sister Julia, TM attends dancing classes

1890

Easter	confirmation in the Marienkirche
April	Heinrich leaves the bookshop to work in Berlin for the publisher Samuel Fischer
April 12	Karl Viktor Mann born
May 23	centenary of firm
Dec.	Elisabeth Mann (née Marty) dies, age seventy-nine

1891

June 30	Senator Mann changes his will and
July 2	undergoes an operation
Oct. 13	Senator Mann dies, age fifty-one
winter	the firm is liquidated, and Frau Mann moves with the younger children into a house in Roeckstrasse; the house in Beckergrube is sold

1892 TM's first experiences of Wagner operas in Lübeck

1893

Easter	living with Professor Hempel
spring	Frau Mann moves to Munich with the three younger children; they live in Rambergstrasse.
May	TM edits and writes pseudonymously for the school literary magazine *Der Frühlingssturm*
Oct.	TM's poem "Zweimaliger Abschied" ("Double Leavetaking") appears under his own name in the magazine *Die Gesellschaft*

1894

March 16	TM leaves school without his *Abitur* and leaves Lübeck to join his mother in Munich

CHAPTER THREE

April	TM starts working for an insurance company, the Süd-deutscher Feuer-Versicherungsbank
Aug.	finishes first act of verse play *Der alte König* (*The Old King*); leaves insurance company and, because his mother wants him to have a career in journalism, he
Nov. 4	starts attending lectures at the Technische Hochschule
Nov. 29	submits his story "Der kleine Professor" to Richard Dehmel for the new quarterly *Pan*

1895

Jan.	joins Ernst von Wolzogen's dramatic society, the Akademisch-dramatischer Verein
Feb.	working on *Der alte König* (*The Old King*) and story "Walter Weiler"
March	thinks of moving to Lausanne to escape the distractions of Munich
April	intends to leave Munich in late summer for either Lausanne or Berlin; Heinrich takes over from Friedrich Lienhard as editor of *Das Zwanzigste Jahrhundert*
May	summer term begins at the Technische Hochschule
May 15	submits the story "Walter Weiler" to Dehmel
June 15	plays old Werle in the German premiere of Ibsen's *The Wild Duck* at the Akademisch-dramatischer Verein
June	writes reviews for *Das Zwanzigste Jahrhundert*

CHAPTER FOUR

July 12	leaves Munich to meet Heinrich in Rome. They leave immediately for Palestrina
Aug.	TM's first contribution to *Das Zwanzigste Jahrhundert* published
end of Sept.	the brothers return to Rome
end Oct.	return to Munich
Dec.	TM writes "Der Wille zum Glück" ("The Will to Happiness")

1896

Feb.	reads Paul Bourget, and Fontane's *Effi Briest*
March	intending to visit Italy alone, as Heinrich is moving to Zurich
May	Heinrich is in Munich, TM helps him with editorial work and starts work on "Der kleine Herr Friedemann" ("Little Herr Friedemann")
	Planning a year or more of traveling with Heinrich—to Corsica, Sicily, possibly North Africa, Naples, Rome, and Switzerland

June	spends three weeks in Vienna
Aug.-Sept.	"Der Wille zum Glück" ("The Will to Happiness") appears in *Simplicissimus*
Oct. 10	TM leaves Munich to spend three weeks in Venice.
Nov. 1	leaves Venice to spend two days in Rome and the rest of the month in Naples, where he writes "Enttäuschung" ("Disillusionment")
Dec. 3	returns to Rome and takes a room in the Via del Pantheon
Dec.	spends time with Heinrich and submits "Der kleine Herr Friedemann" to the *Neue Deutsche Rundschau*. The editor, Oscar Bie, is enthusiastic. TM works on collection of short stories

CHAPTER FIVE

| winter 1896–97 | collaborates with Heinrich on *Bilderbuch für artige Kinder* (*Picture Book for Good Children*) |

1897

Jan.	starts reworking "Walter Weiler" as "Der Bajazzo" ("The Clown")
Easter	confirmation of Carla Mann
April 5	"Der Bajazzo" ("The Clown") is complete
May	Samuel Fischer accepts the collection of stories *Der kleine Herr Friedemann* (*Little Herr Friedemann*) for publication and invites TM to write a long prose work
July	after being delayed by Heinrich's illness, the brothers leave for Palestrina together; TM reads Johann Peter Eckermann's *Conversations with Goethe*. Writes "Luischen," which is to be the first story in his second collection, and works on "Tobias Mindernickel"
Aug.	preparatory work on *Buddenbrooks*
Sept.	"Der Bajazzo" ("The Clown") published in the *Neue Deutsche Rundschau*

CHAPTER SIX

| end of Oct. | they return to Rome, where they live together in the Via di Torre Argentina, where TM starts writing *Buddenbrooks* |
| Dec. | is already working on the fifteenth chapter |

1898

| Jan. | "Tobias Mindernickel" published in the *Neue Deutsche Rundschau* |

spring	publication of *Der kleine Herr Friedemann* (*Little Herr Friedemann*), collection of short stories
April	brief stay in Florence; return to Munich, where, after staying for a few days in his mother's apartment, he moves
May 1	into one of his own, at 82 Theresienstrasse, but soon moves to 69 Barerstrasse
late Oct.– early Nov.	starts working for *Simplicissimus*
Nov.	moves to 5 Marktstrasse in the Schwabing
Nov. 23–29	writes story "Der Kleiderschrank" ("The Wardrobe")

1899

	friendship with Kurt Martens
June	moves to 5 Feilitzschstrasse
	"Der Kleiderschrank" ("The Wardrobe") published in the *Neue Deutsche Rundschau*
late Aug.	goes on holiday, revisiting Lübeck
Sept.	goes on to Copenhagen and Aalsgard, where he stays (September 11–16) at the Badehotel
autumn	reads Schopenhauer; friendship with Paul Ehrenberg begins

CHAPTER SEVEN

1900

June	call-up papers arrive
July 18	finishes *Buddenbrooks*; writes poem "Monolog"
Sept. 20	Story "Der Weg zum Friedhof" ("The Way to the Churchyard") published in *Simplicissimus*
Oct. 1	leaves *Simplicissimus* and begins military service
Oct. 9	Julia Mann marries Josef Löhr
Oct.-Nov.	inflammation of a tendon in his right foot confines him to bed in the infirmary
Oct. 26	Fischer asks for *Buddenbrooks* to be cut to half its present length; TM replies, refusing to make cuts.
Dec.	given leave in anticipation of discharge from the army

1901

Jan.	gives public reading of stories including "The Way to the Churchyard" at the Akademisch-dramatischer Verein
Feb. 4	Fischer agrees to publish *Buddenbrooks* without cuts
Feb.	researches into Renaissance and Savonarola
Feb. 19	takes part in carnival with Paul Ehrenberg
March	Paul paints his portrait
March 26	Fischer signs a contract giving him royalties of 20 percent for five years

CHAPTER EIGHT

end of April	to Florence, where he meets Mary Smith and makes notes on Savonarola
May 20	leaves Florence for Venice
June	back to Munich
July 10	leaves with Heinrich for sanatorium in Mitterbad
end Aug.	returns to Munich
Oct. 1	*Buddenbrooks* published in two volumes
Oct.	working as editor for Albert Langen
Nov. 20	stays at von Hartungen's sanatorium, the Villa Cristofero in Riva
Dec. 19	returns to Munich
1902	
Jan. 1	moves again—to 24 Ungererstrasse
Sept. 1	gives up Ungererstrasse apartment, moving into the Pension Gisela
Oct. 2	leaves for Riva
Nov. 15	returns to Munich, moving into apartment in Konradstrasse
Dec.	finishes "Tonio Kröger"
1903	
Jan.	"Die Hungernden" ("The Hungry Ones") published in *Die Zukunft*

CHAPTER NINE

Feb.	"Tonio Kröger" published in the *Neue Deutsche Rundschau*, cheap edition of *Buddenbrooks* and story collection *Tonio Kröger* on sale; TM gives readings in Berlin
mid-May	goes to Tegernsee
summer	stays with Kurt Martens
July	joins mother in Polling
Aug.	returns to Munich and begins to woo Katia Pringsheim
Oct. 3	in Düsseldorf attends first night of *Kabale und Liebe* with Carla as Luise. Stays at Park Hotel
Oct.	writes "Ein Glück" ("A Moment of Happiness")
end Oct.	gives reading in Königsberg and goes on to give one in Berlin, where he meets Gerhart Hauptmann and Gabriele Reuter
late Nov./ early Dec.	writes "Das Wunderkind" ("The Infant Prodigy")
Dec. 11	reading in Munich

CHAPTER TEN

1904

Feb.	first meeting with Katia
Feb. 14 & 17	TM's article on Gabriele Reuter published in *Der Tag*
April 16	he leaves for Riva
May 7	returns to Munich, and settles into new apartment in Ainmillerstrasse
June 21	reading at Göttingen
mid-July	Katia leaves Munich for summer
early Aug.	he joins his mother and Viktor in Utting

CHAPTER ELEVEN

1905

Jan.	finishes *Fiorenza*
Feb. 11	TM marries Katia Pringsheim; honeymoon in Switzerland
Feb. 23	they return to Munich
March	he writes "Schwere Stunde" ("Hour of Gravity")
May	"Hour of Gravity" published in *Simplicissimus*; he plans a novel about Frederick the Great
summer	visit to Berlin, where he starts to write "Wälsungenblut" ("The Blood of the Walsungs")
Sept.	revisits Potsdam and Sans Souci
mid-Oct.	*Fiorenza* published in book form
Nov.	*Buddenbrooks* mentioned in a Lübeck lawcourt
Nov. 7	"Ein Nachwort" ("A Postscript") published in the *Lübecker General-Anzeiger*
Nov. 9	Erika born
Dec. 9	TM leaves for readings in Dresden and Breslau

1906

Jan.	reading in Basel
Feb. 15 & 16	"Bilse und Ich" published in the *Münchener Neueste Nachrichten*
Feb. 21	baptism of Erika Julia Hedwig Mann
March 5	"Thomas Mann und die Renaissance" by Richard Schaukal published in the *Berliner Tageblatt*

CHAPTER TWELVE

March 10	new contract with Fischer for six years with royalties of 25 percent

March 31	Heinrich's reply to Schaukal appears in *Die Zukunft*
April 14	TM and Katia go to Oberammergau to find a villa for their summer holidays
May	reading in Dresden; stay in sanatorium Der Weisser Hirsch
mid-June	TM and Katia leave for Oberammergau, where they stay till mid-September
Nov. 18	Katia gives birth to a son, Klaus Heinrich
Dec.	starts writing *Königliche Hoheit* (*Royal Highness*)

1907

Feb.	writes "Versuch über das Theater" ("Essay on the Theatre") for *Nord und Süd*
May 11	premiere of *Fiorenza* in Frankfurt
May 23	goes to last of six performances
end June	statement on working methods for *Mitteilungen der literaturhistorischen Gesellschaft* in Bonn
July–mid-Sept.	stays in Seeshaupt with Katia and children
Aug.-Sept.	has written about a third of *Königliche Hoheit* (*Royal Highness*)
Oct. 14	Fischer visits TM in Munich and offers 6,000 marks plus royalties of 25 percent on the first 10,000 copies as soon as he receives a complete typescript of *Royal Highness*
Dec.	TM has written about half; "Im Spiegel" ("In the Looking Glass") published in the *Literarische Echo*
Dec. 17	*Fiorenza* staged in the Residenztheater, Munich

1908

Jan.	"Über *Fiorenza*" in the *Münchener Neueste Nachrichten*
Feb. & March	"Versuch über das Theater" ("Essay on the Theatre") published in *Nord und Süd*
April	Heinrich and Ines come to Munich
May 2	TM and Katia leave for Verona
May 4	TM and Katia meet Heinrich, Ines, and Carla in Venice
summer	visit to Tölz
Sept. 28	building of house begins in Tölz
end of Sept.	back to Munich
Nov.	working on final chapter of *Royal Highness*
end of Nov.	goes to Vienna; meets Schnitzler, Hofmannsthal, and Wassermann
early Dec.	visits Hofmannsthal in Rodaun; reading in Vienna; writes "Das Eisenbahnunglück" ("The Railway Accident"); returns to Munich

CHAPTER THIRTEEN

1909

Jan.-Nov.	installment publication of *Royal Highness* in the *Neue Rundschau*
Feb. 13	finishes *Royal Highness*
March	"The Railway Accident" published in the *Neue Freie Presse*, Vienna; "Little Herr Friedemann" reissued in a cheap edition with "Hunger" and "Das Eisenbahnunglück" ("The Railway Accident")
March 27	second son born—Gottfried Angelus Thomas (Golo)
spring	makes plans for a trip to Livorno with Heinrich
May	in Dr. Bircher's sanatorium, Zurich
June 5	returns to Munich
June	house built in Tölz; idea for a story or novel about a confidence trickster, Felix Krull, originally seeing it as augmenting *Royal Highness*
June	friendship with Max Reinhardt begins
mid-July	moves into house in Tölz
Aug.	in Bayreuth for *Parsifal*; works on essay "Geist und Kunst" ("Mind and Art") and plans a historical novel
Oct.	*Royal Highness* published
Oct. 26	TM and Katia meet Heinrich in Milan and go on with him to Nice for a brief holiday

1910

Jan.	abandons essay and starts work on "Felix Krull" story
Jan. 28	begins to correspond with Ernst Bertram about *Royal Highness*
March 1	"Der Doktor Lessing" in the *Literarische Echo*
March	quarrel with Kurt Martens
April 1	"Berechtungen" ("Justifications") in the *Literarische Echo*
June 7	second daughter born—Monika
summer	in Tölz
July 7	reads first chapter of "Felix Krull" to his family
July 30	Carla commits suicide

CHAPTER FOURTEEN

Aug.	writes essay on Fontane
Sept. 2	celebration of Prof. Pringsheim's sixtieth birthday in Tölz
Sept. 12	meeting with Gustav Mahler after the first performance of his Eighth Symphony
Oct. 1	moves into larger apartment in Mauerkircherstrasse, in the Herzogpark; "Der alte Fontane" ("The Old Fontane") published in *Die Zukunft*

Oct. 6	Monika baptized
Nov.	reading in Weimar, reunion with Count Vitzhum von Eckstadt
Dec. 11	reads "Wie Jappe und Do Escobar sich prügelten" ("How Jappe and Do Escobar Fought") to his family
Dec.	writes essay on Chamisso and his "Peter Schlemihl" is published
Dec. 25	in the *Berliner Tageblatt*

1911

Jan. 12–26	readings in Koblenz, Düsseldorf, Bielefeld, and Münster
Feb.	"How Jappe and Do Escobar Fought" published in the *Süddeutsche Monatsheft*
end March	ill and depressed, considers going back to Dr. Bircher's clinic
mid-May	trip to Brioni
May 18	learns of Mahler's death
May 26	goes to Hôtel des Bains on the Venice Lido
end May	writes on Wagner
June 2	returns to Munich
June	works on Chamisso essay; reading from *Fiorenza* in the Kutscher circle

CHAPTER FIFTEEN

June-Oct.	in Tölz
July	starts working on "Der Tod in Venedig" ("Death in Venice")
Sept. 2–19	Katia in Sils Maria to take the cure
Oct.	Chamisso essay published in the *Neue Rundschau*
Nov.	reading in Brussels
Nov. 20	attends first performance of Mahler's *Das Lied von der Erde*

1912

Jan.	readings in Heidelberg, Bremen, and other towns
Feb.	meets Hans von Weber to discuss publication of "Death in Venice" by Hyperion
March 22	Katia at Dr. Jessen's Waldsanatorium in Davos
May 15– June 12	TM stays in the sanatorium to be with Katia
June 13	TM returns to Munich
June 14	visits the Pringsheims to report on Katia's condition
June 15	goes to Tölz with the children and his mother
July	finishes "Death in Venice"
July 22	his review of Georg Hirschfeld's novel *Der Kampf der weissen und der roten Rose* (*The War of the White and Red Roses*) published in the *Münchener Neueste Nachrichten*
Sept. 25	Katia returns from Davos

autumn	resumes work on second volume of *Felix Krull*
Nov.	production of *Fiorenza* planned for December at the Berlin Kammerspiele; as a member of Munich's censorship advisory board, TM becomes involved in a dispute with Frank Wedekind
Nov. 27	visits possible site of new house with architect
Dec. 7	writes a conciliatory letter to Wedekind
end Dec.	attends a rehearsal of *Fiorenza* in Berlin
1913	
Jan. 3	*Fiorenza* premiered at the Berlin Kammerspiele, where it runs till January 6
Feb.	TM goes to Tölz, where he stays most of the time until autumn; "Death in Venice" published
mid-Feb.	first meeting with Ernst Bertram

CHAPTER SIXTEEN

Feb. 25	buys site in Poschingerstrasse
March 18	reading in Basel
April 30	writes a defense of Frank Wedekind's *Lulu*
May 15	makes a graveside speech at the funeral of Friedrich Huchs
May 26	resigns from censorship advisory board
June 19–	
July 12	holiday in Viareggio
July	preparatory work on *The Magic Mountain*
Sept.	preface to Erich von Mendelssohn's *Nacht und Tag*
Sept. 9	starts drafting *The Magic Mountain*
Nov. 12–13	lecturing in Stuttgart
Nov. 15–	
Dec. 21	Katia in Merano to take the cure
Dec.	TM reviews Bruno Frank's *Requiem* in *Zwiebelfisch*
Dec. 4–8	readings in Vienna and Budapest
1914	
Jan. 4–	
May 12	Katia being treated in Arosa
Jan. 5	TM and children move into the new house
Jan. 19–21	readings in Zurich, Lucerne, and Saint Gall
Jan. 30	reading from *The Magic Mountain* in Munich
Feb. 13	attends a lecture by Karl Kraus
Feb. 18	invites Ernst Bertram to a dinner party
spring	joins committee to organize celebration of Wedekind's fiftieth birthday
May	writes essay on Wedekind
May 12	Katia returns from Arosa

CHAPTER SEVENTEEN

July	"Über eine Szene von Frank Wedekind" ("On a Scene from Frank Wedekind") published in *Der Neue Merkur*
July–mid-Sept.	in Tölz
July 15	reading in Freiburg
Aug. 1	war breaks out
Aug.	Viktor is called up
Aug. 2	Viktor marries Magdalena Kilian
Aug. 12	Heinrich marries actress Mimi Kanova
Aug.-Sept.	TM in Tölz
Aug. 22	starts article "Gedanken im Kriege" ("Wartime Thoughts")
Sept. 12	finishes it and returns to Munich
Sept.-Dec.	writes essay "Friedrich und die grosse Koalition von 1756" ("Frederick and the Great Coalition of 1756")
Oct.	*Das Wunderkind* (*The Infant Prodigy*) published, a collection of short stories
late Dec.	to Tölz
1915	
early Jan.	resumes work on *The Magic Mountain*
mid-Feb.	reads "Wartime Thoughts" in Munich
May 11	*Svenska Dagbladet* publishes his reply to criticism of "Friedrich und die grosse Koalition" in answers to a questionnaire
June	Klaus ill with peritonitis, has five operations; Katia ill
Aug. 3	war article in the *Frankfurter Zeitung*; TM expresses his intention to put *The Magic Mountain* aside in favor of a political book
Aug. 5	to Tölz
end Sept.	Motz put down
?	return to Munich
early Nov.	wounding reference to TM in an essay on Zola by Heinrich in the *Weissen Blätter*; TM starts work on *Betrachtungen eines Unpolitischen* (*Reflections of a Nonpolitical Man*)
1916	
Jan.	TM reads Heinrich's Zola essay; writes article protesting against the suppression of Maximilian Harden's *Zukunft*; submits article unsuccessfully to the *Frankfurter Zeitung*

CHAPTER EIGHTEEN

March	TM ill with flu and erysipelas
April 6	goes to Tölz
mid-May	returns to Munich

May-June	Ernst Bertram pays frequent visits, helping with *Reflections of a Nonpolitical Man*
mid-July	back to Tölz; gets a new dog, Bauschan
Aug.	ill again, TM stops working for a week
Sept.	writes an essay on Joseph, Freiherr von Eichendorff's *Aus dem Leben eines Taugenichts* (*From the Life of a Good-for-Nothing*), which had come out in a new edition during 1914
mid-Sept.	back to Munich
Oct. 5	reads from *Felix Krull* in Munich
Oct. 23	and in Breslau
Nov. 5–10	in Berlin; reads from *Felix Krull* at the Sezession and the Deutsche Gesellschaft
Nov.	article on *Good-for-Nothing* published in the *Neue Rundschau*
Nov. 11	given another medical examination but exempted from active service
Dec. 24	TM's article on Thomas Carlyle's six-volume biography of Frederick the Great published in the *Frankfurter Zeitung*

1917

early Jan.	spends a few days with his family at the Tegernsee
Jan. 20 & 21	Article "Musik in München" published in *Der Tag*
Feb. 19	Heinrich's play *Madame Legros* premiered simultaneously in Munich and Lübeck
March	"Einkehr" ("Self-Communion"), a chapter of *Reflections of a Nonpolitical Mann*, published in the *Neue Rundschau*
April	deterioration in his eyesight makes TM start using reading glasses; eight-day holiday in Mittenwald
April 6	United States enters the war
May 13	Aunt Elisabeth dies in Dresden
June 12	premiere of Hans Pfitzner's *Palestrina* in Munich's Prinzregententheater, TM sees it five times
June 15	Pfitzner and his wife spend an evening with the Manns
ca. July 9	sells house in Tölz; spends last summer there
July	finishes chapter "Tugend" ("Virtue"); goes to Tölz for last time
Aug.	frequent visits from Ernst Bertram; TM writes chapter "Einiges über Menschlichkeit" ("A Few Things about Humanity") before interrupting his work on *Reflections of a Nonpolitical Man*
Sept. 10	back to Munich
Oct.	ill with bowel infection; reads Adalbert Stifter and Tolstoy's *War and Peace*
Dec. 25	working on last chapter of *Reflections*
Dec. 27	article in *Tageblatt*
Dec. 30	Heinrich attempts reconciliation

1918

Jan. 3	TM rebuffs Heinrich's overtures

Jan.	readings in Essen
Jan. 9	reading in Brussels, where the third act of *Fiorenza* is staged in the Théâtre Royal du Parc
Jan. 11–17	readings in Hamburg, Rostock, and Lübeck
March 16	finishes *Reflections*
March 18	begins "Herr und Hund" ("Master and Dog")
April 24	birth of youngest daughter–Elisabeth Veronika
June	Monika ill with Spanish flu
mid-July	to Villa Defregger on the Tegernsee

Chapter Nineteen

Aug.	working on "Master and Dog"
mid-Sept.	back to Munich
early Oct.	*Reflections* published
Oct. 4	new government formed with Prince Max von Baden as chancellor
Oct. 14	TM finishes "Master and Dog"; TM's obituary of Eduard Graf Keyserling in the *Frankfurter Zeitung*
Oct. 23	Elisabeth baptized
Nov. 2	TM starts prose draft of poem in hexameters, "Gesang vom Kindchen" ("Song of the Little Child")
Nov. 9	von Baden resigns in favor of Friedrich Ebert, who proclaims a republic
Nov. 10	Kaiser Wilhelm flees to Belgium
Nov. 11	armistice signed
1919	
Feb.-April	revolution in Munich
March 25	TM finishes "Song of the Little Child"–977 lines
March	short holiday in Feldafing by the Lake of Starnberg
April	"Herr und Hund" ("Master and Dog") published
April 9	unpacks manuscript of *The Magic Mountain*
April 12–13	the councils are overthrown
April 19	TM resumes work on *The Magic Mountain*
April 21	birth of youngest son–Michael
May 9	signs declaration in *Münchener Neueste Nachrichten*
June	Hedwig Dohm dies, age eighty-six
June 16	TM makes after-dinner speech at Pfitzner's fiftieth birthday party
mid-July	goes on holiday in Glücksburg as Fischer's guest
Aug. 2	receives an honorary doctorate from Bonn University
Aug. 5	returns to Munich; Katia goes on holiday with the four younger children to Stock on the Chiemsee.
Oct.	"Tischrede auf Pfitzner" ("After-dinner Speech on Pfitzner") published in the *Süddeutsche Monatsheft*; TM goes back to Feldafing on the Lake of Starnberg

Nov. 16	interrupts work on *The Magic Mountain* to write essay on Fontane, celebrating 100th anniversary of his birth
Dec. 4–19	stopping en route to give a reading in Nuremberg, TM travels with Bruno Walter to Vienna, where *Fiorenza* will be staged.
Dec. 10	return to Munich
Dec. 25	"Song of the Little Child" published
1920	
Jan.	Bauschan put down because of distemper

CHAPTER TWENTY

Feb.	TM in Feldafing again
March	Katia ill with flu
April 22	reads from *The Magic Mountain* in Augsburg
May	plans to found a periodical, *Futura*, with Hofmannsthal, Wassermann, Keyserling, and Ricarda Huch
May–June	Katia convalescing in Oberammergau
June 3	takes Erika and Klaus to *Die Walküre*
mid-July	spends a few days in Feldafing
mid-Aug.	in Garmisch
Sept.	back to Munich
Nov. 2–20	readings in Mühlheim, Duisburg, Dortmund, Bochum, Elberfeld, Cologne, Bonn, and other places
Dec. 7	in Wiesbaden
1921	
Jan. 17– Feb. 3	readings in Winterthur, Zurich, Aarau, Bern, Saint Gall, Lucerne, and Davos, where he spends four days in the sanatorium
Feb.	preface to special issue of *Süddeutsche Monatsheft* dealing with Russian literature
Feb. 11–22	readings in Coburg, Gera, Weimar (where he meets Nietzsche's sister, Elisabeth), Jena, and Berlin
April	writes preface for his collection of essays, *Rede und Antwort* (*Speech and Answer*)
May	eight days in Feldafing; completes "Walpurgisnacht" ("Witches' Sabbath"), the last chapter in the first volume of *The Magic Mountain*
May 29	*Vossische Zeitung* publishes his review of Hermann Ungar's short story collection *Knaben und Mörder*
June 6	celebrates his forty-sixth birthday by taking Erika, Klaus, and Golo to *Carmen*
June 10	starts preparing a lecture on "Goethe und Tolstoy" for the Nordic week in Lübeck
Aug. 8–23	holiday with Ernst Bertram in Timmendorf

Aug. 24–
  Sept. 2   week on Sylt; finishes lecture
Sept. 2–8   stays with Ida Boy-Ed in Lübeck
Sept. 4   delivers lecture
Sept. 10   repeats it in Berlin
Sept. 12   returns to Munich and to work on *The Magic Mountain*
Oct.   writes letter in defense of Oskar Schmitz's *Das rätselhafte Deutschland* for *Neueste Nachrichten*
Oct. 31   repeats lecture in Munich
Nov. 6–12   in Zurich: gives a reading and visits Poliklinik as part of his research for *The Magic Mountain*
Nov. 30   *Neue Zürcher Zeitung* publishes his review of Kurt Martens's *Schönungslose Lebenschronik*
Nov.   *Rede und Antwort* published
mid-Dec.   works on an essay about Franco-German relations to answer an essay by André Gide in the November issue of the *Nouvelle Revue Française*

1922
Jan.   *Der Neue Merkur* publishes TM's essay "Das Problem der deutsch-französischen Beziehungen" ("The Problem of Franco-German Relations"); travels with Katia to deliver the Goethe-Tolstoy lecture in Prague, Brno, Vienna, and Budapest, where he meets Georg Lukács

CHAPTER TWENTY-ONE

Jan. 21   returns to Munich; reconciliation with Heinrich, who nearly died of peritonitis; corresponds with André Gide
Jan. 29   *Prager Presse* publishes TM's review of Knut Hamsun's *Die Weiber am Brunnen*
Feb. 27–
  March 3   in Frankfurt for Goethe week
March 4   in Lübeck for opening of the Buddenbrook Bookshop on lower floor of old family house in Mengstrasse
March 19–20   readings in Berlin
April   short stay in Feldafing
Apr. 16   *Frankfurter Zeitung* publishes his review of Hans Reisiger's translations of Walt Whitman
June   Katia takes the children to the island of Reichenau on Lake Constance
June 24   Walther Rathenau assassinated
early July   TM repeats Goethe-Tolstoy lecture in Heidelberg
July   starts working on a speech about the German republic for celebrations of Hauptmann's sixtieth birthday; com-

	pletes the fourth of the eight sections in the long sixth chapter of *The Magic Mountain*
Aug.	holiday in Ahlbeck (Baltic), where Heinrich spends a few days with him. TM works on speech "Von deutscher Republik" to be delivered in Berlin for Hauptmann's sixtieth birthday
Sept.	TM in financial difficulties because of inflation
Oct. 6	Heinrich present at a private reading of "Von deutscher Republik" ("On the German Republic") in TM's home
Oct 11–13	in Berlin, where he delivers lecture "On the German Republic" in Beethovensaal
Oct.	gives readings in Hannover, Münster, Düsseldorf, Cleve, Nijmegen, Utrecht, Amsterdam, and other Dutch cities
Oct. 31	reading to an audience of 2,500 people in Frankfurt
Nov. 3	returns to Munich
Nov.	"Von deutscher Republik" published in *Neue Rundschau*
Dec.	"German Letter" published in *The Dial*, New York
Dec. 20	takes part in a séance at the house of the Freiherr von Schrenck-Nötzing, and returns in January for two more (January 6 and 24)

1923

Jan.	French troops occupy the Ruhr
mid-Jan.	readings in Chur, Zurich, and other Swiss towns
Jan. 31	delivers Goethe-Tolstoy lecture in Tübingen
mid-Feb.	reading in Dresden
Feb.	to Berlin for discussions about a film of *Buddenbrooks*
Feb. 27	reading in Augsburg
March 11	Julia Mann dies, age seventy-three
March 25–	
April 3	readings in Austria, Hungary, and Czechoslovakia
April 19–	
May 23	Sails with Katia to Barcelona. They go on to Madrid, Seville and Granada, to Santander in the north, then through the Bay of Biscay to Hamburg

CHAPTER TWENTY-TWO

early June	finishes seventh of the eight sections in Chapter 6
June	speaks to republican students in Munich on "Geist und Wesen der deutschen Republik" ("Spirit and Essence of the German Republic") for anniversary of Rathenau's death; second "German Letter" in *The Dial*
Oct.	third "German Letter" in *The Dial*; holiday in Bolzano, where Hauptmann is staying in the same hotel; TM decides to use him as model for Mynheer Peeperkorn in

	The Magic Mountain; collaborates with his brother Viktor on a *Tristan und Isolde* screenplay
Nov. 8	Hitler attempts putsch
Nov. 15	inflation stopped by introducing the Rentenmark
Dec.	TM approached by the painter Hermann Ebers, who wants a preface for a series of paintings he has done based on the Joseph story in the Old Testament
Dec. 12–14	reads "Okkulte Erlebnisse" ("Occult Experiences") in Berlin and Lübeck
Dec. 25	*Frankfurter Zeitung* publishes his review of a script by Ernst Tröltsch; the *Berliner Tageblatt* publishes "Europäische Schicksalsgemeinschaft" ("Europe's Common Destiny")

1924

Feb. 6–10	reads "Okkulte Erlebnisse" ("Occult Experiences") in Heidelberg, Mannheim, and Frankfurt
Feb.–March	Ill, and with a broken foot, Katia convalesces for six weeks in Clavadel, outside Davos, leaving TM alone with the children
March 9	*Allgemeine Zeitung* publishes his essay on Spengler's *Untergang des Abendlandes*
early April	TM has flu; Katia returns to Munich
late April	decides how to end *The Magic Mountain*
May	travels to Holland and England
May 2–4	in Amsterdam; talks on democracy
May 5	goes to London, where he's the PEN Club's guest of honor
May 12	visits Oxford
mid-May	returns to Munich via Southampton, Hamburg, and Berlin, where he sees Erika, who has been employed by Reinhardt as a small-part actress
July 13	reads from his work in a broadcast from Frankfurt
July 18	*Frankfurter Zeitung* publishes his tribute to the poet and literary historian Ricarda Huch on her sixtieth birthday
late July	holiday in Kloster on the Hiddensee with Gerhart Hauptmann
to Aug. 16	continues holiday in Bansin, and
Aug. 18–25	goes on to Ahlbeck
Aug. 18	makes speech at Stralsund in memory of those killed in the war
Sept.	Erika in Berlin; Klaus employed by the *12-Uhr-Mittags-Blatt* as drama critic
Sept. 28	celebrates completion of *The Magic Mountain*

Chapter Twenty-three

Oct.	ten days in Sestri Levante with Katia, Elisabeth, and Michael; Ernst Bertram stays with them for the first few days
Nov. 4	TM makes speech at a musical celebration for the eightieth anniversary of Nietzsche's birth
Nov. 8	reads Peeperkorn episode in the Galerie Caspari
Nov. 12–26	readings in Stuttgart, Freiburg, Dresden, Hannover, and Berlin
Nov.	works on collecting essays for the volume *Bemühungen*
Nov. 28	*The Magic Mountain* published in two volumes
Dec. 14–23	readings and lectures in Denmark; reading in Aarhus
Dec. 18	delivers Goethe-Tolstoy lecture to students in Copenhagen
Dec. 20	reads from his own work in Riddersaal at first meeting of "Freunde der deutschen Literatur"; returns to Munich via Berlin
Dec. 31	Takes Elisabeth and Michael to Humperdinck's *Hänsel und Gretel*
1925	
Jan.	revises the Goethe and Tolstoy essay for the volume *Bemühungen*
Jan. 11	to Dresden
Feb. 4	outlines preliminary plans for *Joseph* novels
Jan. 12–13	lectures on Goethe and Tolstoy at the university in Breslau
Feb.	starts work on foreword for new edition of Goethe's *Wahlverwandschaften (Elective Affinities)* and on a short story; buys a car
March 6	*Frankfurter Zeitung* publishes his obituary for Friedrich Ebert
March 2–25	Mediterranean cruise
April	writes story "Unordnung und frühes Leid" ("Disorder and Early Sorrow")
May 9–16	in Florence as German delegate to International Culture Week
May 17–25	in Venice
June 6	celebrates fiftieth birthday; celebration in Munich's old town hall
June 7	celebration matinee in the Residenztheater; TM crowned with a laurel wreath
June 8–12	festival in Vienna
mid-June	library is reorganized
July	plans *Joseph* novels as a trilogy; motors to Lake Constance, where Monika and Golo are at school and where a classmate with Spanish blood serves as model for the young Joseph

Aug.	finishes "Die Ehe im Übergang" for *Das Ehe Buch,* edited by Keyserling
Aug. 20–30	at Salzburg Festival
early Sept.	corrects proofs of *Bemühungen*
Sept.	holiday with Elisabeth and Michael at Casamicciola on Ischia
Oct.	*Bemühungen* published
Oct. 9–10	belated birthday celebrations in Lübeck; *Fiorenza* staged
Oct.	portrait painted by Max Liebermann in Berlin; Fischer arranges ten-volume edition of collected works
Nov. 8	makes speech at opening of Book Week in Munich
Nov.	starts preparatory work on *Joseph* trilogy

1926

Jan. 12–18	readings in Heidelberg, Marburg, Cologne, and Mainz, where Katia comes to meet him
Jan. 19–28	in Paris
Jan. 20	lectures at the Carnegie Institute on "Les Tendences spirituelles de l'Allemagne d'aujourd'hui" ("Spiritual Tendencies in Germany Today")
early Feb.	ten days in bed, ill with flu while Katia suffers from bronchitis
April	"Disorder and Early Sorrow" published in book form; TM starts preparing speech for celebration at Lübeck—700th anniversary of the city's foundation
May 6–28	stays with Katia in sanatorium at Arosa; finishes speech
May–July	"Pariser Rechenschaft" serialized in the *Neue Rundschau*
May 30– June 2	in Munich
June 3–9	in Lübeck
June 15	reading in Vienna
June 28	Katia returns from Arosa
July 26	Erika marries the actor and director Gustaf Gründgens
early Aug.	preparatory work on *Joseph* novel
Aug. 31– Sept. 13	holiday in Forte di Marmi; writes foreword to Conrad's *The Secret Agent* and article "Die Unbekannten" ("The Unknown") for the *Berliner Tageblatt*

CHAPTER TWENTY-FOUR

Sept.	joins the Committee for Pan-European Union
end Sept.	eight-day visit with Katia and Ernst Bertram to Lausanne, where Monika is studying the piano
Oct. 18–21	in Berlin
Oct. 19	TM gives a broadcast talk on Joseph Conrad

Oct. 21	*Münchener Neueste Nachrichten* publishes his obituary for Berthold Litzmann
Oct. 21–24	in Hamburg, where he visits Klaus and is
Oct. 27	enrolled as a member of the Prussian Academy of the Arts
Nov. 2	makes speech at the inauguration of the Munich Association
Nov. 18	makes speech at Prussian Academy
Nov. 20	makes speech in honor of Gerhart Hauptmann after his play *Dorothea Angermann* is staged at the Munich Kammerspiele
Nov. 23/24	becomes a "senator" of the Prussian Academy
Dec. 7	*Vossische Zeitung* publishes his article "Bleibt München Kulturzentrum?" ("Is Munich still a cultural center?")
Dec. 12–13	lectures in Heidelberg and Cologne
Dec.	Writes "Höllenfahrt" ("Journey to Hell") Prologue to *Joseph* novel

1927

Jan. 7	*Literarische Welt* publishes "Wörte an die Jugend" ("Words to Young People")
late Jan.-mid-Feb.	with Katia and the two young children in the Klosterhotel at Ettal
Feb.	writes foreword for a novel by Hugh Walpole–first in a series, "Romane der Welt," edited by TM and Hermann Scheffauer
March 6	in Berlin for a session of the Prussian Academy's literary section, he reads out Heinrich's protest against the law on censorship being prepared in the Reichstag
March 8–15	in Warsaw as guest of the Polish PEN Club
March 16	reads in Danzig
March	writes on Franco-German relations for Jacques Mortane's book *Das neue Deutschland* (Zurich, 1927)
May 4–7	reads "Disorder and Early Sorrow" in Essen and Heidelberg
May 6	day in Königswinter; expedition to Grafenwerth, an island in the Rhine
May 10	TM's sister Julia kills herself
mid-July	completes first section of *Joseph* while spending ten days on his own at Kreuth
Aug. 10–Sept. 11	summer holiday in Kampen on the island of Sylt with Katia and the three youngest children; falls in love with seventeen-year-old Klaus Heuser, son of Professor Werner Heuser, director of the art academy in Düsseldorf.
Sept.-Oct.	writes essay on Kleist's *Amphitryon*
Oct. 10	lectures on *Amphitryon* before a festival performance at the Schauspielhaus

CHAPTER TWENTY-FIVE

Oct. 20–28	in Berlin, Stettin, and Frankfurt reading from "Disorder and Early Sorrow" and lecturing on *Amphitryon*
Nov. 8	reading in Munich from *Joseph*
Nov. 30– Dec. 10	lectures in Karlsruhe, Wiesbaden, Achen, München-Gladbach, Krefeld, Düsseldorf, Trier, and Frankfurt
Dec.	the *Neue Rundschau* publishes "Höllenfahrt"

1928

Jan. 10	in Berlin for meeting of the academy
Jan. 12	reads from *Joseph* in Berlin
early Feb.	reads from *Joseph* in Vienna
Feb. 24	*Literarische Welt* publishes "Thomas Mann gegen die *Nachtausgabe*" ("TM versus the *Nachtausgabe*")
Feb.-March	works on *Joseph*
March	writes "Kultur und Sozialismus"
March 12	attends inauguration of new members at academy in Berlin
April	*Preussische Jahrbücher* publishes "Kultur und Sozialismus"; motoring trip to Zurich, Geneva, Neuchâtel, Aix-les-Bains, Grenoble, Cannes, Saint-Raphaël, Marseille
May 20	Reichstag elections: shift toward the left, though Nazis win twelve seats
May 21–24	reading at Frankfurt University; visits international press exhibition with Ernst Bertram in Cologne; reading in Düsseldorf
June	publication of *Süddeutsche Monatsheft* (July issue) that contains an open letter from Artur Hübscher, attacking TM for falsifying *Reflections of a Nonpolitical Man* by abridging it
late June	works on *Joseph*
July	visits Dürer exhibition in Nuremberg
Aug. 1–30	returns to Kampen for summer holiday; Ernst Bertram visits him there
Oct. 1	makes speech at Reclam's centenary celebrations in Leipzig
Oct. 31– Nov. 9	readings from *Joseph* in Vienna, Lübeck, Basel, and Lucerne
Nov. 25– Dec. 12	readings from *Joseph* in Duisburg, Cologne, Hamburg, Lübeck, Magdeburg, Liegnitz, and Berlin

1929

Jan. 2–ca. 17	in Ettal; prepares lecture on Lessing for
Jan. 21	celebrations at academy for bicentenary of his birth
April 10	makes speech at dinner for Jakob Wassermann after a lecture by him in Munich
April-May	interrupts work on *Joseph* to write lecture on Freud

May 16	lectures on Freud in Auditorium Maximum
May 25– June ?	convalescing in Gastein; Heinrich stays with him there; visit to Katharineum in Lübeck
July 8	finishes "Rede über das Theater" ("Speech on the Theatre")
July 21	*Neue Freie Presse* publishes his obituary of Hugo von Hofmannsthal, who died on July 15
July 20	makes his speech on the theater at opening of Heidelberg Festival
July 29– Aug. 23	summer holiday with younger children in Rauschen, Samland
Aug.	works on "Mario und der Zauberer" ("Mario and the Magician")
Aug. 29	reading from *Joseph* in Königsberg
Oct.	arrangements to film Heinrich's *Professor Unrat* as *Der blaue Engel*
Nov. 12	receives telegram to say he has won Nobel Prize
Nov. 16	reads "Mario and the Magician" at Nobel Prize ceremony held by Bavarian authors' group Schutzverband deutscher Schriftsteller
Nov. 19	speaks on "Bürgerlichkeit" at Munich's Rotary Club
Nov. 26–30	readings in Bochum, Duisburg, Cologne, and Bonn
Dec.	*Die Literatur* publishes his review of Gide's *Si le grain ne meurt*
Dec. 9–20	to Stockholm with Katia to receive Nobel Prize
Dec. 12	reads "Felix Krull," "Tonio Kröger," and "The Infant Prodigy"
Dec. 14	to Copenhagen
Dec. 16	reads from *Buddenbrooks* and *Joseph*
Dec. 18	PEN Club banquet for him in Berlin
Dec. 20	broadcasts and gives private reading in aid of a Jewish old people's home
Dec. 20–23	in Copenhagen
Dec. 23	returns to Munich; ceremonial dinner in town hall
1930	
Jan.	a fortnight in Ettal, works on "Lebensabriss" ("A Sketch of My Life")
early Feb.	finishes it
Feb. 11	silver wedding
mid-Feb.– mid-April	traveling in Egypt and Palestine
March 18	reception at literary club in Cairo
March 26– April 1	ill with dysentery in a Jerusalem hospital
April 18	returning through Italy
May 18	speech to Pan-Europe congress in Berlin
June	takes part in International PEN Club congress in The Hague

June–July	writes introduction to collected works of Theodor Storm
July 7	reads from *Joseph* novel at Munich University
July 16– early Sept.	holiday in new beach house at Nidden
Sept. 2	Prof. Pringsheim celebrates his eightieth birthday at the new house
Sept. 13	TM speaks on the intellectual situation of the contemporary writer at a regional conference of the Rotary Club in The Hague
Sept. 15	general elections: Nazis get larger share of the vote
Sept.	reads from *Joseph* novel in Geneva
mid-Sept.	prepares lecture on Platen for the Platen Society
end Sept.	Ernst Bertram comes to Munich; political arguments with Bertram
Oct. 4	attends meeting of Platen Society in Ansbach and gives talk
Oct.	*Die Förderung des Tages* published—essays
Oct. 15–19	in Berlin
Oct. 15	reads from *The Magic Mountain* and the *Joseph* novel
Oct. 17	"Deutscher Ansprache—ein Appell an die Vernunft" ("German Address—an Appeal to Reason") speech in Berlin against Nazism
Oct. 19	reading from the *Joseph* novel
end Oct.	finishes first volume: *Die Geschichten Jaakobs* (*The Tales of Jacob*)
Dec.	abandons plan to write a book on Goethe during 1932; writes "Das Bild der Mutter" ("Portrait of the Mother") which
Dec. 11	appears in the *Illustrierte Leipziger Zeitung*
Dec. 12	*Literarische Welt*, Berlin, publishes his review of Heinrich's novel, *Die grosse Sache* (*Serious Matters*)
end Dec.	visits Ernst Bertram in Berlin

1931

Jan. 27	Heinrich elected chairman of literary section of Prussian Academy
Jan. 28– Feb. 12	TM at Saint-Moritz; meets Jakob Wassermann; works on essay "Die Wiedergeburt der Anständigkeit" ("The Rebirth of Decency")
March	beginning of friendship with Erich von Kahler; *Der Staat seid Ihr* publishes "Die Wiedergeburt der Anständigkeit"
March 27	Heinrich's sixtieth birthday; celebration in the academy; Thomas gives speech

CHAPTER TWENTY-SIX

April 4	he sends Ida Herz the Passover section of the *Joseph* novel
April 8	has written six hundred pages of the novel sequence
May 5	lecture in Strasbourg on the intellectual situation of the contemporary writer
May 6	to Paris for publication by Fayard of *The Magic Mountain* in French
May 6–12	stays in Paris; lectures at the Institut International de Coopération Intellectuelle and at the Sorbonne; meets André Gide
June 11	lectures in Erlangen on Europe as a cultural community and
June 12	gives the same lecture in Munich
June 13	rejects an invitation to go on a lecture tour of Switzerland; he wants to finish the *Joseph* sequence by the autumn of 1932
early July	Gide spends a few days in Munich, goes with the Mann family on a trip to the Lake of Starnberg and attends a reading by Thomas at the university
July 6–8	in Geneva for a conference of the Comité Permanent des Lettres et des Arts; Paul Valéry is among the delegates; Thomas makes closing speech
mid-July– early Sept.	holiday in Nidden
Sept. 3	lectures on Goethe and Tolstoy in Königsberg
Sept. 4	reads from his novels in Elbing
Sept. 7	in Lübeck to make a speech at the 400th anniversary of the Katharineum
Nov.	*Corona* publishes "Jaakobs Hochzeit" ("Jacob's Wedding"), an excerpt from the *Joseph* novel
Dec.	ill with chronic catarrh and gastroenteritis
1932	
Jan.	over 6 million people in Germany are unemployed
early Jan.	TM has the flu
mid-Jan.	works on essay "Goethe als Repräsentant des bürgerlichen Zeitalters" ("Goethe as a Representative of the Bourgeois Epoch")
Feb. 5–24	in Saint-Moritz; works on lecture "Goethes Laufbahn als Schriftsteller" ("Goethe's Career as a Writer")
Feb. 25	lectures in Bern on "Goethes Laufbahn als Schriftsteller"
Feb. 26	repeats the lecture in Lucerne
March 13–22	lecture tour
March 15	in Prague as guest of the PEN Club; lectures on Goethe
March 18	centenary of Goethe's death; lectures at academy: "Goethe als Repräsentant des bürgerlichen Zeitalters" ("Goethe as a Representative of the Bourgeois Epoch"); receives Goethe Medal

March 21	in Weimar to lecture: "Goethe's Career as a Writer"
April	holiday in Lugano; the *Neue Rundschau* publishes "Goethe as a Representative of the Bourgeois Epoch"
May 10	in Nuremberg; lecture: "Goethe as a Representative of the Bourgeois Epoch"
May 12–14	In Frankfurt for conference of the Comité Permanent des Lettres et des Arts on Goethe
May 14	speaks at opening of enlarged Goethe Museum in Frankfurt; returns to Munich via Heidelberg and Stuttgart
June 8	lectures in Munich to audience of about 1,600 people: "Goethe's Career as a Writer"
June	(probably) finishes *Der junge Joseph* (*Young Joseph*)
July 2–	
Sept. 4	holiday in Nidden, spending the first two weeks there with Hans Reisiger; Katia and the children don't come till July 15; works on third novel in *Joseph* sequence.
ca. Oct. 20–25	on tour, giving six lectures in five days

1933

Jan. 1	Erika opens a cabaret *Die Pfeffermühle* in Munich
Jan. 2	starts work on a lecture, "Leiden und Grösse Richard Wagners" ("The Suffering and Greatness of Richard Wagner"), for the fiftieth anniversary of Wagner's death on February 13, 1883
Jan. 20	TM decides against addressing the Socialist Kulturbund in Berlin on February 19, but sends the speech he has completed, "Bekenntnis zum Sozialismus" ("Affirmation of Socialism"), so that it can be read out at the meeting
Jan. 29	completes Wagner lecture
Jan. 30	Hitler becomes chancellor
Feb.	*Corona* publishes "Goethe's Career as a Writer"; *Sozialistische Bildung* publishes "Bekenntnis zum Sozialismus" ("Affirmation of Socialism")
Feb. 10	delivers Wagner lecture at Munich University
Feb. 11	goes to Holland with Katia
Feb. 13	lectures on Wagner in Amsterdam
Feb. 14	in Brussels, where he repeats the Wagner lecture in French
Feb. 18	repeats the lecture twice in Paris, first at the Théâtre des Ambassadeurs and then in the Foyer de l'Europe
Feb. 26–mid-March	with Katia in Arosa
Feb. 27	burning of the Reichstag; warnings from Germany that his safety isn't guaranteed
March 12	Nazis force minister-president of Bavaria to resign; Klaus and Erika return briefly to Germany and telephone their parents to warn them not to come home

March 7–24	"improvised stay" in Lenzerheid; meetings with Hermann Hesse
March 24	except for the Social Democrats, all parties agree to declare a state of emergency, which gives Hitler dictatorial powers

CHAPTER TWENTY-SEVEN

end of March–early April	in Linzer Heide and Lugano
April 16–17	Munich, the "Richard Wagner city," protests against TM's Wagner lecture
Apr. 25	TM instructs Golo to send on all the *Joseph* material to him in Switzerland; Ida Herz supervises the packing of the library
May 10–June 17	TM and Katia stay in the Grand Hôtel at Bagnol on the French Riviera
May	Erika rescued the *Joseph* manuscript and others in Munich; she takes it to him in the south of France, and he resumes work
June 18–Sept. 20	in Sanary-sur-mer
Aug.	reads chapter about Jacob's wedding to about twenty people in his garden
Sept. 21	beginning of judicial hearing about the burning of the Reichstag
Sept. 27	TM and Katia settle in 33 Schiedhaldenstrasse, Küsnacht, outside Zurich
Oct. 10	First volume of *Joseph* series is published: *Die Geschichten Jaakobs* (*The Tales of Jacob*)
Nov.	supports appeal to the Rockefeller Foundation for the Jewish philosopher Heinrich Hellmund
Nov. 8	reads from the *Joseph* novels at the University of Zurich
Nov. 25	furniture arrives from Munich
Dec. 4	gives two readings from the *Joseph* novels for students in the Zurich Polytechnikum
1934	
Jan. 1	Erika's cabaret *Die Pfeffermühle* opens in Zurich
Jan. 15	TM delivers his Wagner lecture in the Zurich Schauspielhaus
mid-Jan.	preparations for publication of *Der junge Joseph* (*Young Joseph*)
Jan. 27	starts corresponding with Karl Kerényi
Jan. 28–Feb. 9	lectures and readings in nine Swiss cities

Feb. 26– March 18	holiday in Arosa; works on "Die Feste Zel," last section in first chapter of *Joseph in Ägypten (Joseph in Egypt)*
March 21–22	in Basel to deliver the Wagner lecture
April	*Young Joseph* published in Berlin
April 2	applies for renewal of passport and repossession of house in Munich with library and other contents
April 5–6	in Locarno for seminar; lectures on Wagner
April 23	reading in the Zurich Schauspielhaus
April 30	lectures on Goethe in Basel
May	makes headway with *Joseph in Egypt*
May 17–18	to Paris and Boulogne
May 19–29	crossing the Atlantic for first visit to the United States, invited by Alfred Knopf for the publication of *The Tales of Jacob* in English; reads *Don Quixote* on the boat
June 1	delivers Goethe lecture at Yale University
June 6	"Testimonial Dinner" in the Plaza with Mayor La Guardia and three hundred guests
June 9	leaves New York
June 30	"Night of the Long Knives," Hitler's longtime associate Ernst Röhm executed with several hundred other senior SA men—all accused of plotting against Hitler; Schleicher and wife also murdered
early July	TM working on *Joseph in Egypt*
July 23	Austrian chancellor Dollfuss murdered by Nazis
end of July	TM takes part in international art congress in Venice
Aug. 2	Hindenburg dies and Hitler, abolishing the presidency, declares himself Führer and Reichs Chancellor
Sept.	TM writes "Meerfahrt mit Don Quijote" ("Voyage with Don Quixote"); visited by Emil Preetorius
Oct.	holiday in Lugano
Oct. 15	Samuel Fischer dies
Oct. 22	TM broadcasts on Swiss radio–"Grüss an die Schweiz" ("Greeting to Switzerland")
Oct. 28	the *Basler Nachrichten* publishes "In Memoriam S. Fischer"
Nov.	Hans Reisiger pays another visit
Nov. 5–15	*Neue Zürcher Zeitung* publishes "Voyage with Don Quixote"
mid-Nov.	resumes work on *Joseph in Egypt*
Dec.	the *Neue Rundschau* publishes an extract from *Joseph in Egypt*
Dec. 25	TM and Katia are given a sheepdog for Christmas
1935	
Jan. 19	leaves to give lectures and readings in Prague, Brno, Vienna, and Budapest
Jan. 27	meets Kerényi in Budapest
Feb.	in Saint-Moritz. Meets Bruno Walter

April 1–3	congress of the Comité Permanent des Lettres et des Arts in Nice; TM's paper "Achtung, Europa!" ("Attention, Europe!") is read in his absence
March 28	collection of essays, *Leiden und Grösse der Meister* (*Sufferings and Greatness of the Masters*), published in Berlin
late April–mid-May	the Pringsheims come on a visit to Küsnacht; TM ill
mid-May	holiday in Nice, with René Schickele and Heinrich
May 26	celebration of TM's sixtieth birthday at the Corso-Theater, Zurich, where Act 3 of *Fiorenza* is performed
June 6	family celebration with Bruno Frank, Hans Reisiger, and other friends

CHAPTER TWENTY-EIGHT

June	Erika becomes a British citizen by marrying W. H. Auden; she is stripped of her German nationality
June 9	TM and Katia in Paris, en route for the United States
June 10	they board the SS *Lafayette*
June 20	TM and Einstein given honorary doctorates at Harvard
June 22–29	TM and Katia stay with Hendrik van Loon in Connecticut
June 30	they fly for the first time—from New York to Washington, where they dine in the White House with the Roosevelts; after a few days in New York they sail on a Cunard liner
July 12	arrive in Cherbourg
July 13	back to Küsnacht
July	reading Proust's *À la recherche du temps perdu*; works on scene between Potiphar and his wife
July 15–28	Pringsheims visit them in Küsnacht
Aug. 17–29	TM and Katia in Salzburg and Innsbruck
Sept. 19	Hitler's Nuremberg decrees deprive Jews of their citizenship, barring them from the professions and public employment
Oct.	TM recommends that the Nobel Peace Prize be awarded to Carl von Ossietzky, a former editor of *Die Weltbühne* imprisoned in a concentration camp
Nov. 8	reading from *Joseph in Egypt* in Winterthur
Nov. 17	reading in Zollikon
Nov. 20	makes after-dinner speech at Eduard Korrodi's fiftieth birthday party
Dec.	Bermann Fischer visits TM, wanting to publish from Switzerland
Dec. 11–14	readings in Solothurn and Bern

1936

Jan.	Bermann Fischer establishes the company in Vienna
Jan. 10	reading in Basel
mid-Jan.– early Feb.	TM and Katia stay in Arosa
Feb. 3	open letter to Eduard Korrodi protesting his article equating emigrant writing with Jewish writing
Feb.	writes preface for collection of stories in English translation—*Stories of Three Decades*
Feb. 27	writes tribute to Bruno Walter for inclusion in *Für Bruno Walter* (edited by Paul Stefan, Zurich, 1936)
March 7	violating the treaties of Versailles and Locarno, German troops occupy the Rhineland
March 13	TM writes tribute to Heinrich for *Die Neue Weltbühne*, Paris, March 26, 1936
April– early May	writes lecture "Freud und die Zukunft" ("Freud and the Future")
May 8	lectures on Freud in Vienna at celebration of Freud's eightieth birthday
ca. May 9– 15	repeats lecture in Prague and Brno
June 5	leaves for Vienna, and is driven from there to Budapest, where he's the guest of Lajos von Hatvany
June 8–12	attends conference of Comité Internationale pour la Coopération Intellectuelle in Budapest
June 9 & 13	reads from *Joseph in Egypt* in Budapest and Vienna
June 14	visits Freud
July	works on final chapter of *Joseph in Egypt*
late July	a few days in Sils-Barseglia
Aug.	Bermann Fischer publishes "Freud and the Future" in Vienna
Aug. 23	finishes *Joseph in Egypt*
Aug. 27– Sept. 23	motoring holiday on Riviera—visits Schickele in Saint-Cyr and Heinrich in Le Lavandou, where he's taken ill with angina; suffers a recurrence of erysipelas after returning
Oct.	works on *Lotte in Weimar* (*The Beloved Returns*)
Oct. 12	speaks at memorial service for Jakob Wassermann in Zurich
Nov. 19	granted Czech citizenship
Dec. 2	loses German citizenship effective retroactively to July 1933
Dec. 19	stripped of Bonn doctorate
Dec. 30	writes to dean at Bonn University

CHAPTER TWENTY-NINE

1937

Jan. 7–15	readings in Prague, Budapest, and Vienna, where TM visits Freud
Jan. 21	goes with Katia to Arosa, where he works on *The Beloved Returns*
Feb. 8	to Zurich for negotiations over setting up *Mass und Wert*, a bi-monthly, co-editor with Konrad Falke; Ferdinand Lion is managing editor
March	TM talks on anti-Semitism and reads from *Joseph in Egypt* to the Jewish group Kadimah
April 7	sails from Le Havre on the *Normandie*
April 12	arrives in New York, invited by the New School for Social Research
April 13	delivers his Wagner lecture
April 15	lectures on "The Living Spirit" at New School celebration of fourth anniversary of its Graduate Faculty of Political and Social Sciences
April 20	makes speech at ceremony for foundation of American Guild for German Cultural Freedom and German Academy in New York
April 21	speaks in Mecca Temple at memorial service for victims of fascism
April 23	sails from New York on the *Île de France*
April 27	Guernica destroyed by German bombers sent to help Franco
April 30	returns to Küsnacht after short stay in Paris
May	ill with sciatica; writes foreword for first issue of *Mass und Wert*
June 10–30	with Katia in Ragaz for cure
Aug. 1	concentration camp opened in Buchenwald
Aug.	TM works on *The Beloved Returns*; first issue of *Mass und Wert* (dated September-October) published; Kerényi comes to Küsnacht
Sept. 15–Oct. 7	convalescing in Locarno and preparing a new Wagner lecture
Nov. 16	delivers Wagner lecture at Zurich University
Nov.-Dec.	second issue of *Mass und Wert* contains third chapter of *The Beloved Returns*
Dec.	prepares lecture on "The Coming Victory of Democracy" for a spring tour in the United States
Dec. 18	awarded the Czechoslovakian Herder Prize for exiled writers

1938

Jan. 10–31	in Arosa, working on *The Beloved Returns* and an introduction to a new American edition of Schopenhauer's work

Feb. 12	embarks on the *Queen Mary* for transatlantic crossing
Feb. 21	arrives in New York
Feb. 25	makes speech at opening of the Thomas Mann Collection at Yale University
March 1	starts lecture tour at Northwestern University, Chicago
March 3	University of Michigan, Ann Arbor
March 9	lectures in the afternoon at the Institute of Arts and Sciences in Brooklyn, New York, and in the evening at Constitution Hall in Washington, D.C.
March 11	German troops march into Austria
March 13	Anschluss (annexation of Austria) announced
March 14–29	in Philadelphia; Tulsa, Oklahoma; University of Utah, Salt Lake City; and San Francisco
March 21	decides to make his home in the United States
April 1	in Los Angeles; start of long stay in Beverly Hills; starts writing "Brother Hitler"
April 29	in Urbana, Illinois

CHAPTER THIRTY

May 5	official immigration into United States through Canada
May 5–31	in New York
May 6	gives lecture in Carnegie Hall
May 7	writes foreword for Erika's book on education in Nazi Germany, *Zehn Millionen Kinder*
May	accepts offer of a chair at Princeton, where he's to give three public lectures and conduct seminars on *The Magic Mountain* and Goethe's *Faust*
June 1	honorary doctorate at Columbia University
end May– June 19	stays at Caroline Newton's house in Jamestown, Rhode Island; works on Schopenhauer essay and on *The Beloved Returns*
June 29	embarks on the SS *Washington*
July 11	back in Küsnacht
July	works on *The Beloved Returns* and *Faust* lecture
mid-Aug.	eight days in Sils-Barseglia with Erika
Sept. 13	farewell reading from *The Beloved Returns* in Zurich Schauspielhaus
Sept. 14	to Paris
Sept. 16	Neville Chamberlain visits Hitler in Berchtesgaden
Sept. 17	embarkation on the SS *New Amsterdam* in Boulogne
Sept. 25	arrival in New York
Sept. 26	addresses mass meeting on Czechoslovakia in Madison Square Garden

Sept. 28	TM and Katia move into 65 Stockton Street, Princeton
Sept. 29	Conference at Munich–Hitler, Mussolini, Chamberlain, and Daladier
Oct. 1	German troops march into Czechoslovakia; TM writes "Dieser Friede" ("This Peace"), which becomes the foreword to a collection of political essays, *Attention, Europe!*; inaugurated at Princeton as lecturer in the humanities
Nov. 9	"Kristallnacht" ("Crystal Night")–all over Germany synagogues are burned, Jewish homes and shops wrecked, Jews beaten up and taken to concentration camps
Nov. 28–29	two-part lecture on *Faust*
Dec.	resumes work on *The Beloved Returns*
end Dec.	writes an anti-Nazi manifesto for publication with support from other people, but one of those asked to sign, the novelist James T. Farrell, immediately denounces it in the press; TM then withdraws it

1939

Jan. 17	gives public lecture on Wagner at Princeton University
Feb. 9	British government announces distribution of free air-raid shelters
Feb. 13	TM gives public lecture on Freud

CHAPTER THIRTY-ONE

March 8– mid-April	lecture tour with Katia and Erika on "The Problem of Freedom"
March 15	German army marches into Prague two days after Hitler had issued an ultimatum demanding a change of government and payments to Germany
April	TM addresses meetings of American Committee for Christian German Refugees in Beverly Hills and Chicago
May 1	House of Commons legislates for conscription
May 8	TM addresses world congress of writers in New York
May 10	lectures on *The Magic Mountain* at Princeton
May 18	awarded honorary doctorate at Princeton
May 22	Germany and Italy sign "Pact of Steel"
June 2	League of American Writers elects him as president, and he speaks on "Writers in Exile" at their congress
June 4	offered guest chair at Princeton for second half of 1939–40
June 6	leaves for European holiday with Katia and Erika
June 13	they arrive at Le Havre
June 16– early Aug	in Noordwijk, writes an introduction to an American edi-

	tion of Tolstoy's *Anna Karenina* and works on *The Beloved Returns*
July	Germans smuggle arms and military instructors into Danzig; Chamberlain promises to help the Poles if Germany uses force against them; Golo takes over as managing editor of *Mass und Wert*
Aug. 7	TM and Katia leave for Zurich
Aug. 18	they fly to London
Aug. 21	to Stockholm as German delegate at a PEN congress, which is canceled
Aug. 23	nonaggression pact between Stalin and Hitler
Sept. 1	German troops march into Poland at 5:45 A.M.
Sept. 3	Britain and France declare war on Germany; TM and Katia fly back to London
Sept. 9	sail for the United States from Southampton
Oct.	TM finishes *The Beloved Returns*
Oct. 24	Hitler makes a bid for peace without offering to withdraw from Poland or Czechoslovakia
Nov. 2	TM lectures on *The Magic Mountain* at Columbia University
early Dec.	*The Beloved Returns* published; writes "This War"
1940	
Jan. 5	starts work on *Die vertauschten Köpfe* (*The Transposed Heads*)
late Jan.	lecture tour in Canada and Toledo, Ohio–"The Problem of Freedom" and "This War"
Feb. 8–21	lecture tour in Delaware, Iowa, Chicago, Minneapolis, Topeka, Dallas, and Houston–"The Problem of Freedom"
Feb. 22–28	in San Antonio
early March	back to Princeton, working on lectures, including one on "The Art of the Novel"
March	public lecture on Goethe's *Werther* at Princeton
April 9	Germany invades Norway
April 10	TM lectures on "The Art of the Novel"
end April	visits the Meyers in Washington
May 2–3	lecture in two parts "On Myself" in seminar on German literature of nineteenth and twentieth centuries
May	German armies march into Holland, Belgium, and France
May 10	Winston Churchill takes over from Chamberlain as prime minister
May 28	Belgium and Holland surrender
June 4	Allied forces evacuated from Dunkirk
June 6	sixty-fifth birthday marked by a symposium in the *Neue Volkszeitung*, New York
June 11	Mussolini declares war on the Allies
June 12	TM reads to friends from *The Transposed Heads*
June	TM and Erika join Frank Kingdon's Emergency Rescue Committee
June 22	France surrenders

CHAPTER THIRTY-TWO

June 28	TM visits the Meyers in their country house in Mount Kisco, New York
July 5– Oct. 6	summer holiday in Brentwood, near Los Angeles
July 26	ill with inner ear infection
July 31	birth of first grandchild, Fridolin, son of Michael and Gret
early Aug.	finishes *The Transposed Heads* and resumes work on *Joseph* tetralogy
Sept.	*Mass und Wert* reappears; Golo and Heinrich arrive in Lisbon
Sept. 7	Air forces wage "Battle of Britain" as Blitz on London starts
Sept. 23	Monika and her husband, Dr. Lanyi, are traveling on a British evacuee ship, which is torpedoed; he drowns in front of her
late Sept.	TM buys site in California to build a house
Oct. 3	After-dinner speech on "War and Democracy" in Los Angeles
Oct. 5	TM and Katia leave Brentwood; stay for a few days in Chicago with the Borgeses
mid-Oct.	return to Princeton
Oct.	TM begins series of monthly broadcasts to Germany for the BBC
Oct. 13	refugees from France arriving in the United States include Alfred Döblin and Franz Werfel
Nov. 5	Roosevelt reelected president
Nov. 14–27	TM and Katia in Chicago, waiting for Elisabeth to give them their second grandchild
Nov. 30	the baby is born, a girl named Angelica
Dec. 28	TM and Katia return to see her in Chicago
1941	
early Jan.	TM and Katia visit the Meyers in Washington
Jan. 12	TM lectures on "The War and the Future" in Washington
Jan. 14–15	TM, Katia, and Erika are guests of the Roosevelts in the White House
Jan. 15–21	lecturing on "The War and the Future" in Atlanta and Athens, Georgia; on *The Magic Mountain* in Durham, North Carolina, at Duke University
Jan. 22	lectures in New York on "The Rebirth of Democracy" at the Federal Union Dinner
Jan. 23	back to Princeton
mid-Feb.	two days in New York; broadcasts in series: "I Am an American"
March 11	Roosevelt signs Lend-Lease pact with Britain
March 17	TM and Katia move out of the Princeton house
mid-March– mid-April	lecture tour in the West with new version of "The War and the Future"

March 20   visit to the Borgeses in Chicago
March 22–24 in Colorado Springs and Denver
March 26   lecture in Los Angeles
March 27   in Berkeley: awarded an honorary doctorate at the University of California and accepts the Phi Beta Kappa order; lectures on "Thinking and Living"
April 8   they move into 740 Amalfi Drive, Pacific Palisades
April 17   Germans take Yugoslavia
April 27   British pushed out of Greece
end April   TM makes headway with *Joseph* novel
May 2   speaks at celebrations for Heinrich's seventieth birthday
early June   addresses Emergency Rescue Committee in San Francisco
June 30   breaking the nonaggression pact, Germany invades Russia
July   Alfred Pringsheim dies, age ninety; building work starts on new house
early Aug.   TM writes introduction to collection of Martin Niemöller's sermons
Aug. 14   after a secret meeting Churchill and Roosevelt proclaim Atlantic Charter
Oct. 3   finishes section about Joseph's wedding to daughter of High Priest
Oct.   Michael and Gret bring Fridolin to stay at Pacific Palisades
Oct. 14–
  Nov. 27   lecture tour in the South, East, and Midwest: "The War and the Future"
Oct. 16–27   in Austin, Texas; New Orleans, Louisiana; Birmingham, Alabama; Clear Point on the Gulf of Mexico; and Mobile, Alabama
Oct. 28–29   in Greensville, South Carolina, and Greensboro, North Carolina
Oct. 31–
  Nov. 1   visit to the Meyers in Washington
Nov.   Agnes Meyer arranges for TM to be appointed by the Library of Congress as consultant in Germanic literatures at an annual salary of $4,800
Nov. 2   Chicago
Nov. 4   Indianapolis, Indiana
Nov. 7–16   in New York, except for two days (November 11–12) at Amherst College, Massachusetts
Nov. 17–26   Philadelphia, Princeton, New York, and San Francisco
Nov. 27   back to Pacific Palisades
Dec. 6   committee meeting of German-American Congress for Democracy
Dec. 7   Japanese planes attack Pearl Harbor
Dec. 8   United States declares war on Japan
Dec. 11   Germany and Italy declare war on the United States

CHAPTER THIRTY-THREE

Dec.	TM works on fifth chapter (Tamar)
1942	
Jan. 16–20	in San Francisco: lecture on "How to Win the Peace"
early Feb.	move into new house, 1550 San Remo Drive
Feb. 15	Japan takes Singapore
Feb. 21	ideas about *Doctor Faustus*
March 7	summoned before Tolan committee to take American citizenship
March 28	RAF bombs Lübeck and destroys the *Buddenbrooks* house
April 18	United States planes bomb Tokyo
May	Heinrich stays for fourteen days
May 5	working on Joseph's reunion with Benjamin
mid-May	lectures on Fontane's *Effi Briest*
May 31	about a thousand RAF planes drop two thousand tons of bombs on Cologne
June 2	TM writes foreword for *Order of the Day*, his collection of political speeches
July 11	finishes chapter in which Joseph rejoins his father
Aug. 18	interrupts work on novel to prepare lecture on it
Sept. 2	S.S. troops complete the slaughter of fifty thousand Jews in Warsaw ghetto
Sept. 15	TM writes foreword for collection of his first twenty-five BBC broadcasts
early Nov.	British Eighth Army under General Montgomery wins Battle of El Alamein
Nov. 8	goes to Chicago to stay with the Borgeses
Nov. 14	to Washington, staying with the Meyers
Nov. 17	lecture on *Doctor Faustus* at Library of Congress
Nov. 25	visits Alfred Knopf in Purchase, New York
early Dec.	TM revisits Princeton
Dec. 10	speaks on "The Peace of Washington" at Nobel anniversary dinner
Dec. 12	returns to Pacific Palisades
Dec. 19	starts last chapter of *Joseph the Provider*
1943	
Jan. 4	finishes *Joseph the Provider*

CHAPTER THIRTY-FOUR

Jan. 5	starts preparatory work on new story "Das Gesetz" ("The Tables of the Law") in lieu of an introduction to *The Ten Commandments*
Jan. 24	broadcast to Germany at the end of the Nazis' first ten years in power

Jan. 25	starts writing "The Tables of the Law"
Jan. 31	the Germans surrender at Stalingrad
March 13	TM finishes "The Tables of the Law"
March 14	clears all biblical material from his desk
March 15	looks at old notes for a Faust story
late March	uncertain whether to give *Felix Krull* priority
April 10	decides to write *Doctor Faustus*
mid-April	Germans crush Jewish uprising in Warsaw ghetto
mid-May	in the Atlantic war the Allies begin to get the upper hand
May 23	TM starts drafting *Doctor Faustus*
June 18	gives talk in San Francisco on "The Fall of the European Jew"
June 28	first four chapters completed; first reading to family
July	Theodor Adorno becomes "helper, adviser and participating instructor"
July 23	Allies take Palermo
July 24	Katia's sixtieth birthday
July 25	Mussolini deposed
end July	TM interrupts work on the novel to prepare lecture on "The War and the Future"
Aug. 19–27	writes lecture
Aug. 27–8	spends two successive evenings with Schoenberg and Stravinsky
Sept. 8	Italy surrenders unconditionally
Sept. 13	lectures on "The Problem of Humanity in Our Time" to Hadassah, a Jewish women's society, in Los Angeles
late Sept.	completes Chapter 8 and discusses it with Adorno
early Oct.	after Adorno explains and plays Beethoven's Opus 111 Piano Sonata, TM spends three days reworking the chapter
Oct. 9	TM and Katia leave for lecture tour ("The War and the Future") starting in Los Angeles
Oct. 12	they stay with the Meyers in Washington
Oct. 13	TM delivers the lecture in the Library of Congress
Oct. 16	delivers lecture at Hunter College, New York
Oct. 17	gives same lecture under the title "The Order of the Day" in Boston
Oct. 18	"The New Humanism" in Manchester, New Hampshire
Oct. 22	in New Bedford
Oct. 25	delivers lecture twice in Montreal
Oct. 30	in New York, broadcast to Germany through BBC, London; refuses to join Brecht and Reinhold Niebuhr in the "Free Germany" movement
Nov. 7–11	lectures in Chicago and in Lewiston, Maine
Nov. 16	lectures on "The War and the Future" at Columbia University, New York
Nov. 27	participates in celebration at the New School for Alvin Johnson's seventieth birthday

Nov. 30	lectures in Cincinnati, Ohio
Dec. 4–5	in Kansas City
Dec. 8	back in Pacific Palisades
Dec.	*Joseph the Provider* published by Bermann Fischer in Stockholm
end Dec.	reworking Chapters 8 and 9 of *Doctor Faustus*

CHAPTER THIRTY-FIVE

1944

Jan. 5	TM and Katia interrogated for American nationality
Jan. 22	Allied landings in Anzio, thirty miles south of Rome
early March	TM finishes Chapter 13 of *Doctor Faustus*
March 19	Allied troops land in Burma by glider behind Japanese lines
March 22–April 5	TM and Katia staying with the Borgeses in Chicago to see their new grandchild, Domenica (born March 6)
May	breaks off broadcasts to Germany for BBC
end May	TM refuses to sign the manifesto of the Council for a Democratic Germany
June 3	De Gaulle's Committee of National Liberation in Algiers names itself as provisional French government
June 4	Rome liberated by Allies
June 6	D-Day: British and American troops land on Normandy coast
June	TM ill but goes on working
June 14	London attacked by flying bombs
June 23	TM and Katia take their oath as American citizens
July 1	*Joseph the Provider* chosen by the Book-of-the-Month Club
July	controversy with Henri Peyre over TM's essay "What Is German?"—Peyre regards it as a plea that Germany should be given a soft peace
July 29	writes to President Beneš explaining preference for American nationality
Aug. 25	Paris liberated
end Aug.	after writing Chapter 22 (on twelve-tone music) TM takes a break from novel
Aug. 31	Russians capture Bucharest
Sept. 9	London attacked with silent V-2 rockets
Oct. 11	"The Tables of the Law" published; starts Chapter 23 of *Doctor Faustus*
Oct. 20	troops under General MacArthur land in the Philippines
Oct. 29	TM makes election speech for Roosevelt
Nov. 1	attack of flu
Nov. 7	Roosevelt reelected

Nov.	prepares Washington lecture
Nov. 16	cancels it
Nov. 26	resumes work on novel
mid-Dec.	starts Chapter 25—conversation with the Devil
Dec. 16	Nelly Mann commits suicide
Dec. 19	Germans launch successful surprise attack in the Ardennes

1945

Jan. 1	resumes broadcasts to Germany
Jan. 6	Heinrich comes to stay
Jan. 9	Germans being pushed out of the Ardennes
mid-Jan.	TM resumes work on Chapter 25
Feb.	writes "The End" for *Free World*
Feb. 12	Churchill, Roosevelt, and Stalin meet at Yalta
Feb. 14	Dresden devastated in night and day of relentless bombing
Feb. 20	finishes Chapter 25 and interrupts work on novel
Feb. 22	seven thousand bombers raid German communications
Feb. 27	starts to write lecture "Deutschland und die Deutschen" ("Germany and the Germans")
March 3–8	Destroying bridges, the German army withdraws to the east bank of the Rhine
March 20–30	using diaries from 1914, TM prepares a chronological summary for the rest of the novel
March 25	Allies establish a bridgehead on the east bank of the Rhine
April 12	Roosevelt dies
April 22	speaks at inauguration ceremony of the Independence Movement
April 25	delegates from forty-six states meet in San Francisco to found United Nations; TM writes on the concentration camps
April 26	resumes work on the novel
April 30	Hitler found dead in bunker
May 7	Germany surrenders unconditionally
May 25–26	TM and Katia travel to Chicago, where they stay with the Borgeses
May 29	lecture at the Library of Congress
June 3–4	in New York
June 6	seventieth birthday celebrations; news leaked about division of Germany into zones
June 8	lectures at Hunter College
June 13–24	at Lake Mohawk, Ulster County
June 21	news of Bruno Frank's death
June 25	dinner of the *Nation* associates in TM's honor

CHAPTER THIRTY-SIX

June 26	reading from *Doctor Faustus* to friends in Hotel St. Regis
June 29	celebration in Chicago
July 4	back to Pacific Palisades
July 5–17	writes introduction to Dial Press edition of six Dostoyevsky stories
July 21	works on Chapter 27
July 31	at Potsdam new British premier, Clement Attlee, and new U.S. president, Harry Truman, meet Stalin, who vetoes free elections in East European countries
Aug. 6 & 9	atom bombs dropped on Hiroshima and Nagasaki
Aug. 10	Office of War Information passes on open letter from Walter von Molo in the *Hessische Post*, asking TM to settle in Germany
Aug. 13	memorial service for Bruno Frank in the Manns' house
Aug. 14	Japan surrenders
Aug. 18	*Münchener Zeitung* publishes "Die innere Emigration" by Frank Thiess in support of von Molo
Aug.	completes Chapter 28 in ten days and starts Chapter 29
Sept. 7	TM sends reply to von Molo
Sept.	reaches Chapter 30
Oct.	honorary doctorate from Hebrew Union College, Cincinnati; new edition of *Buddenbrooks*, a collection of essays titled *Adel des Geistes*, and a selection of stories published in Stockholm
Oct. 25	works on Chapter 31
Nov.	writes Chapter 32 in twenty days
Nov. 20	trial of war criminals begins at Nuremberg
end Nov.– Dec.	bronchial catarrh, low blood pressure, and loss of weight
Dec. 7	lectures on Dostoyevsky at University of California
Dec. 27	completes Chapter 33
Dec. 30	enlists Adorno's help for description of Adrian's oratorio
1946	
Jan.	collaboration with Adorno on novel
Jan. 18	X-ray reveals a shadow on his lung
Feb. 2–6	writes "Bericht über mein Bruder" ("Report on My Brother") for *Freies Deutschland*
mid-March	works on Nietzsche lecture
March 20	film rights of *The Magic Mountain* sold for $10,000
March 21	Heinrich's seventy-fifth birthday
March 28	takes Heinrich's doctor, Frederick Rosenthal, as his doctor
mid-April	to Chicago for lung operation
April 24	cancer discovered
May 14	first time out of doors in wheelchair
May 20	discharged from hospital, stays in hotel

May 25	to Los Angeles
May 28	back to Pacific Palisades
May 30	resumes work on novel
June	two excerpts from the novel published in the *Neue Rund-schau*

CHAPTER THIRTY-SEVEN

early Sept.	ill with erysipelas
Oct. 1	Nuremberg tribunal sentences twelve Nazis, including Göring, to death; Hess gets a life sentence, five others are jailed, and three are acquitted
Oct. ??	*The Beloved Returns* published in Berlin
Oct. ?–25	stays in San Francisco with Michael, Gret, and children
Oct. 15	Göring kills himself with cyanide to escape execution
Oct. 16	the other war criminals are hanged
Nov. 8–13	TM writes a statement on world government for a meeting of Chicago students on Thanksgiving Day
Dec. 10	Nobel Prize awarded to Hermann Hesse at TM's instigation
Dec. 12	reading of Chapters 44 and 45 to family
1947	
Jan. 25	renewal of honorary doctorate at Bonn University
Jan. 29	finishes *Doctor Faustus*
Feb. 3	U.S. Senate told Russia has secret of atom bomb
Feb. 7	celebration in Alfred Neumann's house
Feb. 9	starts preparatory work on Nietzsche essay
Feb. 17–	
March 17	drafts it
March 12	wanting to provide military and economic aid for Greece, Truman initiates "positive" anticommunism by pledging U.S. support for "free peoples who are resisting attempted subjugation by armed minorities or by outside pressures"
April 1	TM addresses World Federalists of Southern California
April 22	TM and Katia leave for Chicago, where they stay with the Borgeses
April 28–29	TM and Katia stay with the Meyers in Washington
April 29	Nietzsche lecture at the Library of Congress
April 30–	
May 11	in New York, where he gives the lecture at Hunter College
May 11–16	TM and Katia cross the Atlantic on the *Queen Elizabeth*
May 16–24	in London, staying at the Savoy Hotel
May 20	delivers Nietzsche lecture at King's College, London University

May 23	writes message to German people, explaining exclusion of Germany from his lecture tour
May 24	to Zurich
May 28	hostile articles by Manfred Hausmann appears in the *Weserkurier*
June 3–4	attends International PEN Congress in Zurich
June 5	U.S. Secretary of State George Marshall announces plans for aid to Western Europe
June 8	reads from *Doctor Faustus* in the Schauspielhaus
June 12–16	delivers the Nietzsche lecture twice in Bern, reads in Saint Gall and gives the lecture in Basel
June 20–July 20	holiday in Flims, Grisons
June 25	writes "Briefe in die Nacht" in reply to German attacks on him
July 7	*Neue Zeitung*, Munich, publishes "Briefe in die Nacht"
July 20	back to Zurich
July 23	meets Hermann Hesse in Lucerne
July 30–Aug. 3	in Meina near Arosa on Lake Maggiore as guest of Italian publisher Mondadori
Aug. 5	reading from *Doctor Faustus* in Amriswil
Aug. 10–18	in Amsterdam
Aug. 18–28	holiday in Noordwijk
Aug. 29–Sept. 8	TM and Katia return to New York on the Dutch steamer *Westerdam*
Sept.	"Nietzsches Philosophie im Lichte Unserer Erfahrung" ("Nietzsche's Philosophy in the Light of Our Experience") published in the *Neue Rundschau*
Sept. 14	back to Pacific Palisades

CHAPTER THIRTY-EIGHT

Sept.	works with Klaus on Goethe anthology for Dial Press
Oct. 6–Nov. 23	writes introduction
Oct. 17	*Doctor Faustus* published in Stockholm
Nov. 18	arrives in San Francisco to give Nietzsche lecture
Dec.	writes introduction to a chapter of *Buddenbrooks* in the anthology *The World's Best*, published by Dial Press
Dec. 21	back in Pacific Palisades, he starts preliminary work on *The Holy Sinner*

1948

Jan. 21	starts drafting *The Holy Sinner*

Feb. 8	finishes introduction for one-volume edition of the *Joseph* novels
Feb. 22	resumes work on *The Holy Sinner*
Feb. 26	breaks his shoulder bone
Feb. 27	Communists seize power in Czechoslovakia
end Feb.	*Nietzsche's Philosophy in the Light of Our Experience* published in Berlin
March 10	Jan Masaryk commits suicide or is pushed from window
March 25	protests against U.S. support for creation of Israel as a state
March	writes foreword for one-volume U.S. edition of the *Joseph* novels
April	resigns from the Authors League of America
May 14	independent state of Israel founded
June	*Neue Studien*, a collection of five essays published in Berlin
June 6	TM addresses the "Peace Group" in Hollywood
June 7	President Beneš resigns
June 8	eighty-three-year-old Richard Strauss cleared by a denazification court in Frankfurt
summer	the anthology *The Permanent Goethe* published by Dial Press
June 30	Berlin airlift begins
July 10	Klaus attempts suicide
July 21	interrupts work on *Der Erwählte (The Holy Sinner)* to start *Die Entstehung eines Romans (The Genesis of a Novel)*
Oct. 21	finishes it
late Oct.	resumes work on *The Holy Sinner*
Oct.	donates all new German royalties to the maintenance of the Memling altar in Lübeck and the rebuilding of the Marienkirche
Nov.	Book-of-the-Month Club edition of *Doctor Faustus*
Nov. 3	Truman reelected president
1949	
Jan. 1	letter from Schoenberg and reply from TM appear in the *Saturday Review of Literature*
Jan. 5	starts work on the lecture "Goethe und Demokratie" ("Goethe and Democracy")
Feb. 8	resumes work on *The Holy Sinner*
Feb. 14	show trial of Hungarian primate, Cardinal Mindszenty
Feb. 24	TM elected honorary president of the literary section of the Bavarian Academy of the Arts
late Feb.	awarded Merit Medal of American Academy of Arts and Letters
March 18	North Atlantic Treaty Organization (NATO) formed
April 21	death of Viktor Mann, age fifty-nine
April	*The Genesis of a Novel* published
April 26	TM, Katia, and Erika leave for Chicago
May 2	lecture on "Goethe and Democracy" at the Library of Congress
May 3	TM told he has been awarded the Goethe Prize in Frankfurt

CHAPTER THIRTY-NINE

May 3–10	in New York, where TM delivers lecture at Hunter College
May 10	flies to London
May 10–18	stays at Savoy Hotel
May 12	Berlin blockade ends
May 13	TM receives honorary doctorate at Oxford
May 16	TM delivers Goethe lecture in Senate House of London University
May 19–31	in Sweden and Denmark
May 21	Klaus kills himself in Cannes, age forty-two
May 23	German Federal Republic created
May 24–27	TM delivers Goethe lecture in Stockholm and Copenhagen
May 31	honorary doctorate in Lund University, Sweden
June	BBC broadcasts talk "Goethe the German Miracle"
June 1–26	in Zurich
June 7	Goethe lecture in Schauspielhaus
June 14	reading in Küsnacht
June	lecture in Bern, readings in Zurich and Basel
June 27– July 18	holiday in Vulpera-Schuls in the Engadine
June 30	Truman tries to quell anti-Communist hysteria in the United States
July 19–22	TM and Katia arrive in Zurich
July 23	they arrive in Frankfurt
July 25	speech in Paulskirche for Goethe celebrations
July 27	TM and Katia to Munich
July 30	to Weimar
Aug. 2	they return to West Germany
Aug. 5	they embark at Le Havre on the *New Amsterdam* and
Aug. 13	arrive in New York
Aug. 19	back to Pacific Palisades
Aug. 28	awarded Goethe Prize in Frankfurt *in absentia*, and given freedom of the city of Weimar
Sept. 15	Konrad Adenauer elected chancellor of Federal Republic
Sept. 23	Russia tests atom bomb
Oct. 10	TM gives lecture in Berkeley
Oct. 12	Stalin establishes German Democratic Republic
Nov. 1	meets Jawaharlal Nehru
1950	
Jan. 21	Alger Hiss, former State Department official accused of espionage, condemned to five years of imprisonment for perjury
Feb.	Joseph McCarthy, a junior senator from Wisconsin, claims to have names of fifty-seven card-carrying Communists in the State Department

Feb. 3	Klaus Fuchs, nuclear scientist, charged with espionage
Feb. 15	Stalin and Mao sign pact of friendship
Feb. 25	TM interrupts work on *The Holy Sinner* to start preparation of lecture "The Years of My Life"
March 2	Heinrich dies shortly before his seventy-ninth birthday
March 21	TM finishes writing lecture
March 28	writes article on Klaus for *Die Welt*; Library of Congress cancels lecture arranged for April 25
April 21	TM and Katia arrive in Chicago
April 22	lecture at University of Chicago: "The Years of My Life"
April 26	in New York for lecture: "Meine Zeit"
May 1	flies to Stockholm
May 3	gives the lecture for the Swedish Academy; gives lecture in Lund
ca. May 8–15	in Paris, where he gives the lecture at the Sorbonne
May 16–23	in Zurich
May 24–30	in Lugano; visits Hesse in Montagnola
May 31	to Zurich
June 5	gives the lecture in the Schauspielhaus
June 6	celebrates seventy-fifth birthday with family and friends
June 9	Katia goes into clinic for hysterectomy

CHAPTER FORTY

June 10	TM gives the lecture in Basel
June 15	broadcasts lecture over South German Radio
June 23–July 14	in the Grand Hotel Dolder, Zurich
June 25	Communist North Korea invades independent southern half
June 27	United Nations Security Council supports the South
July 5	American troops do badly in first Korean engagement
July 14–17	in Sils Maria
July 17–Aug. 8	with Katia in Saint-Moritz
July 21	TM starts writing on Michelangelo poems
Aug. 11–17	in Zurich
Aug. 17	to London, staying at Savoy
Aug. 20	they fly to New York and stay at the St. Regis for two nights
Aug. 23	they visit the Thomas Mann exhibition at Yale University
Aug. 29	to Pacific Palisades
Oct. 26	TM finishes *The Holy Sinner*
Nov. 7	starts work on a thirty-minute talk on Bernard Shaw for the BBC

| Nov. 18 | finishes it |
| Nov. 26 | China enters Korean war |

1951

Jan. 8	TM resumes work on *Felix Krull*
Jan.	TM's thirty-minute talk on Bernard Shaw broadcast by BBC; review of Wagner's letters (new edition) in *Neue Schweizer Rundschau*
Jan. 26	U.N. troops halt Chinese advance in Korea
Feb. 6	MacArthur asks for invasion of China
Feb. 25	United States threatens to bomb mainland China
March	*The Holy Sinner* published
March 30	Julius and Ethel Rosenberg found guilty of atomic espionage; backed by many Republicans, MacArthur threatens to invade China
April	controversy with the editor of *Freeman*, Eugene Tillinger, who accuses him of pro-Communist tendencies
April 5	the Rosenbergs condemned to the electric chair
April 11	Truman dismisses MacArthur
May	TM pays tribute in *Aufbau* to Johannes Becher on his sixtieth birthday
May 12	first hydrogen bomb tested
June	TM attacked because of Becher letter in the *New Leader*
June 18	attacked in House of Representatives

CHAPTER FORTY-ONE

July 4	TM and Katia go to Chicago
July 9	they visit New York
July 10	they sail for Europe and
July 19	arrive in Le Havre, where Erika meets them and drives them via Dijon and Paris to Zurich
July 21–26	in Zurich
Aug. 1–11	in Ströbl on the Wolfgangsee
Aug. 11–15	in Salzburg
Aug. 15–Sept. 5	TM takes cure in Gastein
Aug. 22	his article on Gide appears in *The New York Times Book Review*
Sept. 8–13	in Lugano
Sept. 13–29	in Zurich
Sept. 29	they fly to New York
Oct. 2–5	in Chicago, where TM pays two visits to the Museum of Natural History
Oct. 6–7	they return to Pacific Palisades
Oct. 25	Conservatives win general election; Churchill to be premier at seventy-seven

Nov. 20	two chapters of *Felix Krull* published in the *Neue Rundschau*
Nov. 23	truce line established in Korea, roughly along 38th parallel
Nov. 30	TM becomes full member of American Academy of Arts and Letters

1952

March	working on "The Artist and Society," a program for the BBC
May 16	interrupts work on *Felix Krull* to write story "Die Betrogene" ("The Deceived," translated as "The Black Swan")
May 28	"The Artist and Society" broadcast on the Third Programme
June 12	awarded Italian Prize for Literature—5 million lire (ca. $8,000)
June 24	TM and Katia move out of Pacific Palisades
June 24–26	in Chicago and
June 26–29	New York
June 29–30	they fly to Zurich, where they stay at Hotel Baur au Lac
July 8	to Kandersteg
July 16	TM and Katia move into the Hotel Viktoria
July 31–	
Aug. 2	in Lugano
Aug. 2–8	in Hotel Baur au Lac, Zurich
Aug. 8	to Munich
Aug. 9–11	in Salzburg, where he gives lecture on August 10
Aug. 11–19	in St. Wolfgang
Aug. 20–	
Sept. 10	in Gastein
Sept. 10–	
Dec. 24	based in Zurich, staying in the Waldhaus Dolder
Sept. 17	reads from *Felix Krull* in Zurich Schauspielhaus
Sept.	lecture on "The Artist and Society" at UNESCO conference in Venice
Sept. 29	lecture on "The Artist and Society" in Schauspielhaus
Oct. 3	Britain tests first atomic bomb
Oct. 17–21	visit to Munich with Erika
Oct. 19	reading from *Felix Krull* in Kammerspiele
Oct. 23–24	in Bern
Nov. 4	Dwight Eisenhower elected president of United States
Nov. 9	TM speaks in memory of Hauptmann at Frankfurt
Nov. 10	reads from *Felix Krull* at Frankfurt University
Nov. 17–26	in Vienna, where he reads from *Felix Krull* in the Mozartsaal
Nov. 25	lectures on "The Artist and Society" in Konzerthaus
Nov. 30	United States tests first hydrogen bomb
Dec. 2	TM rents house in Erlenbach, outside Zurich
Dec. 4	Antonio Borgese dies
Dec. 16	French government awards TM cross of the Légion d'honneur

| Dec. 19 | he accepts an offer of $50,000 for the house in California |
| Dec. 24 | Thomas and Katia move into rented house in Erlenbach |

CHAPTER FORTY-TWO

1953

March 5	Stalin dies
March 14	Khrushchev emerges as new leader
March 13	reading of "The Black Swan" in Zurich
March	essay collection *Altes und Neues* published
April 11	resumes work on *Felix Krull*
April 17	Settling in Switzerland, Chaplin says he'll never return to United States
April 20–30	TM in Rome, where Pope Pius XII gives him a private audience
June 3	flies to London
June 4	awarded honorary doctorate at Cambridge University
June 5–7	in London
June 7	to Hamburg
June 8–9	reads from *Felix Krull*
June 10–11	to Lübeck and Travemünde
June 15	Chinese launch new Korean offensive
June 17	workers' uprising in East Berlin
June 19	Julius and Ethel Rosenberg electrocuted
June 24	Katia's seventieth birthday
July 31	rejects offer of East German national prize
Aug. 14	Russia claims to possess hydrogen bomb
Sept.	"The Black Swan" published in book form
Sept. 10–14	looking at houses in Geneva, Lausanne, and Vevey
Sept. 15	to Lugano
Oct. 1	back to Erlenbach
Dec. 18	in Weimar
Dec. 27	takes part in radio discussion on language and humor in his work

1954

Jan. 2/3	he completes Part One of *Felix Krull*
Jan. 4	radio adaptation of *Royal Highness* broadcast by Südwestdeutscher Rundfunk
Jan. 27	TM and Katia buy house in Kilchberg on Lake Zurich
Feb. 4–5	they are in Rome
Feb. 6–21	in Taormina, Sicily
Feb. 22–28	they return to Switzerland, stopping in Rome, Florence, and Fiesole, where they see Elisabeth
March	TM writes foreword to collection of letters by resistance martyrs
March 23– April 15	TM and Katia stay at the Waldhaus Dolder

March 25	TM and Katia give up rented house and move into the Waldhaus
April 15	they move into the new house in Kilchberg
mid-April	starts correcting proofs of *Felix Krull*
May	writes essay on Kleist as introduction to new U.S. edition of stories
June	starts working on play *Luthers Hochzeit* (*Luther's Wedding*)
Aug.	TM, Katia, and Erika spend two days in Saint-Moritz and two weeks in Sils Maria
Aug. 23	TM and Katia leave Erlenbach for Cologne and Düsseldorf
Sept.-Dec.	works at essay on Schiller
end Sept.	Part One of *Felix Krull* published
Nov.	first 20,000 copies have sold out, second impression not yet ready
Nov. 30	lectures on Kleist at Eidgenössische Technische Hochschule, Zurich
Christmas	finishes Schiller essay
Dec. 2	McCarthy condemned by Congress
Dec.	TM records talk on Chekhov in English for the BBC

1955

Jan. 16	TM and Katia leave for Arosa
Jan. 22	TM succumbs to virus infection
Jan. 27– Feb. 7	in hospital at Chur after collapsing
Feb. 11	golden wedding celebration in Kilchberg
Feb. 27	talk on Chekhov broadcast by BBC
March 3	TM accepts honorary citizenship of Lübeck
mid-March	working on *Luther's Wedding*
March 22	delivers Chekhov lecture in a Zurich hotel for the local writers' association
March 24	accepts honorary membership of the German Academy of Arts, Berlin
April 18	Einstein dies in Princeton, New Jersey
May 5	sovereign status restored to West Germany
May 7	to Stuttgart for the Schiller celebrations
May 8	delivers lecture in the Landestheater
May 10–13	resting in Kissingen
May 13	to Weimar
May 14	signing of Warsaw Pact, forming Eastern bloc nations into a military alliance; TM lectures on Schiller in Weimar
May 15	accepts honorary doctorate at Jena before returning to West Germany
May 16	to Lübeck
May 20	accepts honorary citizenship in town hall
May 21	reads in Stadttheater
June 4	eightieth birthday celebrations in Zurich; honorary doctorate at Eidgenössische Technische Hochschule

June 5	Bruno Walter, Therese Giehse, Albrecht Goes, Gottfried Bermann Fischer, and TM participate in celebrations at Schauspielhaus and in Zunfthaus zum Rüden
June 6	celebrations at the house in Kilchberg and, hosted by Knopf, in Hôtel Eden au Lac
June 30	to Amsterdam
July 1	gives press conference and delivers Schiller lecture at university
July 2–4	in The Hague, where he delivers the lecture on July 3
July 11	audience with Queen Juliana
July 18	pains in left leg
July 21	examined by Prof. Mulder from Leyden—thrombosis suspected
July 23	flown to Zurich for treatment by Prof. Löffler in canton hospital
Aug. 10	awarded highest German order: Pour le Mérite
Aug. 12	TM dies

EPILOGUE

| Aug. 16 | funeral |

Sidestepping Happiness

THOMAS MANN'S WORK is full of self-portraiture, and none of his characters tells us more about him than Aschenbach in "Death in Venice" ("Der Tod in Venedig"). "Since his whole nature was oriented towards fame, he showed himself, though not really precocious . . . to be ready at an early age for prominence, and to be well suited to it." His Venetian holiday is intended as an antidote to the daily routine of "rigid, cold and passionate duty." The combination of coldness with passion is characteristic of both character and writer, as is their division of working time between fanatical pursuit of perfection in their prose and assiduous cultivation of their reputation, partly through correspondence. Their fame is something that can't be left to take care of itself.

Mann had six children, and it was assumed that his marriage, which survived for over fifty years, was happy. Making his acquaintance through novels, stories, essays, photographs, public appearances, broadcasts, articles, the world took him to be self-controlled, elegant, dignified, self-assured, dispassionate, detached, and rather aloof. Wanting this image to survive his death, he incinerated most of his diaries and stipulated that the five thousand manuscript pages he'd spared should be kept under seal for twenty years after his death.

The release of this material had the effect of sabotaging what would have been the longest biography of him ever written. Published in 1975 to coincide with the centenary of Mann's birth, Peter de Mendelssohn's first volume contained 1,181 pages of smallish print but covered only the period 1875 to 1918. Unfortunately for Mendelssohn, the twenty-year ban on the diaries expired the same year, and writing without access to them, he'd had little evidence about Mann's friendships with young men and the interest he took in boys. According to the first volume of the biography, "Death in Venice" is "biographically indecipherable," and other relationships are depicted with a discretion that borders on dishonesty.

The surviving diaries cover the periods 1918–21 and 1933–55, but in them Mann sometimes recalls moments of passion from the first forty-three years of his life, and sometimes makes new comments on old diaries he's just reread. He also demonstrates that his private life was at odds with his public image. He was prone to fits of nausea, nervous trembling, and convulsive sobbing.

When his novels are reread in the perspective of the diaries, new meanings emerge, new interconnections between the problems of the characters and those of the author. To bring his first volume into line with the new information, Mendelssohn would have had to change it radically, and, though he didn't die until 1982, he preferred to concentrate on editing the diaries, which were published, one volume at a time, from 1977 onward. Since 1982 they've been edited by Inge Jens. The final volume, covering 1953–55, will appear in 1995, and, thanks to the generosity of Mann's publishers, Fischer Verlag, I've been able to read it in proof.

The diaries reveal that there were no limits to Mann's self-absorption. They contain an extraordinary mass of detail about minor physical symptoms, about what he ate and drank, how well he slept. One of his underlying concerns was with normality. Finding, when he was in his fifties, that surges of homoerotic desire were less intense, he wrote: "This is indubitably the normal pattern for human affections, and thanks to this normality I can believe more strongly that my life conforms to the scheme of things than I do by virtue of marriage and children."

It had never conformed to the scheme by which we're attracted to the opposite sex. The diaries show him to be uninterested in his wife's clothes, or the changing expressions on her face, or the way her body moved. They show how much he enjoyed catching sight of "a very handsome young man" or a pair of "fourteen-year-old boy twins . . . who interest me because of their charming symmetry." He feels "great pleasure and emotion" when he sees a young man bare to the waist in a market garden, and he praises German movies for "the pleasure they take in human, especially male, bodies in their nakedness . . . whenever opportunity offers, nude young men are shown in attractive, tender photographic illumination." One night in 1920, unable to make love, he wrote: "It can hardly be a question of actual impotence. . . . What would happen if a young man were at my disposal?"

His attitude to normality changed as he developed. At first it seemed that literary activity was incompatible with happiness. "Literature is death," he wrote in 1896 when he was twenty-one, "and I shall never understand how one can be a slave to it without hating it." Seven years later, his story "Tonio Kröger" questions whether an artist can be fully human. "An honest, healthy, decent man certainly doesn't write, act or compose."[1] Literature, says Tonio, is a curse, not a profession. If the writer becomes emotionally involved in what he's saying, he'll lose control.

Emotion—warm, heartfelt emotion—is always banal and unusable; only the irritations and cold ecstasies of our corrupt artistic nervous system are artistically productive. One needs to be something extra-human and inhuman, to have a strange, distant and detached relationship with all human activities before one wants to enact them, or is able to play with them, depict them effectively and tastefully. The gift for style, form and expression implies a cool, fastidious relationship with human activities, together with a certain human impoverishment and desolation. The fact remains that healthy, strong emotion is always insipid. An artist is done for as soon as he becomes human and begins to feel.[2]

In criticism, as in fiction, Mann was often thinking of himself when writing about other people, and in 1911 he discussed writers who, wanting to be recognized in their work, concern themselves less with fame, form, perfection, and posterity than with putting private life into the public realm, disguising its surface while confronting the reader with their own experience, their own suffering. He was never unconcerned with fame, form, and perfection, but he was compulsive about confronting the reader with his own experience, though he seldom stepped into his fiction without wearing a mask.

He mentioned masks in an 1897 letter to the closest of his former schoolfriends, Otto Grautoff: "For some time I have been feeling as if I could move my elbows freely—as if I had found ways and means of speaking out, expressing myself, moving outwards into artistic life, and whereas I previously needed a diary to unburden myself *in camera*, I am now finding *novelistic* forms and masks which can be displayed in public as a means of relaying my love, my hatred, my sympathy, my contempt, my pride, my scorn and accusations I want to make."[3]

In the theater, the mask releases inhibitions by concealing the face. The liberated actor can give away his darkest secrets: The man he's exposing is someone else. Mann overcame literary inhibitions by speaking freely about his inner life through characters apparently dissimilar to himself. The short story that made him feel he could move his elbows freely was about a hunchback; in subsequent stories he identified with a variety of repulsive and solitary characters—a shabby old man who dresses so oddly that children follow him mockingly in the street, a fat businessman with an unfaithful wife and a compulsion to humiliate himself, a black-clad religious fanatic, a Puritanical eccentric. Reshuffling his own characteristics, he was experimenting with makeshift viewpoints while deepening his self-knowledge.

He was twenty-one when he suffered what he called a "late and violent outbreak of sexuality." "What am I suffering from?" he asked in November 1896. "From sexuality . . . is it therefore going to destroy me?—How I hate it, this knowledge that forces even art to join in. How I hate it, sexuality, which claims to be responsible for everything beautiful as its product and consequence. Oh, it is the *poison* that lurks in all beauty! How can I free myself from sexuality? Eat nothing but rice?"[4]

Using a hunchback as an alter ego is scarcely less drastic than starving himself of protein. The story pivots on the arousal of the deformed creature through Wagner's music and the beauty of a woman who seems sympathetic. When she rebuffs and humiliates little Herr Friedemann, he experiences "an access of self-disgust, a craving to annihilate himself, to tear himself to pieces, to blot himself out." And he promptly commits suicide. The story declines into melodrama after a comically sophisticated opening which displays a talent for pastiche and parodies the naturalism that was current. Quasi-objective explanations were provided for all deviations from normality, and "Little Herr Friedemann" ("Der kleine Herr Friedemann") opens with a witty attribution of his deformity to the alcoholic addiction of a nurse who let him fall off his swaddling table as a baby.

Based on aspiration to scientific precision, Naturalism had originated in France during the 1860s, and toward the end of the century spread to Germany—where Ibsen's *Ghosts* influenced the avant-garde, partly because of the emphasis on heredity in its treatment of a taboo subject, venereal disease. The first German Naturalist play was Gerhart Hauptmann's *Vor Sonnenaufgang* (*Before Sunrise*), which was banned by the censor and privately staged in Berlin by the Verein Freie Bühne in 1889. Addiction to vulgar luxury and alcohol causes degeneration in the family of a Silesian farmer enriched by the sale of mineral rights.

But instead of achieving ironic detachment from fin de siècle decadence, most of Thomas Mann's early stories conform to the fashion for distasteful subject matter. The middle classes were struggling with an identity crisis which encouraged gloomy predictions that the world was going to end with the century, while artists and intellectuals were perversely celebrating the prospect of extinction by focusing on decay, death, corpses, morgues, and suicide. It would be grossly impertinent, said Oscar Wilde, to stop a man who wanted to throw himself into a river, and Joris-Karl Huysmans, whose novel *A Rebours* (*Against Nature*) became a bible for self-styled decadents, complained that "the disgusting monotony of landscapes and skyscapes has finally proved too much for sensitive spirits." Before the central character, Des Esseintes, finally collapses in neurasthenia, he indulges his Epicurean relish for deformity and monstrosity as he moves from one eccentric fancy to another in his search for pleasure. The cult of decadence had flourished in France during the 1880s and spread across Europe; in Wilde's 1891 novel, Dorian Gray pursues his decadent tastes while decaying psychologically and physically, the deterioration being visible only in the portrait.

Crude and callow though it is, "Little Herr Friedemann" represents a turning point in Thomas Mann's development: He could go on releasing guilt feelings by offloading them on characters. The story also announced the theme that was to be a leitmotiv throughout his work. "The principal figure is someone who has been treated by Nature as if she were a wicked stepmother, but he knows how to reconcile himself with his destiny in a way that is clever, mild, peaceful and philosophical, and has devoted his life entirely to relaxation, contemplation and peace." Friedemann means "man of peace." "Passion breaks into this sheltered life with the appearance of a woman who is remarkably beautiful, but also cold and cruel. His routine is overturned and the quiet hero is himself destroyed."[5] Many of Mann's fictions take the form of variations on this theme. In "Death in Venice," passion disrupts the central character's peaceful life after the appearance of a remarkably beautiful boy.

Incorporating the first statement of this theme, "Little Herr Friedemann" gave the twenty-one-year-old writer space to discover a new way of using the gift for mimicry he often exploited in conversation. Dapper, dignified, and charming, he made a good impression socially, presenting a facade that had little to do with the emotional turmoil in which repressed sexuality, guilt feelings, and literary ambitions were bubbling like ingredients in a witch's cauldron. He could be himself only in private. In public, he impersonated a man who naturally made a good impression; the story was an experiment in mimicking a man incapable of making a good impression. At last Thomas Mann could measure the distance between the elegance he affected and the chaos he concealed, while confessing how much he had in common, or believed he had in common, with a hunchback. No one would recognize the confession for what it was.

An 1897 story partly inspired by the opera *Pagliacci* and named after its German title, "The Clown" ("Der Bajazzo"), opens with an explicit statement of self-hatred: "At the end of it all, and as the worthy conclusion of everything is the disgust which life—my life—inspires in me . . . this disgust which suffocates me, drives me to frenzy, convulses me and then paralyses me, and which perhaps will sooner or later give me the necessary impetus to finish off the whole absurd and worthless business."[6] We don't yet know who's speaking. As we learn more about the anonymous narrator, we find that in some ways he's quite unlike the author, while in others they're indistinguishable. The character not only has the same family background and many of the same childhood experiences, he expresses the uncertainty Mann felt about whether he'd ever be more than a decadent dilettante with enough money to idle his life away and enough talent to show off at social gatherings.

In these early stories he gives the impression of putting himself on trial and making a strong case for the prosecution. This was partly due to the influence of Nietzsche: "[W]hat I saw above all in Nietzsche was the man who conquers himself."[7] Nietzsche held that for men capable of greatness, considerations of pleasure and pain should be secondary: "Isolated though I was, I took sides *against* myself and *for* everything that would hurt me, *me* especially, and come hard to me."[8] He tried to make things as difficult for himself as they'd ever been for anybody. "Only under this pressure do I have a *clear* enough conscience to possess something few men have ever had—*wings*, so to speak."

Mann was only twenty when he set his sights on something few men have had—greatness. It's common for adolescents to fantasize about distinguishing themselves, but "Monolog," a poem by the twenty-year-old Thomas Mann, shows an unusually deep fixation on the ambition to get people talking about him and to be crowned with laurels for the work he has done. He was twenty-two when he started an exceptionally long and ambitious novel, *Buddenbrooks*, and he soon realized there was a genuine prospect of fame. "It was always my secret and painful ambition to achieve greatness. The more I wrote in this way, the more respect I felt for what I had done, and I made even greater stylistic demands on myself. It is good that the beginning is so modest, and by the end it is something quite different from an ordinary novel, something perhaps rather rare. Sometimes my heart begins to beat faster at the thought."[9]

What helped ambition to work as an antidote to self-disgust was the excitingly Nietzschean idea that starving himself of pleasure would help him toward fame. He could conquer himself by setting himself difficult tasks. Aiming at greatness meant learning how to play a public role from his desk. When he described Aschenbach's methods of managing his fame, Mann was thirty-five, and had been using similar methods since his early twenties. He knew he must cut a certain figure in society, present a certain image, make sure he was written about and talked about in a certain way. He must make new friends and encourage old friends to write about him in newspapers.

In October 1901, when *Buddenbrooks* came out, Grautoff was reviewing for both the *Münchner Neueste Nachrichten* and a Hamburg paper, *Der Lotse*. Mann briefed him on how to present the novel: "emphasise, please, the *German* character of the book. As two genuinely German ingredients that at least emerge strongly in the second volume (which on the whole is probably the more significant) mention *music* and *philosophy*." *Buddenbrooks* was "genuinely German in its whole bearing (intellectual, social) and in its material: in the relationships between fathers and sons in the different generations of the family." Grautoff was also instructed to discuss the exceptional energy behind the writing, the epic scope and the Wagnerian elements.[10] Obediently, he worked most of these phrases into his review: artistic energy, musical and philosophical, Wagnerian, epic, genuinely German.[11]

Aware of having "a certain regal talent for playing a role," Mann used it consistently. His essays, autobiographical sketches, and even most of his letters had been written guardedly to reinforce the impression he gave of extreme rectitude. He always locked his diaries away, and he was twenty-one when he made the first of his destructive onslaughts on them. "It became awkward and uncomfortable for me to have such a mass of secret—*very* secret—writings lying around." Having left Germany shortly before Adolf Hitler became chancellor in 1933, Thomas Mann did not return to Germany, even on a visit, until 1949. But, having left his diaries behind, he was terrified they might fall into Nazi hands. "Something terrible, even fatal, may happen." As the most prominent of the émigré German anti-Nazis, he was sometimes called Hitler's worst enemy, but had the Nazis found his diaries, they could have ruined his reputation.

IN MAY 1934, thinking about Joseph and Potiphar's wife while working on his sequence of biblical novels, he read passages in the diaries for 1901–1902 about his friendship with a young painter, Paul Ehrenberg. He congratulated himself: "I have lived and loved. In my way, I have been human and paid the price. . . . I actually knew happiness, held in my arms someone I really longed for." An entry made in 1936, when he was sixty-one, shows that when he declared his love to Paul, the excitement was greater than any he had experienced with anyone else, male or female. "The early A.M. and W.T. experiences belonged still to my childhood. . . . They lacked the youthful intensity of feeling, the wild surges of exultation and deep despair of that central emotional experience at twenty-five."

Armin Martens and Willri Timpe were fair-haired schoolboys who'd aroused his adolescent passion. Hans Hansen, the beautiful blond boy in "Tonio Kröger," is modeled mainly on Martens. Mann's friendship with Paul Ehrenberg lasted for less than five years—from the end of 1899 to 1904; to call it his central emotional experience was to depreciate his marriage, which survived from 1905 until his death fifty years later.

Throughout the first winter after he met Paul, crisis followed crisis. Passionate love and ecstatic happiness alternated with a recrudescence of the self-disgust that had provoked such a fruitful combination of comfort and discomfort when he slipped into the hunchback persona. He told his brother Heinrich: "Really severe depressions with plans for self-destruction that were intended perfectly seriously have alternated with an indescribable, pure and unexpected heartfelt happiness, with experiences that cannot be discussed, and even to hint at them would sound like boasting."[12] A fortnight later he said he'd been "going to pot," and had "basically wanted nothing more than a solid typhus with a satisfactory outcome."[13] Writing to Heinrich again in April, he promised not to "do anything stupid. . . . My gratitude knows no bounds. My sentimental need, my need for enthusiasm, devotion, trust, handclasps, loyalty, had been starved to the point of wasting away and becoming atrophied, but now it is feasting."[14]

Neither before nor after his marriage to Katia Pringsheim could she have made him so happy or so desperate. He liked her and admired her, but he wasn't in love with her. Excited by the prospect of becoming her husband, he couldn't afford to tell her that connubial bliss wasn't what he had in mind. He was longing to have her as his wife, not longing to be her lover. As he confided to Heinrich,

> It's all alive only in my imagination, but it is too daring, too new, too colourful, too superbly like an adventure for me to withdraw from it yet. The *possibility* has offered itself, and makes me feverish. I can think of nothing else. . . . But I can say this straight away: it is pointless to ask whether I would be happy. Am I striving for happiness? I am striving for—life: and *in that sense*, probably for my work.

Belonging to one of the richest and most admired families in Munich, Katia could enhance his status and give him financial security— her father made him a regular allowance. She had a boyish figure and many boyish traits, having a twin brother, three other brothers, and no sisters. But in marrying her he was building a dam to divert the course of his sexual energy, sacrificing his natural inclinations on the altar of his public image. Uncertain about the extent of his "abnormality" and eager to make his life conform to conventionality, he went all out to put on a show of normality as a paterfamilias. He succeeded in deceiving the public but not in deceiving himself. "Someone like me," he wrote, " 'ought' not to bring children into the world." The single quotes around the word *ought* fail to deprive it of its force.

Mann was twenty-five when he finished *Buddenbrooks* and twenty-nine when he became engaged. An alert reader of the novel wouldn't have expected the author to marry for love. Great stress is laid throughout on the importance of keeping up appearances. The theme is connected with that of responsibilities to family traditions. When Thomas Buddenbrook arrives at the deathbed of Gotthold, the uncle to whom he transferred the office of consul which he could have assumed on his father's death, he recognizes, after watching the old man's death-throes, that Gotthold has consistently subordinated pleasure to respectability. Instead of marrying a shopgirl, he has kept up appearances. Thomas silently asks the corpse: "Would you have liked a different life from the one you had? Though you were proud and probably believed this pride was idealistic, there was little aspiration or imagination in your soul, and little of the idealism that enables a man to pursue or cherish or defend with silent enthusiasm—sweeter, more enchanting and more satisfying than secret love—some abstract good or ancient name or trademark, wanting to bring it honour, power and lustre."[15]

Thomas Buddenbrook has more imagination than his uncle, but though he wouldn't have fallen in love with a shopgirl, his motives for marrying aren't romantic: He's concerned with "honour, power and lustre." "Bachelordom," he tells his sister, "always carries the implication of loneliness and idleness, and I have ambitions, as you know. . . . A man does not win the world's respect until he becomes the head of a household and a family."[16]

Nothing mattered more to Thomas Mann than to win the world's respect, and the influence of Schopenhauer combined with that of Nietzsche and with his own revulsion against sexuality. Nietzsche was ambivalent about abstinence. He took the mad Hölderlin and the deformed Leopardi to task for "contradicting the simplest facts, e.g., that a man sometimes needs a woman, just as he sometimes needs a well-cooked meal." But his concept of *Verinnerlichung* (internalization) suggests the process by which libido is turned inward, and he equates this with the development of "soul":

> this secret self-ravishment, this artistic cruelty, this lust to impose form on oneself as on a tough, resistant, suffering material, cauterising into oneself a will, a criticism, a contradiction, a contempt, a negation; this uncanny, weirdly enjoyable labour of a voluntarily divided soul making itself suffer out of pleasure in causing suffering, finally this whole, *active* "bad conscience"—you can guess already—as the true womb of all ideal and imaginative experience.[17]

Schopenhauer, who had a stronger distaste for sexuality, regarded the genitals as the focal point of the will—the blind man that carries everything on its back, including the lame man, intellect. Will is fundamentally appetite for life, which involves us in painful conflict with people whose drives run counter to ours. As a diminution of the suffering that results, happiness is negative, while pain is positive. The only escape from suffering is in the use of the intellect, first to understand the will and then to suspend it.

The ambition to marry Katia Pringsheim derived partly from the books of Nietzsche and Schopenhauer that had most influenced the young Thomas Mann. Magnetized by the regal glamour of the family's lifestyle, he was simultaneously indulging his lust to ravish himself secretly, to perpetrate artistic cruelty, to impose form on himself by embracing a will, a criticism, a contradiction, a contempt, a negation. He was volunteering to divide his soul, and if a bad conscience was the true womb of all ideal and imaginative experiences, he would conscientiously cultivate one. He might have to inflict suffering on Katia, but at least he'd already inflicted some on himself by giving up the relationship that had mattered more than any previous one.

In the bedroom he used his regal talent for role-playing, and at first he seems to have given a good performance as a husband. Onsets of connubial impotence seem to have been rare, and he sometimes indulged in what he termed "sexual excess." He was usually convinced by his own performance in the role of devoted father, but even in the privacy of the diaries he was liable to overact: "Alone with the beloved little one who had kicked her blankets off." "Full of love, I brought her home and carried her to her cradle." When his eldest son was fourteen, Mann, who was forty-five, found he was "in love with Klaus." But everything could be turned into literature: "germ of a father-son novella."

His preoccupation with the problem of his own "normality" helps to explain his preoccupation with the theme of disease, but this, too, derived partly from Nietzsche, who was plagued throughout his life by headaches, stomachaches, and other painful symptoms. The sick man, Nietzsche contended, being more aware of what he lacks than the healthy man of what he possesses, is better placed to understand health. Writing, he thought, was bound up with self-conquest, and in his battle to achieve this, headaches and nausea were his allies: "I have never felt happier with myself than in the sickest periods of my life, periods of the greatest pain." What Nietzsche would have found intolerable—unlike the pain—was to think that his life would make no difference to other people. The only way to represent the conscience of the modern soul is to be possessed of its consciousness, and this is impossible without concentrating all the disease, poison, and danger that modern times have produced. The man who's more than an ordinary individual will be more diseased than any ordinary individual.

Mann's 1895 story "The Will to Happiness" ("Der Wille zum Glück") centers on a young painter who marries in spite of severe cardiac illness. What has been keeping him alive is the drive for sexual fulfillment, and he dies after his wedding night. At the funeral, the bride's expression is like the sick man's: both faces signaled "the solemn and intense seriousness of triumph." This is reminiscent of Nietzsche's reference to what Socrates said on his deathbed about owing a cock to Asclepius. This being the sacrifice conventionally made on recovering from illness, his implication was that life had been a disease.

Like Hauptmann's *Vor Sonnenaufgang*, *Buddenbrooks* is about the degeneration of a family, and, unlike *Vor Sonnenaufgang*, it is obviously about the author's family. Mann characterized it as decaying and himself as decadent. For generations the family has thrived on business. Two of its late-born members turn to the arts, but their creativity is connected with a deficiency in their will to live.

In 1912, when Mann started planning *The Magic Mountain* (*Der Zauberberg*) after a visit to the Davos sanatorium where Katia was being treated for tuberculosis, he was protesting against glib optimism and facile socialistic reformism. In the early stages of writing the novel, he used disease as a metaphor for the artist's need to distance himself from everyday materialism. The mountain sanatorium is a refuge from the commonplaces of life on the Flatlands. He intended the novel as a bildungsroman in which the hero, Hans Castorp, would be brought to an enlightenment deeper than that of the "enlightened" humanitarians who preached progressive liberalism.

But Mann was still working on the novel when war broke out, and it forced him into involvement with public issues. As he became less individualistic, more humanitarian, the disease became more representative. Since we all have to participate in contemporary history, our health is undermined. How can we live positively if the zeitgeist provides no motivation for activity, no answer to the question "What for?"

Before finishing the book—twelve years after he started it—he claimed in a 1921 lecture on Goethe and Tolstoy that disease was an "aristocratic attribute." If neither Schiller nor Dostoyevsky had survived into old age, it was because of their spiritual "disjunction from nature." But Mann's postwar intellectual development carried him beyond his preoccupation with decadence, and Hans Castorp learns a great deal about the nature of reality from his stay in the sanatorium. "What develops in the young man, from experience of disease, death, and decay, is the idea of man, the 'sublime structure' of original life . . . an inkling of a new humanity."

The writing gains some of its intensity from Mann's excitement at the idea that nothing is more normal than deviation from the healthy norm. Explaining the basic bodily processes, Dr. Behrens, medical director of the sanatorium, says life is "mainly oxidisation of the cellular albumen, which gives us that beautiful animal warmth we sometimes have in greater quantities than we need. Well, living consists in dying, no point in beating about the bush—*une déstruction organique*." Later, when the beautiful Clavdia Chauchat is caressing the close-cropped hair at the back of Hans's head, he talks to her in French: *"Le corps, l'amour, la mort, ces trois ne font qu'un. Car le corps, c'est la maladie et la volupté, et c'est lui qui fait la mort, oui, ils sont charnels, tous deux, l'amour et la mort, et voilà leur terreur et leur grande magie!"* The probability that Hans will be killed in the trenches is prefigured by an account of masonic initiation rites. After being instructed, the novice is eventually led to the tomb, "the place of corruption" which is also "the receptacle in which the material is prepared for its final transformation and purification."

Though most of his behavior gave no indication of his preference for male beauty, and though the stories he wrote before 1910 contain little evidence of homoeroticism, he'd never lost his relish for the young male body, and in two stories written between 1910 and 1912, "How Jappe and Do Escobar Fought" ("Wie Jappe und Do Escobar sich prügelten") and "Death in Venice," he succumbed to temptation, luxuriating in memories of his love for Armin Martens and Willri Timpe and in persistent observation of a beautiful young Polish boy staying at the same hotel on the Venice Lido.

On the surface, the story is about a Dionysian lapse from the Apollonian self-discipline that an aging writer has inflicted on himself. The name Aschenbach implies an anomalous combination between cinders and moving water. He's apprehensive that his time might run out before he has fulfilled his literary potential, and though his work has already brought him fame and success, he takes little pleasure in it, feeling troubled by its lack of spontaneity. The narrative seems to be designed partly as a portrait of the artist as an older man. What will he be like in fifteen or twenty years if he goes on strangling his spontaneity? Although Aschenbach is a widower, and the story contains no explicit references to bisexuality, it looks as if Mann, still using characters as masks and talking cryptically about his own experiences, was equating spontaneity with homosexuality and questioning whether he'd been right to impose form on himself in such a drastic way, giving success priority over sexual passion.

Once Aschenbach heard someone saying: " 'You see, Aschenbach has always lived like this'—and the speaker tightened the fingers of his left hand into a fist—'never like this,'—and he let his open hand hang comfortably down over the arm of the chair. The point was valid, and the moral courage involved was that he did not have a robust constitution and his nature could not have been less suited to the constant tension he imposed on it."[18] Forty pages later we're reminded of this image of the open hand after Aschenbach escapes from the cholera-stricken city but returns because he can't bear the idea of never seeing Tadzio again: "Then he raised his head and with both arms hanging slackly over the arms of the chair, he made a slowly rotating lifting movement, the palms of his hands turning forwards, as if to signal an opening and widening of the arms."[19]

The story works in two ways. It can be read as an expression of regret that the author has made too many sacrifices to Apollo and too few to Dionysus, but it exemplifies the way order can be imposed on unruly material. Excited though Mann had been on his own Venetian holiday by the presence of a beautiful boy, he had jeopardized neither his reputation nor his health. It might have been harder for him to control himself if he hadn't had fiction as a safety valve. The anarchic impulses are projected onto a character and passed on to us as part of a carefully structured and highly polished narrative. In a letter written ten years after he published the story, he distinguishes three strands in the writing. One is symbolical, with the boy as Hermes, the messenger of the gods who guides souls: Aschenbach is being led toward a higher form of life. But Mann wasn't sufficiently detached from Naturalism not to view the "case" as pathological, while the third strand derives from his "Protestant and puritanical ('bourgeois') nature," which he passes on to Aschenbach, making him take a basically mistrustful and pessimistic view of passion. "The real subject of my story was passion as a distraction and as destructive of dignity."[20] Which had been the subject of the much simpler tale "Little Herr Friedemann."

Possibly Mann wouldn't have written such a good story as "Death in Venice" had there been no chance that his feelings would get out of hand; but the story would not be so good if he hadn't gained control over them and over the rest of his material. Even if he was reproaching himself for making his life into something more like a closed fist than an open hand, he made no attempt to change it. He was twenty-nine when he stopped seeing Paul Ehrenberg; he didn't fall in love again until he was fifty-two.

In the summer of 1927, holidaying in Kampen on the Baltic island of Sylt, he met a seventeen-year-old boy, Klaus Heuser, son of Professor Werner Heuser, director of the art academy in Düsseldorf. Klaus then visited Mann in Munich, and Mann went to see him in Düsseldorf. In 1934, looking back on the relationship and comparing the boy with Paul Ehrenberg, Mann decided "the K.H. experience was more mature, more controlled, happier," but less intense. Thinking about Klaus, Mann still felt "deeply agitated, touched and moved by the memory of this experience," which he had cherished "proudly and gratefully because it was the unhoped-for fulfilment of a lifelong yearning, it was 'happiness' as written in the book of mankind, though not of the commonplace kind." All his earlier feelings of love were "subsumed in this late, astonishing fulfilment."

WITH THE FOUR *JOSEPH* NOVELS he widened his perspective to take in the whole of humanity: He called them "a humourous and mythical poem about mankind." Analyzing his motives for using biblical material, he cited his interest in the history of religion, his predilection for Egyptian culture, and the pleasure of looking for human impulses that were invisible on the surface. Beyond this the work gave him a sense of looking for the origins of human behavior. To make stories from the books of Genesis and Exodus into material for a novel was to search with modern eyes for the beginnings of human behavior—the first cases of sibling rivalry, the first murders, the first confusions of identity. Joseph and his brothers are seen to be repeating patterns that had already been acted out by their ancestors, but the relationships between the variations are clear, because they all come so close to the beginning of the human story.

Here Mann has no desire to be recognized personally in his work, no interest in confronting the reader with his own experience, his own suffering, though one of his starting points was the love he'd felt for his eldest son. In July 1920, Klaus had suddenly seemed terribly handsome in his bathing trunks, and a few days later his father was disconcerted to find the boy lying on his bed, shirtless and tanned. Later the same day Mann asked himself whether he'd finally lost interest in heterosexual lovemaking, and a few months later, according to his diary, he could no longer bring Katia to orgasm.

In the novel, Joseph is first seen in a position probably inspired by that of Klaus when he was lying on his bed. Joseph has lowered his coarse linen shirt, and his brown skin gleams in the moonlight. With its high, square, Egyptian-looking shoulders, his torso seems full and heavy in relation to the childish head. Displaying his half-nude young body to the moon in the hope of charming her, he incurs the wrath of his father, whose piety is offended, but the author goes on taking pleasure in the beauty of his hero. At seventeen, we're told, a boy can be lovelier than either a man or a woman, and can attract both women and men.

Doctor Faustus (*Doktor Faustus*) contains more autobiographical elements than the *Joseph* tetralogy, but at the same time it is Thomas Mann's most political novel, representing the farthest point reached in a slow drift toward political commitment. In 1914 he'd felt obliged to put fiction aside in order to perform what he called "war service with the weapon of thought." In his first piece of propaganda in support of the kaiser's war, he attacked the civilization of the allies as something that involved softening, while German culture depended on an almost tribal sense of unity, strength, form, and energy. When he decided to develop his arguments into a book, he called it *Reflections of a Nonpolitical Man* (*Betrachtungen eines Unpolitischen*). "I hate democracy," he wrote in 1916, "and I hate politics, for they are one and the same to me."

It was impossible for him not to champion democracy during the Hitler period, but he didn't like being diverted from his work as a novelist. "No more hack work," he resolved at the end of 1937. "No more pronouncements and answers! Why provoke hatred? Freedom and serenity! Time to insist on my right to them." And in 1938 he promised himself to withdraw from political activity: "Away, away! Confine myself to the personal sphere, the inner life . . . I must not let myself be dominated by impotent hatred." But when he was working on *Doctor Faustus*, he felt more deeply involved than he'd ever been: He found he could write simultaneously about himself and about Germany. For Tonio

Kröger, literature had offered an alternative to life in bourgeois society; forty years later the alternative seemed diabolical—fascism. One of Mann's notes runs: "The bursting of civil restraints which proceeds in a pathologically infectious and disintegrating way at the same time *political*. Intellectual-spiritual Fascism, rejection of the humane, use of violence, blood-lust, irrationalism, cruelty; Dionysiac denial of truth and justice, regression to the instincts and uncontrolled 'life', which is really *death*, or if it is life is *only the Devil's work, the result of infection.*"

The artist's inner world is infected, too. Instead of offering to renew the composer's youth, the Devil offers to reinvigorate his creativity, and though they have a conversation in what seems to be a fantasy, the pact is sealed when Adrian deliberately infects himself with syphilis by sleeping with a prostitute who has warned him about the disease. At the same time, Mann is dealing, half-parodically, with the problem of his parody. Simultaneously worried and pleased that so much of his own work rested, like James Joyce's, on parody, he condemned Adrian to start off by writing nothing but parodic music, which could only be of limited interest: He needs help from the Devil if he's to be capable of original or spontaneous work.

Though not devoid of comedy, *Doctor Faustus* isn't primarily a comic work, and in 1954, when the unfinished novel *Confessions of Felix Krull, Confidence Trickster* (*Die Bekenntnisse des Hochstaplers Felix Krull*) was published, critics were surprised that a man of nearly eighty could be so full of comic zest. Some of them noticed how easily Mann could identify with a con man. Perhaps he was giving voice to feelings of fraudulence he'd been harboring throughout his life. If it had been all too easy to make the public believe in him as a bourgeois paterfamilias, had it been equally naive to accept him as a great writer? His irony had always disguised a basic nihilism and an inability to put forward positive values. Perhaps he was making the same point in *Felix Krull* that Chekhov made when he asked himself: "Am I not fooling the reader since I cannot answer the most important questions?"

From "The Clown" onward, Mann had thrown out hints of believing his basic talent was for mimicry and comedy. His essay on Chekhov refers to "the primitive origin of all art, the impulse to mimic, the jester's wish and talent to entertain." If he'd made himself out to be greater than he was, some guilt feelings would be inevitable, but he could use them as raw material in his impersonation of the con man. Nothing was unusable.

Of all the tricks he played in the book, the neatest was to recycle the guilt feelings that had plagued him for nearly fifty years about the successful performance he was giving as husband and father. Felix Krull's sexuality is central to his adventures, but this is comedy, and there was even less risk of self-exposure than in "Death in Venice." Mann could easily afford to identify with a con man who dodges military service by feigning epilepsy so well that he surprises himself, lives on the earnings of a young Hungarian prostitute, and, while employed in a luxurious Paris hotel, first as an elevator boy and then as a waiter, breaks the hearts of a young Birmingham heiress and a homosexual Scottish peer.

Admired all over Europe and America, showered with honors, feted as a great writer, Mann kept his secret until twenty years after his death. All he had needed to do was to go on using the trick he'd explained to Grautoff, finding "*novelistic* forms and masks which can be displayed in public as a means of relaying my love, my hatred, my sympathy, my contempt, my pride, my scorn and the accusations I want to make." If the Nazis had been able to expose his bisexuality, he'd never have risen to such heights of eminence. His lifestyle was always Apollonian, but in his last unfinished novel, which is like a comic counterpart to "Death in Venice," he relishes the Dionysiac blows dealt to the social establishment by the comic con man.

Part
One

Like a Prince

In 1875, when Thomas Mann was born, the German Reich was only four years old. Austria had dominated the loose confederation of states established in 1815 by the Congress of Vienna, just before Napoleon was defeated at the Battle of Waterloo, and in 1849 it was still too early for Germany to extricate itself from the Austrian empire. At the end of March, the German National Assembly proclaimed a constitution and elected Frederick William IV of Prussia "king of the Germans," but, wanting to receive the crown from the princes, he refused to accept it from the people, and the National Assembly took his vague answer to be a refusal. In May, Prussia, Saxony, and Hannover formed a Three Kings' League to promote closer unity, but Austria refused to recognize it, and Saxony later withdrew. In June, when the army broke up the National Assembly, it killed all hope of uniting Germany by parliamentary means.

It could be united by force, as Bismarck saw when he took over the government of Prussia in 1862: If he could achieve military superiority, he might be able to achieve a hegemony and exclude Austria. After occupying Schleswig, Holstein, and Hannover in 1866, he went on the next year to take Mecklenburg, Saxony, and Darmstadt into the confederation, which he extended in 1870–71 to include Bavaria, Baden, Württemberg, and other southern states, besides taking possession of Alsace and Lorraine. Excluded from the Reich, Austria settled with Hungary into a Dual Monarchy, which survived through the forty-three years of peace in which Bismarck's frontiers remained unchanged. Although there were Danish and French minorities in the Reich, and German minorities outside, its integrity rested on the principle of nationality. More than ever before, Europe was a continent of nation-states, and Bismarck survived as chancellor till March 1890, when Thomas Mann was fourteen.

The Liberals were nervous that Bismarck's enlarged army might be used as an instrument of internal repression, but he split them by allying himself with the Junkers, the landowning class that dominated the Prussian civil service and the commissioned ranks in the army. He was only half Junker by birth, but he called himself a Junker, dressed accordingly, and spoke with affected Junker brutality. As a concession to the workers, he introduced insurance against accidents, illness, and old age, but parliamentary democracy failed to develop. Landowners had so much power over laborers that in 1908 an English historian wrote: "Though the name of serfage is no longer used, this condition exists in spirit and to some extent in fact."[1]

The more Germany prospered, the easier it was for Bismarck to fend off challenges to his authority, and the economic policies of Rudolph von Delbrück, head of the Bundeskanzleramt, tended to increase spending power throughout society. With a bigger population than France or Austria-Hungary, and with enormous natural resources, Germany made rapid industrial progress as iron ore from Alsace and Lorraine was used in the Ruhr and the Saarland. Development of the railway system helped trade to expand, and duties were reduced on imports from foreign manufacturers. The sense of affluence spread to farmers, shopkeepers, and workers. Big cities grew, and money changed hands rapidly as more and more people could afford to buy quick gratification. Prostitution thrived; entertainment in theaters, vaudevilles, and cabarets became more vulgar and sensational; wine bars and beer halls luxuriated. The endemic greed for mindless self-indulgence was culturally destructive, and Nietzsche, though he'd at first been enthusiastic about Bismarck's success, predicted that "German spirit" (*Geist*) would be extirpated in favor of the German Reich. As he said, it had become "almost fashionable and patriotic" to question whether the disappearance of German "profundity" shouldn't be welcomed.[2] Without mentioning Bismarck by name, Nietzsche's 1886 book *Jenseits von Gut und Böse (Beyond Good and Evil)* makes a caustic comparison between the genuine greatness of the idea that imparts quality to an action or a thing and the meretricious greatness of the statesman who builds a new tower of Babel, "a monstrosity of imperial power which impresses the populace." His leadership had forced the Germans to "sacrifice their old well-tried virtues for the sake of a new and dubious mediocrity."[3]

In building his imperial juggernaut, Bismarck had given Germany a political center of gravity. Berlin, formerly the capital of Prussia, became the capital of Germany, and in the next twenty years its population doubled, but it didn't become a center of artistic activity until much later. It wasn't in Bismarck's interests to encourage freedom of expression. He favored newspapers that supported him, giving them postal concessions and priority when official information was released, but generally the press had less freedom than in France or Britain, and numerous libel suits showed how morbidly sensitive he was to personal criticism. He tried to encourage national consciousness and to abort any social conscience that might have been critical. Giving the police and the bureaucracy greater power than they had in other Western countries, he kept rigid control over the educational system. Thomas Mann wasn't alone in hating the narrow-mindedness of authoritarian schoolteachers and the oppressive gloominess of vaulted Gothic classrooms.

The Reich now consisted of nineteen states, including four kingdoms, a grand duchy, and three free cities—Hamburg, Bremen, and Lübeck. While the federal government controlled foreign and economic policy, individual states had jurisdiction over matters affecting the daily life and welfare of their citizens. Education, public health, and policing were the responsibility of the separate states, and the three free cities were treated by the federal government in much the same way as the larger political units. Lübeck didn't lose its autonomy until 1934.

Founded in 1143, Lübeck had been partly independent since 1226, when it became an "imperial city." Linked to the sea by the River Trave, and positioned forty miles from Hamburg near the Baltic corner of the neck that lifts the head of Denmark from the shoulders of Germany, Lübeck had been the greatest port in the Hanseatic League, the confederation of Dutch and North German cities formed in the thirteenth century to develop trade relations with Scandinavian and Slavic countries. In its prime, the League incorporated 150 cities, and by monopolizing Baltic trade, it gained enormous wealth and power; but by the mid-seventeenth century, the only remaining members were Lübeck, Hamburg, and Bremen.

Today it's hard to believe such a small city as Lübeck could become so important. Situated on an isthmus formed by two rivers, the Trave and the Wakenitz, and surrounded by walls that were built in the thirteenth century and renewed before the Thirty Years War, Lübeck was confined to a space only two kilometers in length by one in width until the nineteenth century, when the walls were mostly taken down. Originally protected by an imposing castellated gateway, the Burgtor, which is still standing, the isthmus was cut by a canal connecting the two rivers, and the old part of the city is like an island, ringed by water and linked to the mainland only by bridges. But the narrow, hilly space in the center still has the character of an old walled city where rich burghers built massive churches, roads curving bonily down to the water like ribs from a spine, tall, pointed fountains, elaborate complexes of arcades and turrets. Spires, towers, and belfries poke insistently heavenward, some still vertical, some not quite, a lot shaped like candlesnuffers. Many houses have elaborate stepped gables. Steep roofs are characteristic: most of the houses are narrow because merchants tried to combine a maximum of storage space with a minimum of horizontal square footage: they were taxed according to the size of the site. They also wanted to outdo their neighbors by having more windows and more elaborate ornamentation.

Throughout most of the nineteenth century, Lübeck preserved its cultural identity. Annexed by Napoleon in 1810, it became independent again after his defeat five years later. Cut off from the rest of Germany when Schleswig and Holstein belonged to Denmark, the city was effectively protected from the despotic rulers of other German states, but when Bismarck annexed Schleswig and Holstein, it was no longer isolated. The Mann family depended on the corn trade, which was fated to long-term decline, but in 1875, the year Thomas was born, over 10 million kilograms (22 million pounds) of corn, oats, and rye were imported by the family firm, Johann Siegmund Mann, Corn Merchants, Commission and Transport Agents. They bought and sold grain, stored it, and shipped it. Thomas's father, Thomas Johann Heinrich Mann, was the grandson of the firm's founder. Born in 1840, he was known by his third name, Heinrich. In 1878, when Thomas was three, the firm imported 20 million kilograms (44 million pounds) of grain, and business improved again in 1879, with warehouses spread over more than a hundred floors in thirty buildings. But while constitutional changes were putting a belated end to the power of the guilds, Germany was exporting less food and importing more. And as Lübeck was gradually displaced by Hamburg and Stettin as Germany's principal Baltic ports, Heinrich found his business becoming less active.

Taken away from school at the age of fifteen to start work in the business, he was only twenty-two when his father died. Suddenly head of the family, he wasn't immediately head of the firm, only half of which was left to him, the other half being left to a head clerk, whom he succeeded in buying out. He then had to run the business and take his father's place, inheriting not only the title of consul to the Netherlands, which had been handed down from his grandfather, but also the confidence of his fellow citizens. In 1877, when Heinrich was thirty-six, he was elected to the Senate, and proved his political competence. Initially given responsibilities in town planning, indirect taxation, and city fortifications, as well as being appointed to the committee for trading and shipping, he was elected, in 1885, as chairman of the committees controlling taxation and economic planning. As a free city, Lübeck was in some ways like a Greek city-state, and in governing it, Heinrich Mann was second in importance only to the Bürgermeister. In 1945, when Thomas Mann was about to celebrate his seventieth birthday, his elder brother, Heinrich, made a speech recalling their father's reaction to being nominated, once again, for membership on a committee: "Yes, I am always on hand when nothing is to be gained."

The family business might have done better had he devoted more of his time to it. It didn't expand during the twenty-five years that he ran it, though he was well liked by people who did business with him. Farmers would come out to greet him when they heard the clatter of hoofbeats announcing the arrival of the rented carriage, and the deal would be made immediately. They trusted him.[4]

He put himself under constant strain, sitting on committees and taking the chair at meetings. It was his duty to keep up appearances: His concern about the grandeur of his house, his clothes, his coiffure, and his mustache (which was waxed and perfumed) were inseparable from his responsibilities to the business and the city. As described by his elder son, he was at this time a handsome and proud man who always seemed to be on the crest of life. He wore suits of soft cloth, low collars, and combed his hair forward like Napoleon III. He strode confidently about like a captain on his ship.[5]

In *Buddenbrooks*, Thomas and his sister Antonie, are aware of the part played by inheritance in making them what they are. In the family portfolio Tony finds a phrase her father has written: "like a link in a chain." Seeing her life as a new link in the old chain, she abandons the man she loves for a marriage apparently beneficial to the family business. Thomas Mann couldn't help seeing his life as a new link in an old chain. When he was a schoolboy wandering through the streets of Lübeck, citizens who raised their hats to him were saluting his family. Taking their place among the patricians who ruled Lübeck, his great-grandfather, his grandfather, and his father had prepared the way for him. He was what he was because they had been what they were, while their identity had been determined similarly by ancestry. "How often in my life have I not been amused to notice that the personality of my dead father was controlling both the actions I took and those I avoided, was serving secretly as their model? Often I caught myself literally in the act."[6]

By May 1890, when the company celebrated its centenary, Thomas had decided against going into the business. Though proud of being a Mann, he was following the example of his elder brother, Heinrich, whose literary ambitions had diverted him from the family's mercantile tradition. Both sons benefited from growing up in one of Lübeck's patrician families, and both had difficulty in mustering courage to defy paternal expectations—*Buddenbrooks* pivots on this insecurity. Thomas's original intention had been to center the novel on his own deviation from family tradition, and to set the action not in Lübeck but in Bavaria, where he was living. But wanting to tell the story from the beginning—*ab ovo*, as he put it—he studied the history chronicled in family records, which went back to 1644. It wasn't only the dates of births, marriages and deaths that had been recorded in the family bible but other details too, while many documents had been preserved in a leather portfolio. Gradually shifting the balance of the story to make it deal mainly with his ancestors, Thomas ended up with an action that stretches between 1835 and 1877.

The story spans three generations, and in reality Thomas belonged to the third generation of the family that had run the business, though he could trace his family history back to the great-grandfather of the firm's founder, Johann Mann, born 1644 in Parchim on the Elbe. He became a town councillor in Grabow, and a member of the drapers' guild. He "stood very well" until he lost everything in a fire. His son Siegmund, who set himself up as a draper in Rostock, was the father of Joachim Siegmund Mann, Thomas's great-great-grandfather, who started the chronicle in the family Bible.

Born in 1728, Joachim Siegmund was nearly killed in childhood, when a barrel of wine fell on top of him at his sister's wedding. Three subsequent escapes from drowning intensified his faith in the God who had apparently intervened four times to save him. Becoming a merchant and brewer, he married into a firm of shipowners and ship builders.

Joachim's son, also named Johann Siegmund, was only fourteen when, at the Rostock Whitsun fair, he made a good impression on a Lübeck merchant named Kaselan, who then took him home as an apprentice. Johann Siegmund was twenty-eight when, in 1790, his benefactor helped him to establish his own business, dealing in grain. Four years later he was granted Lübeck citizenship.

Johann Siegmund Mann's son, Thomas's grandfather, who was given the same names, Johann Siegmund, wrote elaborate autobiographical notes in the family Bible. Some of these described his travels. He was twenty-seven when he married Emilie Wunderlich, a girl who wasn't yet eighteen. She gave birth to five children before dying at the age of twenty-six. His second wife, Elisabeth, Thomas's grandmother, was the daughter of a Swiss grain dealer, Johann Heinrich Marty, whose ancestry could be traced back to the fourteenth century. Leaving Switzerland, Marty lived in Russia before settling in Lübeck. He was rich enough to keep a private coach and make a substantial contribution to the Mann family firm as his daughter's dowry. Johann Siegmund quarreled with the parents of his first wife, and his two surviving sons by Emilie were disinherited in favor of Heinrich, the elder of his two sons by Elisabeth.

When Heinrich was nearly twenty-nine, he married Julia da Silva Bruhns, who was not yet eighteen. Her father was a successful Lübeck planter who had settled in Brazil and married a woman who was half-Brazilian though descended on her father's side from four generations of Lübeck merchants. The fourth of five children, Julia was in her fifth year when her mother died in childbirth. A year later her father brought all five children back to Lübeck without telling them he was going to leave them there and return to Brazil. They wouldn't even have their black nurse, Anna, who had looked after them on the journey. The three eldest children were to be brought up by their grandmother and

the two youngest by the hunchbacked Therese Bousset, who was helping her elderly mother run a small boardinghouse. It was only on Sundays that the younger children went to their grandmother's house. At
school and on holidays with the shabby, ill-favored Therese Bousset,
living an impoverished life, Julia constantly yearned for something better. She would have liked to go on the stage, but she was discouraged,
and when she fell in love at the age of sixteen with the younger brother
of her sister's bridegroom, Heinrich Stolterfoht, she wasn't allowed to
marry him.

After her grandmother's death Julia had gone to live with an uncle
and aunt, but it was only in June 1869, when she married Heinrich
Mann, that she returned, finally, to the moneyed bourgeois lifestyle
that early childhood had seemed to promise. At first they lived with his
mother at the house in Mengstrasse, which is described, with no disguise and no change of address, in *Buddenbrooks*. It had a large flagged
hall with a white-painted gallery, and on the wallpaper of the main living room white gods and goddesses were portrayed against a blue background.

In 1870 they moved into a rented flat on Breite Strasse, and it was
here that their first son, Luiz Heinrich, was born on March 27, 1871.
Just over four years later, on June 6, 1875—two years before Heinrich
was elected to the Senate—their second son was born in a suburban villa
they'd rented for the summer. They called him Paul Thomas, the name
Thomas being taken from one of Heinrich's English business friends.[7]
Luiz Heinrich was fair and Paul Thomas dark.

The Manns entertained on a grand scale, following fashions that had
emanated from the court of Napoleon III. There were masked balls at
which quadrilles and gallops were danced. Although Julia Mann was
still only twenty-five when her husband was elected to the Senate, his
position involved both of them in a busy life. They attended social
gatherings of every kind, and entertained guests every Thursday
evening—the two boys looking on shyly from the background while officers from the garrison danced on the parquet floor with daughters of
local patricians.[8] The scene is described in a story by Heinrich: After
seeing his mother costumed as the Queen of Hearts for a fancy-dress
ball, a seven-year-old boy gets out of bed to peep at "the bare shoulders,
suffused with mellow light, people's hair glinting like jewels, shimmer-
ing with life, effortlessly turning as they danced. My father was costumed as an officer in a foreign army, with a sword. He was powdered
and I was very proud of him. Mother, the Queen of Hearts, was paying
court to him more than ever."[9]

But several men were paying court to her, and her husband's long ab-
sences in the Mengstrasse offices and the town hall left her with a great
deal of time on her hands, especially as she had a nurse to help with the

children. When her older son Heinrich was in his seventies, he did a lot of drawings showing scenes from his early life. One of them shows Julia in her boudoir, making up in front of the mirror on her dressing table; another, dated 1875, shows her in the garden, leaning flirtatiously back in a rocking chair and fanning herself, while her other arm is stretched out across a table toward the officer sitting well forward in his chair, gazing at her intently. The young Heinrich is lying on the grass not far away from them, and the baby, Thomas, is in his cot. But his parents are holding hands in Heinrich's representation of another incident that occurred in 1875. Julia is trying to comfort her husband, while he, holding his head in his free hand, talks about the disaster that has overtaken him. Heinrich also described what happened. Normally, when his father came into a room, it started to vibrate with activity, "but one day there was silence. . . . He groaned, which made me shudder. The man who was always bright and happy gasped out the names of people who had gone to pieces, lost all they had, including his money. . . . This was my first realisation that luck could change. My father needed the rest of his life to regain what had been lost in a few days."[10]

In August 1877, just over two years after Thomas was born, Julia gave birth to a girl, who was named Julia Elisabeth Therese; another daughter, Carla Augusta Olga Maria, was born in September 1881. Of the two boys, Thomas was his mother's favorite; like her and Heinrich, he knew this.

The brothers seldom played together. Many of Thomas's toys were inherited from Heinrich, and, like many younger brothers, he wasn't always prepared to wait for the moment when a once-precious possession would be handed magnanimously on. They had lead soldiers, two toy lambs, one of them on wheels, and an old, stuffed rocking horse with wide nostrils, glass eyes, pony fur, and a saddle and stirrups. Thomas was given a little shop with a counter, miniature scales, and groceries in the drawers. There was a granary of the same type his father had, and a crane, manipulated by a crank, for lifting sacks and bales; a complete knight's armor was made out of iron-gray cardboard, with a visored helmet, a tournament lance, and a shield. He also had a hussar's uniform, made to measure for him by a tailor.[11]

The toy that caused the greatest bitterness was a small russet-colored violin with real catgut strings. It was given to Heinrich, who kept it in his little polished desk, and one day in the nursery, Thomas, although he wasn't tall enough to reach the desk, played it without Heinrich's permission. One of the grown-ups must have given it to him and then put it back with a string broken. It may have been one of the maids—Heinrich never found out—or it may have been their mother, who always seemed to side with his younger brother against him. On the day he opened his desk to find the string broken, he burst into tears. She tried to comfort him, but only halfheartedly. "You see?" she demanded. "Whether it was just yours or belonged to both of you, it's broken now."[12]

While Julia tried to make the brothers love each other, most of her efforts were counterproductive, and for a year of their childhood the boys didn't speak to each other. This early rivalry had its effect on their relationship as they matured and on the way Thomas remembered his childhood. Like Marcel Proust, who revenged himself retrospectively on his younger brother by eliminating him from the fiction based firmly on memories of boyhood, Thomas erased Heinrich from nearly all his autobiographical sketches and reminiscences, and in *Buddenbrooks* Hanno has no brother.

The one toy they shared happily was a puppet theater, which had been given to Heinrich by their grandmother Elisabeth.

> At the beginning of our biography stands a miniature magic temple, reddish gold and many-coloured, made from pasteboard and glue, with its indoor and outdoor backdrops and gesticulating characters, in a darkened room, artificially lit, the puppet theatre, this dramatic organisation at which, under the influence of full-scale theatrical experiences we had thrown ourselves enthusiastically into being directors, singers, actors, producers, conductors and curtain-pullers. We needed no audience for the loud improvisations we carefully put on: we were also the audience and gave ourselves prolonged applause.[13]

One of the pasteboard puppet characters was Bismarck in the uniform of a cuirassier. Scripts had been provided, including a version of *Cinderella* and an adaptation of Heinrich von Kleist's historical drama *Das Käthchen von Heilbronn*. With his precocious gift for drawing and painting, Heinrich added to the backdrops and made new puppets, and both boys exerted themselves to write new plays, which they sometimes performed, with musical accompaniment, to an indulgent audience made up mainly of uncles and aunts. Heinrich was about fourteen when he lost interest in the puppet theater and handed it over to his younger brother. In Thomas's short story "The Clown" ("Der Bajazzo"), the narrator says that until his thirteenth or fourteenth year his puppet theater gave him more pleasure than any of his other toys.

Puppet theaters were popular with children during the eighteenth and nineteenth centuries. It was in the nursery that Goethe first encountered the Faust story, and that Ibsen became interested in theater. Playing with his puppets, Thomas was both apprenticing himself to the art of storytelling and developing his innate skill as a mimic. He later maintained that the primitive origin of all art was the instinct to copy and imitate. His daughter Erika, who inherited his talent for mimicry, described him and herself as monkeys.

Thomas's relationship with his mother was a very close one. Her

Bechstein grand piano stood by the bay windows of the drawing room, and the boys sat in the quilted armchairs while she played Chopin studies and nocturnes to them or sang songs by Schubert, Schumann, Brahms, and Liszt.[14] She told them about her childhood in Brazil, about black slaves and poisonous snakes on her father's plantation. She entertained them with stories she knew by heart or made up as she went along. In the evening, sitting by the lamp on the table in the living room, she read fairy tales from the Brothers Grimm and Hans Christian Andersen, and stories in Mecklenburg dialect by Fritz Reuter. Later on she read from *Don Quixote*, Hoffmann, Dickens, Tolstoy, and Goethe's *Dichtung und Wahrheit*. She also read from *The Land of the Pyramids*, an illustrated history of Egypt, and from a collection by Nosselt of stories from classical mythology. The book, which had a picture of Pallas Athena on the cover, strongly influenced Thomas, who called his rocking horse Achilles, and found both Homer and Virgil more exciting than stories about Red Indians. Phrases from the book became embedded in his memory.

> A specially sharp impression was made on me by the "sickle which cut as sharply as a diamond" and was wielded by Zeus in the battle against Typhon. I kept repeating this passage to myself. And I was as much at home outside Troy, on Ithaca and on Olympus as my young contemporaries were in the land of the leatherstockings. And what I absorbed so greedily, I also performed. I hopped through the room as Hermes with paper shoes that were wings. As Helios I balanced a shiny gold helmet of rays on my head. As Achilles I inexorably pursued my sister, who for better or worse was standing in for Hector, three times around the walls of Troy.[15]

Writing about childhood games, Thomas was looking at the earliest stages in his development as a writer. Though he may have been emphasizing the games that involved imaginative creativity, his instincts had been leading him to give himself an elementary education in the art of storytelling. Like all children, he was heroic in his imaginary activities, and there was no limit to the self-aggrandizement possible in fantasy. Deciding to be an eighteen-year-old prince called Karl, he could sustain the idea while having lessons, being taken for a walk, or listening to fairy tales. "I dressed with a certain genial grandeur and went around, proud and happy with the secret of my nobility."[16]

In another fantasy game he was a prince or the kaiser.

> Sitting in a little basket-carriage, in which my nurse carried me around over the garden paths or in the entrance hall, I for some reason pulled my mouth downwards as far as possible, so that my upper lip lengthened, and slowly blinked my eyes, which reddened and

filled with tears, partly because of the irritation and partly because of my inward excitement. I sat silently in the little carriage, impressed by my greatness and dignity, but my nurse was obliged to tell everyone who approached about the situation. "I'm taking the Kaiser for a walk here," she announced, pressing her flat hand authoritatively against her temple, and everyone bowed to me.[17]

He was lucky to be surrounded by so many people willing to join in these self-aggrandizing games, which implied his preeminence over his elder brother.

There must have been a time when nothing seemed more desirable than winning the love of the big brother, but Heinrich, deeply hurt by their mother's undisguised preference for his rival, became intolerant of parasitic affection and made Thomas the victim of his sharp tongue. The younger boy had to retreat into fantasies in which he was the only son. The boys had been sharing the same bedroom in the Breite Strasse house, and in the spring of 1883, when their father moved them into the bigger house that had been built for him, they were again given a room to share. The house at 52 Beckergrube had belonged to a merchant, Alexander Grammann, whose wife was Emma Marty, the senator's aunt. They were both dead, and their children had left Lübeck. The senator bought the house in 1881 for 30,000 marks, and spent about the same amount of money on demolishing it and erecting a new one with three floors.

The ground floor was for the use of the firm, with cashiers on one side and management offices on the other; the family's reception rooms were on the second floor. The living room had furniture with olive-green ribbed silk and a round table, with a gas lamp hanging from the ceiling above it. Julia Mann's Bechstein was in the drawing room, which had bay windows decorated with potted palms. The other side of the drawing room was used as a dining room, and there was an adjoining smoking room. The biggest room, which was used for balls, had four large windows overlooking the garden. The low, heavy sofas were burgundy red, matching the curtains, and there was an artificial coal fire in the grate.

The bedrooms were on the top floor, and the two boys were given no more territorial rights than they'd enjoyed previously. They had to play games and do their homework in their bedroom. Thomas's favorite room was the drawing room, where his mother entertained him and Heinrich with music, stories, and readings. It was there, too, that he had his music lessons, taught by one of his mother's admirers, the twenty-three-year-old conductor and composer Alexander von Fielitz, who was a frequent visitor. "I got my first impressions of modern music," Thomas wrote later, "from Fielitz's elegant and sensitive compositions."

He was eight when, at Fielitz's suggestion, he started taking violin lessons.

At about this time the senator bought a steamship, extending his interest in Baltic shipping. All over Lübeck, people raised their hats to him in the street, and many addressed him as "Your Excellency." The two boys were dressed in accordance with his status. Childhood pictures show them in suits and white collars, thick ties, and three-quarter-length boots. But for the sons of Senator Mann, "keeping up appearances" involved more than clothes. They weren't allowed to play with children below a certain level, and some boys they befriended at school were never invited to the house. Thomas's closest friend was one of these. His junior by a year, Otto Grautoff was the small, bespectacled son of a bookseller who went bankrupt and later hanged himself. "We were really intimate. We felt no embarrassment with each other intellectually. . . . We understood each other in every respect."[18]

This was not enough to make Otto acceptable as a visitor to the senator's house, but what drew him and Thomas together was an affinity based on a temperament that couldn't thrive in a school run by disciplinarian and nationalistic teachers. Both boys were highly intelligent, both resorted to mockery when forced onto the defensive, both were profoundly unhappy.

Decaying Family

IN 1882, Thomas was sent to a preparatory school run by Dr. Bussenius in Fleischhauerstrasse. It was known as the Novices' School because there were so many ecclesiastical novices among the rapidly changing staff of teachers. From the beginning, he says, he hated school and found he couldn't do what was required of him.

> I knew that the teachers were not my educators, but mediating officials, and that I had to look elsewhere for my educators, to wit in the world of spirit and poetry. Schooling coincides with childhood, and so it afforded plenty of space for happiness. But school did not contribute to it.[1]

This is confirmed by a classmate, Hermann Pagels, who said that from the outset Thomas was shy with the other boys. During break he didn't fool around, and in the classroom he seemed uninterested in what was going on. When teachers called on him for answers, he put on a thoughtful expression that gained him a reputation for playacting. Though he never exerted himself, some of his classmates believed he could have done better if he'd wanted to, and, so far as Pagels could remember, he never handed in an outstandingly bad piece of work. But instead of reaching the standard required to move on to a gymnasium at the end of his sixth year, he had to spend an extra year at the school.

He made friends with the red-haired young Count Hans Kaspar von Rantzau, who often came to the house in Beckergrube, where they did their homework together. The boy is portrayed in *Buddenbrooks* as Count Kai Mölln, who always appears in shabby clothes with buttons missing and a patch on the seat of his trousers. His narrow, elegant hands are always dirty, and his reddish blond hair uncombed.

In 1881, the year Thomas's sister Carla was born, their father bought the land in the Beckergrube for the new house. He was having trouble with his younger brother, Friedel, who was a liability as a partner. Heinrich encouraged him to start a business of his own in Hamburg, but to finance it Friedel kept drawing money out of the company.

*   *   *

BETWEEN 1882 AND 1891 the boys spent their summer holidays in the fashionable seaside resort of Travemünde, twelve miles north of Lübeck on the estuary of the Trave. The family regularly spent four weeks there between mid-July and mid-August, staying in one of the two Swiss-style chalets that belonged to the spa. The sand was white, there were cabins on the windy beach, and the boys could go on donkey rides. An old wooden bridge led to the bathing-station, and by jumping on it they made it swing from side to side. The old pump room was in Biedermeier style, and in *Buddenbrooks* Hanno spends holidays at Travemünde. Waking up on the first morning, blissfully aware that four indolent seaside weeks are stretching ahead of him, he hears a man raking gravel paths and the buzzing of a fly trapped between the windowpane and the blind. Hanno loves the beach, where he sits at twilight on the end of the breakwater, gazing out at the horizon and waving with his handkerchief to passing ships. Lulled by the sound of waves slapping softly against the stones, he feels at one with the space surrounding him. In the evening he has supper in his room, drinks his milk, and settles down on his little bed between the soft old linen sheets, knowing he'll soon fall asleep. The happy moments he recalls have more to do with solitary relaxation than playing with other children. Children, in any case, could have had only a limited amount of fun on a beach where formality was solemnly preserved. Seaside photographs taken at Travemünde before the turn of the century show men, women, and children trying to enjoy the sun by sitting or standing on the sand fully dressed and wearing hats. Many of the men carry umbrellas or sticks.

It was in Travemünde, at the age of eight, that Thomas had his first experience of orchestral music. In the pavilion the little conductor

> with flowing hair and a gipsylike manner used to conduct his orchestra. I crouched on the steps in the summery scent of the beech tree, insatiably sucking music—my first orchestral music—into my soul. . . .
> In this place, in Travemünde, the holiday paradise, where I have indubitably spent the happiest days of my life, the days and weeks of deep satisfaction—of wishing for nothing at all—were not surpassed or pushed into oblivion by anything in my later life.[2]

This is typical of his boyhood reminiscences in excluding the brother who was only four years older, but the estrangement may have been beneficial to the development of the younger boy's imagination and to his talent as a performer. According to Heinrich's schoolfriend Ludwig Ewers, who often came to the house, the senator, himself a good storyteller, used to call on his younger son to complete an anecdote or mimic someone they knew. Instinctively Thomas developed talents that helped to focus the adults' attention on him. His gift for mimicry made it easy for him to clown. At the bandstand he would pick up two sticks, and holding one against his chin as if it were a violin, he'd move the other as if it were a bow. Later he'd draw on this memory when describing the childhood that served as foundation for the training Felix Krull gave himself as a confidence trickster.

Thomas also enjoyed playing the violin. His teacher was Herr Winkelmann, first violin of the orchestra that von Fielitz conducted. For ten or eleven years the violin played a major role in the life of the young Thomas Mann. He often played sonatas—especially Beethoven's—with his mother, but he never had piano lessons.

The fair-haired Heinrich and the dark-haired Thomas both assumed that the physical dissimilarity between their parents corresponded to their temperamental dissimilarity. The warm blood of the south seemed to run in her veins. She loved playing the piano and singing; she could paint, draw, tell stories, and recite poetry. Her husband's success in business and local politics gave her the right to live happily in a dream-world of the senses. Unlike her, the senator had a strongly developed ethical sense. He had all the virtues of the good burgher. Though not a religious man, he was conscientious, diligent, energetic, and eager to improve the quality of life in the local community.

But he didn't have enough time for his elder son, who, needing more love than he was getting from either parent, gradually became alienated from both. His literary ambitions seem to date from a holiday he had in St. Petersburg at the age of thirteen with his aunt Olga and her husband.[3] He kept a diary, wrote poems, plays, and stories, and, judging from his septuagenarian drawings, started frequenting the brothels of Lübeck when he was seventeen, possibly in the company of his dissolute uncle Friedel. A drawing dated 1886 shows the fifteen-year-old Heinrich writing at a table while a woman leans over to press her ample bosom against his back; one dated 1888 shows him coming down a staircase in what looks like a brothel, holding the arm of a woman nude from the thighs upward, with two other bare-breasted women looking on. Letters to Ewers between March and October 1890 describe sexual experiences, and an 1891 letter recommends a Lübeck brothel opposite the Aegidienkirche.[4] It may have been because of sexual misdemeanors that Heinrich left school early: By the autumn of 1889 he was in Dresden, apprenticed to a bookseller.

Thomas, who should have started at the Katharineum when he was eleven, was finally admitted to the school in the spring of 1889, when he was nearly fourteen. Unlike Heinrich, he didn't rebel outwardly, but he must have been influenced by his brother's example. In the early summer of 1889, two of Heinrich's stories appeared anonymously in the *Lübecker Zeitung*.

Now expected to follow in their father's footsteps and take over the family firm, Thomas began to watch his parents as if a choice had to be made between two styles of living. His mother was happier and more self-indulgent, enjoying the pleasures of their privileged lifestyle, but his father had vastly more power. "I saw men go away from him with beating heart and burning eyes, while others seemed broken, quite desperate. For it sometimes happened that, together with my mother and sisters, I was made to witness such scenes, possibly because he wanted to inculcate in me the desire to be as successful in the world as he was, or possibly, I suspect, because he wanted an audience."[5]

Thomas made little effort to do well at the Katharineum. Having spent seven years, instead of the usual five, at preparatory school, he spent five years, instead of three, in the middle school. In the lower third class the form master was Dr. Hupe, who was a kindly, blond, bearded man with gold-rimmed spectacles, but the authoritarianism of some teachers had a political tinge to it. If the boys were rowdy, they were told not to behave like Social Democrats.[6] It was only after two years in Dr. Hupe's class that Thomas was promoted to the upper third. After a year there, he was moved up into the lower second, where he spent two years. In both classes the form-master was Herr Baethcke, who taught German, French, and Latin. Talking about Schiller's ballads, he said: "You are not only reading the best there is but the best you could possibly read."

Interested in artistic expression and aesthetic experiences, Thomas cared little for the rewards and incentives the school offered, or for the values of the other boys, which derived from the nationalism that had surged since Bismarck's success in uniting Germany. "The ideals of the victorious, united fatherland were those of a rather coarse masculinity; its youth spoke a jargon that was both brisk and slovenly; the vices condemned most categorically were softness and dandyism, the virtues that were most admired were prowess in drinking and smoking, physical strength and athletic accomplishment." The headmaster, Dr. Julius Schubring, had tried to imbue the school with the Prussian virtues. He's portrayed in *Buddenbrooks* as Dr. Wulicke: "The concepts of authority, duty, strength, service and career were given the highest value and the 'categorical imperative' of our philosopher Kant was the banner our headmaster Wulicke forbiddingly unfurled at every speechday. The school had become a state within the state, and the Prussian discipline of service prevailed so forcefully that not only the teachers but also the pupils saw themselves as officials." Thomas particularly hated the physical training. The red-bearded instructor had a pince-nez and a stentorian voice; the boys had to wear starched shirts with stiff collars.[7]

The school day, which began at eight, finished at one. Thomas, who had breakfast when he got up and took sandwiches to school with him, was given a second breakfast when he got home. He then left for his violin lesson, and came back in time for dinner, which was served at four. The senator went to the Exchange at midday, going on afterward to various business meetings, returning home by four.

Thomas was barely into his teens when he made his first attempts at writing. He says his first lyric poems were inspired by the blue-eyed blond friend who is depicted as Hans Hansen in the story "Tonio Kröger." The original of Hans was Armin Martens, the pretty, snub-nosed son of a merchant and sawmill owner who lived in Fleischhauerstrasse. Though Armin was a year younger than Thomas, the boys were classmates for two years in the lower second, and Thomas not only wrote poems but confessed his love to Armin, who didn't know how to react. At the end of his life Thomas admitted: "He was really my first love, and a more tender, more pleasurably painful love was never to be granted to me again. Something like this is unforgettable, even if seventy eventful years supervene. It may sound ridiculous, but I cherish the memory of this innocent passion like a treasure."[8]

In the story, Tonio is fourteen when he suffers because of Hans and learns that whoever loves more is at a disadvantage. Tonio loves Hans not only because of his beauty but because he seems to have all the enviable qualities Tonio lacks. An outstanding pupil, a fine horseman, a good gymnast, an excellent swimmer, he can win popularity among both classmates and adults, whereas Thomas, like Tonio, had become even more unpopular when his classmates found out that he wrote poems. He also enjoyed music and reading poetry—especially Schiller and Heinrich Heine—while most of the boys took no interest in the arts. Tonio "made no attempt to become like Hans Hansen. Indeed his wish to resemble him may not have been entirely serious." The story reflects Thomas's isolation, and apparently none of his teachers ever encouraged his literary inclinations.

Thomas's first extant letter, written on October 14, 1889, when he was fourteen, to Frieda Hartenstein, who had presumably been one of his nannies, is signed Th. Mann, Lyric-dramatic author. It mentions a play he has written, "Aischa," and he seems to be alluding to this when he asks her how she liked the farewell scene at the railway station. "It was moving, wasn't it?"[9]

In his first year at the Katharineum Thomas wrote "an anti-clerical play" under the title *Die Priester*. His grandmother, who was deeply religious, worried about his skepticism. Unlike Heinrich, who moved from prose to verse, Thomas started by writing verse. The first girl to inspire poems from him was one of his partners when, in the winter of 1889, dance classes were held in the ballroom of the Manns' house by Rudolf Knoll, balletmaster at a theater in Hamburg, the Deutsches Schauspielhaus. Thomas and his twelve-year-old sister Julia attended these classes, as did Armin Martens and his sister Ilse. Thomas fell hopelessly in love with a brown-haired girl who in the story became the blond Ingeborg Holm. Tonio has seen her hundreds of times without falling in love, but one evening, while she's talking to a friend, he notices her way of tossing her head to one side with a saucy laugh, and raising her hand to smooth her blond hair, letting her sleeve fall away from her elbow. There's a delicate hint of freckles across the bridge of her nose, and he's haunted by the warm timbre of her voice. Unlike Thomas, Tonio doesn't address poems to her, but she makes him think of a line from a Theodor Storm poem: "I long to sleep, to sleep, but you must dance."

On April 12, 1890, preparations were already under way for the celebration of the firm's centenary when the thirty-eight-year-old Julia gave birth to another son. He was given the names Karl Viktor. By now Heinrich was nineteen and Thomas nearly fifteen. The senator wasn't yet fifty, but his health and spirits were poor—partly because the strain of his life had begun to tell on him, and partly because of the trouble he was having in the family. His relationship with his wife was deteriorating, and his eldest son was becoming thoroughly alienated. Heinrich complained of "the stink of prosperity" in Lübeck,[10] and at the Dresden bookshop he was less deferential than his employer expected. At the same time, his father was still quarreling not only with his ne'er-do-well brother Friedel but also with his half-brothers and even with his mother, who withdrew capital from the company for her brother, Heinrich Marty. In February 1890 there was a scandal in the family when Guido Biermann, the husband of his niece Alice (daughter of his elder sister, Elisabeth), was charged with fraud and sentenced to two years in prison.[11] By now the senator's face was lined and his hair had thinned, but he was still elegant with his waxed mustache, his expensively tailored suits, his gold watch, and his diamond ring.

It hurt him deeply that neither of his two eldest sons would continue the family tradition by coming into the business, and it was like a public insult to the family and its past when Heinrich stayed stubbornly in Dresden instead of appearing at the centenary celebrations. Though everything else went well, it must have spoiled the senator's enjoyment of the day. Thomas's presence would have consoled him if only the boy were willing to fill the gap left by his errant brother. "Looking at my father," he wrote, "the man of the day, whom I admired and loved with nervous tenderness, I saw him as experienced in the ways of the world and representing a century of bourgeois excellence, and my heart was heavy. . . . I knew then that I could not be the successor of my father and my forefathers, at least not in the way that was being tacitly demanded of me, and that I would not lead the old firm into the future."[12] But the senator had to celebrate with his fellow citizens. His employees were being given a holiday, flags were being flown all over the city and in the harbor, where the company's boat, the *Alpha*, was moored at the quay below the Beckergrube. A deputation came to the house, bringing congratulations from the Chamber of Commerce, while the local paper, the *Lübeckische Blätter*, paid tribute to the "universal respect and esteem" enjoyed by the firm, which deserved "a long and prosperous future."[13]

At the end of 1890 the senator's mother died at the age of seventy-nine in her Mengstrasse house, which he decided to sell, and in the spring he quarreled with his eldest son. Having no real interest in becoming a bookseller, Heinrich wanted to give up his job in the Dresden shop. In April he moved to Berlin, where he started working as an unpaid assistant to the publisher Samuel Fischer on the magazine *Freie Bühne (Free Stage)*, the organ of the theater where the Naturalist plays of Henrik Ibsen and Gerhart Hauptmann were being staged.

The senator's health went on deteriorating. Stones had formed in his bladder, and surgery was necessary. Since there was no hospital in Lübeck with an operating theater, the surgeon arranged to operate on the senator in the ballroom of his house on July 2, 1891. On June 30, Heinrich Mann had altered the will he'd made two years earlier, before he knew that neither of his elder sons was prepared to take over the business, and the alterations were vindictive. If Julia had failed to give him the loyalty and support he expected of her, and if his eldest son had publicly insulted him by staying away from the firm's centenary celebrations, he could punish them posthumously, taking vengeance for all the family's shortcomings. Julia was to have no say in what happened to her husband's assets, and wasn't even to be given a free hand in bringing up her children. Two guardians were appointed—Consul Hermann Fehling and Krafft Tesdorpf—and she was obliged to make a quarterly report on the children's upbringing to Judge August Leverkühn.

The estate would be controlled by executors, who were instructed to liquidate the company, to sell the ship and all the stock, as well as the house and the furniture, within a year. It was almost as if the senator wanted to liquidate the family as well as the business. Julia and her five children would be forced into exile from both houses—the one in Mengstrasse, which was already on the market, had been like a second home. The will issued an explicit warning to her. She was to be firm with the five children and keep them dependent on her. If ever she felt tempted to waver, she should read *King Lear*. The next day he added a postscript which makes it even clearer that he had little confidence in her. The children, it said, dearly loved each other and her. "I build all my hopes on that. They will be justified if my wife does not show herself to be weak."

The estate was worth about 400,000 marks, and Julia was the only heir, but she had no control over the capital. Only the income was hers, and from it she had either to support the children or give them monthly allowances. The alterations to the will showed less faith in Heinrich than in his younger brother. The new guardians were asked to influence both sons in the direction of a "*practical* education" and to oppose Heinrich's "inclinations towards so-called literary activity." He's described as lacking "the prerequisites for solid, successful work in this direction," being prone to "dreamy self-indulgence and inconsiderateness towards other people, perhaps through lack of reflection." But Thomas is praised as having "a good disposition" and being "responsive to gentle admonition." The will predicts that he'll find his way to a practical vocation and be a support to his mother.[14]

The senator survived the operation, but it showed the growth to be cancerous. A few days later he was able to get up. Ilse Martens remembered seeing him walking slowly up and down the garden in a long coat. In September he had a last holiday in Travemünde. One of Heinrich's drawings shows his father hunched in a basket chair on the beach with a rug over his knees and a walking stick in his hand.

By the beginning of October it was clear that the fifty-one-year-old paterfamilias was dying. The street was covered in straw to mute the noise of traffic. There was a deathbed reconciliation between the father and his eldest son. Another of Heinrich's drawings shows him kneeling by the bed and kissing the dying man's hand. According to Viktor, their father predicted the date and time of his death in a feverish delusion: "He imagined himself to be at a sitting of the senate, addressing it about an important problem. Clearly and emphatically he ended with the words: 'Gentlemen, on the thirteenth at half past five I will line up for a tour of inspection.'"[15] When the vicar of the Marienkirche, on his knees beside the bed, was praying in a loud voice, the dying man gestured uneasily with his hand and said: "Amen." The interruption had no effect on the prayer, but Thomas felt certain his father had meant "Stop it."[16] According to Viktor, the dying man told his wife: "I would so much have liked to stay with you."[17]

He died on October 13, 1891. Flags were flown at half mast all over Lübeck, and so many people attended the funeral that Thomas could report "the whole town came to see him into his grave." But in none of his autobiographical statements—and they are legion—did he mention the contents of his father's will. There has been some speculation about whether, knowing the cancer would kill him, the senator took poison. In his autobiographical sketch, Thomas ascribes his father's death to blood poisoning,[18] and soon afterward Heinrich failed to dissuade his mother from reading a book on the subject. She was only forty when her husband died, and since the contents of the will couldn't be kept secret, her reputation was inevitably tarnished. Townspeople became less friendly and respectful. The senator had been popular, and they began to turn against a family willing to flout the opinion voiced in the *Lübeckische Blätter* that the firm which commanded "universal respect and esteem" should have "a long and prosperous future." The family's loss of local popularity was exacerbated by the clergyman who'd preached at the senator's funeral, Pastor Ranke, vicar of the Marienkirche: He spoke openly of "this decadent family."

Unable to stay in her home, and no longer wanting to live in the same part of the city, the young widow moved into a smaller house in Roeckstrasse, which is outside the old walls. She kept only the two girls and the baby with her. Heinrich went back to Berlin, and though the house was quite big enough to accommodate four children, the sixteen-year-old Thomas lived there only until Easter 1892, when he was sent to a boardinghouse that had recently been taken over by Dr. Hupe, who had been his form master. With her confidence shattered by the will in which her husband had almost publicly punished her, Julia no longer wanted the responsibility of bringing up her second son, though it was cruel to make him feel excluded from family life when he'd only just sustained the loss of his father and his luxurious home in Beckergrube.

Dr. Hupe, the man she chose to look after Thomas, was ill suited to the anxieties of running a boardinghouse, and he died after only six months. Thomas then moved to one run by another teacher, Herr Timpe. At night, when a light under the door showed that his young lodger was reading in bed, Timpe would shout: "Thomas, it's eleven o'clock."[19]

The teacher's fair-haired son, Willri, provoked another crisis of adolescent infatuation. Eight years later, Thomas not only remembered this passion but used it as a yardstick for measuring current feelings toward a young man liable to provoke "a revival of the Timpe period."[20] The one thing Thomas didn't hate about physical training was Willri's presence in the class.[21] But his mother moved him to another boardinghouse, and he saw less of the boy.

He later claimed to have happy memories of his last year in school, but the four moves must have been destabilizing, though he got on quite well with the other paying guests of his new landlord, Herr Hempel, sometimes "taking part with affable condescension in their premature drinking sprees."[22] He didn't do enough homework to stop him from going to the opera almost every night, and he became addicted to Wagner, whose music helped him to sublimate erotic passion.

In Easter 1893 he should have been promoted to the top class, together with Otto Grautoff, but both boys had to stay in the lower sixth, though the intention, it seems, was that they'd be awarded their *Abitur* at the end of the year. During May, together with some friends in the upper sixth, they started a literary magazine, *Der Frühlingssturm (Spring*

Storm), as a "monthly magazine for art, literature and philosophy." Their idea was to be revolutionary and moderate at the same time. In the first issue the editorial by Paul Thomas—he used his two Christian names as a pseudonym—declared: "Spring storm! Yes, like a spring storm in a dusty landscape, we want to assail with words and ideas the mass of intellectual dustiness and ignorance and narrow-mindedness, the overblown Philistinism that confronts us."

Ending with this manifesto, the editorial begins more like a short story or a prose poem:

> It was the middle of the day. After school. Between one and two o'clock. I had no wish to go home yet, and with my Caesar under my arm and an Italian cigarette between my lips, I strolled through the streets and out through the city gate. Where? First of all, that does not matter, and, secondly, I do not know, for I was not paying the least attention to where I was going. I wandered quite mindlessly— one is always in that state after coming out of school—into the uncertain, and all I know is that after a while I found myself on a bench, with a wide expanse of grass spreading out in front of it.

The vegetation looks parched, and the day is windless. Lübeck is like an airless grassy area that needs a spring storm.

Thomas used the same pseudonym for his other contributions to the magazine, which survived for only two issues. He wrote a story, some verse, a review of Ibsen's *The Master Builder*, a review of a musical comedy, and an article on Heine, defending him against a patronizing piece in the *Berliner Tageblatt*, which portrayed him as a good man and a Lutheran who'd made a deathbed decision to go back into the Jewish fold.

Called "Vision," the story was dedicated to Hermann Bahr, who, in 1891, had published *Die Überwindung des Naturalismus (The Defeat of Naturalism)*, an essay calling for Naturalism to be replaced by a "Literatur der Nerven." "Vision" follows in the wake of Bahr's attempts at a literary impressionism in which dream images, moods, sense impressions, colors, and mental states are enervatingly juxtaposed. Like the editorial, "Vision" starts with a cigarette. The smoke forms letters in the air until languor is dispelled by a salvo of febrile staccato sentences. "Frenzied activity in all the senses. Feverish, nervy, crazy. Each sound jangles." The ensuing vision is based on a picture that reemerges from oblivion— a girl's hand. A bubble rises in a glass of champagne, and when it bursts, the vision fades. The narrative ends in lame sentimentality: "As I lean back wearily, pain twitches up. But I know it now as clearly as then. You did love me. And that is why I can now weep."

Thomas's poems in *Der Frühlingssturm* were all derivative. The best of them, "Double Leavetaking" ("Zweimaliger Abschied"), was written in blank verse under the influence of Schiller and Theodor Storm. Afterward he submitted it to *Die Gesellschaft*, which had published Heinrich's first poem in November 1890. Thomas's appeared in the October 1893 issue.

WHEN JULIA MANN moved to Roeckstrasse, she may already have made up her mind not to stay in Lübeck much longer, and after a year in the new house she decided to settle in Munich, where she'd enjoyed herself during Bavarian holidays with her husband. In the spring of 1893 she took an eight-room flat with a terrace and a walled garden.

In contrast to the senator, who'd done his best to discourage Heinrich from pursuing a literary career, Julia wanted him to enjoy literary success. Feeling guilty about the rebellion which may have eroded his father's desire to live, Heinrich developed lung trouble, which climaxed in a hemorrhage. He was admitted to a clinic in Berlin. After visiting him there in February 1892, his mother arranged for him to be transferred first to Wiesbaden and later to Lausanne. Recovering, he wrote an autobiographical novel, *In einer Familie*, and when he failed to find a publisher for it, she paid for it to be privately printed.

Thomas claims that he wasn't unsettled by the uncertainty of his future, and resigned to the impossibility of making him cooperate, his teachers were putting him under less pressure. In *Buddenbrooks*, Hanno, though he hates his authoritarian teachers, thinks they're right to set a low value on him.

> I get so tired. I'd like to sleep and never wake up. I'd like to die, Kai. . . . No, I'm useless. I can't want anything. I'll never be famous. I'm afraid of it, just as if it would be unfair! Nothing will become of me, you can be sure of that. Recently after the confirmation class, Pastor Pringsheim told someone there's no hope for me—I come from a decaying family.[23]

Failing to get into the top class or to obtain his *Abitur*, Thomas could never be a full-time student at a university. This was an extraordinary setback for a boy of his intelligence, and he may have felt tempted to drop out of the school. But if he completed his *Sekunda* he'd have to do only a single year of "voluntary" service in the army instead of three. The whole of Germany was now subject to the Prussian system by which this partial exemption was granted to all educated young men who could pay for their own uniform, rations, and equipment, provided they'd achieved the required standard at school.

But when Thomas left the Katharineum on March 16, 1894, three months before his nineteenth birthday, at the end of the school year, it was under humiliating conditions. His last-minute promotion to the upper second had been a matter of form, and his grades—"partly satis-factory" and "barely satisfactory"—were only just adequate to qualify him for his *Abgangszeugnis* or school-leaving report. The word *good* ap-peared on the final report only as a description of his conduct, and even here the original "good" had been crossed out and replaced by "on the whole good." He was glad his school career was over, but he had lit-tle reason to feel glad otherwise. Leaving Lübeck to join the family in Munich, he knew he'd be in no hurry to return.

Looking back at the age of twenty-two on his school career, he was highly critical of the system: "In my view school is capable of destroy-ing everything good and tender that has been planted in the boy's soul at home. Whatever a young man has by way of taste, morality, good manners, courage, kindness, everything, all the culture he has, he owes to his home. But everything that school teaches him can be regarded as preparation for life: competitiveness, cringing, deception."[24] His subse-quent development goes a long way toward substantiating this stricture: No one could have guessed from his achievements at school that he had one of the best brains in Germany, and it took him a long time to discover the qualities that teachers could already have encouraged him to develop.

In Munich he got some comfort from reading and writing, but his depression is reflected in the 1903 story "Tonio Kröger," in which Tonio can give no answer when asked what he intends to do with his life.

> And he left his home town with its winding streets and its gabled roofs lashed by the damp wind, left the fountain and the walnut tree in the garden, the trusted companions of his youth, and he also left the sea, which he had loved so much, and he felt no pain. For he had grown big and clever, and he was full of contempt for the crude and inferior existence that had surrounded him for so long.

He surrenders himself passionately to "the power of intellect and words," which sharpens his perceptions, making him aware of how hu-man behavior is motivated. "But what he saw was this: absurdity and suffering, absurdity and suffering."[25]

Stormy Spring

MUNICH, THE BAVARIAN CAPITAL, is only about thirty miles from the Alps. Thomas arrived there during March 1894, a year before the first electric tramway was installed, and two years before a new review, *Jugend*, made the city into the center of the Jugendstil, the German equivalent of Art Nouveau. Founded in the ninth century near a Benedictine abbey, the original village identified itself by taking the name of the monks—*Muniche* in Old High German. Since then, the town's emblem has been the little monk who has become familiar through the beer Münchener Kindl. During the Thirty Years War the city was the principal bastion of German Catholicism. The vast Gothic Frauenkirche with its twin domes and the sixteenth-century Michaelskirche, a Jesuit sanctuary, survived, as did two of the great Gothic churches, the Heiliggeistkirche and the Petruskirche.

With its population of half a million, Munich was over ten times the size of Lübeck, and it made an enormous impact on the boy who'd never been outside his native city except for seaside holidays at Travemünde. His ambivalence about cultural life in Munich is evident from his irony in praising the large proportion of the population which takes an active interest in literature and the arts. Music floats out from open windows; people stroll about with literary periodicals in their pockets; artists roam the streets looking for inspiration; books about art are on sale together with high-quality reproductions, while shopkeepers can talk knowledgeably about Donatello.

> Art flourishes, art holds sway, art smilingly stretches its rose-entwined sceptre over the city. Prevalent everywhere is a respectful concern that it should thrive, and everyone works diligently in its service, wholeheartedly cultivating line, ornament, form, the senses, beauty. . . . Munich gleams. Above the festive squares and white colonnades, the neo-classical monuments and baroque churches, the leaping fountains, the palaces and the parks of this capital city was spread a shining heaven of blue silk, and the broad, bright vistas, tree-lined and well proportioned, lay in the sunny haze of a beautiful day in early June.

The chatter of birds and a mysterious jubilation floating out over all the alleyways. . . . And over the squares and terraces the leisurely and humorous life of the beautiful and easy-going city rolls along, floating and buzzing.[1]

The city could hardly have been more different from Lübeck, a town dominated by the Lutheran upper middle class. Munich was still predominantly an agricultural market town, virtually untouched by the industrialization that had altered the appearance of the Rhineland. Apart from a few breweries, the city had few large-scale industries. Even the richest of the brewers still seemed to belong to the lower middle class, and whereas most of the people in Lübeck had been there for generations, there was less stability in the population of Munich.

Julia Mann's apartment was in Rambergstrasse, a small street close to the Schwabing, the artistic and literary district then enjoying its heyday. The apartment contained a great many of the family belongings that had given the Lübeck houses their character. The green upholstered furniture had found its way into the living room, and in the dining room was a huge sideboard with feet like lions' paws. Frau Mann had brought the lofty bookcases, the heavy curtains, the oak furniture, the oil paintings of ancestors, and the stuffed Russian bear. Her grand piano stood in the drawing room, where she played on it nearly every day, and this was where she had her walnut desk. There were portraits of ancestors on the walls, but generally the domestic atmosphere was more relaxed than it had been in Lübeck. When Thomas arrived in March 1894, his mother was forty-two, his sister Julia was sixteen, Carla twelve, and Viktor just four. He called Thomas "Onkel Ommo," and Heinrich, who now wore a pointed beard, "Onkel Heini." Among the many painters and musicians who came to the flat was Alexander von Fielitz. In his book about the family, *Wir waren Fünf,* Viktor describes him as having a pointed beard and a long dangling mustache. Misleadingly, Viktor says he was a distant relation: This may be a way of covering up embarrassment over intimacy between von Fielitz and his mother.[2]

Though she was helping Heinrich in his literary career, she tried to discourage Thomas. She secured an unpaid job for him as an apprentice in a fire insurance bank, the Süddeutscher Feuer-Versicherungsbank, whose director had been a business friend of the senator's. Thomas started work on April 1, 1894, hoping the job would be temporary. "A strange episode. Among snuff-taking officials I copied out lists of securities and at the same time secretly wrote my first short story at my sloping desk."[3]

Following the senator's instructions, Krafft Tesdorpf kept the family permanently short of money, forcing the widow and her children to live on interest without ever touching the capital. Julia had an annual income of about 12,000 marks, paid in quarterly installments, while Thomas received about 600 marks each quarter. This was enough for him to live comfortably, though he paid over half of his income to his mother as a contribution toward his board and lodging. He could still afford to buy clothes that reinforced the impression made by his well-groomed mustache—that he was a well-to-do burgher.

When Heinrich, who'd been in Italy, spent May and June in Julia's new flat, he got on better than he ever had in Lübeck with his younger brother, who told Grautoff they were at last enjoying real "brotherly intimacy."[4] Returning to Munich at the end of the year, Heinrich wrote a couple of stories Thomas admired. "Evident in the two stories is how much he can achieve with his fine and discreetly elegant language and with his outstanding psychology."[5]

Written during June or July 1894, Thomas's story "Gefallen" reflects the way Heinrich had been talking to him about love affairs. It's about one between a medical student and an actress. The title plays on the double meaning of the German word, which is a verb in its own right, meaning "to please," and the past participle of the verb *fallen*, meaning to fall. As an adjective, *gefallen* can have connotations of moral abjection.

The main story is told within the framework of a conversation between four men about women. Laube denounces the double standard by which a woman is regarded as "fallen" as soon as she has had an affair, while a man is not. Another of the men, Dr. Selten, talks about an innocent medical student who falls in love with Irma, a beautiful young actress in a mid-German university city. A cynic, Rolling, encourages the student to send Irma a letter, visit her in her home, and become her lover. They're happy till he calls unexpectedly one morning to find her with an old man who paid to spend the night with her. After ejecting him, the student ironically covers her face with "mad, cruel, lashing kisses." "Perhaps he learnt from this kiss that for him, from now on, love would be hateful and his only lust would be for wild revenge."

The student is depicted as an innocent driven into cynicism by a single experience, which is presented as if it contains sufficient evidence to overturn Laube's argument about double standards. This problem isn't squarely confronted, and the action doesn't validate the doctor's conclusion: "If a woman gives in today out of love, she'll give in tomorrow for money." Unmistakably, this is a story about a love affair by a young man who has never had one. Instead of emulating his brother, who'd had plenty of sexual experiences by the age of nineteen, Thomas had recoiled in the opposite direction.

The story seems to have some of its roots in his conversations with Heinrich, some in his fantasies, and some in his reading. As Hermann Bahr argued in *Kritik der Moderne*, "Gefallen" represents a movement away from Zola's deterministic Naturalism toward what Thomas called the "learned and delicate psychology of Paul Bourget."[6] This phrase echoes Nietzsche's description of Bourget as a "delicate psychologist." *Physiologie de l'amour moderne* and his novels *Le Disciple* and *Mensonges* had been available in German since 1891–92, while his 1892 novel *Cosmopolis* had just appeared in a German translation. When he was twenty, Thomas, who could also read him in French, listed Bourget as one of his five favorite writers.[7] He'd absorbed many of the ideas stated in his *Essais de psychologie contemporaine. Cosmopolis* attacks the notion of decadence and dilettantism, proposing instead a kind of intellectual epicureanism. "It is not so much a doctrine as a mental attitude. Highly intelligent at the same time as being highly sensuous, it consistently inclines us toward the heterogeneous forms of life, encouraging us to lend ourselves to all these phenomena, without giving ourselves to any of them."[8] In an 1894 notebook Thomas copied out Bourget's attack on two fashionable attitudes. "The young man of 1889 is warned against two contemporary types: the cynical and willfully jovial man whose religion consists of a single word, pleasure, and the more refined intellectual epicurean, aristocratic in both nervous and intellectual reactions."[9]

Thomas's ambivalence toward decadence was rooted in that of Nietzsche, who took decadence as beginning in an aristocracy's loss of faith that society is there to serve it. Aristocratic himself in his nervous and intellectual reactions, and aware of his inability to rise above the decadence that was endemic, Nietzsche tried to take pleasure in it. It is only as aesthetic phenomena, he said, that existence and the world are permanently justified. He also viewed decadence, accurately, as a soil that could produce great art. Poets, he said, "avenge themselves in their work for an all-too-persistent memory, often bogged down and almost enamoured of the muck, becoming will-o'-the-wisps around the swamp, pretending to be stars. People call them idealists." Tortured by incurable disease, he converted his suffering into an asset, and described the intellectual heroes of the period—including himself—as "the bravest spirits who must be the conscience of the modern soul, and so must be its consciousness, concentrating all the disease, poison and danger that only modern times could have produced." Qualified by their misfortunes, they would be the poisonous antidote to public poison.

One of the reasons school had failed to release Thomas's creativity was that it failed to excite him in the way Nietzsche did. Heinrich had been passionate about Nietzsche without sharing his anti-feminism. Thomas did share it and disapproved of Heinrich's sexual adventures. Writing to Grautoff in the spring of 1895, he said he'd almost been making himself into an ascetic. "At my best moments I am in raptures about purely aesthetic sensuality, the sensuality of the spirit, for the spirit, the soul, the mind in general." Though he was keeping himself on a tight rein, he told Grautoff there was no need "to despise the lower half of the body (*Unterleib*) utterly. Though you *may* very well do that. In fact I myself do." He'd picked up the word *Unterleib* from Nietzsche: while making notes on *Zur Genealogie der Moral*, one of the sentences he copied out was "The lower half of the body is the reason man does not so easily mistake himself for a god."[10] But he acknowledged that the lower half contained "a whole lot of poetry. All you have to do is develop it nicely with intelligence and enthusiasm."[11] He didn't yet own any books by Nietzsche: The first he bought was volume four of *Morgenröthe*, and the date written with his name on the flyleaf was 1896. But Heinrich had told him about Nietzsche's books, and lent him heavily annotated copies.

There was an autoerotic element in his artistic sublimation of sexual energy, and it was connected with the fascination Wagner's music had held for him since 1892, when *Tannhäuser* and *Lohengrin* were staged in Lübeck at the Stadtheater. *Lohengrin* had brought him to an almost feverish pitch of emotional excitement, and in Munich he rarely missed a new production of a Wagner opera. The sensuality of Wagner's music seems to have had a catalytic effect on Thomas's youthful sexuality, at once intensifying the flow of desire and helping him to sublimate it dreamily into the kind of fantasy he could distill into fiction.

Thomas submitted "Gefallen" to Michael George Conrad for publication in the review *Gesellschaft*, which was based in Leipzig, and, appearing in the October issue, it made an impact which helped to liberate its young author from office work: His mother let him give up the job on condition that he prepare himself for a career in journalism by sitting in on relevant lectures at the university and the polytechnic. He neither wanted to be a journalist nor believed he had the right qualities, but he expressed misgivings only in his letters to Grautoff. During August 1894, after five months of working in the office, he left.

From the beginning of November Thomas attended courses on culture and world history, political economics, German mythology, foundations of aesthetics, and Shakespeare's tragedies. He spent four hours a week on each of the first three. His notebooks show how much harder he worked than he had at school. The lecturer Karl Haushofer aroused his interest by arguing that political economy was a moral science, involving discrimination between right and wrong ways of making money. Thomas was also attracted to *Hamlet*, readily empathizing with a prince who found it hard to embark on adult life so soon after his father's death. Enjoying the lectures on aesthetics, Thomas augmented his notes with his own reflections on whether things can be intrinsically beautiful or ugly.

On November 5 he received a congratulatory letter from the writer

Richard Dehmel, who'd seen "Gefallen" in *Gesellschaft* and read it aloud to his wife. He was on the editorial board of a new arts quarterly, *Pan*, and invited Thomas to submit stories, offering to pay him at the rate of 10 to 15 marks per printed page. Heinrich was full of envy. "Has anything like that happened to you?" he asked Ludwig Ewers. "Not to me either."[12] Dehmel was not the only reader to be impressed, and Thomas took refuge in comic exaggeration when he told Grautoff about his success: "Here in Munich at least, everybody is talking to me about the story. . . . When I go into the academic reading room, where I am a member, everyone steps aside out of awe. Which makes me feel right in my element. You know how childishly vain I am."[13] But the underlying self-confidence was genuine. When one of the editors at *Gesellschaft*, Ludwig Jakobsky, responded to a short story he'd submitted with the comment "What a gifted creature you are!" Thomas found his surprise naive.[14]

He promised to send Dehmel another story as soon as he could, but he was working on a fairy play, *The Old King (Der alte König)*. He finished the first act in August 1894, but never completed the play. In November he finished another story, "Der kleine Professor," and sent it to Dehmel, who found it unsuitable for *Pan*. It was subsequently rejected by *Gesellschaft*, though the poetry editor, Hans Merian, accepted one of his poems for the January 1895 issue.

In January he joined the Akademisch-dramatischer Verein, a dramatic society run by Baron Ernst von Wolzogen, who'd founded a literary café in Berlin. In Munich he was staging two plays a year, the casts consisting mainly of students and the audiences mainly local aristocrats. Thomas, who spoke up in favor of putting on Ibsen's 1885 play *The Wild Duck*, which had never been staged in Germany, was rewarded with the part of old Werle, and though the production was scheduled for June, rehearsals started in January. "They take a lot of time," Thomas wrote. "Yes, if that were all! But there's the active inactivity in cafés, theatres and concerts–I am always away from my writing desk for three quarters of the day and three quarters of the night."[15]

His story "Der kleine Professor" had been completed in November 1894, but by the beginning of March he'd written nothing else except poems. "For poems, of course, neither hard work nor tenacity is required," he told Grautoff. "I usually write them while dropping off to sleep. . . . My muse is not a giant maiden who lays about her angrily; she is a gentle girl who binds garlands and sings softly."[16]

He registered for lectures during the summer term, but gave up political economy and failed to work as hard as he had during the first term, though he had close friendships with neither men nor women. "I have so many, many acquaintances here," he wrote to Grautoff, "but I have only been really friendly, really intimate with one person, and that was you. By chance, perhaps. But elective affinity was also involved."[17] He was alluding to Goethe's 1809 novel *Die Wahlverwandschaften (Elective Affinities)*, which suggests that mutual attraction is governed by a chemical formula. Looking back analytically on their friendship, he tempered affection with irony, writing about Grautoff in the third person. Surrounded by strangers, Thomas suddenly understood how much there had been between them. Or so he said.

> We were really intimate. In each other's company we were ashamed of nothing, mentally–that was so pleasant and comfortable. We never dissembled except as a joke. We understood each other in every subtle detail. When I recall this or that intimate conversation with him, in which we communicated exclusively through the oddest sounds and words that nobody else would have understood, discussing the most delicate intimacies–my heart laughs inside my body, even now.[18]

But they were less intimate when together than when writing to each other.

THOMAS WAS DUTIFULLY DECADENT, but not consistently. He alternated between cultivating his lethargy and trying to discipline himself. He even started to study shorthand, as if still thinking of a career in journalism. "My mother wants me to have a secure, hard-working occupation, and possibly she is quite right. To avoid frittering one's life away, perhaps one needs a fixed position, a controlled activity. Until I started learning shorthand, I was always sleeping in till midday and sometimes till three in the afternoon. That is appalling, but who can fight his decadent nature without external support?"[19] The support often felt inadequate: On the day he wrote this letter, he canceled his shorthand lesson and breakfasted in the Central Café, where he sat, smoking and reading.

His uncertainty about decadence was inseparable from uncertainty about his family: If it was in decline, was he partly responsible or helplessly caught in an irreversible trend?

> My father was a businessman, practical, but with a penchant for art and extra-curricular interests. The eldest son (Heinrich) is already a creative writer but also a "man of letters" with a strongly *intellectual* talent, well read in criticism, philosophy, politics. Next comes the second son, (myself) who is only an artist, only a creative writer, only a man of moods, intellectually feeble, socially useless. It will be no wonder if the third, late-born son devotes himself to the vaguest of the arts, which is at the furthest remove from the intellect, depending

entirely on the nerves and the senses and not the brain—music. This is called degeneration. But I find it diabolically nice.[20]

It was too early to assess the potential of five-year-old Viktor, but this was the first formulation of an idea that would be seminal. Thomas's school career had left him feeling insecure: Perhaps his achievement would never do justice to his talent, possibly because his vital resources were inadequate. Putting himself in a family perspective and assuming that a vortex of decadence was dragging him downward, Thomas expected to achieve less than Heinrich, who'd written several impressive stories. Thomas especially admired "Das Wunderbare." "It is a work of art for which all words fail me."[21] Now almost twenty, Thomas considered himself "a bit more mature than I was when my diary might just as well have been that of a boyishly frivolous and falsely sentimental pseudo-Parisian."[22] But how much could he expect of himself? Would he ever be more than a dilettante?

Dilettantism was connected with degeneration, decadence, and nihilism. Thomas's next story, "Walter Weiler," was about a useless and decadent dilettante, modeled partly on Grautoff and partly on himself. Grautoff was told he had some resemblance to the "unfortunate dilettante and Eichendorff-like good-for-nothing."[23] Freiherr Joseph von Eichendorff, the son of a noble landed family whose fortunes were declining, had published *Aus dem Leben eines Taugenichts (From the Life of a Good-for-Nothing)* in 1823. Driven out by his father, the central character drifts from one lowly job to another, eventually marrying a porter's daughter.

Thomas enjoyed the final weeks of rehearsal for *The Wild Duck*, which opened on June 15 and had another performance on June 23. Wearing both Wolzogen's fur coat and his spectacles, Thomas played old Werle "as a superior man of the world (with a bit of the rogue in him). He reacts to his overstressed son by shrugging his shoulders."[24] Thomas's performance was mentioned favorably in the *Münchener Neueste Nachrichten*.

Between the two performances he took a short holiday in the Alps. Before leaving Munich he'd been staying out at night till four or four-thirty in the morning,[25] and, returning, he resumed the same indolent life: "lazy and self-indulgent, drinking wine with other people in the Cafe Luitpold, going to bed in the small hours and getting up at midday. For weeks I have not written a line of prose."[26]

But he was planning a new story about "two kinds of love," and in it he'd use some of his "current social sensations."[27] Hoping to get "Walter Weiler" published in *Pan*, he had sent it to Richard Dehmel in mid-May, saying some of his friends thought it better than "Gefallen," while others disagreed. What did Dehmel think? Dehmel's answer was that he'd picked it up, intending to read only the first page, but had been unable to stop reading. He would recommend it for publication in *Pan*, he promised, and when he came to Munich at the end of June, he met Thomas and said he could be Theodor Fontane's successor. (Fontane's best novel, *Effi Briest*, had just come out.) But the story, which never appeared in *Pan*, hasn't survived.

Grautoff, too, was writing stories, and, criticizing them, Thomas was partly talking to himself about his own work. In November 1894, after reading "Spring" ("Frühling"), he complained that the reader didn't get to know the hero, couldn't see him at all from outside and could catch only glimpses of him from inside. The reader "knows nothing about his character, his attitude, his origins, his development—knows only that an indefinite young man feels unhappy in his practical career."[28] In a later attempt to tutor Grautoff in the art of fiction, Thomas used "Gefallen" as an example: "At least something was going on, at least it contained something in the way of plot, movement, dialogue, shape, climax, conclusion—all of which did not exclude the possibility that mood and psychology were also present."[29]

What he knew about psychology had mostly been learned from Goethe and Nietzsche. Impressed by Wagner, Thomas had to confront Nietzsche's abrasive criticism of the man he'd formerly loved like a father. "In one word," Thomas wrote, "what I saw above all in Nietzsche was the man who conquers himself; with him I took nothing literally, I *believed* almost nothing, but this gave two levels to my passionate love for him, gave it depth."

Thomas was so short of money that, not wanting to pay more than the minimum postal rate, he rationed himself to writing short letters. "I am not a rich man; if I am decaying, it is not the result of wealth."[30] Heinrich invited Thomas to Italy. But Thomas said he was reluctant to leave Munich and Julia wanted him to stay, though she said she didn't have room for him in her flat. So Thomas set off on July 12 to meet his brother in Rome.[31]

Nothing but Rice

THOMAS'S FIRST IMPRESSIONS of Rome were distilled into his next story, which he called "The Will to Happiness" ("Der Wille zum Glück"), referring to both Nietzsche's title *The Will to Power* (*Der Wille zur Macht*) and to Schopenhauer's concept of the *Wille zum Leben*, the will to life—the unreasoning drive to go on living and have children. Thomas's narrator wanders through "this exceedingly rich museum of ancient art, this modern metropolis in the south, this city full of loud, brisk, hot, sensual life, where the sultry indolence of the orient is carried across by the warm wind."

But the brothers left almost immediately, traveling by mail coach to Palestrina, birthplace of the composer Giovanni Pierluigi da Palestrina, a small, ancient town in the hills, twenty miles south of Rome. Staying there in April, Heinrich had found a *pensione*, the Casa Bernardini, on the street now named the Via Thomas Mann, and had entered his name in the visitors' book as Enrico Mann; when Thomas signed it, he described himself as "poeta di Monaco," a poet from Munich.

The brothers were given such a spacious living room that they could both work in it. It had a stone floor, two windows, wicker chairs, and horsehair sofas. Heinrich sketched and Thomas wrote. He completed a short story, "Moonlight" ("Das Mondlicht"), but it hasn't survived. Their mother was sending them between 160 and 180 marks a month, and the exchange rate was in their favor.

Heinrich felt at ease in Italy, finding everything less formal and purposeful than in Lübeck. In the city, as in the country, everything seemed more spacious and relaxed, while the heat made the beauty of nature more luxuriant. Before returning to Germany in May 1894, he had been writing happily and fluently. Before going south again in January 1895, he'd agreed to edit a reactionary monthly, *Das Zwanzigste Jahrhundert* (*The Twentieth Century*). Concerning itself with social life, politics, science, art, and literature, it directed its "special attention to the anti-semitic tendencies of our time."[1] Heinrich's appointment was announced in the February 1895 issue, which said editorial principles would remain unchanged. Later, needing to explain why his normally progressive brother had adopted such reactionary ideas at the age of twenty-four, Thomas maintained that Heinrich had taken the job only because he needed money and more freedom of movement, but he edited the magazine from April 1895 until December 1896, and had little apparent difficulty in expressing a nationalistically anti-Semitic viewpoint. In an article on "Jüdischen Glaubens" ("Jewish Faith") he said

> they are not persecuted because of their religion, for to be persecuted because of a religion, one must first have one! And they are not persecuted as a people, for they do not deserve this honourable name. Rather, they are persecuted because they incarnate the negation of both nationality and faith. So they are persecuted less on their own account than as a concept, as a visible sign of everything that destroys and debases. They are in many respects our bad conscience. . . . Everyone guided by a national and social conscience will for that reason be an anti-semite; but the suppression of Judaism signifies for him not the object and goal of his strivings, but only the simplest of their sequels.[2]

This eight-page article by Heinrich was published in August 1895, when the brothers were in Italy together.

Heinrich commissioned Thomas to write for *Das Zwanzigste Jahrhundert*. His first piece was about Oskar Panizza, a writer who was being sued for blasphemy. Thomas sided with the prosecution, and the article was published in the August issue. Thomas went on to contribute six book reviews and another polemical article. He also helped Heinrich with the editorial work. His last piece appeared in November 1896. "I enjoy it," he said, "though it is all quite pointless."[3]

To congratulate their mother, whose forty-fourth birthday fell on August 14, and their sister Julia, who was going to be eighteen on August 23, and to ask, urgently, for money, the brothers jointly wrote a jokey letter in which Heinrich referred to Thomas as his older brother, and Thomas declared: "How spry you still are!"[4] They sent the letter to Starnberg, a fashionable lakeside town sixteen miles from Munich, where Julia had taken the three younger children for their summer holiday. She sent the boys the money they needed to continue traveling. They went on to Salerno and Anzio. They knew the bay of Salerno from a painting that had moved with the family from Beckergrube to Rambergstrasse, and while they were in Salerno, Thomas wrote a story, "Meeting" ("Begegnung"), but it is no longer extant.

At the end of September they went back to Rome, where Thomas stayed in Heinrich's lodgings at a former palazzo in the Via di Torre Argentina behind the Pantheon. Ruins from an ancient wall still stood in the courtyard. "I find Rome exciting," he wrote on October 5. "I will stay here as long as possible—probably till mid-November."[5] He enjoyed mass as performed by Cardinal Rampolla in San Pietro, and he preferred the classical art of the Vatican to the Renaissance paintings in the galleries. "The Last Judgement overwhelmed me as an apotheosis of my mood, which was thoroughly pessimistic, moralistic and anti-hedonistic."[6] He stayed in Rome only till the end of October.

At home he worked harder than before the holiday. In November he wrote "On the Psychology of Suffering" ("Zur Psychologie des Leidenden"), which hasn't survived, and, in December, "The Will to Happiness." The central character, Paolo Hofmann, is given the Italian version of Thomas's first name, and the same surname as E. T. A. Hoffmann, a writer he liked. Paolo is the first of many characters to be given an artistic sensitivity that derives (as Thomas assumed his own did) from a mixed ethnic and cultural heritage. Paolo's North German father had owned a plantation in South America and had married a woman born there. Paolo resembles her. Like his friend, the anonymous narrator, he feels alienated at school. Toward their mediocre teachers and classmates they feel "the *pathos of distance* which is familiar to everyone who secretly reads Heine at the age of fifteen." The phrase "pathos of distance" comes from Nietzsche's *Zur Genealogie der Moral (On the Genealogy of Morals)*. The story spans ten years of Paolo's life. He becomes a painter, while the narrator, not talented enough to keep pace, subsides into the role of biographer.

Paolo becomes puppyishly infatuated with a pretty girl at a dancing class, as Thomas had, and as Tonio Kröger will. Paolo's artistic sensitivity is associated with physical frailty, and when he has a heart attack, he believes he can choose whether or not to survive. What keeps him alive is his will to happiness, which he achieves in marriage with a beautiful young baroness "of at least partly Jewish extraction." She has dark hair, white skin, and soft hands. The characterization of her parents may have been influenced by Thomas's association with *Das Zwanzigste Jahrhundert*. When her father, the Freiherr von Stein, appears, the narrator asks: "Is he a Jew?" He's "an elegant, heavy-set gentleman, with a bald pate and a grey pointed beard"; his elevation to the rank of Freiherr may have involved the sacrifice of a few syllables from his surname. His wife is "just an ugly little Jewess in a grey tasteless dress. Big diamonds sparkled in her ears." Thomas hadn't actually met any families like this, but according to Paul Bourget's *Cosmopolis*, industrialization had enriched some middle-class families while helping to bankrupt others belonging to the landowning nobility. The novel features a bankrupt prince and a repulsive Jewish businessman with an almost saintly daughter. In Thomas's story the von Steins have no connection with the old nobility, but affluence and education have given them entrée to high society.

The ailing Paolo is attracted by Ada's healthy appearance. "The egoistic instinct of the sick man had kindled a desire for union with blooming health." But marriage consumes what's left of his strength, and he dies on the morning after the wedding night. At the funeral the bride's face wears the same expression the narrator had seen on the sick man— "the solemn and intense seriousness of triumph." Thomas has announced a theme that will continue to preoccupy him: opposition between ailing artist and healthy normality.

Thomas's tendency to withdraw explains why the phrase "pathos of distance" appealed to him. In December 1895 he tried to describe his own temperament when answering a questionnaire in the album of Ilse Martens, the younger sister of Armin Martens. Ilse had been at school with Julia Mann and had attended dancing classes with her and Thomas. She could sing and play the piano, but, aware of her good looks, refused to wear glasses even though she was so shortsighted that she couldn't see the stars without using opera glasses. In her album Thomas characterized himself as contemplative, Hamlet-like, and sicklied over with the pale cast of thought. His "idea of happiness" was "to live independently on terms of understanding with myself," while his idea of unhappiness was to be "without means and therefore dependent." He'd have preferred to be alive at the beginning of the century. His favorite writers were Heine, Goethe, Nietzsche, Paul Bourget, and Ernest Renan, while alongside Wagner and Richard Strauss, his favorite composers were Edvard Grieg, Fielitz, and Lasse, a composer of popular music sung by both Ilse and Thomas's mother. He felt "insuperable antipathy" toward "Kant, the categorical imperative and the philosophy of state officials." The qualities he most valued in women were "beauty and virtue," and in men intellect and spirituality.[7]

IN JANUARY 1896, Thomas was approached by Otto Erich Hartleben, who'd read "Walter Weiler" when he was on the editorial committee of *Pan*, and had since been appointed by the publisher Albert Langen as one of the editors of a new magazine, *Simplicissimus*. The son of a rich industrialist, Langen had failed as a painter and decided at the end of 1893 to found a publishing house. Before he came to Munich, Hartleben wrote to Thomas, addressing the letter to Herr Theodor Mann. Thomas therefore missed the opportunity of meeting him, but later, on hearing about *Simplicissimus*, he submitted his new story to Langen, who accepted it, and early in February Thomas called on him. "I must make sure he remains well disposed; later on he could publish a collection of my stories."[8]

Thomas was soon working on a new one he called "completely psychopathic."[9] This was "Little Herr Friedemann" ("Der kleine Herr Friedemann"). Like Paolo and the heroes of earlier stories, Herr Friedemann has a family background similar to Thomas's. His father, a consul, died before his son was born, while the family house is modeled partly on Frau Mann's house in Roeckstrasse and partly on Thomas's earlier homes in Breite Strasse and Beckergrube. Situated near the north gate of an old, scarcely middle-sized merchant city, the house is gray and gabled, with a walnut tree in the garden. Herr Friedemann's three spinsterish sisters derive from the three daughters of Thomas's uncle Johann Siegmund.

Herr Friedemann may have been modeled partly on a hunchbacked cousin in Lübeck, but the character is an alter ego. It's no accident that Thomas's work on this story coincided with his "late and violent outbreak of sexuality" and with his decision to burn all his diaries and some of his stories. "Why? Because they were burdensome to me," he told Grautoff,

> bulky, and besides . . . You think it is a pity? But where should I leave them if, for example, I went away for a long time?. . . It would be painful and awkward for me to have such a mass of secret—very secret—papers lying around. . . . You would be well advised to make a similar purge. It has done me a lot of good. One is literally liberated from the past to live light-heartedly and harmlessly in the present and the future.[10]

Thomas and Heinrich were returning to Italy in the autumn for a longer stay, and it might have been hard to keep the diaries hidden while he was away from Munich. The outbreak of sexuality had come when he had no partner, and the diaries possibly contained evidence of autoerotic practices. Toward the end of his life, he wrote that he never allowed himself to start masturbating without a full erection; the habit probably began at the time of his "late and violent outbreak of sexuality." The hatred of sexuality that made him think of dieting on rice was hatred both of Heinrich's sexuality and his own. Though more intense, perhaps, because the "outbreak" came so late, the self-disgust derived mainly from the usual frustration of an adolescent without a partner. But, as Howard Nemerov has suggested, he may have felt that art, "a kind of ideal equivalent or substitute for sexuality (perhaps at once the equivalent and the antithesis of masturbation?), is the possibility of escape from the world, a transcendence of it if not its redemption."[11]

Like his diaries, Thomas's fiction gave him a space in which he could talk to himself about the problem of having fulfilled only part of his potential. "All my previous writings now strike me as grey and boring compared to the strange things I have in my head."[12] Dissatisfaction with himself spilled over into a sense of disillusionment with Munich, which had seemed at first to be vibrant with artistic activity. "Is it not the *unliterary* city par excellence? Banal women and healthy men—God knows what a lot of contempt I load into the word 'healthy'!"[13] He was looking forward to going away with Heinrich, but on April 4, when the first issue of *Simplicissimus* appeared on the bookstalls, priced at 10 pfennigs, he felt excited, knowing his story would soon appear in it.

The publisher, Albert Langen, was only twenty-seven, and the weekly paper was slanted to a youthful outlook. Whereas *Das Zwanzigste Jahrhundert* had been reactionary, *Simplicissimus* became a platform for the dissidents and rebels who wanted to cock a snook at the bombast and traditionalism of Bismarckian Germany. The paper took its title from the 1668 novel *Der abenteuerliche Simplicissimus Teutsch* by Johann Jakob Christoffel von Grimmelshausen, who created the character Mother Courage and influenced Brecht's well-known play. The symbol of *Simplicissimus*, a red bulldog, scowled at passersby from posters on hoardings all over Munich. The dog was the work of Thomas Theodor Heine, the cartoonist who contributed most of the weekly's illustrations, helping to evolve its distinctively savage satirical tone. Langen was competing with Samuel Fischer, but while his review, the *Neue Deutsche Rundschau*, was decorously literary, *Simplicissimus* was deliberately brash and irreverent. Though it published unsatirical stories such as "The Will to Happiness," the cartoons, ballads, jokes, articles, and anecdotes hit out raucously at almost everything, and a lot of space on the large pages was taken up by advertisements for a variety of products, including motor cars and Kodak cameras. By associating himself with *Simplicissimus*, Thomas took a major step toward changing his image.

Describing the hunchback's sufferings, he uses many of the words and images he'd used in letters to Grautoff, detailing agonies and characteristics that had, since his school days, made him cultivate aloof isolation. Finding he can't join in games with classmates who seem embarrassed by his presence, the cripple falls back on solitary activities, such as reading, and he enjoys playing the violin—as Thomas did. Friedemann's isolation even has a Nietzschean dimension. At the age of sixteen, after his equilibrium had been unsettled by a classmate's blond sister, he finds her kissing another boy, and, knowing he stands no chance with her, decides to avoid emotional entanglements. "He had made a renunciation, a permanent renunciation."

This doesn't stop him from pursuing an Epicurean ideal in which the avoidance of pain is no less important than the quest for pleasure. Nietzsche, who had little success with women, said the search for happiness was nonsensical. The aim was to avoid suffering, though this ideal, he said, was decadent.[14] The hunchback's withdrawal from sexuality is presented in the perspective of Thomas's alienation, which rested partly on memories of not joining in games at school and on a sense of the artist's difference from other people, but also on the aestheticism and dilettantism that were fashionable. The story cantilevers out from personal problems toward a modish attitude. Its "keynote," said Thomas, was "yearning for a neutral Nirvana, peace and decline into sexuality."[15]

In this story Wagner's music makes its first appearance in Thomas's fiction. Herr von Rinnlingen, who has an upturned mustache, brings his beautiful wife to a performance of *Lohengrin* in the city theater, where odors of gas lamps and scent mix with the buzz of conversation. Friedemann's box is next to that of the Rinnlingens. The woman's dress is slightly décolleté, and, during the prelude, noticing how voluptuous her figure is, he stares at the pale blue veins running through the bare arm resting on the red plush balustrade. "The violins sang, the trombones blared, Telramund fell, jubilation prevailed in the orchestra, and little Herr Friedemann sat motionless, pale and silent, his head low between his shoulders, a forefinger in his mouth and the other hand at the lapel of his coat." Based on a medieval High German epic about chivalry and courtly life, the opera presents a heroic world: When Telramund charges the Queen of Brabant with fratricide and inchastity, the Knight of the Swan appears and, defending her honor, defeats her accuser.

After the intermission, when Friedemann's eyes meet Frau von Rinnlingen's, he has to look away. Before the end of the act, she drops her fan beside him, and they both stoop simultaneously. For a moment he catches the warm fragrance of her breast. His heart throbs so violently that he can't breathe, and he leaves the theater, "pursued by the clangour of the music." Because his sensuality, like Thomas's, has been intellectualized, he's defenseless against the simultaneous assault of the fragrant breast and the orgasmic music. Though they haven't spoken to each other, he's emotionally involved. Later, by sympathizing with him, speaking of her own unhappiness, she releases all the energy and yearning that have been repressed. He shudders, sobs, moans, experiencing love as if it were the onset of a disease. Quivering convulsively, he buries his face in her lap. She doesn't immediately push him away, but when she does, hatred for her is inseparable from self-disgust and an urgent craving for self-annihilation.

The other Wagnerian element in the story is the use of leitmotivs. Wagner had taken the idea, without acknowledgment, from Schubert's songs; Thomas copied Wagner. Friedemann is recurrently subject to twitching, which indicates both nervous tension and the life force that runs through him. The same words are used to describe the movements of water and of plants in the garden when stirred by the wind. Another leitmotiv is the red that features in descriptions of Frau von Rinnlingen, while the twitching assertiveness of the force in animal and vegetable life works like an orchestral accompaniment to the growth of passion.

The story fails to sustain the comedy of its parodistic opening, which pokes fun at Naturalism by attributing the deformity to the negligence of a drunken nurse. Thomas later liked to quote Goethe's definition of irony as "the grain of salt without which we couldn't enjoy the food set in front of us. Irony, it seems to me, is the spirit in art which draws a smile from the reader or listener, an intellectual smile, I might call it, while humour induces the laughter that wells up from the heart."[16] From the beginning, Thomas felt he could win the reader over by eliciting intellectual smiles, but the irony fails to inform the structure of the story.

COMING OF AGE on June 6, 1896, he became more solvent. Three hundred and nineteen marks were paid over to him once he'd rebuffed Krafft Tesdorpf's attempt to retain control over savings that had accumulated, and at the end of July, Thomas left for Vienna. He stayed at a fairly simple hotel, the Klomser, and returned to Munich early in August. In late August and early September "The Will to Happiness" was serialized in three issues of *Simplicissimus*, bringing Thomas his first fees for fiction. Calling at the office, he received the money in gold coins from the twenty-three-year-old journalist and short-story writer Jakob Wassermann, one of the magazine's editors.

Thomas had been working simultaneously on "Little Herr Friedemann" and another story, "Death" ("Der Tod"), which he finished by the end of September.[17] It's written in the form of sixteen diary entries spread over thirty-three autumnal days. Setting the action by the sea, he makes atmospheric and semisymbolic use of wind howling in the chimneys and waves whipped by storms that increase in violence as death approaches. Feeling alienated from the rest of humanity, the aristocratic diarist, a forty-year-old count, wants nothing banal to encroach on his last days. "The Will to Happiness" had suggested there might be an element of free will in dying; taking up this idea, the new story shows that Thomas was thinking about his father's death. After feverishly predicting the hour of his death, the senator had died on October 13. Believing that he's attracting death to him, and can control the speed of its approach, the count wants to die on October 12. When death approaches on the tenth, suggesting it would be as well to get things over, he dismisses it. It's as prosaic, he finds, as a dentist. Like Paolo Hofmann's love for his wife, the count's love for his young daughter, Asuncion, encourages him to keep death at bay: Only after the child has predeceased him is he willing to die.

In September, when *Simplicissimus* was running a competition for a short story with no sexual content, Thomas submitted "Death" and felt hopeful of winning the prize. But he was accused of plagiarizing Jakob Wassermann. Instead of defending himself, he withdrew the story, apologizing for the "dastardly" plagiarism he'd unwittingly committed, and—adding the vaguest of explanations—that Wassermann's influence was "generally in the European atmosphere."[18]

Thomas then made his second polemical contribution to *Das Zwanzigste Jahrhundert*–a critical article titled "Criticism and Creation" ("Kritik und Schaffen"). Alfred Kerr, the young drama critic for the Berlin daily paper *Der Tag*, had savaged a farce by Richard Skowronnek, who challenged him to a duel only to find that Kerr refused to fight. Reprimanding him for insulting Skowronnek, Thomas dismissed all critics as dilettantes, constantly on the lookout for an artistic personality into which they could vanish. "Georg Brandes, regarded as a private personality, is a wholly uninteresting liberal Jew, but in certain circumstances he may succeed in dissolving himself and being Heine or Mérimée or Tieck, or someone else."

ON OCTOBER 10, 1896, Thomas and Heinrich left Munich. Heinrich went to Rome and Thomas to Venice, where he stayed about three weeks. His impressions of the Piazza San Marco are recorded in a story he wrote the following month, "Disillusionment" ("Enttäuschung"):

> Only a few people were walking around, but on the broad square flags were flapping in a light sea-breeze in front of the wonderful colours and shapes which stood out with opulent and legendary contours and golden finery in enchanting clarity under a tender, pale blue sky. Directly in front of the main entrance a huge crowd of pigeons had gathered around a young girl who was scattering maize, while still more were swooping down from all sides.

The story is about an encounter with a disenchanted man. "I stepped outside of this famous life, full of greed for just one experience that would correspond to my yearnings." Convinced that nothing will measure up to them, he's waiting for death, expecting it to be no more than another disappointment.

Most of the story was written in Naples. Thomas left Venice on November 1, traveling by boat to Ancona, and going on to Rome, where "with a profound enthusiasm" he revisited the places that had impressed him most the previous year. But, impatient for unfamiliar territory, he stayed only two days. "After all the exhausting and harrowing experiences in which I steeped myself with deplorable energy in the hope of coming to terms with my youth, I had a strong instinct to distance myself as far as possible from German life, German concepts, German 'culture.'"

Leaving Heinrich in Rome, he went to Naples, expecting a combination of Roman and oriental ingredients. He wasn't disappointed. "The oriental note sounds here distinctly–though this almost excludes the aristocratic pride which is characteristic of Rome–that majestic city *par excellence*. Naples is more plebeian, but in a way that is naive, sweet, gracious and amusing. . . . For four days I have been studying the city's physiognomy; its sensual, sweet, southern beauty touches me more and more." He enjoyed watching the primitive and uninhibited activity in the streets. "This is no longer Europe. Finally I am outside Europe. On the far side of the bay, Vesuvius begins to glow as I write."

Elated though he was, he felt uncomfortable in his role as detached onlooker. "I observe everything, silently, reflectively and a little weary of solitude. My thoughts are gliding backwards and forwards like that light on the water which seems to be searching for something on the dark surface. I think about my sufferings, about the problem of my sufferings."[19] The pleasure to be had from writing letters (or stories) was distinct–if not entirely distinct–from the pleasure of leading his life. He had a central, if unheroic, role in a drama that was endlessly suspenseful, and if he was in full control of neither events nor feelings, he was in command of the way he presented both. He wrote this letter to Grautoff before dinner, afterward adding a long postscript. Drinking his coffee, he'd thrown lumps of sugar to ragged young beggars, had watched policemen breaking up a knife fight, had listened to pimps offering young girls and boys to anyone who could pay. "They do not know one is almost determined to eat nothing but rice just to be liberated from sexuality."

Rice was cheap, too. He might still win the *Simplicissimus* story competition, but the odds were against him, and he'd be glad to earn 50 marks with "Little Herr Friedemann," which he'd taken to Rome and sent to the *Neue Deutsche Rundschau*. Four years ago Heinrich's former employer, Samuel Fischer, had made *Freie Bühne* into a literary review, ensuring that it made an impact by publishing the work of well-known playwrights, including Ibsen, Hauptmann, and Björnson. Thomas, who stayed on in Naples till the end of November, received a letter from the editor, Oscar Bie, who not only praised and accepted the story but also asked him to send everything he'd written. Heinrich, though he'd worked for Fischer, was never invited to do this.

Rounding Up the Dogs

ON DECEMBER 3, 1896, Thomas returned to Rome, where Heinrich was staying in the Via di Torre Argentina. Instead of moving in with him, Thomas rented a room nearby in the Via del Pantheon, and the brothers spent a lot of time together. Besides writing and doing his editorial work, Heinrich was painting, while Thomas was reading Russian and Scandinavian novels, including work by Jonas Lie and Alexander Lange Kielland, who wrote family sagas in the modern manner. Partly because of Ibsen and partly because of ethnic affinity (or an illusion of it) Scandinavian literature was fashionable in Germany. The brothers usually ended the day together, eating at a small restaurant, Genzano, which did good chicken croquettes, before going on to a café, where they played billiards and drank punch.[1]

When Thomas asked himself whether he was happy, the answer was negative. "I am to a sufficient degree enervated, gloomy, exhausted."[2] But in another January letter he said his life in Rome was the most pleasant, relatively, that he could have. His one anxiety was that he might have to do military service when he returned to Munich, where his mother had given up her eight-room flat in Rambergstrasse, moving with the three younger children to an uncomfortable house, which Viktor describes as "not at all beautiful," in Gabelsbergerstrasse.

The fifteen-year-old Carla was to be confirmed on Palm Sunday, and her two elder brothers decided to collaborate on a literary present for her. Writing rhymes and drawing pictures in the cartoonish style of *Simplicissimus*, they prepared a hand-lettered and hand-colored *Picture Book for Good Children* (*Bilderbuch für artige Kinder*). Though they were obviously aiming to have it ready by Palm Sunday, it contains a reference to a story that Thomas didn't write until July 1897, "Luischen," giving the main character Heinrich's first name, Luiz, in a feminine form. The book may have been posted to Munich in time for the confirmation and posted back so that they could go on adding to it.

Bound in cardboard and linen, it had an ink drawing by Thomas on the cover—a head sticking out of a marshy pond and looking mournfully out at a moonlit landscape. He also contributed drawings that were stuck together until there were twenty-eight colored pictures and what looked like forty-eight engravings representing the whole of society "from the Kaiser to the Pope, from vulgar workmen to beggars in the street," while Heinrich's pictures were mostly caricatures. The brothers wrote sixteen poems and a lot of captions satirizing the morality being drummed into children. Ostensibly, the editor of the collection was a formidable senior teacher, Dr. Hugo Giese-Widerlich, who was portrayed with spectacles, a beard, and a malevolent expression. Schiller was parodied in a poem called "The Murderer Bittenfels Overpowered by Sunset," which was accompanied by an exaggeratedly pedantic commentary, and, referring to "Luischen," one of the pictures was described as coming "from the charming novella by the much loved poet Thomas Mann, which is heartily recommended to the German public." The picture of Mother Nature makes her fat, old, and obscene, with disheveled hair, piglike features, and a malicious grin. A drawing of Viktor showed him alone in a railway carriage: At the age of four he had suggested that his parents should take him on holiday to the Baltic; told to be quiet, he had tearfully threatened to go by himself.

For Thomas, though, the winter was unproductive, partly because he couldn't yet exercise his talent for satire and parody in his serious fiction. At the beginning of the new year, 1897, wanting to remind Fischer of his existence by sending a new story, he warned Grautoff that for a time he'd be obliged to work "instead of writing letters, which I much prefer."[3] Nine days later he complained about having to start his story all over again because the foundations were so flawed.[4] Toward the end of January he said the story had "been given a painstaking reworking under a new title and it is being reorganised (probably in the form of a diary)."[5] But it wasn't until April 5 that he announced the completion of this thirty-page story.

The new title, "The Clown" ("Der Bajazzo"), echoes the German title of Leoncavallo's opera *Pagliacci*. The main character is a performer in private life, good at entertaining people. He charms them with mimicry, clowning, and musicianship, but has no deep commitment to any of the arts. As in "Little Herr Friedemann," the self-disgust that runs through the narrative corresponds to Thomas's sense of inadequacy, but the act of telling the story was therapeutic, and he took pride in his ability to doctor himself:

An evil impulse cannot be uprooted with a single stroke . . . one only slips back more desperately into it. Slowly and carefully one must let the drive weaken and dry up; doing this it can be useful to employ all the clever intellectual tactics which are available and which suggest the instinct of self-preservation. Ultimately one is too much of an *homme de lettres* and psychologist not to take superior pleasure in such autotherapy. At your age there is no justification for any kind of despair. You have enough time, and the dogs of the subterranean depths will be rounded up by your striving for serenity and self-satisfaction.[6]

Taking a similar interest in autotherapy, the "Clown" buys a notebook intending to write his story down, and "at certain moments enjoy a kind of lofty detachment from myself, together with something like indifference."

In "Little Herr Friedemann" and "Walter Weiler," Thomas had been rounding up the dogs by writing in the third person about characters with experiences and impulses that corresponded to his; in "The Clown" he's confident enough to use the first person and start with a declaration of self-disgust. No straightforward equation can be drawn between the narrator's attitude to himself and the author's, but Thomas gives the character a background similar to his own. The "little old town" is obviously Lübeck, with its narrow angular streets and gabled houses, its Gothic churches and fountains. Like Paolo Hofmann (and Thomas), the anonymous clown grows up in a patrician house which has been inhabited by four generations of merchants. The mother plays the piano; the father is influential in public affairs. The boy thinks about the contrast between the dreamy, artistic woman and the powerful man of action. She encourages her son in his artistic pursuits, while the father, critical of the boy's failure at school, says he has no more than "a kind of Pagliaccio talent."

As a boy, he loves playing with his puppet theater, and shows some aptitude for the arts. He takes a dull job in a timber business, but, after his father's premature death, leaves his native town to travel in Italy. Sitting at a piano in a Palermo *pensione*, he impresses the other guests by improvising a music-drama in the Wagnerian style, and an old man says he should become an actor or a musician. He's twenty-five when he returns to Germany, settling in a big city, where he lives lazily, rising at ten and frittering the day away playing the piano, reading, sketching, smoking, writing letters, lunching in a restaurant, and going to a concert or a play in the evening. Sometimes he envies people who can't afford such a leisurely existence. Having no friends and belonging to no social circle, he feels isolated and frustrated. He could be happy, he believes, if only he were capable of artistic expression, but his unproductive brain is full of half-formed thoughts and fancies. He feels superior to the people in the streets, to shopkeepers and workers lacking in taste, but, while enjoying landscapes or works of art or food and drink, he knows his pleasures are those of the consumer. Thomas is translating into fiction an idea he'd formulated in a letter to Grautoff: "[T]he useless decadent soon gives up the notion of amounting to something in the world, finding it enough to let the world be something for him."[7]

The narrator's equilibrium, like Friedemann's, is upset by a woman who rebuffs his gauche advances, but he doesn't kill himself. More subtle in its handling of self-hatred, this story makes a verbal connection between self-disgust and self-destruction, but doesn't let the character act out the violence he contemplates. The narrative ends with a reiteration of the feeling expressed at the beginning. Even suicide, he decides, would be too heroic for a joker like him. "What will happen, I fear, is that I will go on living, eating, sleeping, doing a bit of this and a bit of that, gradually and dim-wittedly accustoming myself to being an 'unhappy and ridiculous figure.' "

Deriving from comic stories by Gogol and Dostoyevsky about outsiders forced to recognize their existence as superfluous, "The Clown" also owes something to contemporary ideas of decadence, but its energy comes from Thomas's depressive uncertainty about his talent. Successful though his stories have been, he hasn't proved himself. Like the clown, he's rarely had a job, and he doubts whether his intrinsic qualities justify the respect and privileges he's given. Like his character, Thomas knows some people float through life as if the gods loved them. "Children of light, with the radiance of the sun reflected in their eyes, they flirt their way through life in an effortless, confident and amiable way, while everyone surrounds them, admires them, flatters them, envies them, loves them, because even envy is incapable of hating them." Thomas would have liked to be one of these children of light; he had innate dignity, but he didn't know whether he would sustain it, or become a great artist.

By the spring of 1897, he was being spurred on by sibling rivalry. After *Simplicissimus* had accepted his story "Das gestohlene Dokument," Heinrich quickly wrote four more, and Albert Langen offered to publish the collection as a book in a series—Langens Kleine Bibliothek. This prodded Thomas into offering Fischer a collection of stories. Not wanting to submit "Gefallen," which he regarded as a piece of juvenilia, he offered "Little Herr Friedemann," "Death," "The Will to Happiness," "The Clown," and "Disillusionment." At the end of May, agreeing to publish the collection in a pocketbook series, Fischer offered only 150 marks, but promised a more generous fee if Herr Mann sent him a larger prose work, perhaps a novel.

This gave him the nudge he needed, but before settling down seriously to preparations for a novel, he wrote two more stories, "Tobias Mindernickel" and "Luischen." He was more cheerful by the end of April. The weather had improved, and he could go out into the Campagna to "sit down in an osteria and drink a wine that is sweet as Malvasier, or one sits down, one is so indolent, in front of a café on the

Corso, drinks a vermouth with seltzer water, smokes a cigarette, watches people and feels ready to persuade oneself for ten minutes that life is a thoroughly pretty thing."[8]

Written in Rome during July, "Luischen" was "a strange and ugly tale which corresponds to my present world and my view of humanity."[9] The central character, Jacobi, belongs with Friedemann, the anonymous clown, and Tobias Mindernickel in the gallery of unattractive men who are disgusting or self-disgusted or both. The clown says the only real unhappiness is dissatisfaction with oneself; there can be little doubt that Thomas was dissatisfied with himself. Even without his obesity, Jacobi would have been repulsive on account of his abjection. He never tires of disparaging himself and he talks sentimentally about his love for his beautiful wife, Amra, who's carrying on an affair with a pianist, Lautner, who also composes music. To humiliate her husband, Amra organizes a party at which she requires him to dress in a frock and perform a popular song, "Luischen," with new music composed by her lover. Lacking the willpower to resist, Jacobi complies, only to die in the middle of his performance from a cerebral hemorrhage, brought on by the realization of what has been going on between his wife and the pianist. None of the characters is sympathetic. Lautner is prostituting his creativity to satisfy the whim of a vindictive and superficial woman, while Jacobi, believing his love for her to be pure, debases it by consenting to the vulgar performance.

The brothers had been planning to spend another summer in Palestrina, and they'd have left Rome by the middle of July had Heinrich not fallen ill.[10] He recovered in time for them to travel before the end of the month, and "Tobias Mindernickel," which features a dog, was probably written in Palestrina, where Thomas acquired the first of the many dogs he owned. One day when he and Heinrich were out walking, they found a stray, short-haired puppy lying on a haystack. It was a hunting dog, black, with a white patch on its chest. Thomas adopted it, called it Titino, and enjoyed its dependence.

Tobias Mindernickel enjoys the dependence of the dog he adopts, and it's no accident that he's given the same initials as the author, though Tobias, who shamefully abuses the defenselessness of his dog, is just as grotesque as Friedemann. Tobias isn't deformed, but his appearance is so odd that children run after him in the street, jeering. He wears an old-fashioned top hat with a curved brim, an ancient frock coat, and shabby trousers which are too short. "He seems to be lacking in the natural, physical superiority with which the normal perceptive individual looks out at the world of appearances; he seems to feel worsted by every phenomenon, and his restless eyes sank to the floor at each confrontation with men or things." As in the story about the hunchback, Thomas could explore the contrast between the glamorous image he

presented to other people and the uncouth, unlovable self he believed–
or half-believed–to be concealed behind the facade.

The story is like a fictional gloss on the point Nietzsche made in
Menschliches, Allzumenschliches about weak people who have power to inflict pain, and then feel sorry for their victims. Mindernickel asserts
himself only once in dealing with the children who pursue him in the
street. This is when a boy hurts himself. Mindernickel consoles him,
bandaging his bleeding head with a handkerchief. After this, the man
buys a dog, and beats it when it disobeys him. When it's ailing, he feels
sorry for it and treats it well; but when it's full of health and high spirits, he treats it badly, finally killing it, only to be overcome by remorse.
Returning to the theme of sickness and health, Thomas dramatizes his
own anxiety that self-disgust could culminate in destructive violence.
The innocent dog is sacrificed to the man's self-hatred.

"For a long time I myself had really not believed I would be able to
find the courage for such an undertaking," Thomas wrote in August
when he started preparations for a novel. "But now I have rather suddenly discovered a subject, made a decision and think that I will soon,
after reflecting for a while, make a start on the writing. The novel will be
called *Abwärts* [*Downwards*]."[11] The subject he'd chosen was his decadent deviancy from family tradition. Here he was, in the sunny south, a
refugee from the materialism and hard work of the austere north. Para-
doxically, though, the decision to write *Downwards* marked a reversal of
the downward drift. Cultivating his decadence and contemplating no
literary activity more taxing than that involved in writing stories and
poems, Thomas had surrendered to the same inertia that had characterized his school days. Now he was committing himself to a sustained effort that would involve discipline. Instead of acting out his decadence,
he was going to analyze it.

THOUGH PREOCCUPIED with the ideas of decadence, decay, dilettantism, and nihilism, Thomas had come to grips with them only briefly and
impressionistically in stories. Autobiographical though these were in reflecting feelings about himself and facts about the family, he hadn't
tried to isolate the causes of the decadence in himself or in his family,
though he believed, as he'd indicated in his May 1895 letter to Grautoff
(see pages 111–12), that he could see his father, Heinrich, himself, and
Viktor as representative of four stages in the downward trend. As Heinrich suggests in a memoir, the hostile clergyman Pastor Ranke, who disparaged the Manns as "a decaying family," may unintentionally have
been helpful to Thomas, and the idea of charting a family's decline
may have roots in Hauptmann's play *Vor Sonnenuntergang*. But by writing
a novel, Thomas could go more analytically into the causes of the decay.

He hadn't wanted to embark on a detailed study of family history: He'd planned to write a short novel of about 250 pages, focusing on his own experiences. But as he accumulated more information about the past, he became more ambitious. Instead of concentrating on "the story of the sensitive latecomer, Hanno, and perhaps on Thomas Buddenbrooks," Hanno's father, he found that "everything I had been expecting to use as pre-history took on a very independent, very autonomous form, and my concern about the way the material was growing rather reminded me of Wagner's experience with *Der Ring*, which had grown from his idea for 'Siegfried's Death' into a cycle of four operas with *Leitmotifs* running through them."[12]

Making notes about his family while he was in Palestrina, Thomas was looking at an accumulation of memories and facts, all associated with Lübeck, in an environment that encouraged detachment. He learned something about the evolution of his own personality by comparing himself with Heinrich, who was more enamored of Mediterranean life. "What I myself was," wrote Thomas, "what I wanted and did not want—not the aesthetic posturing of the South but the ethics, the music and the humour of the North—what I felt about life and death: I discovered all that in the process of writing."[13]

His novel was going to be a fictional history of German burgherdom from its heyday to the *Gründerzeit*—the period between 1871 and 1873 when so many bogus companies were floated—and the fin de siècle, the decadence in which the fabric of art seemed to be rotting. What encouraged him to be ambitious was the absence of social realism from nineteenth-century German literature. By studying French, English, Russian, and Scandinavian fiction, he could import something new into the tradition. Of the novels currently influencing him, the most important was by two brothers—*Renée Mauperin* by Edmond and Jules de Goncourt. He read it again and again, "delighting in the lightness, sureness of touch and precision of this work, which is written in quite short chapters. My admiration for it was productive, making me think that after all something of this kind must be feasible."[14] At first it seemed like a good idea to emulate the brevity of their chapters: Most of his experience had been in writing stories, some of them—"Little Herr Friedemann," "The Clown," and "Death"—made up of extremely short sections. But as he gained confidence and the novel gained momentum, his chapters became longer.

He was also influenced by the Jonas Lie novel which had been translated into German under the title *Ein Mahlstrom* (*A Whirlpool*). It deals with the downfall of a rich, highly respected mercantile family, and the main character's sister, a generous, resilient woman deeply concerned about the welfare of the family, is called Antonie—the name Thomas used for the equally resilient and good-hearted character he based on his aunt.

Conflicting claims have been made about who contributed the name "Buddenbrooks." Heinrich may have suggested it when Thomas was "searching for some kind of Low German name that would therefore sound serious, or it may have been Ilse Martens, who had "distant relations, so-called relations, Buddenbrook. That sounds like something, Buddenbrook! And he immediately liked the name very much."[15] " 'Brook' obviously means stream, and 'Budden-brook suggests a low, flat moorland. I have always taken the name to be middle-class, in contrast to 'Buddenbrock.' "[16] But in Fontane's *Effi Briest*, which Thomas had read, as he mentioned in a February 1896 letter to Grautoff, Herr Buddenbrook is a nobleman.

He wrote to question his father's cousin, Consul Wilhelm Marty, about the atmosphere in Lübeck before Bismarck, the old and new currencies, the movements of grain prices, the street lighting in the old city, and possible causes for the decline of a grain company. Meticulously answering his questions on the stationery of the Portuguese vice consulate in Lübeck, Marty provided a lot of information that could easily be converted into fiction. In the area, he said, it was unusual for a firm of grain merchants to buy a crop before it was harvested, though this was done in Hesse, where many of the farmers had borrowed from Jewish moneylenders. On the other hand, the Manns had often made advance payments to farmers they knew to be reliable.[17]

Thomas was to base an important episode on this information. Wanting to help her friend Armgard von Schilling, whose husband, a landowner, is being harassed by creditors, Tony Buddenbrook asks her brother, Thomas, to contravene the company's normal practice and buy a crop which is still unharvested. At first he refuses, saying his great-grandfather, his grandfather, and his father had never done business that way. Thomas draws directly on Marty's letter when he makes Thomas Buddenbrook talk about deals of this kind in Hesse, where many of the landowners owe money to Jews. Eventually Thomas Buddenbrook acts against his better judgment, sustaining a heavy loss which contributes to the decline of the family firm.

Thomas also asked his nineteen-year-old sister Julia to collect as much information as she could about their aunt Elisabeth, her two marriages, and the fraud perpetrated by the husband of her daughter Alice. Julia's twenty-eight-page reply started by begging him to be careful with the facts she was sending: "It feels as if each word is an indiscretion." But the letter provides a lively minibiography of their aunt Elisabeth. When Thomas approached her directly, she answered all his questions, including some about her son-in-law. The character of Tony is closely modeled on Elisabeth, and at first Thomas plotted the novel to parallel events in her life: Tony's two marriages are as disastrous as their aunt's. But her second was so much like a reprise of her first that he deviated from her life story to introduce some variation. Elisabeth had two children from each marriage; Tony has only one in her first, a girl she calls Erika, and Thomas models this character on Alice, the daughter of Elisabeth's second husband. Erika, like Alice, married a swindler.

Thomas also enlisted his mother's help. As Viktor Mann testifies, Julia lent her son "all the old family papers, yellowing records, letters, souvenirs and deeds." She also gave him recipes from the family's cookery books. Soon, emulating the precision of the Goncourts, he compiled genealogies and chronological tables covering over a hundred years. The Buddenbrooks firm was founded in 1764—later he changed the date to 1768—and Hanno was to die in 1877. The family's decline was illustrated almost diagrammatically in a table showing the reduction of the company's capital; Thomas also noted down phrases that could work like leitmotivs.

If he'd written "The Clown" partly to warn himself against squandering his talent on a dilettante life, he benefited from the caveat. Though only twenty-two, and inexperienced as a novelist, he couldn't have started work on *Buddenbrooks* in a more businesslike way. He filled two notebooks with jottings, and over a hundred loose sheets of various sizes. The notes he made in Palestrina show he was in no danger of letting personalities get bogged down in family history. Under the heading "Psychological Points" four characters begin to emerge: Thomas, Christian, Tony, and Hanno. They don't exactly correspond to his father, Heinrich, himself, and Viktor as described in the letter to Grautoff about decadence in the family, but the plot is patterned on this formulation: a mercantile family sinks into decadence as its last man of action dies prematurely after marrying a woman with an artistic temperament, and his sons gravitate toward art and irresponsibility.

Thanks partly to research done by Julia, Tony Buddenbrook soon came alive for Thomas. Many of his notes were made on folded sheets of foolscap sent to him from Munich. One of these is headed "Anecdotes, Characteristics, Turns of Phrase" with the subheading "The Old Buttenbrooks." But instead of making notes on earlier generations, he collected ideas for characterizing Tony. She's to be "intelligent, industrious, but because of wild behaviour has to be moved several times from one school to another." She will be good-looking, with "a fine, narrow face, very delicate colouring, a rather prominent upper lip, greyish blue eyes, ash blond hair. The scene in front of the mirror when, because of the heat, she combs back her hair, which at that time was worn with a parting, flat over the ears, giving an old-fashioned appearance."

At the same time, Thomas was planning the structure. Among his preliminary notes is a provisional listing of fourteen chapter titles:

1. The new house. Banquet. Letter from Gotthold.
2. Birth of Maria. The Children.
3. Antonie's First Engagement. Christian to London.
4. Birth of Erika and Antonie's First Divorce.
5. Thomas and Maria Marry.
6. Antonie's Second Engagement. Christian at Home.
7. Antonie's Second Divorce.
8. Birth of Little Johann and Th's Election as Senator.
9. Erika Marries.
10. Celebration of the Company's Centenary.
11. Trial and Arrest of the Director.
12. Death of the Frau Consul. The House Is Sold.
13. Thomas Dies.
14. Little Johann Dies.

Without sticking rigidly to this scheme, Thomas preserved the basic structure.

He worked consistently hard to root the fiction solidly into fact. Planning Hanno's death from typhoid fever, he copied out an entry in an encyclopedia. "Typhoid fever begins with a general feeling of being unwell, mental depression, extreme exhaustion, loss of appetite . . ." Eventually, describing Hanno's final illness, he achieved the detached tone he wanted by incorporating the passage almost verbatim. This was one of his earliest experiments in what he later called collage: Reinforcing fiction with fact, he borrowed the language of the authority he was drawing on. Economizing in time and effort, he also enriched his fiction with a tone that suggested authenticity.

Meticulous in researching family history, he was equally careful to avoid inconsistency. Among the preliminary notes are separate pages headed "Age Tables," showing the ages of the characters year by year.

The first name to appear in the notes is that of Christian, Thomas's brother. Even if he hadn't been spending so much time with Heinrich during the early work on *Buddenbrooks*, Thomas would have wanted to focus on sibling relationships, a theme he hadn't treated in any of his stories, though he'd copied Heinrich and competed with him since childhood without any apparent chance of catching up with him. After publishing his first novel in 1894 and his first collection of stories in 1897, Heinrich felt more invigorated than Thomas did by Italy and, working on his second novel, *Im Schlaraffenland* (*In the Land of Cockaigne*), put on an impressive spurt at the end of the year. "I was overwhelmed by the awareness of talent," he wrote. "I hardly knew what I was doing. I was intending to make a pencil draft, but instead wrote almost the entire novel. My talent was born in Rome after three years of absorbing the city's influence."[18]

Thomas started more tentatively and progressed more slowly, but he now had a theme that pushed him into writing about fraternal tensions and drawing on the nervous energy he'd accumulated from years of making adjustments to the presence of a sibling. In *Buddenbrooks* it's the elder brother who's called Thomas, and though Christian Buddenbrook is modeled partly on their uncle Friedel, and is characterized, like the clown, as a charming scapegrace, talented but lacking in willpower, squabbles between the fictional brothers echo real ones. The younger Buddenbrook brother makes up his mind not to display any animosity, silently acknowledging the preeminence of Thomas, his superior capacity, earnestness, and respectability. Instead of being gratified, Thomas is irritated: Such casual acknowledgment of his superiority suggests that his brother sets no value on it. Christian complains that he has always felt cold in his brother's presence, always been frozen out with a stream of icy contempt. If he has no brotherly love to spare, he should at least have Christian love. When Thomas answers by blaming all of Christian's sufferings on his vices and his idleness, his younger brother accuses him of being self-righteous, ruthless, and egoistic, pushing aside everyone and everything that could disturb his equilibrium. "I have become what I am," answers Thomas, "because I did not want to become like you. If I have inwardly given you a wide berth, it was because I had to protect myself from you, because your being and your personality are a danger to me."[19] This is the elder Buddenbrook brother speaking to the younger, but the function of the passage was obviously to express the resentment of the younger Mann brother, who thought he had found his identity by going out of his way to bypass the example set by his elder sibling.

During the early stages of work, Thomas had made elaborate financial calculations, showing fluctuations in the capital possessed by the principal characters. Thomas Buddenbrook starts out with 157,000 talers. He makes 350,000 out of dowries on his two marriages and a trading profit of 42,000 before he has the big house built, spending 100,000 on it, but recouping 40,000 from selling the small house and 22,000 from selling a part of the big house. He then suffers a business loss of 80,000, which reduces his capital to 432,000. Most of these figures came from family accounts, and the figure of 432,000 corresponds roughly to the value of the estate when Johann Siegmund Mann, Corn Merchants, was liquidated.

Thomas set great store by the mathematics of novel-writing. In 1903–1904, when he was working on his abortive *The Loved Ones (Die Geliebten)*, one of the characters was going to be an inferior writer, "too weary, not energetic enough to concern himself with the many trivialities, mathematical and arithmetical, which are part of the process of making a book."[20] Scrupulous preparatory accountancy made it possible to write confidently about the Buddenbrook business. When Thomas takes it over, heavy financial losses have been sustained, partly because of the 1848 revolution and the subsequent war, but the accrued profits of fifteen years have amounted to 30,000 talers, and the assets add up to 700,000 marks. Thomas knows the family fortunes have taken a downward turn. "What is success?" he asks.

> A secret, indescribable strength, resourcefulness, preparedness . . . consciousness of being able to exert pressure on the movement of life around me by my very existence. . . . Belief in the willingness of life to put itself at my disposal . . . Happiness and success are in us. We must grip them: firmly and profoundly. As soon as, here inside us, something begins to let go, to slacken, to feel tired, then everything outside us will be free to resist, to rebel, to escape from our influence. . . . One thing comes after another, one failure after another, and that is the end. . . . I know that often the outward visible and tangible signs and symbols of happiness and success do not appear until in reality everything is already in decline.[21]

The young novelist understands how loss of stamina can conspire with adverse events. Gradually losing his grip on actuality, Thomas Buddenbrook regrets his extravagance on building the new house, and soon he's making economies, giving up summer holidays, simplifying family meals, reducing the size of the staff, changing his shirt only every other day.

This involves no loss of elegance. He prides himself on his appearance and takes trouble to look his best, but the strain has begun to tell on him.

> When he was alone, his face changed almost beyond recognition! Otherwise disciplined and forced into meek subservience to the incessant exertions of his willpower, the muscles of the mouth and the cheeks slackened into flabbiness. The appearance of alertness, concern, benevolence and energy, which had for a long time been sustained only artificially, fell from this face like a mask, to be replaced by a tortured weariness.[22]

The suggestion of performance is later made more explicit: "Really Thomas Buddenbrook's existence was no different from that of an actor, whose whole life has become a production, down to the most trivial and commonplace detail."[23]

But the decline of Thomas Buddenbrook isn't left at the level of personal history or family history. Later, when Thomas Mann accused himself of having slept through the deterioration of German burgherdom into the German bourgeoisie, he was being grossly unfair to himself. The deterioration couldn't have been chronicled better than it is in the eclipse of the Buddenbrooks' patrician culture by the vulgar materialism of their business rivals the Hagenstroms, who become increasingly powerful in the city as the Buddenbrooks lose their supremacy. Certainly, the pride of the Buddenbrooks had been underpinned by tough commercialism, but the Hagenstroms represent a vulgar economic opportunism that has nothing to do with tradition or morality or good taste. When the house in Mengstrasse is finally sold to them, the feeling is comparable to that achieved by Chekhov in *Three Sisters* as their sister-in-law, Natasha, gradually but irresistibly assumes command of the house. Something coarse and insensitive is taking over a home where life had been lived more stylishly, more scrupulously, and more generously.

6

Establishing Himself

AT THE END OF OCTOBER 1897, after three months at the Casa Bernardini, the brothers left for Rome, where they lived together in Heinrich's third-floor apartment on the Via di Torre Argentina. Settling down to draft the novel, Thomas knew he had to make his narrative entertaining. "Psychology alone," he reminded himself, "would infallibly be depressing; it is the coquetries of the literary forms of expression that keep us alert and perceptive." He managed to combine psychology with coquetry.

Being even farther away from Lübeck than he would have been in Munich, he depended on correspondence when he needed to check facts. In the first of the chapters that are set in Travemünde, he depicted the town in 1845–about forty years before he'd first seen it. Needing to know when the first trains ran between Lübeck and Travemünde, he wrote to ask Wilhelm Marty, who said the line had opened in 1882. But Thomas was wrong to let Tony Buddenbrook see basket chairs on the beach and the Swiss-type chalets. The chalets weren't built until 1861, and the chairs didn't appear until the end of the century.[1]

Thomas was no longer spending much time on letters, but it wasn't just the novel that kept him busy. While working on the fifteenth chapter he felt "intoxicated with material for stories."[2] Before the end of the year he'd seen advance copies of his first collection, *Little Herr Friedemann* (*Der kleine Herr Friedemann*), but the book wasn't due to be published till the beginning of February 1898.[3] In fact, publication was delayed until May.

Besides thinking about stories, he was thorough, almost creative, in his reading of Goethe. In his copy of Johann Peter Eckermann's *Gespräche mit Goethe* (*Conversations with Goethe*) he made careful pencil markings and notes like an index, telling himself where to find references to such topics as "the weaknesses of our century," "poets and patriotism," "nature and art," "truth, reality, deception and art," and "European degeneration."[4]

Working in Rome on the novel, he realized it had to be quite long. "There is something highly remarkable about this wilfulness of a work which should come into existence, which is really already there in its ideal form, and the author himself has the biggest surprises while letting it materialise. A first work, what a school of experience for a young artist—objective and subjective experience! . . . I found out what the epic element really is, for it carried me along in its wake."[5] What was coming into existence, he believed, was "a spiritual history of the German bourgeoisie," but his narrative style was, as he knew, conditioned by a host of cultural influences—"French naturalism and impressionism, the gigantic moralism of Tolstoy, Wagner's *Ring* with its *Leitmotifs*, Lower German and English humorous writing, Schopenhauer's philosophy of suffering, Henrik Ibsen's dramatic skepticism and symbolism." He'd been reading *Anna Karenina* and *War and Peace* with the idea of fortifying himself for the task at hand.

In April 1898, taking the dog Titino, he returned to Munich with a manuscript that had already "swollen beyond all expectations." He'd spent ten months on it, including the three months of preliminary work in Palestrina, but *Buddenbrooks* wouldn't be finished until July 1900.

He wasn't sorry to be leaving Italy. Looking back just over a year later on the eighteen months he'd spent there, he said that toward Italy he felt a mixture of indifference and contempt: "It is a long time since I deluded myself that I belonged there. . . . Velvety blue skies, hot wine and sweet sensuality . . . In short I do not like it. The whole *bellezza* makes me uneasy. And I cannot bear all those fearfully lively people down there with their dark animal glances. Those Romans have no conscience in their eyes."[6]

THE ITALIAN who interested him most was fanatically conscientious— Girolamo Savonarola, a fifteenth-century Florentine monk who'd been a forerunner of the Reformation. From a marginal annotation ("Savonarola!") in his copy of Nietzsche's *Zur Genealogie der Moral* we know Thomas had thought of the Florentine monk while reading the book. The third essay answers the question "What is the meaning of ascetic ideals?" and the eleventh section deals with "the ascetic priest," who takes pleasure in inflicting pain on himself and regards life as a wrong road on which one must finally walk back to the beginning, or as a mistake that can be corrected by action. His aim is to achieve mastery over life itself. Through self-mortification and self-flagellation, he uses force to block the sources of force. Since there have been ascetic priests in each society and each period of history, it must be in the interest of life that the type survives with its belief that triumph lies in the ultimate agony.

Savonarola appealed to the pessimistic, moralistic, antihedonistic side of Thomas. Having never visited Florence, he stopped there on his way home in April 1898. All his earliest jottings for his play *Fiorenza* are about Savonarola. One describes him as a natural sinner who sided against himself and got defeated in the conflict; another says he could understand why his torturers took sensual pleasure in their work.[7]

Back in Munich, Thomas stayed for a few days with his mother, who'd moved with the three younger children and some of the old furniture into a small apartment in Herzogstrasse, in the Schwabing. Julia was now an attractive woman of twenty-one, and in the recollection of Viktor (who was then eight) the seventeen-year-old Carla was highly flirtatious. But it was the forty-six-year-old widow who drew a lot of male admirers to the apartment—bankers, lawyers, painters, musicians, actors—though she dressed mainly in black. She seems to have oscillated between flirtatiousness and prudery. When a portrait of her made her dress more décolleté than she thought it ought to be, she blacked out some of her own flesh.

Though the house in Roeckstrasse hadn't been too small to accommodate Thomas, the apartment was. Renting furnished rooms in Theresienstrasse, he settled in before the end of April. At the beginning of May, wanting to make contact with his old school friend Korfiz Holm, who'd worked with him on *Der Frühlingsturm* and was now working for *Simplicissimus*, Thomas invited him to call, promising him a copy of *Little Herr Friedemann*. When Holm responded by suggesting he should call at the office, Thomas said that first he must buy some new clothes. "As soon as my appearance is reasonably bourgeois, I will have the honour of accepting."[8] In Palestrina and Rome, going all out to make headway with the novel, he had neglected his wardrobe, and one of his first appointments in Munich was with his tailor.

The rooms in Theresienstrasse were adequate, and he told Grautoff: "I am glad to have my library intact again, and within my four walls I feel comfortable with my dog, my pictures, my grand piano and my violin—in so far as a poor neurasthenic can feel comfortable."[9] He was still there in the middle of May,[10] but soon afterward moved to two small, expensive rooms on the first floor of a building in Barerstrasse. They'd have been more suitable, he thought, for a banker.[11]

Reviews of *Little Herr Friedemann* were generally favorable. Writing in *Gesellschaft*, the Austrian poet Richard Schaukal said: "Since the debut of D'Annunzio, Nansen and Chekhov, no book has made such an impression on me. This author must be noticed: he is an artist with purity, sureness of touch and expertise."

He worked hard at the novel throughout the summer. By October 25, he was expecting it to consist of five or six hundred printed pages and was hoping to finish it by the following year. He'd completed the first half, reaching the eighteen fifties, and gained enough confidence to lean less heavily on family history. Herr Permaneder, Tony's second husband, was inspired by a caricature in the November 1897 issue of

Simplicissimus. A fat and irascible Bavarian is sitting drunkenly at a table in a tavern while a waitress hurries to pour more beer for him. By the end of 1898 two thirds of the book were in existence: Thomas had written over two hundred pages in the eight months since he came back to Munich, and was planning to follow the novel with another collection of stories.[12]

After about six months in Barerstrasse, he moved again in November, settling into an apartment on the fourth floor of a house on Marktstrasse in the Schwabing, close to his mother's home. He could easily cycle over for meals. A craze for cycling had spread like an epidemic, and though Thomas had to carry his bicycle all the way up the stairs, he cycled almost everywhere he went, wearing a cape and galoshes when it was raining. In the morning, when he ended his stint of writing, he stood his bike on its saddle and cleaned it lovingly.[13] He even gave up his little dog, Titino, now that he cycled around Munich instead of walking. He'd thought of raising cash by selling Titino, but Viktor was so fond of the dog that Thomas gave it to him.

According to Viktor, the apartment in Marktstrasse was cheerful, with strawberry red chairs and white walls partially covered with avocado green burlap. The picture of Tolstoy on the green-topped work table was decorated with a laurel wreath, and the manuscript of *Buddenbrooks*—sheets of paper filled with precise, steep handwriting and neatly stacked—sat next to a heavy lamp.[14] Thomas kept his violin on the rented piano, and, showing his mother and Viktor around, he laughed when he pointed out the piece of burlap that stood in for the missing back of the wardrobe in the bedroom.

This strange piece of furniture, which belonged to his landlady, appears in the short story he wrote in the last week of November, "The Wardrobe" ("Der Kleiderschrank").[15] Like Paolo in "The Will to Happiness" and the count in "Death" ("Der Tod"), the central character, Albrecht van der Qualen, is suffering from a lethal illness. "Qualen" means pain or suffering. Traveling on the Berlin-Rome express, he wakes up when it stops at a medium-sized station and gets off as impulsively as he'd got on. The narrative is at pains to establish his indifference to time and place. He carries no watch and prefers not to know which day in the week it is or which month in the year. Though he has a ticket for Florence, he stays in this anonymous north German town that is modeled on Lübeck. The old gate with two massive towers is unmistakably the Holstentor, and he crosses a bridge with statues on the railings. The long wooden boat, ancient and disintegrating, and the man with a long pole look backward to Charon and the Styx, forward to the morbid gondolas in "Death in Venice" ("Der Tod in Venedig").

Walking along wet black pavement without knowing where he is, van der Qualen thinks no one has ever been more solitary or more detached. He has no obligations and no objective. Reaching the edge of the town, he finds a house where rooms are available on the third floor. The one he takes is low-ceilinged, with straw matting on the walls. The window is shrouded with muslin; in the bedroom three pink chairs stand out against the white walls like strawberries in whipped cream, while the wardrobe has a piece of burlap hanging where the back should be. During the night a beautiful naked girl appears in the wardrobe and offers to tell him a story. It has a sad ending, one of the lovers stabbing the other. She tells him sad stories every evening until she disappears, and when she returns, she tells no more stories. The implication is that masturbation fantasies inhabit the same corner of experience as the fantasies that give rise to literature. "The Wardrobe" ends not sadly but indecisively. We're left uncertain whether van der Qualen, after he woke up on the train, went back to sleep and dreamed everything else that happened.

For his apartment in the Marktstrasse, Thomas bought furniture in Munich shops and got some from his mother. The big mahogany bed was the one he'd been born in, and he lacquered the chairs pink. On his second visit, Viktor noticed the smell of smoke from cigars and Egyptian cigarettes. Having associated these with their father, he formed the impression that the senator's spirit had settled into the apartment.

In late October or early November 1898, Thomas gave up his freelance life, accepting a job on *Simplicissimus*. The review had been plunged into crisis after publishing a caricature of the kaiser, who'd made a voyage to Palestine, and a satirical poem by Frank Wedekind, who was writing under a pseudonym. Copies of the issue were seized by the police, and orders went out for the arrest of the publisher, the cartoonist, and the poet. Albert Langen escaped to Zurich, went on to Paris, and stayed in exile for five years. The cartoonist, Thomas Theodor Heine, was arrested, while Wedekind, who surrendered to the authorities, was imprisoned for about six months. Within a few weeks the circulation of *Simplicissimus* had rocketed from 15,000 to 85,000, but it had to survive without Langen, its chief cartoonist and one of its principal contributing editors. Meeting Thomas in the street, Korfiz Holm offered him 100 marks a month to work as reader and editorial assistant for both *Simplicissimus* and Langen's publishing house.

This involved him in several editorial jobs and in reading manuscripts. An 1899 letter complains about "stupid editorial work (you would not believe how time-taking this nonsense is!). I am left with only two poor hours a day to keep my novel bouncing further along in front of me, so I have to reject even the most pleasant distractions."[16] But, needing the money, he kept the job for two years. "I worked in the elegant offices in Schanckstrasse as reader and sub-editor. In fact I had to make a first selection of all the fiction manuscripts submitted to *Simplicissimus*, and then to obtain a final decision about my proposals from my superior, Dr. Geheeb, brother of the country school-teacher."[17] Geheeb was, necessarily, more selective than Thomas, who tended to be overgenerous. He had his own office but didn't have to stay in it all day: He could take work home with him. The writer Ludwig Thoma, who was now a colleague, remembered him as very shy and soft-spoken,[18] but in the evenings he often drank with other members of the staff—writers, editors, cartoonists—at the table in the Café Luitpold that was reserved for *Simplicissimus* or at the Odeon Bar in the Wittelsbacher Platz. Suddenly life was less solitary, and his social self-confidence increased. As Viktor remembers, Thomas took part in the *Fasching*, the carnival, wearing swallow-tails, buttoned patent-leather boots, white gloves, bow tie and high collar, and an opera hat over the mask that covered the whole of his face. It had the squint eyes, the low forehead, the snub nose, the thick gaping lips, the wild hair, and the horselike teeth of a young moron. Sometimes raising a gloved finger to scratch at the wide nostrils of the mask, Thomas threw himself into playing the idiot.

In June 1899 he moved again, settling in Feilitzchstrasse, near the English Garden. Again he chose a fourth-floor apartment. Though the job subsidized his freelance earnings, he didn't want to spend much on rent. One of his friends spoke derisively of his "paltry little room" in a house no better than a "poor folks' home."[19]

Through *Simplicissimus* Thomas made friends with the novelist and playwright Arthur Holitscher, who could accompany him on the piano in violin sonatas. When Holitscher finished his novel, *Der vergiftete Brunnen (The Poisoned Well)*, he submitted it to Langen, and Thomas championed it. It was published in 1900. Alternately confiding in Holitscher about his life and reading from *Buddenbrooks*, Thomas showed how memories of embarrassment were finding their outlet in irony. One day, according to Holitscher, he looked back after leaving Thomas's apartment to see his friend watching him through opera glasses,[20] but according to Katia Mann, this story is a fabrication. Holitscher served as the model for Detlev Spinell in Thomas's 1903 story "Tristan." Though Spinell is in his early thirties, his hair is graying. No beard grows on his round, white, puffy boyish face—only a few downy hairs. His nose is thick and fleshy, his upper lip arched and porous, his teeth large and carious. A malicious friend calls him "the putrefied infant." Though unsociable, he's roused to such transports of joy by anything beautiful that he's liable to fall on the neck of who-ever's with him.

Like Holitscher, the writer Kurt Martens was slightly older than Thomas. He came from a patrician family and had established himself as a spokesman for the decadent movement with his novel *Roman aus der Decadence* and his collection of stories, *Katastrophen*. He submitted a new story, "Der Geiger John Baring" ("The Fiddler John Baring"), to *Simplicissimus*, and it was Thomas who wrote the letter of acceptance, inviting him to send more work. When Martens, who'd read pieces by Thomas in *Die Gesellschaft*, invited him to pay a visit, "He actually came. Extremely modest, almost shy, but carrying himself well, a serious, slim young man stepped across my threshold. Clever, reflective, steeped in mild melancholy, his conversation enchanted me as nobody's ever had before."[21]

They often visited each other after this, and Martens introduced Thomas to a number of writers and artists, including the painter Alfred Kubin. Thomas let himself be persuaded to join the literary society which had been formed by Ernst von Wolzogen, a comic novelist who also ran a cabaret. Though five years were to elapse before Thomas and Martens addressed each other in the second person singular, a certain intimacy developed. Thomas played the violin to his new friend, and read from *Buddenbrooks*, while Martens, already believing in Thomas's future greatness, deferred to him as if he were the older man. Martens, who had a wife, a child, and a summer house outside Munich, tried to involve Thomas more fully in what he "smilingly called 'crude' life, not merely to have him at my side but because I thought his art and his not very broad horizons might benefit. But he always resisted, instinctively or obstinately. He became attached to nothing that did not emanate from himself."[22]

Planning a holiday at the end of August, Thomas decided to spend some time in Denmark, and, on his way there, to refresh his memories of Lübeck, which he hadn't seen for five and a half years. He was preparing to write the sequence in which Elisabeth Buddenbrook dies and the old house has to be sold, just as the Mengstrasse house had been sold after the death of his grandmother. Another reason for going northward was that he felt in need of an antidote to southern *bellezza*. While Heinrich believed Rome had made him into a novelist, Thomas felt himself to be a northerner. In the story "Tonio Kröger," which had roots in this journey though it wasn't written until 1902, Tonio visits Denmark. He spent his boyhood close to the frontier but has never crossed it, "though I always knew and loved Denmark. I probably get this northern proclivity from my father." He speaks affectionately about "the books that get written up there, so profound and pure and humorous," and about "the incomparable Scandinavian meals that can be digested only in a strong salty air."[23]

In Lübeck, instead of staying with any of his relations, Thomas booked a room at the Hotel Stadt Hamburg, but didn't make himself known to the proprietor, who had gone to school with his father.

Thomas didn't even contact Johann Marty, who'd been so helpful in providing information for the novel.

In "Tonio Kröger" the Mengstrasse house is conflated with his parents' home in the Beckergrube. Tonio's heart beats anxiously as he walks up the steep draughty street toward his former home. He takes a deep breath before going inside. He's half expecting a door to open and his father to emerge in his office coat, with a pen behind his ear. As if having a dream in which obstacles dissolve to let him advance unimpeded, Tonio hears his own footsteps on the square flagstones in the big entrance hall. The large cupboards and the carved chest that had once stood outside the kitchen have disappeared. Climbing the imposing staircase, he touches the solid old handrail, hoping to reestablish familiarity with it, but he's distracted by the sign "Public Library." Books have been installed in what used to be the breakfast room on the mezzanine floor. His grandmother and father had both died in the adjoining room, which is now full of bookshelves. A seedy-looking attendant sits at a desk in the room which had once been Tonio's. With a pang of grief he looks through the window at the old walnut tree in the garden, which is neglected and overgrown.

On his last day in Lübeck, Thomas wanted to leave the hotel after lunch and travel by steamer to Copenhagen before going on to Aalsgaard, a seaside resort near Elsinore. But he was delayed by policemen on the lookout for a confidence trickster who was also traveling from Munich to Denmark. They interrogated Thomas, who had trouble proving his identity. Son of a Lübeck senator but estranged from his native city, Tonio is questioned by a helmeted policeman in front of the hotel proprietor. Unable to produce any papers except the proofs of something he has written, Tonio can't prove he isn't the confidence trickster—a man of unknown parentage and no fixed address, wanted in Munich for fraud and other offenses. Tonio could have established his identity by revealing who his father was, but he's reluctant to do this. Besides, he feels partially in agreement with "these representatives of middle-class society": As an artist, he's a deviant from their norms, a criminal adventurer.

Like Thomas, Tonio goes on to Copenhagen. With a guidebook in his hand, he spends three days exploring the city, impressed by its resemblance to Lübeck. Many of the houses have ornamental pierced gables, and, striking him as familiar, the names by their front doors seem to contain a kind of reproach, a nostalgic reminder of something he has lost. After a few days he goes northward, as Thomas did, sailing up the coast of Zealand to Elsinore, and making the last part of his journey by coach. It takes him along a coast road to Aalsgaard, where the season is ending. Thomas spent five days at the Aalsgaard Badehotel from September 11. Tonio stays at a similar small hotel, white with green shutters and a wood-shingled tower. Surrounded by low-lying houses, it looks out across the sound toward the Swedish coast. He enjoys the noise of the surf and the desolate cries of crows. He feels lethargic and forgetful, as if floating disembodied above space and time, but sometimes he's stricken by grief. Thomas was reading Goncharov's *Oblomov*, which may have contributed to Tonio's sense of detachment.

While Thomas was at the hotel, a dance was held, and this gave him the idea for a sequence in the story (see page 175). He knew he was going to draw on his experiences in Aalsgaard: Grautoff was instructed not to lose the letter of September 9 which describes them.

KURT MARTENS was right to characterize Thomas as resistant to anything that emanated from outside himself. He was constantly on guard against new emotional commitments. With Martens he was in no danger, but his equilibrium was upset toward the end of 1899 after he met Paul and Carl Ehrenberg, sons of a Dresden painter and art historian. Paul was twenty-three and Carl two years younger. After losing their mother, the boys had partly been brought up by the Distels, distant relations of the Manns, and Thomas may have met the brothers through Hilde Distel, who was friendly with his sister Julia. An art student at the academy in Munich, the fair-haired, good-looking Paul reminded Thomas of both Armin Martens and Willri Timpe.

The Ehrenberg brothers were talented musicians, and music played a big role in their friendship with Thomas. They often came to his mother's apartment. According to Carl, "The evening mostly began there with music, then we read—in other words Tommy read from Tolstoy, Knut Hamsun or his own work. After that there was music again till late in the evening, and if our staying-power was remarkable, so was that of the Manns, who put up with these orgies of music. Piano trios and violin sonatas by Haydn, Beethoven, Schubert, Brahms, Grieg were played, and I contributed my 'Improvisations' for violin and piano, a piano trio and a few 'Intermezzi' for two violins and piano, so that we also had something to play without a piano."[24]

Thomas, who'd been neglecting his violin, was so eager to take part in this music-making that he resumed serious practice. By June he could tell Paul: "The violin now gives me a lot of pleasure, and that is unquestionably thanks to you. I practise a little every day and play regularly once a week with Ilse Martens, apart from the times when she comes to us in Herzogstrasse."[25]

Thomas and Paul often went together to Wagner operas—*Parsifal*, *Tristan*, *Götterdämmerung*—and Thomas encouraged Carl to play Wagnerian themes on the piano. He played music from *Tristan* while Paul painted a portrait of Thomas. The three of them met for meals and long bicycle rides. Unlike Thomas, Carl rarely cleaned his bike, and they called it the cow, because its nether parts were always filthy. Thomas, who rarely used the second person singular and rarely relaxed in mindless pursuits, called both brothers "*Du*" and joined in when they threw stones at empty bottles. He'd often go to what Paul called his "den," "where for most of the time he would see me only through a haze of tobacco smoke."[26] "Gently and tactfully," Thomas wrote, "they overcame my gravity, diffidence and irritability by accepting them frankly as concomitants of talents they respected."[27]

On March 6, Thomas sent a photograph of himself to Paul, inscribing it with a quotation from Joseph, Freiherr von Eichendorff:

> *When two people truly accept and complement each other,*
> *The happy work of the muses grows unobtrusively.*

Just as Tonio tries in vain to interest Hans Hansen in Schiller's *Don Carlos*, Thomas tried in vain to interest Paul in Nietzsche. But Paul succeeded in persuading Thomas to take more interest in the visual arts. In 1895, asked to name his favorite painters, he'd listed Polycletus (a Greek sculptor of the fifth century B.C.), Guido Leni, and Gustav Lembach, but now he began going to galleries. He hung a painting by Paul on the wall of his workroom, and when Paul was away from Munich, Thomas sent long letters describing exhibitions in local galleries as well as performances of Wagner operas. Thomas was ambivalent about the conductor Hermann Zimpe, who'd been appointed as court orchestral director in 1900. "In certain cases (*Tristan*) Fischer's *Germanic* gravity (Zimpe is obviously Jewish) is more sympathetic." In fact, Zimpe wasn't Jewish.

Friendship with Paul provided a strongly positive surge of feeling, but it coincided with the negative surge provoked by Schopenhauer's philosophy. Thomas had bought the second volume of *Die Welt als Wille und Vorstellung*, which is usually translated as *The World as Will and Representation*, though *Vorstellung* can also mean "performance." He'd bought it in the Brockhaus edition at a reduced price, and the pages had remained uncut for a long time, "but once I started to read, I read day and night in the way one reads only once in a lifetime." The impact, he said, could be compared with that of sexuality when he'd belatedly become aware of it at the age of twenty.[28] Seventeen years after reading Schopenhauer for the first time, he could still recall how he "lay stretched out all day on the oddly shaped chaise-longue or sofa," reading. "Solitary and undisciplined youth, longing for life and death—how it gulped down the liquid magic of this metaphysic, which is rooted in eroticism, recognising it as the spiritual source of Wagner's *Tristan* music!"

Schopenhauer starts with the assertion that the world as perceived is the creation of the perceiving mind. For Kant there had been two worlds: the world of phenomena or appearances, and the noumenal world, which is real—the world of the *Ding an sich* (thing in itself). Schopenhauer reinterprets the Kantian division of mind into the part that perceives and the part that thinks. Thinking is establishing relations between ideas, while nothing but the self can be known directly. Aware of our body as an object extended in space and time, we're in contact with a world of sensations and desires. For Schopenhauer the body is the phenomenal form of the will, while will is the noumenal form of the body. Will is identical with the inner world—the only world we know—and the single insight that, according to him, constitutes the whole of his philosophy is: "My body and my will are one." This made Thomas regard thinking as a physical process.

Kant, like Hegel, had written from a Christian standpoint; Schopenhauer was the first great German philosopher to deny that the universe had been created by a benevolent deity and that human behavior was motivated principally by rational intelligence. Anticipating Freud's account of the unconscious, he depicts the will as a blind man carrying the lame intellect on his back.

Wagner, who'd drafted the libretto of *Der Ring* before reading Schopenhauer, arrived at a new interpretation of his own text. Siegfried had been intended to represent the possibility of a future existence devoid of pain, while Wagner thought he'd instinctively "grasped the essence and meaning of the world in all its possible phases, and I had realised its nothingness."[29] After Schopenhauer made him intellectually aware of what he'd known intuitively, he displaced Siegfried from his central position in favor of Wotan, the god who longs for his own annihilation: "Whatever I love I have to abandon, those whom I woo I murder, deceitfully betray whoever trusts me . . . destroy what I have built . . . I want only one thing, the end. . . . What profoundly disgusts me I give you as your inheritance—the futile splendour of the divine."

For Wagner, Schopenhauer was the first philosopher who'd understood all the implications of Kant's philosophy. "His main idea, the final denial of the *will to life*, is frighteningly austere, but altogether salutory. When I remember the turbulence in my heart . . . I have found only one sedative which finally helps me to sleep during my restless nights: it is a sincere and profound longing for death, the total lack of sensation, complete non-existence, the disappearance of all dreams—the only ultimate salvation!"[30] In *Tristan und Isolde* he suggested that in death the lovers achieve the transcendent bliss of permanent oneness.

Thomas, while excited by Paul Ehrenberg, was also thinking about Schopenhauer.

And what a piece of luck that instead of having to keep the experience to myself, I had a beautiful opportunity to testify for it and express my thanks, having suitable poetic accommodation ready for it! Only two steps away from my sofa was the impossibly and impracticably proliferating manuscript . . . which had just reached the point where Thomas Buddenbrook was to meet his death. To the man who was triply related to me—as father, offspring and *Doppelgänger*—I gave the precious experience, letting him make the great discovery of his life just before it ended: I incorporated it into the story because it seemed to belong to him, the suffering man who had confronted life so bravely, the moralist and "militarist" of my heart, the latter-day, complicated citizen, nervously ill at ease in this sector of life, an aristocrat in a municipal democracy . . .[31]

But Thomas was partly misreading Schopenhauer, and, while preparing for death, the senator misreads him completely, finding comfort in what's not intended to be comforting. To the surprise of his staff, he's seen during office hours pacing up and down the garden with his hands behind his back. Sometimes he sits in a rocking chair inside the pavilion on the terrace, staring across the garden, knowing he must arrange everything before it's too late. From the bookcase in the smoking room he has taken out a big book, poorly printed on cheap paper, and inadequately bound. It pleases him to find that a philosophical mind can master the mocking thing called life. The senator has always concealed his sufferings, as if he hadn't been entitled to them, but now he sees they were justified.

Schopenhauer demonstrates that what he'd taken to be the best of all possible worlds was actually the worst. Without understanding all he reads, he finds his experience has unaccountably expanded. Overpowered and incapable of thought, he goes to bed early and for three hours sleeps more deeply than ever before. Waking abruptly, he feels almost as if he has fallen in love. The wall of night seems to part in front of him, revealing boundless light. He will live, he believes, because *it* will live, and the mistake which will be exposed by death is that this *it* is not himself. Death was such a profound joy that it could be apprehended only in moments of revelation like this one. Nothing was going to be lost, except his body—an odious encumbrance that had stopped him from being different and better. Death subsumes all separations, redeeming the prisoner from the need to stare out despairingly through the barred window of his personality. Pressing his face into the pillows, the senator weeps in transports of joy. Nothing begins or ends: There's only an infinite present, and he'll always have access to it through the power in him that loves life.

One of the wheels had come full circle. Thomas's idea of death had derived mainly from the experience of losing his father when he was sixteen. Writing and thinking about death and decadence in the nineties, he'd already absorbed some of Schopenhauer's ideas at second hand. No one had influenced him more than Wagner and Nietzsche, who'd both been profoundly influenced by Schopenhauer, and now, at the age of twenty-four, after reading *Die Welt als Wille und Vorstellung*, Thomas tried to put his father's death into a Schopenhauerian perspective. He couldn't have written *Buddenbrooks* if the senator had still been alive; if he hadn't revisited Lübeck and read Schopenhauer, he wouldn't have been able to make Thomas Buddenbrook's death so different from any previous death in German literature. In Theodor Fontane's last novel, *Der Stechlin*, which came out in 1899, after Thomas had started *Buddenbrooks*, the dying Dubslav von Stechlin sits in his armchair, looking out on his veranda and garden. With him are his former batman and a little girl, Agnes, who brings in snowdrops. The dying man comforts himself with the idea that an eternal law is fulfilling itself. Thomas Buddenbrook dies alone, without any comparable consolation. He tries to recover his faith in a personal God, tortures himself for days with anxiety about what happens to the soul after death. He even thinks of going to ask the pastor, but he doesn't, and on his way home from a visit to the dentist, he decides to stop at a bar for a brandy. Suddenly his brain feels as if it's being gripped and swung around in circles, more and more quickly, until it smashes against a stony center. Performing a half-turn, he collapses on the wet pavement with outstretched arms. A pool of blood begins to form as his hat rolls down the steep road. There's slush on his fur coat, and in their white kid gloves, his hands have fallen into a puddle. He lies there until some passersby turn him over.

Lust for Fame

THOMAS WAS TAKING NO INTEREST in politics. Like many young people of his generation, he believed the best things in life could be enjoyed separately—music, metaphysics, philosophy, ethics, and cultural idealism had nothing to do with politics. It was only later that he maintained: "[T]he German citizen was in error when he believed that one could be cultivated and unpolitical."

Progress on *Buddenbrooks* had been slowed down by the work for *Simplicissimus* and the need to spend time with colleagues and friends. The writing must also have been affected by the way he kept exposing the unfinished manuscript to reactions from other people. He gave readings from it not only to Ilse Martens and his sisters but—without putting on evening dress—to Holitscher and Martens. Their laughter and their obvious enjoyment of the fiction helped him to think of it as an entertainment, and he made changes on the basis of their reactions.

Since his school days, he'd been fascinated by the polarity between temperaments like his own and those of ordinary middle-class people with a talent for practicalities. The structure of his novel had been influenced by Nietzsche's analogy in *Götzendämmerung (Twilight of the Idols)* between a degenerate young man—effete, prematurely aged—and a degenerate people. It isn't viciousness and luxury that cause decadence: The growing need for strong stimulants is the result of physiological deterioration in the race, just as the young man's sickness is the consequence of hereditary exhaustion.[1] The decline of the Buddenbrook family is accelerated by Thomas's marriage to a woman whose children have inherited her predisposition to the arts. Just as Heinrich and Thomas were the first Manns who refused to become businessmen, Hanno is the first Buddenbrook who would have been unable, even if he had survived, to go into the business. But the Thomas who wrote the final chapters shortly before and after his twenty-fifth birthday no longer took the same view of solitude and the specialness of the artist as the twenty-one-year-old author of "Little Herr Friedemann." Working on the history of his own family, he'd arrived at a different perspective on the problem of the outsider. The twenty-one-year-old had been using fiction as therapy and learning to live with his sense of shame. But within four years he'd matured into a novelist who could look at Thomas Buddenbrook from Hanno's point of view and at Hanno from his father's. The boy

> saw not only the assured charm his father could exercise on every-one, he saw also—saw with curious, painful penetration—what a strain it was to do this. . . . To little Johann, putting in appearances, talking, behaving oneself, activity, discussion between human beings seemed less like a spontaneous, natural and half-unconscious way of han-dling interests one has in common with some people and not others, but as a kind of end in itself, consciously and artificially strenuous, demanding not a straightforward and simple involvement but a fear-fully complex and exhausting virtuosity. And at the thought that he too would be expected to appear in public and, exposed to the gaze of everyone, talk and gesticulate actively, Hanno shut his eyes with a shudder of apprehensive resistance.[2]

He is condemned to be an outsider, and there will be no reprieve. His father had been trying to make him more self-confident and practical. When food and drink give the boy pleasure, Thomas makes such re-marks as "You seem to enjoy the good things of life, my dear, so you had better become a good businessman and earn a lot of money. Would you like to do that?"[3]

When Hanno is eleven, his father blames his lack of assertiveness on the influence of the women in the household. From now on, Thomas decides, he'll play a greater part in his son's life, "to draw him over to his side and neutralise the feminine influences that had been dominant with masculine counter-pressures." Hanno must be toughened up till he can fulfill the family's expectations and occupy the place that will be waiting for him.[4]

The young novelist's ideas about the family's decadence and Hanno's lack of masculine willpower were related to guilt feelings about letting his father down, to the feelings of self-disgust that had filtered into his early stories, and to the weakness he felt when attracted to healthy fair-haired boys who seemed full of vitality. Before succumbing to the illness that will kill him, Hanno talks to Kai about his lack of faith in himself. Kai strikes him as being livelier and braver.

The magnetism of Wagner's music derived partly from its power of suggesting death, decline, isolation, and autoerotic indulgence. The magic fire music in the *Ring* and the *Liebestod* in *Tristan und Isolde* seemed to promise both a forbidden pleasure and a refinement incom-patible with life, while Thomas's prose was at its best when he made music seem life-threateningly dangerous. As Hanno succumbs to ty-phoid fever, he uses the last of his strength on improvising at the pi-ano. The theme is pitifully simple, a single resolution—one note melts yearningly and painfully into another. Developing the theme, he introduces syncopation and repetitions that suggest a shrieking soul tormented by knowledge it can't conceal. The curdled accumulation of present participles—"questioning, complaining, protesting, demanding," "crowding, swelling, wandering, vanishing," and "bursting, tinkling, foaming, purling"—is itself suggestive of frantic, greedy, thrusting pressure toward an ecstatic climax. The piano music is described as if a whole orchestra were involved in a strenuously daring foray into forbidden territory. Bursting beyond admonitory chords, the music launches a cacophonous assault on the impossible. Insistently, urgently, relentlessly, the prose thrusts its pounding way toward a climax that can't come until the musical spasms have reached the point at which release can be postponed no longer. The vulgar little theme seems to weep and shiver in tremolo as the last drop of sweetness is squeezed from it. The final arpeggio suggests weariness after excess, and Hanno, pale, with burning eyes and weak knees, has to rest on the chaise longue.

THOMAS COULDN'T HAVE invested so much time and energy in the novel without using the idea of greatness to spur himself on. At school he hadn't exerted himself because he hadn't been attracted by the rewards that were on offer, but the idea of fame excited him. Keeping his ambition secret, he was slightly ashamed of it, and in a poem he wrote on July 18, 1899, he tried to distance himself from his own lust for fame. His sleep is disturbed, he says in "Monolog," by dreams of a narrow laurel crown that will one day be placed on his brow

> *as a reward*
> *For something or other that I did well.*

The poem, which was published in *Die Gesellschaft*,[5] was a comic apology for his self-absorption, but he was shrewd enough to know it would also serve to advertise him as a writer of fiction.

With his flair for self-promotion, he knew it was dangerous to let too much time elapse between one story and the next. Writing to Martens about "Revenged" ("Gerächt"), which was to be published in *Simplicissimus*, he said: "It has little value . . . but until the novel is finished I must keep myself somehow or other in the public eye."[6] The joke conceals a genuine anxiety.

The main character, Anselm, is named after Anselmus in "Der goldene Topf" ("The Golden Pot"), E. T. A. Hoffmann's story about a young man who discovers his poetic vocation while copying out stories. Now that fairy-tale phenomena around him have begun to make sense, he feels able to marry the beautiful little "snake," Serpentina. Thomas's twenty-year-old Anselm, who tells his story in the first person, meets the unattractive Dunja Steegemann in a boardinghouse. She writes a column on books and music for an inferior newspaper, and he enjoys engaging her in the kind of intellectual conversation he often has with male friends. One night, after drinking a lot of wine, he tells her he finds her physically repulsive. Without seeming upset, she talks about a love affair she had. Her account of it induces physical desire which takes him by surprise, but when he propositions her, she rebuffs him.

In earlier stories Thomas had developed themes corresponding to his perversity, but he'd largely ignored this in the novel. For a young man of twenty-four he was exceptionally inexperienced and ill at ease with women. He felt threatened and intrigued, and though he could seem self-assured in stories such as this one, the only exploration was literary. As in "Gefallen," ignorance about female sexuality was being camouflaged with cynicism based partly on conversations with Heinrich and the determination to be different, partly on the self-hatred that arose from frustration and sexual guilt, and partly on uneasiness about his perception of differences between himself and other young men of his age. He didn't know whether to trust his feelings of inferiority or his conviction of being superior.

THE TWENTIETH CENTURY began badly for Thomas, with news that only 413 copies of *Little Herr Friedemann* had been sold. Fischer tried to soften the blow by adding in his letter that he was waiting in suspense for the novel.

In May 1900, Thomas wrote a Schopenhauerian story, "The Way to the Churchyard" ("Der Weg zum Friedhof"). Only eight pages long, it is bizarrely allegorical and heavily symbolical, contrasting fertile fields with gnarled branches of old beech trees, and establishing the grave as the goal of life. The central character, Lobgott Piepsam, is another of Thomas's solitary and grotesque old men. *Loben* is to praise, while *piepen*, the verb used of birds and mice, is to cheep or squeak. Increasingly isolated since he lost his wife, his children, and his job as a copyist, Piepsam has been depending on alcohol. The color of his nose proclaims his addiction. Wearing a top hat and black gloves, he's on his way to visit the graves of his family when a blond cyclist overtakes him, riding on a gravel path where no cycles are allowed. The cyclist "came along, like life, and rang his bell; but Piepsam did not move out of his way by a hair's breadth. He stood there and looked at life impassively."

The equation between the cyclist and life is made insistently in phrases such as " 'I don't know,' said Life." The cantankerous old man orders Life off the road, threatening to inform the authorities, and when Life defies him, Piepsam works himself up into an apoplectic rage, which kills him. The corpse is carried away as Life proceeds on its journey.

The recurrence of solitary old men in these stories reflects Thomas's isolation, which had increased since he left Lübeck in 1894 at the age of eighteen. Until he met Paul Ehrenberg toward the end of 1899, his only close friend had been Grautoff, who often came to Herzogstrasse. Viktor remembered him as having "broad shoulders which carried a mighty head with large features, while a premature formation of baldness increased the dimensions of his forehead to excess."[7] But, finding he had more fun with Paul, Thomas told him Grautoff was "overflowing with knowledge of art history," and that when they went to the Hoftheater together, Grautoff always wore a black dinner jacket and a red bow tie.

On June 6, 1900, Thomas celebrated his twenty-fifth birthday, but the euphoria was dispelled by the arrival of call-up papers. He had already been exempted twice from military service on medical grounds, but "their lordships of the Higher Reserve Commission" had finally classified him as "fit for all branches of the services. It follows that on 1 October, to the dismay of all the Fatherland's enemies, I shall be shouldering a rifle."[8]

Like Proust, who was equally ill-equipped for a military career, Thomas tried to believe army life would be beneficial. It might do him good to be shouted at by sergeants: Perhaps it would cure his excessive twitchiness. "If my civilian endeavours are delayed by a year, I am convinced that this year will add ten others to my life." Or possibly he'd get treated so roughly that he wouldn't be able to stand it. In which case he'd be useless as a soldier, and the authorities would be obliged to release him after a few weeks.[9]

On July 18, when he finished *Buddenbrooks*, he was expecting to spend at least three months on revisions. After all, he'd been only twenty-two when he started. "I see it coming that whole chapters at the beginning, which now seem to me repulsively stupid, will have to be reworked."[10] But rereading these chapters, he was satisfied, and on August 13, without even making a copy, he wrapped his bulky manuscript in brown paper, tied it with string, and burned himself badly with sealing wax before posting the parcel to Fischer in Berlin. Had it been lost in the post, more than three years of work would have been wasted. Marking the package "Manuscript," he insured it for 1,000 marks.

Samuel Fischer was in the Tyrol, but the letter Thomas enclosed was forwarded, and he replied promptly. He was looking forward to reading the novel, he said, and would be glad to meet the author in the interim. Thomas was invited either to join him and Arthur Holitscher for a few days in the Tyrol, or to meet Fischer in Munich at the end of the month. Nervous about making a bad impression, and thinking a brief meeting would be safer, Thomas opted for Munich, and they arranged to meet for dinner on August 29.

Reporting afterward to Grautoff, Thomas said the conversation couldn't have been more futile, and it would have been better if they hadn't met. "I will write to him in order to bring my literary personality back to the foreground of his imagination and make him a bit more forgetful about the physical and social aspects (which are always unavoidable). The murky problem is what is to become of my novel."[11]

A man of forty, Jewish, and Hungarian by origin, Fischer had started his working life as an assistant in a Viennese bookshop. He'd moved on to a Berlin bookshop and, at the age of twenty-seven, established himself as a publisher. He'd brought out books by Henrik Ibsen, Hugo von Hofmannsthal, Arthur Schnitzler, Gerhart Hauptmann, and Hermann Hesse. Fischer was subject to deep depression and, as Thomas later put it, "to a religiously coloured melancholia."[12] Thomas was impatient to be told his three years of hard work hadn't been wasted, but Fischer was in no position to give a verdict.

On September 1, before presenting himself at the infantry barracks, Thomas took care to dress elegantly. He was told to come back in two days for another medical examination, but he didn't go. Having been warned by Kurt Martens against the drill he'd have to do in the infantry, he preferred the idea of joining a cavalry regiment. "I have nothing against riding and shooting. I hope they still have spaces."[13] But they didn't, and there was no alternative to the infantry.

He liked the uniform, which was blue, with a red collar, silver braiding, shiny buttons, and a black swordbelt. He wore it on October 9 at the wedding of his twenty-three-year-old sister Julia. An affair she'd had with Armin Martens had caused such a scandal that he'd been obliged to leave Lübeck at the beginning of 1899. He'd gone to Africa, where he died. Julia had always been attracted to the bohemian life, and, answering the questions in Ilse Marten's album, she said the mistakes she forgave most readily were those that came from passion.[14] But in nineteenth-century Lübeck, passion was a luxury available to few men and fewer women. Julia had surrendered by agreeing to marry a thirty-eight-year-old Frankfurt banker, Josef Löhr, a doctor of law with an annual income of 30,000 marks. According to Katia Mann, he'd been hesitating between Julia and her mother, who at forty-nine was closer to his age than her daughter was. According to Viktor, his mother had asked Julia: "Child, do you really love him?" But he couldn't hear how his sister answered.[15]

Thomas approved of the marriage, but dedicated to Julia Book Three of *Buddenbrooks*, in which Tony, submitting to her parents and to what seems like commercial expediency, marries a man she doesn't love. Thomas has involved the reader's emotions in opposition to the match: We're disappointed when Tony overrides her own instincts, and not surprised when the marriage fails. But Thomas, who hadn't decided whether marriage should to be based on love, was looking at Julia's decision in a different perspective. To Paul Ehrenberg, who begged her not to marry Löhr, Thomas wrote: "Actually, was that very intelligent of you? One must not be too idealistic about these things. With every kind of respect for 'love,' one makes more headway without it. A prudence, incidentally, which to me personally is rather repulsive, but on this inferior planet, what can we do?"[16] Heinrich's attitude was less muddled: Disapproving of the match, he stayed in Italy, though he, as head of the family, should have given his sister away. Thomas did this at the white wedding which was followed by a glittering reception at the Hotel Vier Jahreszeiten.

Thomas made a good impression in his uniform, but he was to spend little time wearing it. He hated the discipline and discomfort of army life, the insistence on immaculate appearances, the obligation to salute officers, the constant shouting and drilling on the parade ground, the noise in the barracks, the squandering of precious time. Twelve years later he could recall "the sensation of being helplessly cut off from the civilised world, of a frightful, overpowering external pressure, and, connected with it, an extraordinarily heightened enjoyment of inner freedom, so, when I had to clean my rifle in the barracks (which I never learnt to do) I whistled something out of *Tristan*."[17]

A tendon in his right foot became severely inflamed, but he had to undergo a lot of pain before it was properly examined. He was sent to the sick bay in the barracks, and then transferred to the infirmary, "the unhealthiest and most disgusting place I have seen in my life."[18] He spent two weeks in bed there, wearing a dressing that neither eased the pain nor cured the inflammation.

Grautoff brought his mail every day, but there was no news from Fischer. Holitscher was going to Berlin, and Thomas asked him to press for a decision.[19] He came back with a letter, half typed and half handwritten. Fischer had read only half the novel, but had received a report on it from his reader, Moritz Heimann. If Thomas could cut the novel to about half its present length, Fischer suggested, he'd be willing, in principle, to publish it. "I do not believe that many people would muster the time and the concentration to accept a work of fiction as long as this. I know that I am making a monstrously unreasonable demand, and that for you this perhaps means rewriting the book completely, but as a publisher I cannot resolve the question in any other way." Perhaps the narrative had taken too much material into its compass, he said, and perhaps a greater concision would be advantageous. He was sorry to hear Herr Mann was in an infirmary and offered to send books that would help him pass the time.[20]

Replying promptly and courageously—in pencil—he refused to cut *Buddenbrooks*. The final stages of writing had been exhausting, and he felt incapable of reworking it. He was willing to accept deferred payment, and he was unconcerned about how many copies were sold. What mattered was to have the novel published intact. Besides, he had a lifetime of writing ahead of him: Fischer must either invest in his talent or reject it.[21]

The day after he wrote this letter to Heinrich about the letter he'd written to Fischer—it is no longer extant—Thomas was sent back from the infirmary to the sick bay at the barracks, and had to lie there, still in pain, knowing neither how Fischer would respond nor how long he'd be at the mercy of army doctors. "The life I have been compelled to lead for four or five weeks is ridiculous and revolting."[22]

In early November, after a week in the sick bay, he was again transferred to the infirmary.[23] Having been discharged, he soon found himself back in the sick bay, where he spent another week in bed. After this he submitted to a few days of drill, but then reported sick again, "partly because I really was, partly to make people think they ought to release me."[24] The junior medical officer in charge of his case was a captain who didn't hide his disgust at the foot he had to examine. Unless he lit a cigar, he said, he'd faint.[25]

After weeks of being shunted while in pain between sick bay and infirmary, Thomas decided to enlist the help of his mother, whose doctor, Hofrat May, was friendly with the chief medical officer, a major. Examining Thomas's right foot, the Hofrat felt sure they could secure his demobilization, and promised to intervene as soon as Thomas reported sick again. Confident of being free by the end of the year, he began to think of going back to Italy with Heinrich.[26] Hofrat May spoke to the major, who examined Thomas's foot and arranged for a print of it to be taken on carbon paper. While the captain was in the infirmary with Thomas, his cap on his head, the major came in, planting himself in front of the captain and staring at his cap until he snatched it off and stood to attention. The major then showed him a paper. The captain clicked his heels, and from that moment, knowing Thomas had connections, treated him more respectfully.[27]

In December, declared unfit to be in the infantry, he was given leave in anticipation of his discharge. Though he still had to report to the barracks at regular intervals, he could wear civilian clothes. He was liable to be recalled for service in the artillery, but after his experiences in the army, there was nothing he wanted less. Later he claimed that his determination to free himself had "assumed a deadly and irresistible character."[28]

Glad though he was to be free, he couldn't settle down to a steady routine of writing. He still didn't know what would happen to *Buddenbrooks*, and he felt envious of Heinrich, whose novel, *Im Schlaraffenland (In the Land of Cockaigne)*, was being favorably reviewed. The first edition, which consisted of two thousand copies, sold out within a fortnight of publication. "How well people are looking after you," Thomas wrote, "and how brightly your star is beginning to shine!"[29]

His own star began to shine when he gave the first of his public readings. He'd already found it was both enjoyable and helpful to read from work in progress, even when the audience was very small. In January 1901, when he accepted an invitation from the Akademisch-dramatischer Verein and read some of his stories, including "The Way to the Churchyard," he found he was giving a performance, impersonating the characters. He was encouraged by the presence of Georg Stollberg, the director from the Schauspielhaus, who was laughing appreciatively and applauding demonstratively. At the end, when Thomas bowed in his direction, he bowed back.[30]

Thomas went on seizing–and creating–opportunities to perform his work in public and in private, sometimes to a sizable group of friends, sometimes to a small family circle. In this way he got a regular diet of gratification and encouragement, continuing in adult life the games that had started when other people played along with his make-believe about being the kaiser, and when servants, together with members of the family, gathered to watch him and Heinrich play with their puppets. Forty-two years later he wrote: "I am at my best if I can give a performance; on such occasions I stand up surprisingly well, but at other times I am nothing much to boast about."[31]

We can form some impression of his readings from the account he gives in *Joseph in Egypt (Joseph in Ägypten)* of the way Joseph reads to Potiphar. The voice is measured and agreeable, the tone practiced and level. Joseph is fluent, precise, unaffected, moderately dramatic, and so familiar with his material that he can give the most intricate literary syntax a conversational ring.

Though Thomas had plenty of ideas for stories, he was making little headway with the play on Savonarola. Its provisional title was "The King of Florence" ("Der König von Florenz"). Besides studying Jakob Burckhardt's *Die Kultur der Renaissance in Italien*, Pasquale Villari's *Savonarola und seine Zeit*, and Giorgio Vasari's *Lives of the Most Eminent Painters and Architects*, Thomas wanted to do more research in Italy, but the beginning of the new year found him short of money. Without the *Simplicissimus* salary he was earning little, and his mother was deducting expenses of over 200 marks from his allowance for each quarter. Leaving rent and unpaid tailor's bills out of account, he'd have to survive for three months in Munich on 240 marks.[32] There was no prospect of leaving for Florence till the beginning of April, and though Heinrich hadn't intended to be in Italy then, Thomas urged him to prolong his stay for another month.

* * *

THOUGH HE'D KNOWN the Ehrenberg brothers since the autumn of 1899, it wasn't until late 1900 or early 1901 that Thomas entered what his diary describes as "that central emotional experience at twenty-five." Belatedly, his relationship with Paul had become intense, though they saw little of each other while Thomas was in the army and Paul was traveling from place to place. Uncertain how much time they'd have together, especially if he went to Italy, Thomas oscillated between elation and suicidal depression. In January he'd already put up with more than ten weeks of silence from Samuel Fischer when he attended a party given by Korfiz Holm, who made the point that Langen had nothing against novels in two volumes and would pay a generous advance. This prompted Thomas to demand a decision from Fischer, who replied on February 4, apologizing for the long delay and agreeing to publish the novel as it was, probably in three volumes. He also invited Thomas to send another volume of short stories.

He was elated, but his happiness depended more on Paul than on literary success. On February 13 he wrote:

> When spring comes, I shall have behind me a winter that inwardly was infernally turbulent. . . . But they have proved one thing for me, these very unliterary, very simple and lively experiences: namely that there is still something honest, warm and good in me, and not just "irony," something which has not been devastated, over-refined and eaten away by that accursed literature. . . . The last and best thing it taught me is this: how to reach through death towards its antithesis, *life*. I dread the day, and it will soon come, when I shall be shut up again in isolation with it, and I am afraid that the egoistic devastation and over-refinement will then make rapid progress.

This letter to Heinrich reflects his anxiety that by giving in to the ironic attitude he found comfortable, he was cramping his capacity for enjoying life. Up to this point he hasn't even mentioned the good news about *Buddenbrooks*, and when he does, he goes on triumphantly, though ironically: "I shall have a photograph taken, my right hand in the waistcoat of my dinner-jacket and my left resting on the three volumes; then I can really die happily.—No, it really is good that the book is going to see the light. It contains so much that is personally revealing that it will really give me a profile at last, especially for our esteemed colleagues."[33] Like many writers—Kafka is another example—Thomas assumed that the more personal information his readers absorbed, the more likely they were to sympathize. What he wanted most was to be loved, not for his literary skill or his talent as an entertainer but for his human qualities. What he wanted least was to be condemned as cold, detached, unloving, unlovable.

If Fischer had refused to accept his terms, Thomas would have rejected Fischer's, and his subsequent career might have been quite different. To some extent he'd been living the decadent pattern he had described in *Buddenbrooks*: His portrait of Hanno had been, in essence, a self-portrait, but if the love he felt for Paul was comparable to a disease, it also gave him good reasons for staying alive.

In February he was planning to dedicate either a part of *Buddenbrooks* or his next collection of short stories to Paul, whose name keeps recurring in his letters to Grautoff. "This dedication has gradually become a fixation: I am set on it passionately." He wanted to show he could make Paul's name glitter. "This is mad and ridiculous! I am writing nothing but 'he' and 'him' and 'his.' The only thing left is to write it in big letters and surround it with a golden frame." He was nervous of becoming as obsessed with Paul as he had been with Willri Timpe.[34]

We don't know when his suicidal feelings were at their most acute. Writing to Heinrich in March, he promised not to kill himself, and gave only vague indications of why he'd thought he didn't want to live.

> It is all a matter of metaphysics, music, adolescent eroticism: I never seem to emerge from my adolescence. Grautoff too was very worried about it, but there is no urgent problem, the thing is growing roots so slowly, and, there is at the moment so little practical reason to take it seriously that you need have no anxiety. Admittedly, I cannot vouch for what will happen in the future, and whether I, with my obsession for "the wondrous realm of night" in my heart, could, for example, survive the next bout of military service, is a question that unsettles me. . . . It is not a love affair, at least not in the usual sense, but a friendship—one which is, to my astonishment, understood, reciprocated, rewarded, which, I admit without affectation, at certain times, especially during solitude or depression, involves rather too much suffering. Grautoff says I have simply fallen in love like a schoolboy. . . .[35]

The mixture of openness and evasiveness is characteristic; the headlong emotionality is not. He is neither analyzing nor giving an account of what's happening, but celebrating the unfamiliar sensation of feeling totally at ease with someone who attracted him.

Paul was painting another portrait of Thomas, and they were spending so much time together that Thomas kept postponing his departure to Florence. In the middle of December he had planned to spend February and March there. In a letter he posted on January 8 he told Heinrich he couldn't leave before the beginning of April, contradicting himself a few paragraphs later to say he'd leave on March 15. His letter of April 1 starts: "No, I cannot possibly come now, although the cinque-lire *pensione* is certainly very tempting." The first reason he gives is shortage of money; the second is that both the portrait and the short story he's writing are still unfinished; the third is: "I am feeling much too good here at the moment. Really I go on writing negatively and ironically only because the habit is deep-seated, but at the same time I enthuse, love and live, and now that spring has come, life is like a celebration. . . . I want to hold on to it till the last moment." He rarely sent out such signals of being happy. Less than two years earlier, when he was with Kurt Martens, he'd seemed intent on being self-sufficient, but Paul was bringing out desires that had been repressed and potentialities that had been hidden: "My gratitude knows no bounds. My sentimental need, my need for enthusiasm, devotion, trust, handclasps, loyalty, has been starved to the point of wasting away and becoming atrophied, but now it is feasting."[36]

Fischer's letter of February 4 had implied a strong interest in publishing Thomas's work without making any financial proposals for *Buddenbrooks*. The offer, when it came in a draft contract posted on March 23, was better than Thomas had expected. He was to receive a 20 percent royalty on the shop price of each copy sold, and for the next six years Fischer would have the right to publish all his other work on the same terms. Telling Heinrich about the draft contract, Thomas said: "If he reduces the 6 years to 3 or 4, I will sign. If he will not, I will sign anyway."[37] The novel was scheduled for publication in September 1901, but no payment would be made until twelve months later, when he would receive about 2,000 marks if the edition had sold out.

When the contract was drawn up and sent to him on April 17, the six years had been reduced to five. He finally left for Italy at the end of the month.

8

Fair Hair and Blue Eyes

HEINRICH HAD BOOKED INTO a *pensione* run by a Signora Fondini on the third floor of a house in the Via Cavour. Though he was still in Florence when Thomas arrived at the end of April 1901, he left shortly afterward for Naples, returning to Florence before his brother left on May 20. Thomas described the city as "the most pleasant in the world. Everything smells of flowers and cakes, and one goes around all the time in such a good mood that it is as if one were celebrating a birthday. What is more, nowhere else are so many beautiful things to be found in such a small space."[1]

Sharing a table with the two brothers in the *pensione* were two English sisters, Edith and Mary Smith. The four of them became friends and played cards. Edith, the elder sister, was dark; Mary, the younger, blond. Mary, "who looked as if she were by Botticelli, started off by being a happy-go-lucky flirt, but later she became quite remarkably serious—and indeed (of all amazing things!) this was reciprocal. Our leavetaking could almost have been put on the stage."[2] On her birthday Thomas presented her with a basket of candied fruit and they even talked about the possibility of marrying. "But now, I believe, I am becoming too melancholy for her." In this letter to Heinrich he says: "She is so very clever"—these five words are written in English—"and I am so stupid that I always love those who are clever, though in the long run I cannot keep up with them."[3]

If they were temperamentally incompatible, the differential was more likely to have been a matter of brightness than cleverness. An ambiguous entry in his notebook may be relevant: "You arrived with so much vitality, it made me shy, at one blow it reduced me to desperation and to a full hour of silence, unlovable and hopeless. I cannot join in."[4] This could refer either to the friendship with Mary, which came to nothing, though they went on exchanging letters, or to the relationship with Paul. Thomas hadn't grown out of his boyhood sense of inferiority to fair-haired "children of light."

This is one of the underlying themes in his preparations for a fiction he was going to call *The Loved Ones (Die Geliebten). Geliebt* was the word he'd used to describe Armin Martens. In a section of this notebook which seems to date from the middle of 1901, he jotted down fragments of dialogue, story ideas, and scraps of psychological analysis. One observation is about the common experience of feeling indifference or contempt toward the people who give signs of being attracted, while feeling despair at the real or apparent indifference of those who seem most glamorous. "To go on longing for love all one's life and yet to despise those who love one. Happiness is *not* being loved: that is a gratification, which is mixed with disgust, for one's vanity. Happiness is to love and to steal slightly closer to the beloved object."[5] Of the glamorous children of light, Paul was the only one who invited him closer.

The notebook also contains jottings on Savonarola. Thomas drew inspiration from the clay bust of Lorenzo de' Medici, from a portrait by Ghirlandaio of Lorenzo's mistress, Giovanna Tornabuoni, and most of all from Fra Bartolommeo's portrait of Savonarola in the Museo San Marco. Thomas kept a reproduction of this on his desk. Writing *Buddenbrooks*, he'd depended heavily on facts and memories but hardly at all on pictures, except when a cartoon gave him the idea for Herr Permaneder; what he formed now was a habit of collecting visual information that could be translated into words. He used files for postcards, brochures, and clippings from newspapers, magazines, and travel books. The file he used for the *Joseph* novels contained over three hundred pictures, and the *Felix Krull* file over five hundred.[6] Just as his fiction depends less on his imagination than on his genius for making new structures from old fragments of reality, his descriptions depend partly on a talent for making verbal transcripts of images he had in front of him.

Although he didn't complete his Savonarola play until 1905, he tried out some of the themes in "Gladius Dei," a story dedicated to Mary Smith. In 1482, transferred by his order from Brescia to Florence, Savonarola had been enchanted by the city's beauty but disgusted to find that under the Medicis, the cultured citizens were spiritually moribund. Enraged by the corruption and sensuality, Savonarola passionately denounced both from the pulpit. When he gained ascendancy in Florence, which became a Christian republic, stringent laws were passed against gambling, vice, and frivolity. Rich people flocked to the Piazza della Signoria to surrender jewelry and fine clothes, which were sacrificed by Savonarola's followers in the "bonfire of the vanities." One of his visions was of a hand in the sky holding a sword inscribed "Gladius Domini supra terram cito et velociter" ("Sword of the Lord over the earth, take action and swiftly").

Thomas's "Gladius Dei" pivots on an equation between contemporary Munich and quattrocento Florence. Since the reign of Ludwig I, an admirer of classical antiquity who wanted to make his capital the most beautiful city in Europe, Bavaria's cult of the Italian Renaissance had centered on Munich, where architects had used Florentine and Venetian models. The main character in the story, Hieronymus—the name is a variant of Girolamo or Jerome—has something of his namesake's temperament. Thomas describes the city ironically.

> Munich gleamed. Above the festive squares and white colonnades, the neo-classical monuments and baroque churches, the leaping fountains, the palaces and parks of this capital city was spread a shining heaven of blue silk, and the broad, bright vistas, tree-lined and well proportioned, lay in the sunny haze of a beautiful day in early June.
>
> The chatter of birds and a mysterious jubilation floating out over all the alleyways . . . And over the squares and terraces the leisurely and humorous life of the beautiful and easy going city rolls along, floating and buzzing.[7]

Music pours from open windows. "Art flourishes, art dominates, art stretches her rose-entwined sceptre over the city and smiles."[8] But Hieronymus is striding down the Schellingstrasse—a haggard young man shielding his face from the sun with the hood of his black cloak. In an empty church he sprinkles his forehead with holy water and genuflects in front of the high altar before joining the crowd that has formed outside an art shop. Photographs are on sale of a provocatively sexy Madonna painting, which has been bought by the city's principal gallery, the Pinakothek.

Believing God wants the shop owner, Herr Bluthenzweig, to destroy the photographs he's selling for 70 marks, Hieronymus enters the shop to denounce the decadent art that celebrates sensuality. Knowledge, he says, is the bitterest of torments, a purifying anguish, the fire of purgatory, while art is "the sacred torch that probes into the most fearful depths, the shameful holes and corners of life with merciful illumination; art is the divine flame applied with redeeming compassion to make the world ignite and vanish with all its disgrace and agony."[9] But the art purveyed in Wilhelmine Munich and in Herr Bluthenzweig's shop is less austere. Commanded to burn all the pictures, statuettes, busts, and ornaments he's trying to sell, Herr Bluthenzweig loses his temper, and after being thrown out by a giant packer, Hieronymus has a vision of God's sword in the sky.

Like other black-clad characters, such as Tobias Mindernickel and Lobgott Piepsam, Hieronymus is meant to seem absurd, but the ambivalence underlying his tirades suggests that Thomas was asking himself whether Savonarola would have condemned his fiction. Certainly it didn't just reflect the surface of fashionable Munich life. According to Schopenhauer, the visual arts, which reproduce the world as *Vorstellung*, are inferior to music, which can penetrate wordlessly to the inner life of the will or self. Thomas, whose writing often aspires to the condition of Wagnerian music, agrees with much of what Hieronymus says, but the story doesn't throw its full weight behind him. Knowing he'd return to these themes in his play, Thomas was content to be inconclusive, and his ambivalence is based partly on uncertainty whether his style of living was superior or inferior to that of people less intelligent but more full-blooded. Hieronymus's *saeva indignatio* derives partly from sexual frustration, and his equation of art and knowledge with a sacred torch suggests that illumination overlaps with destruction. While exposing the absurdity of ascetic priests who denounce the pleasure from which they feel excluded, Thomas is deliberately exposing some of the ambiguity in his own position. Art makes the spirit visible, but only by introducing an element of corruption that needs to be burned away.

Waiting in Munich for his return were galley proofs of *Buddenbrooks*. Because the compositors had been working from a handwritten manuscript, the proofs were full of mistakes, which he had to correct during his six weeks in the city, though he'd have preferred to work on "Gladius Dei." Suffering from stomach pains and digestive troubles, he left with Heinrich on July 10, wanting to take the cure at a Tyrolean sanatorium in Mitterbad, south of Innsbruck and close to the Italian border. Heinrich had stayed there in 1893, when high blood pressure had prompted him to consult the Austrian doctor who ran it, Christoph Hartung von Hartungen. Suffering from both nervous and bronchial disorders, Heinrich had often gone back to him, sometimes staying at Mitterbad and sometimes at his other sanatorium in Riva, near Lake Garda. The doctor appears in Heinrich's novel *Die Göttinnen* (*The Goddesses*) as Dr. von Manningen.

The brothers spent their first Tyrolean night at Bolzano, a picturesque little town, full of tourists.[10] In the morning, after traveling by train to Lana, they had a three-hour ride on horseback into the mountains.

Von Hartungen's patients were subjected to morning gymnastics and ten hours of exercise, including mountain climbing in the bracing air,[11] but Thomas took no pleasure in enforced activity. He used a clinic as a setting for a story he'd started in February, "a burlesque named 'Tristan.'"[12] There are two puzzles here. One is that he venerated *Tristan* and never missed a new production in Munich. He had an almost erotic relationship with the opera. "It was a *rapport*—sceptical, pessimistic, enlightened, almost hateful, but at the same time totally passionate and indescribably vivacious. Wonderful hours of profound solitary happiness amongst the theatre crowds, full of shuddering and short moments of bliss, full of the lust of the nerves and the mind, of insights into moving and great truths, such as can be offered only by this insurpassable art."[13] Nor is the opera burlesqued in the final version of the story.

The other puzzle is that Thomas had obviously done a lot of work on "Tristan" before arriving at Mitterbad, though he'd had little experience of sanatorium life, and couldn't have gained much insight into the subject from Heinrich's letters. The story, which is like a preliminary sketch for *The Magic Mountain* (*Der Zauberberg*), seems to derive mainly from his Mitterbad experiences, which he obviously found stimulating. He succeeds brilliantly in evoking the atmosphere of a sanatorium. With its slate roofs, its spacious gardens, and its views of the mountains, Einfried—the name is reminiscent of Wagner's home, Wahnfried—has a large drawing room with an elegant fireplace in which glowing red paper is pasted over pieces of imitation coal. Dr. Leander, who has thick glasses and a curly, two-pointed black beard, rules tyrannically over patients too feeble to evolve their own discipline. The two principal male characters are Herr Klöterjahn, whose name derives from a Low German dialect word for "testicles," and the writer Detlev Spinell. Though modeled mainly on Holitscher, he derives partly from Heinrich and Thomas, who later said he'd been parodying "an undesirable element" in himself—"that moribund preciosity of the aesthete." Like Hieronymus, Spinell pontificates about the nature of beauty, but, unlike "Gladius Dei," this story makes its points more through action than explication.

A rivalry develops between the frail Spinell and the burly Klöterjahn, whose wife, Gabriele, seems to have used up the last of her strength about ten months earlier in giving birth to their sturdy little son, Anton. After leaving her in Einfried, Klöterjahn returns occasionally for a brief visit. A wholesale merchant who enjoys eating, drinking, and womanizing, he uses his business as a pretext for spending little time at the sanatorium, and in his absence the shy, nervous, gauche Spinell courteously makes friends with the delicate Gabriele, who seems wasted on such a coarse husband. She comes from an old bourgeois family, and the *Buddenbrooks* theme is reprised when Spinell maintains that artistic transfiguration can be produced by the decline of a family founded on business.

As her health deteriorates, excitement could be dangerous, and she's told not to play the piano. But Spinell tempts her into disobeying orders when the doctors and most of the patients are sleigh-riding in the mountains. She plays music from *Tristan*. Ridiculing the bourgeois characters incapable of appreciating art, Thomas writes admiringly of the music and the woman's artistry. A subtly parodistic variation on the *Liebestod* theme is developed as the man who can't seduce her lures her into an artistic communion that damages her fragile constitution. The scene is reminiscent of the sequence in which Hanno Buddenbrook's wild improvisation turns out to be valedictory, and it's oddly close to an 1898 story Heinrich had set in a sanatorium, "Dr. Biebers Versuchung" ("Dr. Bieber's Temptation"). At the climax the doctor plays music from *Tristan* on the piano.

Thomas's story is more interesting, and he poises Spinell uncomfortably between artistry and bourgeois mediocrity. Unlike Klöterjahn, who possesses a beautiful woman but can't appreciate beauty, Spinell is a connoisseur, but, like The Clown, essentially a dilettante—undisciplined, uncommitted. He can function only as a catalyst: He makes Gabriele overcome the will to live and achieve artistic excellence, but he's sterile as a writer, and unworthy to be united with her in a *Liebestod*.

She's the only tragic figure in the story. Klöterjahn is entirely comic, while Spinell is often ridiculous. Before she dies, he sends Klöterjahn an abusive letter. Like Hieronymus, Spinell tries to make his weakness into a weapon. "Let it be understood, sir, that I hate you, you and your child, as I hate life itself, the vulgar, ridiculous but triumphant life that you represent, the eternal opposite and deadly enemy of beauty."[14] But assaults like this have no impact on the thick-skinned Klöterjahn, and the final confrontation is between the discomfited Spinell and the robust infant, Anton, who seems to be laughing at the black-clad figure in front of him. We're reminded of the fatal confrontation between the blond cyclist, "Life," and the apoplectic Piepsam.

In a later essay on Schopenhauer, Thomas points to the possibility of writing in the spirit of a philosopher without accepting his ideas; the story presents variations on both Schopenhauerian and Wagnerian themes. Coupling the German word for "one" with the word for "peace," the name "Einfried" suggests peaceful integration, but this is achieved neither by any of the characters nor by Thomas. Like Hieronymus, Gabriele is partly a self-portrait. He saw himself both as the antihedonistic solitary and the frail beauty whose artistic talents exceed her vital resources.

DR. VON HARTUNGEN advised him to stay at the sanatorium in Riva. Before doing so he went back to Munich at the end of August. He'd sent "Gladius Dei" to the Insel Verlag from Mitterbad in mid-August, but it wasn't published until July 1902, when the first of two installments appeared in the Viennese review *Die Zeit*. By the middle of August 1901 he'd started working for Albert Langen as an editor; another reason for wanting to delay his departure for Riva was that Paul Ehrenberg was in Munich again.

> He is his old self. . . . I too am my old self, still permanently weak, so easily seduced and unreliable and not to be taken seriously in my philosophy as I seize life's hand the moment it is laughingly held out to me. Strange! Every year at the time when nature freezes up, Life

breaks into the summery freezing and desolation of my soul, and pours streams of feeling and warmth through my veins! I am letting it happen. I am artist enough to let everything happen for I can use everything.[15]

Simultaneously admitting weakness and claiming exceptional strength, Thomas confronts both the female and the male components in his psyche. He seems to take pleasure in picturing himself as easily seduced, but in claiming to be so virile and creatively robust that he could find literary uses for all his experiences, he was neither deceiving himself nor expecting to deceive the friend he was confiding in, Grautoff. But this notion served as a constant excuse for inconsistency and for postponing commitment. How did he really want the relationship with Paul to develop? If Paul had suggested that they should live together, Thomas would almost certainly have demurred. He didn't want a scandal, and, living on his own, had more time for his writing. Though it was uncomfortable to be kept in ignorance of how much Paul cared, the ignorance was acceptable, not merely because he could use it in the novel but because, perversely, he found it pleasurable. As a child, Thomas had been treated by his father to an alternation of affection and absence; Paul was repeating the pattern.

COSTING 6 MARKS EACH, the two volumes of *Buddenbrooks* appeared in the shops at the end of October. Only a thousand copies had been printed: The high price would discourage buyers. Few of the first reviews were enthusiastic, but in the *Berliner Tageblatt*, defending the novel against accusations of formlessness, Samuel Lublinski predicted it "will grow with time and still be read over many generations."[16]

Thomas finally left for Riva on November 20. At the Villa Cristofero the doctor prescribed a regime of physical exertion and mental relaxation: Thomas was allowed neither to read nor to write. He'd brought with him a story he'd intended to call "Literature" and eventually called "Tonio Kröger," but did no work on it, though, disobeying orders, he wrote some letters. One was to Grautoff, briefing him on what to say in his critique of *Buddenbrooks*.

Reviewing it in *Das literarische Echo*, Kurt Martens praised the intensity of feeling underneath Thomas's descriptions of physical sufferings and mental repercussions. The reviewer in the *Bremer Tageblatt* was Rainer Maria Rilke, who announced: "One will certainly have to make a note of this name." Thomas had told a story that spanned four generations in such a surprising and interesting way that, although it takes days, one reads the two hefty volumes page by page attentively and with suspense, without wearying, without skipping, without the slightest sign of impatience or haste. One has time, one must have time, for the relaxed and natural sequence of events, precisely because nothing in the book seems to be there for the reader, because nowhere does a reflective writer seem to be leaning across the incidents toward a reflective reader to persuade him and carry him along. . . . Rilke called the novel "an act of reverence towards life."

After returning to Munich before Christmas, Thomas moved again on New Year's Day. His new apartment was on the second floor of a house in Ungererstrasse. Writing to Paul at the end of January 1902 and enclosing a review of *Buddenbrooks*, he said he was collecting all the favorable ones as a compensation for being starved of human affection. This starvation, he grumbled, was damaging his creative powers. "*Where* is the man who says yes to me, when I am not very likeable, moody, self-torturing, sceptical, irritable but sensitive and extraordinarily hungry for sympathy?" He felt isolated, misunderstood, depressed. "I would almost have said 'Come and see me' if I somehow felt entitled to assume that you were *not* one of those who have a high regard for the talent and none for the man."[17]

Paul responded promptly to this self-pitying appeal, calling on his friend two days after the letter was written.[18] "Pact of friendship. Promise of loyalty. He occasionally signs himself 'Once and for all—yours' . . . It is half joke, half solemnity."[19] But Thomas would have found it intolerable if Paul hadn't been half-joking and half-serious. As it was, he could enjoy both the evidence of Paul's affection and the self-torture to be had from questioning the degree of his commitment to other relationships while using the novel to record and explore pleasure and pain.

Thomas was working simultaneously on *The Loved Ones* and on the story "Tonio Kröger," which wouldn't be completed till December 1902. In an 1899 notebook he'd made the entry: "Tonio Kröger. Some people go astray knowing that they cannot avoid it, because no right path exists for them." By using the new notebook as both a diary and a space for notes toward the two stories, he was encouraging himself to blend fiction with autobiography. Reading the notebook today it's hard to differentiate between factual and fictional entries. "What lasted so long? Numbness. Boredom. Ice. And reflection! And art! Here is my heart, and here is my hand. I love you! My God . . . I love you! Is it so beautiful, so sweet, so lovely to be human?"[20]

In *The Loved Ones,* translating his relationship with Paul into Adelaide's with the violinist Rudolf, Thomas is assigning himself the female role. This accords with the assumption that Paul had more initiative than he did, and later, in *Felix Krull*, when he portrays the homosexual Scottish lord by describing his own features, Thomas refers to "feminine lips." In *The Loved Ones,* he finds it easy to identify with Adelaide.

"Moments of unprecedented happiness when she succeeded unexpect-edly, through some chance word or some intimate play of the features in winning his confidence, and he almost yielded to her. . . . "[21] Thomas is fueling the fiction by spying on himself. Upset by what keeps happening, he rushes home to jot down details about gestures, fa-cial expressions, feelings. It was like the excitement of poisoning butter-flies and knowing he could pin them down on paper. In becoming a possessable object, the living thing becomes less exciting, but the action makes it possible to live with frustration. Sometimes he sinks into ba-nality while trying to make his discomfort into literature. "The suffering in the yearning for togetherness on days when she does not see him. . . . To know that the other lives, laughs, talks, works, keeps himself busy, without having anything to do with all that, and having at the same time to live on one's own two legs . . . each action seems just *like a betrayal of love*–and he too, oh dear, must be feeling that."[22] Any frus-trated lover can indulge in autoerotic fantasy that feels like a betrayal of love; the writer feels entitled to assume that any notes he makes may come in useful.

At other times Thomas seemed to think sublimation could be achieved partly through fiction and partly through the special quality of their relationship.

> We talked about sexuality, about the precarious situation when one doesn't like tarts, but at most ladies, and an appetizing relationship is too expensive; also that we have both been medically advised to have a relationship with a married woman. Which made me want to explain my feelings for him, to tell him (even if it is not true) that this friendship is something beneficial for me, also from the psychi-atric viewpoint, that it has worked on me as a purgative, as a cleanser and solvent of sexuality.[23]

Sometimes thoughts of cutting himself off from sexuality went even further than this. One of the questions Tonio Kröger asks is whether a male artist is really a male. Isn't he more like a *castrato*? "We sing like angels, but . . ."

Paul was going to leave Munich again at the beginning of May, and the prospect of separation reduced Thomas to frantic insecurity. He'd be alone for several months, but, far from abandoning "The Loved Ones," he decided to expand it into a novel, introducing new characters and widening the focus. He went on making notes for it until the end of 1903.

The same depressive mood filters into his story "Die Hungernden," which centers on an artist Thomas calls Detlef, though he distances himself less than he had from Detlev Spinell. Detlef loves a woman, Lily, who prefers a young painter. Detlef's sense of being superior to other people makes it hard for him to live with the knowledge of being excluded from their pleasures. With his dreams, insights, and inexorable creativity, he can neither settle for the life that to them seems satisfactory nor suppress the jealous suspicion that the "children of light" feel glad when they're liberated from his oppressive presence. "We poor ghosts of life . . . we all entertain a surreptitious and hectic yearning for the harmless, the simple, the vivacious, for a little friendship, devotion, intimacy, human happiness. . . . We sneak along after you, profound imps that we are, insightful monsters, we keep our distance, and our eyes burn with a greedy curious longing to be like you."[24]

Half in love with Lily and half contemptuous, knowing she'll always be transparent to him, Detlef believes he could bring the world to ridicule her shallow pleasures. But understanding is no compensation for being unloved, and he seems to inspire only disgust in the overheated faces of the dancers at the party he leaves. Outside in the darkness, he sees a hungry man in tattered clothes, leaning against a lamppost. They're both outsiders. This is a theme that will be articulated more forcefully in "Tonio Kröger."

Making little progress with this story, Thomas kept changing his plans for the summer. With Carl Ehrenberg he cycled out to Starnberg, where they each rented a bungalow, intending to move in on July 1 for three months, but Thomas stayed in Munich, leaving only for a brief stay at Kurt Martens's summer house in Kreuth on the Tegernsee. In late August or early September he met Samuel Fischer, who was again passing through Munich on his way to the Tyrol. Though the first edition of *Buddenbrooks* hadn't sold out, he promised to bring out a cheap edition, admitting that had he done so at the outset, it would by now be in its fifth or sixth edition.[25] Offering a first payment of 1,000 marks whenever Thomas asked for it, Fischer also wanted to bring out a second volume of his stories.

By now Thomas had decided to spend six weeks at the Villa Cristofero in Riva. On September 1 he gave up his Ungererstrasse apartment, but instead of going straight to the sanatorium, he moved into a boardinghouse, the Pension Gisela. His sister Carla, who was twenty-one on September 23, had secured her first acting job at the Stadttheater in Zwickau, fifty miles south of Leipzig, and he didn't want to miss the party for her at the end of the month.

On October 2 he left for Riva. The day started at seven with a session of gymnastics before breakfast. At eight he sat down to write, but worked for only half an hour, taking a break when the mail arrived. It was still warm, and at nine he stuffed a book into his pocket and wandered down to the lake, where he'd rented a boat for the month, but spent as much of his time in it reading as rowing. A heavy lunch was followed by a siesta, and the doctor gave each of his patients a massage.

Afterward Thomas went for a long walk—sometimes two hours—and before dinner put in some practice on the violin.

The routine left little time for writing, and he probably didn't complete "Tonio Kröger" before returning to Munich on November 15, when he moved into the "pretty little flat" he'd found in September.[26] It was on the ground floor of a house on the corner of Konradstrasse and Friedrichstrasse. He must have finished the story by the end of the year, for it appeared in the February 1903 issue of the *Neue Deutsche Rundschau*, which was on sale by mid-January.

If there are passages in the notebooks which could be either diary entries or notes for stories, the stories contain passages that look like undisguised excerpts from a diary. Developing the idea he'd jotted down in his 1899 notebook about people for whom there's no alternative to going astray, Thomas contrasts Tonio's gait, which is awkward, with Hans Hansen's, which is rhythmic and "elastic." Tonio "went the way he had to go, a little carelessly and unsteadily, whistling to himself, with his head tilted sideways and staring into the distance. If he went astray, it happened because for some people no right way exists. When asked what in the world he wanted to become, he gave different answers, for he used to say (and had already written it down, too) that he carried within him possibilities for a thousand forms of existence, together with the secret knowledge that they were all quite impossible."[27] This gives him an affinity with Robert Musil's Man without Qualities, who feels "like a stride that could be taken in any direction, but which leads from one instant of equilibrium to the next."

Tonio's friendship with Hans derives partly from recent events involving Paul, and sometimes, when describing Tonio and Hans at the age of fourteen, Thomas imposes an adult sophistication both on their behavior and on Tonio's reflections. When Hans pretends he hadn't forgotten his promise that they'd walk home together, Tonio realizes his friend attaches less importance than he does to their conversations *à deux*, but appreciates that Hans, regretting his absentmindedness, is trying to make peace. Knowing that suffering is unavoidable for the one who loves more than the other, Tonio has to be grateful for any conciliatory gesture. This looks more like a transposition of what kept happening with Paul than a memory of what had once happened with Armin Martens and Willri Timpe, but Thomas also tries to introduce behavior characteristic of fourteen-year-old boys. Standing on the bottom rail of a gate, Hans swings to and fro on its creaking hinges. But Thomas is again writing about his friendship with Paul when jealousy of other people he liked is reflected in Tonio's jealousy of Erwin Jimmerthal, the classmate who interrupts their serious conversation to chat about horses and riding lessons.

The most directly autobiographical of Thomas's stories, "Tonio

Kröger" shows he no longer felt oppressed by the anxieties visible in earlier stories. In 1896 he'd still been pessimistic about life in general and his own in particular. Heinrich had brought out a novel and had a volume of stories accepted by Langen, while Thomas was uncertain whether he'd ever be more than a talented dilettante.

Yet by the age of twenty-seven, he had proved that he had all the qualities he'd seemed to lack throughout his school career. He'd mustered enough self-discipline to work extremely hard for three years on *Buddenbrooks*, which had brought immediate fame. In "Tonio Kröger" he not only discards the grotesque masks he'd needed but celebrates his freedom by painting a self-portrait. In "Tristan" he'd made the man of letters look ridiculous, but comedy in the new story rarely works against the central character except in moments of clumsiness and confusion during the dancing class. In fact, Thomas identified with him sufficiently to sign some of his letters "Tonio Kröger."[28]

Unlike Julia Mann, Tonio's mother remarries after her husband's premature death. Otherwise Tonio's childhood parallels Thomas's. Herr Kröger is not only a senator but a grain merchant: The firm's name is printed in big, black letters on sacks of grain that are driven through the streets on drays. The name of the city isn't mentioned, but the gabled houses, the narrow streets, and the strong damp breeze make it recognizable as Lübeck, while the Krögers live in a big ancestral mansion, the city's grandest house. Consul Kröger comes from the north, while Tonio's beautiful, dark-haired, piano-playing mother is unlike any of the local ladies: The consul had fetched his bride-to-be from "somewhere at the bottom of the map." Tonio writes poetry and, after learning to play the violin, finds he can draw uniquely tender notes from it, but at school he's lethargic and inattentive. The alienated teachers write unfavorable reports, which worry his father but not his mother.

Thomas even introduces the main theme from *Buddenbrooks*. The old Kröger family has been disintegrating, and Tonio's personality is generally regarded as symptomatic of the decline. Thomas also makes Tonio resemble him physically, with dark hair, slanting brows, and sharp, clear-cut features. Tonio wears a mustache, parts his hair simply and correctly, and dresses punctiliously, saying that though he's an adventurer in his inner life, he likes to keep up appearances and behave like a respectable citizen.

Later Thomas denied that the story was autobiographical, complaining about critics who'd "thoughtlessly" quoted his description of Frau Consul Kröger as if he'd been portraying his mother,[29] but, like Jean-Paul Sartre, he kept slipping compulsively back into the autobiographical mode. Sartre said: "You cannot put life into perspective while living it—it steals up on you from behind and you find yourself inside it"; Thomas's autobiographical writing was partly an attempt to stop life stealing up from behind, and partly a series of attempts to plan his future. He also wanted to refute adverse criticisms of his weltanschauung. The adult Tonio, in conversation with Lisaveta, a young painter, rejects what has been written about him—presumably by book reviewers: "It has been said, it has even been written and printed, that I hate life, or fear or despise or abominate it. I was pleased to hear this, it was flattering, but that doesn't make it less untrue. I love life."[30]

Written as if Thomas were interviewing himself about his beliefs, the long sequence with Lisaveta incorporates formulations he'd made in conversation with Paul. He took tremendous trouble over this undramatic sequence, rewriting it again and again. Tonio complains that he's tired of portraying humanity without participating in human experience. He assumes that the artist can function only if he sets a low enough value on himself to withdraw from life, giving up all hope of sexual fulfillment and using his feelings merely as raw material.

Thomas was plagued at this time by digestive troubles that kept sending him back to von Hartungen's sanatoria. Prone to overinterpret physical symptoms, Thomas believed his artistry had improved as his health had deteriorated. When Tonio argues that literary language eliminates emotion, that words put our passions in cold storage, he's expressing a view that derives partly from guilt feelings about using literature as a refuge from—or an outlet for—the passion Paul inspired. Though "Tonio Kröger" is based partly on Thomas's holiday in Aalsgaard before they met, the feeling was in line with previous feelings, and the story was designed as a safe area.

The story highlights blond hair, blue eyes, and fair skin, not simply because Thomas, as an adult, was still attracted by these features, which link his Aalsgaard experience with the frustrated love he'd felt as a schoolboy for Armin Martens, Willri Timpe, and a brown-haired girl he met during the winter of 1889, when the balletmaster Rudolf Knoll was teaching dance and deportment to children of the best families. The parents took it in turn to let their houses be used for the classes. Ingeborg Holm, the girl at the dancing class in the story, is blond, with narrow-cut blue eyes, and Tonio can hardly bear it when he catches a fragrance from her hair or the delicate white material of her dress. But, like all the other children, she laughs at him when, confused by the intensity of his emotion during a quadrille, he joins in a *moulinet des dames*, a movement that should be executed only by the girls. Striking a balletic pose to express stylized horror, Herr Knaak flaps a yellow silk handkerchief at him, addressing him as Fräulein Kröger. He retreats to the corridor, hoping in vain that Inge will come after him, put her hand on his shoulder, persuade him to come back, and declare her love. But the only girl to sympathize is the clumsy Magdalena Vermehren, who keeps falling over when trying to dance. Reproducing the excruciating embarrassment of the fourteen-year-old boy, Thomas makes good use of what seem to be accurate memories—talcum powder scattered on the floor, wine jellies in clinking glass cups, mothers and aunts watching the lesson through lorgnettes.

The story distinguishes between two kinds of people. There are those who write poetry and read lyrical stories about unattainable love; there are those who never look into things deeply enough to let life become complex and sad. The unintelligent people are the ones who look charming and are loved. To Ingeborg, who watches Herr Knaak with rapt and smiling attention, Tonio will always be an outsider and a stranger.

This is confirmed by what happens in Aalsgaard. When a dance is held at the hotel, a blond couple saunters into the dining room holding hands—Ingeborg Holm and Hans Hansen. She's wearing a thin, light-colored frock with a floral pattern, and her wonderful blond tresses are wound around her head. Broad-shouldered and narrow-hipped, Hans is wearing a close-fitting jacket with gold buttons and carrying a sailor's cap. Tonio's heart leaps with joy as he catches sight of them. He loves the race and the type, the radiant blondness, the steely blue eyes, the appearance of untroubled purity and lightness of heart. It was for them, he thinks, that he wrote his works, although they don't read. He wishes he could be like them—happy, healthy, normal, liberated from the curse of intelligence and the torment of creation. When their eyes meet his, their indifference is close to contempt, but he feels happy, and goes back to his room without speaking to them.

Themes are reprised, like leitmotivs, from the earlier dance sequence. A quadrille is danced, and, catching a fragrance from Inge's hair or her white dress, Tonio remembers his humiliation at the hands of Herr Knaak. Again there is a girl who seems interested in him; again she's clumsy enough to fall over in the dance. After helping her to her feet, he withdraws, and again entertains the fantasy that Inge will follow him, persuade him to come back, declare her love. But he goes to bed without having spoken to her, just as the diffident Thomas had remained incognito in Lübeck on his way to Aalsgaard. But Tonio feels happy after his wordless encounter with Inge and Hans. In bed he

whispered two names into the pillow, these few chaste northern syllables, which represented his genuine and original way of loving, suffering and being happy. He looked back over the years that had intervened. He thought about the profligate adventures of his senses, his nerves and his mind, saw himself devoured by irony and intellection, devastated and paralysed by insight, half ruined by the fever and frost of creativity, ceaselessly and contritely tossed about between crass extremities, between abstinence and rutting, refined, impoverished, etiolated by coldly and artificially cultivated ecstasies, lost, ravaged, tortured, unhealthy–and he wept with remorse and homesickness.[31]

The vicarious self-pity in the writing is balanced by the passion and precision.

As an adult, though proud of the fame he'd achieved through literature, Tonio is uncertain, as Thomas was, whether the price has been too high. The urgent underlying question in the story is whether he's still fully alive. The story's divided into nine sections. The last sentence in the first begins with the phrase "His heart was alive at that time . . ."[32] This phrase is repeated toward the end of the second section. The implication is that it's not alive now, but three pages before the story ends, we read: "His heart was alive," as if the encounter with the blond couple has brought it back to life. The previous years, in which he became what he now is, were years of "paralysis; sterility; ice; and intellect! and art!"[33]

The story ends with the affirmation that Tonio's bourgeois conscience has made him fall in love with respectability and mediocrity. Standing between the bourgeoisie and the artists, he is at home with neither, but if anything, he declares, can make a man of letters into a good writer, it's nostalgia for the bliss of the commonplace. He's confident he'll write better in the future than he has so far.

> I am looking into an unborn and shadowy world that wants to be ordered and shaped. In the swarm of shadows I can see human forms which are beckoning me to deliver them with a spell–tragic and ridiculous and those who are both at the same time. I am very drawn to these, but my deepest and most secret love is for the fair-haired and blue-eyed, the bright and lively ones, happy, lovable and ordinary.[34]

Like a great actor, Thomas could find his way instinctively to equilibrium between self-exposure and discretion. The emotion is never naked, but it looks naked, and the resonance he achieves is due partly to the hidden content of his narrative. The accidental involvement in the *moulinet des dames* provides only a delicate Freudian hint of feminine traits in Tonio's personality, but his love for people with fair hair and blue eyes is partly the admiring envy of a man who knows himself to be excluded from the pleasures of ordinary heterosexual love. Later, in "Death in Venice," Thomas makes Aschenbach believe that a fiction can achieve deep and lasting influence only if founded on a "secret affinity and congruence" between the writer's personal destiny and that of his contemporaries in general. Here there is a secret and accidental affinity between Thomas's sense of being an outsider and everyone else's. He writes in such a way that the most dissimilar readers find Tonio's story to be *their* story. Without being fixated on a youngster of the same sex or being an artist or an intellectual or a highbrow or being stranded between two classes, any reader, male or female, can identify with Tonio. In one way or another, we all feel ourselves to be outsiders, ambivalent, caught between conflicting loyalties. After "Tonio Kröger" appeared in 1903, it became the classic statement about the discomforts of being on the outside.

Kafka, who responded to Thomas's "extraordinarily profitable love of contradiction," read the story at least twice, as did Arthur Schnitzler.[35] The critic Georg Lukács admitted that "the Tonio Kröger problem" had been "a major influence in determining the main lines of my own early work,"[36] and Nathalie Sarraute said she felt she was related to Tonio Kröger, who had made her want to become a writer.[37] These are just four exceptionally articulate examples of countless readers who had the impression of reading a story about themselves. "Tonio Kröger" achieved a popularity unequaled even by "Death in Venice," while *Buddenbrooks* would eventually achieve sales of 1.3 million, making it the most popular novel in pre-Hitler Europe apart from Erich Maria Remarque's *Im Westen nichts Neues* (*All Quiet on the Western Front*). Here, too, there was a congruence between the personal and the generational. Writing about the decay of his own family, he was writing about the decline of the European bourgeoisie. The novel conveys an exceptionally strong sense of what Georg Lukács calls "bourgeois patrician dignity: the dignity that derives from the slow movement of solid wealth." The novel, like the Mann family, could hardly have been rooted more deeply in Lübeck, a small city which has preserved many signs of its Hanseatic past and could hardly be less representative of the modern port. But the critic Albert Guerard found the Lübeck of *Buddenbrooks* "no stranger than Mauriac's Bordeaux. The commercial background reminded me at times of [Gustav Freytag's] *Soll und Haben*, at times of *Dombey and Son*, at times of *The Forsyte Saga*." Guerard concludes: "Thomas Mann is Europe."[38]

Writing My Life

COSTING 6 MARKS in hardcover and 5 marks in paperback, the cheap edition of *Buddenbrooks* came out at the beginning of 1903. By the end of the year over 10,000 copies had been sold, and by the end of 1906, 37,000. By 1918 sales had passed 100,000 copies. Reviewing the six stories in *Die Gegenwart*, Otto Grautoff could say: "The number of those who have not yet read Thomas Mann's novel *Buddenbrooks* is beginning to dwindle; for this beautiful, melancholy book has penetrated in the course of two years to the widest circle of readers." It wasn't one of the books that made an immediate impact, only to be forgotten quickly: "[I]t has made its way quite slowly, gradually breaking through to serious significance and general approval."[1] As Thomas wrote, "It was fame. I was caught up in a whirl of success. . . . Letters flooded in, and so did money, my picture appeared in the illustrated papers, a hundred pens wrote about the work I had produced in seclusion, the world embraced me amid praise and congratulation."[2]

After having to live on 200 marks a month, plus earnings from periodicals, he received a royalty of a mark on each copy sold. The two-volume edition had brought in a total of 2,400 marks, but from 1903 onward the cheap edition earned him at least 13,000 marks a year, while fame enabled him to command high fees for lectures, readings, contributions to newspapers, magazines, and radio programs.

No one could have predicted that such a novel could become so popular, but twenty-nine years later he went some way toward explaining its success when he quoted Goethe's comment on the popularity of his early play *Götz von Berlichingen*: "There is a strangely comforting sensation that a whole people can experience when a man succeeds in calling up its history strikingly and sympathetically. It celebrates the ancestral virtues and smiles at the ancestral shortcomings as at bygone events. A work of this sort is bound to arouse sympathetic applause."[3] In Theodor Fontane's *Der Stechlin*, the old man's decline has little historical resonance; the decay of the Buddenbrook family is the decay of a society, a way of life. Here was a narrative that defined decadence without being either decadent or avant-gardistic. Like the Forsytes, the Buddenbrooks belonged to the same class as most of the book's readers, and, as their social superiors, could arouse envy and pity at the same time.

IN FEBRUARY 1903, Thomas paid his first visit to Berlin. "The Hungry Ones" ("Die Hungernden") had been published at the end of January in *Die Zukunft*, and "Tonio Kröger" appeared in the February issue of the *Neue Deutsche Rundschau*. Six stories collected under the title *Tonio Kröger* were on sale at the same time as the cheap edition of *Buddenbrooks*, which allowed readers to compare a massive novel with six small-scale fictions. As Hermann Hesse, then an assistant in a Basel bookshop, wrote in a Zurich paper, *Buddenbrooks* had shown its author to be an athlete, capable of running long distances, while the stories showed he was also a juggler, a master of the bagatelle.[4] He struck Fischer's wife, Hedwig, as "a little aloof, somewhat incommunicative, with the elegant certainty of pose which betrayed the good breeding of his Hanseatic patrician background."[5]

Richard Schaukal's reaction was similar. "The impression of his outward appearance conforms with that of his writing: distinguished and simple, reserved and temporising composure. The melancholy, sincere eyes are German, profound, intense; the steep brow stands nakedly above them, and a fine, nervous nose. A soft moustache that tries in vain to look north German and military. Parted, towering hair, chestnut-brown, brushed outwards from the sympathetic temples."[6]

He did well at the readings he gave in Berlin, sharing the platform with Jakob Wassermann at the Lessing Gesellschaft on February 4, and appearing alone the next day at the Verein der Berliner Presse. Invited to Fischer's home in Fasanenstrasse, he met one of his favorite composers—Richard Strauss. Thomas seems generally to have impressed the people he met; the one old friend to be upset was Arthur Holitscher, who'd recognized himself in "Tristan" as Detlev Spinell—"this maliciously caricatured figure." But it wasn't until several months later that he protested at the abuse of "living models."[7]

No one could have shamed Thomas into desisting from this practice, which was essential to his way of recycling experience, and he could afford to let several of his relationships deteriorate—even the one with Heinrich, who was living in Italy. His ambitious novel *Die Göttinnen*, which had come out at the end of 1902, won extravagant praise from many writers and critics, including Gottfried Benn and Erich Mühsam, but Thomas went out of his way to attack it obliquely in a book review for a Munich weekly. Discussing a novel by Toni Schwabe, he praised her for her delicacy: "No breathlessness. No ferocious and desperate attacks on the reader's interest." Her subtlety was "roughly the opposite of that puffed-up pseudo-poetry which during the last few years has been brought in from the beautiful land of Italy."[8]

In mid-May Thomas went to stay by the Tegernsee with Kurt Martens, who'd written a rave review of "Tristan" in the *Literarische Echo*, ranking Thomas as one of the best German storytellers; younger colleagues would recognize him as "a master of their art." Walking with him in the woods outside Kreuth, Martens talked about his years in the cavalry. One of the stories he told would appear in Thomas's story "A Moment of Happiness" ("Ein Glück"), but the only jotting about it in his notebook is: "Casino story: baker-boy—riding on the pavement—pistol-shooting in the marketplace."[9]

Heinrich still hadn't read Thomas's review of Toni Schwabe's novel when the brothers both took a summer holiday where their mother was staying, outside Weilheim, thirty-four miles southwest of Munich, on the Würmsee, not far from the Bavarian Alps. Polling was a deconsecrated Benedictine monastery. Its owner, Max Schweigart, was farming the estate and supplementing his income by taking summer boarders. Under the Gothic arches, baroque furniture and sculptures mingled with paintings and books inherited from the monastery. Julia had stayed there during the summer of 1899 as the guest of her future son-in-law, Josef Löhr. She and Viktor liked Polling so much that they went back regularly, and in the summer of 1903 it was the scene of a family reunion involving Thomas, Heinrich, and Carla, who'd left the theater at Zwickau and was due to join a company in Düsseldorf when the new season began in the autumn. In March, Julia had been thinking she might rent a seven-room apartment, keeping two of the rooms for Thomas and two for Heinrich,[10] but nothing came of this plan to reestablish concord between the brothers and unity in the family.

After arriving at Polling during July, Thomas stayed till the end of August. Heinrich was there till early September, and, judging from entries in Thomas's notebook, their conversations were not devoid of friction:

> Hatred makes me *suffer* more than any other feeling. In comparison with the refined, cold H. I am a soft-hearted plebeian, but equipped with much more thirst for power. It is not for nothing that Savonarola is my hero. . . . I should not hate you because my role is to love you? No, I hate you all the more passionately . . . because I hate no-one more than those who alert me to weaknesses in my character through feelings they arouse in me.[11]

Of the people who knew both brothers, few would have called Thomas more soft-hearted and plebeian, but the analysis is accurate in linking hatred of Heinrich with heightened awareness of his own weaknesses.

It was in 1903, taking only a few months over it, that Heinrich wrote a novel he didn't publish until the summer of 1904, *Die Jagd nach Liebe* (*The Hunt for Love*). The action centers on an unsuccessful actress, Ute, rather like Carla, on whom he'd been emotionally fixated for several years. She was only thirteen when she inspired his sequence of poems "Mysterium," and, according to Viktor, she was still a young girl when she had "great success with the young men of the neighbourhood."[12] The suicidal fifteen-year-old girl in Heinrich's 1894 story "Contessina" had been modeled on her, and by the time he wrote *Die Jagd nach Liebe*, she was twenty-one. Though Ute's rich admirer, Claude, isn't her brother, they behave as if there were an incest taboo between them, especially when he forces his way into her room, threatening to take her by force. When she read the novel, Carla understood its secret meaning, but she said only that she had more in common with Ute than Heinrich realized. "I can play only women who break down either mentally or physically. Or of course all those who are inclined from the beginning to hysteria or some form of sickness. And I believe Ute is like this—isn't that right?"[13]

HEINRICH WAS BEING phenomenally prolific, and Thomas was probably thinking of him when he made one of the characters in his Savonarola play, *Fiorenza*, argue that all good work is produced effortlessly. The play itself was being written slowly, with enormous effort, partly because Thomas had no previous experience of the dramatic form. As with the elaboration of Tonio Kröger's credo, he worked tirelessly when he came up against difficulties.

Throughout 1903, Thomas's main project was his abortive novel *The Loved Ones* (*Die Geliebten*). Together with numerous jottings for scenes between Rudolf and Adelaide, his notebook contains diaristic entries about conversations and moments of shared experience with Paul. Many of these could easily be fitted into the story. Some of the dialogue in the notebook seems to come directly from actual conversations, while other passages seem to depart from what had actually been said. It's dangerous, of course, to develop a novel and a relationship in tandem. You may misinterpret your lover's behavior to suit a pattern that's emerging in the fiction, or you may find yourself fanning the flames of a quarrel to provide the story with a good climax.

Often jealous of Paul's involvements with other people—a young baroness, for instance—Thomas would usually be reassured by demonstratively affectionate behavior—Paul's arm around his shoulder, or a prolonged handclasp.

Incidentally he is born for flirtation and not for love or friendship. Our friendship is also a flirtation, and I am quite sure it would have less appeal for him if it were not. . . . It is astonishing how closely he observes each nuance of my behaviour towards him. I should be grateful for this. . . . In the evening he found me in the drawing-room alone at the piano when he came and greeted me with a movement and a smile I found touching and heart-warming. No, it is true! He greets no-one else in the way he greets me—neither women nor chums. He *is* my friend.[14]

Thomas couldn't understand why he squandered so much time on letters to Paul and Carl. He justified it by telling himself that since he never worked on fiction in the afternoons, he couldn't be spending the time better than on the five-finger exercises involved in writing to the brothers. "Besides, I am not a man of letters but a serious writer who is working on his life. And in so far as I am *building beautiful bridges* between my artistic isolation and that bit of the world, I am writing my life."[15]

The relationship with Paul was often painful: In his notes, Thomas writes in the third person, making Rudolf behave badly and Adelaide suffer. "He comes to have tea with her at five and says he has promised to be somewhere else between half past five and six, which simply is not true. Then stays till six, an enchanting indication that he stayed here as if bound by chains, that the others can wait. It belongs to his social technique." "Feverish night of love after being unhappily together: a consequence of boisterous short dreams in which he is always there and shows himself to be cold and suspicious or talks to her hurtfully—to clear the air—about his connections with others. In between she is constantly waking up, getting up, putting the light on. 'My God, my God, how is this possible! How is so much torture possible.' "[16] Most of the notes seem to be intended for the period before Rudolf and Adelaide become lovers, and there's no knowing how Thomas, if he'd completed the novel, would have integrated these with the notes (presumably more fictional) for the later period of their relationship.

Everything was going to change, and the break, when it came, would come suddenly, but the buildup to it was slow. Thomas began to take an interest in the twenty-year-old Katia Pringsheim long before he channeled all his energy into wooing her. The daughter of an exceptionally rich professor and a beautiful ex-actress, Katia not only looked like a princess but behaved like one. Son of a Silesian railway entrepreneur who'd made a fortune in the early days of industrialization, Alfred Pringsheim belonged to a Jewish family that had converted to Protestantism. Since 1886 he'd been professor of mathematics at the University of Munich, and his forty-nine-year-old wife, the former Hedwig Dohm, was one of the city's most fashionable hostesses. At twenty-three she'd given up a promising career in the troupe run by the duke of

Saxe-Meiningen to marry Alfred Pringsheim, who was now fifty-four. His mistress, the singer Milka Ternina, was accepted by his wife and received as a regular guest in the house.

Katia was dark-haired and pretty. For at least a year, without trying to meet her, Thomas, who was still involved with Paul, went on taking an interest in her from a distance, although several of his friends knew her parents, and he could easily have got an introduction. But it was characteristic of him to hold back from action when he was most emotionally excited. In the Kaim-Saal, the concert hall, where her father had subscription tickets for six seats in the second row, Thomas often saw Katia, her mother, and her four brothers. One of them, Klaus, was her twin. Sitting in the gallery, Thomas focused his opera glasses on "the silver shawl on her shoulders, her black hair, the pearly paleness of her face down there, her appearance of wanting to hide her awareness that many people were looking at her."[17] He also saw her in the theater, at the opera, at parties, and sometimes on a tram.

He didn't at first realize she was the girl in a picture he'd cut out at the age of fourteen and pinned above his desk. It featured her and her four brothers dressed as Pierrots in white costumes with page-boy haircuts, frilly collars, black stockings, black pompoms on their tunics, and tall white hats. The girl was six and the youngest of the boys was her twin; the eldest was ten. The photograph, which had appeared in several magazines, was of a picture, "Kinder Karneval," painted in July 1888 by court portraitist Friedrich Kaulbach, a friend of the family giving the party, a fancy dress ball for children.

The first evidence of Thomas's interest in Katia appears in a letter to Grautoff drafted in a notebook on August 29, 1903. Having confided in his friend the previous evening, Thomas made no attempt to conceal his elation: "[I]f you knew what wonders and wild stories I've been letting myself dream up in the last few days–and nights! What a fool! A jackanapes! It would be better to get down to some hard work and produce something good, instead of giving way to fairy stories." He cryptically mentions "the ancient garden with the international public," probably meaning a garden party at which he'd seen Katia, and he goes on to compare the "miracle" with one that occurred at school in Grautoff's presence–presumably an encounter with Armin Martens or Willri Timpe. Thomas was confident of having made a good impression on the people he met in the "ancient garden." "And what if it was only the cut of my frock-coat that attracted so much attention? I do not believe that. I do not need to."[18]

In the same way that his friendship with Paul had been interwoven with work on an abortive novel, he went on sketching out the novel that would eventually be called *Royal Highness* (*Königliche Hoheit*) as he was getting to know Katia. Just before the draft of his letter to Grautoff, he made the jotting: "You are Emperor (Czar)—live alone! Epigraph to *Royal Highness* (Pushkin)" and a couple of pages after the draft of the letter, under the heading *Royal Highness*, he makes his first notes for the novel. A prince, being constantly under observation, must constantly be presentable. A prince, Thomas notes, is a lieutenant at sixteen and a captain at twenty-five. After referring to Tamino, the prince in Mozart's *Die Zauberflöte*, he writes preliminary notes about the prince in his new novel—his way of sitting in a car and his connection with an American millionaire.[19]

A few days after making these jottings Thomas went to Düsseldorf, where Carla was playing a leading part, Luise, in Schiller's *Kabale und Liebe*, which opened at the Stadttheater on October 3. At the palatial Park Hotel, Thomas had his first taste of the luxury offered by grand hotels, and it gave him some ideas for the novel. He watched the elevator-boy with his cap fastened to his thigh, and noticed how visitors preserved their dignity by remaining silent while being waited on. He looked appreciatively at white marble floors and pillars, luxurious beds, white lacquered double doors with brass handles and bolts. In the afternoon, refreshments were served on a tea tray—fruit in a silver basket, biscuits on a plate with a doily and a finger bowl. He noticed the quietness of life in the hotel as people walked about on carpet. There were rubber wheels on the trolleys used for luggage. In the prince's life the silence would be broken only occasionally, by applause or cheering. These notes were made on October 6 in an address book Thomas had taken to Düsseldorf; back in Munich he transferred them to a notebook.[20]

Observing rich hotel guests and their reactions to deferential treatment, he felt ambivalent, as he did when thinking about the Pringsheims. He'd have preferred to be unimpressed by wealth and the privileges it bought, but he was avidly collecting impressions that could serve as raw material for a novel in which his portrayal of a royal family would derive from observations of the Pringsheims and the hotel guests, though in the novel he introduces a polarity between the royal court, with its dignified rituals, and the family of the American millionaire, Samuel Spoelmann, and his daughter, Imma, who are modeled on Alfred Pringsheim and Katia.

At the end of October, Thomas left Munich again to give readings in Königsberg and Berlin, where he learned that sales of the one-volume *Buddenbrooks* had passed the ten thousand mark, and met some of Fischer's authors, including Gabriele Reuter and Gerhart Hauptmann. Now forty-four, Reuter had made her name in 1895 with the novel *Aus guter Familie*, about a woman from a good family who tries unsuccessfully to make contact with social reality by breaking through the conventional barriers. Frau Reuter's subsequent fiction had focused on obstacles to female emancipation. In the first sentence of a long essay he later wrote on her for a Berlin newspaper, Thomas betrayed one of his own anxieties: "Every artist must be fearful of being overtaken by the sad fate that threatens, if only from afar: to remain until death and for posterity the author of a successful first work." Thomas also appears to be thinking more about himself—he even uses the masculine pronoun—than about Reuter when he analyzes the writer's division of interest between developing his artistic potential and ameliorating the human condition. "Seriously, it is only too probable that he believes in nothing on earth except his own talent."[21]

The forty-one-year-old Hauptmann was impressive. "I would have been a long way from expecting so much magic to go out from his personality as it actually exudes."[22] Hauptmann was in Berlin for the premiere of his play *Rose Bernd*. Eager to be liked and unable to gauge what the playwright felt about him, Thomas was probably more optimistic than he made himself out to be. Hauptmann, "always victorious, will have formed the impression of confusion, conflict, awkwardness, and extreme exhaustion. . . . The others, who have regarded my person with curiosity, will just be bitterly disappointed. Perhaps I also compensate them through the assiduously crafted symbol of my life, which is less uninteresting than my mustachioed personality."[23]

Wanting to learn about royal etiquette, he was reading Herr von Holten's memoirs of the Danish court, but what proved more fruitful, as Thomas went on living his fiction and writing his life, was his ability to empathize with a prince. "Love and tenderness for his own exquisite person," runs one note under the heading *Royal Highness*. "Looking after his body. Rubbing his pale skin." The more Thomas thought about it, the more affinities he found between himself and his hero. Like the prince, the artist—or at least *his* kind of artist—is isolated, remote, deprived of the facile pleasures of shoulder-rubbing familiarity with ordinary people. The basic assumption of distance from mediocrity is the same as in "Tonio Kröger," but there is less emphasis on deprivation, and more on privilege. The blond Hans Hansens and Inge Holms, who look so ordinary, have been displaced by an extraordinary dark girl who looks like a princess. Imma also looks rather like photographs of Julia Mann as a girl.

At the beginning of December, Thomas wrote: "The artist invariably finds direct personal intimacy and communicativeness unsatisfying and trivial because he habitually represents his life in symbols (works of art). He leads a symbolic, representative life—like the prince!"[24] Another note runs: "Looking into the interior of a ground-floor flat on the corner of Friedrichstrasse. *That* is American. In comparison my room is royal."

Though he was venturing into new subject matter, he'd written so much about tensions and contrasts between artists and the bourgeoisie that he felt entitled to regard this territory as his own, and Heinrich appeared to be invading it in *Die Jagd nach Liebe*. Thomas must also have realized that it was a novel about Carla and Heinrich's feelings for her, but he says nothing about this, though the letter is more aggressive than any he'd previously written. He starts with a statement about being depressed: "I am working with disgust and without the slightest satisfaction. I give away the filth in the deepest of despair, and then I get letters, money, praise. People shake my hand and 'admire' me. Everyone enjoys it except me. Which is unfair." But he goes on to launch a fierce attack on his brother, accusing him of striving ambitiously for effect. Heinrich had always seemed to be a man of distinction, "full of discretion and culture." "Instead of which we now have what? These contrived jokes, these wild, horrible, hectic, contorted violations of truth and humanity, these desperate bids for the reader's interest!" The treatment of sexuality was crude and the novel was determined less by a hunt for love than a hunt for effect. The constant smell of flesh was exhausting, and everything was garish, strident, exaggerated.[25] While attacking Heinrich for faults he was well aware of having himself, Thomas was also making accusations against himself.

Another letter written on the same day indicates a different mood, though it also voices misgivings about his fame. "One feels as if one were exposed in the beam of a gigantic searchlight, one's whole body visible in public, burdened with responsibility for disposal of the gifts one was imprudent enough to reveal." He wrote this to Walter Opitz, a writer who'd come to Munich after reading "Tonio Kröger" and, meeting Thomas, had been disappointed at his failure to strike up a friendship. Thomas tried to console him by making out that he always held back from personal contact: "No-one can come closer to me than those who, like you, read 'Tonio Kröger,' and if you found me very reserved personally, that may be because one loses the taste for personal communication when one forms the habit of expressing oneself symbolically." The letter goes on to make the comparison Thomas had made in his notebook between the writer and the prince. Both lead a "representative" life, and the prince, Klaus Heinrich, is named after his brother.[26]

He develops this idea in *Royal Highness*, making the prince's tutor, Dr. Überbein, explain that formality and intimacy are mutually exclusive. Leading, as he must, a formal existence, Klaus Heinrich has to keep his distance from people who would like to be his friends. His function is to stand for the many by being himself, to be the exalted and self-disciplined representative of the masses.

Thomas couldn't devote all his working time to the novel. He was eager to finish his Savonarola play; the *Neue Freie Presse* had sent a telegram asking for a story; he'd just finished an article for the *Neue*

Rundschau (which had changed its name, leaving out the word *Deutsche*) and he'd been asked to review some books for *Der Tag*. By now he'd written "A Moment of Happiness," but didn't think much of it.[27] It begins, gauchely and self-consciously, with the author's apologies for being so busy that he can't spend much time on his character, the baroness. He's on his way back from ancient Florence, has been dealing with serious matters, and may be on his way to court—perhaps a royal castle.

After this unpromising start, Thomas succeeds in building Kurt Martens's anecdote into a moving story about cavalry officers who are being entertained in the presence of their wives by an itinerant group of female singers called the Swallows. The sensitive Baroness Anna is watching her profligate husband, Baron Harry, with a young Swallow, Emmy, who's unexceptional but attractive, with childlike arms and black strands of hair framing a wide sensual face. She's less attracted to the vain, insensitive, self-confident baron than to a young cadet he humiliates. The cadet had been at the piano, accompanying the Swallows, until the baron shouted across the room, abusing him for playing badly and ordering him to let a lieutenant take over.

Watching her flirtatious husband with Emmy, Anna realizes that she likes the girl more than he does, and when he pulls off Emmy's ring, giving her his wedding ring in return, Anna gets up to walk out of the casino, only to be intercepted by the girl, who apologetically and respectfully kisses the baroness's hand as she returns the ring. There's a moment of genuine happiness in the contact between the two women, but Thomas leaves this theme undeveloped. The story was written in October 1903 and published at the beginning of 1904 in the first issue of Fischer's magazine under its new title, the *Neue Rundschau*.

Piano-playing features again in "The Infant Prodigy" ("Das Wunderkind"). At the Munich conservatory Thomas had attended a piano recital by a nine-year-old Greek boy, Loris Margaritis; the nine-year-old pianist-composer in this satirical story is called Bibi Saccellaphylaccas, but the satire is aimed mainly against his public. Having found it so easy to arouse audiences to enthusiasm during his readings, Thomas was drawing on the mixture of gratitude and contempt he felt toward people who applauded him.

In the first paragraph he uses the word *Leute* (people) seven times and the neologism *Leutehirn* (collective brain) twice. The story reflects his uneasiness about the relationship between the artist and the machinery that controls his contact with the public, while itself being controlled by the profit motive. The nine-year-old Greek boy, who's dressed entirely in white silk and has learned a number of tricks from his impresario, enjoys applause and knows how to prolong it. His favorites among his own compositions aren't the same as the public's favorites, and Thomas harshly contrasts the individual performer with his audiences, which collectively have only a "heavy, dull, mobile soul." Not expecting them to appreciate nuances, Bibi caters with precocious cynicism to their appetite for vulgar effects, while the narrative, taking us inside the mind of a few spectators, shows how irrelevant their thoughts are to the music that is being performed. At the end of the performance, the boy is introduced to an elderly princess, and the reader, by way of contrast, is introduced to an elegant, exquisitely beautiful young lady, who's being helped into her evening cloak and fur shoes by her two brothers, both lieutenants.

Giving a reading in Munich on December 11, Thomas started with "The Infant Prodigy," which was well received, though, writing to Heinrich, Thomas said he had shamelessly written both stories to commission for the money. Heinrich, naturally enough, had responded angrily to Thomas's letter about *Die Jagd nach Liebe*, but Thomas was keen to make peace before Christmas. "It is better for us both when we are friends—certainly for me. I never feel worse than when I am hostile to you."[28]

Heinrich wasn't ready to make peace, and Thomas sent another letter in January, complaining that Heinrich misunderstood him, rather like Uncle Friedel, who'd failed to understand that in *Buddenbrooks* Thomas had involved himself "better, longer and more passionately" in Christian, the character modeled on him, than in anyone else. He and Heinrich should let their relationship mature. They were both at an age "where it is easy to mistake what is only Pathos for Ethos and where one is always inclined to believe one's present condition will continue throughout eternity."[29]

The new year had begun well for Thomas. Over fourteen thousand copies of *Buddenbrooks* had been sold, and a new literary society in Lübeck invited him to give a reading. Keen though he was to appear there, he was apprehensive; perhaps his chances of a friendly reception would be greater if the reading were deferred until later.[30]

Deciding to make peace, Heinrich sent a typescript of his latest story, "Fulvia," which is about a love affair during the Risorgimento of 1848. Thomas's reaction could hardly have been more effusive. He called it "a brilliant little thing, firm, noble, masterly, and with that romantic intensity of style which is so entirely your own. It made me think, once again, that today you are really the only writer who can still write stories, adventures, authentic novellas—the only one who is really inspired."[31]

Without quite stepping into irony, the tone brinks on it, and Thomas is self-consciously damning himself by praising his brother as the only inspired writer who can still tell stories.

Heinrich had moved significantly to the left since he gave up editing *Das Zwanzigste Jahrhundert*, and Thomas was uncertain how to take the evidence of his new liberalism in the story.

It must make you feel unexpectedly young and strong? Really I would interpret your liberalism as a sort of consciously mastered youthfulness if it did not, more probably, simply signify "maturity." Maturity! Will I ever achieve it?

First of all I understand little about "freedom." It is for me a purely moral and intellectual concept, synonymous with "honesty." (In me some critics call it "coldheartedness.") But I have no interest at all in political freedom. The most powerful Russian books were surely written under monstrous oppression. Would perhaps never have come into existence without this oppression? Which at least means that the battle for "freedom" is better than freedom itself. What exactly is "freedom"? Simply because so much blood has been shed for the notion, it has for me something uncannily *un*free about it, something quite medieval.[32]

This studied indifference to political freedom derived from Nietzsche, who'd expected the growth of socialism to be culturally damaging. The Europeans of the future would probably be "talkative, weak-willed, and highly employable workers, who need masters, leaders, as badly as they need daily bread. The democratisation of Europe is conducive to the production of a type prepared for slavery in the finest sense."[33] The imperatives of the herd morality were based on timidity. "Sooner or later we would like a world in which there is *nothing left to be afraid of*. In modern Europe everything that tends *in this direction* is called progress."[34]

Underlying Thomas's antipathy to political freedom was a fear of personal freedom, but he couldn't afford to scrutinize this, though he was becoming more alert to the Nordic strain in his temperament, more aware that, unlike Heinrich, who seemed to have inherited their mother's predisposition to a Mediterranean outlook, he was gravitating toward their father's austerity. In January 1904, answering a questionnaire in *Die Zeit*, he wrote:

To use the words of the young Nietzsche, I love and affirm in "the atmosphere of ethics, the Faustian flavour, the cross, death and the grave."[35] In art I believe in pain, experience, recognition, love, profundity, and confront all superficial beauty with either irony or impatience, as seems appropriate. . . . Wherever they come from, Protestant, moralistic and Puritanic inclinations are deep-seated in my blood, and as I nourish a mild contempt for the Southern orientation, every specific vulgarity that unambiguously derives from Italianate taste in art provokes in me an instinctive and nervous displeasure.[36]

Part Two

Like a Princess

THOMAS'S DECISION TO GET MARRIED was like a punishment he imposed on himself, not arbitrarily but despotically, during February 1904. For over four years his life had revolved around Paul Ehrenberg, and recently nothing had mattered more than indications that Paul genuinely cared; nothing had been more alarming than evidence of his interest in another man or woman. But in February 1904, Katia displaced Paul as the person Thomas thought about most. There was no quarrel with Paul, no negotiation, not even a discussion. Thomas simply started wooing Katia as if an order had been issued by a god he couldn't question.

The long-delayed introduction to Katia had been effected between February 7 and 23–shortly after an incident on a tram. She usually cycled to her classes at the university, where she was studying math with her father and experimental physics with Wilhelm Röntgen, the man who had discovered X rays. But when it rained, she made the journey by tram, and one morning, when she threw her ticket away before getting off at the corner of Schellingstrasse and Türkenstrasse, the conductor tried to make her buy another ticket, She lost her temper, and Thomas was impressed by her refusal to be bullied.[1]

In her book *Unwritten Memories* (*Meine ungeschriebenen Memoiren*), she describes the Manns of Lübeck and the Pringsheims of Munich. The Manns, she says, were "somewhat anti-Semitic and conservative–that's the way it was in Germany." The Pringsheims were rich and cultivated, she says, without mentioning their Jewishness, and she'd been brought up in ignorance of it. That's the way it was in Germany.

It may have been through Fischer that Thomas got to know Max and Elsa Bernstein, who were both writers, though he was better known as a lawyer; under a male pseudonym, Ernst Rosmer, his thirty-seven-year-old wife had scored a success with a fantasy play, *Die Königskinder* (*The King's Children*), which had incidental music by Engelbert Humperdinck. It was probably the Bernsteins who got Thomas invited to the Pringsheims' house in Arcisstrasse. "One day I found myself in the Italian Renaissance salon with its Gobelins, its Lenbachs, its door carvings in *giallo antico*, and I accepted an invitation to the big ball that was to be held there the next evening. 150 people, literary and artistic."[2]

Placed at the same table as Frau Bernstein, he felt the strain of acting up—like a prince—to the expectations of admirers. By now *Buddenbrooks* had sold over eighteen thousand copies, and people crowded around, staring at him, wanting to meet him, and listening respectfully to everything he said. The experience was unpleasant but not unwelcome, since it offered insight into the feelings of royalty regularly surrounded by curious onlookers.

On his first visit to the Pringsheims' house, Thomas had spoken only briefly to Katia; their first conversation was at the ball. He went back to the house a week later, returning a book Hedwig Pringsheim had lent him, possibly to give him a pretext for coming back. She was alone when he was shown in, but she called Katia, and the three of them chatted for an hour over tea. Two days later Katia's twin brother, Klaus, a musician, called on Thomas, bringing a visiting card from his father, who was too busy to come himself. Klaus was "an extremely pleasant young man, soigné, educated, considerate, with north German manners. No thought of Jewishness occurs in the company of these people; nothing but culture is in evidence. We chatted about all kinds of things—art, his music, his sister."[3] Thomas habitually thought in terms of polarities, and the antithesis between Jewishness and culture is revealing. In this letter to Heinrich, he described Katia as "a miracle, something indescribably rare and precious, a creature who through her mere existence has more cultural value than the output of fifteen writers or thirty painters."[4]

Aware as she was of being stared at in the street and in the theater, Katia didn't consider herself to be pretty. And her paternal grandmother kept telling her she'd never be on a par with her mother, who was regarded as a great beauty. The Pringsheims entertained frequently and lavishly, holding regular Sunday tea parties. The elegant Hedwig Pringsheim, dressed in Chinese or Indian silk, presided charmingly, pouring tea from a heavy silver teapot. Their house and lifestyle reminded Thomas of his parents' home in Lübeck and the parties that had been a regular feature of his childhood.

His courtship of Katia was assiduous, but he was less in love with her than with her background and the adventure of wooing a young woman so much like a princess. Her style, her clothes, her self-confidence, her pride, and her family's position in local society made people deferential to her. To woo her was to enter into a relationship with the family, and Thomas, with traumatic memories of having his family sent into exile by his father's will, needed a new father figure and a new family. In the questionnaire he'd filled out at the age of twenty-four for Ilse Martens, he'd equated happiness with independence and living in harmony with himself. Eight years later he was less ambitious.

Alone with Katia he felt reasonably comfortable, though less relaxed than he'd been with Paul and Carl Ehrenberg. He'd felt more at ease with them than with any previous friends, and nothing in his new life would replace the hours the three of them had spent together. He knew this, but the opportunity seemed too good to miss. As he told Heinrich,

> nothing has actually *happened*. It's all alive only in my imagination, but it is too daring, too new, too colourful, too superbly like an adventure for me to withdraw from it yet. The *possibility* has offered itself, and makes me feverish. I can think of nothing else. . . . But I can say this straight away: it is pointless to ask whether I would be happy. Am I striving for happiness? I am striving for—life: and *in that sense*, probably for my work. And something else: I am not frightened of wealth.[5]

At one time he'd thought of his predilection for irony as something that steered him away from living life to the full. Now, introducing a polarity between life and happiness, he's setting his sights on a future that gives him freedom to develop his literary potential. The indifference to happiness is bizarrely characteristic, and so is the failure to ask himself whether Katia was equally indifferent to it, and, if not, whether she'd achieve it as his wife. Like Klaus Heinrich, he was resigned to leading what he called a *representative* life, but was that what he expected her to want?

The letter goes on to describe an encounter with Albert Langen, who was now Heinrich's publisher. Meeting him at a party. Thomas put in a good word for his brother, predicting that he'd eventually "have a great success." Langen said he intended to keep Heinrich on his list. But this long letter didn't satisfy Thomas's need to confide in his elder brother. A month later, congratulating Heinrich on his thirty-third birthday, Thomas suggested they should spend a fortnight together in Riva during April.

Katia was being courted by several of the regular guests at the Pringsheims', including a university professor and a good-looking student, but, enjoying her life as it was, she was in no hurry to marry. She had her studies, her concertgoing, the companionship of her brothers, tennis at the local club, and cycle rides with the student. Her mother's bookseller predicted that Thomas would become as great as Gottfried Keller, but her father didn't want a writer as his son-in-law, thinking a professor would be preferable, while her brothers, amused by the erectness of Thomas's stance and the pride he took in his appearance, dubbed him "the liverish cavalry officer." But her mother made Katia take him seriously,[6] and, writing to Heinrich again at the end of March, he reported that Hedwig Pringsheim smiled encouragingly whenever he felt relaxed enough to say "Katia," instead of "Fräulein

Katia" or "your daughter."[7] At the beginning of April he told Kurt
Martens he was making such "gigantic strides" that he might prefer not
to leave Munich.

There was an element of game-playing in his campaign, as there was
in his writing. He'd always thought of himself as a kind of prince, and
identification with Klaus Heinrich was like a continuation of his childhood fantasy. Identifying with his hero, he was indulging in an adult
version of the same game, and when he thought about a bride for the
prince, he pictured Katia. He used her as the model for Imma Spoelmann, the American millionaire's daughter, emphasizing Imma's darkness. This is a common denominator between the Pringsheims'
Jewishness and the southern exoticism Thomas associated with his
mother, contrasting it with the blond, blue-eyed Aryan quality his father had. One of the leitmotivs in *Royal Highness* would be references to
blue-black hair and dark eyes that gaze searchingly at the prince. Another quality Imma shares with Katia is freedom from self-consciousness: She isn't nervous about the prince's reactions, or anyone else's.

Katia had an appealingly boyish body, and as the playmate of a twin
brother and three other brothers who weren't much older, she'd grown
into more of a tomboy than she might have done if she'd had a sister or
two. Had she been more womanly, she'd have been less like the boys
and young men who preceded her in Thomas's amorous fantasies. The
novel never focuses on Imma's femininity, and she's never made to
seem seductive or sexy. Her figure is childlike, and though her arms are
well developed, her shoulders and wrists are those of a child. Neither
her legs nor her breasts are mentioned or even indicated, except in a
sentence which says her figure is well shaped yet childlike. There's also
something childlike about her way of speaking, and some of the sounds
she utters are distinctly childish. In moments of affection Klaus Heinrich inwardly calls her "Little Sister." Thomas couldn't confide in Katia
as he had in Grautoff, Heinrich, and Paul, but he felt a strong urge to
possess her.

Working on the novel, he could identify with both the prince, whose
rank is hereditary, and the Spoelmanns, who, like the Pringsheims, are
richer than the Manns had been but resemble the Buddenbrooks as
burghers who have achieved not only wealth but power and prestige
through mercantile success. This gives the two real and two fictional
families something in common with the Medicis, and in *Fiorenza* the
dying Lorenzo talks to his sons, Piero and Giovanni, about the family's
rise to political power through commercial acumen. The Magnifico,
who secretly despises the citizens he rules, warns Piero and Giovanni to
be aloof and stern with themselves. The crowd needs to pay homage—
homage is easy to pay—but the Medicis' supremacy depends on the ability to win power afresh every day.

The play echoes *Buddenbrooks* and the history of the Mann family. Ever since Grandfather died, the Medici family has been decaying, and according to Giovanni, even sparrows on the treetops know this. The brothers quarrel, and Lorenzo makes no secret of his dissatisfaction with them both. It's their fault that Savonarola has won effective control of the city. The play is awkwardly written, with too little action, too many long speeches, and too much argument. Like Hieronymus in "Gladius Dei," Savonarola is ugly, with a big, hooked nose; thin, compressed lips; a sallow, woebegone face; and a small sickly body. He's fanatically hostile to the sensual art that celebrates the beauty of women, costumes, colors, and surfaces. Infected with this killjoy Puritanism, the repentant Botticelli (in an offstage climax) destroys one of his paintings, while another artist, who has used his mistress as a model for the Virgin, is beaten by a crowd intoxicated with Savonarola's rhetoric.

In writing the play, Thomas depended as never before on pictures. His description of Savonarola derived mainly from the painting on wood Thomas kept on his writing table; he also owed a great deal to Giorgio Vasari, Villari, Jakob Burckhardt, and *Die Mediceer* by Eduard Heyck (1897), as well as to photographs he cut out of newspapers, magazines, and travel books.[8]

One of his concerns was to differentiate between the functions of art and literature. The artist mirrors things without analyzing them, while literature is based on opposition, irony, and nihilism. The writer can't let himself be conquered by facts and phenomena. Savonarola interested Thomas as a "born protestant"—a man with a physiological need to protest, regardless of the situation in which he finds himself.[9]

Without understanding how closely his characterization of Savonarola reflected the streak of asceticism in his own nature, Thomas threw himself into the pursuit of Katia. Hearing she enjoyed cycling, he suggested a bicycle ride, and took her by surprise when he turned up at the house one morning, saying she'd promised to go cycling with him. They rode to a lake in the English Garden, and, finding her American bike, a Cleveland, was faster than his, she pedaled defiantly ahead, not letting him catch up.

Toward the end of March she went into a private clinic for a minor operation on her foot. Her mother advised Thomas to send flowers, and, partly to thank her for helping, partly to carry the courtship a stage further, he introduced both mother and daughter into a story. Titled "At the Prophet's" ("Beim Propheten"), it's set on Good Friday in an attic apartment on the outskirts of the city, where "Proclamations" by an eccentric writer, Daniel, will be read aloud. In reality, on the evening of Good Friday, April 1, 1904, Hedwig Pringsheim and Thomas were at a poetry reading in the apartment of Ludwig Derleth, a member of Stefan

George's circle. Derleth's *Proklamationen*, a collection of verse, was published four years later. Like Hedwig Pringsheim, Derleth passionately admired Napoleon, and he came to her Sunday afternoon tea parties with his sister, who lived with him. In the story, Daniel's sister receives the guests, who include a rich lady and a successful young novelist. The novelist, who has a carefully trimmed mustache and wears a bowler hat, has fallen in love with the lady's daughter, a girl described in the terms Thomas had used when describing Katia to Heinrich. In the novelist's eyes she's "an incredible windfall of creation, a marvel of all-round education, a living cultural ideal." Just to pronounce her name gives him "an indescribable pleasure."[10]

Her mother is described in more detail. She lives in a splendid house with Gobelin tapestries on the walls and doorframes painted in *giallo antico*. Having been driven to the suburb in her silk-lined coupé, she appears in the doorway, "beautiful, sweet-scented, luxurious, in a blue woollen dress with yellow embroidery, a hat from Paris on her reddish-brown hair and a smile in her Titian eyes." Surprised to see her there, the novelist thanks God that he's looking presentable. "How beautiful she is! he thought. She is worthy to be the mother of this daughter. . . ."

An inflammation on her daughter's foot has been lanced in a clinic. Not content to send greetings through her mother, he accepts the suggestion that he should send flowers.[11] After being interrupted by the arrival of Daniel's "disciple," who reads the "proclamations," the lady and the novelist resume their conversation, and instead of saying "Fräulein Sonia" or "your daughter," the writer tentatively uses just the Christian name. The mother "set a high value on his books, and so she tolerated it, smiling."[12] Before publishing the story, he submitted it to Hedwig Pringsheim, who raised no objections.

Intrinsically unimportant, it shows how radically Thomas's image of himself had changed with the shift of allegiance from Paul to Katia. (This is not to say that the shift was the cause of the change: It may partly have been the result.) In early stories he'd identified with outsiders who either had no interest in the arts or no more than a dilettante's interest. Unlike the Clown and Spinell, Tonio has proved his seriousness and achieved fame but has remained an outsider to bourgeois society. Though he dresses carefully and keeps up appearances, he frequents artists' studios and garrets such as the one featured in "At the Prophet's," but the novelist in the story ventures only rarely into bohemian territory. Thomas is no longer presenting himself as isolated from the bourgeoisie.

The beautiful Hedwig Pringsheim had shown herself to be his ally, but her husband was still opposed to the marriage, and Katia was still undecided. While she was in the clinic, Thomas was invited to spend an evening with the family. Suffering from a headache and a sore throat when he arrived, he didn't conceal his malaise. When Hedwig Prings-heim advised him to make a cold compress, the professor, who was suf-fering from stomach trouble and lying on the sofa, got up to fetch a piece of gutta-percha from the closet, explaining how it should be used. Writing to Katia about it, Thomas was delighted to have evidence of her father's friendly concern.[13]

His jottings for *Royal Highness* contain material that seems no less di-aristic than the notes he'd made for *The Loved Ones:*

> Detail for a love story. As passion wanes, there is an increase in one's ability to conquer, to make oneself loved. For days he had suffered frightfully over her, full of yearning, weak, disoriented, broken down, ill. Then, after seeing her again in a big hat which did not specially suit her, he suddenly felt healthier, fresher, more free, more forward, less full of yearning, stronger, more "egoistic," able to challenge, score points, pay court, make an impression.[14]

The next entry in the notebook is: "Sunday 9 April–big discussion with K.P."

He now felt confident enough to leave Munich for three weeks. He went to Riva on April 16. A postcard to Carl Ehrenberg about rowing, cycling, and breathing the good air doesn't mention Katia, but he wrote to her several times, and complained about her slowness in replying: "Waiting is frightful. Fate should not be encouraged in its evil habit of letting good things happen only after one has waited for them so long that apathy has set in." But he was glad to hear she was no longer giving priority to her studies at the university.[15]

Restless throughout his six years in Munich, he'd already had five apartments, but after returning on May 7, he moved into the sixth in Ainmillerstrasse. Nine days later he had a "second big discussion with K.P.," and "the period of waiting began on Thursday 19 May."[16] But he didn't have to wait passively: He was a persistent and persuasive letter-writer with a flair for self-promotion, as he'd shown when telling Grau-toff how to review *Buddenbrooks.* "I am quite aware," he told her, "of not being a man who arouses simple and instantaneously safe feelings. . . . To prompt mixed feelings and 'perplexity' is after all–forgive me!–a sign of personality. Someone who never provokes doubts, never aston-ishes, never . . . causes a slight feeling of dread, someone who is always simply lovable is a fool, a phantom, a figure of fun."[17]

Uncertain of her feelings, and worried about "a sort of awkwardness or something" when they were together,[18] she said they should get to know each other gradually, but etiquette prevented them from being left alone together. As a chaperone, her twin brother, Klaus, was toler-ant. He knew when to turn his back and if he'd previously felt posses-sive about his twin sister, he quickly adapted to the new situation.

Afterward he claimed credit for bringing them together. But Thomas resented the waste of evenings they could have spent on getting to know each other better. In her presence he sometimes felt tongue-tied, but in his rather formal letters he was eloquent, even in describing aspects of himself that eluded definition: He was aware, he said, of causing the "sort of awkwardness"

> through my "lack of spontaneity," of ingenuousness, of unself-consciousness, all the nervousness, artificiality and difficulty of my nature, hinders everyone, even the most well-meaning people, from coming closer to me or even dealing with me in a bearable, comfortable way; and that troubles me all the more when I detect in people's behaviour towards me that warmer interest which is called sympathy, and in spite of all the obstacles, this happens with quite incredible frequency. . . . You know that personally, humanly, I could not develop like other young people, that a [talent] can function like a vampire—bloodsucking, parasitic. You know what a cold, impoverished, merely representative, merely symbolical life I have been living for years, know that for many years, *important* years, I regarded myself as nothing, in human terms, and wanted to be considered only as an artist. . . . Only one cure is possible for this attachment to the representative and artistic, this lack of instinctive trust in my personal and human side: through happiness; through *you*, my clever, sweet, good-hearted, beloved little queen . . . Be my affirmation, my justification, my fulfilment, my salvation, my—*wife*.[19]

Glossing over all the strong emotions he'd felt toward boys and young men, he was presenting his past life as more ascetic than it had actually been, but without taking her into his confidence about his ascetic plans for the future. His implication here is that he wants happiness and believes in it as something they can share.

He was still addressing her as "Sie," but within a few days, when they were together after dark in the garden at Arcisstrasse, he was rewarded with an embrace. On June 6, his twenty-ninth birthday, he wrote rapturously to her about feeling her "sweet, sweet little head" against his cheek.[20] Having to wait several days for an answer to this letter, he thought he'd offended her by using "certain possessive pronouns and nouns."[21] His words had been more possessive than his behavior.

He needed a male confidant, and instead of turning to Heinrich or Grautoff, he talked to Kurt Martens. They'd arranged to go on a Tyrolean trip together, to the Brenner Pass, but on June 9, Thomas reneged: "You know how strong the chains are that bind me here, and how they cut into the flesh at every attempt to escape."[22] Martens responded by advising him to give her a deadline: "What kind of weakling are you? . . . She constantly puts your patience on trial, fends you off, plays with you. . . . Let her see you are a man. . . . You are bound to seem less and less desirable to her, the longer the thing is dragged out."[23]

It would have been dangerous to act on this well-meant advice. Martens knew nothing about Katia's upbringing, or her combination of decisiveness and hesitancy. "To display manly strength by forcing the girl to a decision now would mean forcing her to say No, which we would both regret; for thanks to the quite exceptional form of her development, she cannot yet bring herself to say Yes."[24] The bonds that tied her to her parents could not have been thrown off abruptly.

All the same, his impatience had been sharpened by Martens's letter, and one day, unable to bear the strain of waiting passively, he clambered onto his bicycle and pedaled furiously for two hours without knowing where he was going. He passed through unfamiliar villages, skirmishing in one of them with a butcher's dog. When he returned to Ainmillerstrasse, dusty and disheveled, a letter was waiting. It struck him as sweeter and more confiding than any she'd previously written. It said she was afraid he might be overestimating her, that he had expectations she couldn't fulfill.

He was well equipped to rebut such arguments. He exploited Martens's advice, not following it but using it as an example of what people were saying about them, and giving the impression he'd reprimanded Martens sharply.

> Silly little Katia. Still carrying on about "overrating," and insisting you will be unable to "be" for me what I expect you to be. But I love you. Good God! Do you not understand what that means? What else is there to expect and to be? My wife is what I want you to "be," and in that way to make me absurdly proud and happy. After all, what I "make of you", the meaning I give you—which you have and will have for my life—is my concern, and it gives you no bother or responsibility.[25]

Though he was trying to be tender and teasing, the tone is still characteristically formal.

In late June and early July, when they were going for cycle rides together, he took a keen interest in the weather, tapping the barometer as if auscultating it.[26] Though she enjoyed his company, she kept pleading for more time, saying everything was happening too fast. In the summer her father fell ill, and went to take the cure at Kissingen. Her mother accompanied him, and when Katia joined them, she was ambivalent about leaving Munich. When Thomas wasn't pressing her for a decision, she felt everything between them was going well, but each time the question of marriage came up, she looked at him "like a hunted doe."[27] Meeting him every other day before she went, she was warm and affectionate. On the last day, Klaus left them alone together for half an hour. "There was an indescribably sweet and painful parting, which is still present in all my nerves and senses."28

Nothing was harder than to do nothing, but he had no alternative. Partly to give himself the illusion of making headway, he consulted a neurologist, Dr. Seif, who recommended tact and restraint. There might be a morbid element, he said, in Katia's fear of making a decision, but it would be dangerous to apply pressure. Thomas bought flowers to see her off at the station and, when Klaus took a considerately long time to pay the porter, she squeezed Thomas's hand.29

They were separated for most of the summer. She'd arranged to spend three weeks in Kissingen, returning to Munich for only a few days before going to Switzerland with her mother. In the autumn she was to stay with relations in the north of Germany. Thomas still couldn't concentrate on work. He was due to give a reading in Göttingen on June 21, and though he wanted to see *Parsifal* in Bayreuth, he'd gladly stay in Munich to see Katia. "You cannot believe how much I love this creature. I dream about her every night and wake up with my heart hurting all over. I have tasted too much of her to be able to withdraw."30

He'd been planning to spend six weeks with his mother, who'd given up Polling in favor of a villa at Utting on Lake Ammer, twenty-five miles west of Munich. After enjoying his encounter with interested academics and students at Göttingen, he spent a few days in Berchtesgaden, on the German side of the border near Salzburg. He wrote to Katia about snow-covered peaks floating above mists against the blue sky. "I am by no means a zealot about 'nature', but there are spectacles that move me."31

At the beginning of August he went to join his mother and fourteen-year-old Viktor in Utting. They were now living in Augsburg, where he was at the Gymnasium. Heinrich must have been one of the main topics in Thomas's conversation with his mother, though he was again feeling hostile toward his brother and the novels he produced:

The sentiment his artistic personality arouses in me is as remote as possible from contempt. It is rather hatred. His books are bad, but in such an extraordinary way that they provoke passionate opposition. I am not speaking of the *boring* shamelessness of his eroticism, or the mindless and soulless way his sensuality reaches after tactile effect. What infuriates me is the aestheticising deathly coldness that his books exude.32

So often accused of coldness himself, Thomas was seizing the opportunity to accuse someone else, but, recognizing an overlap or affinity between his own work and Heinrich's, he was attacking both at the same time. Unlike Heinrich, though, he couldn't be accused of turning out too many books. In his notebook, under the heading "Anti-Heinrich," he wrote: "I find it immoral to write one bad book after another from fear of suffering idleness."[33]

Heinrich's feelings about his brother were sardonically expressed in the autobiographical sketch he wrote for his publisher's catalogue when *Die Jagd nach Liebe* was advertised:

> Everyone knows all about my background from my brother's famous novel. After we had been Hanseatic merchants for two thick volumes, we finally arrived at art, thanks to an admixture of Latin blood, which, according to Nietzsche, invariably produces neurasthenics and artists. . . . Isolation between two races strengthens the weakling, making him ruthless, hard to influence, obsessed with building for himself a little world and a home he would not otherwise have found. . . . Since he nowhere finds a public with quite the same instincts, he narrows his need for communicating till he is his own audience."[34]

Heinrich was thinking of his reasons for living in Italy, but his generalizations about "isolation between two races" could be applied to the brother who now had a very big audience. Thomas said nothing about Heinrich in his letters to Katia, and these were what mattered to Thomas more than anything else. At twenty-one—she'd celebrated her birthday in July—she was closer in age to Viktor than to him, and he was a long way from thinking of her as his equal. In a notebook entry he said: "Her naivety is extraordinary—supreme and dumbfounding. This strange, kind-hearted and yet egoistic little Jew-girl, polite and without a will of her own! I can still hardly believe she will ever bring the word Yes to her lips." He also refers in his notebook to her "small child's handwriting,"[35] and one of his letters mentions her "rather childlike scrawl." But in letters to her he did his best to write as if he regarded her as no younger, no less experienced, intelligent, or sophisticated than he was. He couldn't help sounding pedantic when he tried to influence her way of thinking, but he was judicious in blending didacticism with self-recommendation and declarations of love.

Instead of assuming that love was a matter of letting feelings speak for themselves, he suggested, they should discuss everything, calmly, rationally, sensibly. Repeating what he'd said in a letter to Samuel Lublinski, the critic who'd called him the most important novelist of the modern movement, Thomas said there were only five or six people in Germany who understood that irony wasn't the product of cold-heartedness; it was more a matter of pungency and economy.[36]

In a late August letter he tried to analyze the way she'd made him change his position since he'd defined it in "Tonio Kröger." Equated with blue eyes and blondness, the "life" Tonio loved was commonplace; the love, which had an element of mockery in it, couldn't have been reciprocated. But a new and exciting possibility had emerged: Perhaps he could have his love returned by a superior creature, intelligent, kind, and sweet.[37]

She still thought he was overrating her. When she wrote to insist that she was "stupid," he said he was stupid, too, and glad to be, since stupidity was the opposite of cleverness, which pivoted on caution and the regularity of routine. " 'Stupid' is everything naive, noble and devoted, every bold enterprise on earth. *Let us be* stupid, my Katia!"[38]

These letters made an impact. According to her memoirs, he "wrote me wonderfully beautiful letters—he *did* know how to write—which naturally impressed me but which I didn't answer quite so beautifully."[39] Sometimes she must have felt thoroughly confused. In one letter her suitor confessed to weeping like a child with a letter from her in his hand;[40] in another he said that though he was never conscious of his value when he was with other people, he expected them to be aware of his importance and regarded their conduct toward him as a criterion of their inner cultivation.[41] He also told her about his prince fantasy. The reason they suited each other so well, he said, was that she belonged to neither the bourgeoisie nor the Junker class, while he'd always seen himself as a sort of prince. In her, therefore, he'd found his predestined bride.[42]

During ten weeks of communicating only by letter, he made more progress than he might have done had they been seeing each other. Her letters must have boosted his confidence, for during the second half of September, when she was back in Munich, he wrote: "I believe you feel as strongly as I do that it is high time to put an end to this in-between state! Do you not think that once we belong together in the eyes of the world, the relationship will be much more clean-cut and comfortable?"[43]

The next time he went to Arcisstrasse, he was allowed, on the pretext of seeing her library, to go up to her room, where they were alone together. When he took her in his arms, he was half-surprised she neither pushed him away nor called for help.

They were engaged on October 3. "You can have no idea of my condition," he wrote two days later. "It consists of an extraordinary mixture of disturbance, happiness and exhaustion."[44] Kicking down the barricade he'd erected to protect his solitude, he was uncertain whether he was lapsing from dutiful dedication to his art or committing himself dutifully to deeper immersion in life. He still believed in a polarity between the two, though he wouldn't have wanted to symbolize it in a tussle between a blond cyclist and an apoplectic old man. "My conscience is still unsettled, because I am more than a little afraid of 'happiness', and I am still in doubt about whether my surrender to 'life' is something highly moral or a sort of dissipation."[45]

He said this in a letter to Philipp Witkop, a professor in Freiburg, without explaining the pricking of his conscience and the sense of surrendering as due partly to misgivings about the allowance he'd agreed to accept from Alfred Pringsheim. The success of *Buddenbrooks* had raised Thomas's standard of living without making him rich enough to give Katia as stylish a life as the one she'd been having. To accept regular financial help from his father-in-law was to put himself in a subordinate position. He accepted when Alfred Pringsheim offered to find an apartment for them to live in. He chose one in the Schwabing, on the fourth floor of a house in Franz-Joseph-Strasse—within easy reach of Arcisstrasse, which meant Katia could visit her parents every day, and they could easily come to see her. The professor took charge of decorating and furnishing the apartment, selecting antique furniture from an expensive shop, Bernheimers, and with the exception of three Empire chairs, he rejected all the furniture from Thomas's bachelor apartment in Ainmillerstrasse, not even letting his future son-in-law make his own arrangements for his study. Thomas accepted all these decisions meekly.

Giving Myself a Constitution

IN ALL THESE MONTHS of wooing and campaigning, Thomas seems to have thought little about what married life would be like. He had wanted Katia as his fiancée, he had wanted to be accepted by the Pringsheim family, and he was willing to accept what Alfred Pringsheim was prepared to give him. If it had seemed like an adventure story, he'd brought it to a happy ending, and now he felt triumphant. The engagement, he said, was the crown of his life. "Without it everything else I have achieved would have no value for me."[1]

It might have been possible to continue the friendship with Paul on a different basis if one or the other of them had taken the initiative to arrange a meeting, but they both let the opportunity slip by. Over the last six months they'd had no contact, and for some time after the engagement, Thomas didn't even get in touch with Carl. Within less than a year, Paul married.

Thomas had been due to give a reading in Berlin on October 27 and one in Lübeck two days later. He'd promised to deliver *Fiorenza* by the beginning of November, and its publication in the *Neue Rundschau* had already been announced, though he hadn't completed it. But he enjoyed reading from unfinished work to small audiences: at the Pringsheims' house on November 16 he read from the play, which was still unfinished twelve days later, when he and Katia left Munich. They traveled with her mother to Berlin, where he met members of their family and gave a reading from *Fiorenza* at the Verein für Kunst. The chairman, Herwarth Walden, a musician and husband of the painter Elsa Lasker-Schüler, had composed a piece he titled "Thomas Mann," but Katia, who found it no more than "a strange buzzing on the cello," was reduced to fits of giggles.[2]

After being taken to meet her uncle Hermann Rosenberg, president of the Berlin Bank Society, who gave a dinner in honor of the engaged couple, Thomas was introduced to her paternal grandparents, whose first question was what he'd like them to give him. He asked for a watch.

Going on without the Pringsheims to Lübeck and wanting to avoid the hotel where he'd been cross-examined by the police, he accepted an invitation to stay with the motherly Ida Boy-Ed, a popular novelist who had been brought to the city in 1865 as a child of thirteen and had lived there ever since. Thomas had known her when he was a schoolboy, and she had been corresponding with him about his visit. He had a large audience, which was enthusiastic about his story "The Infant Prodigy" and less enthusiastic about the excerpts from *Fiorenza*. At the end of his reading he was ceremonially given a laurel wreath with a bow in the city's colors. No one appeared to be harboring resentment about the way he'd depicted Lübeck and its citizens in *Buddenbrooks*, but the local newspaper's reporter went out of his way to attack the novel: "We regard this kind of artistic creation as tasteless . . . for the people concerned, who are completely defenceless against such a work, cannot but feel hurt when they are described in the novel with their failings, big and small."[3]

On December 23, Hedwig Pringsheim and Katia went to Augsburg, where they met Julia and Viktor Mann, who were invited to Arcisstrasse on the day after Christmas, together with the Löhrs and Grautoff. According to Katia, Julia was no longer beautiful, but her fine features showed that she had been.[4] Instantly disliking the Pringsheims and noticing that the professor was holding hands with his daughter throughout most of the evening, she concluded that Katia was going to marry Thomas only to please her parents, who seemed interested in him mainly as an acquisition for the family. "So much wealth makes people frigid, demanding and hard-hearted," Julia told Heinrich, who was still in Italy, "and leads them to expect more consideration from other people than they reciprocate. . . . There are plenty of other girls, nice, sweet and less spoilt, who would have loved him more deeply and more faithfully, and looked after him better. . . . I am sorry to make so much fuss, but if only Tommy were free again (I mean his heart!) I think it would relieve me of a great burden."[5] Ignorant of her misgivings, Thomas wrote to Heinrich exuberantly: People were saying he'd become more worldly, and he was wearing a light gray velvet waistcoat with silver buttons under his dinner jacket.[6]

The wedding was fixed for February 11, 1905, and, wanting Heinrich to come, Thomas wrote as persuasively as he could. But though Heinrich was head of the family, he was less interested in making his presence felt than his absence, as he had when Julia married Josef Löhr. From Heinrich's point of view, Thomas was opting for a society too close to the one he'd satirized in *Im Schlaraffenland* (*In the Land of Cockaigne*). It's about the adventures of a provincial student, Andreas, who penetrates into the world of the nouveaux riches by seducing the wife of a Jewish financier. She makes him rich and sets him up in a luxurious flat, where he starts an affair with her husband's vulgar seventeen-year-old girlfriend. All ends badly when the youngsters are forced to marry each other and ejected from the society in which they'd wanted to live.

Heinrich snubbed his younger brother in two ways. He stayed away from the wedding and failed to send a separate present. Carla, who also absented herself—she was working at the Oberschlesischen Volkstheater in Königshütte, Upper Silesia—sent a present which was meant to be from her and Heinrich, who never saw what she'd chosen.

Thomas and Katia were married in the register office on Marienplatz. The reception in Arcisstrasse was a small one. The guests included Julia, who tried to disguise her misgivings about her new daughter-in-law, Viktor, the Löhrs, and Grautoff, but none of Thomas's other friends— not even Kurt Martens. Wanting to start a new life, he also wanted to consolidate his success, to take full advantage of the "increased self-respect, the higher level of taking oneself seriously, the inclination to re-gard oneself an important element in national history . . . the per-spective of literary history, etc."[7]

A last-minute spurt had carried him to the end of *Fiorenza* before the wedding, though his concentration had been imperfect. He and Katia honeymooned in Zurich at the Baur au Lac, where they had a suite with a magnificent view of the lake, the private park, and the Alps. The hotel, which was sixty years old, had been luxuriously renovated at the end of the century. Local citizens considered it to be the unapproachable residence of princes and royal families. Wilhelm II used to stay there, as did the empress of Russia, the king of Sweden, and the khedive of Egypt. Liveried servants stood on duty, waiting to open doors for guests, and Thomas, who'd felt like an outsider at the Parkhotel in Düs-seldorf, where he made notes for use in *Royal Highness*, could now feel like an insider. From now on, subsidized by his father-in-law, he would al-ways be able to stay in the most expensive hotels.

Though he must have resented the snub from Heinrich, he decided to be conciliatory, and within the first week of the honeymoon he wrote a long letter, thanking him for his share of the present, and using Heinrich's word *Cockaigne* (*Schlaraffenland*) to distance himself, almost apologetically, from the luxury in which he was living. "Neither my stomach nor my conscience are entirely in order," he admitted, "and I not infrequently long for a bit more cloistered peacefulness and . . . mental activity." He was suffering from constipation; he didn't explain what was troubling his conscience, but he wrote about the marriage as if he'd had no more say in it than a character has in a story: "The whole thing was a strange and bewildering occurrence, and I was wondering all day what I had let myself in for."[8]

The ambivalence was genuine, although he had seized his opportu-nity to reverse what could be called the Buddenbrooks syndrome. If his novel had been partly a response to his father's vindictive will, the mar-riage had forged an alliance with a family with an even higher social standing than the Manns. The idea of bourgeois society was closely associated in Thomas's mind with the idea of family life. No longer an outsider, he could start a family of his own, while the marriage stood a better chance of surviving if Katia was preoccupied with motherhood. His notebook contains addresses for three doctors in Zurich. We don't know which of them he consulted; we do know Katia saw a gynecologist who advised her to let three or four years go by before having a baby, but either this advice came too late, or it was ignored. She conceived during the honeymoon: The baby was to be born in November.

Without children she might have wanted a husband who was also an ardent lover; as it was, their relationship settled down comfortably into something resembling close friendship, Thomas replacing the father who'd been so close to her. Though they often made love and sometimes indulged in what he called "sexual excess," he'd never taken much interest in the female body, and he didn't begin to. But they enjoyed each other's company, and always had plenty to talk about.

After returning to Munich on February 23, they moved into the apartment, which was small but pleasant, overlooking the gardens of the Prinz Leopold Palace. Thomas's study, the drawing room, and the dining room were at the front of the apartment, with his bedroom, her room, the bathroom, the spare bedroom, and another small room on the other side. In the drawing room was a baby-grand piano, at which he often improvised on Wagnerian themes. For the study, his father-in-law had chosen a new writing table and an armchair covered in pink and gold velvet.

Thomas's enjoyment of his new life was marred by constipation, which persisted, although he consulted several doctors and tried different remedies. He even underwent electric-shock treatment of the stomach, hoping to get himself into the right physical state for starting a new novel.[9] A note he made under the heading "Maja" may have some bearing on his life with Katia: "the writer who is 'going to ruin' with his young wife. She has never understood that happiness is out of bounds for him, though she had given signs of acquiescence. How he finally confirms to her, after a prolonged moral struggle: the soft voluptuousness (with a feeling of contradiction and going to the dogs), the half true statement 'I am happy.' "[10]

That the artist should renounce happiness is an idea that recurs in a piece on Schiller commissioned by *Simplicissimus* for the centenary of the writer's death in May 1805.[11] Thomas started work on it in mid-March. After studying Schiller's letters, his massive historical play *Wallenstein*, the new biography by Ernst Müller,[12] and an article by Adolf Baumeister in the *Marbacher Schillerbuch*, Thomas wrote a short story, "Hour of Gravity" ("Schwere Stunde"). Formerly an intellectual freebooter, Schiller has settled into a bourgeois marriage, and the story centers on his difficulties in writing *Wallenstein*, which struck Thomas as paralleling his own difficulties with *Fiorenza*. Apart from the description of the cheerless six-sided room in Jena, virtually everything in the story refers as much to himself as to Schiller. He even interweaves fragments of Schiller's letters with fragments of his own, drawing especially (with Katia's permission) on one to her in which he'd quoted Flaubert's line: "Mon livre me fait beaucoup de douleurs" ("My book causes me a lot of suffering"). Neither Schiller nor Goethe is named, though Thomas plants clues that make their identities unmistakable.

Goethe is credited with knowing how to live and create without abusing himself; unable to go on working, Schiller gets up from his frail writing table, trying to distance himself from his work and himself. For the last five years—ever since he contracted catarrhal fever and inflammation of the lungs—he has suffered from a piercing, stabbing pain in his chest, but hasn't consulted a doctor. Nothing that involves suffering, he believes, can be either useless or evil. It costs him a great effort to construct a sentence or follow a thought to its conclusion. It's auspicious that the unfinished manuscript is causing him so much trouble. For him, writing has never been effortless; talent is a permanent dissatisfaction which cannot produce its best fruit without discomfort. Everything extraordinary is egoistic in proportion to the pain it causes. His passion for his own ego burns insatiably. Thinking about his hand fills him with a tender passion for himself, but his egoism is only superficial: He's sacrificing himself for a great ideal. Freedom is partly freedom from happiness, the most insidious of constraints. Going to the bed where his pretty, dark-haired wife is sleeping with parted lips and a ringlet of hair straggling across her cheek, he feels fond of her, but doesn't want her big, searching eyes to open, doesn't want her to make him happy and unable to go on working. He kisses her gently, but turns back to the outer room.

The disorders in Thomas's stomach weren't irrelevant to the disorders in his conscience. He might have felt less uneasy had there been no financial fibers in the marital rope holding him in *Cockaigne*. He may have been worrying about his loss of independence, his sexuality, about promises he'd explicitly or implicitly made to Katia, about the pregnancy that contravened the doctor's advice, about tension that would be inevitable since he'd accepted that happiness—even if it was desirable—was inaccessible, while she'd been brought up to assume it was her hereditary right. He may also have felt uneasy about her twin brother, Klaus, who might have been the subject of anguished entries in diaries later destroyed; few comments on him survive, but he must have featured in Thomas's thoughts before and after the marriage. Though Klaus had been friendly and encouraging, Thomas understood ambivalence. At first he'd been an unprivileged outsider to the intimacy the twins had shared since infancy; Thomas's success with Katia was success in displacing a male who gave no sign of regarding him as a rival. But Klaus might be concealing his hostility, while Katia, who still held hands with him and looked at him adoringly, would inevitably be comparing the two men. Thomas must have felt apprehensive, guilty, and confused—jealous of Klaus, nervous that Klaus was jealous of him, and possibly dazzled by Klaus's charm and good looks, as he'd been by Paul's. Thomas may, for a time, have felt more attracted to Klaus than to Katia, or felt equally attracted to both. In his new story, "The Blood of the Walsungs" ("Wälsungenblut"), each twin is the "darkly beautiful counterpart" of the other.

Thomas may have conceived the story in an attempt to exorcise these anxieties. It's partly about the lifestyle of a rich Jewish family, partly about an incestuous brother and sister, nineteen-year-old twins ironically named Siegmund and Sieglinde Aarenhold, partly about the awkward position of Sieglinde's gentile fiancé. Thomas started the story in Munich before he left with Katia at the beginning of August for their first summer holiday together. He'd thought of taking her to Travemünde, but she didn't want the holidaying citizens of Lübeck to see her in her pregnant state. She and Thomas finally opted for another little town on the Baltic coast, Sopot, where Katia, who was in her sixth month, could go for long walks. But a spell of rainy weather and rumors of cholera in nearby Danzig made them retreat to the Tiergarten district of Berlin, where they spent a week in the villa of her relations, the Rosenbergs.

They visited Katia's maternal grandmother, Hedwig Dohm, who'd been active as a campaigner for women's rights. According to Katia, she asked Thomas whether he wanted a boy or a girl, and he was tactless enough to answer: "A boy, of course. After all, a girl isn't to be taken seriously."[13] According to him, he made this remark not to Hedwig Dohm but to someone else: It was reported to her, and she reprimanded him, looking at him severely with her big gray eyes.[14]

After revisiting Potsdam and the castle of Sans Souci at the beginning of September, he was intending to write a novel about Frederick the Great and read Carlyle's biography. Thomas wanted to focus on the Emperor's relationship with his brother, the Prince of Prussia, "a dreamer who was ruined by 'emotion.' " "The brother problem constantly stirs me up." He consulted Heinrich on whether to tackle the subject. "I am now thirty. It is time to think about a masterpiece."[15]

For more than a year his creative energy was to be divided between the abortive Frederick novel and *Royal Highness*, which he'd conceived as a story. After he started it, late in 1905 or early in 1906, it evolved gradually into a novel, which he finished in 1909. In comparison with *Buddenbrooks*, it's thin-textured and almost novelettish, partly because he wasn't trying to write a masterpiece. "It is a children's game," he told Heinrich, "in comparison with the new project"—meaning the plan to write about Frederick.[16] He went on feeling excited about this, though Heinrich advised him not to attempt a historical novel. It wasn't so much a historical novel, he explained, as an attempt to portray greatness, and "for that one needs knowledge of greatness, experience, personal experience *in* greatness." He believed he could do something that had never been done before, "portraying a hero as human and *all too* human, writing sceptically, *maliciously*, with psychological radicalism and yet positively out of my own experience."[17]

In March 1906, when Fischer signed a new contract, giving Thomas a royalty of 25 percent (instead of 20 percent) on everything he wrote—better terms than any other author had in Germany—Thomas was doing research on Frederick.[18] Though he went on making notes until 1911 or 1912, he never found the energy he needed to write the novel. In 1906 the main deterrents were bad health and the distractions of luxurious living. Most of his notes were made during the spring; after this he gave *Royal Highness* priority.

In Berlin, at the Villa Rosenberg, he basked in the luxuries. "We are enjoying a sheltered and exquisite life. Oh, wealth is certainly a good thing, whatever people say. I am enough of an artist, and corruptible enough to be enchanted by it. And incidentally the contradictory proclivities to asceticism on the one hand and luxury on the other are probably characteristic of the modern soul: you see this on the grand scale in Richard Wagner."[19]

But the negative side of his ambivalence prevailed in "The Blood of the Walsungs." Though he didn't finish the story till the end of October, he worked on it during the week with the Rosenbergs, modeling the Aarenholds partly on them and partly on the Pringsheims. He was going to upset both his pregnant wife and her family. She and Klaus were unmistakably the models for his incestuous twins, and it's puzzling that neither he nor Hedwig Pringsheim objected when Thomas read the story to them. Klaus admits to feeling flattered. The twins take mutual delight in the expensive, pampered, well-groomed smell they exude. At dinner with their parents, their brother, their sister, and Sieglinde's non-Jewish fiancé, von Beckerath, she sits between him and Siegmund, who holds her hand out of sight. "Sometimes their gaze found each other's, melting together, forming a concord to which there was no access from outside."[20] Though Siegmund has always been the dominant partner, he hasn't opposed the match, but he despises himself for not having done so. Von Beckerath comes from a good family, but in every other way he's their inferior.

Sieglinde has a girlish figure, and in describing her Thomas uses several phrases he also uses about Imma: Both have sparkling black eyes, dark hair, childish shoulders and arms, skin the color of smoked meer-schaum—hydrated magnesium silicate used in manufacturing pipes. Both girls are sharp-tongued, and so is Siegmund. Though the twins are pampered and secure, they talk as if they've cultivated merciless critical acuity as a weapon of defense. "They always contradicted, as if they found it impossible, shameful, ignominious not to."[21]

Drawing on observation of the opulent Pringsheim and Rosenberg households, Thomas describes the Aarenholds' luxurious furniture, the tapestries and paneled walls, the lavish meals, with several servants in attendance, the books specially bound for the family in embossed leather, the time and effort indolently squandered on hesitating be-tween different brands of cigarettes, soaps, scents, clothes. The twins are compared to self-centered invalids who get absorbed in trivialities, while Siegmund, who complains that his life is too comfortable for him to be creative, takes over Thomas's fear that luxury will destroy the need to write.

At a performance of *Die Walküre*, the twins hear the lonely Siegmund singing of his yearning for human company. During his Tonio Kröger phase, despite his Wagnerian sense of superiority to ordinary people, Thomas had yearned for company and hated loneliness, but his ideal partners, male and female, were always blond. Now, married to a dark Jewish girl who was as exceptional as he was, he'd not only found re-demption from loneliness, he had a vantage point from which he could write knowingly about both outsiders and insiders. As a gentile he was an outsider among the Pringsheims, though more of an insider in Ger-many than they were. Having once written as an outsider about the need to maintain an appearance of bourgeois respectability, he could empathize with Siegmund Aarenhold, who has to take more trouble over his appearance than the blond citizens, who go around in elastic-sided boots and turnover collars.

Marriage to a Jewish girl might seem to indicate that Thomas had re-solved his ambivalence about Jewishness, but he hadn't. Like Baron Stein's wife in "The Will to Happiness," Frau Aarenhold is ugly, over-dressed, and undignified. She eats greedily and introduces vulgar Yid-dish phrases into mealtime conversations. The Aarenhold children despise their father for his origins, for the blood that runs through his veins, and for the way he earned his fortune. Staring into a mirror, Sieg-mund looks for racial characteristics in his face—the slightly drooping nose, full lips that rest softly on each other, high cheekbones, thick black curly hair, black eyes that glow with weariness and suffering. Spell-bound by the music Wagner wrote for their incestuous namesakes, the twins make love, and Thomas ends the story by letting Siegmund gloat in Yiddish over the non-Jew he has cuckolded before the wedding. Without running the risk of infuriating his father-in-law by reading the story to him, Thomas both prepared him for it and implicated him by questioning him about suitable Yiddish words. After paying a literary obeisance to the Pringsheims in "At the Prophet's," which he wrote before they'd accepted him, Thomas was making a spiteful declaration of independence.

He was so familiar with *Die Walküre* that if he'd ever suspected incest between Klaus and Katia, he'd have thought of Siegmund and Sieglinde. The equation between the dark and the fair twins would have been complicated by Alfred Pringsheim's idolization of Wagner. In spite of the composer's well-known anti-Semitism, the professor admired him sufficiently to fight a duel with a man who talked about him derisively. When Thomas, after Klaus's first visit to his apartment, said the idea of Jewishness never came to mind when he was with the Pringsheims, only the idea of culture, he was revealing distaste for traits he regarded as characteristically Jewish. But though the twins in the story are more sympathetic than Frau Aarenhold, they have many of these traits, and the idea of Jewishness had come strongly to mind when Thomas was with the Pringsheims.

Simultaneous with the recoil against them was a rapprochement with Heinrich in mid-October, when *Fiorenza* appeared in book form. Heinrich sent a eulogistic letter which "has more than once brought tears of joy into my eyes."[22] And it was Heinrich that Thomas consulted when Oscar Bie, editor of the *Neue Rundschau*, balked at the final paragraph. Heinrich was against changing it, but Thomas wrote a new ending which is slightly less offensive, though it fails to provide a strong conclusion. Siegmund talks patronizingly about the non-Jewish fiancé: "He should be grateful to us. He'll lead a less trivial existence from now on."[23]

Whatever she felt about the story, Katia was preoccupied with preparations for giving birth. She wanted to have the baby in the apartment. Labor pains lasted for forty hours before a little girl was delivered on November 9. Katia felt totally exhausted—almost dead. "I had impressions of both life and death," Thomas wrote, "but what birth is I did not yet know."[24] Feeding the baby at her breast, Katia "herself still looked like a lovely child."[25] But the letters to Heinrich and Ida Boy-Ed show Thomas to be less interested in her forty-hour ordeal than in his own reactions. He'd been "deeply shaken" by watching the birth. He was disappointed not to have a son, who would have been more like "a continuation and new beginning of myself under new conditions," though perhaps a daughter would involve him in "a closer relationship with the 'other' sex, of which I really, though now a husband, still know nothing." (As a writer, he should not allow himself to remain ignorant about it.) It looked as if the little girl, Erika, was going to be very pretty.

"At moments I believe I can see a little bit of Jewishness peeping through, which always makes me feel very cheerful."26

Arriving back in Berlin on an overnight train from Breslau, he found Klaus Pringsheim waiting at the station. Later in the morning Klaus called at the apartment to warn him about an impending scandal. Rumors were circulating that he'd written an anti-Semitic story, and if it appeared in print, it would provoke gossip about the family. With the revised ending, the story was to appear in the January issue of the *Neue Rundschau*, and copies had already been printed. But Thomas was in such a strong position vis-à-vis Fischer that he could insist on withdrawing the story, even though the copies would all have to be scrapped. "I must acknowledge," he told Heinrich, "that humanly and socially I am no longer free. . . . Up to now, frankly, I have never escaped from a feeling of constraint, which is very oppressive during periods of hypochondria, and you will certainly call me a cowardly bourgeois. But it is easy for you to talk. You are a despot. But I stopped to give myself a constitution."27

He probably wouldn't have suppressed the story if he hadn't already had misgivings, thinking of it as a wayward attempt to breach the tacit agreement he'd made with the Pringsheims. He'd been married for eleven months, and he didn't want to lose the income his Jewish father-in-law was providing, but the story reveals intense hostility, although—or perhaps because—Katia was already pregnant when it was written.

The *Rundschau* appeared without the story, but the printed pages that had been discarded were used as packing paper. When a consignment of books from Fischer arrived in a Munich bookshop, an assistant found part of the story, and, when another consignment arrived, he not only pieced it together but circulated it privately until Thomas complained to Fischer at the beginning of February.28

For some time Thomas had wanted to rebut the charge that he was unscrupulously basing fiction on living models. During October 1905 his name had been mentioned in a Lübeck lawcourt when a writer, Johannes Dose, was sued by his cousin for libeling him in *Der Muttersohn*, a novel about an alcoholic. The prosecutor mentioned *Buddenbrooks* as well as a roman à clef which had become notorious, *Aus einer kleinen Garnison* by Fritz Oswald Bilse, a lieutenant who'd been court-martialed and imprisoned for six months after divulging what he knew about corruption inside a garrison town in Lorraine. Dose argued that he hadn't intended to slander anyone and, claiming that specialist knowledge was needed, asked for three writers, including Thomas, to be called as witnesses. Angry at being bracketed with Bilse, a writer he regarded as amateurish and incompetent, Thomas riposted in two newspaper articles, "A Postscript" ("Ein Nachwort") for the *Lübecker General-Anzeiger*29 and "Bilse und ich" for the *Münchener Neueste Nachrichten*.30

His "Postscript" explained that he hadn't read Dose's book, but that if he'd had to give evidence about *Buddenbrooks*, he wouldn't have claimed, like Dose, to be unaware of resemblances between his characters and real people. Before writing his novel he'd looked carefully at various aspects of reality, but he'd added something that was intimately his own. How many of the greatest novelists would pretend that they took nothing from observation of their contemporaries? Had *Werther* involved Goethe in litigation with Charlotte and her husband? Neither of them had been so petty-minded as to resent a literary process that had given them a life more intense, more interesting, and more durable than the one they were living. Was Thomas comparing himself to Goethe? No, but he felt more kinship with him than with Bilse, who was an untalented libelist; *Buddenbrooks*, like *Werther*, was a work of art.

"Bilse und ich" carries the argument further, adducing Turgenev's use of real-life models in *Fathers and Sons* and *A Sportsman's Sketches*, as well as Shakespeare's use of Sir John Oldcastle in characterizing Falstaff. But the crucial point, Thomas argues, is that a good writer transforms the material he takes, giving it something of his own, deepening it, implanting in it a new soul, filling it with his own breath and being. Having little talent for fabricating new material, he contends, many of the greatest writers preferred to lean on given realities. Though he could have argued that *Buddenbrooks* didn't reproduce family history for its own sake but used it to illustrate ideas about degeneration and decay, it was disingenuous to maintain that Lübeck had nothing to do with the city he portrayed. Undeniably, he was in Italy when he started the novel, but he's overstating his case when he says that for him, Lübeck was no more than a dream. He doesn't admit to revisiting the city in 1899 before he finished the novel.

He contended that he'd reduced members of his family and other models to masks through which he dealt with problems that were his—not theirs. It's true that a writer never stops using himself as a model, but, like an actor, he presents personalities which are composites, based on fusion. Thomas also introduced his theory that the writer lives a representative life. The poet and the prince derive an "austere happiness"—a phrase Thomas borrowed from *Die Jagd nach Liebe*—from standing for many people by being themselves. In his painting "Ceci n'est pas une pipe," Magritte was wittily making the point that a pipe in a painting isn't identical with a real pipe; Thomas was neither so witty nor so wise when he asked: "If I make a thing into a sentence, what does the sentence have to do with the thing?" Nor was it true that the complaints about his work were like the questions put to him when, as a child, he drew pictures of little men, and adults asked who they were.

Uncomfortable over rumors circulating through Munich about "The Blood of the Walsungs," he argues that a writer of fiction is entitled to use people close to him. However many details and characteristics he reproduces, the result will differ substantially from the source. As if to appease his father-in-law, Thomas even works in a reference to Shylock. It might look as if Shakespeare had despised the Jew, but there is a "profound and fearful solidarity" between playwright and character.

While there was no question of betraying Katia with another woman, Thomas had betrayed her by writing "Blood of the Walsungs," and he was disloyal in telling Heinrich he shouldn't have committed himself to marriage and domesticity. He couldn't fulfill his potential as a writer with so many restrictions on his liberty. He sometimes felt, he said, as if he were chained with a golden ball on each leg, and though Katia was intelligent enough to take over some of his business correspondence as well as dealing with babies and household affairs, he didn't share his inner life with her.

She couldn't even comfort him when he felt wounded by criticism. To reward Richard Schaukal for his favorable review of *Buddenbrooks*, Thomas dedicated the story "Luischen" to him, but in March 1906 Schaukal attacked *Fiorenza* in the *Berliner Tageblatt*, accusing Thomas of lacking versatility. Furious, Thomas wrote to Heinrich, saying the review would harm him, and that of all his friends and admirers "no-one had felt sufficiently alarmed to challenge this limited and self-righteous jackanapes publicly or even privately."[31] Heinrich's response was to write a thousand-word article vilifying Schaukal as an untalented novelist who couldn't be taken seriously as a critic. After underlining the parallel between the decaying Buddenbrooks and the degenerate Medici, Heinrich explained how writers project their own destiny on that of their characters. Thomas, who arranged for the article to be published in the March issue of *Die Zukunft*, felt as grateful to his elder brother as if he'd been defended against a bully in the school playground.[32] Julia was delighted that her two sons were allies again.

Representing Other People

THOMAS HAD BEEN WRONG to assume his friends would all ignore Richard Schaukal's attack on him. By the time Schaukal had replied to Heinrich and Heinrich had replied to the reply, Kurt Martens had written an article on the Mann brothers for the *Leipziger Tageblatt*, but it characterized them both as aloof—icily hostile toward humanity and likely to arouse more respect than love. Though Heinrich was a master of caricature, he was the "most repulsive of all German writers to the average reader," partly because he was a ferocious enemy of the bourgeoisie from which he came. He was more objective than Thomas, whose nature was softer, but both brothers had exposed the motivation of the human psyche, submitting its most delicate fibers to closer scrutiny than they'd previously received.

It was a pity that both brothers used living models. Thomas's arguments in "Bilse und ich" would convince no one, and people would inevitably be alienated by social recklessness. The article concluded that Heinrich was temperamentally stronger, more open-minded, and more widely educated, but that Thomas had tenderer feelings and a deeper understanding of human nature.

If Martens had been hoping to please his friend, the article was badly misjudged. Struggling to keep his anger under control, Thomas defended himself against the imputation of icy misanthropy and lovelessness toward flesh and blood. Describing himself as a "lyric poet of the heart," he called inventiveness a talent of secondary importance. His work was no more autobiographical than Tolstoy's. Besides, "You must acknowledge that I have a gift for detail, liveliness and modernity, one or two shafts of perception and *power of vision.*"

As always, he was irked by the imputation of coldness. He was ascetic, he said, only insofar as his conscience dictated an ethic of achievement. No one was strong enough to be both an artist and a *bon viveur*. A choice had to be made. Nor was it true that readers felt more respect than affection for his work. "*Buddenbrooks* and 'Tonio Kröger', those articulations of my self, are *loved*, believe me, and to an extent that might disturb me." What aspects of his image would offend posterity? "I was a placid, well-behaved man who achieved a degree of prosperity by the work of his hands, took a wife, had children, attended first nights and was a good enough German to be incapable of going abroad for more than four weeks at a stretch. Is it absolutely essential, on top of all that, to go bowling and drinking?"[1]

Frederick the Great had often been accused of coldness, and in characterizing him, Thomas could defend himself vicariously. He made copious notes. "Frederick's tenderness and nervous sensitivity . . . Says in a complaining tone he has too much feeling, more than anyone else. . . . His softness outwardly hardened through his contempt for humanity and his duties. Reproaches of coldness: once again ridiculous."[2] Thomas used himself as a model when describing Frederick at work in Potsdam: "The painfully absorbing sensation of being sunk while working . . . Work is always solid and severe . . . and he lets it become heavy, with no enjoyment of surroundings and circumstances."[3]

The confrontation with Martens failed to kill their friendship. After being sent his latest novel, *Kreislauf* (*Circulation*), Thomas read it during an April holiday with Katia in Oberammergau, where they were hoping to find a villa to rent for the summer. Though he rated *Kreislauf* "an extraordinarily respectable novel," he couldn't deny his lack of enthusiasm, and pleaded in extenuation that "by now I am applying a desperately exacting criterion, which one of these days will probably stop me from producing anything at all."[4] The anxiety was genuine. His ironic intellect always seemed to be in danger of outstripping and negating his creativity.

All this time Thomas was in poor health. During January he said the whole of his neurasthenia was concentrating on his stomach.[5] At intervals of about two months he had periods of eyestrain, depression, and insomnia, while, at its worst, the abdominal pain would lead to vomiting. Afterward he'd feel "very weak and gentle, as if transfigured,"[6] and, unable to work, he'd have to rest or doze. He thought the malaise was nervous in origin, and even if there was a constitutional cause for it, it was obviously exacerbated, as it recurred throughout his life, by nervous tension.

IT MAY HAVE BEEN IN 1906 that Thomas read the memoirs of George Manolescu, alerted to them by a review in the March issue of the *Neue Rundschau*. *A Prince of Thieves* and *Ruined: From the Spiritual Life of a Criminal* had originally been published in French, and a two-volume German translation appeared in 1905. A Hungarian confidence trickster and womanizer who operated in hotels as a jewel thief, Manolescu must have reminded Thomas of the 1899 incident in Lübeck, when the police had mistaken him for a confidence man. Liking the directness of the autobiographical form, Thomas thought it would be enjoyable to write a first-person narrative in which he transposed some of Goethe's self-portraiture onto a criminal plane. In between a note for *Royal Highness* and one for the Frederick novel Thomas wrote: "For the Confidence Trickster. At dangerous moments he instinctively feigns a fit of coughing: the man who suffers is innocent, suspicions of a sick man soon fade away."[7]

The main starting point for the story was (as Hans Wysling has shown) taken from J. J. Davids's recently published story "Die Weltreise des kleinen Tyrnauer" in *Wunderliche Heilige*.[8] A noble dragoon, Poldi Kirchnegger, who doesn't want to be parted from his soubrette, employs a minor official to assume his identity traveling around the world. Poldi supplies the man with money, a passport, tickets, letters of recommendation, travel books, and so on. After reading the story, Thomas made an entry toward the beginning of a notebook he started in 1906:

> The confidence trickster meets a young count who is having an affair and his family, wanting to extricate him from it, have arranged for him to travel round the world. They send him a large sum of money for it and demand letters from the places he stays at. Felix proposes that they should change places. He is given the money, together they write letters out of Baedeker and Felix travels as the count, posting the letters at the various places while the real count stays with his sweetheart.[9]

Applying the technique he'd used when writing *Fiorenza*, Thomas collected pictures and kept them in folders to give him ideas for a narrative about a confidence trickster—pictures of health resorts, hotels, elegant gardens, prisons.[10] But mainly because of malaise, listlessness, and depression, Thomas made no progress with the story.

In May 1906, after being involved in a minor railway accident on his way to a reading in Dresden, he withdrew to a nearby sanatorium, the Weisser Hirsch. After three weeks there, he felt no better, and left to visit Samuel Fischer at his new house in Berlin-Grünewald. Exhausted when he got back to Munich, Thomas sank into lethargy. "How little it is to conceive an idea!" he wrote to Heinrich. "One does not realize that until the strength, the courage, the desire to *work* are lacking."[11]

Katia and Heinrich never talked to each other in the second person singular. She describes him as "very formal . . . I could imitate his slightly affected, precise tone well, and I always loved doing do. One of my lines was, 'Ah, the rich! How well off they are.' "[12] Only vaguely aware of how important the brothers were to each other, she didn't know how confessional Thomas became in letters to Heinrich.

After writing so derogatorily about Heinrich's fiction in notebooks and in letters to Ida Boy-Ed, he was surprised to be impressed by a story Heinrich published in *Simplicissimus* and dedicated to him—"Abdankung" ("Abdication"). It's about a schoolboy, Felix, who has enough willpower to tyrannize over his classmates until he falls in love with the most subservient, a fat boy called Hans Butt. Suddenly eager to be submissive, Felix makes Hans his adjutant and courts humiliation. The climax comes when Felix interprets an outburst of anger as an order to commit suicide. The story is suspiciously similar to Robert Musil's novel *Die Verwirrungen des Zöglings Törless* (*Young Törless*), which had just been published, but Thomas felt almost as if he'd written "Abdication" himself.13 What he didn't see was that Heinrich had been referring to him. Not only had the younger brother risen socially above his sibling, he'd achieved greater fame and a higher income. But when Heinrich had been offensive, Thomas had been conciliatory, betraying both Katia and himself by confiding in his brother.

Thomas didn't understand the implications of "Abdication" until he reread it in the book *Stürmische Morgen*, which reprinted four of Heinrich's stories. Not without irony, Thomas wrote to congratulate his brother on "a brilliant book that displays all your virtues, your overpowering tempo, your famous 'verve', the enchanting pithiness of your language, your quite astonishing virtuosity, to which one surrenders, because it undoubtedly comes directly from passion."14

Heinrich not only ignored the irony but chose this moment to confide in Thomas about the affair he was having. In March 1905 he'd been on his way to Florence when he met the twenty-one-year-old Ines Schmied in Milan. His junior by twelve years, she was attractive, temperamental, and ambitious, wanting to make her name as a singer or an actress. By June they'd become secretly engaged. The liaison had rescued Heinrich from a long period of solitude. He hadn't yet met Ines when he wrote his novel *Professor Unrat*—*Unrat* means excrement—about a tyrannous schoolteacher who loses his respectability and his job when he gets involved with a singer at a low cabaret called Der blaue Engel. The name became famous, and so did Heinrich, when the novel was made into a movie starring Marlene Dietrich. He claimed that previously the only woman in his life had been Carla. Certainly, he'd had enough experience with prostitutes to produce a dichotomy between emotion and sexuality.

Thomas, who'd heard rumors about the liaison with Ines but had never discussed it with Heinrich, tried rather gauchely to comfort his brother by comparing his problem with the totally dissimilar one Thomas had once had with Katia: "You are united, you are sure both of yourselves and of each other—that is really a more favourable situation than ours was at that time. . . . I see here many opportunities of happiness—for me too; for it would not be out of the question for you to live for at least a part of the year with your wife in Munich." But if Ines was pursuing a career on the stage, Heinrich might have to travel more than he'd wish to. "Though I find a certain amount of mobility, freedom, restlessness, insecurity desirable . . . I believe from what I remember that you have in you a desire for stability and a great need for bourgeois comfort." In the meantime, perhaps Heinrich would like to visit him and Katia in Oberammergau.[15]

They left Munich on June 15, and while they were staying at the villa they'd rented, enjoying the mountain air and the peacefulness of their routine, Thomas's spirits improved. Working on *Royal Highness*, he wrote to tell Fischer he was no longer depressed.[16] Later on in the summer, Heinrich and Carla both came to visit him. Carla was twenty-four and beautiful, but unhappy. She stayed at the Flensburg theater for only one season, moving on to Göttingen, where she met the thirty-four-year-old Theodor Lessing, who was working as a theater critic. They went for walks together and had long chats, but neither became important to the other. She was resigned, he says, to a "chaise-longue life, which she filled out with heroic yearning for a millionaire, manicuring her very beautiful hands and reading a lot of novels."[17]

FOR *ROYAL HIGHNESS*, as previously for *Buddenbrooks*, Thomas did a lot of research, amassing formidable quantities of detail that could be presented realistically. But in both novels, as in stories such as "Tonio Kröger," his prime concern was to make a statement about what it was like to be Thomas Mann—a latecomer in a decaying family, a bohemian homesick for bourgeois *Gemütlichkeit*, and, in the new novel, a prince among commoners, condemned to isolation on a higher plane.

By the time he got down to serious work on the novel, he'd allowed over six years to elapse since finishing *Buddenbrooks*. He'd made notes for novels he never even started to draft; it was only now that he committed himself fully, and, though *Royal Highness* is less substantial than *Buddenbrooks*, the task was again going to take three years. Staying with Katia in Oberammergau until mid-September, he went on making notes; after returning to Munich he started drafting the narrative.

In the Bismarckian Reich, there were several kings, princes, and a grand duke with no real power. It suited Bismarck to let them keep their titles: Their existence camouflaged the hegemony of Prussia, and while he played off the various states against the Reichstag, the kings, princes, and the grand duke of Baden had no option but to act as agents of Prussia in the government of the empire, just as they'd previously been co-opted as agents of Napoleon. It was coincidental that the grand duke was responsible for Bismarck's downfall. Kaiser Wilhelm II, who wasn't yet thirty when he came to the throne in 1888, trusted the grand duke, who encouraged him to distrust Bismarck. Believing the seventy-five-year-old chancellor was mentally unbalanced, Wilhelm dismissed him.

All over the world, observers of the political scene were astonished; the cartoon in *Punch* was captioned "Dropping the pilot."

Prince Klaus Heinrich has a withered arm, like the kaiser, but Thomas had the grand duchy in mind—a small and impoverished south German state where people were resistant to the authoritarian industrialism of the Reich. Though Baden retained its parliament, the Landtag, it had little power. In the fictional state, a population of a million is spread over an area of 3,200 square miles. The country is undeveloped, and what the royal family has in common with the predominantly peasant population is poverty. The state owes 600 million marks, and royal castles are falling into ruin.

In the Grand Duchy of Baden, elaborate court rituals still survived, and Thomas had been collecting information about them, taking clippings from newspapers, and making contact with two men who had experience of court procedures, the Freiherr Alexander von Bernus, who'd served in Karlsruhe, capital of the grand duchy, and Dr. Robert Printz, who'd been in the diplomatic corps. Both men were generous in giving time to Thomas's questions, and many of their answers are incorporated almost verbatim into the narrative.

But he worked so slowly that Fischer, who'd sold almost fifty thousand copies of *Buddenbrooks* and wanted another popular success, came to Munich during October, when Katia was in the final month of a pregnancy that had begun only a couple of months after the birth of her daughter. On the fourteenth, after Thomas had read him a chapter of the manuscript, Fischer tried to speed him up by offering to pay a preliminary 6,000 marks plus royalties on the first ten thousand copies as soon as he received the completed typescript. At 25 percent, assuming the book was priced at about 5 marks, the advance on royalties would amount to 12,500 marks.

Thomas's financial prospects were improving just as his family was on the point of increasing. Katia gave birth to a boy on November 18, and this time her labor was much easier. She and Thomas were both delighted to have a son. "I have always been annoyed when it was a girl," she said after having three children of each sex. "I don't know why."[18] The baby was given the same names as the prince in the novel, Klaus Heinrich.

Much of the narrative pivots on the analogy between the writer and the prince, whose function is to represent other people. Another premise is that both roles preclude happiness. Klaus Heinrich realizes he exists to be stared at and cheered: The people, seeing him as an idealized version of themselves, are applauding themselves when they applaud him. As his mentor Dr. Überbein explains, formality and intimacy are mutually exclusive. At school the prince feels envious of Anselm Schickedanz, who has a reputation for devilry, and it's frustrating to be told: "You should see what he's like when you're not there." But while princes and dignitaries can never find out how other people behave in their absence, the question is even more tantalizing to novelists, with their professional need to speculate about other people's behavior.

Thomas's urge to dramatize his own situation was so strong that, not content with having a prince as his alter ego, he introduced a writer, Axel Martini, who has no function in the story. He owes his Christian name to *Axel*, the best-known play by the nineteenth century symbolist Villiers de l'Isle-Adam, famous for the line: "Living? Our servants can do that for us." Though uncertain whether his talent justifies the time and energy he invests in writing, Martini feels unsuited to any other occupation. Like a decadent hero in a play by Oscar Wilde or Villiers de l'Isle-Adam, he claims that for people like himself, lack of experience is advantageous. Hygiene is indispensable, and nothing is more unhygienic than life. His pact with his muse involves him in isolation and unhappiness. Having written a poem in praise of life, he knows he'd despise his existence had he actually sampled the pleasures he celebrates, and he envies an acquaintance who drives around in a racing car, seducing peasant wenches. While conceding that Martini doesn't have an easy life, Klaus Heinrich finds him rather repulsive. As Thomas admitted, he was under the influence of Ibsen's play *The Pretenders*, which contains a similar interview between Earl Skule and a writer.

Like Martini, all the main characters in *Royal Highness* are cut off from ordinary people. Though the prince has to enter into occasional conversations with veterans, marksmen, athletes, peasants, victims of disaster, and so on, he takes little interest in them. He has been taught by his tutor to adopt a Nietzschean, anti-egalitarian aloofness. In this commonplace world, says Überbein, a man with spiritual needs will search for the exceptional and will love it wherever he finds it. Having extraordinary gifts and obligations, he's entitled to despise ordinary people. He shouldn't regard himself as no better than citizens who play skittles in shirtsleeves.

Thomas doesn't distance himself from this attitude, which the prince shares, assuming the common man to be dull-witted and preoccupied with petty, money-grubbing problems. Nor does Thomas ever connect this assumption with the allegation of coldness that's often leveled against Klaus Heinrich. Defending him, as he'd intended to defend Frederick the Great, against the charge, Thomas is defending himself. Klaus Heinrich notices that even his most loyal supporters tend, after spending a certain amount of time with him, to become irritable and exhausted, as if they can no longer breathe in his presence. This saddens him, but he doesn't ask himself what he could do to make them feel more relaxed.

Instead of writing about Frederick the Great's relationship with his brother, Thomas gives the prince an elder brother modeled partly on

Heinrich. Their father, the grand duke, Johann Albrecht III, has a Schopenhauerian death like Thomas Buddenbrook's: He ends up feeling "sick to death of the whole thing." In the boyhood section of the narrative, little is said about the elder brother, except that he looks unapproachable and aristocratic, making his sibling feel almost plebeian in comparison. At their father's funeral, Albrecht seems shy and awkward, constantly looking down and sucking his lower lip, unable to conceal his disgust at having to participate in the ceremony. After his accession, he grows a pointed beard, as Heinrich had, and resents the duties that stop him from going south in the summer.

In February 1907, Thomas interrupted his work to contribute a short article for a symposium in *Nord und Süd* on the cultural value of theater. The question concerned him because rehearsals had started in Frankfurt for a production of *Fiorenza*. Heinrich urged him to arrange for Carla to play Fiore, but Thomas refused, saying the enterprise was already riskier than he would have liked. The director, Carl Heine, kept postponing the opening, and when *Nord und Süd* contacted him, he was pressing Heine to stop procrastinating. Insecure about the play, and wanting to believe it measured up to the standards of classical drama, he spent several weeks on his "Versuch über das Theater" ("Essay on the Theatre"), which contends that in classical drama, as exemplified by Jean Racine and Pierre Corneille, language matters more than story. (*Fiorenza* might have been a better play if Thomas had paid more attention to story and less to language.)

At the same time he wanted to defend the novel against the German tendency to regard only poetry and drama as literature. Later, writing to Hugo von Hofmannsthal, he said: "[T]here is no better way of elevating the novel than by making it into a construct which contains ideas."[19] Both theoretically and practically, he tried throughout his life to steer the novel away from the naturalism in which the writer did no more than serve up slices of reality.

In this essay he tries to demonstrate both the novel's superiority to drama and drama's superiority to theater. Of all the arts, he says, theater is the most naive, childish, and popular. Its essence is its direct appeal to the senses. For Thomas, drama is part of literature, while theater is a building in which even dramatic literature doesn't feel at home. But drama is eclipsed by the novel, which is more profound, more precise, more complete, more conscientious: The writer can express himself not only through characters but through objects and atmosphere, while a play may be no more readable than an opera libretto.

Not long after finishing the article, Thomas left with Katia for a reunion with Heinrich and Carla in Venice. It would have been hard to stay on good terms with both Heinrich and the Pringsheims, and by now even Hedwig Pringsheim, who'd been such a good ally, was disenchanted with him. In March she'd told a friend that Katia was "living rather quietly, because her husband is a real fusspot, and there's a lot that he refuses to put up with. She's blissfully happy with her two children and I believe motherhood is what she is most suited to."[20]

Staying on the Lido at the Grand Hotel, the fusspot found it pretentious and overpriced, but he enjoyed Heinrich's company. Once again, the brothers achieved more of a rapprochement than either had expected, and they were getting on so well that Thomas refused to cut the holiday short when he heard *Fiorenza* was going to open on May 11. He and Katia attended the last of the six performances in Frankfurt on May 23, staying at the Frankfurter Hof–"a really grand hotel . . . you know what you are paying for and that gives me a kind of happiness."[21]

The actors were mediocre—except the one who played the cardinal—but the audience gave Thomas an ovation when he shared the curtain calls with the cast and, at the end, he took a solo bow. "The performance, however inadequate it mostly was, has shown me that the play, as a play, is not by any means so impossible as almost everyone believed."[22]

FOR THEIR SUMMER HOLIDAY Thomas and Katia chose Seeshaupt, a fashionable resort at the southern end of the Lake of Starnberg. They rented a villa, but when Heinrich accepted the invitation to join them, he had to stay at a nearby boardinghouse. Believing, mistakenly, that Heinrich was editing a series of Flaubert translations, Thomas asked him to give Katia one of the novels: She'd do it just as well as the average translator, if not better.[23]

By the end of June, Thomas had been invited to a symposium at Bonn University, where Professor Berthold Litzmann, founder and editor of *Mitteilungen der literarhistorischen Gesellschaft Bonn*, was planning a Thomas Mann issue. At the symposium several writers were going to make statements about aims and methods. Thomas could hardly refuse, but, not wanting to give up as much time as he had for his "Essay on the Theatre," he set himself a deadline of two weeks for writing his paper.

His method, he said, was to write a sentence every morning, but, needing to feel perfectly fresh, he never attempted any sentence of importance when he'd been working for more than two hours. "It is a matter of being patient, staying idle half the day, going back to sleep and waiting to see whether things will go better the next day, with the brain rested." Later on in the essay he changed his mind about patience. What was needed, he said, was a combination of doggedness, obstinacy, and self-control, which were almost unimaginable; the nerves should be stretched to the point at which it was impossible not to cry out.[24]

Having started his novel at the end of 1906, he'd written only about a third by the end of August 1907, and about half by the end of the year.[25] He'd broken off once again, briefly, to write a self-portrait under the title "In the Looking Glass" ("Im Spiegel") for the December issue of the *Literarische Echo*. In it he wryly predicted that if his body held out, he'd be at his best between fifty and sixty.

At home he wasn't entirely neglecting his two-year-old daughter. As Erika later recalled, "He took trouble at that time not only to teach me how to talk but also to differentiate between things. He carried me about on his arm and took me for instance over to a row of books and said again and again: 'That is the green book and that is the red book.' And then I had to repeat: 'Green book—red book.'"

In February 1908, leaving Katia and the children in Munich, he went to stay with his mother in Polling, where he spent two hours each morning at a writing desk, but "I sometimes feel quite stupid. My way of working makes me obstinate and apathetic. Freshness can probably be achieved only in the opposite way—by improvising and writing occasional verse."[26]

At the beginning of April, Heinrich came to Munich with Ines, and after her first meeting with her prospective daughter-in-law, Julia described her as "of medium build, dainty, golden blond hair with golden brown eyes, complexion like milk and blood, amiable, like a good fairy."[27] Viktor, who first saw her in the foyer of a variety theater, said she was "a woman of such beauty that it gave me a shock."

Heinrich and Ines arranged a holiday with Thomas and Katia in Venice, where Carla was to join them. Thomas and Katia left for Verona on May 2, and two days later met the others at the Grand Hôtel des Bains on the Lido. For the first ten days the weather was fine, but Ines was liable to be upset by such trivial confrontations as when Thomas asked her to return a book he'd lent her. In the middle of the month the sirocco set in, "a depressing, enervating kind of wind."[28]

Back in Munich, Thomas settled down to a regular schedule of work, but without any enthusiasm: He was "boring himself to death."[29] He and Katia were planning to spend the summer in Tölz, on the river Isar, just over thirty miles to the south of Munich, near the Lake of Starnberg. On the way they visited the Löhrs in Starnberg, only to find that Julia, who'd aged, was in an exhausted state. Though he'd been in favor of the marriage, Thomas put the blame on her "mean little man, whose favourite topics are, as is well known, war, cancer and starvation. In short Lula deserves a lot of sympathy."[30]

After arriving in Tölz with Katia and the children, Thomas thought the atmosphere was doing him good. Hearing a piece of land was on sale at a bargain price, they went to see it. It had views of the town, the Isar, and the mountains. Without needing any more financial help from the Pringsheims, Thomas bought it, taking out a mortgage to have a house built.

He'd intended to finish the novel during the summer at Tölz, and it was announced that serialization would begin in the October issue of the *Neue Rundschau*, but once again progress was slower than he'd expected. He was still in Tölz at the beginning of September when Ida Boy-Ed arrived in Munich hoping to see him. He made excuses: He'd recently found it painful to interrupt work on the novel for a trip to Munich, and Katia, who was already pregnant with their third child, "can bear neither railway journeys nor being left on her own."[31]

In the first half of the novel (about 150 pages) there are seven chapters; in the second half, the same number of pages is taken up by two chapters, both about Klaus Heinrich's relationship with Imma. Laying himself open again to the charge he'd tried to refute in "Bilse und ich," Thomas didn't try to camouflage the resemblance between Imma and Katia, and he borrowed the letters he'd sent her, though letter-writing doesn't feature in the prince's protracted wooing of Imma.

Thomas hadn't forgotten Katia's defiance of the tram conductor. This is developed into an incident illustrating Imma's audacity. A crowd has gathered outside the royal castle to watch the changing of the guard, and Imma, wearing a toque and a fox fur jacket, is hurrying toward the university. Unwilling to wait till the ceremony is over or detour around the band and the crowd, she walks between the double rank of soldiers, pushing aside the sergeant who tries to bar her progress with his rifle. She can't bear to be ordered about. Her nostrils are distended; her dark eyes blaze with indignation. Watching from a window, the prince is impressed, and he goes on thinking about her.

The cycling episode is also used, with the bikes transformed into horses. Klaus Heinrich goes out riding with Imma, who is chaperoned by Countess Louewenjoul. After warning the prince not to overrate the effect he has on her, Imma kicks her horse into a gallop. Neither Klaus Heinrich nor the countess can keep up with her. Amused, she waits for them at the edge of the woods.

Another incident that echoes actual events is the first kiss. Saying he has never visited Imma's study, the prince asks to see her books. Given half an hour alone with her, he goes down on his knees, throwing his arms around her slender body. She reprimands him for lacking self-control, but then kisses his hand. "Little sister," he says—a phrase he repeats on the evening of the ball, when she's presented at court, and they agree to become engaged. Thanks to information from Robert Printz, the formalities of the presentation are described convincingly, but the ensuing offer of marriage is subject to the proviso that her father will subsidize the state, and it's hard to believe Imma would be as happy about this as we're told she is.

The buildup has been central to the structure of the novel. Thomas has been at pains to establish the country's economic backwardness, and it has been predictable that the American millionaire will solve all the financial problems. Here, Thomas, who'd been so meticulous in the arithmetic he did for *Buddenbrooks*, goes wrong in leaving the national debt at the same level for about twenty-five years. If it was 600 million marks just before Klaus Heinrich was born, Thomas should have either made it greater by the time of his engagement, or explained how it had been kept at the same level.

The Spoelmanns aren't Jewish, but, wanting to introduce racial impurity, Thomas makes them of partly Indian descent. The only Jewish character is a doctor, Sammet, who's described as being ill-fated insofar as he was born a Jew. Explaining why her father was glad to leave the United States, Imma says: "[T]here's something wrong with us." Her grandfather married the daughter of a white and a half-caste, and in the States, where Indian blood, she says, is considered a blemish, their origin was a handicap. This pleases Klaus Heinrich because it helps to explain the sharpness of her tongue. Like Sieglinde in "The Blood of the Walsungs," Imma keeps people at a distance by speaking mockingly and sarcastically, as if she were incapable of accepting a compliment or agreeing with anyone else's opinion. As the daughter of a millionaire she has been pampered and indulged, but she has also been the object of mockery. Her habitual irony had looked aggressive; now he can see it was developed as a form of self-defense.

The characterizations of Imma, of the twins in "The Blood of the Walsungs," and (later) Naphta in *The Magic Mountain* suggest that Thomas associated sharpness of the tongue with Jewishness, and this is confirmed by a statement he made in 1907 on "the Jewish question." Known everywhere as a stranger, he says, the Jew "carries the pathos of exceptionality in his heart" and stands out from the norm "in a sublime or offensive way." A permanently frustrated desire to conform produces the characteristically Jewish combination of contrasting qualities—revolutionary tendencies and warped snobbism, gregariousness and individualism, insolence and insecurity, cynicism and sentimentality, sharpness and melancholy.[32]

Ambivalence was often apparent in his behavior toward Katia, but negative feelings are eliminated from the portrayal of Imma. Never having been exposed to coarseness or vulgarity, and conditioned by her privileged upbringing, she has grown to resemble a princess. She had to sit conspicuously in a box at the opera because the family needed to be seen in public, but she has led a sheltered, isolated life. Instead of being intimidated by the prince, she's almost condescending, and when she praises him for making a favorable impression on Countess Louewenjoul, he takes more pleasure in being patronized than in everyone else's subservience. He and Imma can be honest with each other because they live on a higher level than the rest of humanity.

Professor Pringsheim was an art collector; Mr. Spoelmann collects fine glass. Neither enjoys good health, and the Arcisstrasse tea party Thomas attended in Katia's absence is almost exactly duplicated when the prince comes at teatime to the castle the millionaire has bought. Mr. Spoelmann is lying on a couch beside the table, wrapped in a fur-lined cover of green silk. Learning that Klaus Heinrich has a sore throat, he recommends cold compresses and gets up to fetch a piece of gutta-percha. Four and a half years after the incident, Thomas is still celebrating what he'd seen as a turning point in his relationship with Alfred Pringsheim.

But the professor hadn't been forgiven for rejecting all the Konrad-strasse furniture except for three chairs. When Mr. Spoelmann arrives at the Eremitage to see whether any of the prince's furniture is good enough for the mansion being prepared for the bride and groom, he rejects all the sparsely cushioned sofas, the stiff-legged table, and the white corner tables, accepting only three mahogany chairs upholstered in yellow satin.

The theme of emotional coldness is taken up several times. During the horse-riding sequence Imma reports that though the countess is impressed, she finds him so harsh and stern that he has a chilling effect on her. He asks Imma whether she, too, finds him chilling, but she sidesteps the question, and later on, when he wants to know why she doesn't confide in him, she says she can never let herself go in his presence. His manner of speaking and his way of looking at people are inhibiting. He carries himself well and always asks appropriate questions, but seems to have no deep convictions, and no concern for anything but his dignity. Awkwardness and embarrassment would always be barriers to intimacy, she says. He tells her he cares for her so much that he's certain to win her confidence in the end, but she refuses to promise that she'll stand by him and laugh at both of them whenever he makes her feel awkward.

Though Thomas thought he was writing a love story, he succeeds neither in making the prince appear to be in love nor in showing what makes Imma change her mind. Perhaps Thomas never understood how much pressure Hedwig Pringsheim had exerted on her daughter—at the end of her long life Katia said she had never been able to do what she'd wanted to do.[33] Certainly, he writes unconvincingly about the prince's sudden success in wooing Imma. There's a long and effective conversation between him and the minister of state, Baron von Knobelsdorf, who favors a marriage with the daughter of a millionaire because the country could benefit from a generous dowry consisting of investments. But the narrative subordinates emotional aspects of negotiations between the lovers to political and ceremonial aspects. After the session with the minister, the prince takes a sudden interest in political economy, avidly studying books bought from an academic bookshop. Imma seems to be teasing when she invites him to bring books next time he visits her, but when he starts to teach her what he has learned, she becomes more relaxed, gaining confidence in him through studying public welfare. This leads up to the implausible sequence in which she agrees to marry him, happy at the austere prospects. Neither of them will ever be frivolous or selfish; they'll look at their own interests in the perspective of the general good.

Thomas still hadn't finished the novel when, after two months in Munich, he left for Vienna, arriving on November 24 and staying at the Hotel Klomser. He was due to read a chapter of *Royal Highness* on November 26 in a bookshop. The arrangements had been made by Jakob Wassermann, whose latest novel, *Caspar Hauser*, had impressed Thomas when he read it in Venice. Wassermann introduced him to the forty-six-year-old Arthur Schnitzler, a doctor who'd been successful as a playwright for over ten years and had recently completed the first of his two novels, *Der Weg ins Freie*, portraying a society in which moneyed middle-class Jews mingle with liberal-minded aristocrats.

A few days later, Schnitzler, Thomas, and Wassermann went to Semmering, where they met Hugo von Hofmannsthal. If Hauptmann had reminded Thomas of a priest, Hofmannsthal seemed more like a prince. "And the prince type is what specially interests me at the moment."[34] To another friend, Thomas described Hofmannsthal as "a charmingly intense little man who lives on a high level. I have a weakness for such lives."[35] Hofmannsthal and his wife, Gerty, then invited the three writers to visit their country home in Rodaun, "a small, old baroque palace with suitable furnishings."[36]

In Vienna, Thomas wrote the very short story "The Railway Accident" ("Das Eisenbahnunglück"). He told Heinrich his intention had been to earn the 300 marks he needed for Christmas presents.[37] The story was based on an experience he'd had two and a half years previously, traveling to Dresden on an overnight train that was derailed in a collision. In the story the anonymous novelist is carrying his manuscript in a suitcase he leaves in the luggage van, and it looks as if he'll never get it back. In May 1906, Thomas hadn't started drafting his novel, and it was only preliminary notes that were at risk, but now, writing the story in December 1908, he could ask himself how he'd feel if the whole of his unfinished novel were destroyed. Possessing no copy of his work, the anonymous novelist agonizes over what he'll do if his manuscript is lost. "My beehive, my artifact, my warren, my pride and pain, the best of myself . . . I cross-examined myself and saw that I would start again from the beginning . . . and perhaps this time the going would be a little easier."[38]

13

Marxist Fairy Story

EACH YEAR, CHRISTMAS was becoming more of a family occasion. Erika was three and Klaus two. At the end of 1908 their father
told Heinrich: "[T]he children were charming, just as they are in books,
when the presents were given out; but now they are twice as naughty as
they used to be."[1]

In January, when the *Neue Rundschau* started serializing *Royal Highness,* it was still unfinished, and Thomas was displeased with the first installment. No book, he told Korfiz Holm, could be less suited to
serialization.[2] On January 7, Robert Printz made final suggestions about
ways the millionaire could subsidize the state, and on February 13,
Thomas completed the final chapter.

He'd come close to fulfilling a fantasy based on equating himself
with a prince and Katia with a princess. In 1895, helping Heinrich edit
the anti-Semitic *Das Zwanzigste Jahrhundert,* he wasn't expecting to
marry a Jewish girl, but her privileged upbringing and exceptional qualities had made her seem superior to every other girl he'd met. Success in
wooing her had seemed to validate the princely equation, but the
process of validation wouldn't seem complete until the novel was finished. It still wasn't published, but at least he'd done everything he'd
been driven to do. With his writing table finally cleared of the *Royal
Highness* material, he could feel a new period dawning.

On the afternoon of March 27, in a clinic, Katia had enormous difficulty in giving birth to their third baby, another son. The labor lasted
for seventeen hours, and the doctors were on the point of intervening
with forceps, for the baby's heartbeat was weakening. He was named
Gottfried Angelus, but he was known as Golo.

Fischer, who'd never seen Paris, was planning to motor there, taking
four days for the trip, and he invited his best-selling author to join him,
but on April 20, after a lot of hesitation, Thomas said he wasn't well
enough. "What I need is rest, quiet life and strong air."[3] He would have
liked to spend a few weeks with Heinrich in Livorno, partly because he
was worrying about his treatment of the brother theme in the novel.
Making public appearances in lieu of his gauche and diffident elder
brother, Klaus Heinrich becomes more popular than Albrecht in a way

that parallels Thomas's eclipsing of Heinrich's reputation. Heinrich would read the serialization in the *Neue Rundschau*, and Thomas wanted to avert another quarrel. "I always think siblings should not fall out," he wrote. "They laugh at each other or scream at each other, but they do not break off the connection with each other. Just think of No. 52 Beckergrube! Everything else is immaterial!—This may all seem like good-natured gush, but there is some truth in it, believe me! . . . Farewell, dear Heinrich, I am hoping to hear from you soon in a friendly vein."[4]

Heinrich's scribbled reaction on the letter was: "Why all reproaches for me? The bad behaviour is wholly one-sided." Thomas was assuming that reproach was the best form of self-defense. Heinrich would have come to Livorno, but Thomas wrote again on May 10, saying he'd decided instead to spend three or four weeks at the Bircher-Benner clinic. He left Munich the next day, and, from Zurich, sent a picture postcard to Walter Opitz: "Cordial greetings from a grass-eating Nebuchadnezzar who goes into the 'air-bath' on all fours."[5] He was referring to a 1795 watercolor by William Blake showing the mad Babylonian king on all fours. Shadrach, Meshach, and Abednego had told him he was like a dog: this is how Blake depicted him.

Founded in 1897, the clinic had moved in 1904 to a position in the foothills of the Alps, with a superb view of the city, the gardens, the lake, and the mountains. In the evening, when the lights came on, the beauty of the scenery was extraordinary. At first Thomas chafed against the austere discipline: patients had to get up at six and put their lights out at nine, dividing the day between "air-baths," sunbathing, water therapy, and gardening, while living on a diet of vegetables, fruit, and nuts. For five days he hesitated about whether to leave, but when his digestion began to improve, he was glad he'd stayed.[6]

THOMAS'S EXPERIENCES IN THE CLINIC had seemed relevant to the prison experience his confidence trickster, Felix Krull, would have. "Even in gaol he sleeps like a child" runs one note, and another points to the possibility of letting the prison doctor give him a note suggesting he should work in the garden.

After returning to Munich on June 5, Thomas became more interested in theater, and struck up a friendship with the director Max Reinhardt, whom he'd seen during 1903 in Berlin, when Reinhardt was only thirty but was playing old characters at the Deutsches Theater under Otto Brahm. Normally reluctant to admit outsiders to rehearsals, Reinhardt broke his rule for Thomas. Alongside the work of Ibsen, Schiller, and Shakespeare, Reinhardt directed plays by Hauptmann and Hofmannsthal. "Nothing has interested, excited, stimulated me so much for a long time. This is the very essence of modernity—naive, bold, unreflective. Reinhardt, this strange, quiet, solid, little man . . . is the incarnation of encouragement for every modern artist who has doubts about approaching big subjects."[7] Even after moving into the house at Tölz when it was ready in mid-July, Thomas kept making the thirty-four-mile journey to Munich for evenings in the theater.

Early in August he paid his first visit to Bayreuth for a performance of *Parsifal*. He felt at first as if he'd gone to Lourdes or to a fortune-teller, but then found he was deeply moved by musical and dramatic climaxes. Wagner, he decided, was still at the highest point of modernity, and Richard Strauss had failed to overtake him.[8] "The accents of contrition and anguish, on which W. worked throughout his life, achieve here their final intensity. Tristan's yearning is really eclipsed by this, with its profound details, its ardent cruelty. To be sure, it is another question whether there is still a future for all this thoughtfulness and good taste, or whether it now belongs to history."[9] It seemed unlikely that Wagner exerted much influence on the younger generation.

Planning a critical essay on modern culture, Thomas took many of his bearings from Wagner. With the novel finally out of the way, Thomas wanted to divide his time between the essay, which would be called "Mind and Art" ("Geist und Kunst"), and a story that would be complementary to the novel, though different in atmosphere, possibly having something of the eighteenth century in it.[10] He hadn't decided against the novel on Frederick the Great, but didn't intend to work on it yet. In June he complained of having so many commitments that he didn't know where to begin[11]; in fact, he was working on the essay, which he planned as the centerpiece in a new collection containing "Essay on the Theatre" and other contributions to newspapers and reviews.[12]

"Mind and Art" would develop the argument advanced in the essay on theater. Literature should be considered as no less respectable, no less important than art or music. Hadn't Pascal, Montaigne, Rochefoucauld, and Nietzsche been artists?[13] Wagner, though his handling of music had been literary, had encouraged Germans to feel less respect for the man of letters than the French felt for the *homme de lettres*.[14] Thomas reiterated this in March 1910, responding to a questionnaire on the situation of the German writer. But "Mind and Art" was to remain unfinished, causing him nothing but anxiety. "Every morning I lacerate my nerves on it so badly that in the afternoon I am closer to inanity than to letter-writing. . . . The subject is so ticklish and intricate."[15] He wrote seventy-five pages of notes and collected forty-seven newspaper clippings, but never started to draft the essay.

Mainly because of consistently bad weather, Thomas and Katia didn't enjoy their first summer in the new house. The building had a red roof with a weathercock on it. On fine days they could eat on the spacious south-facing veranda that led out into the garden. The ground floor was divided between the kitchen, the dining room, Thomas's small workroom, which faced toward the east, and a south-facing living room used mainly by Katia. It overlooked the mountains and the garden, which had apple trees, an enormous chestnut tree, and a bed of asters. Contiguous with it was a virgin forest of tall slim pine trees: Used by no one else, it was like an adjunct to their property.

The bedroom on the second floor had French windows leading out onto the large balcony above the veranda. There was a small bedroom for Erika, a larger one for the two younger children, and one for the nanny. On the third floor were two guest bedrooms and a maid's room. There was only one bathroom, but each bedroom had a washbasin.

It was probably during August that Heinrich came to stay with them, and some photographs survive. In one the thirty-four-year-old Thomas, wearing a stiff-collared shirt and a suit with a waistcoat, is holding his pigtailed four-year-old daughter in one hand and his three-year-old son in the other, while the twenty-six-year-old Katia stands next to him, holding the baby, Golo. Also in the picture is their collie, Motz.

The family didn't return to Munich until October 22, just after *Royal Highness* had appeared in the bookstores, and four days later they left again to meet Heinrich in Milan and go with him to Nice, a town he'd enjoyed the previous year. The three of them had a brief holiday there together.

The first reviews of *Royal Highness* had already appeared, based on the serialization, which had been completed in September. In the *Lübeckishe Blätter*, Ida Boy-Ed praised the novel as "monumental"—an important contribution to cultural history. For the second time Thomas Mann had created a form of his own for a subject that was uniquely his. Gratified, he wrote to thank her: "How perceptive you are when you say that the vitality of a work consists less in superficial vivacity than in that organic coherence which is a matter of memory, planning and conscientiousness."[16]

Sales surpassed both his expectations and those of Fischer, who'd printed ten thousand copies; by Christmas another ten thousand were ready, and by the end of 1910 about 25,000 had been sold. But no English translation appeared until 1916, when *Buddenbrooks* was still unknown in the English-speaking world. By the end of 1909 about thirty reviews of *Royal Highness* had appeared in German and Austrian papers, but Thomas was dissatisfied with the intellectual level on which these were written.[17] Though Alfred Kerr never devoted a whole review to the book, he sniped at it in other articles, or, as Thomas put it, "spat at me a few times."[18]

Hermann Hesse, now co-editor of the bimonthly *März*, wrote a discerning review, characterizing Thomas as a noble, astute, highly complex man, consummately stylish but ashamed of his artistry, "a mental attitude that drives him to melancholy and, because he is intelligent and on the defensive against himself, often to irony." *Buddenbrooks* had been "as natural and convincing as a natural phenomenon," but *Royal Highness* was more contrived. "For though Thomas Mann has the tastefulness that comes from the highest cultivation, he lacks the somnambulistic security of naive genius. . . . He is a talented storyteller, possibly even a great one, but he is also, and perhaps even more emphatically, an intellectual." While a naive writer such as Balzac or Dickens could give the impression of never thinking about his public, a distrustful intellectual like Thomas tried to keep the reader at a distance by treating him ironically and "pretending to oblige him, to make things easy for him." Thomas had been abusing his art by playing up to the public. Hesse was attacking him for doing the opposite of what Rilke had praised him for doing in *Buddenbrooks*, which had seemed to ignore the reader.

Concerned that this might seem offensive, Hesse sent an apologetic letter, which Thomas answered, saying he hadn't been playing to the gallery. If the book gave this impression, it was a "consequence of my long-standing, passionate and critical admiration for the art of Richard Wagner—that art which is as sophisticated as it is demagogic, and which may have permanently influenced, if not corrupted, my ideals, my ambitions." What he meant was that Wagner appealed to the crudest as well as the most refined taste. Thomas had never had a high opinion of writers whose work appealed only to an educated coterie. "I need the ignorant too."[19]

Hermann Bahr was going to review the novel in the *Neue Rundschau*. Remembering how he'd once imitated Bahr's style, Thomas waited impatiently, only to be disappointed when the review appeared in the December issue, spread over six large pages. Bahr called the novel a Marxist fairy story. "Just as fairy stories let people vanish into humanity, here the prince Klaus Heinrich and the rich Fräulein Spoelmann vanish into their class. They are only figures of their economic situation . . . he is the prince of our time, she is the rich girl of our time without any personal features."[20] Heinrich was delighted with this interpretation of the novel.[21]

Both reactions would be incomprehensible if democracy hadn't been such a burning issue. Long before the end of the nineteenth century it had been obvious that the spread of education would produce new challenges for the ruling classes. As Nietzsche had said, "If you want slaves, you are foolish to bring up masters." Though universal suffrage had been introduced in Austria, it was only after the general election of 1907 that Germany seemed likely to follow suit. In the autumn of 1908 the kaiser had aroused a storm of protest by declaring in an interview with the *Daily Telegraph* that his friendly feelings toward England were shared by only a minority of the German people. What he said was no more arrogantly imperialistic than many of his previous pronouncements, but in the endemic nervousness about the collapse of domestic stability, he was caught in the crossfire between the progressives, who blamed him for preserving Bismarckian autocracy, and the antidemocratic Junkers, who accused him of lapsing from Bismarckian authoritarianism. When Prince von Bülow, the Chancellor, encouraged the uproar in the Reichstag, Kaiser Wilhelm had to promise he'd respect his constitutional obligations. Bismarck's unification of the empire had been founded on autocratic monarchy; this had now been weakened, but there was nothing to replace it. Most of Germany's eminent writers had signed an appeal in the *Berliner Tageblatt* for electoral reform, but Thomas had remained aloof, and it was in this climate of uncertainty that he and Heinrich argued about democracy.

Though they got on well enough in Nice during November, tension between them was acquiring a political dimension. Just before *Royal Highness* came out, Heinrich's new novel, *Die kleine Stadt* (*The Little Town*), was published by Insel Verlag, and he thought it was his best work so far. Ines was his model for Flora Garlinda, a singer in a touring opera company visiting a small Italian town, but with its wide-angle focus, the narrative pays almost as much attention to the other members of the company and the townspeople. Thomas's reaction was: "The whole thing reads like an ode for democracy, and one gets the impression that great men are to be found only in a democracy. That is not true, but under the influence of your narrative, one believes it. One is also inclined to believe in 'the justice of the people', though that is still less true."[22] Aware that the gap between them was widening, Thomas called Heinrich "a passionate democrat of the newest type . . . So far as I can see into my future writing, it has nothing in the least to do with democracy."[23]

None of this stopped Thomas from offering financial help. Though *Die kleine Stadt* was favorably reviewed, less than a thousand copies were sold during the first two months. "I see more and more clearly," Heinrich wrote, "that my connection with the Insel Verlag was a serious mistake. With Langen my failure never reached such depths."[24] At the end of 1909, saying he could easily spare a couple of thousand marks, Thomas offered his brother a share in "the economic fruits of *Royal Highness*."[25] Heinrich hesitated, but in February he accepted 2,000 marks, using some of this money for his journey back from Nice to Florence.[26] Thomas went on to advance another 4,000 marks. But in the spring of 1910, Heinrich left Insel Verlag to sign a contract with Paul Cassirer, who guaranteed him an annual income, and by June he'd returned 1,000 marks to Thomas.

In the story about the confidence trickster Felix Krull's family is decaying in a much more vulgar way than the Buddenbrooks family did. Until the father, who makes inferior sparkling wine, goes bankrupt and kills himself, the garden is ornamented with china dwarfs and a chiming device plays the first bar of "Wine, Women and Song" whenever the door opens. At parties, which turn into sexual romps, Felix's plump mother and sister flirt shamelessly with guests. But Felix knows he's made of superior stuff. With his light, silky hair and blue-gray eyes, his golden-brown skin, his well-shaped hands, and his pleasing voice, he has the kind of good looks Thomas enjoyed describing, and he plays the kaiser game, exactly as Thomas had, with grown-ups in supporting roles. His godfather, an artist, often uses Felix as a model, sometimes in the nude, encouraging his vanity, and sometimes in costume, encouraging his talent for dressing up. Ordinary life seems dull after the bouts of self-transformation.

Giving a comic twist to the Nietzschean idea of self-conquest, Thomas makes Felix cultivate an expertise in physical self-control. He teaches himself to dilate or contract the pupils of his eyes. Together with the skill he acquires in forging his father's signature, this talent stands him in good stead when he wants to avoid going to school: If the doctor is called in, Felix can confuse him by inducing shivers and making his teeth chatter. His mother encourages these performances, which are given an extra dimension when Felix is taken to a theater and goes backstage to find that the leading man who seemed so glamorous under the lights is charmless and repulsive, with suppurating pimples all over his body. What looked like a glorious butterfly is a repulsive worm.

Thomas's identification with Felix is apparent in the emphasis on powers of concentration and in the insistence on having a deeper truth at the root of every deception. Each one should arise from a lively imagination which hasn't yet produced a harvest of material success. Even faked illness is partly genuine when the imagination has been exercised strenuously enough to produce tension which is almost painful.

All this was by way of preparation for adventures that were still unwritten when Thomas got embroiled in controversy with Theodor Lessing, the doctor who'd tried to befriend Carla and who wrote about culture and philosophy. He disliked the crippled critic Samuel Lublinski and now published a scurrilously anti-Semitic attack on him. "The secret," wrote Thomas, "is that I could not get started on the 'Confidence Trickster'; tormented by inactivity I hit out."[27]

On January 20, 1910, the weekly *Die Schaubühne* had published Lessing's article "Samuel zieht die Bilanz oder der kleine Prophete" ("Samuel Draws Up the Balance, or the Little Prophet"). Lessing, a baptized Jew who'd become a Zionist and returned to the Jewish faith, repeatedly used the abusive and untranslatable word *mauscheln*, which refers to speaking in a Jewish way. He sneered at Lublinski's "little, globular body" and his "spongy little stomach," calling him "Talmud progeny whose faculties of speaking and writing have degenerated into hypertrophy."[28]

A protest, signed by thirty-three writers including Stefan Zweig, was organized by Otto Falckenberg, a director at the Munich Kammerspiele. Invited to sign, Thomas opted for independent action. Both in his review of *Buddenbrooks* and in his 1904 book *Bilanz der Moderne*, Lublinski had shown himself to be perceptive and well disposed. After Lessing had refused to write an apology, Thomas showed his talent for invective in an article for the *Literarishe Echo* of March 1. It described Lessing as "a disadvantaged dwarf who ought to be glad that the sun shines on him too." His article was a "calumniating caricature, and it is hard to imagine anything cruder or more insipid." The whole thing was "so bad, so stupid, so full of misapprehensions" that it had "absolutely nothing" to do with Lublinski as a writer or a man. Quoting the proverb about not throwing stones if one lives in a glass house, Thomas pointed out that Lessing couldn't pose as a good example of Aryan masculinity. "The man who scuttles through life as a fearful example of Jewish racial inferiority shows something worse than imprudence—he shows an obscene self-contempt if he accepts payment for lampoons in which every third word is 'mauscheln'."[29]

Lessing sent a telegram, threatening to challenge Thomas to a duel. After consulting his father-in-law, he replied that the telegram was in breach of convention and was incomprehensible. Lessing retaliated by publishing statements in both *Die Schaubühne* and *Literarische Echo* on March 3. Saying Thomas had refused to fight a duel, Lessing called him a liar and a falsifier. His answer, "Justifications" ("Berechtigungen"), appeared in the *Literarische Echo* on April 1. "Must I say that I am disgusted by the idea of breathing the same air as this creature, that I want nothing to do with him?" It was like the story about the man with a dwarf clinging to his back. Lessing wanted "to have his name put next to mine as often as possible for as long as possible. But I am shaking him off, I do not acknowledge him. . . . In me he does not have an opponent."[30]

Lessing riposted by issuing a privately published pamphlet under the title "Samuel zieht die Bilanz und Tomi melkt die Moralkuh oder der Sturz zweier Könige" ("Samuel Draws Up the Balance and Tommy Milks the Moral Cow or the Collision of Two Kings"). The cover announced contributions by Thomas Mann and Samuel Lublinski. Lessing had reprinted all the articles with a misleading, one-sided commentary.

If Thomas hadn't joined in the controversy, he might have given more time to his story. By April he had a provisional title for it—"Confessions of the Thief and Swindler Felix Krull" ("Bekenntnisse des

Diebes und Schwindlers Felix Krull"). The first friend to be told the title was the writer Walter Opitz, who wanted Thomas to visit Paris, but the answer was: "I cannot travel now because I shall shortly become a father for the fourth time. (If it happens a fifth time, I shall pour petrol over myself and set light to it.)"[31]

At seven in the morning on June 7 the twenty-seven-year-old Katia gave birth to a daughter, whom she thought "the prettiest baby of all four." They called her Monika. Writing to Ida Boy-Ed, Thomas reiterated his determination not to have any more children. "The margin of the ridiculous has, I fear, been reached."[32]

Trying to concentrate on the story, he found himself in trouble. Writing to Lublinski on June 13, he complained about the problems of being frivolous and moralistic at the same time, skeptical and passionate. He was involving himself both sensually and intellectually, he said, at the cost of putting his artistic strength and his conscientiousness under enormous strain. "What is the artist! This mixture of Lucifer and clown . . ."[33] Just over three weeks later, after dinner in his apartment with Katia and his parents-in-law, he read some of the story.

At the end of June, needing distraction from it, he wrote to the editor of *Die Zukunft*, Maximilian Harden, offering to review a collection of Theodor Fontane's letters.[34] Jewish, and formerly an actor, Harden was a friend of the Pringsheims who'd been involved in a scandal during 1907 when he wrote an article in *Die Zukunft* making accusations of homosexuality against the German ambassador to Vienna, Kaiser Wilhelm's protégé Prinz Phillip von Eulenburg, and several of his friends, including Count Kuno von Moltke, who sued Harden for defamation. Thomas, when asked for his views by a Berlin monthly, had sided with Harden, who now commissioned him to write on Fontane.

But after moving to Tölz with Katia and the four children on July 17, he had the worst kind of distraction at the end of the month. At four o'clock in the afternoon of July 30, Carla, who was staying with their mother at Polling, killed herself with cyanide. She was nearly twenty-nine.

Her relationship with Heinrich had been stressful. Only ten when her father died, Carla had looked up to her twenty-year-old brother, and had been confused by the fictions that expressed his incestuous longing for her. Both her emotional life and her acting career had been full of disappointments, but she'd recently got close to happiness. She was engaged to a young Alsatian industrialist, Arthur Gibo, who lived in Mulhouse, and, having triumphed over his family's resistance to the marriage, she relished the prospect of severing herself from Germany and the German language, bringing up her children to speak French. But a former lover, a doctor, forced her back into his bed by threatening to tell Gibo about their affair if she refused. Though she gave in, the malicious doctor got in touch with Gibo. Carla asked Heinrich to send Gibo's mother a reassuring letter, but the irate fiancé arrived in Polling to cross-examine her. After telling him the truth, she hurried past her mother with a smile and locked herself in her room. The last sound she was heard to utter was gargling as she tried to cool the burning in her throat. Then she lay down on the chaise longue. She was found dead with dark spots on her hands and face. In her hand was a note saying: "Je t'aime. *Une fois* je t'ai trompé, mais je t'aime." ("I love you. *Once* I deceived you, but I love you.")35

As a girl she'd kept a skull on the dresser and given it a name, Nathanael. She also had cyanide in her possession; she boasted to her friend Liane Pricken about owning enough to kill a regiment. Seven years earlier, in *Die Jagd nach Liebe*, Heinrich made his heroine play with poison and a skull, and Thomas, in his rather callous summing up, said she must have bought the poison "as a kind of aesthetic caprice . . . And then she played with the idea too long, grew accustomed to the idea of taking it at the first provocation. . . . Apparently it never entered the poor child's head what she would do to us all, how it would damage our lives if she destroyed hers."36

Even in later letters to Heinrich, Thomas shows little empathy or sympathy: He thought of the suicide as something that had happened *to him*. "It is the bitterest thing that could have happened to me." He condemns Carla for thinking of no one but herself. She "should not have cut herself off from us. In this act she had no sense of family solidarity, no feeling for the common destiny of our family. She acted, so to speak, *in breach of a tacit agreement*. It is unspeakably bitter. In Mama's presence I control myself. Otherwise I weep almost all the time."37

According to Viktor, their mother never entirely recovered from the suicide. She survived her daughter by thirteen years, but, unable to settle anywhere, kept on the move. Concerned about her suffering, Thomas now brought her back to stay at Tölz.

Heinrich was more deeply stricken, but didn't acknowledge any guilt. He probably didn't come back to Germany, even for the funeral, and wrote in his notebook as if he felt entitled to a detached viewpoint:

To the body what is the body's, quick accesses of love, which are despised. Exaltation which is not quite trusted. Consciousness of not being united with another person, and of artificiality. Proud of it, despises self-deception, weakness, sentiment; disengagement from *life*. Also *cheerful* out of disengagement . . . She chooses her first love in a new world, France, speaks her first true words of love in a new language, wants to be a human being under a different nationality, her children will never understand the words of her earlier existence.

She has the artist's contempt for reality. "She pays no attention to meanness or danger, instinctively she scarcely treats anything alien as real, she is *still* alone and at the deepest level untouchable. Warmth is not for her, she is not made for happiness, sociability, for *life*."

Arthur Gibo had begged her on his knees not to see the doctor again, and if she hadn't been in possession of the poison, she might never have been unfaithful. She told a girlfriend that she'd take the cyanide if Arthur found out. It had given her the security of knowing she could end everything at a moment's notice. "Her deepest instinct," Heinrich wrote, "is always to be free. Lies bind people together, the truth separates them. People must be able to lie if they want to live. Carla is not capable of living."[38] He may have been thinking that since he wanted to survive, he ought to tell himself lies about the role he'd played in her life.

Leading Man

LOOKING BACK on her childhood, Erika Mann said her father didn't work in order to live but lived in order to work. His daily routine had been evolved out of an assiduously cultivated self-discipline. Without being called, he was always awake by eight, and after getting out of bed, he drank a cup of coffee with Katia before taking his bath and dressing. At eight-thirty, still unshaven, he breakfasted with Katia, and at nine he started work. After he closed the door of his study, he was unavailable for visitors, telephone calls, or children.

Though his desk was large, he allowed himself only a small working space, surrounded by holders for pens and pencils, framed photographs, flowers in a vase, ornaments, boxes, and knickknacks, including a tobacco box made of tortoiseshell inlaid with gold. It had belonged to his father, and Thomas, though he never used it, enjoyed having it on his desk. It was almost as if he wanted to feel cramped by the objects surrounding him as he committed himself to a draft he wouldn't feel free to change:

> I need white, perfectly smooth paper, fluid ink and a new, smooth-flowing pen. Outward irritations cause inner ones. I need legibility since I rework nothing but newspaper articles, handing over the one and only draft of longer manuscripts to the printer. . . . Concentration depends on the well-being of body and soul, of sight and hearing, so that from one's inner resources something emerges that arouses pleasure and hope, making me believe that if I treat it in the right way, something remarkable might be developed out of it. Invariably the conception is very small and modest. I start things because I imagine they can be completed quickly and easily.[1]

He smoked while he was writing, but never more than twelve cigarettes and two cigars a day. He enjoyed the first cigar after lunch in his study, sitting in a corner of the sofa and reading newspapers, periodicals, and books till he went upstairs to lie down for an hour. But on Sundays, when the family always lunched with the Pringsheims and stayed to tea, he was deprived of his afternoon rest. On weekdays he reappeared at five for tea, afterward settling down to write letters, reviews, or newspaper articles, and while doing this kind of work, he didn't mind being interrupted by visitors or telephone calls. He often took another walk before dinner, which was served at seven-thirty or eight. Sometimes there were guests. After the meal, if he was alone with Katia, they read or played gramophone records till about midnight, when they retired to their separate bedrooms, with books.

Though steadfastly faithful to his daily routine, he had misgivings about its rigidity. In the 1901 story "Tristan," Detlev Spinell confesses that he gets up early because his natural inclination is to stay in bed. He's swindling his conscience by putting in long hours at his desk. "Conscience, dear lady, is a bad business. I and people like me use it to push ourselves around. . . . We're useless creatures. . . . We hate what's useful, knowing it to be vulgar and unbeautiful . . . but conscience goes on gnawing at us so fiercely that nothing of us remains intact." Their whole way of life is so unhealthy that they need "a certain standard of good behaviour and a hygienic strictness in time-tabling our lives. Getting up early, cruelly early, taking a cold bath and a walk in the snow— that makes us feel rather pleased with ourselves for perhaps an hour."2 The emphasis on hygiene is reminiscent of Axel Martini in *Royal Highness*. Like "Hour of Gravity," the semi-autobiographical story about Schiller, his review of Fontane's letters was partly about himself. He was writing both fiction and nonfiction as if the notion of living a representative life entitled him to draw equations between himself and everyone he wrote about. Like an actor who can't help making all his characters look like himself, he was content that his prince, Karl Heinrich, and the writers he took as subjects should emerge with an undisguisable resemblance to himself. In *Buddenbrooks*, identifying mainly with Hanno, he'd made his entrance in the final chapters, and in his early stories he'd disguised himself as bizarre old men. But as if to reward himself for all those years of hard work as a character actor, he was now taking the stage as leading man.

The review reads as if he'd gone through the letters, looking for common denominators between Fontane and himself. He found plenty. Fontane had a nervous constitution which made him alternate between animation and melancholy. Constipated and unable to sleep properly, he often felt exhausted and depressed. As he explained during his seventies in a letter to his wife, he felt incapable of being "considerate, vivacious, adaptable and charming" when making no headway with his work. He regarded himself as having a poetic nature but not a free-flowing poetic talent. "It only dribbles along."

Titled "The Old Fontane" ("Der alte Fontane"), Thomas's twenty-page review depicts a man who was never young. Feeling ill at ease in Paris when he was thirty-seven, Fontane attributed this to indifference toward gambling, womanizing, smoking, and billiards. In the same year, 1856, he said he must be getting old because he was beginning to enjoy music. The face in his youthful portraits is insipid; the old man has a splendid head with merry, penetrating eyes.

When Fontane was seventy-nine, he thanked a critic for saying he "took the field not only against other people but also against myself. . . . Despite all one's unavoidable vanities, one comes to regard oneself as something fairly questionable. 'Thou comest in such a questionable shape.' " (This was one of Thomas's favorite quotations from *Hamlet*.) And at sixty, Fontane declares his envy of "the lieutenants, the six-foot Junkers and . . . all the other attractive, laughing, clean-looking conquerors of girls' hearts. The intellectual, however decent and clever he is, appeals only to himself and a small handful of others. . . . When I was young, I thought differently: appearance counted for nothing–talent, genius for everything." Thomas's quotations approximate to the attitude expressed in "Tonio Kröger," though it was only in his old age that Fontane had admired the attractive nonentities Thomas had admired in his youth.

As a writer, he envied Fontane's skill: "This expansive prose, easygoing, lucid, with the same quality as the ballad; easy to speak and elliptical. Notwithstanding its appearance of effortless spontaneity, it has loftiness, roundness and fullness. . . . In fact it is closer to poetry than its modesty and simplicity would make you think." This could not be said of Thomas's prose, which is usually subtle and often elegant but always prosaic.

Posting the review on August 21, he expressed dissatisfaction: probably it was too long and unsuitable for *Die Zukunft*.[3] Surprisingly, Harden replied by attacking Fontane, and especially his attitude to Bismarck. Thomas had quoted several of his comments on "the greatest disregarder of principles that ever lived . . . a genius, a saviour of the state, emotionally an arch-traitor . . . This constant inclination to deceit, this consummate underhandedness offends me profoundly." When Harden accused Fontane of the same deceit and underhandedness, Thomas defended not his review but its subject.[4] The piece was finally published in the October issue.

On September 2, Alfred Pringsheim celebrated his sixtieth birthday, and a party was held on the previous evening at the Landhaus Thomas Mann in Tölz. The band from the spa played in the garden, Thomas made an after-dinner speech, and singing schoolchildren marched in a torchlight procession.

Because the Pringsheims knew Gustav Mahler, Thomas and Katia attended both the final rehearsal and the first performance of his Eighth Symphony. They also had tea with Mahler and his wife. On the way home Thomas said: "That was probably the first time in my life that I had the feeling of encountering a really great man."[5] Afterward he sent

Mahler a copy of *Royal Highness* with a letter acclaiming him as the man "in whom, as I believe I recognise, the most serious and holy artistic will of our era is incarnate."[6]

By now the flat in Franz-Joseph-Strasse was too small: Thomas and Katia had four children, a governess, a nanny, and two servants. Though they were staying on in Tölz till the beginning of November, they devoted the first week of October to moving things from the old apartment into the new home they'd found for themselves in Mauerkirchenstrasse on the other side of the river Isar, where they were taking two interconnected four-room apartments on the third floor of a house in Herzogpark, the district adjoining the ducal park. A bridge across the Isar led to the English Garden. What had once been the village of Bogenhausen was now a suburb.

At the beginning of November, Thomas left Munich again to read from the unfinished *Felix Krull* in Weimar, where he stayed with his old schoolfriend Hermann Graf Vitzhum von Eckstadt, who'd grown fat, become a gentleman of the bedchamber at the imperial court, and married a countess. Though Heinrich had invited him to Berlin for the premiere of three one-act plays on November 21, Thomas went back to Munich, wanting to concentrate on writing a short story commissioned by the Viennese paper *Neue Freie Presse* and an article for the *Berliner Tageblatt.*

Called "How Jappe and Do Escobar Fought" ("Wie Jappe und Do Escobar sich prügelten"), the story was written quickly. It's about a fistfight between two fifteen-year-old boys on a sand dune. Possibly the reunion with Vitzhum in Weimar had revived memories of school and Travemünde, while the story foreshadows "Death in Venice," providing plentiful evidence of how Thomas responded to the boyish body. The most attractive of the boys he described is an English boy, Johnny Bishop, based on Thomas's Manchester-born classmate John Eckhoff. Johnny Bishop is small, finely made, and physically childlike, with friendly blue eyes. The word *pretty* is employed repeatedly—to describe his eyes, his soft blond curls, his mischievous little sister, Sissie, who's as pretty as he is, his enunciation, and his little head, while his accent is twice called "charming." The narrative focuses sharply on his clothes and the way he wears them. The best-dressed boy in town, he's distinctly aristocratic and elegant in his English sailor suit. Resting on the sand with his arm over his head, he looks "like a slim little Cupid."

The antagonists are physically contrasted. Jappe, the German, is broader in the shoulders, fair-haired and red-cheeked, with a turned-up nose and a saddle of freckles. Do Escobar—Thomas had heard his mother mention the name—is of Latin origin, and he speaks Spanish. He's dark, with thick black hair on his yellow arms, and extremely vain.

The dancing-master, Herr Knoll, who appeared in "Tonio Kröger" as

Herr Knaak, reappears under the same name to umpire the fight. Plump, especially around the hips, he's rumored to wear a corset. Far from being passive and detached, the narrator feels apprehensive, shy, and ashamed, nervous of being drawn into the fight and exposed as lacking in manly courage. He keeps empathizing with the antagonists, visualizing the moment of provocation and imagining the lust for revenge. "Brought to the extreme point, transported beyond all anxiety, I fought myself blind and bloody with an equally dehumanized opponent, drove my fist with all the strength of my being into his detested mouth, breaking all his teeth, received in return a brutal kick in the stomach and went under in a sea of blood."[7]

After the fight, which lasts only about ten minutes, the audience wants more. Two other boys should fight—any two who want to prove they are real boys. "Nobody came forward. But why did this summons make my heart begin to beat like a little drum? What I had feared had happened: the challenge was reaching into the audience. . . . Why did I feel singled out to meet the challenge, feel excitedly obliged to overcome my diffidence by making a tremendous and dreamlike effort and draw everyone's attention to me by stepping heroically into the arena?"[8] Thomas had found a new way of indicating the contradictory inclinations in the artist whose capacity for empathy makes him want to be involved, conditioned though he is to remain a spectator.

Not knowing what to write for the *Berliner Tageblatt*, Thomas discussed a luxury edition, published in 1908, of Adelbert von Chamisso's 1814 story "Peter Schlemihls wundersame Geschichte" ("Peter Schlemihl's Wonderful Story") with illustrations by Emil Preetorius, a young painter who'd contributed to *Simplicissimus*. The story is about a man who barters his shadow for a magically inexhaustible purse. After throwing it away, he discovers a pair of seven-league boots, which he uses when devoting himself to scientific research. Encouraged by the illustrations to reread the story for the first time since leaving school, Thomas interpreted the shadow as bourgeois solidity, and shadowlessness as the condition of the artist or outcast. After reading the article, Fischer, who was bringing out a new edition of Chamisso's work, commissioned Thomas to write an introduction.

Writing to congratulate Heinrich on his fortieth birthday, which was on March 27, Thomas complained that in the last two months he'd achieved almost nothing. He'd been suffering from what had looked like inflammation of the appendix but had been diagnosed as exhaustion of the central nervous system.[9] He thought of going back to the Bircher-Benner clinic, but decided not to, partly because he and Katia were planning a holiday in May.

They stayed off the Dalmatian coast on the island of Brioni, where Heinrich joined them, but there were no sandy beaches, and they didn't enjoy themselves. The weather was cheerless, and the archduchess of Austria was staying at the hotel, which obliged all the other guests to stand up each time she made her belated entrance into the dining room, and again when she made her exit.

On May 18, while the Manns were at the hotel, Gustav Mahler died at the age of fifty-one, after returning from an American tour. Thomas clipped the photograph and obituary from a newspaper. "His princely progress towards death in Paris and Vienna, which was reported, step by step, in the papers, made me decide to give the hero of my story the passionately strong features of this artist whom I knew." Aschenbach is described as being of less than average height, dark, and clean-shaven. The lenses of his rimless gold spectacles cut into his strong, nobly curved nose. Graying at the temples and thinning at the top, his hair frames a high, deeply lined, scarred-looking forehead. His large mouth is often relaxed but frequently becomes tense and narrow. The cheeks are lean and furrowed, the well-shaped chin slightly cleft. Aschenbach is also given the same first name as Mahler—Gustav.

Not wanting to stay on in Brioni, the Manns decided to continue their holiday on the Venice Lido, a slim little island formed mainly of silt carried down from the Dolomites by three rivers. The Lido boasts fine beaches, unlike Brioni and the city of Venice. Thomas booked a room at the Hôtel des Bains, which is where Aschenbach stays.

On his previous visit to Venice, the city he praised as "incomparable, fabulous, like nothing else on earth," he and Katia had arrived by train; this time they sailed from Pola on a steamer, and in the story, Aschenbach tells himself that to travel by rail is like entering a palace through the back door. The proper approach to Venice is by sea.

It was three years since Thomas had been here, and his pleasure is apparent from Aschenbach's reactions. "So he saw it again, the most astonishing landing-place, that dazzling group of fantastic structures which the Republic set up to meet the reverent eye of the approaching seafarer: the airy magnificence of the palace and the Bridge of Sighs, the columns with lion and saint on the shore, the glorious projecting flank of the legendary temple, the vista of the gateway and the gigantic clock."10

Real events incorporated into the narrative include an encounter with a dandified old man on the steamer from Pola, the experience of being ferried across the lagoon by a gondolier who behaved oddly, and an outbreak of cholera. The old man was trying to fraternize with a group of boisterous youngsters. Sporting a light yellow suit, extravagantly cut, a rakishly tilted Panama hat, and a scarlet tie, he had rouge on his cheeks, a wig, and false teeth.

At that time gondoliers were allowed to ferry passengers across the lagoon from the landing-stage by the Piazza San Marco to the Lido, and the Manns' luggage was passed to a gondolier who seemed exceptionally surly. Thomas always felt ambivalent about traveling in

> that strange vehicle, which has come down from ballad times quite unchanged, and so extraordinarily black, like nothing else in the world except a coffin—it is reminiscent of silent and criminal adventures in the plashing night, still more reminiscent of death itself, the bier and solemn rites and the last soundless journey! And has it been noticed that the seat in such a bark, this coffin-black lacquered armchair with dull black upholstery, is the softest, most luxurious, most soporific seat in the world?[11]

When they arrived at the Lido, the gondolier loaded their luggage onto a trolley, then disappeared before Thomas could change money to pay him. His license had been canceled, and he'd left quickly to evade the policemen waiting on the landing-stage.

The hotel was crowded, "and in the dining room," writes Katia, "on the very first day, we saw the Polish family, which looked exactly the way my husband described them." Aschenbach first sees the children in the foyer with their governess. The eldest of the three girls is virtually grown up, but they all wear unbecoming slate-colored half-length dresses with white turnover collars. Stuck back firmly to their heads, their hair makes them as expressionless as nuns. But the son is obviously treated differently.

> With astonishment Aschenbach noticed that the boy was perfectly beautiful. His face, pale and pleasingly reserved, ringed with honey-coloured hair, with the rather straight nose, the charming mouth, the expression of gracious and godlike seriousness, was reminiscent of Greek sculpture of the noblest period, but together with the perfection of form there was such extraordinary personal charm that the onlooker thought he had seen nothing more consummately achieved in either nature or art.[12]

His hair, which looks as if it has never been cut, falls in curls over his forehead, his ears, and still lower over his neck. He's wearing an English sailor's suit with lanyards, bows, embroideries, and full sleeves tapering down to fit the fine wrists of childlike but slender hands. It's not only the sailor's suit that makes him reminiscent of Johnny Bishop, the English boy in "How Jappe and Do Escobar Fought." Dealing with Imma and other women in stories and novels, Thomas hadn't written in such loving detail about their physique or clothing, and had never made any of them sound so glamorous as these two boys.

The Polish boy's relaxed posture contrasts with the servile stiffness of his sisters, and his complexion is so white that Aschenbach wonders whether he's in poor health. Later, seeing his teeth are rather jagged and bluish, Aschenbach predicts that he'll have a short life. In reality, Wladyslaw Moes, who had a punctured lung, was here because a Viennese specialist had prescribed sea breezes. He was allowed to stay in bed as long as he liked in the mornings, and generally he was accustomed to preferential treatment, not only from his family but from strangers. Women wanted to kiss him on the promenade. The son of Baron Moes, who'd sent his wife and children to Venice without him, Wladyslaw had been leading a pampered life in a château on a large estate in the south of Poland, where his family owned a paper mill.

He was born on November 17, 1900, which means he was ten and a half when Thomas saw him. His age in the story is given as about fourteen, while Katia, compromising tactfully in her memoir between the truth and her husband's fiction, says he was about thirteen. She reports that he "caught my husband's attention immediately . . . and my husband was always watching him with his companions on the beach." The Polish boy who played with him, Jan Fudakowski, was a few months younger. Thomas calls this boy Jaschiu, which is his phonetic spelling for Jasio, a Polish diminutive for Jan, and the story makes him into a sturdy lad with brilliantined black hair. Like Johnny Bishop, Wladyslaw was small for his age. Writing nine years later in defense of loving protectiveness toward boys, Thomas said: "That mature masculinity reaches out its arm, showing itself to be tender towards masculinity which is softer and more beautiful—I find in this nothing unnatural and a great deal that is edifying, a great deal of high humanity."[13]

Thomas was only thirty-five, but in later life Wladyslaw Moes remembered the "old man" who'd been watching him wherever he went. He recalled an especially intent look when he and the man were together in the elevator, and he told his nurse it was another gentleman who liked him. Jan also remembered being watched by an old man when he was playing with Adzio, and the two boys talked about it.[14]

In 1923, reading the story in a Polish translation, Moes noticed how accurately Thomas had described the striped linen suit he wore with a red tie, and his favorite blue jacket with gold buttons. He says Thomas had been equally observant about his characteristic way of moving, and the story reports the processional entrance the family always made into the dining room—the baroness leading, followed by her three daughters in order of age, followed by the governess, and the boy last of all.[15]

Though the story is based mainly on incidents during the holiday in Venice, the holiday wasn't seminal. Some of the story's roots go back to 1905, when Thomas had jotted down an idea: Success boosts a writer's self-esteem, encouraging him to take himself seriously as a figure of national importance. The jotting was probably inspired by guilt about his self-importance, but he didn't intend to be a character in the story. "What must be shown is the suffering and the tragic aberration of an artist with enough imagination and 'serious playfulness' to be destroyed by the ambitious pretensions to which success leads him, but for which he is insufficiently mature."[16] This note prefigures the characterization of Aschenbach, but Thomas had also made jottings for a story about the way Goethe jeopardized his dignity in Marienbad during 1823, when, at the age of seventy-four, he proposed to the seventeen-year-old Ulrike von Levetzow.

Many of Thomas's fictions are indebted to Heinrich, and both these story ideas may derive partly from *Professor Unrat*, the 1905 novel about the teacher and the cabaret singer. Six years later, after seeing the Polish boy, Thomas thought of centering his narrative on a passion that could be neither reciprocated nor consummated. But this wasn't the first or the last time he was fascinated by a boy on a beach. His daughter Monika describes his interest in a tanned, athletic boy who was running, jumping, turning cartwheels, and throwing the discus. He called the boy "Body Joy."[17]

As we know from the diary entry of May 1934 (see pages 411–12), the moments of passion he treasured most were moments of hugging young men and declaring his love to them. With the schoolboys, Armin Martens and Willri Timpe, he never went as far as hugging or declaring his passion, though he considered his love for Armin Martens to have been more delicious and more blissfully painful than any other love he'd felt. Incomparably more passionate—and more believable—than Karl Heinrich's love for Imma, Aschenbach's love for Tadzio pivots on the inaccessibility of the object, and climaxes in a vehement declaration of love made in the boy's absence. After an encounter with Tadzio, who smiles at him, the man retreats to the darkness of the park behind the hotel. " 'You mustn't smile like that! Listen, you must never smile at anyone like that!' He flung himself on a bench, he deliriously inhaled the nocturnal smell of the plants. And leaned back with dangling arms, overwhelmed and quivering all over his body, he whispered the standard formula of intense desire—impossible now, absurd, abject, ridiculous, but still sacred, and honourable even now: 'I love you!' "[18] This in the only time he ever speaks to Tadzio—who is out of earshot.

Though Thomas's feelings for the ten-year-old Polish boy were like a rebirth of his schoolboy passion for Armin Martens, Aschenbach's solitary declaration of love seems to derive from a declaration made to Paul Ehrenberg, as recorded in diary entries he later reread: ". . . the overwhelming intensity in certain notes of the P.E. period, this 'I love you. My God, I love you!'—an ecstasy of the kind suggested in the fragmentary poem 'But listen, Music! A shiver of sound wafts rapturous about my ears'—has occurred only once in my life. . . ."

* * *

"Death on the Lido" is a title that would have appealed more to Agatha Christie than to Thomas, but during this visit, he spent little time in the city. After the first rapturous salutation of the Doge's Palace and St. Mark's cathedral, the narrative seldom focuses on churches, palaces, or statues. On journeys across the lagoon, Thomas couldn't have failed to enjoy looking at the round Church of Santa Maria della Salute, which was designed (by Baldassare Longhena) to look like a crown dedicated to the Virgin, but there's no mention in the story of the allegorical figures on the high altar. On the left of the Virgin and Child, Venice is praying; on the right, an angel is chasing away the plague. Even when Aschenbach makes what he intends to be his last journey along the Grand Canal, we get only a perfunctory mention of the Public Gardens, the princely charm of the Piazzetta, the great row of palaces and the splendid marble arches of the Rialto.

Thomas was back in Munich for his thirty-sixth birthday on June 6. It seems to have made him reflect more than his thirty-fifth had about being *nel mezzo del cammin* ("at the middle of the journey"). In the story Aschenbach (who is over fifty) is scared of dying before he has fulfilled his potential. He has given priority to his work, and, like Thomas, never traveled outside Europe, but in spite of his success, he feels dissatisfied, knowing he has never lived his life to the full. The risks he now takes are aimed simultaneously at compensating himself and punishing himself. He's indulging himself by doing what he wants to do, regardless of the consequences, and this recklessness also serves as expiation for his sins of omission. But he's not entirely conscious of his own motivation. In a 1925 interview in *La Stampa*, Thomas admitted the direct influence of Freud on "Death in Venice": The death wish is present in Aschenbach's consciousness though he's unaware of it, and the word *Ich* is used in the Freudian way to indicate a part of the personality that makes demands in conflict with instinct.[19] (Freud always uses the word *Ich*; the Latin *ego* was introduced by his English translator.)

The story also has a bearing on Thomas's feelings about his own sins of omission. Opting for marriage and living behind the facade of respectability as a bourgeois paterfamilias, he had turned his back on passion. If the two stories centered on boys represent a swing back toward preoccupations he'd tried to put behind him, the swing must be viewed in the perspective of his deepening friendship with the young Ernst Bertram, a *Privatdozent* in German literature; lecturing at Bonn University, he was paid only out of student fees for his courses. He had read two papers to the Literaturhistorischen Gesellschaft about Thomas's work, and in 1910 had sent him a copy of the second paper, a perceptive twenty-three page analysis of *Royal Highness*, delivered on November 16, 1909. Writing to thank him, Thomas said it had brought tears to his eyes,[20] and they went on corresponding. Bertram was in his late twenties, and when he came to visit the Manns in Tölz, Golo thought he looked like a bespectacled student.[21]

Bertram's lover was Ernst Glöckner, a member of the male group that surrounded Stefan George, usually addressing him as "Meister" and supporting his efforts to renew German civilization through the cult of youth and the creation of disciplined poetic beauty. Ludwig Derleth, whom Thomas had portrayed as Daniel in the story "At the Prophet's," was a member of this group, and Thomas, who especially disliked the glorification of self-sacrifice, had been writing satirically. George was a standing joke in the Mann household, where certain lines of his verse were regularly quoted for comic effect, but there are some affinities between "Death in Venice" and the verse George dedicated to the fifteen-year-old Maximin, who was so handsome and well built that until his premature death only a year after they met, George saw him as an incarnation of the godhead.

Although Aschenbach isn't depicted as frustrated, he has lived alone since the premature death of his wife, who gave him a brief period of happiness. Thomas playfully identifies with him by crediting him with several of his own unfinished works, including a novel about Frederick the Great, the essay "Mind and Art," and another novel called *Maja*. Aschenbach, we're told, had completed all these books. He has also written a story about a "semi-rogue" who sounds like Felix Krull. Despite the differences of age and marital status, Aschenbach is unmistakably a self-portrait. Neither writer is prolific: both have a creativity which, in Fontane's word, only "dribbles," and Thomas describes Aschenbach's malaise in terms similar to the ones he used for his own, which was inseparable from a distaste for his own work.

At the beginning of the story Aschenbach has to go out for a solitary walk because his writing has overstimulated him. He's in the middle of something which demands care and circumspection. Increasingly subject to fatigue, he needs to sleep every day after lunch, but today he couldn't halt the rhythm that his writing had set up in his brain, though, far from enjoying his work, he's continuing it only out of obstinacy. A daily battle is fought between his willpower and his refractory material. His constitution is far from robust, and he's been pushing himself into work that doesn't come naturally. When he feels a craving for distant places, it's partly a matter of wanting to run away from his work.

The story implies connections between the malaise, the overcast weather, and the threatening political situation. In May 1911, Russia demanded the withdrawal of Turkish troops from the Montenegro frontier; at the beginning of July, the arrival of a German gunboat in Agadir created international tension; and nine days later, Germany was warned that Russia supported France in the Moroccan crisis. To set the mood for the story Thomas starts the action at the beginning of May 19–, "when for months our continent had looked so threatening."22 After a protracted spell of cold, wet weather, high summer has set in prematurely, and though trees are only just bursting into leaf, the English Garden is as sultry as in August. A storm seems to be brewing.

After returning to Munich at the beginning of June, Thomas intended to stay no longer than a couple of weeks. Though he wasn't running away from his work by spending summers in Tölz, where he kept to the same routine as in Munich, he'd habituated himself to traveling around Germany and neighboring countries to give readings and to welcoming commissions that would sidetrack him from the main task at hand. He'd promised to contribute an article to the Bayreuth issue of the Viennese paper *Der Merkur*, and to write a short piece on Wagner. To test his current feelings about the operas, he went to a Munich production of *Götterdämmerung* and felt more resistant than ever to both the music and the cult of Wagner. "Only a barbaric and intellectually half-blind nation could build a temple for the production of such work."23

Before he could settle down to write the Venice story, he had to rework his Chamisso review for Fischer, and he spent most of June on this. Less penetrating than his piece on Fontane, the essay devotes a lot of space to summarizing Chamisso's life and his plots. Once again Thomas finds common denominators between himself and his subject. At school Chamisso had put less energy into working than into writing poetry; after a bohemian period, he achieved equilibrium in bourgeois domesticity. Though there's relatively little autobiography in Chamisso's work, the essay groups him with the writers who are less concerned with posterity than with telling the world about their life and their suffering. But here too Thomas was talking about himself.

Mountain Air

THOMAS DIDN'T SPEND MUCH TIME with the four children. Erika was six; Klaus five, with curly blond hair reaching down to his shoulders; Golo three; and Monika not quite two. Though their lives were dominated by his presence and governed by domestic routines geared to his convenience, "Pielein" seemed remote and unavailable—unlike their mother, whom they called "Mielein," and their governess. The affectionate nicknames are at odds with the household strictness. The children weren't allowed to make any noise between nine in the morning and twelve, when he was working, or between four and five in the afternoon, when he took his nap. If they disturbed him, they'd hear him clearing his throat angrily, and if this failed to silence them, he'd come storming out of the study or the bedroom. They were more scared of him than of their mother, who could usually be softened by persuasion, even when she was trying to be firm.

They saw their father at mealtimes, and he sometimes took the older ones with him when he went out walking. He never raised his voice, but they had to respect his aversion to dirty fingernails and bad table manners. They couldn't go into his study without an invitation, and they dreaded the silences that ensued when they offended him. Their mother's anger was predictable: They'd be told off if they ate sweets before dinner or messed up their clothes, but it was harder to know what would upset him, and sometimes he interfered in their relationship with her. Monika never forgot how he'd stopped her from sitting on her mother's lap in the evening.[1]

Klaus's memories of him at this period centered on

the ticklish touch of a moustache; the aroma of cigars and eau de Cologne; a smile thoughtful and absentminded. "Father" means a placid, sonorous voice; the long rows of books in his working room—a solemn, suggestive sight. And music . . . yes, his image and name invoke harmonies; floating, saturnine sounds; the wistful fragment of melody he used to play at the piano. Shortly before supper, after his evening walk, he would withdraw into the darkening drawing room, and then the fatherly tune would waft, soft and low, through the house, up to the second floor where we sat with our governess. . . . It always was the same rhythm, at once drawling and violent; always the same desperate tenderness; always that swelling, weeping, jubilating song: it was always Tristan.[2]

Klaus, who shared a bedroom with Erika and later with Golo, suffered from a recurring dream about a decapitated man: The head, which he carried under his arm, could grin and wink. Klaus confided in their governess, Anna, and when she consulted Thomas, he paid one of his rare bedtime visits to the children. He advised Klaus either to ignore the ghost or ask it politely to go away. "Tell him that a children's bedroom is no place for a decent phantom to hang out and that he should be ashamed of himself. . . . You may warn him that your father is very irritable and just doesn't like to have ugly spooks in the house. At this point he'll disappear without making any more fuss. For it is a well-known fact in ghostly circles that I can make myself very unpleasant indeed." Impressed, Klaus took this advice and found it worked.[3]

He remembered Erika as having disorderly dark hair and scratched knees. She was the most active and athletic of the children, good at gymnastics, and she often joined in fights. Thin, dark, and pretty, she looked like a gypsy, and strangers sometimes took her for a boy.

She was about seven when she got into the habit of telling lies. "I lied very gladly and very often, whether it was because I found it amusing or necessary." Eventually Katia referred the matter to Thomas, who astonished Erika by inviting her into his study. What would happen, he asked, if everybody told lies? Communication would be impossible because people would no longer believe each other. She came out of the study intending to go on lying, but found she couldn't.

Walking in the street with their governess and their collie, Motz, the children attracted attention, partly because of the heavy, embroidered linen jackets and knickerbockers their mother chose, and partly because of Motz, who, though gentle and obedient at home, was noisy and hysterical when taken out.

The least attractive of the four children, Golo made the strongest impression. Erika remembered him as looking rather Chinese or like a young Eskimo. If she and Klaus bossed the younger children about, Monika seemed to submit out of weakness, Golo out of masochistic relish for humiliation. But he could become spiteful, quarreling with Erika, though he got on well with Klaus, who took him for long walks in the garden and told him stories. Golo developed more slowly than the others. After starting to sing when only ten months old, he didn't talk till he was nearly two. He was frightened by loud noises and given to running up and down the room with clenched teeth and bobbing head. Most of the time he'd let his little sister tell him what to do, only occasionally threatening her with violent reprisals. He became the most talkative of the children, chattering endlessly about dreams and imaginary friends, giving them such names as Dr. Klauber, Dr. Londoner, and Frau von Loon. He afflicted them with outlandish illnesses, but any who died were soon replaced.

AFTER THEIR RETURN FROM VENICE, Thomas and Katia spent only about a fortnight in Munich, leaving in mid-June for Tölz, where they stayed till mid-October. From the beginning of July he gave most of his working time to "Death in Venice." He'd planned it as a short piece, suitable for *Simplicissimus*, but, finding the story needed to be told at length, he started dividing it into chapters. (These remain in his final version of the story, but not in the authorized English translation.) As with his novels, he made elaborate notes and collected clippings from papers, including one about the cholera epidemic in Palermo. He calculated that if Aschenbach was fifty-three when he died in 1911, he'd have been born in 1858, but his age is never mentioned. Another note shows how the timing of his stay in Venice differs from that of Thomas, who spent only eight days there, leaving on June 2. According to the note, Aschenbach arrives in Brioni on May 22, leaves for Venice on June 2, and he's still there at the end of the month, when the cholera breaks out.

Some if not all of Thomas's notes for the story were written after he read Georg Lukács's book of essays *Die Seele und die Formen* (*The Soul and Forms*), which was published in 1911. In Budapest, Thomas had stayed with Lukács's rich father, Josef von Lukács, but hadn't met the son, who first read "Tonio Kröger" when he was still at school and later said it had determined the essential features of his early writing. There was a two-way flow of influence between the two men. What Lukács called his "Tonio Kröger experience" shaped the ideas he advanced in several of his essays, especially the one on Theodor Storm, subtitled "Bürgerlichkeit und *l'art pour l'art*." The underlinings and marginal markings in Thomas's copy of the book show how carefully he read this essay. What especially appealed to him was the equation of bourgeois life with asceticism. According to Lukács, the bourgeois way of life depends on a renunciation of all brilliance, a reductionist approximation to the holy simplicity that's nostalgically associated with the past. Describing the bourgeois way of life as an unappealing form of servitude that involves unnatural restraint and discipline, Lukács was describing a style of living that Thomas would have associated less with the average citizen of Lübeck than with the kind of artist he wanted to be.

The main thrust of the essay is ethical, and in spite of the aversion he'd professed in 1895 to categorical imperatives, Thomas welcomed a formulation of principles he had either instinctively adopted or inherited. For the young Lukács, burgherdom was a "whip" that could galvanize those who had negative feelings toward life. Though the order and discipline of bourgeois life masked the anarchy of the self, it was possible to achieve mastery over life by working systematically, subordinating mood to discipline. The artist is bound by the same rules as the old craftsmen who never strained to go beyond the frontiers of form. In the middle of the last century there were still towns on the edge of Germany—the allusion was to Lübeck—where the old burgherdom still existed in its pure form, and artists emerged who were capable of representing the old values, because they longed for the holy simplicity that could be forced back into existence "by the ultimate frantic energy of a diseased nervous system." By sacrificing splendor and brilliance in life, they can transfer it into their art. This could be read like a sermon addressed personally to Thomas, and he took it seriously.

"Death in Venice" probably owes its mythological dimension to Lukács. Another of his essays, "Yearning and Form" ("Sehnsucht und Form"), contains numerous quotations from the Platonic dialogues in Rudolf Kassner's translations, and it gives an un-Socratic twist to the argument about love, stressing that the object of desire nearly always remains out of reach. Socrates sometimes managed to impart a spiritual dimension to physical love, but few poets can emulate him successfully. "The object of their yearning has a gravity of its own and a self-involved life. Their aspiration is always tragic: the hero and fate must be converted into form. . . . In life yearning has to remain love: that is its happiness and its tragedy."[4] This seemed like tailor-made support for a story dealing with a passion that could be neither reciprocated nor consummated, and, as T. J. Reed has pointed out, Thomas's ending echoes Lukács's formulation.[5] "Passion is our edification, and our yearning has to remain love—that is our pleasure and our shame . . . we are incapable of spiritual ascent, only of aberration."[6]

Looking at problems of the modern artist, Lukács discusses connections between Eros, Beauty, and Transcendence. He takes keen interest in a point made by Diotima in the *Symposium*—that love for someone beautiful can grow into love for physical beauty in general, and then into love for spiritual qualities. In one of his notes Thomas says Eros guides the artist toward spiritual beauty, and a sequence in the story seems to derive from the idea, common to Plato and Plutarch, that love can teach the poet how to write.

The story would have been less important to Thomas if it hadn't forced him to reassess his experience of love. Had he exerted too much control over himself? Been too wary of letting himself go? Love is the friend of courage and achievement. Like Hercules, the bravest men were the ones most given to love. The Greeks knew that contact with the gods could be made only through madness or psychological imbalance.

Had he tried too hard to keep his balance? He was warning himself, in the story, against the dangers of reining himself in too tightly.

The writer's main consolation for the rigors of his work is the continuity between thought and emotion: ideas become feelings, feelings ideas. Nature is convulsed with rapture when the mind defers to Beauty. Though Eros encourages idleness, erotic excitement stimulates Aschenbach to write. Answering a questionnaire on "a certain important cultural problem," he works on it in Tadzio's presence, so that his prose will take its flavor from the boy's beautiful body. "Never had he found the pleasure of words sweeter, never been so certain of Eros's presence in them as during the dangerous and delicious hours when at his crude table under the awning, seeing his idol and hearing the music of his voice, he used Tadzio's beauty as a model for his short essay, those one and a half pages of exquisite prose whose clarity, nobility and vibrating emotional tension would soon have many admirers."[7]

AT TÖLZ in the middle of July 1911, Thomas received a visit from Fischer. To celebrate his twenty-five years in publishing, he was going to bring out a book containing extracts from works-in-progress by his most important authors. Thomas contributed a chapter from *Felix Krull*.

By July 24—Katia's twenty-eighth birthday—it was apparent that she and Thomas should have paid more attention to the Zurich doctor who had advised her against an early pregnancy. In five years she'd given birth to four children, and before her last two children were born, she'd had two miscarriages.[8] The four children were all healthy, but she had been feeling ill and suffering abrupt changes of body temperature ever since Monika was born. Her doctor recommended mountain air, and on September 2, leaving Thomas—not without help—to look after the children, she went with her parents to the Swiss Alps, where they stayed in Sils Maria till September 19. She seemed slightly better when she came back, but she still wasn't well.[9]

By the beginning of 1912, she was so ill that he sent her to a sanatorium outside Munich. The director, Dr. Ebenhausen, diagnosed pulmonary catarrh, but failed to cure it, and when her condition deteriorated,[10] he recommended a cure in Davos, an Alpine village which had been fashionable since the eighteen seventies on account of its air, which was reputed to be especially pure and bracing, with properties that healed tubercular lungs. When Katia left for Switzerland on March 10, it wasn't Thomas who accompanied her, it was her mother.

They traveled by train to Chur, where they spent the night. The next day, wrapped in furs and blankets, Katia was taken on a sleigh up to Davos, where they stayed at the Hotel Ratia. They had intended to book her into the sanatorium run by the well-known Dr. Turban, but, following advice they were given in the hotel, they opted for the newer Waldsanatorium, run by Dr. Friedrich Jessen. She moved in on March 22.

Depending mainly on their mother, the children were badly affected by her long absence, though it made Thomas pay more attention to them. He even thought of featuring them in a story. He didn't finish it until thirteen years later, but he wrote about them at length in letters to Katia. On Monika's second birthday, June 7, Golo refused to clink glasses with the other children to toast their mother's recovery. He wasn't strong enough, he said, and when the others were talking critically about the Munich zoo, he joined in, complaining about the lack of cannibals.

Thomas, who didn't enjoy the Sunday lunches with his parents-in-law even when Katia was with him, sometimes took Golo along as a distraction in her absence. For the boy it was less boring when Erika and Klaus were there and the children could sit at one end of the long table, talking quietly without trying to follow the adult conversation.[11]

WHEN KATIA LEFT MUNICH, Thomas had already spent nearly nine months on a story that would run to only about seventy pages. Without abandoning the Platonic idea of physical love as a step toward spiritual love, he was interweaving private and public themes. The love—and this is more of a love story than *Royal Highness*—can neither be reciprocated nor consummated. The secretiveness of a distinguished man obsessed with the beauty of a young boy is counterpointed against the secretiveness of civic authorities trying to quell rumors of a cholera epidemic and concerned only about the danger to the tourist trade. Thomas plants a trail of clues that leads to the truth.

> "They're hushing it up!" thought Aschenbach excitedly as he threw the newspapers back on the table. "They're hushing it all up!" But at the same time his heart filled with satisfaction over the adventure that was going to implicate other people. For everyday security and well-being are inimical to passion, as they are to crime, and passion must welcome each loosening of the bourgeois framework, each disaster and subversion of the world, hoping to turn them to its advantage. So Aschenbach felt a dark satisfaction at the concealment in the dirty alleys of Venice—this sinister secret of the city which melted together with his own inmost secret, and exposure of the truth would have been disadvantageous to him. For this man who was in love, nothing was less desirable than that Tadzio should leave, and he realised with horror that he would be unable to go on living if that happened.[12]

No other city could have served so well as the setting for a story combining these two themes, and Thomas is supremely successful in rendering the atmosphere of decay. In 1911, Venice's beauty already seemed precarious. Palaces, churches, bridges seemed to exude confidence in their own permanence, but under the glittering surface of the canals the process of disintegration was at work: The buildings' foundations were rotting like the *bricole*, the wooden posts that stuck up out of the lagoon. Oppressed by the atmosphere and apprehensive about the effects of the sirocco, Aschenbach decides to leave, but gets no farther than the railway station. Appalled by the prospect of never seeing Tadzio again, he succumbs to temptation. Under pretext of waiting for luggage that has been sent to the wrong destination—this, too, is something that happened, but to Heinrich, not Thomas—Aschenbach returns to his hotel.

> The air was stagnant and smelly, the sun burned heavily down through haze that made the sky look like slate. Water slapped sobbingly against wood and stone. The call of the gondoliers, half warning and half greeting, was distantly answered through the silent labyrinth in accordance with some strange convention. Out of small, highly sited gardens umbelliferous flowers, white and purple, smelling of almonds, were hanging down disintegrating walls. The turbid water reflected the shapes of Moorish windowframes. The marble steps of a church climbed above the surface with a beggar crouching on them, showing off his wretchedness, holding out his hat and displaying the whites of his eyes as if he were blind. An antique dealer in front of his den made obsequious gestures to invite passersby inside, hoping to swindle them. This was Venice, the ingratiating and suspect beauty—this city, half legend, half man-trap, in whose putrid air art once blossomed luxuriantly and musicians found melodies that could both lull and arouse sensuality. To the adventurer it felt as if his eyes were drinking in all this voluptuousness, as if his ears were being wooed by these melodies. He remembered too that the city was sick and concealing it out of cupidity.[13]

Inside the hotel again, Aschenbach becomes reckless, stopping outside Tadzio's bedroom to lean ecstatically against the door. After a life of Puritanic self-control, he's finally neglecting Apollo in favor of Dionysus. The collapse of his willpower and the surrender of his formidable intellect to self-indulgence and self-sacrifice constitute a crisis which gains so much resonance from the narrative context that the sick city becomes representative of a sick civilization.

Thomas might have achieved less resonance if he'd felt less implicated, as he would have done if the narrative hadn't brought him so close to revealing his darkest secret. Tonio Kröger in the 1903 story remains unimpeachably heterosexual, even if the blond Hans fascinates him as much as the blond Ingeborg. But "Death in Venice" comes close to revealing his bisexuality. One reason for taking so long over the story was the difficulty of quantifying the risk.

He was also struggling to balance positive and negative feelings toward Aschenbach. On one level the story explains literary genius. "If I scrutinise myself carefully," he wrote to the Austrian translator and cultural historian Paul Amann, "this and nothing else was always the object of my 'creativity': to invade the consciousness of a master. When, as a boy, I played at being a prince, it was to invade the princely consciousness. Working as an artist, I won access to the existence of the artist, indeed the great artist." But there was also a parodistic element in the writing. "It involves a kind of mimickry which I love and practise involuntarily. I once tried to define style by calling it a secret adaptation of the personal to the objective."14

The original impulse was positive and possibly lyrical. In a 1920 letter to a young poet, Carl Maria Weber, Thomas described his Venetian holiday as "a personal-lyrical travel experience,"15 and, as T. J. Reed has argued, he may have intended to write the narrative in hexameters. Working on "Tonio Kröger," he had written a fragmentary draft in verse. With his strong need to think of himself as a *Dichter*–the word implies that only a poet can be a serious creative writer–he tells Weber the story had a *hymnic* origin and remained hymnic at its core. He then quotes seven lines of a poem he'd written later, "Song of the Little Child" ("Gesang vom Kindchen"), the seventh being: "Look, your *drunken song* turned into a *moral fable*."

Contrasting Dionysian lyrics, which are spontaneous outpourings, with Apollonian epics, which are more responsible and objective, Thomas tells Weber that the process of objectifying had been imposed on him by the inner necessities of his nature, and that he'd wanted to achieve a synthesis of sensuality and morality. He felt critical of himself for being too inhibited–for living more like a closed fist than an open hand–but his cautious nature made him more critical of Aschenbach's recklessness than he'd originally felt.

TUBERCULOSIS was often treated with injections of arsenic. Dr. Ebenhausen never used it, but the Waldsanatorium offered a course of arsenic injections, and Katia thought it might expedite her reunion with the children. In fact it harmed her, and she was told in April that she'd have to stay on for at least another six months.

Planning to visit her in May for about three weeks, Thomas was hoping to have the story finished.16 But the ending caused problems that, by the end of April, he still hadn't solved. "Perhaps the change of air in the middle of May will help me."17

He traveled to Davos on May 15. His weeks in the sanatorium provided material for *The Magic Mountain* (*Der Zauberberg*) and, as he said later, its first chapter gives "a fairly exact description of our reunion in this sphere and my own curious impressions," which "became stronger and deeper" during the weeks he spent there.[18] The central character, Hans Castorp, has to change trains at Landquart, a small Alpine station. Inside a gray-upholstered compartment in a narrow-gauge train, with his traveling rug and his alligator-skin bag, wearing his silk-lined summer overcoat while his winter overcoat swings from a hook, he's carried upward along a wild and rocky route. As the train, vomiting smoke, climbs through narrow passes, speeding him into a phantasmagorical world of towering peaks, he finds that the change of air alters him, jerking him away from the rhythms, routines, and preoccupations that had filled his life. His character will find it has a similar effect on them.

Thomas was met at the station, Davos-Dorf, by Katia; Hans is met by his cousin Joachim, who says he'll find it hard to acclimatize himself. Appearances are deceptive here, and time passes in a different way: Three weeks seem like a day. Joachim, though he's looking well, will be here for at least another six months, and he shows Hans a flat curving bottle of bluish glass with a metal cap. Nearly all the patients carry one around—for sputum.

Thomas took unmistakable pleasure in describing symptoms of disease, the sanatorium, and the routine imposed by the medical director, Dr. Behrens, who combines the roles of paterfamilias and benevolent despot, making rules, fixing bedtimes for patients as if they were children, and controlling what they eat. Protected and relieved of responsibility, they've become passive consumers of food and medicine. Never needing to take the initiative, they rest, chatter, play games, convalesce—committed to nothing but the attempt at recovery.

Thomas was reminded of previous stays in clinics—Dr. von Hartungen's in Mitterbad and Riva, Dr. Bircher-Benner's in Zurich; he even gives the assistant medical director, Dr. Krokowski, the same beard he'd given to Dr. Leander in his 1901 story "Tristan"—dark and forked. Once again Thomas enjoyed deviating from his normal routine to conform with the rules imposed on patients, whose day was programmed, with fixed times for eating, resting, taking exercise, and going to bed. Once again he was stimulated by an ambience in which sickness was the norm. Describing it, he could make the setting into a magnifying glass for studying processes of physical decay. While *Buddenbrooks* interweaves moral degeneration and disease, *The Magic Mountain* uses a background of disease to explore possibilities of moral rehabilitation.

In "Tristan," when Gabriele asks Spinell why he's staying in the clinic, his answer is "Because of the style."[19] He likes the building, which was formerly a castle, and the straight lines of the furniture. "This brightness and hardness, this cold, harsh simplicity and diffident austerity give me self-confidence and dignity, dear lady, they continually make me feel refreshed and inwardly cleansed." The Waldsanatorium is also described in terms of hard, clean lines. The corridors are narrow, the walls gleam with hard white enamel paint, and the lightbulbs have white glass shades. The doors are white-enameled, while the rooms have white washable walls, white furniture, clean linoleum, and white linen curtains.

When he's not at Wahnfried, Spinell gives himself a strenuous program of work to distract himself from his uselessness, while the useful world of industry and commerce is represented in the story by the plump, red-faced, short-legged businessman. In *The Magic Mountain*, more subtly, the utilitarian world has been left behind on Hans's journey into the mountains. Joachim tells him: "I often think disease and dying are really not serious, they're more like a kind of idleness. Genuine seriousness is to be found only in life down there."[20] Unlike the story, the novel doesn't use the backdrop of sanatorium life to contrast artistic activity with the productivity of industry and business. None of the main characters in *The Magic Mountain* is an artist, but Hans Castorp finds it's untrue that genuine seriousness is to be found only "in life down there." The experiences he has up here are more intense and more educational than any he's previously had.

The sanatorium is over 5,200 feet above sea level. The snow is permanent, with a glacier visible in the background. There are several sanatoria in the area, and one of the others, the Schatzalp, is so high that in winter the dead bodies are brought down on bobsleds because the roads are always blocked. Though the air is cold, Hans feels as if his skin is burning. He learns that an American woman died in his room the day before yesterday, but it has since been fumigated. He's upset by the sound many of the patients make when they cough—"a coughing without any pleasure in it, and it did not come out with the right pressure behind it, but sounded like a dreadfully feeble stirring in the mush of organic dissolution." It makes him feel as if he can look inside the man, seeing slime and mucus.[21]

The sanatorium is comfortable, and its restaurant provides good food, but Joachim, tired of the cooking and the monotony, is glad to have a visitor. Feeling oddly restless, Hans finds that the rarefied atmosphere seems to make his words tumble over each other. Meeting Dr. Krokowski, who psychoanalyzes the patients, he's asked whether he requires physical or psychical treatment. When he claims to be perfectly healthy, Krokowski says he has never yet come across a perfectly healthy human being.

In his bedroom Hans wants to smoke, but knowing a cigar would be too strong, lights a mild cigarette. Several days later, walking alone on the mountainside, he finds blood pouring from his nose, and it takes almost half an hour to stanch the bleeding. Afterward he has to breathe very slowly. Later on he catches cold, and examining him, Dr. Behrens says he has a moist spot in the upper left lung. If he resumes his life "down there," he'll only have to come back "up here."

Thomas had the same experience—feeling feverish in the high altitude and then catching cold. Patients jokingly said he must be tubercular; he'd no doubt want to stay on with his wife. Letting Dr. Jessen examine him, he was told he had a moist spot in his lung, and when the doctor advised him to stay, he must have been reminded of Dr. von Hartungen, who had suggested he should stay at Riva: He described Dr. Jessen as "smiling profitably."[22] But whereas Hans Castorp meekly accepts the doctor's advice, Thomas ignored it. As he said afterward, it could have changed his life had he been more like his character.[23]

Nothing stimulated his imagination more than the notion of being overtaken by disaster. In the 1907 story "The Railway Accident," he'd asked himself what it would be like to lose the only script of something he'd written, and he was never more inventive than when pondering what might have happened had he stayed on in a situation that became life-threatening. "Death in Venice" has this premise in common with *The Magic Mountain*. In the story he pictured himself failing to escape from a city infected with cholera; the novel shows what might have happened had he been magnetized by the doctor's profitable smile. Staying in the sanatorium, he might have become seriously tubercular.

Work on *Buddenbrooks* and reflections on the family's past had convinced him that Nietzsche was right about the relationship between decadence and degeneration. Just as a young man's disease can be the consequence of hereditary exhaustion, physiological deterioration in the race can produce a need for artificial stimulation. This is the argument of Nietzsche's *Götzendämmerung* (*Twilight of the False Gods*). In *Buddenbrooks* disease runs parallel to decadence, weakening the willpower and strengthening the artistic imagination; in *The Magic Mountain* Thomas comes close to equating disease with intelligence: *la maladie c'est l'esprit*. He obviously enjoyed researching in medical textbooks before writing about Hanno's terminal illness in *Buddenbrooks*, about tuberculosis in *The Magic Mountain*, and about cholera in "Death in Venice." In the story, as in *Buddenbrooks*, he laconically incorporates facts garnered from medical books, scarcely bothering to change the wording. After originating in the Ganges delta, Asiatic cholera had raged with prolonged virulence over northern India, striking eastward into China, westward into Afghanistan and Persia, and following the main caravan routes to Astrakhan. The epidemic had appeared in several Mediterranean ports, including Palermo and Naples, causing devastation all over Calabria and Apulia. Infected through contaminated vegetables, fruit, meat, or milk, victims would become dehydrated within a few hours, their blood thickening like pitch. Caused by suffocation, their death would be accompanied by convulsions and hoarse cries.

Thomas's interest in disease isn't an isolated phenomenon in German literature. In the eighteenth century, Novalis had suggested that disease, like sin, was a means to transcendence, and Friedrich Schlegel had believed the illness which almost killed him had a "mysterious life fuller and deeper than the vulgar health of people around me, who were really dreaming sleepwalkers."24 Nietzsche's illness had pushed him into a closer relationship with his own consciousness and a closer examination of consciousness in general. Another strain of influence had passed from Schopenhauer to Wagner, who married the themes of love and death in *Tristan und Isolde*. The *Ring* is profoundly nihilistic, and it was thanks to his reading of Schopenhauer that Thomas Buddenbrook had been almost happy to die, while two of the main characters in the novel have an artistic creativity connected with a lack of interest in living. Thomas survived to the age of eighty, but never had the Dionysiac energy that empowered Aschenbach to risk his reputation while pursuing the beautiful boy. If Thomas had been in danger at the Lido, the presence of Wladyslaw Moes wouldn't have kept him there.

It was impossible for most English readers to understand the end of "Death in Venice" until a new translation by David Luke appeared in the United States during 1987 and in Britain during 1990. Until then Helen Lowe-Porter had exclusive translation rights to nearly all of Thomas Mann's work on both sides of the Atlantic, and she was responsible for the English version of the twenty-four stories–including "Death in Venice"–collected in *Stories of Three Decades*, which was published in 1936 without identifying the translator. She often failed to notice ironical undertones, and sometimes damaged the text by leaving out phrases when she failed to understand either their function or their meaning. In "Death in Venice," she omits the last sentence of the penultimate paragraph. The dying Aschenbach is on the beach, sitting in a chair with a rug over his knees. After wrestling with the more muscular Jaschiu and being defeated, Tadzio walks off sulkily to paddle. Aschenbach looks up, and in Mrs. Lowe-Porter's version, "It seemed to him the pale and lovely Summoner out there smiled at him and beckoned; as though, with the hand he lifted from his lip, he pointed outward as he hovered on before into an immensity of richest expectation."

Here is the passage in David Luke's translation, with the missing sentence restored: "But to him it was as if the pale and lovely soul-summoner out there were smiling to him, beckoning to him; as if he loosed his hand from his hip and pointed outwards, hovering ahead and onwards, into an immensity rich with unutterable expectation. And as so often, he set out to follow him." As a rendering of Mann's abstract and ironically Goethean "Verheissungsvoll-Ungeheuere," Mrs. Lowe-Porter's "immensity of richest expectation" is neater than Luke's "immensity rich with unutterable expectation." But it's unforgivable to jettison the sentence that gives us a final glimpse into Aschenbach's consciousness and rounds the story off by adding a layer of inevitability to his death. In Venice, casting aside his habitual self-discipline, he has often trailed Tadzio through the narrow streets; finally he's under the comfortable illusion of succumbing to the same temptation–with the encouragement of a signal.

Written after Thomas returned from Davos to Munich, the end of the story was clearly inspired by Lukács's references to the *Symposium*, in which Diotima explains how the initiate of love turns finally to "the open sea of beauty." Thomas underlined these words in his copy of Kassner's translation. This ending is prefigured in the description of the gondola as reminiscent "of death itself, of biers, sombre funerals and the final silent journey."[25]

FIVE YEARS AFTER THOMAS'S PLAY *Fiorenza* had been published in book form, Wedekind wrote about it in *Schauspielkunst* (*The Art of Theater*), saying the final scene between Savonarola and the dying Lorenzo contained the "most sublime, most brilliant and most dramatically effective" writing in German drama.[26] Now, nearly six years after its Frankfurt premier, the play was to be staged in Berlin at Max Reinhardt's theater, but instead of directing it himself, he gave the production to Eduard von Winterstein. In November 1912, preliminary discussions were held with Thomas, who traveled to Berlin at the end of December to see a rehearsal, but came away feeling dissatisfied. The play was certainly too long, but Winterstein had made the wrong cuts, and the confrontation between Lorenzo and Savonarola seemed "thin and disappointing."[27]

Thomas went back to Berlin for the first performance on January 3, 1913. In spite of the cuts, the play ran for three and a half hours. Reinhardt had gone abroad, and, writing to Hofmannsthal, Thomas called the play his "problem child, which can neither live nor die . . . But in spite of all the disappointments, unfruitful excitements and humiliations the theatre has in store for men of my kind, it is still, for the lonely novelist, a strange and intoxicating experience to see his dreams transformed for once into flesh." Unlike Wedekind, most of the reviewers were unimpressed and Alfred Kerr was vindictive: Nothing would bring him more pleasure, he said, than the news that Thomas Mann had retired from authorship.[28]

*   *   *

Death in Venice was published as a book in February 1913, and by the end of the year 18,000 copies had been sold. Before war broke out, about forty major reviews had appeared; by 1918 sales had reached 33,000, and by 1930, 80,000. If *Royal Highness* had laid Thomas open to charges of superficiality, the story vindicated his seriousness. Retrospectively, he saw it as a watershed in his development: "It signified a final and extreme point, a conclusion: it was the most morally and formally pointed and concentrated formulation of the problems of decadence and artistry, on which my output since *Buddenbrooks* had focussed . . . in full correspondence with the detachment and isolation of the collective individuality of the bourgeois century which was working its way towards catastrophe."[29] Or as he put it in a letter, "What acts in it, I believe, as a solvent of art, or a substitute for it, is *Zeitgeist*, the spirit of the times or the burden of the times. (Today one is still proud to be a part of destiny.)"[30]

Not wanting the story to be regarded as immoral or perverse, he could regard it as representative of the immorality and perversity that were endemic.

> Perhaps a war is necessary to a country in which such a story can not only be written but, to some degree, applauded. Ultimately everything comes back to the old dilemma: culture or efficiency? What is required? For it is probably not possible to want both at the same time. For it is not the substance of art that matters. Art itself is suspect—and that is the message of my story. This story could be dangerous to rugged national prowess not because it deals with sick love but because it is too well written. It is really not vanity that makes me say this but a guilty conscience.[31]

Reviewing the story in the June 1913 issue of the *Neue Rundschau*, Ernst Bertram said Nietzsche's poetic vision had been extended into realistic prose by Thomas Mann: "This writer steps forward briskly and bravely into the wholly godless world as the first of those who are called to assume a representative function."[32] Two members of Thomas's family joined in the chorus of critical praise. In *März* Heinrich wrote perceptively about the interweaving of private and public themes, while Katia's indomitable grandmother, Hedwig Dohm, reviewed the story in the Berlin paper *Der Tag* on February 23, 1913.

16

A New Home

ERIKA AND KLAUS were both precocious. Having meals with the grown-ups, they regularly listened to conversations about literature, art, and politics, gradually understanding more of what was being said, and their relationship with their father changed as they were admitted to readings he gave during the early evening. In the absence of friends, he'd often read to Katia, and it was through his readings that Erika and Klaus were initiated into the world of *The Magic Mountain*. Soon Golo and Monika would increase the size of the regular audience.

The more Thomas read his work aloud, whether in private or in public, the more influence the readings were liable to have on the way he wrote. Poets who in mid-career find themselves reading a lot in public sometimes find themselves writing differently to give themselves good material for performance. It's noticeable that in Thomas's early fiction there are fewer long speeches and less dialogue than in his mature fiction, and while it would be simplistic to attribute this change, which is rarely damaging, to a desire for material that can effectively be read aloud, a good mimic can have more fun with dialogue than with anything else, and a good reader makes good use of long speeches.

As the children grew older and more reluctant to share rooms, Thomas and Katia needed a bigger house. Deciding to have one built, they found an architect and started inspecting possible sites with him in November 1912. At the end of February 1913, they chose Poschingerstrasse, on the banks of the river Isar.

It was at about this time that Thomas made friends with Hans Reisiger, a Silesian law student in his late twenties. He'd published short stories in magazines and was undecided whether to abandon the law in favor of a literary career. They met at Samuel Fischer's house in Berlin, and Thomas discovered that after losing contact with the Ehrenberg brothers seven years earlier, he'd at last met someone who could make him relax as much as they had: "scarcely anyone else has made me so alert to the comic side of existence; with no-one else have I laughed in such a carefree way."[1] Golo confirms this: "My father, otherwise so often self-absorbed, came out of his shell the moment Hans Reisiger was there." It was by being such a good listener that Reisiger made himself indispensable, Golo says, to both Thomas and Gerhart Hauptmann: Hearing them read from work in progress, he could understand their intentions, could empathize, criticize, encourage.[2] Reisiger was the only friend with whom Thomas played cards, and they sometimes exchanged stories about experiences of military service.

WITHOUT APPROVING of censorship but believing he could be usefully influential, Thomas had since 1912 been one of the twenty-three writers on a committee that advised the police commissioner about banning plays or passing them, subject to cuts. The writer most consistently at loggerheads with the committee was Frank Wedekind, who'd had several plays banned and others subjected to substantial cutting. His admiration for *Fiorenza* didn't make Thomas like him: Unfairly, Wedekind had held him personally responsible for cuts made in his play *Franziska*, but in April, when the Artistentheater in Munich wanted to present two of his plays, *Erdgeist* (*Earth Spirit*) and *Pandoras Büchse* (*Pandora's Box*) under the title *Lulu*, Thomas supported the proposal, having attended two private performances of *Pandoras Büchse*. In 1904 the shocked public had protested vociferously, but in 1910 the audience was respectful and impressed. Thomas was in favor of licensing an uncut performance of *Lulu*, but he was outvoted. The negative verdict was then condemned in a "unanimous resolution" by the German Writers' League, which was under the sway of such radicals as Erich Mühsam. Thomas, who was serving on the league's executive committee but hadn't participated in the resolution, was irked to find that a "unanimous" verdict had been announced, and that his dissenting voice on the censorship committee had been ignored. The only possible response, he decided, was to resign from both the board and the league.[3]

In mid-June he and Katia left for a three-week holiday in Viareggio on the Ligurian coast of Italy. Though he found the holiday refreshing,[4] he decided to postpone *Felix Krull*, on which he'd been working since he finished "Death in Venice," in favor of the sanatorium story that would in some ways counterbalance the Venice story. "In style it is quite different, relaxed and humorous (though again there is sympathy with death); but that makes it no easier. On the contrary, I find tragedy is easier."[5] The Venice story had grown about ten times as long as he'd first intended it to be; the sanatorium story would grow into a 950-page novel. By mid-September, sketching out a background for Hans Castorp, who comes from Hamburg, Thomas needed to inform himself about the training available there in engineering, and he posed questions in a letter to Ludwig Ewers, who was working there as an editor.[6] Thomas's original title for the story was "The Enchanted Mountain" ("Der verzauberte Berg").

In "Tristan" he'd made fun of doctors who ran clinics and conde-scendingly advised patients to invest in expensive courses of treatment. Among his preliminary notes for the new fiction is a reference to oper-ations in which ribs are cut out: "50 percent used to be 'left on the op-erating table' and the patient still often dies in consequence—totally unnecessary torture of people who should be left to die in peace. But the operations costs 500 to 1000 francs."[7]

The notes show how self-conscious he was about the "sympathy with death" that led him "to recognise morality not in intelligence and breeding but in surrender to what is injurious, so that one has the power to recognise it as ethical. Christian sympathy with suffering, also with morality. Ethically it stands above virtue."[8]

As he worked on the story, Thomas's intentions changed. At first he saw it as a quick by-product of his investigation into the swindler's mentality and as a "satyr play to follow the tragedy of disgrace" he'd written in the Venice story. "The fascination with death, the victory of extreme disorder over a life founded on order and dedicated to order were going to be ridiculed and transposed into comedy."[9] Like Aschen-bach, Hans Castorp leaves his normal environment for what he intends to be just an interlude. Ignoring the patients who advise him to go home, he gets trapped—partly, like Aschenbach, by passion—in a place which is dangerous. Castorp's passion for Clavdia Chauchat is exciting in proportion to its irrationality, and, like Aschenbach, he's content for a long time to worship the beloved from a distance. Love and disease are intimately connected in both fictions, but in *The Magic Mountain* it's deliberately left unclear which is the cause and which the effect. All we know is that Castorp (like Aschenbach when he loses his luggage) is glad to have a pretext for staying on.

Thomas had plenty of reasons for staying on in Tölz, not just for the summer but most of the autumn and part of the winter. The new house in Poschingerstrasse was nearly ready, but Katia, who was coughing end-lessly and feeling exhausted, couldn't have coped with the strain of moving, while the seven-year-old Klaus, who seemed to have inherited her weak lungs, was suffering from bronchial catarrh. In the autumn, Thomas's depression was exacerbated by financial anxiety—building a new house was costing more than he'd anticipated.

He took little cheer from fame that brought invitations from all over Europe. After reading in Basel during March, he was invited to Zurich, Budapest, and Russia; he'd already accepted invitations to Stuttgart, Vi-enna, Lübeck, and Berlin. Thinking the right moment had come for a book on his work, Fischer was looking for a suitable writer, and Thomas would have liked the job to be done by the Berlin critic and playwright Julius Bab, who'd written on *Buddenbrooks* in the *Neue Rundschau*. "I would be glad to see you write later on about the whole of my work, about my restless hero-type of which Thomas B., Lorenzo de' Medici, Savonarola, Klaus Heinrich and the one I now have in hand (a confidence trickster!) are only various individuations."[10]

But in November, writing to Heinrich, he complained about

the constant pressure of exhaustion, over-scrupulousness, weariness, self-doubt, a rawness and weakness that give any difficulty the power to prostrate me; quite apart from the inability to commit myself spiritually or politically, as you have done; and my deeply innate predilection for death, which is growing stronger: my concern always gravitated towards decay, and that is probably what stops me from being interested in progress. . . . It is bad to feel oppressed by the whole misery of the era and the fatherland, without having the strength to depict it. But that is probably a precise symptom of the misery of the era and the fatherland. Or will it be depicted in *Der Untertan* (*Man of Straw*)? I take more pleasure in your work than in my own. You are spiritually better off, and that is what matters.

My best days are behind me, I think. Probably I should never have become a writer. *Buddenbrooks* was a bourgeois book, and those are no longer valid in the twentieth century. "Tonio Kröger" was just maudlin, *Royal Highness* pretentious, "Death in Venice" half formed and artificial.[11]

This was partly a demand for reassurance, and, trying to provide it, Heinrich elicited the confession that Thomas had long entertained the fantasy of writing "a great and faithful book of life, a continuation of *Buddenbrooks*, the story of us five brothers and sisters. We deserve it. All of us."[12] He might have invited Heinrich to Tölz had Katia been in better health, but the next day he took her to see a doctor. She didn't want to go into a clinic unless the doctor insisted, but he did, and on November 14, accompanied by Thomas, her parents, and her brother Peter, she set out for Merano. Seven years later, Kafka was to go there. "Half of Western Europe has more or less defective lungs," he wrote, trying to reassure another sufferer, Milena Jesenska.[13]

Thomas went back to work on the sanatorium story in Tölz until he left on December 4 for a four-day trip to read in Vienna and Budapest. In Vienna he lunched with Arthur Schnitzler and visited him in his villa; in Budapest, Thomas was received by the minister of culture and generally acclaimed. "I have never had so much fuss made of me in my life."[14] Having made the outward journey in a sleeping-car, he traveled home on the Orient Express.

Though Katia came home for Christmas, she wasn't well enough to move into the new house with the family. Advised to stay in the mountains for the rest of the winter, she left on January 4, 1914, for Arosa, and the next day Thomas took possession of the newly built house.

Looking out over the river, it had three stories, with stone steps leading down into the big garden. The central part of the building was turret-shaped, and the front door was at the back. The Russian bear from the house in Beckergrube stood in the entrance hall, holding a wooden tray for visiting cards. To one side of the hall was the drawing room, with a grand piano in it and Katia's books; on the other side was the dining room. Between the two rooms was Thomas's large study, which had French windows opening onto the garden steps. His writing desk was in the round alcove, which gave him light from three angles. In this room were the bookcases from Lübeck and the Empire armchair his father-in-law had spared from banishment.

Above the study was the room where Katia would sleep and do secretarial work for him. It had French windows opening onto a balcony. Next to it on one side was the room where the children had their breakfast and their supper; on the other was Thomas's bedroom with its white-lacquered furniture. There were two other bedrooms on this floor for the children. The three rooms on the top floor were left empty at first. The kitchen was in the basement, as were rooms for the cook and the maid.

The area surrounding Poschingerstrasse is more urban today than it was then. Dominated by the huge trunks and small leaves of the trees—ash, silver poplar, birch, and willow—the landscape, as Thomas later explained in his story "Master and Dog" ("Herr und Hund"), never ceased to affect him. Going out every day before lunch for a forty-five-minute walk with the collie, Motz, he soon became familiar with the scenery, but still felt transported to another geological period or to the bottom of the sea—an impression strengthened by the fact that water had once stood in the low-lying meadow basins. Festooned with creepers that seemed almost tropically luxuriant, the trees struck him as forming something more like an enchanted garden than a wood or a park.

> The ground is uneven, constantly rising and falling, which creates the effect of enclosure, for the view is restricted on every side. . . . Only the ear is reminded—by rhythmic whispering from the west—of the invisible river's friendly proximity. . . . There are gorges, stuffed with elder, privet, jasmine and wild cherry bushes, so that on misty June days the scent is overwhelming. . . . It is my park and my solitude; my thoughts and dreams are mixed and intertwined with glimpses of it as the tendrils of climbing plants are with the branches of trees.[15]

On his daily walks Thomas noticed seasonal changes in the landscape and watched Motz's reactions to noises, sheep, birds. The dog's companionship bulked larger in Thomas's life than that of the children: Monika said later that she'd never had a single intimate conversation with him and never seemed to exist for him.[16] Reading or writing as he sat in the corner of the garden wall or on the lawn with his back against a tree, he'd interrupt his concentration to address Motz, repeating his name in different tones and watching the galvanizing effect it had: Reminded of his identity, the dog whirled around, barking excitedly. Sometimes Thomas tapped him gently on the nose, watching him snap back with no intention of biting, and sometimes an approximation to a smile passed over the dark inhuman features. Thomas enjoyed his superiority, not with the sadism of Tobias Mindernickel but as a benevolent despot who'd enjoyed owning dogs for over twenty years.

Among his new neighbors was the conductor Bruno Walter, who rang up one day to complain that on the way home from school Klaus had been pulling the hair of his daughter Gretel. Thomas's junior by a year, Walter had read much of his work, and soon became friendly with him and Katia, while Gretel and his other daughter, Lotte, spent time with Erika and Klaus. Far from finding Thomas cold or aloof or condescending, Walter admired his warmth, his moral strength, and his humanity.[17] Katia has described how enthusiastic Walter always was about the music he worked on. "He treasured it, loved it, admired it, became excited . . . played for hours on the piano, sang as well, explained plots and pointed out specially beautiful passages." He was impressed when Thomas noticed a mistake he'd made in the second act of *Tristan*, leaving out the soft E-flat of the trumpet at the words "Das bietet Dir Tristan." And Thomas, convinced that a literary idea was "nothing more than the product of a rhythmic need," liked to think that, given another life, he could be an orchestral conductor.[18]

Life in the new home was clouded by financial anxiety. As Klaus later put it, the house "was somehow strained and burdened by a mysterious blot called 'mortgage'. A certain scarcity of funds seemed to result from this weird condition."[19] Writing in early January to Heinrich about invitations he'd accepted to give readings in Zurich, Lucerne, Saint Gall, and Frankfurt, Thomas explained that it brought some money in,[20] and at the end of the month, when he wanted to buy a painting by Ludwig von Hofmann, he told the artist he couldn't afford it: "Like a real new German, I live above my income. The building of the villa has impoverished me."[21] Hofmann then reduced the price.

Either on his way back from Switzerland or later in the year Thomas paid a brief visit to Katia in Arosa, and he reported on her condition in letters he wrote during late April: Still suffering from high temperatures, she had to stay in bed.[22] At the risk of provoking his parents-in-law by refusing to wait for her return, Thomas decided, by way of housewarming, to give a *Herrenessen*—a dinner party for men. The guests included Ernst Bertram, Bruno Frank, Professor Pringsheim, and Maximilian Brantl, who was Heinrich's lawyer. The children were allowed to come downstairs in their pajamas to see the sumptuous spread on the dinner table. Afterward, Ernst Bertram was invited to either lunch or dinner at least once a month. According to Klaus, he was neither amusing nor boring, but soft-spoken and modest. He made graciously pedantic gestures as he talked.

Working on *The Magic Mountain*, Thomas claimed in June to be making "the usual cautious but rather regular progress."[23] By now he knew it was going to be "pretty long. The thing has several layers of meaning. I am setting all kinds of hopes on it."[24] He was enjoying the work, and, as usual, continued his Munich routine in Tölz, when he and Katia moved there in the third week of July, just over two months after her return from Arosa.

As in "Death in Venice," he created tension for himself by testing how far he could go toward revealing his secret. The theme of forbidden love is central to the novel, and though its object this time is a woman, passion for her is linked to memories of adolescent passion for a boy. Like Tadzio, both Pribislav Hippe and Clavdia Chauchat are Slavic. In "Hippe," the last chapter Thomas wrote before putting the novel aside in 1915, Hans remembers a schoolboy infatuation. Hippe is blond with prominent cheekbones under slanting eyes. Without being his friend or even speaking to him, Hans thinks about him for over a year, looking forward to watching him and hearing his husky voice. Though there's no mention of masturbation or fantasy, it's clear that the boy remains central to Hans's imaginative life. Given no release in action, the tension goes on mounting until Hans makes contact by asking to borrow a pencil. Sharpening it, he hides the shavings in his desk and keeps them, like a fetish, but once the pencil has been returned, the boys never speak to each other again.

Later, talking to Clavdia, Hans says he's not passionate but does have passions—phlegmatic ones. Thomas characterizes himself in the same way when he talks of "the patience imposed on me by my natural slowness, a phlegm that could perhaps better be called a restrained nervousness."[25] Dealing with Hans's two experiences of love, he links them together by making both Hippe and Clavdia Slav, narrow-eyed and broad-cheekboned. For a long time Hans stares at Clavdia and thinks about her obsessively without making any attempt at getting into conversation with her, but he dreams about borrowing a half-length red pencil from her and being told in her pleasantly husky voice that he mustn't fail to return it.

Thomas had intended not only to make fun of his sympathy with the death wish but to satirize the bildungsroman—the novel in which the hero matures through learning by trial and error how life should be lived. But in its final form, *The Magic Mountain* has little comedy in it, and it's more like a bildungsroman than a parody of one, while in the first part of the novel Thomas fails to distance himself from the "sympathy with death," which is no less prominent than in "Death in

Venice." Without any explicit reference to Freud or his death wish, Dr. Krokowski lectures the patients on the instincts, which he divides into two opposing groups—drives associated with love, and those (such as shame and disgust) which push the subject in the opposite direction. Suppressed, love works its way covertly through the system to emerge in the form of disease. "A symptom of disease is the activity of love in disguise and all disease is love transformed."26

Later a connection will be implied between sexual love and tuberculosis when Hans learns from reading a book on pathological anatomy that disease is only a form of life, which is itself only an infection, a sickening of matter. Infectious tumors are luxuriant forms of tissue in an organism which has been perversely hospitable to them, and parasites produce organic combinations which are toxic to the cells that have supported them. Reacting to the stimulus of foreign bacilli, the cells produce tumors, while nerve centers are poisoned by toxins which the bacteria release. But just as disease in the organism is only an intoxicated heightening of its physical state, life is only an infection of matter. In origin, procreation is no more than growth produced by morbid stimulation.

Throughout the process of anatomical enlightenment, Hans is fixated on Clavdia, and when they finally make love, he tells her in French that the body, death, and love are indistinguishable. "For the body is disease and pleasure, and that is what causes death, yes, they're both carnal, love and death, which is their terror and their great enchantment!"27 And while this whole treatment of the physical takes its tone from the location of the action in a sanatorium, the underlying attitude derives partly from a situation in which Thomas, unlike Aschenbach, was giving himself no chance to become passionate. Talking to Clavdia during celebrations for Shrove Tuesday, Hans not only identifies his love for her with the disease that made him stay on in this place, but insists it was love that brought him here. When she tells him this is madness, he says "love is nothing if it isn't madness, an insensate and forbidden thing, an adventure in evil."28 His love for her is like Aschenbach's for Tadzio and Thomas's for all the beautiful boys and men he could never possess.

Part Three

17

World War

AFTER JULIA AND JOSEF LÖHR moved into the house next door in Tölz with their three daughters, Eva-Marie, Rose-Marie, and Ilse-Marie, Thomas's four children often played with their three girl cousins, who struck them as pretentiously elegant, always wearing silk bows in their long hair, always dressed in pretty frocks, always curtsying or coming out with a pat "Guten Tag, Tante Katia, Guten Tag Onkel Tommy."[1] The eldest, Eva-Marie, was four years older than Erika, and during the summer of 1914 the seven children rehearsed a play they were going to stage as a surprise for the grown-ups.

With Eva-Marie as director, they were rehearsing under the chestnut tree in the Manns' garden when the governess came out to say they might as well abandon the production because no one would be interested. War had been declared on Germany and Austria. The kaiser had taken over supreme command of the army and navy. The children went to consult Thomas and Katia, who were on the terrace. A newspaper was spread out in front of her like a map, while he was leaning against a balustrade, staring at the mountain peaks silhouetted against the sunset. Neither of them noticed the children. "Before long," he said, "a bloody sword is going to appear in the sky."[2]

The governess was wrong about who had declared war. Since dismissing Bismarck in 1890, Kaiser Wilhelm had been aiming at world leadership, and he saw Russia's growing military strength as a threat. After an ill-judged attempt in 1908 to ally himself with Britain, he'd become increasingly isolated. By 1914 he'd promised support to Austria-Hungary in what was intended as a preventive war. Both the kaiser and the emperor thought they could keep the fighting to a small scale and win quickly. But a European war became unavoidable on July 23, when the Austrian government delivered an ultimatum to Serbia, alleging Serbian complicity in the assassination of the heir to the Austro-Hungarian throne, Archduke Franz Ferdinand, who'd been shot in Sarajevo on June 28. On July 26, Serbia mobilized its army, and Russia threatened to intervene if Serbian territory was invaded, as it was on July 27 by Austrian troops. When the tsar ordered the mobilization of 1.2 million troops, the kaiser threatened to mobilize the German army, and rejected Britain's offer to mediate. On August 3 the kaiser declared war on France. Ignoring Belgian neutrality and Britain's commitment to guaranteeing it, Germany invaded Belgium on August 4. Within two days Austria had declared war on Russia, and Serbia on Germany.

In the spring of 1913, after reading Jakob Wassermann's novel *Der Mann von vierzig Jahren* (*The Man of Forty Years*), Thomas had written to praise him for depicting war as "a crisis of moral cleansing, a grandiose transcendence of all sentimental distraction by seriousness."[3] Toward the end of July 1914 Thomas tried to assure his mother that war would be avoided. "They will go to the brink and then somehow reach an agreement."[4] A few days later, on July 30, he heard the German army was being mobilized. "I feel shattered and shamed by the fearful pressure of reality," he wrote to Heinrich. "Until today I was optimistic and incredulous—one's disposition is too moderate to believe something so atrocious can be possible. And I still incline to expect that things will be driven only to a certain point. But who knows what madness will break loose once Europe is swept off its feet?"[5]

Their brother Viktor was among the first to be called up. Twenty-four and engaged to a girl of nineteen, Magdalena Kilian, he decided to marry her before leaving to serve in the artillery. The ceremony took place in Munich on August 2, and Thomas came from Tölz to act as witness. The railways were so chaotic that the thirty-four-mile journey took four hours. He never forgot the "hurly-burly in the packed railway stations in the summer heat, the hubbub in the crowd simmering with anxiety and excitement."[6] Viktor recalled that "Thomas was very serious, but deeply impressed by the attitude of the people."

Contemplating the future, he couldn't separate his own prospects from those of Western civilization:

> I still feel as if I were dreaming, but it is shaming not to have believed it possible that the catastrophe would come, not to have seen it had to come. What an affliction! What will Europe be like, inwardly and outwardly, when it is all over? Personally, I must prepare myself for a complete change in the material foundations of my life. If the war lasts for long, I shall certainly be what is called "ruined". In God's name! What does that matter in comparison with the upheaval—especially spiritual—that must follow in the wake of such great events! Should one not be grateful for the wholly unexpected when one has to experience such great events? My chief feeling is enormous curiosity—and, I admit, profound sympathy for this despised and enigmatic Germany, which is ruled by fate, and though it has not so far set the highest value on "civilisation", it has at least taken on the task of destroying the vilest police state in the world [tsarist Russia].[7]

By September it was clear Thomas wouldn't be ruined, but neither would he be so well off. His allowance from his father-in-law was halved, while Fischer, whose turnover was shrinking, paid only a small proportion of the advance he'd promised on *The Magic Mountain*. At any other time, Thomas could have raised money by selling the house in Tölz, but no one would want to buy it now. He and Katia failed to conceal their anxiety from the children. To Klaus, his father seemed "distrait" in a dignified way, while his mother made less effort to appear calm. She economized by sacking one of the maids and—to the children's delight—the governess.[8] Katia stopped serving puddings, and the two older children, taken away from their expensive private school, were sent to the Gebele-Volkschule in Bogenhausen.

Thomas asked for some of the money he'd lent Heinrich, who was even worse off than before, though *Zeit im Bild* had been publishing *Der Untertan* in installments. Two thirds of it had already appeared when, in early August, nervous of censorship and knowing patriotic readers found the satire offensive, the editor suspended the serialization. In spite of this setback and in spite of the war, the forty-three-year-old Heinrich got married on August 12 to Mimi Kanova, a pretty twenty-eight-year-old Czech actress who rather resembled Carla and played the character modeled on her in his play *Die Schauspielerin* (*The Actress*).

In April, when Wilhelm Herzog, editor of *Das Forum*, had wanted to convene a conference of intellectuals to speak out against the danger of war, both Thomas and Heinrich were on his list of names,[9] but the political divergence between them was widening. At the end of August, Heinrich described a visit he'd paid to Thomas, who admired the surge of patriotism and didn't feel pessimistic about the war. "My brother enjoys it aesthetically," Heinrich said, "as he enjoys everything."[10]

Jakob Wassermann's sister-in-law, Agnes Speyer, described a day when she and her husband, Emil Ulmann, were with the brothers in Heinrich's Leopoldstrasse apartment. The men had "the most animated political argument about the war. Heinrich pro-French. My husband and Thomas pro-German. The most violent conflict of opinions—finally: breach between the brothers. From this day on, they no longer spoke to each other. Did not once greet each other in the street." Probably writing long after the event, she was mistaken in saying this happened at the end of July, when neither Thomas nor Heinrich was in Munich, but it could have happened later,[11] though Heinrich's wife, Mimi, later gave Golo a different account of the last wartime confrontation between the brothers. Heinrich was speaking quietly: "Don't you understand that Germany will lose the war, that the ruling classes are mainly responsible, that it will end in the fall of the monarchy?" At which Thomas stormed out of the room.[12]

In the brothers' correspondence the first evidence of a rift occurs in Thomas's letter of August 7. Promising to be a witness at Heinrich's wedding on the twelfth, he'd written to say he'd probably travel to Munich on the previous day. But on the seventh, complaining that the chaos on the railways could last for several weeks, he asked Heinrich either to use someone else as witness or to postpone the wedding.[13]

Inwardly at least, he must have been prepared for the cataclysm—or so he told himself. Otherwise, how could the outbreak of war have provided the conclusion *The Magic Mountain* needed? It could end with the hint of a new beginning, for war would wipe out a world that didn't deserve to survive.

> Had we not all had enough of it? Had it not been decaying with luxury? Was it not festering and stinking with effluents from the decomposition of civilisation? I confess that right up to the last minute I did not expect war . . . but if I could not see its political inevitability, I sensed the moral and psychological need for it, and most Germans will have failed to share the feeling of cleansing, exaltation, liberation, that took hold of me when what I had thought impossible was really there.[14]

He volunteered for active service, but at the medical examination, the staff doctor recognized him and patted his bare shoulder. "You will be left in peace," he said.[15]

Prominent German and Austrian writers, including Hauptmann and Robert Musil, made patriotic declarations. Published by Fischer and edited by Oscar Bie, the *Neue Rundschau* had always been progressive, but in September 1914 the regular contributors joined the chorus of support for the war, idealizing the conflict into a confrontation between German *Geist* and enemy materialism. As Musil pointed out in a *Rundschau* essay on "Europäertum, Krieg, Deutschtum," literature and intellectuality had both been minority affairs, directed against the mainstream of German life, but now that war was bringing national unity, the writer was finally at one with his compatriots.

Thomas could enjoy a new sense of solidarity with the community. Marriage had saved him from feeling stranded, as he did when he wrote "Tonio Kröger," between bohemians and the bourgeoisie; now, instead of feeling he belonged to a privileged minority, he could say "we" and mean the whole of Germany. This was a luxury he'd never have dared to expect. On August 22 he put *The Magic Mountain* aside to start an essay, "Wartime Thoughts" ("Gedanken im Kriege"), which he completed on September 12, just before returning from Tölz to Munich. He wanted to perform "a war service, using thought as a weapon."

The essay pivots on a distinction between culture and civilization.

Four years earlier he'd used these two words as if they were synonymous: making notes for his essay on "Mind and Art," he'd drawn up a list of "opposites," including: "Culture (Civilisation) and Art."[16] But now, by contrasting culture with civilization, he provided an argument for use against journalists who mocked Germany for rejecting civilization in favor of militarism and barbarism. Civilization, he argued, has never mattered so much to the Germans as culture, which is a matter of exclusiveness, style, form, attitude, taste, while civilization depends more on intelligence, enlightenment, refinement, morality, skepticism, analysis. While the "enlightenment" of the allies involves a softening form of relaxation, German culture rests on an almost tribal sense of unity, strength, form, energy. Through devotion to a higher cause, the war would purify the spirit and cleanse Germany of the inner hatred that had been fomented by the comforts of peace. "German militarism is the true expression of German morality." Borrowing some of Nietzsche's ideas and turning them into propaganda, he conceded that German irrationalism was offensive to more superficial nations, while militarism and moral conservatism contained elements of the demonic and heroic.

When he started the essay, German troops were engaged along a front of 150 miles from Mons to Luxembourg, while the Russian army had penetrated 50 miles into Prussia; when he finished it, the Germans had taken Rheims, Lille, and Ghent, and before it appeared in the November issue of the *Neue Rundschau*, planes had dropped bombs on London and Paris, the Belgian government had been evacuated to Paris, and Turkey had attacked Russian ports and ships in the Black Sea. Thomas received letters from officers and men all over the front, thanking him for giving them strength and encouragement. Implicitly contradicting what Heinrich had written in an essay on Voltaire and Goethe, Thomas praised Frederick the Great for ordering his army to march on Saxony, and for ignoring Voltaire's *Questions encyclopédiques*, which listed the evils of war. Frederick's action was a triumph of genius over intellect, of clouded destiny over dry lucidity, of heroic duty over bourgeois good breeding. "Today Germany is Frederick the Great. It is his battle we are fighting to an end. The coalition has changed a little . . . but it is his Europe that will not tolerate us . . . and his soul that has reawakened in us."

Pleased with the analogy and keen to develop it, Thomas spent nearly three months on a forty-six-page essay, "Frederick and the Great Coalition of 1756." Returning to notes he'd made and books he'd bought while planning a novel about Frederick, he worked some of the material into the new essay, which appeared in the January and February issues of the *Neue Merkur*. Toward thought, it argues, Frederick had felt a mixture of love and contempt, enjoying it while recognizing its impotence. "He had to do wrong and live his life in opposition to ideas. Unable to be a *philosophe*, he had to be a king, so that the earthly mission of a great people could be fulfilled."

It was better for Thomas to believe he'd been expecting war semiconsciously. Born four years after the armistice of 1871, he'd experienced nothing but peace, and this was how he explained his failure to see that the archduke's assassination had made a European war inevitable. But he was glad, he said, to have been wrong. "It is not good when people no longer believe in war. Then they soon stop believing in many other things in which they must believe if they are to be tolerable."[17]

Soon after Christmas he returned to Tölz, where throughout January it snowed torrentially. "Never had I seen so much snow in my whole life, and really it was the first time I became acquainted with this element."[18] Resuming work on his Davos story, he wrote part of what would eventually be the section titled "Snow" in the sixth chapter of *The Magic Mountain*. "The rarefied air tumbled into turbulence, swarming so thickly with snowflakes that you could not see what was only a step away from you. Squalls strong enough to bang the air out of your lungs whisked the flurries of snow wildly sideways, tossed it upwards from the bottom of the valley, whirled it madly into an anarchic dance—it was no longer a snowstorm but a chaos of white darkness."[19]

LIKE OTHER WRITERS, Thomas benefited from the demand for cheap paperbacks that could be sent to soldiers on active service. This boosted sales of *The Infant Prodigy*, the collection of five stories Fischer had published before Christmas in an edition costing only 10 pfennigs. The most recent of these stories, "How Jappe and Do Escobar Fought," had been written in 1910, and the other four between 1903 and 1905. The first edition consisted of 22,000 copies, and by the end of the war, 59,000 had been sold.

Thomas wanted his essay on Frederick to be published in book form, but Fischer resisted the idea until May, when *Svenska Dagbladet* printed a letter from Thomas defending his "Wartime Thoughts" against criticism of it in replies to a questionnaire the paper had sent out. His letter rejected allegations that Germany had started the war, and as an example of anti-German feeling he pictured a Senegalese negro, "an animal with lips as thick as cushions," guarding German prisoners and calling them barbarians. Comparing the situation with that of 1756, and praising Frederick for not trying to look innocent, Thomas again asked whether prewar Europe had been worth preserving. Germany, he contended, wanted war only because she'd been forced to want it. To prepare for it was to prepare for her third Reich, which would be "the combination of *might* and *mind*, of might and spirit." This was Germany's highest war aim.[20]

After being reprinted in the *Neue Rundschau*, the letter was published with "Wartime Thoughts" and the essay on Frederick in *Friedrich und die Grosse Koalition*, the fifth book in Fischer's new series on contemporary history. Consisting of ten thousand copies, the first edition came out in June. The book was widely reviewed in the papers, and so popular in the army that another five thousand copies had to be printed before the end of the year.

In March, Thomas tried to resume work on his story—he still didn't know it was going to become a novel—but in mid-May, within forty-eight hours of each other, Golo and Monika developed symptoms that were diagnosed as acute appendicitis. Erika was the next victim. All three had operations at Hofrat Krecke's clinic on the other side of Munich, and when nine-year-old Klaus succumbed, it was hard to believe the four of them hadn't infected each other. Klaus was the unluckiest. "I recall with terrifying liveliness the endless and painful transport from our house to the clinic. . . . My abdomen seemed to burn, to explode, to rave, to burst asunder."[21] Katia's tearful face alerted him to the danger he was in: The abscessed appendix had ruptured. He had an operation on May 24, and two more before June 6, Thomas's fortieth birthday. The abscesses made it hard to intervene surgically, and the boy had two cannulas in his stomach. Thomas, who wasn't expecting him to survive, wondered how Katia would cope if he didn't.[22]

A week later Klaus's heart was still standing up to the strain, and no more abscesses had formed: It seemed he was almost out of danger, but there were complications in the healing process. In the fourth operation, which lasted an hour and three quarters, the whole of his abdominal cavity was opened up and his intestines taken out, laid on a heated table, examined, replaced, and sewn in. Again his heart withstood the pressure, but he suffered intestinal paralysis, and for three days seemed unlikely to recover. On June 23 the surgeon resorted to injecting him subcutaneously with a new senna derivative, which had the desired effect.

For weeks Katia had been shuttled between hope and despair. On the day he began to recover, she had a nervous breakdown.[23] Nor was he out of danger. His digestive system was still paralyzed, and two more operations were performed, while Katia had an appendectomy in the clinic on June 28.[24] Klaus was confined to bed until the beginning of August but discharged from the clinic on the fifth—the day the family moved back to Tölz. "Sprawling on an armchair in the shade of a chestnut tree, I breathe the sultry air of boredom and recovery. I was a hero, for I had survived. Small wonder that I began to look down at my ordinary brothers and sisters who·just 'lived.' . . . Small wonder that I was spoiled and fed with all sorts of dainty and nourishing things."[25]

Besides working at the sanatorium story, Thomas tried to continue the story about the children, and to start one about the Requiem composed by the dying Mozart,[26] but he was distracted by the possibility of another medical examination to check whether he was fit for military service.[27] Once the danger had passed, he thought of developing the sanatorium material into one of his longer stories, the basic intentions "being didactic and political—a young man has to confront the seductive power of death and, in a comic and frightening way, be led through the spiritual issues of humanism and romanticism, progress and reaction, health and disease."[28]

In April 1915 the Germans started using gas on the western front, and in May, London was bombed. On the eastern front in mid-July the Russians were retreating as German and Austrian troops closed in on Warsaw. Another essay by Thomas about the war, "Wartime Thoughts," was published in the *Frankfurter Zeitung* on August 1. Even if fighting still had to be done, he said, Germany had already won a moral victory. Ideologically, the Allies had proved themselves to be in the wrong: they were resisting only out of obstinacy.

He wondered whether to suspend all fictional work to go on writing about the war. The possibility of putting the sanatorium story aside is mentioned at the beginning of August 1915 in a letter to Paul Amann, for whom France still represented the revolutionary principle. But in Thomas's view France had no mission and no purpose. "The battle it is fighting is superfluous from every viewpoint except the heroic one, and all historical justice, all real modernity, the future and certainty of victory are with Germany." Committed to the ideal of legitimacy and to a form of civilization that belonged to the eighteenth century, the Allies were old-fashioned: Sympathy with their declining world was "sympathy with death."[29]

The war didn't make it any easier to make a decision about the collie, Motz, who'd been suffering from a skin disease that turned out to be incurable. He had boils all over his back. "We decided his existence was no longer worthy of him and handed him over to the local gunsmith, who put him down with two good bullets, one in the spine and one, for safety's sake, in the head."[30] Not wanting to be in Tölz at the time of the shooting, Thomas and Katia went to Munich without worrying about whether the children would hear the shots. They did. When they found the freshly dug grave at the bottom of the garden, they put a big stone on it.[31]

Like Proust's *À la recherche du temps perdu*, which would have been neither so long nor so good had it not been interrupted in 1914 by the war, *The Magic Mountain* became longer and better—though less cohesive—

than it would have been if Thomas had worked at it uninterruptedly. Believing in Germany's historic mission, he'd have interpolated argument into the story; it was as well that he shelved the fiction in favor of what he originally intended as an essay—*Reflections of a Nonpolitical Man* (*Betrachtungen eines Unpolitischen*). Among the notes he wrote for the foreword is the sentence: "Origin largely artistic: to avoid intellectual overburdening of *The Magic Mountain* and to make the work of art 'lighter.' "[32]

The decision to write the essay seems to have been taken in Tölz during late August or early September, and Thomas may have started it before he returned to Munich on October 15. By the end of the month he was fully engaged on the new work, "which to me means a great spiritual cleansing,"[33] and by mid-December it was clear that he wouldn't finish it before Christmas. It still had no title: It wasn't until June 1916 that he arrived at *Reflections of a Nonpolitical Man*.[34] At first the essay had nothing to do with Heinrich, but their relationship reached a crisis at the beginning of 1916, after his essay on Zola appeared in the November issue of a new dissident monthly, *Die Weissen Blätter*, founded and edited by the Alsatian writer René Schickele. The issue sold out immediately, and rumors reached Thomas that there were references to him in the essay. On New Year's Eve he wrote to Heinrich's solicitor, Maximilian Brantl, asking to borrow his copy of the monthly, and when Brantl said he'd lent it to Ernst Bertram, Thomas wrote to him, asking for it.[35]

The essay began: "The writer who was going to encompass a greater mass of reality than anyone else was for years just a man with dreams and fantasies. It is the ones likely to dry up young who make their debut in their early twenties with enough self-assurance to confront the world. A creative artist matures late." Taking the second sentence to be about him, Thomas said the essay made him ill for weeks.[36] He kept the text for six months, and when he finally returned it to Brantl in June, he had to apologize for pencil marks he'd made all over it. He'd tried to rub them out,[37] but he'd been too angry to stop the pencil from cutting deeply into the paper, and he'd made forty-four vertical marks in the margins, thirty underlinings, and twenty comments or exclamation marks. The essay struck him as being directed more against him than against Germany.[38]

Taking politics and literature to be interdependent, Heinrich had been uneasy for years about the disjunction in Germany between the activities of the intellectuals and the actions of the state. *Der Untertan* was originally subtitled "Geschichte der öffentliche Seele unter Wilhelm II" ("History of the Public Soul under William II"), and in a 1910 essay on "Geist und Tat" ("Intellect and Action") Heinrich had attacked the passivity of the intellectuals. Though the Germans "thought more deeply" than any other people, they accepted the rule of "God's grace and the fist."[39] Now, unable to criticize either Germany or complaisant intellectuals, Heinrich had found a way of breaking the awkward silence he'd kept since August 1914 by commenting obliquely on the current situation. Attacking France's Second Empire as a state that had come into existence through violence, he praised Zola for realizing that it was disintegrating and for championing Dreyfus, the Jewish officer who'd been unjustly accused of treason. Condemning reactionary French intellectuals who, feeling "a sudden urge to cheer the sabre," sided with the army against the Jew, Heinrich was tilting at German intellectuals who supported the kaiser. Significantly, the essay slips into the present tense and uses the second person plural when it argues that French writers had seemed harmless before the crisis, even if they'd always been skeptical about

> such crude concepts as truth and justice. . . . But we never believed that if the worse came to the worst they could be traitors to intellect and humanity. But now they are. Rather than turn round and step up in front of their people, forcing it backwards, they run alongside it together with its most despicable seducers, encouraging it in the injustice to which it is being seduced. . . . You false intellectuals are turning wrong into right and even into a mission, which is being undertaken by the people whose conscience you ought to be.[40]

In other parts of the essay, Heinrich, who could empathize with Zola, wrote some perceptive literary criticism, but here he's thinking of his brother as representative of the writers supporting the war. Thomas's *Reflections of a Nonpolitical Man* would have been different—and shorter—if he hadn't felt so wounded by Heinrich's attack. The quarrel had some of its roots in sibling rivalry, and there was brotherly jealousy in the comment on writers who achieve success in their early twenties, but there was also a more generous element in Heinrich's attack. More realistic than Thomas about the slaughter and the destruction, physical and cultural, he was challenging those who'd contributed to the war effort.

He considered Thomas to be a solipsist. In a letter drafted when the war was nearly over, Heinrich describes him as "incapable of coming seriously to grips with the reality of another human being's life." In *Royal Highness*, for instance, the "people" had been represented by an unconvincing crowd of extras.[41] But this letter was never sent.

Though Thomas and Katia never argued about the war in front of the children, it was obvious that they disagreed. She rapidly lost faith both in the cause and in Germany's chances of winning, but if he had doubts about either, he seemed to be concealing them even from himself, though not without paying a heavy price.

Breite Strasse in 1880. The family was living at number 36 when TM was born on June 6, 1875, in a suburban villa his parents had rented for the summer. They went on living on Breite Strasse till the spring of 1883. [DrägerDruck GmbH, Lübeck]

Lübeck in 1880, when TM was five. [DrägerDruck GmbH, Lübeck]

Heinrich (*right*) with the twelve-year-old Thomas, Julia (Lula), and Carla (*center*)
in 1887. [Thomas Mann Archive of the Eidgenössische Technische Hochschule]

Town hall and market square in Lübeck.
[Thomas Mann Archive of the Eidgenössische Technische Hochschule]

The beach at Travemünde in 1994. Between 1882 and 1891 the family
spent four weeks here every summer. [Ronald Hayman]

The house at 7 Roeckstrasse. TM's mother moved here after her husband
died on October 13, 1891, but the sixteen-year-old TM was allowed to
live here only till Easter 1892, when he was sent away to a boarding
house run by a schoolteacher. [Ronald Hayman]

"A True Knight Was Fridolin" (*left*) and "The Little Umbrella Man" (*right*).
Two drawings by the twenty-one-year-old TM in the handmade *Picture Book for
Good Children*, which he and Heinrich prepared for the confirmation of their
younger sister. [Thomas Mann Archive of the Eidgenössische Technische Hochschule]

Narrow, winding streets and gabled Lübeck houses as they
appear on the jacket of the first one-volume edition of
Buddenbrooks, published in 1903.

TM in 1893. [Thomas Mann Archive of the
Eidgenössische Technische Hochschule]

TM at the age of twenty-four in April 1900.
[Thomas Mann Archive of the Eidgenössische
Technische Hochschule]

TM in 1900 with Heinrich.
[Thomas Mann Archive of the
Eidgenössische Technische Hochschule]

The seventeen-year-old Katia Pringsheim with her twin brother Klaus.
[Thomas Mann Archive of the Eidgenössische Technische Hochschule]

Katia in 1905. [Thomas Mann Archive of the
Eidgenössische Technische Hochschule]

Son of a Polish nobleman, Wladyslaw Moes was only ten when
TM became sufficiently obsessed to write "Death in Venice."
[Thomas Mann Archive of the Eidgenössische Technische Hochschule]

Katia with (*left to right*) Monika, Golo, Erika, and Klaus in 1915.
[Thomas Mann Archive of the Eidgenössische Technische Hochschule]

TM at his writing table in 1916 (*above*), and in 1925 (*below*). [Ullstein Bilderdienst, Berlin]

(*Left to right*) Erika, Klaus, Golo, Monika, and Elisabeth, with the dog, Bauschan, and their nurse. [Stadtische Bibliotheken, Munich]

(*Left to right*) Katia, Monika, Michael, Elisabeth, TM, Klaus, and Erika at the Hiddensee. [Ullstein Bilderdienst, Berlin]

Number 1 Poschingerstrasse, Munich. TM bought the site in February 1913, had
the house built, and moved in with the children on January 5, 1914.
It was their home till they left Germany in 1933.
[Thomas Mann Archive of the Eidgenössische Technische Hochschule]

His writing table in the Poschingerstrasse house.
[Thomas Mann Archive of the Eidgenössische Technische Hochschule]

Erika and Klaus in 1927, when she was married to the
actor and director Gustaf Grundgens. [Thomas Mann
Archive of the Eidgenössische Technische Hochschule]

Erika and Klaus with Pamela Wedekind (*right*), daughter of the playwright, in 1925.
She'd had a lesbian affair with Erika before the seventeen-year-old Klaus proposed to
her in a letter. She wrote back on a postcard, accepting. [Ullstein Bilderdienst, Berlin]

Nazis and S.A. men distract the Berlin audience at the Beethovensaal
on October 17, 1930. [Ullstein Bilderdienst, Berlin]

TM relaxes on the beach at Nidden in 1932. [Ullstein Bilderdienst, Berlin]

TM on his sixtieth birthday, 1935. His publisher sent an album containing handwritten greetings from Einstein, Shaw, and many others.
[Ullstein Bilderdienst, Berlin]

The house in Küsnacht, a fifteen-minute drive from the center of Zurich.
[Ronald Hayman]

The house in Kilchberg. They moved into it seven weeks before his seventy-ninth birthday. [Ronald Hayman]

The view of Lake Zurich from the house at Kilchberg. [Ronald Hayman]

Last visit to Lübeck. TM and Katia in 1955 outside the remains of the bombed house in Mengstresse, which had belonged to the Mann family since 1841.
[Hans Kripgans, Lübeck]

Outside Lübeck at the border of the Soviet zone, in 1955. [Hans Kripgans, Lübeck]

This wartime father seems estranged and distant, essentially different from the father I have known before those years of struggle and bitterness. The paternal physiognomy that looms up when I recall that period seems devoid of the kindness and irony which both inseparably belong to his character. The face I visualise looks severe and sombre—a proud and nervous brow with sensitive temples and sunken cheeks. . . . I see him leaving his working room—very erect in a tight uniform-like jacket of gray material. His lips are sealed, as it were, over an ominous secret, and his pensive regard goes inwards. . . . What uncanny spell is it that forces him to cloister himself in his library, every day of the year, from nine o'clock until noon . . . to withdraw as soon as breakfast is over, leaving the fragrance of his morning cigar as a familiar token? . . . He becomes impatient when visitors ask him about his forthcoming work. "It's just a book," he says, with a strangely unfocused look in his eyes. "No, not a novel. . . . It has to do with the war." . . . The cruel strain of those days, the bleak seriousness of the author's life, his lack of political training, even the inadequate food and the chilly atmosphere in his studio during the winter months—all these elements work together to create the peculiar climate, the perplexing mixture of violence and melancholy that prevails in the *Reflections*.[42]

None of the children failed to notice the difference in their father. "We had once loved our father almost as tenderly as our mother," wrote Golo, "but that changed during the war. He could still project an aura of kindness, but mostly we experienced only silence, sternness, nervousness or anger. . . . I can still see him, returning from his walk and entering the dining-room at one-thirty in a way that made his presence unmistakable; I can see him going across to his study after the meal and closing the door with a decisiveness that in Switzerland would be described with the phrase 'It's closed now.' "[43]

Thomas had been more seriously wounded by the Zola essay than by any previous criticism. He wasn't exaggerating when he said in the preface that *Reflections of a Nonpolitical Man* was the work of an artist "whose existence was shaken to its foundations, whose self-respect was brought into question and who was so upset that he could produce nothing else." Any attempt at self-justification would be an attempt to refute Heinrich's argument, and in January 1916, when Thomas read from the work in progress, it was apparent to friends that he'd been thrown off balance. "Poor Tom has obviously been very upset by the Zola essay, and in his new work he attacks his brother (whom he does not name) so violently and relentlessly that we felt a little as if we were caught between the two of them."[44]

In the book he keeps coming compulsively back to the man he calls "civilization's *littérateur*." This is the title for Chapter 3, which was written between December 1915 and January 1916, and altogether this phrase is used in the book 172 times.[45] Though Heinrich is never named, there are quotations from the Zola essay among other clues that would make it easy for the informed reader to identify the *littérateur*.

The quarrel had some of its roots in divergence between the brothers' attitude to scenic beauty. For Thomas—so he says—beauty was always something for Italians and "tricksters of the intellect . . . fundamentally it had nothing German in it."[46] He'd listened to the romantic messages of the *Lohengrin* prelude while sitting under palm trees he despised, and under a deep blue sky that irritated him.[47] Heinrich had loved Italy and betrayed Germany, helping to cause the war by speaking up for the values and traditions of the Allies, while underestimating the virtues Germany was defending. This is highly unreasonable, but Thomas is committed to getting beyond reason. The *littérateur* is the archetypal literary man who uses words in the ostensibly reasonable way Western civilization has encouraged; Thomas aligns himself—and German culture—with antirationalism. This gives him the right to ignore facts he'd have to confront if he were trying to be objective.

Though writing about Germany and the war, he ignores the effects of the war on Germany. He says nothing about other people, their reactions to wartime hardships or to news they read in the papers, nothing about the experience of soldiers in the trenches or civilians in the streets. Provoked by Heinrich into questioning his own position, Thomas presents an apologia which is intended to be as self-searching and as open as Rousseau's *Confessions*, but he's too proud and too inhibited to enter wholeheartedly into the confessional mode. The reminiscences are mostly unrevealing, and a great deal of space is taken up with random quotations about politics and national character—from Dostoyevsky, Turgenev, Goethe, Schopenhauer, Fichte, and many other writers. The well-read Ernst Bertram, who paid frequent visits and worked almost as a collaborator, provided much of the material.

Thomas also generalizes about differences between the Germans and other people. He accepts the view of the pacifist Friedrich Wilhelm Foerster that democracy could never thrive in Germany, the Germans being conservative by nature. Though Wagner had believed in brotherhood between nations, the words *foreign, translated,* and *un-German* always had a pejorative ring when he used them, because he hated democracy and politics equally, recognizing the identity between them. The countries in which democracy prospers are, unlike Germany, essentially political countries.

Quoting Dostoyevsky's claim that a genuine Russian is a brother to all human beings, Thomas argues that Germany and Russia belong together: The history of the *origin* of their humanity is the same—a history of suffering. Besides, Dostoyevsky had understood what it was that divided the Germans, "this great and special people," from the people of Western Europe. As the patriotic philosopher Johann Gottlieb Fichte had put it, the German—and no one else—practices art as a virtue and as a religion. This, glosses Thomas, is a valid translation into German of *l'art pour l'art*.

One of his oddest pronouncements is that if it's characteristically German to be a burgher, it's even more German to be something between a burgher and an artist. In "Tonio Kröger" he had tried to analyze what made him different from everyone else. Belonging to both the bourgeoisie and the bohemian fringe, he belonged to neither. But now he was ascribing to everyone the same combination of qualities that made him into an outsider.

At the same time, he reverses his former condemnation of German philistinism. Following Nietzsche and following his natural inclinations, he had attacked the public for its indifference to literature and the arts. Now, suddenly, the Germans are praised for their admirable immunity to ideas promulgated in the democratic west through literature. *Littérateur* is a term of abuse.

18

I Hate Democracy

IN MARCH 1916, introducing an English sentence (with German punctuation) into a letter, Thomas wrote: "I think, we can't win the war."[1] In 1914 anxiety about his earnings had been outweighed by positive feelings—optimism about the cleansing effect of war on a corrupt continent, a new sense of solidarity with the German people, and a confidence, encouraged by reactions to his essays, that he could play an important role. By the spring of 1916 it was harder to believe either in his own contribution to the German war effort or in the prospect of victory.

In Munich the war had produced a severe shortage of food. Constantly hungry, Thomas, Katia, and the children couldn't believe they'd ever again live as well as they had until so recently. "Our food and clothes," wrote Klaus,

> the shoes, the coal, the soap, the writing paper—everything we touched, smelled or swallowed—"ersatz", miserable shoddy stuff. . . . The "artistic outfit" and handsome marine uniforms [Mother] had bought us in 1914 were threadbare and outgrown in 1917. And as for shoes, leather was almost as rare as butter. For a while we wore heavy sandals with wooden soles. But soon we grew tired of them and preferred to walk about barefoot.

They still lunched every Sunday in the Pringsheims' sumptuous dining room, but took along their own bread, and "the festive menu consisted of an emaciated bird—a dubious sort of heron with a disturbingly fishy flavour."[2] Golo has described how at home the boys and girls shared baths to economize with hot water, and how they ate snails they collected in the garden.[3] If Thomas was to go on being productive, Katia told herself, he needed nourishment, and the children noticed that she gave him priority over them with the little food there was.[4]

He seldom went out, except on solitary walks. Occasionally he met Ernst Bertram, Bruno Frank, and Maximilian Brantl at the Odeon Bar in Briennerstrasse. When Maximilian Harden's *Zukunft* was suppressed by the military authorities at the end of 1915, Thomas protested to the *Frankfurter Zeitung*, but the editor didn't publish his letter.[5] In any case, *Zukunft* was reprieved.

Joylessly immersed in his *Reflections*, Thomas felt unwell and dispirited. In March 1916 he canceled a reading in Berlin: He had succumbed to flu and then to erysipelas, or St. Anthony's fire–a painful skin inflammation, which was common and dangerous till sulfonamides were discovered. "I am curious about what will come next after the erysipelas; there are so many possibilities. Perhaps death is approaching."[6] He was forty, and the joke only half concealed the hypochondria.

In the central sector of the western front, the French army checked a fierce assault on Verdun, and on March 20, as food shortages became acute in Germany, rationing began. Writing to Samuel Fischer in mid-April, Thomas deplored the prospect that "democratic progress will be imposed on us from outside . . . through defeat."[7]

Though he went on making sporadic notes for the confidence trickster story and the fiction about the sanatorium, which now seemed likely to be a short novel,[8] he wasn't intending to concentrate on either till he'd finished *Reflections*, and he resumed work on it in April.

EVER SINCE MOTZ HAD BEEN SHOT, Thomas and Katia had talked about buying another dog, and if the story "Master and Dog" ("Herr und Hund") corresponds, as it probably does, to real events, they mentioned their intention, while spending the summer at Tölz, to the landlady of a mountain inn. In July she rang up to say she had a dog they might like. The next afternoon, when they took the children up to the inn, she was cooking in the steamy kitchen, where, roped to a leg of the table, a bony, knock-kneed puppy was shivering. Stooping, they fondled him. She explained that he'd grown up on a farm, and his owners wanted her to find him a good home. The food shortage was so acute that it was hard to keep dogs, even on a farm, and he'd been fed only potato peel. Thomas and Katia could take him and bring him back if they didn't like him: She was sure they would. On the meager body the male sex organ looked absurdly large. They asked how big he'd be when fully grown. About the same size as their collie, she said.

They went away without him, but the children had fallen in love with him, and three days later they bought him for 10 marks. On the way home they had to keep stopping: He had chronic diarrhea. This might be a symptom of distemper, they thought, and at first, too nervous to eat, he sniffed suspiciously at the chicken bones and cheese parings he was offered, but he turned out to be healthy, and attached himself to Thomas. "A deep-seated patriarchal instinct in the more masculine outdoor breeds of dog tells them to recognise and respect the head of the family and the master of the household as their lord and protector, without ever becoming so dependent on the rest of the family."[9] Accepting this vassalage, Thomas allowed him into the study, but he brought mud into the room and damaged the carpet with his claws. Besides, his presence was distracting. Wagging his tail, he'd approach Thomas and put his forepaws on the arm of the chair. He'd sniff at the objects on the desk as if they were food, smudging freshly written words with his paws. Called to order, he'd lie down and go to sleep, but, following the action in his dreams, he'd growl and make running motions with his paws.[10] Taking the name from Fritz Reuter's novel *Ut mine Stromtid*, Thomas called him Bauschan.

In August, when "a really serious nervous crisis" forced Thomas to stop writing for eight days,[11] he regretted starting such an exhausting and enervating book, which made novels seem temptingly "three-dimensional" and "musical." But he'd invested so much time and effort that there was no question of abandoning the book, though it would interest only a small minority. The further he got with it, the more convinced he became that it would provoke the critics and bore the public.[12]

He put it aside in September to write an article on Eichendorff's 1826 story *Aus dem Leben eines Taugenichts* (*From the Life of a Good-for-Nothing*), which had been published during 1914 in a new edition with drawings by Emil Preetorius. A miller loses patience with his lazy son and sends him out into the world. Seeing the good-for-nothing as a genius and an artist, Thomas could identify with his sense of being at home nowhere and arriving everywhere too late. Looking, as he still was, for what could be listed as typically German, he cited the good-for-nothing as an exemplar of German normality, and when Paul Amann disagreed, Thomas pointed to the separation of philosophy from politics that makes him so dissimilar to "civilisation's *littérateur*."[13] The article was published in the November issue of the *Neue Rundschau*, and, reworking it, Thomas used it in the book as a chapter called "On Virtue" ("Auf der Tugend").

In October it again seemed possible that Thomas would be called up. Early in November he went to Berlin, where he read from *Felix Krull* at the Sezession and the Deutsche Gesellschaft before returning to Munich for a medical examination on November 11. Again he was lucky: The doctor decided his nerves and stomach made him incapable of active service.[14]

No longer expecting his book to exert a useful influence, he was still compulsive about condemning tendencies Nietzsche would have condemned. "I hate democracy," he wrote to Paul Amann on November 25, "and with it I hate politics, for that is the same thing. I also hate the jargon of Freemasons and Jacobins, which is becoming the contemporary language. . . . To make Germany literary, radical, political and Western is to make it un-German, and I am letting that happen, but taking no part in it."[15] On the same day, Ernst Bertram was told: "I have believed for a long time that, more for internal than external reasons, no authentic political life can be created in Germany. . . . The basic problem is that we are not a nation. We are more like the quintessence of Europe—being subject to the conflict of Europe's intellectual contradictions without having a national synthesis."[16]

Though he was expecting to forfeit all his chances of influencing current events, Thomas considered it wrong for the writer to intervene in politics.

> No, the intellectual does *not* act—that is forbidden for him. The dichotomy between thought and deed, poetry and reality will always remain wide, and open. A political article can be poetic, and poetry can have consequences in reality, but the writer should have no direct contact with whatever it is that should be affected. . . . The intellectual must produce results without intervening. If he denies this, if his passion leads him into reality, he is slipping into the wrong dimension, where he will behave badly, amateurishly and awkwardly.[17]

After the Austrian president, Count Sturgh, was assassinated by the writer Friedrich Adler, a socialist activist, on October 21, Thomas described the killer as "an intellectual, neurotically tainted, problematic, delicate, with a Nietzsche moustache and the eyes of a fanatic, full of nerves, incapable of speaking in public, for example, and regarding himself as an innocuous writer, shy vis-à-vis reality and diffident, totally unsuited to be a politician or a man of action but as a son of pure spirit incapable of compromising or mediating politically between thought and action."[18]

On October 23, Thomas read from *Felix Krull* in Breslau, returning to Munich on October 25, with nine days in hand before his next reading in Berlin. He prefaced this with a talk, arguing that the novel, with "its mixture of synthetic-plastic and analytical-critical elements," was essentially un-German insofar as it was political and social. But the bildungsroman, which took the individual out of his social context, was typically German, legitimately national. Alongside the tradition of the bildungsroman lay an equally legitimate possibility of subverting it through parody, and this was what he was trying to do in his new fiction. He afterward made the talk into an article for the *Vossische Zeitung*,[19] and he developed his ideas about parody and irony in *Reflections of a Nonpolitical Man*. But even the title was out-of-date. Nietzsche, he conceded, had been right to call himself the last nonpolitical German; the reflections were those of an antipolitical man.[20]

When Heinrich scored a double success in February, it was infuriating to Thomas that the brother who'd sidetracked him into a massive piece of nonfiction was outclassing him creatively. A play Heinrich had written in 1913, *Madame Legros*, was premiered simultaneously in Munich and Lübeck. After reading the script early in 1914, Thomas had called it a very beautiful work, admirably economical in composition and dialogue,[21] but now he disliked it for the same reasons audiences liked it: It corresponded to the general disenchantment with the war. As in his Zola essay, Heinrich had been thinking about Germany while writing about France. In prerevolutionary Paris, Mme Legros is obsessively convinced that a prisoner in the Bastille is innocent. Unable to live with this social injustice, she campaigns indomitably till the wrong is put right. In the audience one evening Heinrich heard a woman say: "At last we can look into each other's eyes again."[22]

Thomas, who didn't go to see the play, complained that Heinrich, who "had already been thoroughly 'Entente' before the war, has written a drama that is thoroughly anti-German."[23] "The brother problem," he admitted on March 11, "is the real—in any case the most serious problem of my life. Such great closeness and such strong inner repulsion are painful. . . . The provocative, intellectual, contrived 'humaneness' of *Legros*—horrible. The blind submissiveness of critics and public—astonishing."[24]

Thomas was sufficiently unpolitical—or antipolitical—to be more interested in Heinrich's attitude toward the French Revolution than in the Russian Revolution. Since the beginning of the year, workers in Petrograd had been striking and rioting against food shortages and the loss of so many lives: In the 1915 offensive on the German front 2 million men had been killed, but instead of responding to popular demands for peace, the tsar had taken personal command of the army. The revolution broke out when breadlines erupted into raids on bakeries. With factories closed through lack of fuel, workers went on strike, demonstrations surged through the streets, and soldiers defected from regiments sent in to quash the disorder. On March 16, Nicholas II abdicated, and in April, Lenin returned from ten years of exile with seventeen other Bolsheviks. By making a secret deal with German ministers, they got themselves transported across Germany in a sealed train. Russia's provisional government was still collaborating with the Allies; the ministers were hoping the Bolsheviks would overturn it and take Russia out of the war.

But if Germany had still had any chance of winning, it vanished when the United States joined the Allies. In early February the Germans had threatened to torpedo neutral ships trading with the Allies, and by the end of the month, they'd sunk 134 ships belonging to neutral countries. After the American *Housatonic* was torpedoed off Sicily, Woodrow Wilson broke off diplomatic relations with Germany. On February 7, U.S. citizens there were held as hostages, and on the twenty-fifth it was disclosed that the foreign minister, Adolf Zimmermann, had secretly asked the Mexican government to declare war on the United

States. Addressing Congress, Wilson asked for an "armed neutrality" to deal with submarine warfare: The idea was that ships should be fitted with weapons. After the American government called up the National Guard and 26,000 sailors on March 26, the German chancellor said he didn't want war with the United States, but on April 6, Wilson signed the declaration of war. Ninety-one German ships were seized in New York harbor, and the first American shots were fired on April 19, when a German submarine was sunk.

For Thomas the war was primarily a confrontation between rival attitudes, and, doggedly abstaining from fiction, he went on with his book. "I am losing this year exactly as if I had been called up. But it brings me a certain clarity, self-knowledge, familiarity with the boundaries of myself."25 The question he put to himself about Russia was how Dostoyevsky would have responded to the revolution. Searching in his political and literary essays for his views on Slavophile and pro-Western attitudes, Thomas found they were "highly interesting in relation to my own intellectual and political position between nationalism and 'nihilism'—I mean between Germanism and Europeanism."26

He was worrying how readers would react to his book, but between March and June he wrote the longest chapter—the one on "Politik," which fills over a hundred pages. He read excerpts from it to Ernst Bertram, who was told: "I am now so sore and irritable that there are few people (and indeed few books) in whose company I can be confident of not feeling angry or insulted."27

What boosted his spirits in June was a new opera, *Palestrina*, by the Munich composer Hans Pfitzner. To help Bruno Walter, Thomas had written a long article for the Berlin paper *Der Tag*, "Music in Munich." As the city's "General Music Director," Walter had provoked controversy and made powerful enemies; Thomas explained how fortunate Munich was to have him. It was Walter who introduced Thomas to the opera that impressed him more than any other new music he'd heard. Even more than most writers, Thomas intertwined new experiences with current preoccupations, and his reactions to Pfitzner were inseparable from ideas about Germany's distinguishing characteristics. Devoid of the sentimentality he associated with Catholicism, France, and Italy, *Palestrina* was intensely *German*, he thought, reminiscent of Dürer and *Faust*, of Schopenhauer and Wagner. Romantic but austere, it was redolent of everything Thomas associated with Nietzsche's phrase "the cross, death and the grave."

The opera was premiered on June 12, and after seeing it for the third time on June 23, he claimed to feel distressed at having to wait six weeks for the next performance.28 Pfitzner and his wife accepted an invitation to dinner, and he arrived wearing a white, raw silk suit, but "I doubt whether he felt at ease, though he drank at least five glasses of Moselle wine and ate a great number of home-made pastries. . . . Probably he was not born to feel at ease—a difficult, sore, ambivalent creature."[29]

But Thomas never forgot a conversation they had at the opera house, during the intermission between the second and third acts. They were sitting on a garden terrace, comparing the opera with *Die Meistersinger*, which ends with the stage crowded and brightly lit, whereas *Palestrina* ends with the composer alone in his half-dark room, under a picture of his dead wife, daydreaming about the past. All through the opera, said Pfitzner, "everything tends towards the past. It is dominated by sympathy with death." His phrase *Sympathie mit dem Tod* was identical with the one Thomas had often used about "Death in Venice" and *The Magic Mountain*.

Devoting most of his chapter on virtue to Pfitzner, he explains why he was astounded to hear these words, and this involves him in summarizing the plot of *The Magic Mountain*. Describing it as a little novel, a kind of educational story, he says the central character is positioned between two equally quaint educators. One is a progressive Italian man of letters, humanist and rhetorician; the other is a reactionary and disreputable mystic, an advocate of irrationalism. The Italian, Settembrini, had already appeared in the chapters Thomas had written, while the mystic hadn't yet made his debut; but, by July 1917, after polemicizing against Heinrich for three years in *Reflections*, Thomas had decided to carry the argument into *The Magic Mountain*. Presumably the Italian, as originally conceived, was less oriented toward Heinrich's values.

SELF-ABSORBED though he undeniably was, Thomas was far from being mean. While investing nearly four years in a book motivated by commitment to the German war effort, he also wanted to help financially, and by the beginning of June he'd made up his mind to sell the house at Tölz[30] and donate the money as a war loan. Early in July he sold the house for 80,000 marks (from which 12,000 went on repaying the mortgage), but in letters to friends he gave different explanations for his decision: They wanted to spend more time in other places, the house was too small for a family with four children, and it had other drawbacks.

Certainly he didn't sell it to raise cash for himself. In spite of the paper shortage, which sometimes stopped Fischer from printing a new impression when one of his books sold out, they were doing well. Between 1914 and 1918, 33,000 copies of *Royal Highness* were printed, 32,000 of *Buddenbrooks*, and 14,000 of *Death in Venice*. Of his short story collections in cheap editions, *Little Herr Friedemann* had sold 49,000 by the end of the war, *Tonio Kröger* 16,000, *Tristan* 6,000, and *The Infant Prodigy* 59,000. The volume of essays, *Frederick and the Great Coalition*, 38,000.

The biographer Peter de Mendelssohn calculates that during the war years Thomas earned between 120,000 and 150,000 marks from German sales. This was an annual income of at least 25,000, which was comfortable, without leaving a great deal of margin for a man with two houses, mortgages on both, and four children.

Klaus was ten and Golo eight when, going out into the garden at Tölz for the last time, they went into the shed where they'd so often played, and took a last look at their wading pool and at the place under the four chestnut trees where they had breakfasted on hot summer mornings.[31] By the end of September, the family was back in Munich, but instead of completing the chapter "On Belief" ("Vom Glauben"), Thomas succumbed to a dysenteric bowel infection. For several days his temperature was uncomfortably high, but when it went down, he could enjoy reading—especially Tolstoy's *War and Peace*, which he'd read only once, as a boy, and works by the nineteenth-century Austrian novelist Adalbert Stifter, who was new to him.[32] He recovered in time to finish "On Belief" by the end of October. The next chapter, "Aesthetic Politics," was completed by the end of November, and the final chapter before Christmas.

For the Christmas issue of the *Berliner Tageblatt*, several writers, including Thomas and Heinrich, were invited to assess the possibility of world peace in the future. Under the title "Leben—nicht Zerstörung" ("Life—Not Destruction"), Heinrich's piece came out on December 25. "Now that we have matured into democracy," he wrote, "we Germans have ahead of us the greatest experience of all."[33]

Thomas's article appeared two days later. He had never tried to insulate himself from the war, he said, and it had shown him that he was more "national" than he'd realized, though he'd never been a "nationalist." He didn't conceal his distaste for democracy: "I know exactly what is appropriate at the moment, but my nature and education prevent me from subscribing to this doctrine or sharing this belief. . . . In its rhetorical and political form, love for humanity is right at the circumference of real emotion, and usually it is expressed most melodiously when weak at the centre." Abruptly, he switches into the second person singular: "Be better to yourself, less harsh, less darkly dogmatic, less aggressively self-righteous before you play the philanthropist." Then he paraphrases a quotation he'd copied from the New Testament into a notebook during 1916. "It can be effective to come out very beautifully with the saying: 'I love God!' But if a man 'hates his brother' at the same time, then, according to the Gospel of St. John, his love of God is nothing but beautiful literature and sacrificial smoke, which fails to rise."[34]

Less than two years ago he'd said the "brother problem" was the most serious in his life; now he was thinking of Heinrich when he used the second person singular and the words *hates his brother*. When Heinrich heard the article read out, it struck him as being addressed to him "almost like a letter." Though he was living in the Leopoldstrasse, less than a mile away from Thomas, they'd had no contact since September 1914, and at the beginning of 1917, when they both attended a lecture by Karl Kraus, they ignored each other. Hoping to renew friendly relations before the war ended, Heinrich now broke the silence, writing as if he were personally being accused of "brotherly hatred." His letter is no longer extant, but the draft is. "In my public statements, no 'I' comes to the fore, and therefore no brother." His writings were aimed beyond his personal situation, and, sometimes at least, he'd proved his goodness by lifting his heart toward love of humanity, which could be translated into political terms as European democracy. He'd read Thomas's work

with the greatest willingness to understand and sympathise. I have long been familiar with your intellectual hostility, and if your wartime extremism took you by surprise, it had been predictable for me. In spite of this knowledge, I often loved your work, and even more often entered deeply into it, frequently praising it or defending it in public, and consoling you like a younger brother when you were troubled by self-doubt. Though I received almost nothing in return, I was not discouraged. I knew that to feel self-confident, you had to set bounds for yourself and even to fend off other people.

The essay on Zola, Heinrich explained, had been written during an international emergency, and had been aimed not just at Thomas but at "a legion" of writers who were "rushing forward to do damage." That legion had been reduced to a handful of desperate people, and Thomas needn't regard his brother as an enemy.[35]

But Thomas, with obstinacy, idealism, and controlled rage, had given more than three years to a sustained attack on his brother's values. It would have been pointless to send Heinrich a conciliatory letter unless he was willing to scrap the book. He did consider this possibility. At the last minute, while copies were being distributed to wholesalers, he sent Fischer an express letter, asking him to hold them up. But it was too late.[36]

What's surprising about the letter he sent Heinrich on January 3, 1918, is its vindictiveness. The passage of time and the long book he'd just finished hadn't taken the edge off his anger. His article for the *Tageblatt* had been controlled and balanced; his letter to Heinrich is neither, though it insists that the reference to fraternal hatred in the article had been mainly "a symbol for more general discrepancies in the psychology of the Rousseauites." Why should he assume Heinrich still hated him after the release of aggression in the Zola essay? But it was frivolous to expect a rapprochement after the "truly French viciousness, slanders and calumnies of that brilliant concoction," which had made him suffer and struggle for two years—in reality it had been longer—condemning himself to silence as an artist and neglecting the projects he cared most about in order to refute the accusations.

Thomas denies that his behavior has been extremist. "Yours was," he says, "and indeed to a degree that was utterly detestable." Heinrich might now feel triumphant, but not a single line of his letter had been "dictated by anything but moral complacency and self-righteousness." Thomas even implies that the world is too small for the two of them. "You cannot see the rightness and the ethos of my life because you are my brother." Richard Dehmel, who'd written from the trenches to congratulate Thomas on his war essays, could still be Heinrich's friend,

> for though you are anything but kindred spirits, you are not brothers, and therefore you can live at the same time.—Let the tragedy of our brotherhood move on towards its conclusion. Pain? That is all right. One becomes hard and apathetic. Since Carla killed herself and you broke with Lula for life, permanent separation is nothing new in our circle. I did not create this life. I detest it. One must do one's best to go on living it. Goodbye. T.37

Before drafting a reply, Heinrich made careful notes. He felt "deep regret" that by expressing his opinion once, he'd made Thomas spend two years on answering him. He didn't intend to read Thomas's book, the reason being that he preferred a natural relationship to a polemical one.

> To me all the evidence seems to suggest that you underestimate your importance in my life so far as natural feelings are concerned, and overestimate it with regard to literary influence. . . . So far as I am concerned, I see myself as a thoroughly independent creature, and my experience of the world is not brotherly but simply mine. You are no obstacle. For example, I should simply be delighted if you were to write something other than nonsense about the activities and qualities of the French. But you—if I wanted to commend the old Prussian, do you know what you would do? Throw all your notes about Frederick the Great on the fire. . . . Stop referring my life and behaviour to yourself, they do not concern you, and would be exactly the same without you.

Heinrich had no trouble in defending himself against the charge of self-righteousness. What he felt was guilt at having been one of those who led his generation into the catastrophe. How could Thomas think he felt triumphant? "Triumphant about what? That everything is going well for me—namely the world reduced to rubble and ten million corpses under the earth." Thomas, who had approved of the war, was still doing so, but literature, even if it couldn't help people to live, shouldn't help them to die. "The hour will come, I hope, in which you can see not shadows but men, and then me too."38

Though Heinrich didn't know Thomas had sold his house in Tölz to raise money for the war, it was true that he was still helping people to die, and though the sacrifice of the house was an act of generosity, he was still siding patriotically with the aggressors. Even in these three letters there's more magnanimity in Heinrich's criticisms of Thomas than in his of Heinrich. But Heinrich was right not to send this letter. Over four years were to elapse before Thomas was willing to make peace.

His excuse for responding only briefly to Heinrich's December letter was that he was getting ready to leave "on a fourteen-day journey which I curse. Its character is ill-suited to my mood."39 He didn't explain why; one of the reasons was that Katia was in the sixth month of her fifth pregnancy.

He left her with the children for seventeen days, traveling from Munich to Strasbourg, where he visited Pfitzner, and from there to Essen, where he read from *The Magic Mountain*. An appearance in Brussels was scheduled for January 9, when his reading was to be followed by the third act of *Fiorenza*, staged by soldiers in the German army occupying the city. The train was so late that the director, Saladin Schmidt, had to take over the reading, but Thomas liked the production. In the morning he breakfasted with the military governor and his staff officers, who wore iron crosses and addressed Thomas as "Herr Kriegskamarad" ("Herr War Comrade").40

He went on to read in Hamburg and Rostock, arriving on January 15 in Lübeck—his first visit to his hometown since 1904. He stayed with Ida Boy-Ed, who was now living in a 1571 brick house adjoining the Burgtor, the fortified tower above the north gate of the city. Thomas raised money for wounded servicemen by appearing in the municipal theater on the seventeenth to read some of his stories.

Expecting *Reflections* to be published in April, he had to work hurriedly on the foreword. Writing preliminary notes, he reminded himself that he'd started the book at the beginning of a war which was nearing its end, but he was only partially aware of differences this had made to the way he'd written it.41 He wanted the foreword to be critical, taking an overall view of the book,42 but his "twelve chapters on politics, morals, art, philosophy, autobiography" struck him as "a ragout of diverse ingredients, a thing belonging to no genre, and without precedent."43

The foreword was still unfinished when he learned that Frank Wedekind had died on March 9 after an operation. He was fifty-four. At the funeral, three days later, when Heinrich was making a graveside speech, Thomas walked off. A radical freethinker throughout most of his life, Wedekind had finally turned to religion.

How did civilisation's *littérateur* begin to excuse him? How did he extricate himself from the affair? "The spiritual commitment," he said at the grave, "that we call religion was obviously something that the deceased was acutely aware of." But we all know what civilisation's *littérateur* means by spirit. He means literature and politics, together with something called democracy. When I heard this unctuous coining of false concepts by a freethinking Sunday preacher, witnessed this attempt to reclaim for politics a soul's last efforts to attain salvation, I put my top hat on and went home.[44]

Thomas added this paragraph after he got home, and finished the foreword by March 14, when he read it out to Ernst Bertram. The enormous manuscript was posted to Fischer on March 16, but publication would have been delayed if Thomas hadn't used his influence to get Fischer supplied with paper. It was thanks to intervention from Walther Rathenau, the Jewish electrotechnician who was organizing German war industries, that the book was treated as helpful to the war effort.

His self-imposed task completed, Thomas was again free to enjoy Munich's cultural life. He started going to theaters and concerts and met friends in the Odeon Bar. He took Erika and Klaus to a performance of Wagner's *Der fliegende Holländer*, after preparing them by explaining the story, whistling themes—he could whistle well—or playing them on the piano.

Giving himself permission to work on fiction again, he settled down to what he called "a kind of idyll, whose prose exudes something of the hexameter spirit."[45] Centering on his relationship with Bauschan, "Master and Dog" shows a remarkable capacity for observing a dog's movements, describing them with precision, and empathizing with a dog's mind. "Nothing was disguised in the characterisation of the dog. For once it would have been possible for a character to be perfectly justified in saying: 'That is me!' And all the Bilses could have confirmed it."[46]

The baby was born on April 24, 1918—another girl, who was named Elisabeth Veronika. From the beginning, Thomas felt a special affinity with her. "The little one is a sensitive little creature, but charming, in my opinion. For none of the earlier children did I feel what I feel for this one. That goes hand in hand with increasing pleasure in nature. Does one generally become more emotional with the passage of time? Or is it the harshness of the period that puts me in this mood, makes me feel *loving*?"[47] They employed a nurse, who kept using the word *Medi* (little girl), and this became Elisabeth's nickname. At mealtimes seven places were now laid at the table.[48]

Thomas had been hoping to finish "Master and Dog" before he had to correct proofs of *Reflections*, but, as usual, he found himself writing at greater length than he'd intended, and the story was only half finished when, early in May, the postman started delivering galley proofs. Bertram, who helped him with them, was invited to make corrections, cuts, and adjustments without consultation. The proofs were ready by June 2, but Fischer hesitated about whether to publish in two volumes, and it wasn't until mid-July that he decided on a single volume.[49] Thomas had resumed work on "Master and Dog" early in June, and, by the end of the month, written three of the five chapters and started the fourth.[50]

He really was taking more pleasure in nature. Neither *Buddenbrooks* nor *Royal Highness* had contained any extensive description of landscape. Even "Death in Venice" says little about the city's appearance, but in the new story he describes woods, fields, hills, and the brook he saw on his daily walks. It was as if the dog's alertness to noises and smells alerted his master to scenic details.

The portrayal of the dog is vivid. Bauschan was mainly a short-haired German pointer. He had a rusty brown coat with black stripes, a slight dewlap, and forelegs that curved gently outward. In the middle of his chest was a small white tuft, and hanging from his muzzle and the corners of his mouth was a hairy growth like a mustache and goatee. Some of the most interesting statements in the story are unintentional: Giving a richly detailed account of interaction between him and the dog, Thomas shows how much he enjoyed an unequal relationship—the one with Paul was his only equal one—in which the other participant was totally dependent. No questions could be asked and the only responsibility of the human was to keep the animal healthy, well fed, and exercised. When Thomas came home late in the evening, the dog was there to greet him, not reproachful but joyfully welcoming.

If Motz, a thoroughbred, had been aristocratic, Bauschan had a peasant soul. Lacking his predecessor's pride, he showed an undignified fear of the dog-whip, and because he had a weak bladder, he slept out of doors in a kennel—a humiliation Thomas would never have inflicted on Motz. But when they were out together, Thomas enjoyed the moments when, after trotting through brushwood, Bauschan stood stock-still, listening with a paw elegantly raised and turned inward. If he started digging to unearth a field mouse, his master would assist him, using his walking stick to dislodge pebbles or pieces of gnarled root. But if Bauschan caught the mouse and gobbled it alive, Thomas slipped back into the role of detached observer.

This was the last summer of the war and the first summer since 1909 they couldn't spend in Tölz. Had he known about Katia's pregnancy in time, he said, he'd have kept the house for at least one more summer,[51] but he rented the big "Villa Defregger" in Abwinkl on the Tegernsee. Taking bed linen and a lot of household utensils, the family moved in on July 12, but on his last day in Munich, Thomas was worrying gloomily about what sort of government Germany would have when the war ended. What kind of restrictions would it impose? Would it have any tolerance or need for artists of his kind?[52]

The villa belonged to a painter who'd been called up. It was attractive, with a big garden bordering on the lake, where the children could swim and row. The beach reminded Thomas of the Lido at Venice. He especially enjoyed the boating and a visit from Ernst Bertram, who came to stay and went to Bad Kreuth with him.[53] While correcting proofs, Thomas was reading works by the eighteenth-century poet and novelist Christoph Martin Wieland, including his essays on the French Revolution. Finding several passages that reflected his misgivings about the dangers of forcing democracy on a defeated Germany, Thomas ended his book with a last-minute addition, written on the proofs. Wieland, he said, had been "national" in the highest and most intellectual sense when he insisted that if the human race was ever to improve, it would happen through change in the individual, not political or constitutional reform. Any German with a spark of patriotic feeling must hate the idea that another nation would use military success to destroy domestic and burgherly traditions by imposing a political delusion. Wieland had promised to go on working with all his strength against the specious and confused concepts of freedom and equality that subverted those traditions. *Reflections* ends with the implicit promise that Thomas will do the same.

Sons of Defeat

ON THE WESTERN FRONT in late June and early July 1918, a flu epidemic caused a lull in the fighting, but on July 15 the German commander Erich von Ludendorff launched an attack across the Marne, optimistically calling it the *Friedensturm*, the peace offensive. But he was halted after a four-mile advance, and when the Allies counterattacked, he had to retreat, leaving 25,000 prisoners.

By July 23, the day he finished correcting proofs, Thomas was consistently pessimistic. "I hear from Berlin that eleven hundred thousand Americans are already in France. What will happen? Do we have to give up Alsace-Lorraine to be accepted into the economic community?"[1] And three weeks later, he predicted that "If we have to give up Alsace-Lorraine, this will not have been the *last* war."[2]

The military situation was deteriorating rapidly. Early in August, with over four hundred tanks spearheading the attack, twenty divisions of Allied troops went into action near Amiens, forcing the Germans back toward the old Hindenburg line, the position they'd held before the spring offensive. During riots in Berlin at the end of the month, pictures of the kaiser were being burned, and in mid-September, Britain and the United States rejected an Austrian peace proposal.

Returning to Munich with the family on September 10, Thomas was still worrying about reactions to his book: "I am compromising myself with it quite differently and much more directly than one does with a novel."[3] But he wanted it to read like a novel–"as the representation of an intellectual destiny, consciously experienced and therefore inwardly distanced already."[4]

After supper on September 18 he finished reading Ernst Bertram's book on Nietzsche. He hadn't expected to feel so involved: He was as proud as if he'd written it himself.[5] To Bertram, three days later, he wrote: "How close it is to me; how my whole being constantly resonates with it!"[6] Without having read "Tonio Kröger" and "Death in Venice," Bertram couldn't have written like this about Nietzsche, and in some ways the book was complementary to *Reflections*. As with Lukács, whom he still hadn't met, there had been substantial interaction. Both through his fiction and through the long conversations they'd had,

Thomas had influenced Bertram, and, through conversation and now the book, had gained not only new ideas and insights but confidence. He found his own ideas and insights carried to a new stage of development or formulated in a way that gave him both encouragement and a firmer grip on his own creative and critical thinking.

An idea crucial to *Buddenbrooks* would be crucial again when he wrote *Joseph and His Brothers (Joseph und seine Brüder)*: that a man's ancestors and predecessors lay down a pathway for him. In "Lübeck as a Spiritual Concept of Life," he claimed to have been "amused" by awareness that actions he took and actions he avoided were determined by the personality of his dead father. Alongside amusement, many other feelings were present, and his novels form a monument to their complexity. The kind of empathic identification that had characterized his critical essays on Goethe, Schiller, Fontane, and Chamisso involved a reversal of the same process. Seeing his own image reflected in theirs, he could see their work as prefiguring his own. Nietzsche had influenced him deeply, and when he was writing *Reflections,* the influence had entered a new phase: The rejection of rational European culture in favor of passion and irrationalism took some of its authority from Nietzsche's vitalism, and by focusing on Nietzsche's ambivalence, Bertram's book invited Thomas to recognize that they had in common an "incurable tragic dualism," or as Thomas phrased it in his appreciative letter, an "antithetical intensity in living." Bertram's book showed Nietzsche to be the active victim of contradictory impulses— torn between Dionysus and Apollo, between religion and skepticism, affirmation and negation, irrationalism and analysis, passion and cerebration. Subtitled "Versuch einer Mythologie," Bertram's book made Nietzsche's life into a "myth of the believing doubter," and in seeing himself as the model through which his friend had come to understand Nietzsche, Thomas could also see Nietzsche as the model through which he had come to understand himself. The passage in Bertram's introduction, "Legende," which bears most closely on this feeling is a passage that probably had roots in conversations between the two men: "[W]e know only what we look at, and we look only at what we are, and because we are that . . . a great or 'significant' man is always, ineluctably, our own creation, just as we are his. If we strive to clarify our impression of a man, what appears in our consciousness is only for today, only for us, only for this moment."7

This helped to vindicate the method Thomas used in his critical essays, treating each subject in terms of common denominators. As he said, "Criticism that is not confessional in character is worthless. The really deep and passionate critique is poetic in the sense of Ibsen: putting oneself on trial."8

One effect of the book was to deepen Thomas's feeling for Bertram, and he got angry with Katia, who bridled when he said he was proud of their friendship. He took no pride in most of his other friendships. He had too many followers whose adherence struck him as degrading: Obliquely, it confirmed all his self-deprecation. Bertram was "almost the only exception."[9]

But he cheered himself up by concentrating on the baby, Elisabeth, whom he adored. He often took her into his room, enjoyed carrying her about, and spent time on trying to keep her entertained. Taking her pot-bellied roly-poly doll, he made it dance on the table for her.[10] She inspired him to write a long poem in hexameters, "Song of the Little Child" ("Gesang vom Kindchen"), which he started drafting in prose on November 2, and his mother, who now seemed fragile, muted, and old, touched him most deeply when she enthused over the baby.[11] The prose was then converted into hexameters, but later, when Thomas asked Hofmannsthal what he thought of them, the answer was: "It's good that you're not any better."[12]

As he'd written when she was born, he and Katia regarded the family as complete; now, suffering from morning sickness, she felt sure she was pregnant again, though her gynecologist, Dr. Hermann Faltin, assured her she wasn't.[13] When he finally acknowledged she was, they agreed she should have an abortion, but after the doctor at the hospital, Friedrich Müller, had provided the necessary certificate, she changed her mind, and Thomas's hesitation was based partly on anxiety that a new baby would "subtract something from the experience" of Elisabeth, whom he regarded "in a certain sense" as his first child.[14] Always superstitious about numbers, he may also have felt nervous of exceeding the quota of children his parents had allowed themselves.

As it became clearer that defeat was imminent, he became more apprehensive about the Allies' intention of rendering their enemy impotent.[15] To bludgeon the country into democracy would be to dismantle the old, romantic, imperial Germany,[16] driving people away from the experience of Goethe, Luther, Frederick the Great, and Bismarck.[17] As a writer, Thomas was rooted in this tradition, and if it was cut off, there might be no raison d'être for his work in the future. Sometimes he thought it would be better to die.[18]

He felt outraged and humiliated by the widespread willingness to admit that Germany had been in the wrong, and he hated the endemic remorse and self-abnegation. He believed the fatherland had heroically preserved its honor throughout an "impossible" war, while the Allies were being "heartless and hypocritical" in their demands.[19] It was absurd to assume the enemy had always been in the right, and that Germany could be reformed by foreigners.[20] Heinrich promulgated this view: In speeches he called the Germans "sons of defeat."21

Published at the beginning of October, *Reflections* aroused a lot of lively interest. Fischer had printed six thousand copies, which were soon sold out, and a new impression was needed before the end of the year. By the end of 1919, fourteen thousand copies had been sold. Press reactions, as Thomas had expected, were generally unfavorable, but he received many approving letters, mostly from strangers. Writing in the *Münchener Neueste Nachrichten*, Kurt Martens predicted that he'd become "still more isolated in his proud solitude," and in the *Münchener Blätter für Dichtung und Graphik*, Paul Amann launched such a devastating attack that sixteen years had to pass before their friendship could be reinstated.

The appearance of this antidemocratic book coincided with the formation of a democratically oriented government. At the end of September, when Ludendorff warned Chief of the General Staff Field Marshall Paul von Hindenburg and Chancellor Count von Hertling that an armistice was urgently needed, he advised them to form a government that would strike the Allies as liberal and representative. Suddenly the three majority parties in the Reichstag—the Center, the Social Democrats, and the Progressives—were "commanded to take over power," as the historian Theodor Eschenburg put it in *Die improvisierte Demokratie*.22 They regrouped under a new chancellor, Prince Max von Baden, and at a cabinet meeting the Social Democrat Philipp Scheidemann said how shameful he found it that the democratic changes his party had consistently advocated were now being made under pressure from the enemy.23

The state's genuflection to liberalism failed to make Thomas recant. In his view, the only hope for the future lay in the possibility of separating cultural and national life from politics. One evening in November, walking home with friends, he deliberately interrupted a political conversation to comment on the beautifully starry sky. Eternity, he maintained, induces a contemplative mood, and what is human is fundamentally alien to politics.24

But politics asserted itself in November, when violence broke out on the streets. Karl Marx had expected a proletarian revolution to start in Germany and spread over Europe, while to Lenin it seemed tragic that none of the parties could lead the German workers into insurrection. Most people, exhausted by over four years of war, had become politically lethargic, and the only party to favor revolutionary violence was the Spartacus Union, led by Karl Liebknecht and Rosa Luxemburg, a Pole intent on the moral transformation of Germany. Even when the shooting began on November 10, the people, according to the diary of the diplomat Harry Graf Kessler, "did not lose their *sang-froid*. . . . A great contrast to 1914, when they were all impatient to sacrifice themselves."25

Von Baden had been negotiating for an armistice, but at the end of October, wanting to avoid ignominious surrender, the naval high command ordered the fleet at Kiel to attack the British navy. This would have been suicidal, and a mutiny broke out, culminating in the creation of a sailors' council, which took control of the big naval base at Wilhelmshaven. Sailors and workers marched on the town hall in Hamburg, and there were scattered uprisings all over Germany. In the north the government could no longer rely on the obedience of the army, while in the south, the surrender of Austria-Hungary and the dissolution of the Habsburg empire made Bavaria vulnerable.

Since 1917 the Independent Socialist Party there had been led by Kurt Eisner, a demagogue who'd been imprisoned for his antiwar agitation. After being released in mid-October, he rallied enough support from soldiers and members of the Bavarian Peasants' League to capture the military headquarters in Munich. Going into town on November 7, Thomas heard shouts of "Down with the dynasty" and "Republic!" The shops were closed, no trams were running, and in the crowded streets a soldier, carried about on people's shoulders, was making speeches. Red flags were being waved, and in the evening intermittent gunfire was accompanied by fireworks explosions, as if people were celebrating the dawn of a new age.[26]

On November 8, Thomas read in the newspaper, which arrived late, that Eisner had proclaimed a Bavarian republic with himself as head of state. In Berlin the Social Democrats were demanding the kaiser's abdication, and on November 9, hoping to fend off revolution, von Baden resigned in favor of Friedrich Ebert, president of the Social Democrats, a forty-seven-year-old trade-unionist and saddle-maker, who was instructed to call a Constituent Assembly with power to decide what form the new state should take. Ebert's instincts were monarchist, but, nervous of being outmaneuvered by left-wing extremists, he supported the republicans. It was announced that the kaiser had resigned—in fact, he hadn't—and that arms would be distributed to workers' and soldiers' "councils," soviets of the Russian variety.

In Munich, soldiers were selling their weapons and their uniforms. Not only shops but barracks were being looted, and food was being requisitioned by the council. In the Pienzenauerstrasse, Thomas read a poster proclaiming the council's authority and calling on workers to form a civil guard. Back at the house he was telephoned by "Citizen Bertram," who said shops were being looted in the city. He could still hear gunfire, and according to a schoolfriend of the children, the son of a policeman, the mob might soon descend on the Herzogpark. In the afternoon Katia and the children emptied the pantry, hiding most of the food in other parts of the house.[27] Expecting a mob of looters to arrive, Thomas prepared a short speech: "Listen—I'm neither a Jew nor a war profiteer nor anything else that's bad. I'm a writer who has built this house from money he earned through brainwork. In my drawer I have two hundred marks. Take the money and divide it between you, but don't destroy my things or my books."[28]

Ambivalent about the revolution and constantly shifting his position, he had bitter arguments with Katia, who was less hostile to democracy and more hostile to the revolution. Sometimes he spoke out against communism, and sometimes defended it, especially when the revolution seemed to be reducing the danger of a humiliating peace settlement. Sometimes he wanted the Reich to disintegrate, and sometimes he said he had nothing against the downfall of the monarchy provided that the unity of the Reich, including German Austria, was preserved. But so many rumors were circulating that he couldn't be sure what was going on. A revolution was said to have broken out in Paris, and shooting was reported in Berlin. Hindenburg and the kaiser were both said to have fled to Holland.[29] This was true. On November 10, twelve cars drove up to the Belgian frontier; the kaiser and kaiserin had arrived with their servants and possessions. To Thomas, it looked as if the future belonged not to democracy but to socialism.[30] Both Munich and Bavaria, he complained, were being governed by Jewish writers— Erich Mühsam was organizing the students on behalf of the council, which had Bruno Frank and Heinrich's friend Wilhelm Herzog among its members. How long would Munich put up with Jews in positions of power?[31]

When the armistice was signed on November 11, Germany promised to surrender all guns, warplanes, and U-boats. The surface fleet was to be interned in British waters. The Allied blockade of Germany was to continue, and Allied troops were to occupy the Rhineland, with Germany paying for their upkeep.

"Something was wrong with the peace," Klaus wrote. "Nobody seemed to like it. In fact, people now looked more apprehensive even than during the war."[32] Ebert's authority was challenged by the councils, by the Spartacus Union (which at the beginning of 1919 was to become the German Communist Party), and by the Independent Socialists, while bands of leaderless troops were wandering about, looting and taking advantage of unarmed citizens. The shortage of coal made it hard to celebrate the first postwar Christmas. Theaters, cinemas, and concert halls couldn't be heated; shop windows couldn't be lit, though shopkeepers were mostly too scared of looters, anyway, to display their goods.

In January 1919, Thomas still believed that if the revolution hadn't broken out, Germany could have won the war. England, France, and the United States had nothing new to offer: Their entire wartime ideology had consisted of scraps left over from the revolution of 1789.[33]

Woodrow Wilson's speeches were "unctious," and the disarmament of Germany was a disgusting swindle.[34]

Turning his back on the chaos to concentrate on the poem about his baby daughter, Thomas was giving himself a holiday from the preoccupations of *Reflections*. As the poem grew, he read it to Katia, who approved, except when he touched on intimate marital details.[35] During the morning of February 21 he was working on the poem when she burst into his room to say Eisner had been killed. It wasn't clear whether the assassin was an army officer or a member of a student fraternity. In fact, it was a young nobleman, Count Arco-Valley. In retaliation a member of the Revolutionary Workers' Council went to the Landtag and shot the Social Democrat leader Erich Auer. The young count struck Thomas as idiotic, but at schools children danced with joy at the news of Eisner's death.[36]

The two assassinations inaugurated a phase of revolutionary violence. Hostility was growing between the Landtag and the councils, which were being infiltrated by Communists. At meetings in beer halls, unemployed workers called for revolution, and the new leader of the Social Democrats, Johannes Hoffman, decided to withdraw the Landtag to Bamberg. On February 22, denouncing him for absconding, the council proclaimed that the Landtag was dissolved and that Bavaria was to be a soviet republic. Thomas, who could hear hand grenades exploding as looters clashed with soldiers, didn't know whether the dissolution of the Landtag was meant to be permanent. He was apprehensive about Bavaria's relations with the rest of the Reich, and about the food shortage, but he was glad looting had become a capital offense and that security guards had been posted. But by Monday, February 24, the moderates seemed to be in the ascendant. The soviet system hadn't been implemented, and workers were no longer being armed.[37]

Though he read newspapers avidly, trying to find out what was happening, Thomas carried on with his routine. Gunfire in the distance didn't stop him from sleeping,[38] but he was annoyed when a seven o'clock curfew deprived him of his evening walk.[39] He worked steadily on the poem, and in early March, wanting to finish it somewhere he could count on being left in peace, stayed at a hotel in Feldafing on the Lake of Starnberg. When the poem was finished on March 25, he counted lines and found there were 977.[40]

In Feldafing he saw the art dealer Georg Martin Richter, who during October had sold him a Dutch painting and a French marble relief, promising to find buyers for them at higher prices. Wanting to build a country house, Richter had bought a piece of land there and invited Thomas to invest in it. For 10,000 marks, a bedroom and a study would be put permanently at his disposal, and there would be a housekeeper to look after him whenever he wanted to stay there in Richter's absence.

By the end of March the deal was done, and the builders started work.

In mid-March, at a memorial service for Eisner, Heinrich acclaimed him as a martyr who had more creative ideas in the last hundred days of his life than other people had in fifty years. "Sickening," commented Thomas.[41] After a soviet republic had been proclaimed in Hungary, and the whole Socialist Party had gone over to communism, Thomas welcomed what he saw as a reaction to Allied imperialism. "Uprising against bourgeois rhetoric! Nationalist insurrection after being worn to a pulp by the cheating phrases of that riff-raff, and, for all I care, in the form of Communism—a new 1 August 1914! I feel like running out into the streets shouting 'Down with the western democracy of lies! Three cheers for Germany and Russia! Three cheers for Communism!' "[42] And in early April, when it looked as if a soviet republic would be proclaimed in Bavaria, allied with the Russian and Hungarian soviets, he wrote: "I almost love communism to the extent that it is aligned against the Entente."[43]

Two days later, when the republic was proclaimed, he thought the rest of Germany might follow suit, which would convince the proletariat in the Allied countries that nothing further was to be gained from the capitalist exploitation of Germany. Workers couldn't be expected to go on believing their interests were identical with those of capital.[44] But he was deeply confused and ambivalent. He was pleased when the soviet government was overthrown on the night of April 12, and the Hoffmann administration regained control, but he thought the old order was finished. He said he'd welcome a socialist revolution so long as it denied the Allies their victory, but two days later he wanted the "Whites" to march in and restore bourgeois order. After another two days, leaflets were dropped from planes sent by the Landtag in Bamberg. The citizens of Munich should hold out. "Our troops are on the way."[45]

In the midst of this turmoil, with a new baby due on the nineteenth or twentieth, few writers could have resumed work on a novel that had been put aside over four years earlier. But as soon as the poem was finished—he had conceived it as an "idyll" to be published with "Master and Dog"—he went back to *The Magic Mountain*. On April 8 he brought manuscript and notes back from the house in Arcisstrasse, where he had stored them, but when he reread the narrative, the "pathological undercurrent" struck him as old-fashioned. While the idylls were imbued, he thought, with the spirit of the future, this was lacking in his prewar work; he was glad he hadn't completed *The Magic Mountain* before he'd understood that the end of the war was the beginning of the Communist revolution. The main focus had been on a conflict between humanistic rationalism, with Settembrini as its spokesman, and reactionary Christianity, which had been represented by a Protestant pastor, Bunge. The old dualism—soul and body, church and state, life and death—had been superseded by a new conception of man as a mind-body entity and a renewal of the *civitas Dei* in a humanist guise. He could see now that Bunge and Settembrini were "equally right and wrong in their viewpoints." But there was plenty of scope for satire on the old epoch.[46]

By April 19, the Saturday of the Easter weekend, he was ready to make a start, though Katia could go into labor at any minute. On Sunday he wrote a new opening to the first chapter, which he wanted to expand by introducing Hans Castorp's grandfather and the symbolic christening basin he'd used in "Song of the Little Child." He decided to rewrite the whole text of the novel on the better-quality paper he'd used for *Reflections*. Copying—and making changes—would be the best way to regain control over his material.[47]

On Easter Monday, April 21, he was awakened at six in the morning by footsteps overhead. Labor had begun, but he left everything to the midwife and Dr. Kockenerger, who'd arrived earlier in the morning. Though the pains were coming so rapidly that Katia expected the baby to be born within two hours, he went back to bed, and found, when he got up at seven, that the pains had slowed down. Waiting for the physician, Dr. Ammann, Thomas opened his mail and read a review of *Reflections* in the *Tägliche Rundschau*. After a great deal of pain, and with the aid of forceps, Katia gave birth to a healthy boy in the middle of the day. Afterward, she had a fit of convulsive sobbing, and in the next few days she wept a great deal. Inflammation had developed on her breast, and she had to stay in bed until May 4. Thomas knew it would give her a psychological boost to have another son, but he couldn't summon up any of the tenderness he'd felt from the first moment for Medi.[48]

With the other children he vacillated between irritability and tenderness. One day he hit Klaus for helping himself to a snack just after he'd been told not to, and a couple of weeks later he got very angry with him for tickling Golo so hard that he screamed. But it was touching that the thirteen-year-old Erika acted as deputy housewife while her mother was having the baby.[49] They decided to call him Michael.

Though Thomas had reservations about the "cultural Hottentotism" of the Communists,[50] at the outset of this new phase of work on *The Magic Mountain* he believed that a Communist future was the synthesis toward which the fictional dialectic must work.[51] But by the end of April, the Communist regime seemed to be disintegrating as government troops moved toward Munich. They encountered little resistance on May 1 as they took control of the city. Thomas, who confessed to feeling liberated and cheerful, was appalled by the Communists' last act of brutality—killing and mutilating a hundred hostages, including titled ladies.[52] Reprisals were brutal: In the White terror that ensued, almost a thousand people were killed, many of them innocent of any revolutionary activity. But by May 5, when the red flags had disappeared from the city, Thomas concluded it was easier to live under military dictatorship than under the rule of the *crapule*.[53]

The name of the Weimar Republic stems from a February 1919 meeting of the National Assembly in Goethe's hometown to lay down the constitutional foundations for a democratic Germany. Undeniably, part of the motivation was to persuade the Allies to grant favorable terms for a peace settlement, but the stratagem failed. At Versailles on May 7 the German delegates were presented with a treaty they found unacceptable. Fighting an election at home, the British premier David Lloyd George had promised to "squeeze the German lemon until the pips squeak," but the French were still more severe, and the final terms were so harsh that Lloyd George said within twenty-five years another war would have to be fought at three times the cost.

On May 20 the deadline for signing was extended, and the Allies' refusal to modify their demands prompted the resignation of the foreign minister, Count von Brockdorff-Rantzau, at the end of May, and the chancellor, Philipp Scheidemann, three weeks later. It was only under threat of military occupation that the German delegates finally gave in, and a treaty was signed on June 20, setting the figure for provisional reparations at 20 billion gold marks, and making Germany give up territory with a population of 7 million. The left bank of the Rhine was to remain under Allied occupation for up to fifteen years. The Germans blamed Woodrow Wilson, who was breaking his promise of peace on the basis of his Fourteen Points. Thomas, who went on despising him, was pleased when he was described (by the cultural historian Rudolf Pannwitz) as "the old washerwoman of the ocean."[54]

At the end of July the deputies adopted the Weimar Constitution, using a basis of universal suffrage and proportional representation, with seats allocated to names on party lists, which meant that membership of the Reichstag would in fact be determined by party activists.

IT'S EASY TO SEE WHY MAY was a difficult month for Thomas, but hard to understand what made him leave Katia on her own for a week with the new baby and the other children. In his diary for May 1 he records "Erotic night." Though he often uses this phrase to mean that he made love to her, he can hardly have done so only ten days after she'd given birth and when she was still so ill. In the entry for May 16 he uses another word, "onset" (*Anfall*), by which he sometimes means intercourse, but it doesn't seem to have that meaning in "A sexual onset yesterday, some time after going to sleep, had very severe nervous consequences: great agitation, anxiety, continuous sleeplessness, trouble in the stomach in the form of heartburn and discomfort. . . . Today very exhausted and ravaged."[55] If Katia was involved in neither the erotic night nor the sexual onset, the reference is to some solitary attempt at relieving sexual tension, and if he was upset, it must have been mainly with himself.

On May 13, Richter had invited him to Feldafing, and on the sixteenth he decided to go. He wanted to leave the same evening, but couldn't get a travel permit till the following day, when he left for a week. Still unwell, but not, apparently, resenting his defection, Katia sent him a loving letter.[56]

In company, they could make it look as if they had an "ideal marriage." This was the impression her brother Peter got when he came back from Australia in late July.[57] In fact, Thomas, who referred in his diary to his "sexual inversion," remembered the relationship with Paul—perhaps inaccurately—as being akin to requited love.[58] Though he was gratefully aware that "poor little Katia" loved him, and though he used the word *love* for his feelings toward her, he loved her, he said, just as he loved the children. Love-making was a source of anxiety: For a few days, once a month, when she was "unwell," he had, as he put it, one thing less to worry about[59]; one concern, when they did make love, was how his nervous system and his ability to work would be affected. After an "erotic night" on June 22 he still felt subdued during the evening of the following day, but refreshed and relaxed. After indulging in "sexual excess" on November 24, he found it "intellectually beneficial"—though subsequent nervous excitement kept him awake.[60]

He was putting less energy into any of his personal relationships than he had when wooing Paul and writing about it in the abortive novel, or when wooing Katia and writing about it in *Royal Highness*. To write well, he had to have an objective other than writing well, and what preoccupied him in the aftermath of the war was the urge to strike a blow for what he thought of as Germanism when the majority of those around him seemed irresponsibly eager to renounce traditions that had nurtured everything he valued in German culture.

He'd started reading Oswald Spengler's *Untergang des Abendlandes* (*Decline of the West*) before replying to a Berlin neurologist who'd written in praise of *Reflections*. The war, said Thomas, had been partly a social revolution from the start. The defeat of Germany had completed the process of "civilising, rationalising, utilitarianising" that had been inevitable in the West, as it was in every elderly culture, and Germany's efforts during the war had been "a gigantic piece of quixotism, a mighty attempt to do battle for the Germanic Middle Ages." The denigration of German traditions, he predicted, would continue but fail to destroy them, though it might force them into a largely romantic role—representing the culture's nostalgia for when it was still young and vigorous.[61]

Spengler had got interested in the problem of time during 1912–13, when it became one of *The Magic Mountain*'s basic themes. Thomas explained this by saying they'd both been sensitive enough to pick up tensions that were still invisible but would surface during the war. It seemed likely that Spengler would have more of an impact on Thomas than any other writer since Schopenhauer.[62] Generally, Thomas thought he'd stand less chance of picking up what mattered if he were more involved in local society. He was often accused of being standoffish, but it was his solitude, he believed, that reached out to the deepest ideas and insights.[63]

Though making progress with the novel, he interrupted his work in early June, 1919, to spend a week on writing an after-dinner speech for Pfitzner's fiftieth birthday celebrations. Incorporating the phrase that had surprised him so much when the composer used it, Thomas contrasted "romantic sympathy with death" and "revolutionary sympathy with the future."[64] This formulation marks a new phase in his increasingly critical attitude to "sympathy for death."

In mid-July, accepting an invitation from Samuel Fischer, he went to stay at the Strandhotel in Glücksburg, a quiet resort near the Danish frontier. He enjoyed the beach, the swimming, and watching the two fair-haired sons of a Hamburg shipowner, who reminded him of the North German boys he used to love. "A thousand boyhood feelings overwhelm me. A pity I have already written 'Tonio Kröger.' "[65]

He was still in Glücksburg when he heard that Bonn University had awarded him an honorary doctorate. The ceremony, which took place on August 2, was already over when the telegram, dated July 28, arrived in Glücksburg. He made no secret of his delight: "With a certain amount of good will, something can be made out of such an honour."[66] Returning to Munich on August 5, he was pleased to find himself in the same railway carriage as a Jewish woman reading *Royal Highness*.

Widely sold all over Germany and Austria, his books were phenomenally lucrative. By the end of 1919, *Buddenbrooks* was in its 112th impression. During June, Fischer and Thomas had signed a new contract, covering the next six years. In 1919 he earned over 100,000 marks, but with inflation and six children to feed, this still wasn't enough. Combined with the unfulfilling marital relationship, the strain of running the household had pushed Katia to the verge of a breakdown, and in early November she was saying she couldn't go on living.[67]

Now able to command a fee of 600 marks for each reading, Thomas started organizing a February tour in the Rhineland and the Ruhr. But he put most of his energy into *The Magic Mountain*. It would be a waste of time, he'd decided, to copy out everything he'd written. Some of the old pages could be incorporated into the new draft.[68] Before breaking off in mid-November to write another essay on Fontane—he'd been rereading *Effi Briest*–he completed four chapters: nearly a quarter of the book. He was depending on Settembrini to provide the only positive moral counterweight to the fascination of disease and death, but was enjoying the "intellectual comedy" that pivoted on the "conflict between the fleshly mystique and political morality."[69] This formulation harks back to his feeling that Goethe's *Wahlverwandschaften*, which he claimed to have read five times while writing "Death in Venice," achieved the perfect "balance between sensuality and morality."[70]

In early December, 1919, a production of *Fiorenza* was due to open at the Volkstheater in Vienna, and Thomas had been invited to give a reading there. After changing his mind several times about whether to go, he traveled with Bruno Walter, stopping en route to read at Nuremberg. The Viennese audience responded enthusiastically to the play, and at the premiere Thomas took several bows with the actors.

The city was suffering acute shortages of fuel and food. Lighting was subdued everywhere because of penalties for consuming too much fuel, but Thomas enjoyed the deferential treatment he was given, and the favorable review in the *Neue Freie Presse* for his reading. He was glad to meet Richard Strauss and Paul Wittgenstein, the one-armed pianist, brother of the philosopher. Thomas saw Hofmannsthal, Musil, and Schnitzler, while in the Hofmuseum he responded warmly to pictures by Brueghel, Vermeer, and Velázquez. One of Velázquez's infantas reminded Thomas of little Elisabeth.[71] After returning to Munich on December 13, he reconstructed his Viennese experiences for Katia by reading from his diary.[72]

Three days before Christmas, Erika, Klaus, and Golo, who in January had formed a "Mimik Bund" (acting club) with their friend Ricki Hallgarten, put on Lessing's *Minna von Barnhelm* at the house of a neighbor, Erich Marcks, a historian. Both Bruno Walter, who was in the audience, and Thomas found the eight-year-old Golo irresistibly funny as the Lady in Mourning. He spoke with a lisp, and his earnest efforts to portray a ladylike melancholy were at odds with the charcoal bosom he'd tried to draw on his décolleté chest.[73]

Christmas was more enjoyable than it had been in 1918. Thomas gave Katia an umbrella, writing paper, a pair of boots, a camera, and the deluxe edition of *Master and Dog*. Elisabeth was delighted by the lights on the Christmas tree and the toys she was given. All the children were showered with presents, and at dinner they had roast goose, chocolate cake, and champagne. The only cause for anxiety was that Bauschan was ailing. Droopily sad, with no appetite for food, he was twitching and whimpering. The physician, Dr. Gruber, thought he had a lung infection and promised to send a vet, who came later in the day. Diagnosing distemper, he held out little hope. Sadly, Thomas fed Bauschan sausage in the warm spot where he liked to lie. After being taken to an animal hospital, he was put down early in the new year. He'd belonged to the Manns only two and a half years, and though no dog has been more securely immortalized, Thomas couldn't get rid of the superstitious feeling that he'd harmed the defenseless creature by bringing him to life "on another plane." In the *Münchener Neueste Nachrichten*, Bauschan was given an obituary with a heavy cross after his name.[74]

Unchartered Love

WHEN GERMANY HAD SEEMED LIKELY to be capsized by a Communist revolution, Thomas had reconciled himself with the idea, but early in 1920, he gladly came around to believing conservatism had suffered only a temporary defeat. When the cultural historian Hermann Graf Keyserling, who was married to Bismarck's granddaughter and admired *Reflections*, sent a copy of an article he'd written for the *Kreuzzeitung*, the newspaper of the Prussian conservatives' radical right wing, Thomas's response was: "Nature somehow reasserts itself in the end, and 'Germans *are* conservative'—Wagner will always be right about that. Therefore nothing is more important than to imbue German conservatism with intelligence."[1] If conservatism could be educated, he wanted to be one of the teachers, though he admired Lenin as "the only real man in the world, a Genghis Khan, the incomparably more powerful opposite of poor Woodrow Wilson."[2]

In Darmstadt, Keyserling had founded a college he called the "School of Wisdom," and, writing an open letter in support, Thomas reiterated arguments from his book: Organic bonds were preferable to emancipation; romantic uncertainty and transgression to the virtues of enlightenment. But he disapproved of the right-wing putsch attempted in March. When the government wanted to disband two of the free corps, their commanders appealed to General Baron von Luttwitz, who tried in vain to get the order reversed. In alliance with a Pan-German agrarian official, Wolfgang Kapp, Luttwitz marched on Berlin. Finding he couldn't count on his troops to fight against their wartime comrades, Ebert withdrew his government to Stuttgart.

Thinking Ebert had "already messed things up too badly," Thomas sympathized with Kapp's intention of reinstating "honour and honesty," but thought the coup premature and likely to be damaging, "seriously compromising the conservative idea, which has been gaining so much ground throughout the country."[3] The Kapp regime collapsed the day after Thomas wrote these words. It couldn't survive the general strike that ensued when Ebert asked the working class to defend the republic.

Working on *The Magic Mountain* in a Reich liable to disintegrate, Thomas couldn't keep up with events. Though he believed his "seismographic sensitivity" had picked up international tensions before the war, he had founded so much of the fiction on prewar Germany that he now regretted leaving the book unfinished for so long.[4] But when he read passages to Katia, her reactions were often helpful. In January she'd approved his decision to reverse the order of the first two chapters, and later he made a "technical" change she suggested.[5] She was still ailing, and what started as a cold in late February kept her in bed through the first half of March. One evening, when she asked him to massage her back, ribs, and breasts, he felt sexually aroused.[6] In April, Dr. Leo Hermanns recommended rest, milk, and sunlamp treatments, and in May she had her lungs X-rayed.[7] Repelled and fascinated by the disease festering inside the body he knew so well, Thomas explored his ambivalence in *The Magic Mountain*. Through illness, Hans reflects, the body asserts its independence from the rest of the self. He feels guilty about falling in love with a woman who's inwardly diseased, and, disapproving of her slapdash behavior, he equates lack of discipline with illness. But he finds Clavdia irresistible.

If she's irresistible to the reader, it's partly because her body, posture, and way of moving are, unlike Imma's, brought graphically to life. We share Hans's annoyance when Clavdia lets the dining room door slam, raises her arms prettily, and glides to her seat; we share his admiration for the line of her thigh, her back, her neck bone, and the arms that press her small breasts together. Unlike the full-breasted Marusja, who attracts Joachim, Clavdia has a boyish figure, and Hans's pursuit of her is reminiscent of the way Aschenbach kept stalking Tadzio through the hotel, shamelessly willing to squander time on waiting about in a foyer or walking up and down a corridor when the loved one was likely to appear.

But the self-betrayal in *The Magic Mountain* is different from the self-betrayal in "Death in Venice": Thomas is more aware of his weakness for it, and more sophisticated when indulging himself. He even theorizes about self-revelation, saying men in Hans's condition crave it, feeling "a drive and pressure to display themselves . . . a blind self-involvement and a desire to fill the world with themselves. How such people start to betray themselves is hard to explain; they seem incapable of doing anything or leaving anything undone unless it betrays them."[8] But Thomas, who wasn't in love, finds subtle ways of betraying himself. His preference for women with boyish figures is almost invisible behind the statement by the doctor, Hofrat Behrens, that the plasticity of the female form consists of nothing but fat. Discussing the doctor, who's also an amateur painter, Thomas is simultaneously discussing the professional writer who's also an amateur of disease. It's advantageous for the artist, says the doctor, if instead of having only a lyrical relationship to his subject, he has scientific knowledge of what's going on under the epidermis. Thomas couldn't have written *The Magic Mountain* without his penchant for disease, and it was helpful that Katia kept bringing him into contact with doctors, clinics, X-rays, and conflicting ideas about how to cure tuberculosis.

Politically, though, she was still at odds with him. Talking to the children about socialism, she took a position which struck him as negatively critical, and she couldn't persuade him to vote in the Landtag elections, which coincided with his forty-fifth birthday on June 6, 1920—the first national poll since the ballot for the National Assembly.[9] The center parties did badly, and the Independent Socialists well, though their success was to be short-lived. The general swing was to the right, and away from republicanism. The Weimar coalition was left in control of less than half the 452 seats. Of the bourgeois parties, the Nationalists became the strongest, and, rather than serve in a new, predominantly bourgeois coalition, Ebert's party withdrew, leaving space for a bourgeois government to be formed.

Against this background, Thomas tried (when writing to Carl Maria Weber in early July) to analyze his attitude to bourgeois values. As a paterfamilias by instinct and conviction, he said, he was typically bourgeois, but not in his eroticism. In *Reflections* he'd said life represents the male principle and mind the female. There can be no union between them, only unresolvable tension. "The mind that loves is not fanatical, it is spirited, it is political, it woos, and its wooing is erotic irony." No reader is likely to take this as confessional, but Thomas calls it "self-betrayal," saying it sums up his own experience of eroticism, and he summarizes Friedrich Hölderlin's poem *Sokrates und Alkibiades*, which justifies and explains "the emotional tendency in question." After quoting the line "Those who have thought most profoundly love what is most alive," Thomas endorses a comment Stefan George had made on "Death in Venice": In it the highest things are dragged down into decadence. Yes, says Thomas, but without denial or denigration.[10]

Sometimes he implies an underground connection between homoeroticism and disease. In the novel, when Dr. Krokowski delivers his Freudian lecture to the patients, he talks about "bourgeois resistance that sets itself against love."[11] His argument is that the compulsive force of love is checked by conformist tendencies that encourage chastity. Once suppressed, the unchartered love can reappear in the form of illness. Sitting behind Clavdia, Hans tells himself it's as senseless to desire a sick woman as it had been to desire Pribislav Hippe. Again and again Thomas comes back to this theme of unchartered love where there can be no union, only unresolvable tension and erotic irony.

Though he was fairly cautious in these chapters and in the letter to Weber, the self-examination may have influenced marital relations with Katia, which became more strained during the summer. In his diary on

July 14 he recorded a "rencontre" in which his failure had probably been caused not by impotence but by desire that went in another direction. What if a young man had been at his disposal?[12]

The next day he took her and the children with him to Feldafing, but she stayed only four days; he stayed on for another five after she'd left and began to find their thirteen-year-old son looked terribly handsome in his bathing trunks. What could be more natural than for a man to fall in love with his son? Klaus was confused and sometimes scared by his father's unpredictable behavior. Sometimes Thomas was almost too affectionate, at others fiercely authoritarian. In October, hearing a noise in the room Klaus shared with Golo, Thomas went in to find Klaus "completely naked in front of Golo's bed, fooling around. Strong impression of his developing, magnificent body. Strong emotion."[13] But, finding Klaus indolent and self-satisfied, Thomas sometimes reprimanded him sternly. "After all, it is one's duty not to protect oneself by sidestepping the unpleasant emotion of anger."[14] Often, though, Thomas would leave Katia to do all the scolding, and would pretend not to know there had been any altercation.[15] She didn't know how much Klaus had guessed about the nature of his father's love for him. Neither of them could talk frankly to their son, or help him. Klaus's homosexuality and drug addiction both had roots in this evasive silence.

The closest he got to articulating a reaction to his father's desire for him was in a 1924 story called "Der Vater lacht" ("The Father Laughs"). The boyish daughter, Kunigunde, bears a physical resemblance to Klaus; the father, who is called Hoffmann, is modeled on Thomas, and when he harangues Kunigunde, the words are probably taken from harangues Klaus had suffered. At the end of the story, she flirts provocatively with her father in a hotel, asking whether he'd like her to dance for him, challenging him to kiss her, questioning whether he's afraid.[16] Klaus, like his phlegmatic father, who kept silent about his passions until he could achieve a literary consummation, was turning to literature—perhaps in the hope that a confrontation would be unavoidable if his father read what he'd written. The confrontation never came.

On July 23, 1920, traveling back to Munich by train, Thomas bought a third-class ticket and found himself sitting next to a young man in white trousers. They got into conversation. At home he felt disconcerted when he saw Klaus lying on his bed, shirtless and tanned. Writing in his diary later that evening, Thomas asked whether he'd finally lost interest in heterosexual lovemaking.[17] Three months later he was still feeling grateful to Katia for her unfaltering love, and though he could no longer bring her to orgasm, she accepted this uncomplainingly.[18] In her letters to him when they were separated, she addressed him with such phrases as "Dear Little Lamb" and "Dear Deer," and signed herself "Little Hare" or "Katiulein."[19]

Less than three months after Bauschan's death, Thomas bought a new dog from a policeman who'd offered to find one for him. It was a small German shepherd, and the price was 750 marks. Using the name that had been Bauschan's before he joined the Mann family, Thomas called the new dog "Lux." He seemed good-tempered, friendly, and alert, but he wasn't properly housebroken, and he made several attempts to run away. Two weeks after buying him, Thomas let him into his room, and had to clean up after him.[20]

THOUGH HE LATER CLAIMED to have cured himself of conservatism by writing *Reflections*, Thomas's viewpoint didn't change after the war ended. In March 1920 he supported the bourgeois republic because Germany couldn't have survived economically without help from the Western democracies, but this was no reason for adopting their political ideas,[21] and in the novel he went on satirizing the humanist liberalism he associated with Heinrich. Offering himself to Hans as a kind of tutor, Settembrini warns him against Russian ideas and Russian phraseology. He should cling to everything that has been sanctified by Western European traditions. Settembrini supports the International League for the Organization of Progress, which has listed all the conceivable projects for human improvement. It aims to combat human suffering in every possible way. By publishing a series of twenty volumes titled *The Sociology of Suffering*, the League will prove that individual suffering is always caused by disease in the social organism. Settembrini's contribution will be to summarize in one volume all the literary masterpieces that depict conflict. But the character isn't based entirely on Heinrich. Thomas takes the opportunity to distance himself from earlier statements of his own. The equation of good writing with clear thinking and commendable behavior occurs in *Reflections*, and a passage in praise of the literary spirit as the noblest manifestation of the human mind is taken verbatim from "Tonio Kröger."

Working on the sequence about the International League in late May, when he called the project a comic bit of rationalism,[22] Thomas was thinking in terms of a polarity between rationalism and romanticism. In early July he read a book on German romanticism by Georg Brandes, the Danish literary historian whose six-volume history of nineteenth-century literature had influenced *Buddenbrooks*. Recognizing that Novalis had articulated some of the ideas featured in *The Magic Mountain*–Thomas hadn't realized that they might not be new–he was looking forward to the disputes he was going to write between Settembrini and Pastor Bunge. Bunge hadn't yet been abandoned in favor of Naphtha, but Thomas was already planning to let the argument culminate in a duel.[23]

Making fun of Settembrini may have helped him to soften his antagonism toward Heinrich, and in mid-December, writing to Philipp Witkop, who was working on a book about contemporary Germany, Thomas asked to be discussed together with Heinrich in the chapter on narrative.[24] More than a year was still to elapse before the brothers were reconciled.

In December he left Munich again with Katia for three days in Berlin, where he took part in a conference on orthographic reform. Prompted by school authorities, the Ministry of the Interior had formed a committee to modernize spelling by simplifying it. The committee, which had been meeting since the beginning of the year, had invited Thomas to represent the writing profession at the December meetings. In Berlin he and Katia stayed at the Hotel Excelsior, visited the Rosenbergs and her brother, went twice to the theater and had lunch with the Fischers. Back in Munich he enjoyed reading to friends from the novel, but the pleasures of Christmas were dulled by influenza, and, exhausted, he felt the need for a quiet spell of work in Feldafing.[25] He was hoping to complete *The Magic Mountain* within the next twelve months.[26]

The quality of a novel depends, as he said in his diary, on the writer's ability to keep the ideas simultaneously in his mind while maintaining control over all the motifs and threads of narrative.[27] It follows that interruptions can be detrimental, but in spite of the 25 percent royalty and the demand for his books in the shops, he couldn't afford to miss opportunities of giving lucrative readings. He also enjoyed reviewing books and writing prefaces.

Nineteen twenty-one started with a performance by the children of Shakespeare's *As You Like It* at the Hallgartens' house, and Erika's acting impressed her father, who found her enchanting.[28] The next day he paid a friendly teatime visit to Paul Ehrenberg, who was married to the painter Lily Teufel. They lived in the Schwabing.[29] But on January 3, Thomas left Munich for Feldafing again, to work not on the novel but on an introduction for a special issue of the *Süddeutsche Monatshefte* devoted to Russian literature. Ever since deciding that Germany was culturally closer to Russia than to England, France, or Italy, he'd felt well disposed toward Russian writers, especially Tolstoy.

After returning to Munich, he left again on January 17 to tour Switzerland. One of the places where he gave readings was Davos, which struck him as dreamlike. After an absence of nine years, it felt odd to be in the place he'd been trying to visualize while writing the novel. He was met at the station by a journalist, Martin Platzer, and taken by sleigh to the pump room, where he met Niddy Impekoven, a German dancer who was going to perform at a banquet after the ice carnival, which they watched in the afternoon. The next day he went for a sleigh ride and spent the evening in the café at the sanatorium. On February 1, before reading in the music room there, he watched a bobsled race in the ice rink. The audience at the reading included Dutch and English people taking the cure. He called on Dr. Jessen at the Wald-sanatorium, met the owner of another sanatorium, and went to see a third, constantly looking for usable details and making notes. On February 2, climbing the Schatzalp with Platzer, he got up to above 6,600 feet. To the west, the blue sky looked almost black, and on the way down Thomas fell, but without hurting himself.

In Davos—if his experiences were assigned directly to Hans—sleighs were jingling up and down the main street, which was lined with luxurious shops and crowded with bronzed people in expensive sports clothes. The four-cornered rink—in summer it was a meadow—was at the bottom of the valley. While a band played in the gallery of the wooden pavilion, professional skaters performed with furred and braided jackets over close-fitting costumes of black tricot. Invalids from the sanatorium were vastly outnumbered by elegant spectators in brightly colored clothes, chatting in various languages, shouting encouragement and bursting into applause. Even the café at the pump room was bustling with activity. Music was supplied by a band in red uniforms, and the dancing became livelier as the evening advanced: Patients from the sanatoria arrived, and visitors from the hotels.

Thomas left Davos on February 3, arriving in the evening at Munich, where Katia was waiting at the station. He allowed only one day to pass before he started revising the novel on the basis of notes he'd taken.[30] He left again on February 11 for a tour in North Germany and Thuringia. In Gera he was met at the station by Grete Litzmann, wife of Berthold Litzmann, a privy councillor and professor of literature in Bonn. On February 16, when Thomas went to Weimar, Nietzsche's sister, Elisabeth, who was in the audience, came up to him afterward. Her eyes were like her brother's. The next day, when he breakfasted with her, the mayor of Weimar, and the mayoress, she talked about the last years in her brother's life. His good manners had survived even into advanced stages of madness.

Thomas went on to Halle, where he saw Frau Litzmann, who turned out to be "terrifyingly, hysterically in love" with him, and insisted the next day on accompanying him as far as Naumburg. He found the reading there strenuous and unrewarding, but in Berlin, where the auditorium was both overcrowded and overheated, the applause was "almost frantic, shattering," and people milled around him afterward, paying tribute and asking for his autograph. He bought dolls for the younger children, and, going home on Tuesday, February 22, he found an embarrassing letter from Frau Litzmann. He read it to Katia.[31]

At the end of February the weather was so mild he could usually take his afternoon nap on the balcony, and he made headway with the

novel, using recent observations and experiences during the ice carnival
and climbing the Schatzalp. But he had to deal with correspondence
that had accumulated, and to sign several hundred sheets for a deluxe
edition of his story "The Blood of the Walsungs."32

His reading covered a wide range of subjects, including biology, and
the seventh section of Chapter 5, which is titled "Research" ("Forschun-
gen"), summarizes what Hans learns from books on anatomy, physiol-
ogy, and biology. Consciousness, he comes to believe, is a function of
matter organized into life, while life is a fever which accompanies the
incessant process of decay, a warmth generated by an instability that
preserves form. When Thomas read this section to the Austrian writer
and translator Emil Alphons Rheinhardt, he "as a medical man raised
various objections."33

In March, when Thomas dipped into *Theoretische Biologie* by Baron
Jakob Johann Uexküll, he noted that interest in biology—even in the
newer, less mechanistic, anti-Darwinian biologists—tended to encourage
conservatism and political rigidity.34 But the insight didn't work as a
solvent on any of his own prejudices. Going for a walk with three
young members of the Werkbund, an association of artists, architects,
and craftsmen trying to raise standards in design, he encouraged them
to talk about their plan to build a sort of monastery for young men,
complete with refectory and cells. Many of their ideas, he noticed ap-
provingly, derived from Goethe and Jean Paul—the pseudonym of Johann Paul Friedrich Richter, novelist, educationalist, opponent of
"poetic nihilism" and "poetic materialism." Thomas sympathized with
the ideas that seemed to have roots in German tradition, as opposed to
"Western European political radicalism."35

His hostility to Heinrich was still partly cultural: He sneered at the
plan to celebrate Heinrich's fiftieth birthday on March 27 with a program of old Italian music. The fancy invitations also promised the
recitation of a sonnet in his praise, opera stars, fanfares, and flour-
ishes.36

Early in May, Thomas was working his way toward the climactic love
scene in the novel. The idea may have evolved out of connecting the
ice carnival in Davos with Fasching, the annual carnival in Munich on
the days leading up to Shrove Tuesday. After a long period of being
silently aware of each other, Hans and Clavdia have a conversation preceded by celebrations which subvert all normal conventions. In the afternoon many of the patients go down to the Platz, where harlequins
are shaking rattles as masked revelers skirmish verbally and throw confetti over decorated sleighs. In the evening, at all seven tables in the
sanatorium's restaurant, patients wear paper hats and blow toy trumpets
or shake rattles bought from the concierge. Paper snakes dangle from
the chandeliers, confetti swims in the sauces, and champagne is mixed

with burgundy. When the ceiling light goes out, the room is illuminated only by paper lanterns. Clavdia's new dress leaves her beautiful arms bare, and after the meal, many of the patients put on improvised fancy dress. Hans, inebriated less by alcohol than by the atmosphere, insists on talking in the second person singular to Settembrini and then to Clavdia. Speaking to her in French helps him to cast off the restraints of normality. At the table, where punch is being poured, Behrens starts a new game, drawing a pig while keeping his eyes shut.

This enables Hans to do what he has dreamed of doing: He gets into conversation with Clavdia by asking to borrow a pencil. There's another hint of autobiographical self-indulgence in the way "Oh my God!" recurs like a leitmotiv in moments of passion. Thomas associated them with Paul, and had already given them to Aschenbach.

As Hans and Clavdia talk, the other patients, losing interest in the drawing game, start dancing, and though she refuses to dance with him, their flirtatious banter goes on so long that as the dancing tails off, the others gradually leave them alone with the musicians, and, later, alone together in an empty room, surrounded by the debris of the partying. Disease is a factor in the intimacy that develops. After asking her to show him her X-ray prints, he lovingly accuses her of causing his temperature to rise and his heart to palpitate. He's desolated to hear she will leave the sanatorium the next day, returning to her husband in Russia. With a mixture of mockery and regret, she says Hans could have spoken to her sooner. He had never wanted to address her in the second person plural, he explains, provoking her to tease him for bourgeois subservience to the rules of the carnival. Later, caressing him, she calls him a pretty bourgeois with a moist spot in his lung, and, as he goes on talking, kneeling in front of her with his body quivering, babbling statements that equate love with disease, Thomas is parodying the didactic discourses delivered by Behrens and Settembrini. But the underlying equation of love with abnormality also refers to Thomas's cravings for young men.

Though "Death in Venice" isn't set during the Venetian carnival, it involves circumstances that slacken the grip of conventionality, while the love scene between Hans and Clavdia would be possible only against a carnival background. When she leaves the room, saying adieu, she calls him her carnival prince and predicts that his temperature will have risen. But he's still in possession of her pencil, and the question of what will happen next is neatly answered when, on her way out of the room, she echoes the only words Pribislav Hippe had ever uttered to him, reminding him to return it. Again Thomas is elaborating a memory of frustrated desire into a story with almost mythical dimensions.

Finishing this chapter, he knew he'd completed a decisive phase in his work, and during the second half of May he took time to find "ornamental" titles for the sections in the five chapters. He calls this section "Witches' Sabbath" ("Walpurgisnacht") and the previous one "Dance of Death" ("Totentanz"). He'd become intensely aware of his involvement with Goethe and the final spasms of Romanticism. The end of the movement, he believed, was expressing itself in a variety of ways, including a progressive weakening of the sexual symbolism that had been central to it. This weakening was visible in *Parsifal*.[37] It seemed to him that in Nietzsche nineteenth-century Romanticism had transcended itself, "joining itself with something new and inexpressible in his death on the cross of thought."[38] Romanticism was also imbued with the same spirit as nationalism, and the concept of sympathy with death was Romanticism's final word.

Straining himself to the uttermost, Thomas felt enervated, irritable, and unwell, troubled with headaches, nausea, and lassitude. The novel would have been hard to write even if he hadn't needed to keep interrupting his work, but knowing he could make lucrative use of a new lecture by repeating it all over Europe, he'd accepted an invitation to speak on Goethe and Tolstoy at Lübeck during Nordic Week, a festival to be held September 2–8. It was typical of him to start work on the lecture in May. He read a three-volume biography of Tolstoy by Pavel I. Biryukov, with the intention of going on to Albert Bielschowsky's 1896 book *Goethe. Sein Leben und seine Werke*. In early June he was feeling "so very much in arrears, so very much in the world's debt and suffering from my inadequate capacity for work."[39]

But he enjoyed the celebrations for his forty-sixth birthday on June 6. Katia, who crowned Elisabeth and the baby, Michael, with garlands of flowers, gave him an elegant-looking water-heating apparatus for the washstand, and he received a lot of presents from family and friends, including Bertram and Witkop.[40] In the evening he took Erika, Klaus, and Golo to *Carmen*. He'd been studying Don José's main aria from the piano score so that he could sing it for himself.[41]

By late June he was drafting the lecture, and in July, when the weather improved, he worked on it in the garden every day after breakfast. It was becoming too long, and when he read it to Katia, he found after two hours that he was still nowhere near the end.[42] One morning he rewrote it completely, feeling pleased with what he'd done until he was distracted by seeing a young, clean-shaven gardener with open shirt and sun-tanned arms.[43] There was no question of taking any action based on desire for the young man: Thomas was a collector of visual memories which he preserved like dead butterflies in his diaries and fiction.

Titled "The Idea of Education in Goethe and Tolstoy" ("Der Idee der Erziehung bei Goethe und Tolstoy"), the lecture contends they were both influenced by Rousseau, whose name evokes the ideas of nature, education, and autobiography. Sensuously physical, both Goethe and Tolstoy rooted their work in natural life, and though this couldn't be said of Thomas, he felt an affinity with their educational and autobiographical preoccupations. Reading and rereading Goethe's work, including *Wilhelm Meisters Wanderjahre*, he was "astonished" to find how Goethean *The Magic Mountain* was.[44] His original intention of parodying the bildungsroman had faded as Hans learned from mentors and experiences in the sanatorium, while the novel's change of direction was encouraged by Thomas's work on the lecture. Only the hero of a bildungsroman can be as retrospectively proud as Wilhelm Meister is of having made it his principal objective to achieve maturity: "from my youth onwards," he says in the *Wanderjahre*, "my purpose and desire was, obscurely, to form myself, exactly as I am." And though Tolstoy never wrote a bildungsroman, his work charts movement toward a mastery which struck many of his contemporaries as godlike. After quoting the critic Dmitri Merezkhovsky, who called Tolstoy's work "an enormous diary, kept for fifty years, an interminable, explicit confession," Thomas praises the quality Goethe called "reverence for oneself," and declares self-love to be at the bottom of all autobiography. Like both predecessors, he possessed this quality in abundance, and he seems to be indulging in self-betrayal again when he says great artists realize they have been teaching while they thought they were learning; through their power over words they have been putting their own stamp on the younger generation. This creative bliss, he maintains, surpasses all the commonplace pleasures of love and paternity.

As in *Reflections*, he struggles to define what is quintessentially German. Discussing Goethe's compulsive renunciation, he says this imperative is the essence of the German spirit, which always has a vocation to perform cultural tasks. Goethe's play *Tasso* is typically German—and schoolmasterish—in renouncing "the advantages of barbarism." Discussing Goethe's "German and Protestant aristocratism," Thomas talks about democracy no less critically than in *Reflections*, saying humanity, civilization, Christianity are all democratic. While the classical foundations of European culture are disintegrating, clues can be found in both Goethe and Tolstoy about more enduring values based on folk wisdom and the old myths.

Goethe had no enthusiasm for democracy, and if France was the country of revolution, Germany preferred things to evolve organically. Tolstoy, knowing the educated classes can't give the masses what they need, rejects European educational ideas and ideals. Lacking faith in liberalism, constitutionalism, and parliamentarianism, while feeling the primitive Russian's resentment of everything that comes from the West, he turns to the Orient, putting his faith in love, mildness, and nonresistance. Thomas sees him as a precursor of the Russian Revolution, which ended the bourgeois, liberal, humanizing epoch. The implication is that the revolutionary movement will spread to Western Europe.

THE FIRST TIME Thomas had thought of taking Katia to Lübeck, she hadn't wanted to be seen there while pregnant, but no longer having a base in Tölz, they could choose a different holiday each summer, and on Sunday, August 7, they traveled by sleeping car to Lübeck. They arrived late the following evening and were met by Bertram, still a professor in Cologne. They went into town together, visiting the Mengstrasse and Beckergrube houses. In the marketplace the architecture now reminded Thomas of Venice, and they had tea at a café facing a church.

Returning to the station with Bertram, they traveled together to Timmendorf, which is on the coast, a few miles to the east of Travemünde. They'd rented a villa there for a fortnight. Bertram was to stay with them for the first week and in fact he stayed for nine days, his departure being delayed by migraine. In the mornings, sitting on his balcony, Thomas worked on Goethe and Tolstoy, and in the evenings he enjoyed conversations with Bertram. What he enjoyed most of all, though, was seeing a well-built athlete from Hamburg, still more of a boy than a man. He looked particularly good when running. "The knowledge that I would never see him again made it hard for me to leave."[45]

On their way to Wenningstedt on the island of Sylt, Thomas and Katia stayed in Hamburg at an uncomfortable hotel—the only one they could find with a vacant room. It was good to see the North Sea again from the island, where they spent a week, staying behind the dunes in a pleasant room at the Haus Erika. On the beach were wicker shelters from which they could step directly into the powerful surf.

From there they traveled back on an overcrowded train to Lübeck, arriving late in the evening and going straight on to Ida Boy-Ed's house. Thomas delivered the lecture on September 4 to a crowded audience in the Johanneum. After visiting relations, laying a wreath in the cemetery, and being interviewed by Swedish and German journalists, he left with Katia on the ninth for Berlin, where he repeated the lecture at the Beethovensaal. The large audience was respectful, and scores of people came up to him. After two visits to the theater and several meetings with Fischer, one over breakfast at the Adlon Hotel, he and Katia returned to Munich in a sleeping car, arriving exhausted on September 13.[46]

Disconcerted by the amount of work awaiting him, Thomas decided to engage a secretary, but instead of leaving himself free to concentrate on The Magic Mountain, he'd accepted an invitation to write "On the Jewish Question" for a special issue of the Neue Merkur. On Wednesday, September 21, he started what was to become a ten-page article in the form of a letter to Efraim Frisch, publisher of the review. Thomas's intention was to show much more goodwill than when he'd previously written about the "Jewish question": "Jews have discovered me, Jews have printed and publicised me, Jews staged my impossible play. . . . And when I travel around the world, visiting cities, it is not only in Vienna and Berlin that it is almost without exception Jews who receive me, give me hospitality, feed me and make a fuss of me."[47] But in his memories of Jewish friends from his school days onward, his attitude was more condescending than he realized, and one evening in late October, when he read the article to Katia and Bertram, who'd been invited to dinner, she objected to his tone.[48] He entered into complicated discussions with Frisch about whether to make cuts or jettison the piece. They agreed to make cuts, but Thomas finally withdrew it.

In November he went to Switzerland again, delivering the lecture in Zurich, where he also went twice to the theater. He returned to Munich exhausted but exuberant about his earning capacity. A single reading could net 4,000 marks, and Eduard Korrodi, features editor of the *Neue Zürcher Zeitung*, had offered 100,000 for the serial rights to the novel. By the end of November it was clear that Thomas's income for the year would exceed 300,000 marks.[49]

But affluence was no remedy for depression. The weather was cold and slushy, Katia was in bed with a cold, while he was suffering from dyspepsia and constipation. His old underwear was too small, which showed he was putting on weight.[50] He was upset to find no mention of his work in a special issue of the *Neue Merkur* dealing with narrative. The June issue had contained an essay by Ernst Robert Curtius on "Deutschfranzösische Kulturprobleme" ("Franco-German Cultural Problems"), which had inspired André Gide to write a positive response in the November issue of the *Nouvelle Revue Française*. Thomas's essay "Das Problem der deutsch-französischen Beziehungen" ("The Problem of Franco-German Relations") reiterates arguments he'd already formulated. Answering French criticisms of *Reflections*, he argues that the contrast between the Entente's moral pretentions and its ruthless behavior proves European humanism to be obsolete and on the point of collapse. Having deeper affinities with Russia, Germany doesn't need to be capsized by the Western crisis.

Though he wanted to work on the sixth chapter of *The Magic Mountain*, he'd committed himself to a lecture tour in Eastern Europe. He took Katia with him. Because trains were canceled, the journey to Prague took thirty-six hours, and they had to spend a night in Kirchenlaibach, near Nuremberg.

In Budapest they stayed, as Thomas had before, with Josef von Lukács in his luxuriously furnished house. Lukács's younger son, Georg, the author of *Die Seele und die Formen*, was living in Vienna. He'd joined the Hungarian Communist Party in 1918 and, after taking part in the uprising of 1919, had escaped to Vienna. Thomas had intervened to save him from being extradited out of Austria to Horthy's Hungary. He'd dropped the *von* from his name and quarreled with his father, but Thomas never forgot the proud and blissful smile that appeared on the old man's face whenever he heard his son's intellectual powers being praised.[51]

In Vienna they stayed at the Hotel Imperial, where their room was burgled. Thomas lost his pearl cuff links, a wristwatch, ties, handkerchiefs, and a leather toilet kit, but the burglar, who may have been disturbed, failed to find either their money or Katia's diamonds.[52]

Thomas, who still hadn't met Georg Lukács, invited him to the hotel. He was now thirty-six and had a steely aristocratic bearing, not unlike his father's. It was hard to picture what he'd been like before his conversion to communism. They talked for nearly two hours in the hotel room, not about the Hungarian events of 1919 but about the current function of literature. Lukács did most of the talking, propounding his theories, and quoting Fichte's phrase "the age of absolute sinfulness" to argue that in such a corrupt period as the present, salvation was possible only in the political realm. "So long as he was talking, he was right. Even if the impression he left was of an almost alarming abstractness, it was also one of purity and intellectual nobility."[53]

Fraternal Armistice

THOMAS'S HOSTILITY TO DEMOCRACY could have only a limited life span. The moment had to come when not to speak out in support of it would have been to condone, and effectively support, the rise of fascism. The movement had been launched in 1919 when the Fascio di Combattimento was founded in Milan—an anti-Socialist militia that took its name from the bundles of rods carried in front of Roman magistrates. In Germany, Munich was, from the outset, a seedbed of Nazism. It was here that in 1919 a thirty-year-old ex-corporal, who was working as an informer for the army and spying for it on the activities of small political parties, joined the reactionary German Workers' Party, which had been founded earlier in the year by a machine fitter named Anton Drexler and a sports journalist, Karl Harrer. It had only 554 members: Adolf Hitler was the 555th. He was responsible for changing its name in 1920 to National Socialist German Workers' Party (NSDAP), and the next year, when he became party leader, his rabid anti-Semitism and his belief in "Aryan" superiority determined all statements of party policy, while his talents as a demagogue were fueled by a resentment he shared with a great many people, including Thomas, against financial and economic burdens inflicted on Germany by the Treaty of Versailles.

There were so many parties in the Reichstag that a majority could be attained only by a coalition, and between February 1919, when Philipp Scheidemann took office as the first chancellor, and June 1928, Germany had fifteen cabinets. None lasted more than eighteen months; some less than three. The failure of Germany's postwar republicanism is often attributed to the economically punitive Treaty of Versailles, but inflation had its roots in a decision taken before war was declared in August 1914 to pay for it not with taxes but with borrowed money. Authorizing the government to borrow up to 5 billion marks, the Reichstag suspended all restrictions on circulating notes not covered by gold reserves. This made it possible to raise money by printing it, and in 1918, when the market came back to life, confidence in the currency slumped, while inflation exacerbated mass unemployment. When Socialists and conservatives both failed to bring the situation under control, Nazism began to seem more attractive. By the beginning of 1922 a pound sterling was worth 32,000 marks, and at the end of January it was calculated that the cost of living in Germany had risen by 73.7 percent in twelve months. But by then Thomas had come to terms with democracy. And with "civilisation's *littérateur.*"

In January 1922, Heinrich was taken into the hospital with acute appendicitis that developed into peritonitis, and there was no alternative to immediate surgery even though he was suffering from bronchial catarrh, which made the doctors nervous of complications with his lungs. After the operation on January 26, the newspapers reported that his situation was serious but not hopeless.[1] After his wife, Mimi, telephoned the house in Poschingerstrasse, Katia went round to see her, and on January 31, Thomas sent flowers with a card: "They were difficult days that lie behind us, but now the worst is over and things will get better for us—together if your heart feels what mine does."[2]

Heinrich responded warmly: Whatever their differences of opinion, they should "never lose each other again." Still cautious, Thomas confided in Bertram: "Moved and happy, indeed fantastically shaken though I am, I have no illusions about the fragility and difficulty of the newly revived relationship. A modus vivendi of a humanly decent kind is the most that can be expected. Genuine friendship is barely thinkable. The memorials of our dispute still stand." Heinrich, who hadn't read *Reflections*, "knows nothing of what I have been through . . . and nothing of the way circumstances hammered me into maturity, nothing of how I developed, becoming the helper and leader of others." Written on February 2, 1922, before the brothers had met, the letter indicates a shift in his political stance: "Perhaps we can after all speak of a certain development towards each other. . . . The really dominant thought in my mind at the moment is for a new, personal fulfillment of the idea of humanity—in contrast, certainly, to the humanitarian world of Rousseau. I shall be speaking about this at the end of the month in the Frankfurt opera house before the performance of *Die Zauberflöte.*"[3] His speech in Frankfurt consisted of an extract from the essay on Goethe and Tolstoy, which had made him start thinking about Rousseau.

The change of attitude may, as he told Arthur Schnitzler, have been partly due to his work on *The Magic Mountain.* Saying he'd been aware for some time of an infatuation with humanism, he described the novel as a kind of bildungsroman in which the hero is led by experience of sickness and death to the idea of man and the state.[4] The narrative reflects the change not by making Settembrini more sympathetic but by seating him on an ironic seesaw. As Thomas said, the kind of irony he liked was the kind that deals cunningly and playfully with both sides of an argument, refusing to hurry toward a conclusion. What he wanted to achieve was not resolution of uncertainty but balance, harmony.[5]

Though Settembrini is at first Hans's only mentor, Thomas had always intended to introduce a rival viewpoint. But the character he'd kept waiting in the wings, Pastor Bunge, was now dropped in favor of a more formidable antagonist, modeled on Georg Lukács. Thomas's first mention of the new character is in a June 1922 letter to Bertram: "Leo Naphta, a partly Jewish Jesuit, has surfaced, and is constantly engaged in sharp disputations with Herr Settembrini."[6] According to Arthur Eloesser, who had a series of interviews with Thomas before publishing the first biography of him in 1925, he spoke of being supplied with Naphta's "symbolic physiognomy" when he met "a small, ugly Jew, a fanatical theoretician of steely logic who once defended every single form of absolutism and anti-individualism, from the Counter-Reformation and Jesuitism to the Communist Revolution and Leninism."[7] Naphta is described as small, thin, ugly, sharp-featured, with pale gray eyes, thick glasses, and a hooked nose. Dulled by a cold in the head, his voice sounds like a knuckle tapping on a cracked plate. But his ideas are based more on Lukács's early writings than on books written after his conversion to communism.

Looking back ironically on prewar optimism, Thomas makes Settembrini deride Naphta for predicting catastrophe, and accuse him of seeing only political trickery in the lofty exertions of democracy. Believing there is no such thing as objective or scientific truth, Naphta equates truth with whatever benefits mankind. While Settembrini believes democracy depends on individual resistance to state absolutism, and that future revolutions will bring freedom, Naphta contends that what people want and need is the kind of terror that enforces discipline, sacrifice, restraint of the ego, curbing of the personality. Thomas doesn't immediately reveal that Naphta is a Jesuit who was Jewish before he converted. What's clear from his first scene is that he favors the irrational in a way that could have made him into a Fascist. The first stirrings of Nazism had convinced Thomas that hostility to democracy was a luxury he could no longer afford: In the impassioned arguments between Settembrini and Naphta he's exploring his ambivalence by developing an antinomy between two viewpoints neither of which he shares. At the same time, he subsumes the less sophisticated argument he'd put forward in *Reflections*, distancing himself from "sympathy with death" when he makes the humanist warn Hans that death, if regarded as something distinct from life, becomes a negative power, dissolving restraint and suggesting a route through evil to salvation. Settembrini tries to discredit Naphta by saying that even if he's a voluptuary, all his thoughts stand under the aegis of death.

Thomas took his first public step toward democracy in a review published on April 16 in the *Frankfurter Zeitung*. His friend Hans Reisiger had been translating Walt Whitman, and Thomas claims that for Whitman democracy was "the same thing that we in our old-fashioned way call 'humanity' . . . I am convinced there is no more urgent task for Germany today than to fill out this word, which has been debased into a hollow shell."[8]

Few deputies in the Reichstag would have accepted this; one who would was Walther Rathenau, who'd been involved in reparations payments since May 1921 and been appointed in February 1922 as foreign minister. In April he negotiated a treaty establishing normal diplomatic relations with Lenin's government and the mutual abandonment of claims for reparations. This infuriated the extreme right, and on June 24, Rathenau was assassinated by a young anti-Semitic nationalist. The killing produced a panic, which affected the value of the mark. Several Nationalists resigned, and a law was passed for the protection of the Republic. Thomas understood the seriousness of the crisis.

> Gradually I am gaining insight into the dangers of history, which through false analogies obscures the singularity of the situation and seduces a certain kind of youth into mad actions. . . . I am thinking of turning a birthday article about Hauptmann into a kind of manifesto addressed to the conscience of the young people who listen to me. . . . I am the last to demand from youth enthusiasm for things they have inwardly outgrown, such as socialism and democracy, but . . . the new humanity may after all thrive no worse in the soil of democracy than in the old Germany. It is a question of shying away from words and rebelling. As if "the Republic" were not still the German Reich, which is in fact more accessible today than it was when dominated by historical forces that had degenerated into banal theatricality—and that is exactly what democracy is.[9]

Without referring explicitly to his comparison of Germany in 1914 with Frederick the Great's Prussia, Thomas had presumably come to think of it as a false analogy, and he no longer wanted to separate culture from politics.

Early in July he went to Heidelberg. He'd been invited to deliver his Goethe-Tolstoy lecture to a group of Swedish students who were at the university for a summer course. After being feted by young Swedish girls in national costume, he was taken to a party where, beneath colored lanterns, Swedish and German folk songs were sung to guitar accompaniment.[10]

For Erika and Klaus, who were now at boarding school, it was pleasant to be in Munich. Thomas and Katia had intended to stay there through the summer, but they took an August holiday in Ahlbeck, and he wrote most of "Vom deutschen Republik" ("On the German Republic"), the speech he was going to deliver in Berlin during October at the celebrations for Hauptmann's birthday. In it he fulfilled the intentions expressed in his letter to Bertram. By saying "we are the state," he did his best to commit intellectuals to the Republic, and, pursuing his point about false analogies, he said it would be wrong for Germany to rearm secretly as Prussia had done after being defeated in 1806. He condemned cultural nationalism and the sentimental obscurantism that disguised acts of terrorism as Germanic passion. The assassination of Rathenau had been enough to drive the most die-hard Romantic in the opposite direction.

Back in Munich and resuming work on the novel, Thomas was plunged into financial trouble that was intensified by the devaluation of the mark. At the end of August, rumors had been circulating that French troops were marching into the Ruhr after Germany's failure to pay a £2 million installment in war reparations, and the mark, which had been falling 30 or 40 points a day against the dollar, was halved in value between August 14 and 24, when it fell over a hundred points in an hour. Thomas's seventy-one-year-old mother, who'd come to recuperate from an illness in his house, insisted on paying for her meals, without understanding that the banknotes she handed over had lost their value.[11] Writing to Fischer, who'd had to raise book prices, Thomas explained that to earn money outside Germany, he'd agreed to lecture in Holland and write for an American magazine, *The Dial*.

At home on October 6, wanting to rehearse the birthday lecture, he read his text to Heinrich and a few friends. Writing to Kurt Martens on the tenth, the day before he left Munich, Thomas admitted he was uncertain how long the Republic could survive. But he wanted to proclaim his loyalty, so that if it disintegrated, none of the blame could fall on him.[12] When he delivered the lecture at the Beethovensaal in Berlin, the audience reacted as if he were campaigning for the president, Friedrich Ebert.[13]

When the lecture was published in the November issue of the *Neue Rundschau*, Ida Boy-Ed was one of many friends and supporters who found him guilty of apostasy and self-betrayal. Defending himself in December, he argued that the Republic he supported was roughly the opposite of the Republic that existed, but it was essential "to breathe something like an idea, a soul, a living spirit into this lamentable state without citizens."[14]

FIVE DAYS BEFORE CHRISTMAS Thomas attended a spiritualist séance. A specialist in nervous disease and sexual pathology, Dr. Albert Freiherr von Schrenck-Notzing had been concerned with occult phenomena for over thirty years. Published before the war, his book *Materialisations-Phänomene* had been ridiculed, but the postwar publication of the second volume had been taken more seriously. Thomas found a zoologist, a well-known actor, and a Polish painter among those waiting for the séance to begin. Speaking with an Austrian accent, the medium, Willi, a dark boy in his late teens, was giving monosyllabic answers to the questions they put. Before the séance started, he changed into a long, dark knitted garment with luminous tapes all over it, and needles with luminous heads were attached to the curtain so that people would see any movements made by him after the lights were put out. Nonstop music was to be provided by the zoologist, who produced a mouth organ from his pocket, and various objects had been collected like theatrical props—a handbell, a bell operated by a button, a slate with a piece of chalk, a typewriter with paper in the roller. Two people were put in "control" of Willi: a woman held his wrists, while Thomas was asked to hold his hands and grip the boy's knees between his. The other spectators formed a chain by making physical contact with each other.

Willi answered questions by pressing Thomas's hand to signal "Yes," moving his hands and his upper body sideways to signal "No." It wasn't until the second half of the session, when another man had taken over "control" from Thomas, that he experienced a feeling like seasickness as spirits began to assert themselves. After being dropped on the floor, the baron's handkerchief rose independently in the air three times, to be thrown finally against the table. The handbell was picked up and rung. An invisible finger pressed the button on the other bell. Two invisible hands worked at the typewriter, producing two lines of nonsense. Convinced that no trickery was involved, Thomas attended two more séances in January 1923, and because of the way he talked about his new interest, the children started holding secret séances.

THE ALLIES had been demanding 20 billion gold marks in reparations by May 1, 1921, but the gold mark was only a notion based on prewar money markets, in which a mark was worth $4. By 1921 the dollar was worth 60 marks. To raise $250 million the German government had to issue newly printed paper currency, which accelerated devaluation, and by November a dollar was worth 310 marks. Inevitably, Germany fell into arrears, and by the end of 1922 the French were intending to occupy the Ruhr, the manufacturing and mining region, on the grounds that Germany had defaulted on shipments of coal and timber.

Depending on France to protect their Middle Eastern interests, the British were in no position to restrain the aggressive Raymond Poincaré, and on January 11, 1923, French and Belgian troops marched into the Ruhr, where the workers launched a campaign of passive resistance. "It is safe to assume," Thomas wrote,

that the details about the Ruhr are not exaggerated but rather fall short of the truth. The anger is fearful—deeper and more united than that which caused the downfall of Napoleon. It is impossible to see what will happen. What is so bad is that a French withdrawal, however desirable that would be, would mean a triumph of nationalism in internal politics. Must the better Germany really be pushed into this dilemma? In 1918 Germany was soft as a jelly, but the others, who thought they were better, have shown little talent for educating.[15]

Ten years had passed since he started work on *The Magic Mountain*, and four since he went back to it after the long interruption, but to concentrate on it he'd have had to give up traveling outside Germany to earn money. "I do not need to tell you," he wrote to Heinrich, "that German lectures are now scarcely worth while."[16] In mid-January Thomas was touring Switzerland with Katia, but she was worrying so much about the plunging mark that she traveled back to Munich alone.[17]

By mid-February, when Thomas earned 50,000 marks for a reading in Dresden, prices had risen so steeply that he'd have made a loss if he hadn't been able to stay with friends, and since he had to visit Berlin for discussions about a film of *Buddenbrooks*, the Dresden fee paid for the journey. Though he'd committed himself to a reading in Augsburg at the end of the month for 25,000 marks, he advised Heinrich never to accept less than 40,000.[18]

In Augsburg it was gratifying to find the hall so full that people were sitting on the podium, but popularity was poor compensation for failing to make headway with the novel. He found time only for an episode based on his séance experiences. Climaxing in the reappearance of Joachim after his death, this would become the ante-penultimate section in the seventh and final chapter, though Thomas was still at work on the sixth. He gives Hans the seasick feeling he'd had himself, and uses many of the details he'd observed. The medium is young, but female; two people "control" her by gripping her knees, hands, and wrists while the other spectators form a chain; nonstop music is arranged; and the spirits play mischievous tricks, one of which is to make a handkerchief rise independently in the air.

Presiding over the séance is Dr. Krokowski, who says the manifestations, which confirm an "ideoplastic" property of nature, are "biopsychical projections of subconscious complexes into temporary reality." Thomas adds imaginatively to the details he took from experience, dovetailing incidents with reactions from characters he has established. Locked into the subterranean room by the doctor, they're nervous of the psychic phenomena. The episode is crowned with a double climax. Joachim appears, chillingly, in the uniform of a war that has not yet begun, and then Hans, at the risk of upsetting the spirits and harming the medium, interrupts the proceedings by making the doctor unlock the door to let him out of the room. This corresponds to Thomas's decision at the end of his third visit to the baron's house that he'd have nothing further to do with spiritualism. He wrote a detailed account of the first séance, "Occult Experiences" ("Okkulte Erlebnisse") for the *Neue Rundschau*,[19] but he stuck to his decision, and when his mother died on March 11 in Wesseling, he made no attempt to get in touch through a séance.

She was seventy-three, and he hadn't been seeing much of her, but it was she who, unlike her husband, had encouraged him and Heinrich to become writers. Without her he felt more isolated. Five days after her death he wrote: "I do not believe I have ever in my life felt so sad."[20] He was glad to be distracted by a trip to central Europe, having arranged to give readings in Austria, Hungary, and Czechoslovakia, but the readings featured "Occult Experiences," which made him think of her often. Staying in Vienna from March 25 to 30, he met Schnitzler, and on April 1 he met Hofmannsthal in Rodaun.

Nor could he settle down to *The Magic Mountain* when he returned to Munich: He left again with Katia on April 19 for five weeks in Spain. To avoid France they took the train to Genoa, and sailed to Barcelona, going on to Madrid, where they were received by the Infanta, Isabella, and to Seville, where they spent Ascension Day. They attended mass in the cathedral, and afterward saw a bullfight. "[O]n the whole the Andalusian south had less meaning for me than the classical region—Castille, Toledo, Aranjuez, King Philip's granite cloister stronghold and that journey, passing the Escorial, to Segovia beyond the snowy heights of Guadarrama."[21] A combination of palace and monastery, the Escorial had been built by Philip II to fulfill a vow after the victory at St. Quentin in 1557. Conceived as a royal necropolis and a center of studies in the service of the Counter-Reformation, the building has a classical severity which is unusual in Spain. Attracted, partly through his own characterization of Naphta, to the spirit of the Counter-Reformation and the Inquisition, Thomas felt he was "in the presence of my old friend Philip II."[22] Clavdia Chauchat will be given the opposite reaction: She calls the Escorial "inhuman" in comparison with the Kremlin, and claims to have got more pleasure from folk-dancing in Catalonia.

Jewish Jesuit

LIKE OTHER GREAT NOVELISTS, Thomas had a knack for integrating recent experiences into his fiction, convincing himself that they'd been just what he needed to carry the action forward, and then using them skillfully enough to convince the reader. Impressions formed in Spain filter into Naphta's arguments about liberating the spirit by chastising the flesh. Once his antihumanist viewpoint has been established, Thomas explains how it was evolved. "Like many clever Jews," we are told, "Naphta was by instinct both a revolutionary and an aristocrat; a socialist—and at the same time possessed by the dream of participating in forms of life that were proud and fine, exclusive and formal."[1]

He was sixteen when, finding himself next to a Jesuit on a park bench, he declared that politics had an affinity with Catholicism, since both aimed at galvanizing everything objective, practical, empirical, and realizable, while Protestantism was more pietistic, having its origins in the mystical. The encounter led to the conversion of the young Naphta and the training, which wasn't interrupted by illness until after he'd finished his novitiate and taken his first vows. It was a moist spot on his lungs that stopped him from working as prefect and preceptor of young pupils in a Jesuit school, which prompts Hans to wonder whether illness disposed Naphta to be more adventurous with ideas.

The structure of the Jesuit order is compared with that of the army, represented in the novel by Joachim, who eventually leaves the sanatorium to rejoin his regiment, defying the authority of the doctors to put himself back under the orders of his superiors. Listening to Naphta, Hans feels confirmed in his values as a civilian and a "child of peace," though at the end of the novel he'll want to fight in the war. Thomas sees a parallel between the instructions Frederick the Great issued to his infantry and the exercises drawn up for the Jesuits by Ignatius Loyola, the Spanish founder of the order. Naphta often uses military metaphors and Spanish phrases: Talking about the enmity between celestial and Satanic forces, he calls Jesus the *capitán general* and Lucifer a *caudillo* or chieftain. Like Frederick, with his motto of *Attaquez donc toujours!*, Loyola commanded his followers to subdue the rebellion of the flesh and assail the foe.

Naphta, who talks with relish about warlike medieval monks, likes bloodshed and torture. The body is a prison, and pain releases the soul. Didn't St. Elizabeth beat an old woman who was too sleepy to make her confession? Naphta blames the Inquisition on the Renaissance spirit of enlightenment: Instead of relying on God to intervene in favor of the truth, people demanded evidence. Guilt had to be proved by confession, and confession extracted by torture. For Naphta, value and dignity reside not in the flesh but in the spirit, which differentiates humanity from the animals. For Settembrini, God and the Devil are two separate principles, fighting for dominion over life, but for Naphta, God and the Devil are equally opposed to the utilitarian values of the bourgeoisie.

Making the disputants reiterate arguments he'd advanced in *Reflections*, Thomas is parodying and relativizing them. The basic insight that had inspired the book was that enlightened cultivation of sweetness and light ignored darker and more sinister areas in human experience; the postwar Thomas is aware that Naphta takes too much pleasure in pain. On the other hand, there's something attractive about his austerity, and it's even possible that Thomas was emulating it when being cruel to his youngest son. Michael had always been scared of crucifixes, hating to think about the pain inflicted on Jesus; Thomas nailed a crucifix on the wall above the little boy's bed, making him scream out in terror and try to hide under the blankets. When Katia complained that it was unfair, Thomas said the children must get used to being treated unfairly.[2]

Making substantial progress with the novel, he was at the mercy of his compulsion to give a compendious account of life and consciousness. Only that which is thorough, he believed, is really entertaining, and since that which seems trivial can turn out to be important, he never dared to leave anything out. Like *Buddenbrooks* and *Reflections*, *The Magic Mountain* was becoming extremely long, and he soon gave up hope of completing it before the end of the year.[3]

At a meeting held on June 24, 1923, the anniversary of Rathenau's death, he addressed students in Munich on "The Spirit and Essence of the German Republic" ("Geist und Wesen der deutschen Republik"). His speech was reprinted on June 28 in the *Frankfurter Zeitung*, but its influence was negligible. The nationalistic and racist associations led by former officers were on the point of forming a militant alliance with the National Socialist German Workers' Party, led by Hitler, who was proving his effectiveness as an orator. The Nazi cause was helped by rising prices—on June 9 an egg cost 800 marks and a pound of tea over 27,000—by the passive resistance of the Ruhr miners, which meant that Germany was producing less coal, and by the aggressiveness of the French, whose troops had seized railways in the Ruhr on June 5. Though many workers became National Socialists, the hard core of the party's leadership was formed by men from the industrial middle classes and the academic professions. The Nazis' program was evolved to cash in on the anxieties and aggressions of the petit bourgeoisie, which had never felt much confidence in the parties purporting to represent its interests, and on the general feeling of dissatisfaction with the existing order. For the people who had given their allegiance to the kaiser, it was hard to accept an ex-saddlemaker as their leader or to believe that he could restore Germany's greatness. On September 2, Hitler launched a ferocious attack on the Republic at the "German Congress" in Nuremberg, and three weeks later Ebert declared a state of emergency.

Like Thomas, Heinrich was using what influence he had to defend the beleaguered Republic. On August 11, four years after the Weimar Constitution had been adopted, he had spoken at a celebration for it in Dresden, and on October 11, addressing an open letter in the *Vossische Zeitung* to Gustav Stresemann, who'd been chancellor since June, Heinrich called on him to take firm action in defense of the constitution. But Stresemann, uncertain whether he could count on the army to support him, was indecisive when a former prime minister, Gustav von Kahr, appointed as general state commissioner in Bavaria with special powers in matters of public security, imposed martial law to quell the unrest.

Thomas left Munich in October to stay at the Hotel Austria in Bolzano, an Alpine resort. Another guest there was sixty-one-year-old Gerhart Hauptmann, an impressive, big-boned man with a weather-beaten face, a deeply furrowed forehead, and a shock of white hair. Ever since marrying a rich woman at the age of twenty-three, he'd been able to live as he pleased. He'd gone on to win the Nobel Prize, and to be paid increasingly generous advances by Fischer. As Thomas reported to Heinrich, "I hobnob every evening with Hauptmann, who is a really good old fellow."[4]

Coincidence was again providing what Thomas needed to carry his narrative forward, but he had to take the kind of risk that had got him into trouble when he modeled characters on people who'd be recognizable. In the essay "Bilse und ich," he'd argued that the gifted writer always implants a new soul in material taken from experience, but the body of Mynheer Peeperkorn is undeniably Hauptmann's body. Their drinking sessions seemed to solve two problems. One was that he needed a character who could emerge as more impressive than either Settembrini or Naphta without outclassing them intellectually. The other was that Thomas wanted to bring Clavdia back to the sanatorium without giving Hans any chance of resuming the affair they'd begun before she left. She'd be unavailable if she came back with a man, but who should the man be? Thomas later told Hauptmann:

I have sinned against you. I was in need, was led into temptation and yielded. The need was artistic. I was searching for a character I had long envisaged as structurally necessary without seeing or hearing or being in possession of him. Uneasy, worried and uncertain, I was still searching for him when I came to Bolzano, and there, while drinking wine, what unconsciously offered itself to me was something I should never, from the human and personal viewpoint, have accepted, but which, in a condition of lowered human responsibility, I did accept, did believe it was right to accept, blinded by the passionate conviction, the prospect, the certainty, that in my translation (for of course it was a matter not of a life but a translation and stylisation of one whose reality was inwardly altogether transformed while the externals became almost unrelated) I could make it into the most remarkable character in a book which, as I no longer doubt, is itself remarkable.[5]

Peeperkorn's appearance and mannerisms are derived from careful observation of Hauptmann. Tall, broad-shouldered, lean, and robust, with a red complexion and a majestic head adorned by a white beard and flowing white hair, Peeperkorn likes to stand with his legs apart and his hands in his trouser pockets. He has big hands, like a sea-captain's, but they move fluidly, as if he were an orchestral conductor. With his thumb and forefinger he keeps forming a circle, poising it above his ear and coyly twisting his head away from it. He's always courteous, with a commanding manner that makes him dominant in any social situation, in spite of his excessive drinking. Thomas keeps reiterating the word *kinglike*, but he justifies it: We are made to believe in Peeperkorn's majestic charisma not only through the way he talks and behaves but through the reactions of other characters, including Clavdia.

Thomas needed a character who, unlike Settembrini and Naphta, rarely advances coherent arguments. Peeperkorn's impressiveness has nothing to do with his intellect. Many of his pronouncements are banal, many of his sentences unfinished. He is never more appealing than during the picnic scene when he talks inaudibly at great length, his words being drowned by the noise of a waterfall, and his prominence in the final chapter is structurally justified by the way he differs not only from Settembrini and Naphta but also from Hans, who shares his author's fascination with death, while Peeperkorn is an exuberant hedonist.

Thomas stayed in Bolzano till the end of October; within about a week of his return to Munich, Hitler attempted a putsch. On November 8, in the city's biggest beer hall, the Bürgerbräukeller, the state commissioner, von Kahr, had just started a lecture on the moral justification for political dictatorship when a gang of men in brown shirts burst in brandishing guns. One of them, a short man with a toothbrush mustache, jumped on a chair, shot at the ceiling, and shouted: "The national revolution has begun." Citizens of Munich were addressed through a special edition of the *Neueste Nachrichten* in which he announced that he had ousted the treacherous government and assumed power. Law and order would be restored as soon as possible. Meanwhile, there must be no gathering of more than three people in public. Encouraged by Ludendorff, Hitler was planning to take over the Bavarian state government, march on Berlin, and establish a Nazi state. But the rebellion collapsed in the Odeonplatz when Bavarian police fired on the procession, killing sixteen Nazis. This enhanced the government's prestige so much that Hitler seemed innocuous, but Heinrich left Munich the same day, not expecting equilibrium to be restored.

Having situated *The Magic Mountain* in the prewar period, Thomas didn't have to think about linking the narrative to the latest political events. In any case, as an intellectual, he had no power comparable with that of the demagogue, and for the creative writer, always obliged to stand on the periphery of the action, it was questionable whether the novel still had a function. Underlying Thomas's work is the uncertainty whether there's anything left for art to do except parody itself. He can also reveal his own perplexity through that of his characters. Settembrini hates the Austro-Hungarian empire but has scruples about expressing support for the Balkan Federation, which is working against it with support from the tsar. The danger, as he sees it, is that the Slavs will destroy European civilization.

In 1914, Thomas had predicted that German *culture* would survive the war, even if European *civilization* didn't. In the book, Naphta takes Settembrini to task for assuming that the Mediterranean, classic, humanistic tradition belongs to the whole of humanity. If it's no more than the intellectual topsoil of the bourgeois liberal age, it could easily be eroded in the near future. But it is no more? Thomas's opinion was different now from what it had been eight or ten years earlier. Clarifying his views on German republicanism involved him in rethinking his outlook on Romanticism and German traditions, and he was influenced by a book he reviewed before leaving Munich to read "Occult Experiences" in Berlin and Lübeck.

In 1922 the historian Ernst Troeltsch had lectured at the Deutsche Hochschule für Politik on "Natural Law and Humanity in World Politics," and when the lecture was printed, Thomas reviewed it for the *Frankfurter Zeitung*. The concept of natural law, Troeltsch said, derived from antiquity, but it had been rejected in the rebellion against bourgeois society launched by German Romanticism, which tried to set up individual impulse as a substitute for moral sanctions. During the war, Thomas had thought he was taking a conservative stance when he championed German irrationalism against French and British moral philosophers of the Enlightenment, but Troeltsch helped him to understand that far from being rooted in the eighteenth century, liberalism and humanitarianism belonged to a much older tradition. Arguing that rapprochement with Western ideas didn't involve betrayal of German culture, Troeltsch helped Thomas to move beyond *Reflections* and to reconsider his intentions in *The Magic Mountain*. In his review he praises Troeltsch for clarifying what had been "an obscure movement in the conscience of many Germans—perhaps even in some who have long been deeply absorbed in the magic mountain of romantic aestheticism."[6]

The magic mountain may be the novel's central symbol, but its connotations had changed as the book grew. At first the mountain had provided an elevated refuge from the lowlands of a superficially healthy normality. But the two immense final chapters—together they fill over 500 pages, while the first five chapters occupy a total of 463—stress the boredom and volatility of patients who have come to represent prewar German society. They are people who respond greedily and superficially to the excitements of Romantic art, while Hans benefits not only from the education he has acquired on the mountain but also from his author's awareness of what lay ahead for Europe. "While I was working I always said: 'I am writing about a young German who before the war is already emerging from the war.' "[7]

One of the main changes that had overtaken Thomas—and the novel—since the summer of 1913, when he'd intended it to be no more than a long short story, was that he'd become more political, more preoccupied with public issues, and more eager to see himself as a leader who could influence public opinion.

In 1916, still working on *Reflections*, he'd insisted that the intellectual must never take direct political action. "If his passion leads him into reality, he is slipping into the wrong dimension, where he will behave badly, amateurishly and awkwardly" (see page 295). Seven years later he saw it as his duty to move into that dimension.

Unless he'd already been trying to detach himself from his "sympathy with death" when he started *The Magic Mountain*, he wouldn't have presented it in a comic focus, counterbalancing the seriousness of "Death in Venice." He claimed later that he'd succeeded in making death into a comic character, but few readers would agree, and though Thomas proved his skill as a comic writer in *Felix Krull*, the comedy in *The Magic Mountain* is peripheral. In spite of Peeperkorn's majestic vitality, the book is dominated by disease and death, although Thomas achieves control over his fascination with them. One gauge of this is the way Naphta's ideas are put into a diminishing perspective. At the same time the scope and substance of the novel help it to transcend any relish for morbidity. The turning point comes in the vision Hans has during the snow sequence. He resolves to keep faith with death in his heart without forgetting that faith with death is hostile to humanity if it's given power over thought and action. He returns to his waking state intending not to let death dominate his thinking.

Working his way through narrative to a new synthesis, Thomas had been trying to pack almost everything he'd experienced and learned into the novel. Reaching far beyond his original intentions, it became a statement not merely about the human organism and its decomposition but about Europe, time, consciousness, love, and war.

BY THE BEGINNING of 1924 the currency crisis was over. In mid-November 1923, Stresemann's government had introduced a new unit of currency, the Rentenmark, worth a billion marks and pegged to the 1914 level of 4.2 to the dollar. This halted the inflation, which had been ruinous for those who kept their capital liquid; others had done better by taking their money out of the country or translating it into solid assets. The book trade had survived, and though Thomas still needed to supplement his income from royalties and advances, he no longer had to travel abroad in pursuit of worthwhile fees. "Germany pays in gold marks," he reported on February 13, "and not at all ungenerously."[8]

His unfinished comic novel was still nagging at him. "I do not know why I got stuck at that time—perhaps because the extremely individualistic and unsocial character of the work seemed unsuitable for the period, perhaps also because I had the feeling of having already said everything that was essential in the first part."[9] What he had to do now was make a final spurt to finish *The Magic Mountain*, and he was pleased that "towards the end events have taken a wonderfully surprising turn—surprising for me."[10] It's easy to see why he wanted the series of long disputes to culminate in a violent climax, but, though he prepares for it carefully, the duel sequence might have been disappointing if he hadn't taken himself by surprise. The twist comes after Settembrini announces that nothing would induce him to shoot at his opponent, and he fires into the air. The saturnine Naphta, who has rebuffed Hans's last-minute attempt at conciliation, points his pistol at his own temple and pulls the trigger.

His death completes the movement toward life that had begun in the snow sequence. Thomas had endowed Naphta's apologias for torture and execution with a formidable cogency. Ever since his appearance, Settembrini had been no match for him. In an essay on Kierkegaard, Lukács argued that the only essential difference between one life and another is whether the mutually exclusive opposites are separated sharply enough. Where most men compromise to convince themselves that opposites are compatible, Kierkegaard insisted on "the duty to go right to the end of each chosen road at each crossroad."[11] Whereas Settembrini, for all his good intentions, comes across as a man who doesn't believe in anything as strongly as this, Naphta is Kierkegaardian in this respect. But his death, having little connection with his beliefs, does nothing toward validating them.

IN APRIL, Thomas's work on the novel was delayed by flu. Staying in bed and recovering slowly, he felt inclined to give fewer lectures and readings.[12] He'd accepted invitations to visit Amsterdam and London with Katia in May, which meant there was no hope of finishing the novel before July. In Amsterdam, as guest of the Letterkundige Kring, he made an after-dinner speech about democracy, and in London he was a guest of honor at the PEN Club, which had been formed in 1921. The first president, John Galsworthy, arranged for the Manns to spend five days in the home of his German-speaking sister, Lilian, who lived in Hendon. Galsworthy spent so much time with them that Thomas thought he lived there. "The knightliness, the moderation, the lovable morality of his nature constitute something like the blossoming of European man." But Thomas didn't think Galsworthy was spiritual enough to deserve the word "gentleman."[13] One evening George Bernard Shaw and H. G. Wells came to dinner. "The dinner in London," Thomas reported, "was a *demonstration*, highly enjoyable, beautiful and moving."[14]

But the high point of his stay in England was his visit to Oxford. "It was really enchanting for me to breathe the atmosphere of English humanism—a specially noble variety, according to Tolstoy."[15] He and Katia traveled back by steamer from Southampton to Hamburg, stopping to see Erika in Berlin.

In general, Thomas had treated her better than Klaus, whose bids for attention were usually counterproductive. The seventeen-year-old boy now proposed marriage to Wedekind's daughter, Pamela, a budding actress and singer who'd had a lesbian relationship with Erika while Klaus had been homosexually involved with Ricki Hallgarten. Pamela idolized her dead father. His death mask hung on the wall of her studio, where she performed his songs, accompanying herself on the guitar that had been his. In the early summer Klaus wrote to her suggesting that it would be rather nice if they got married, and she wrote back on a postcard, accepting. His parents were upset, wanting him to get his school-leaving certificate, but, finding passive resistance was effective, he stopped going to school and refused to see the private tutor who was engaged. Klaus stayed in bed and feigned a psychological crisis. When Katia said she'd always hoped he'd become an architect, he told her he wanted to be a dancer.[16] Thomas tried to reason with him, gave up, and went back to his novel.

But it was still unfinished when he left with Katia on July 19 to spend two weeks with Hauptmann and his wife at the Haus am Meer in Kloster on the island of Hiddensee in the Baltic, where they went every summer. "Life is primitive and shamelessly expensive, but the sea extraordinarily splendid for Baltic relations."[17] Hauptmann loved to perform: He sang for the Manns and read from a novel that wasn't yet published, *Eulenspiegel*. Much as Thomas enjoyed reading from his work, he didn't want to expose a novel that featured his host. The excuse he made was that he'd been overwhelmed by Hauptmann's reading, but the older man insisted. "In my father's house," he said, "are many mansions." Thomas read the section of the seventh chapter that comes before Peeperkorn's first appearance.

At the end of the month the Manns moved on to Bansin, where the children would enjoy themselves more. Thomas went on working at the novel, knowing he had to make only one final spurt. They stayed in Bansin until August 16, and, having agreed to make a speech in commemoration of those killed during the war at Stralsund, which is on the Baltic coast, northwest of Rostock, he took the family to stay for a final week in Ahlbeck. Possibly the last section of the novel was influenced by what he said in his Stralsund speech. The end of the last chapter gives the impression of being written hurriedly: He fails to solve the problems created by moving the action away from the sanatorium where it has been securely lodged for seven hundred pages. The evocation of the war is sketchy, and though the narrator has come into the foreground on previous occasions, he's too conspicuous at the end, and the bantering tone keeps striking false notes, especially when Hans is addressed in the second person singular about the war that has just begun: "Your prospects are poor; the evil dance that has caught you up lasts for many a sinful little year, and we wouldn't like to bet much money on your survival. To be honest, we are not too worried about leaving the question open."

One reason for the awkwardness is that Thomas had been persistently widening the focus: The story had been conceived when he regarded himself as a nonpolitical man. Eight years later, thinking about Goethe, he was also thinking about his own bildungsroman, *The Magic Mountain*, when he cited *Wilhelm Meister* as evidence of the way confessional and autobiographical writing can turn outward as the instinct to educate his public makes the writer more social and political. Thomas is again referring as much to himself as to Goethe when he explains that the impulse to educate derives not from inner harmony but from insecurity, disharmony, difficulty in achieving self-knowledge. While deviating from the norm, the creative writer also believes himself to be representative of humanity, and to bear responsibility.

Widening the focus involved Thomas in problems of how to balance optimistic and pessimistic inclinations. There's an upbeat intention in making Hans decide to leave the sanatorium and volunteer to be a soldier. The intention is to show that though he's "sensually and intellectually in love with death (mysticism, Romanticism) this corrupt love refines itself at least spasmodically, in moments of illumination, into an impression of a new humanity, which he carries in his heart as a germ, while the bayonet attack carries him with it."[18] In a letter to Schnitzler, Thomas said "the book is meant to be a mockery of death, an anti-Romantic disillusionment, and a European call to life." Of all subsequent criticisms, the one that annoyed him most was the aspersion of enmity toward life.[19] The modulation into a major key may take us by surprise, but Thomas had probably lived too long with the idea of concluding the story with the outbreak of war. In a January 1925 letter he says the magic mountain has its magic stripped away by the war.[20] But he fails to show how this happens; perhaps the novel, like the duel episode, needed a final twist in which he surprised himself.

It was on September 28 that he wrote the words *Finis operis*. Most of the text had already been set up in print, and less than a month elapsed between the completion of the book and its publication. It came out in two volumes on October 27. Fischer had printed twenty thousand copies, of which five thousand had been sold before they appeared in the shops. By the end of the first week in December, another impression of ten thousand copies was in hand, and by December 26, Fischer was considering a one-volume edition on thin paper.

Years of Plenty

NOT WANTING TO ATTEMPT anything else on the same scale, Thomas planned to write some short stories.[1] But first he needed a rest. At the beginning of October he left with Katia for ten days in Sestri Levante on the Ligurian coast of Italy, near Rapallo. For the first few days there Ernst Bertram stayed with them.

In November Thomas gave several speeches and readings in Munich and other German cities. After reading a newspaper report of his lecture in Dresden, Ida Boy-Ed protested at his new republicanism. He replied by asking her to believe in his sense of duty and responsibility.

> I must make good use of the confidence I had the luck to inspire in my country. But what is good is to circumvent new catastrophes that would be fatal to our part of the earth. For a long time there has been no hope that Europe would take control. For it merely to survive it needs consolidation, which is attainable only with help from a German democracy, and I would consider that morally and intellectually my behaviour was disgraceful if I worked against this or failed to support it with all my strength.[2]

After a long period of hating democracy, he'd come to believe in it as a lifeline.

Reviewers and friends were almost unanimously enthusiastic about *The Magic Mountain*, but the new year, 1925, began with a panicky attempt to silence the writer Herbert Eulenberg, who was planning a newspaper article about Peeperkorn's resemblance to Hauptmann. Nothing would be achieved, Thomas argued, except a scandal, and he'd concede no more than that he'd borrowed a few of Hauptmann's "external features." None of the reviewers had noticed the resemblance, which would be recognizable to at most two dozen of the people–probably about fifty thousand by now–who'd read the novel. "I urgently and cordially beg you to abstain. . . . Write to him, write to me, as your heart bids you! But do not spoil everything by dragging the thing in front of a public which, as you, like me, so well know, is neither mature enough for it nor worthy of it."[3] The plea was successful: Eulenberg sent a telegram promising not to publish anything.[4]

At first Thomas gave most of his working time to revising the Goethe-Tolstoy script for publication in *Bemühungen* (*Endeavors*). Now, stepping firmly beyond literary criticism into political commitment, he repudiated the position he'd taken in *Reflections*:

> The anti-liberal reaction is not only apparent but crass. It is express-ing itself politically in the way people are disgustedly backing away from democracy and parliamentarianism to turn with dark resolu-tion towards dictatorship and terror. . . . For Germany this is not the time to act anti-humanistically, to follow the example of Tolstoy's pedagogical Bolshevism . . . this is the time to put strong emphasis on our great humane heritage and to cultivate it solemnly.[5]

After all the work on *The Magic Mountain*, Thomas felt entitled to indulge in buying a car. He used a valet as driver. "I have," he told Ernst Bertram, "between ourselves, already earned seventy thousand marks from the sale of admission tickets to my mystical-humorous aquarium, and so I have bought . . . a pretty six-seater Fiat. Our swag-gering Ludwig has already qualified as a chauffeur, so I can make 33 horse-power expeditions into the town, waving condescendingly in every direction."[6]

Michael, who was nearly six, was fascinated by the new car. One day he opened the door and sat down in the driver's seat. When he took off the brakes, the car rolled backward till it hit a stone wall. His punish-ment was to be beaten with his own walking-stick: Because Thomas had one, the children all had sticks of their own. Ever since Michael was four, Thomas had singled him out for harsh treatment, but it was the beating that rankled most in his memory. He didn't forgive his father for over forty years.[7]

Brought up by a series of nannies, the two younger children seldom saw their parents, except at mealtimes, when Thomas sat at one end of the table and they sat at the other with their nanny. They weren't al-lowed to talk unless they were addressed, and weren't allowed to make any noise in the house, except at times—and there were few of these—when he wasn't writing, reading, resting, or writing letters. According to Michael, it was Thomas's modesty, shyness, and uncertainty that made him so unapproachable. While the older children addressed him as "Magician," the two youngest called him "Herr Papale." When Michael wanted to play the violin, he was given Thomas's, and when he wrote stories, Thomas advised him on how to go on with them, but he still seemed remote. During Katia's illness, the children saw more of him. When he read Hans Christian Andersen stories to Elisabeth, Michael was allowed to listen, but he didn't understand all he heard and couldn't ask questions. He felt like an intruder who'd never be ad-mitted to the magical intimacy his sister had with their father.[8]

* * *

THOMAS'S DECISION to go on a Mediterranean cruise might have looked like another piece of self-indulgence, but he had an ulterior motive for accepting the invitation from a shipping magnate, Hugo Stinnes, who assumed that his presence on the liner would pay dividends in the form of publicity. Thomas was mainly interested in seeing Egypt. "I shall catch sight of the desert, the Pyramids, the Sphinx. . . . It may be helpful to certain plans, which I am keeping to myself, shadowy though they are."9 He didn't explain until June that he wanted to write some stories, and even then, he said no more than that they were to center on Joseph, Erasmus, and Philip II.10 His intention was to create a tryptich based on the Bible, the Reformation, and the Counter-Reformation.

The idea had germinated in December 1923, when a painter who knew Katia, Hermann Ebers, had asked him to write a preface for a series of pictures based on the Old Testament story of Joseph. Goethe had found the story "highly attractive, but it seems too short, and one feels called on to sketch in the details." In the evening, Thomas consulted the old family Bible, "in which many underlinings in faded grey ink evidenced the pious study of dead ancestors."

> I did not yet know how important these words from *Dichtung und Wahrheit* were to be as a motto for years of work ahead of me. But the evening was full of groping, tentative, adventurous speculation, and the idea of something quite new: what appealed to me indescribably, both sensually and intellectually, was the idea of moving away from the familiar modern bourgeois environment to penetrate by means of narrative deeply into the human.11

The project would give him a chance to interrogate himself on how much pre-historical man had in common with modern man.

Big enough for 160 passengers, the liner was to sail from Venice, and Thomas enjoyed the slow journey in the gondola from the station to the boat, which was anchored in front of the Piazzetta. "My God, how moved I was to see this beloved city after carrying it in my heart for thirteen years!" The cabin he was given was "a compact and practical space with a writing-table and several roomy drawers under the bed and in the commode. I am comfortable, but not too comfortable, which is fine. My deck-chair for reading is by the door."12

In Cairo, where he was molested by beggars and street traders, he rode a donkey with three names—Bismarck, Maurice, and Dooly; in Capri his donkey was called Michelangelo. He saw Luxor, Karnak, and the royal tombs at Thebes. "I also climbed down with the others into the stifling suite of vaults belonging to the sons of the sun in the mountains on the edge of the Libyan desert," and he stood for a long time in front of the glass-encased mummy of the young king Amenophis IV in his porphyry coffin. He saw a line of camels with turbaned riders against the horizon; he sailed through the Dardanelles and the Sea of Marmara to the city that was still called Constantinople. "The minarets look like Faber pencils with little mastheads." In Athens, visiting the Acropolis, he refused to be photographed like the other tourists in front of the caryatids of the Erechtheon, "but I gallivanted about just as vulgarly and contemptibly as they did between the noble ruins." He also bought a postcard to send Heinrich.13 But in Athens, tired of "all this Flying Dutchmanism," he decided against going on to see Algiers, Málaga, the Alhambra in Granada, and Barcelona. He left the boat when it docked at Naples,14 and he was back in Munich before the end of March, knowing he would develop his idea.

First, though, he must write the short story he'd promised for the special issue of Samuel Fischer's *Neue Rundschau*–a *Festschrift* for Thomas's fiftieth birthday. He went back to an idea he'd had before the war when Katia was in Davos and he was alone with the children—he'd write a story about them. And already they were beginning to fight their way into the limelight. The nineteen-year-old Erika had played a walk-on part in Reinhardt's production of Shaw's *St. Joan*, and the eighteen-year-old Klaus had already had a book of stories, *Vor dem Leben*, accepted for publication. In Thomas's story, "Disorder and Early Sorrow" ("Unordnung und frühes Leid"), Ingrid is eighteen, with theatrical ambitions based on her smile, her voice, and her talent for mimicry, while her blond brother Bert, her junior by a year, seems unprepared for adult life. This worries their father, Professor Cornelius, a historian whose hostility toward current events is counterweighted by affection for Philip II and the Counter-Reformation. Elisabeth was seven and Michael six, but in the story Ellie is five, with a four-year-old brother nicknamed the Biter. Nicknames were important in the family. It wasn't only Katia ("Mielein") and Thomas ("Pielein" or "Zauberer") who had pet names. Mielein's parents were "Ofey" and "Offi," Elisabeth was "Medi," and Michael "Bibi." The nurse who called Elisabeth "Medi" called Michael "Bibi," which means "little boy." In the story the two younger children are "the little folk" and the other two children "the big folk." The Biter is prone to outbursts of anger and tears, but his nervousness and instability are blamed on pressures exerted by the war on family life.

Eight years younger than her husband, the wife in the story, like Katia, is in poor health and subject to fits of giddiness. Her mental and physical resources have been sapped by the constant strain of running a family home when broken washbasins can neither be repaired nor replaced, and feeding a family when a bottle of beer costs 8,000 marks, eggs 6,000 marks each, and no household is allowed more than five a week. While many people can no longer afford a telephone, the Corneliuses still have one, and their three servants include two middle-class sisters who feel humiliated by having to do menial work.

Ingrid and Bert are always playing practical jokes, assuming outlandish identities, improvising loud conversations when traveling by public transport, and ringing up distinguished neighbors, pretending to be shop assistants or titled foreigners. But the main focus is on the sweet-faced Ellie, who has a symbiotic relationship with her father. From the first moment of seeing her, he knew his love for her would be stronger than any other feeling. The action of the story pivots on his temporary displacement in her affections by a charming young man who comes to a party at the house, dances with her, and behaves gallantly, as if she were older than five. But the story ends happily: She'll soon forget the young man. Like "Master and Dog" and "Song of the Little Child," the story is what Thomas called an idyll.

It was embarrassing for Klaus whenever his father read the story out loud in his presence,[15] and in 1926 he retaliated with a story of his own about a family with four children, "Kindernovelle." The most provocative sequence is a flashback in the mother's memory to lovemaking with her husband. "Above her she saw his big face, which had almost scared her, the black, gleaming eyes, the gigantic nose, the sharp mouth, which paid precise and hymn-like homage to her beauty."[16] Like "Der Vater lacht," the story may have been motivated by longing for a candid conversation with Thomas, but if so, Klaus was again frustrated. Writing to Erika, Thomas reported that the story had made him laugh a lot, though "here and there doubt crept in."[17] It was characteristic of him not to be more specific.

Spending an evening with him, Hermann Hesse formed the impression that there was something defensive not only in his behavior but in the way he'd surrounded himself with all the appurtenances of a comfortable bourgeois lifestyle. "I sat at his table till late at night, and he conducted the occasion handsomely and stylishly, in good humor, with a touch of cordiality and a touch of mockery, defended by his beautiful house, defended by his cleverness and good form."[18]

Sometimes he felt glad to be distracted from private guilt feelings by the obligation to make statements about public and political issues, though generally he was more at ease when dealing with personal and domestic themes. On April 23, 1925, in a letter to Julius Bab, who'd written appreciatively about *The Magic Mountain*, he admitted: "My weak side is the social . . . the Zolaesque is weak in me, and that I had to speak out on the eight-hour day feels to me almost like a parody of the social viewpoint."[19]

He also spoke out against the right-wing parties' choice of a monarchist, the seventy-eight-year-old Field Marshal Paul von Hindenburg, as their candidate in the elections held on April 25 to find a replacement for Ebert as president of the republic. In a letter to the *Neue Freie Presse* before the election, Thomas condemned the choice as disastrous and blamed it on "the romantic drives" of the German people. He could only hope voters would refuse to elect "a knight at arms from antiquity." His letter was given the title "Save Democracy" ("Rettet die Demokratie") but wasn't published till the day after the election.[20]

The Communist candidate, Ernst Thälmann, had stood no chance of being elected, but nearly 2 million people voted for him. If half of them had voted for the ex-chancellor, Wilhelm Marx, candidate for the left and center parties, Hindenburg wouldn't have got in, but he defeated Marx by 14,655,000 votes to 13,751,000. Taking his oath to the republican constitution, Hindenburg emphasized that it was democratic, but Harry Graf Kessler, who attended the ceremony, recorded the remark of a friend who said they'd just witnessed the death of the German Republic.[21]

Glad to absent himself from the country that had elected the old soldier as its leader, Thomas spent most of May in Italy, but before leaving Germany he made peace with Hauptmann, to whom he'd written in April pleading for forgiveness. The characterization of Mynheer Peeperkorn had been respectfully in line with the essay in which Thomas had described Hauptmann as the king of the German nation.[22] Less than a month after Thomas wrote this letter, Hauptmann came to Munich for his play *Festaktus*, which he'd written for the opening of the Deutsches Museum. "We pressed each other's hands a great deal, and everything is all right once again. He is such a great man—I love him very much."[23]

After spending seven days in Florence as German delegate to a "week of international culture," Thomas had eight days in Venice, returning to Germany in time to celebrate his fiftieth birthday on June 6. The newspapers paid generous tribute to him, and among those sending congratulations and greetings were Hauptmann, Hofmannsthal, and Stefan Zweig. In the celebration at Munich's old town hall, the most dramatic moment came when Heinrich stood up to speak briefly but emotionally about birthday parties at their parents' home in Lübeck. Since then they'd never celebrated a birthday together until today, when he was ready to rejoice in his brother's fame. Thomas, who walked across to embrace him, wasn't alone in being moved to tears.[24] The next day the Residenztheater presented a matinee performance of *Fiorenza*. He read from "Felix Krull," and a laurel wreath was ceremonially placed on his head.

One former friend who didn't join in the celebrations was the reactionary Hans Pfitzner, and, hearing from him a couple of weeks later,

Thomas tried to be conciliatory about his republicanism. "Please believe at least that it stemmed from good will—and from the feeling of a responsibility which may be stronger than that encumbent on a musician." Perhaps he stood in the same relation to Pfitzner, he suggested, as Nietzsche to Wagner, continuing to love him but forced by conscience to liberate himself from the spell.[25]

Though he was thinking about the *Joseph* stories in July, he hadn't done any serious work on them when he took Katia to the Salzburg Festival for the last week in August, and in early September he had to correct proofs of *Endeavors*. Later in the month they took Elisabeth and Michael to Italy for a holiday. They'd intended to stay in the Grand Hotel in Forte di Marmi, but when they arrived on September 8, they were told their rooms wouldn't be available until the fifteenth. They went on to Casamicciola in Ischia, where Thomas felt almost as if he were in Africa.[26] They made excursions to Rome and Naples, and the children had such a good time that they couldn't believe the holiday would ever come to an end.[27]

Later in the month *Endeavours* was published, and in Lübeck, as a belated birthday celebration, *Fiorenza* was staged on the ninth. Thomas went there, and, before the end of the month, left Munich again for a few days in Berlin, where he had a session with the painter Max Liebermann, who was working on his portrait, and met Albert Einstein, who was impressive for his "sweetness of character, childishness, modesty."[28]

With the prospect of two relatively undisturbed months before the tour of the Rhineland he'd planned for January, Thomas intended to give no lectures or readings. He'd settle down to work like "a historian or half-historian of Jewish-Egyptian events."[29] It was extraordinary, though, that he didn't go to Hamburg in October when the eighteen-year-old Klaus's play *Anja and Esther* was staged with Erika, Klaus, Pamela Wedekind, and the twenty-six-year-old star of the Kammerspiele, Gustaf Gründgens, in the leading parts. There was a simultaneous premiere in Munich, but it was the Hamburg production that attracted big crowds, largely because of newspaper articles about "children of famous poets staging a big show in Hamburg." The *Berlin Illustrierte* published a front-page photograph of Klaus and the two girls. But though the children's upbringing had set a high value on achievement, Thomas adamantly withheld the pleasure he could have given them by sitting in the audience. As Golo put it, "he was a kind of king, someone with sovereign willpower,"[30] and his two eldest children were guilty of lèse-majesté, achieving the kind of theatrical success he'd wanted but never had. His first duty now, he told himself, was to his novel.

The appeal of the biblical material lay partly in the opportunity it provided to write a different kind of fiction, less autobiographical, less personal, more general. Talking about it later in the perspective of Goethe's *Faust*, and calling Faust a symbol of humanity, Thomas said his aim had been to make the *Joseph* material symbolical in the same way. Delving back to where historical knowledge blurred into myth, he could concern himself with beginnings, writing as if each human experience was unprecedented—loving, feeling envious, hating, murdering.

> But this dominant originality is at the same time repetition, reflection, image, the result of rotation of the spheres which brings the upper, the starlike, into the lower regions, carries in turn the worldly into the realm of the divine so that gods become men, men in turn become gods. The worldly finds itself pre-created in the realm of the stars, and the individual character seeks its dignity by tracing itself back to the timeless mythical pattern giving it presence.[31]

In none of his previous work had he tried to analyze man's relationship with the circumambient universe. Now, freeing himself from the need to deal with the circumstantial complications of life in an industrial society, he could look at the natural life of men and planets.

Taking Goethe's idea of fleshing out the story which is told so sketchily in *Genesis*, Thomas applied techniques he'd used in *Buddenbrooks*. The Bible is vague about the passage of time and about the age of the characters at different stages of the story; drawing on the scanty store of knowledge about Israel and Egypt in this early period, on facts archaeologists and anthropologists had accumulated about creeds, customs, and clothes, and on knowledge to be gleaned from coins, sculptures, and illustrations, he did his preparatory work thoroughly. Concerned, as in both *Buddenbrooks* and *Fiorenza*, with a family that had made itself into a dynasty, he could start by calculating the passage of time between key events. One way in which the Bible implies intervals of time is by listing who begat whom. Though he would sometimes place a quasi-biblical emphasis on offspring, and on the proliferation of Jacob's family, Thomas was planning to give himself freedom to invent new details and to be novelistic in detailing what happened during the two periods of seven years in which Jacob had to work for Laban, first to be fobbed off with Leah and then to earn Rachel. Similarly, in giving an account of what went on in Egypt during the seven years of plenty and the seven years of want, he'd flesh out the biblical story with fiction of his own invention.

OVER CHRISTMAS he was thinking about the ten days he'd spend in Paris during January, and the lecture he was to give there at the Carnegie Foundation for International Peace. "But from now on," he told Bertram, "I am resolved to let myself have quite different dreams, and what I look forward to most is talking with you about Abraham and Hammurabi, Joseph and Amenhotep IV."[32]

Katia didn't accompany him on his mid-January reading tour, but after joining him in Mainz, she traveled with him to Paris, where they stayed at the Hôtel Palais d'Orsay. His talk, which he called "Les Tendences spirituelles de l'Allemagne d'aujourd'hui" ("Spiritual Tendencies in Germany Today"), was given on Wednesday, January 20, and he amused his public by starting to speak in French and switching in mid-sentence to German as he looked down at his script. A French translation of his speech was afterward read out to the audience, which consisted mainly of academics, writers, and their ladies. After all his years of hostility toward the Entente, here he was, a kind of cultural ambassador, helping to restore goodwill between France and Germany: Europe, he said, would either survive or fail to survive as a whole.[33]

A reception was held at the German embassy, where the guests included the minister for education, Édouard Daladier; the minister of war, Paul Painlevé; Félix Bertaux, who'd translated "Death in Venice" into French; and Thomas's old enemy, the critic Walter Kerr, who greeted him politely. Because Kerr had been heckled at a provocative lecture he'd given in Paris, the organizers had been careful not to publicize Thomas's appearance. This annoyed the press, and on Thursday morning, newspapers carried such headlines as "Newspapermen excluded from Mann speech." But he and Katia enjoyed their breakfast at Prunier's, where nothing was served but seafood. "On the buffet tables a submarine utopia of lobsters, oysters, caviarre and salt-water fish."[34]

A program of events had been laid on for them by the Foundation, and in the afternoon they were taken to the Union pour la Vérité. "You have the impression of a conventicle, the meeting of a community of gentle conspirators for goodness." Expected to make a speech about Europe and Franco-German relations, he managed to talk extempore for about seven minutes. He and Katia were then taken to the Union Intellectuelle Française, where he again had to improvise, but this time only to express thanks for what was said about him.

The next day they had a meal with the critic Edmond Jaloux, whom he'd met several times; the thirty-two-year-old Richard, Count Coudenhove-Kalergi; and his wife, Ida Roland. Jaloux, who came from Marseilles—a city whose fortunes, like Lübeck's, had declined with those of its port—had been reminded by *Buddenbrooks* of how he'd uprooted himself from provincial bourgeois society. He struck Thomas as a typical French intellectual, while Coudenhove-Kalergi, founder of the Pan-Europa movement, was "one of the most remarkable and incidentally most beautiful people I have come across." The movement was in favor of forming a European federation, excluding Britain and Russia. "Half Japanese, and on the other side descended from an international mixture of European nobility, he really represents a Eurasian type of well-bred world-citizenship, in confrontation with which the average German feels quite provincial."[35]

Before leaving Paris, Thomas gave his Goethe-Tolstoy lecture at the École Normale Supérieur and, when he dined with the International Literary Circle at the Paris PEN Club, met François Mauriac and Jules Romains. Leaving Paris on the evening of January 28, he and Katia traveled on the Orient Express, which he called "an aristocratic train, the king of trains." The journey to Munich took fourteen hours.[36]

The ten days had been so strenuous that when the tension slackened he fell ill with flu, and infected the rest of the family. More vulnerable than the children, Katia soon developed bronchitis. Thomas was so ill that he stayed in bed for nine days, and still felt unwell when he got up, though this didn't stop him from starting a detailed account of his Parisian experiences, "Pariser Rechenschaft."[37] This would run to ninety pages, and he was still working on it in mid-March,[38] when planning a visit to Lübeck in June for the 700th anniversary of the city's foundation.

He'd have preferred to read a short story, but, asked to make a speech, and not wanting to speak extempore again, he decided to talk autobiographically about "Lübeck as form and fate, as intellectual form and literary fate."[39] The title he'd eventually choose would be "Lübeck als geistiger Lebensform" ("Lübeck as a Spiritual Concept of Life").

Katia had to stay in bed for over a month, taking little comfort from such distractions as listening over the telephone to complete performances of operas.[40] She recovered so slowly that her doctor recommended another dose of mountain air, and Thomas decided to travel with her to the Swiss Alps. Not wanting to be seen in Davos, they settled on the Waldsanatorium in Arosa, twenty miles from Chur. They spent most of May there. She was still confined to bed, but while there was snow on the mountains, spring sometimes asserted itself strongly enough for her bed to be rolled out onto the balcony.[41]

It felt strange to be back in the world of *The Magic Mountain*. Thomas worked at the Lübeck speech and caught up on arrears of correspondence. Replying to a letter from Ernst Fischer, editor of the left-wing Austrian paper *Arbeiterwille*, he tried to quantify the political commitment incumbent on "a man naive enough to let the public catch sight of his conscience, provoking the mistaken assumption that he was a born preceptor." Before 1914 it had seemed unnecessary for the writer to choose between "art and socialism," and *The Magic Mountain* had been critical of the "aestheticising" era that had ended with the war, but "Ultimately it is not the novel that is historical–it is I myself. My roots lie in Goethean narrative of autobiographical development, in the bourgeoisie, in Romanticism." His relevance to the contemporary world depended on his absorption of Nietzsche, in whom Romanticism had transcended itself. "What you find fascinating (in the sinful sense) in my works is the critical disintegration of the fundamental instinct: irony. *The Magic Mountain* is a perfectly genuine expression of my being, especially in so far as it displays the parodistic conservatism through which my artistry holds itself in suspense between epochs." He wanted his work to express the crisis which had overtaken art as a form or as an idea.[42]

In the rarefied air of Arosa he felt something of the detachment Hans had felt from the world "down there." Writing about Lübeck on a balcony with a view of the mountains, Thomas produced a speech different from the one he'd have written in Munich. He tried to view his artistic development as that of a Lübecker, and to portray *Buddenbrooks* as "a piece of the history of the soul of the German bourgeoisie." He got closest to his theme when discussing the extent to which he'd inherited his father's ethics, and developed arguments Lukács had put forward in *Die Seele und die Formen*. In contrast to aestheticism and nihilism, morality belonged to *Lebensbürgerlichkeit*. Without a strong drive to improve the well-being of the community, there could be no positive achievement. The artist wasn't exonerated from duties to his family and to mankind. Associating the city with his father, Thomas believed their features to be present in all his work, not through direct description but essentially. Would he, for instance, have responded as he did to Venice had the city borne less resemblance to Lübeck?[43]

Leaving Katia in the sanatorium, he returned to Munich at the end of May, but stayed only three days before leaving for Lübeck, where *Fiorenza* was performed on June 4, the day before he delivered his speech in the Stadttheater. The title of Professor was conferred on him through the Senate, and before returning to Munich, he visited his old school, the Katharineum. Because Hamburg is so close to Lübeck, he'd accepted an invitation to read there on June 8, and he had an audience of sixteen hundred people.

Erika and Gründgens were to be married at the end of July. Klaus described him as "a neurotic Hermes, light-footed in his worn but elegantly shaped sandals, wearing his monocle with striking nonchalance and his shabby leather overcoat with as much sovereign grace as if it were a beautiful antique garment. He was haunted by his vanity and his persecution mania, and a frantic desire to please. . . . His eyes were icy and soft like the eyes of a rare and royal fish who had jewels in place of eyes."[44] The marriage lasted only a year, and Gründgens was later to inspire Klaus's 1936 novel *Mephisto*, the source of István Szabó's 1981 film with Klaus Maria Brandauer.

* * *

After eight weeks in the sanatorium Katia returned to Munich at the end of June. Thomas would have liked to take her on holiday, but both the young children had whooping cough.[45] By the end of July he'd immersed himself in work on the *Joseph* story. "It is the Biblical story itself, which I want to retell objectively and humanistically."[46] Once again, Goethe's influence had been decisive. Nor did Thomas stop working on the story at the end of the month, when he left with Katia, Elisabeth, and Michael for the Forte di Marme holiday they'd postponed from the previous summer.

Even in a seaside resort it was impossible to escape from "the flatulent influence of the Duce."[47] One day on the beach, while the eight-year-old Elisabeth played in the hot sun, they let her keep her wet bathing costume on, but it soon became so stiff with sand they told her to take it off, rinse it in the sea, and put it on again. Some of the Italians were so outraged by the sight of a naked child that an officious man, wearing a suit and a bowler hat, came across to say the indecency had insulted the honor of Italy and the authorities must be informed. An official escorted the entire Mann family to the Municipio, where they were told the offense was *molto grave* and fined 50 lire.

They again had trouble at the Grand Hotel, where an aristocratic Italian family was staying. Elisabeth and Michael were both better, but the seven-year-old boy was sometimes awakened at night by a fit of coughing. Naive enough to believe the sound could infect her children, the aristocratic mother complained to the management, and though the hotel doctor confirmed there was no risk of contagion, the Manns were asked to move into the annex. Instead they moved into the Pensione Regina.

One evening they took the children to an entertainment in a hall normally used as a cinema. Advertised as a traveling conjurer, the performer turned out to be a hypnotist with a sadistic streak. He humiliated several members of the audience, including a waiter who'd befriended the children. Tricked into mistaking the hypnotist for the girl he loved, he gave the man a kiss. When he realized what he'd done, the waiter was so embarrassed that he ran away, and Erika said she wouldn't have been surprised if he'd shot the hypnotist. But the next day, when he waited on them at tea, he was extremely pleased with himself, and full of praise for the hypnotist.[48]

Myth and Madam World

THE MORE HEADWAY Thomas made with the *Joseph* story, the more he found himself being pressed backward into the story of Jacob. After the forty-seven-page prologue, "Journey to Hell" ("Höllenfahrt"), he wrote sixty-two pages featuring the young Joseph, only to retreat into 228 pages leading up to his hero's birth. Writing *Buddenbrooks*, he'd found everything he'd intended to use as prehistory took on an autonomous form, and he'd allowed the material to grow, just as Wagner had let his idea for the death of Siegfried become a cycle of four operas. Once again Thomas was glad to use Wagner as a model while his new novel grew into a tetralogy.

At the same time he was indebted to Ernst Bertram, who'd used the word *mythology* in his title: *Nietzsche: Versuch einer Mythologie*, and had, as T. J. Reed pointed out, given a new dimension to Thomas's realization that Nietzsche was the medium through which he could understand himself. "Not only did he remind Mann of much that reinforced the affinity in his mosaics of quotation, he stated as a method of understanding what Mann had practised instinctively; and he linked it with myth. . . . History is not a report, reproduction or preservation of the past. . . . The historical record is made up of the myths which changing perspectives have created."[1] If it was inevitable, as Bertram argued, that we shape in our own image the great men who are shaping our development, it follows that creators of myth shape their creations in their own image at the same time as being shaped by the myths they create. Bertram, had he been describing the process critically, might have "cut the ground from under Thomas's feet," but he enthuses rhapsodically: "Everything that has happened wants to become an image, every living thing a legend, every reality a myth."[2]

In "Death in Venice," Thomas had given the story of Aschenbach and Tadzio a mythical dimension, but to use biblical material was to immerse himself directly in myth. He was identifying both with Jacob, who stole Isaac's blessing from his elder brother Esau, and with Joseph, whose talent for words and for interpreting dreams is almost a literary talent. He is also perceived as a confidence trickster, the main trick lying in the way he takes advantage of existing myths to make it sound as though he has the sort of powers that are familiar from legends. He gives the impression of being able to survive death, like the god Tammuz, who comes back to life after being torn to pieces. Thomas was also looking ahead to the Jesus story, as he was when, writing of Joseph's birth, he made the mother, Rachel, seem almost virginal.

> For at midday, when the child was born, the sign of the virgin had risen in the east, and, as he knew, it corresponded to the star of Ishtar, the planetary revelation of divine femininity, and he was determined to see in Rachel, the childbearer, a heavenly virgin and mother goddess, a Hathor and Isis with the child at her breast.[3]

At the same time Thomas was playing, neatly and satisfyingly, with a reversal of his own family history. His father's will had been like a curse, punishing the widow and the bereaved children who were turned out of their home; Jacob has a blessing to pass on, and at his death his children will benefit.

Work on the story intensified Thomas's awareness of the political responsibility each generation has to the next. In September he agreed to join the committee of Coudenhove-Kalergi's Pan-Europa movement, but instead of attending the inaugural congress in Vienna, he sent a letter saying that though men in their fifties might never see a Europe fit for their children to live in, they could contribute toward its creation. "We owe something to our children and as a generation we are to some degree guilty in relation to them."[4]

His ongoing problem was how to divide his time between fiction and the various activities through which he could exert influence helpfully. He sacrificed time to reading books sent by friends, acquaintances, and strangers, writing courteous letters in reply, and being polite when refusing most of the other demands made on his time. He hesitated in the autumn about whether to visit Erlangen, where he was invited to lecture on Platen and to be awarded the medal of the Ansbach Platen society. He decided that the medal could be presented to him in absentia. "Once again, forgive me, but one thing leads to another, the months and years slip by, life is drawing to a close, and one has the worrying sense of not having arrived at what is really one's own, purely through weakness and submissiveness to the world."[5]

At the end of September he and Katia motored with Ernst Bertram to Lausanne, where Monika was studying the piano, and to Salem, where Golo was studying for his school-leaving examination. In Schaffhausen, Thomas was fascinated by the noise the waterfall made, and they motored back through the Danube Valley. "There is great magic in this way of travelling."[6]

Like the writing of *The Magic Mountain*, the writing of the *Joseph* novels was disrupted by lectures and readings inside Germany and abroad.

"Madam World always finds pretexts for incessant disturbances."7 But Thomas didn't realize how much time he was jeopardizing when he became involved with the Prussian Academy of the Arts, which had existed for over two hundred years but had concerned itself only with art and music. Now that the painter Max Liebermann was president, the decision was taken to form a literary section. Gerhart Hauptmann and Thomas both agreed to join as founding members. Changing his mind two days before the inauguration ceremony, Hauptmann caused a scandal by resigning, but Thomas, who stayed on, joined a committee to select members for the literature section.

He was planning to take Katia with him to Berlin, but she was ill again, and he went alone. Staying from October 18 to 21, he broadcast a talk on Joseph Conrad, having written an introduction for Fischer's edition of *The Secret Agent*; he went on to spend three days in Hamburg, where he saw Klaus, whose "Kindernovelle" had just been published. At the end of the month Thomas was back in Berlin for what he called "a stupid Academy occasion"8—and was enrolled as a member. Disappointed when Hofmannsthal refused to join, Thomas told him the academy would "have the strength to exert cultural authority."9

Thomas paid a third visit to Berlin on November 18 to speak at an academy celebration. In his "Sketch of My Life," he says it was no accident that he was chosen to speak: "like perhaps no-one else, I had undergone violent internal conflict in submitting to contemporary pressure to make the transition from the metaphysical-individual to the social."10 After agreeing to be one of the twenty-four senators, he gave time to such problems as finding a name for the literary section. Eager to resume work on the *Joseph* story, he turned down an invitation to Vienna,11 but agreed to make a speech at Munich's town hall in honor of Hauptmann, whose play *Dorothea Angermann* was being premiered at the Kammerspiele.

Thomas was also taking time to keep fit. Dr. Arno Lampe, a specialist in internal medicine, had recommended a masseur, Herr Silberhorn, who gave his patients gymnastic exercises. "Among other things he makes me hop forty times, and finally rubs me down with eau de cologne."12 Thomas also took time to prepare for Christmas. For Katia he bought some Murano vases, a platinum wristwatch, a pocketbook, some warmly lined gloves, and a flashlight—so that she could look in on the two young children late at night without waking their governess, Fräulein Kurz.

None of these distractions stopped him from generating momentum in the *Joseph* story:

I am really glad to be writing again. It is only when doing something that one feels like oneself and knows something about oneself. The times in between are gruesome. The Joseph material is growing page by page, even if I am as yet doing no more than amusing myself by laying down essayistic or comic-pseudoscientific foundations. I am having more fun with it than with anything I have ever done. It is for once something new and intellectually remarkable, in that with these people meaning and being, myth and reality are constantly merging, and Joseph is a kind of mythical confidence trickster.[13]

In a letter to Ernst Bertram he called Joseph a "Typhonic Tammuz-Osiris-Adonis-Dionysus figure."[14]

What Joseph has in common with Tammuz/Osiris, Dionysus, and Jesus Christ is the ability to rebound from what looks like death. After being rescued from the pit where he'd been left to die, he rises to power through diplomatic use of a preternatural talent for interpreting dreams; they assert divine powers after being torn to pieces.

Between writing the first and last words of *The Magic Mountain*, he'd let twelve years go by; the last words of the *Joseph* tetralogy were to be written sixteen years after the first, but though intentions and motivations were subject to even more fluctuation than those behind *The Magic Mountain*, one of the main themes in both fictions is the properties of time, while one of the intentions behind the *Joseph* novels is to give a tinge of eternity to the present tense, generalizing the particular and writing about the whole of humanity while telling the story of one man. Incident is transformed into what Thomas calls *mysterium*—in which meaning is indistinguishable from being.

In his prologue, Thomas discusses the nature of time, myths of creation, and explanations of how narrative had originated. He also describes the mixture of anxiety and curiosity he felt at the prospect of descending into the remote past. It felt as if he'd committed himself to a journey backward beyond death. He might lose sight of time. Narrative always involves a sense of being present at the events that are dramatized: This time the sense of being present would fade backward into pre-history.

THE YEAR ENDED with a bout of flu that continued into 1927,[15] but at the end of January, Thomas escaped with Katia and the two young children, now eight and seven years old, to Ettal, a health and skiing resort to the south of Munich, near Garmisch. The Benedictine monastery reminded him of the Escorial, and the mountains looked beautiful under the snow.[16] They stayed at the comfortable Hotel Ludwig der Bayer: "Down with carnival, theatre and society," Thomas wrote on a picture postcard. "Long live nature with hot and cold water."[17]

He enjoyed the reading he was doing for the *Joseph* story. In Hans

Ludwig Held's newly published *Der Gespenst des Golem* (*The Ghost of the Golem*) the chapter that interested him most was about the creation of Adam,[18] and he made contact with Egyptologists and Orientalists at Munich University.[19] Corresponding with a Frankfurt rabbi, Jakob Horovitz, who'd published a book on the *Joseph* story, *Die Josepherzählung*, Thomas made the point that whether the events were historical or legendary, the narrative, which was written in the ancient Oriental literary tradition, would have been tricked out with mythic allusions and loaded with conventional ideas.

> Thanks to my penchant for the history of religion, which constitutes a good deal of my pleasure in the story, it is easy for me to believe that, but I long ago decided to turn the tables and let the characters make the allusions themselves. The Amurru boy, Joseph, who has been brought up in Babylon and Egypt, naturally knows about Gilgamesh, Tammuz, Osiris, and he patterns his life on them. He can be found guilty of a far-reaching and strangely fraudulent identification of his ego with that of these heroes, and I am inclined to think that a prominent feature in the psychology of this whole world was a re-enactment of the essentially timeless myth.[20]

Due to spend the second week of March in Warsaw, Thomas traveled via Berlin for a session of the academy's literary section. He read out Heinrich's protest against the censorship that was being prepared in the Reichstag. In Warsaw, where he was a guest of the PEN Club, he was given a more enthusiastic reception than he'd expected.[21] In the overcrowded foyer of the Hotel Europejski he spoke on freedom and nobility; when he left Warsaw, the secretary of state for external affairs saw him off at the railway station.

In April he tried to economize with time, giving no readings or lectures, but at the end of the month he and Katia traveled down the Rhine from Koblenz to Cologne: "[I]t was beautiful all the way, and our eyes drank what was held in our eyelashes."[22]

On May 10 his sister Julia hanged herself. She'd been a widow for five years, but when Josef Löhr was still alive she'd started taking morphine and had become addicted to it, finding it made it possible for her to sleep with him as often as he wanted her to. He had died at the age of sixty, and inflation had left her without enough money to bring up their three daughters. She'd always prided herself on her position in society; now that she felt déclassée, her dependence on drugs increased. As Heinrich told Alfred Pringsheim, "My sister was conventionality incarnate. What mattered to her more than anything: not to attract attention, to appear *comme il faut*." And he told Golo: "the gruesome contrast was between her superbourgeois public existence and her humiliating secret life." Eva-Maria, now twenty-six, was married, and the twins were twenty. Julia had a lover, but he was unfaithful–Golo often saw him with another woman. Julia wasn't yet fifty when she died. Golo reports that his father "was deeply shaken, not because the death of his sister, long since become an embarrassment, was a loss, but because, as I heard him tell my mother, it was like lightning striking very near him." It was seventeen years since Carla's death: both his sisters had committed suicide. Julia's unfaithful lover came to the funeral, and Thomas wrote a eulogy for it, but didn't read it, leaving everything to the pastor who'd baptized the three girls.23

Soon afterward Thomas spent ten days by himself in Kreuth, twenty miles from Tölz, where he finished the first section of the novel. He was realizing the idea he'd had for a father-son novel when he fell in love with Klaus; Jacob's paternal affection for Joseph also derives partly from Thomas's for Elisabeth. Joseph has a charming, oval face, with gentle slanting eyes. When we first meet him, he's in a position inspired by that of Klaus lying down without his shirt. Joseph has lowered his coarse bleached linen shirt, and his brown skin glistens in the moonlight. With its high, square, Egyptian-looking shoulders, his torso seems full and heavy in relation to the childish head. He likes to display his young body, half-nude, to the moon, hoping to charm her, or the powers above. If circumcision symbolizes a marriage between God and mankind, the bond of faith is sexual in nature, but circumcision suggests emasculation, and Jacob's piety is offended when he sees his son displaying himself to the moon. The beautiful boy, who can chatter appealingly, modulating from vivacity to quiet reassurance, is good at calming his father's anger.

Thomas's emotions found their way into his work long after he'd experienced them. The pleasure of looking at a beautiful boy wasn't entirely divorced from the idea of consummation, but with Klaus, as with the ten-year-old Wladyslaw Moes in Venice, the only consummation Thomas wanted was literary, and it came a long time after the anticipatory pleasure of looking. In *The Age of Innocence*, Newland Archer dawdles over a cigar, making himself late for a rendezvous because he's looking forward to it so keenly. If dilettantism, as Edith Wharton suggests, is the habit of taking pleasure in postponing pleasure, Thomas was an arch-dilettante. Sometimes he confessed his love to the young males who excited him, but more often he hugged it silently to himself. Klaus would have been surprised to learn that his father had ever felt so close to him. Thomas's behavior was always so formal and reserved that the son could only respond in the same way. Trying to make the formality into a joke, Klaus would usually start letters to his father with some such phrase as "Dear and Highly Honoured Mr. Magician"– "Liebe Herr Zauberer hochgeehrt" or "Lieber und verehrter Zauberer."24

To Golo, now eighteen, his elder brother seemed to have an enviably relaxed relationship with their father. "Thomas Mann could be nice, but that was infrequent," Golo said in 1987. "When we were children there was no warm, cordial, relaxed feeling of trust." At seventeen or eighteen, he said, "I started to stammer when I spoke to him, which happened seldom enough. My parents were really frightfully awkward with me when they told me: 'Don't try to join in. Do you think you know better than we do?' After that, of course, I kept silent for six months." He didn't like eating alone with them, and especially hated eating alone with Thomas. Unable to bear long silences, Golo used to prepare himself for these meals by making notes for possible topics. Later, when he told his younger brother, Michael laughed and said he did the same thing. "It didn't occur to Thomas Mann that it might be unpleasant for a child to sit in silence."25

AFTER RETURNING FROM KREUTH, Thomas had less than three weeks in Munich, leaving again on August 11 for a month with Katia and the three youngest children in Kampen on Sylt, one of the North Frisian islands, near the border between Denmark and Schleswig-Holstein. Though the island struck him as extraordinarily beautiful, it was so cold that he couldn't relax. At first he could scarcely read and never write.26 "The charms of this island are chaste and scanty and steer the senses towards rum grog."27 In the evenings, he and Katia drank with a museum director from Lübeck and Werner Heuser, director of the art academy in Düsseldorf.28 But the weather improved while they were there, the sea was spectacular, and Thomas remembered "the soft thunder of the waves."29

Nor did he forget Heuser's seventeen-year-old son, Klaus, a handsome boy who inspired more intense feeling in the fifty-two-year-old man than anyone since Wladyslaw Moes. Thomas had to suffer the painful pleasure of seeing the boy every day without being able to woo him openly, and knowing that the end of the holiday would bring the much sharper pain of separation. Unable to talk about this, he wrote about it a few weeks later when he was generalizing about love in a paper he was going to read at Munich's Schauspielhaus before a special performance of Kleist's *Amphytrion*. No one in the audience would guess that he was talking about recent experience when he started by asking: "What is loyalty?" He answers that it is loving without seeing—conquest over the forgetfulness that might have supervened.

We encounter a face that we love, and after some gazing at it, which consolidates our feeling, we are separated from it. Oblivion is inevitable: the pain of parting is only the pain of certain oblivion. Our sensual imagination, our power of remembering is weaker than we like to think. . . . What remains is nothing but the certainty that each new confrontation with this manifestation of life will renew our feeling, will make us love it again, or rather go on loving it. This knowledge of the law of our nature, and this holding on to it is loyalty. It is love that makes us forget why; it is belief in love that may speak while it is alive, because it is certain to regain life, immediately and according to the law, immediately we see it again.[30]

He made it come back to life by inviting the boy to Munich, and spending a great deal of time with him. He also visited his young friend in Düsseldorf. Certainly they kissed and probably they hugged each other, but it's unlikely that they ever brought each other to orgasm. For Thomas the pleasure in these encounters was more visual than tactile. It was as if he wanted to lay the foundations for what he'd remember. The emotion that came with the verbal reconstitution of the experience may have been stronger than the emotion felt in the presence of the beloved. Or perhaps he could never confront the opportunity squarely until he was certain it was in the past tense. All emotion was retrospective. One event that meant a lot was that Klaus had shed tears on his account.[31]

WHEN TWO OF THE ACADEMY'S literary senators, Josef Ponten and Wilhelm Schäfer, wanted to nominate Thomas as chairman, he'd agreed to stand for election, but while he was on the island, Heinrich, who was also a senator, intervened to dissuade him. The academy, he said, would give German literature its only chance to achieve the social recognition it deserved, and the senate needed a chairman who not only wanted the academy to be powerful but would gladly fight for it, raising money and promoting its interests. This would take more time than Thomas would be willing to sacrifice.[32] Capitulating immediately, he wrote to tell Ponten he'd changed his mind. Heinrich would be the right man, said Thomas in a letter to him, if he could spare enough time.[33]

Returning to Munich on September 11, Thomas failed to regain the momentum he'd lost with *Joseph*: A new interpretation of the Pentateuch forced him to reconsider his treatment of the story.[34] Analyzing his motives in answer to a questionnaire about work in progress, he cited interest in the history of religion, a predilection for Egyptian culture, and the fun of looking for human impulses that were invisible on the surface.[35]

Meanwhile he prepared his lecture on Kleist's *Amphytrion*, which had been published 120 years earlier. It was a reworking of Molière's 1668 *Amphytrion*, based on a comedy by Plautus, and Thomas decided it was the wittiest, profoundest, and most beautiful play ever written. Infatuated with the beautiful Alkmene, loyal wife of Amphytrion, Jupiter can win her only by impersonating her husband. Since the disguise is impenetrable, even in bed, is the deceived wife being unfaithful? The playwright probes provocatively into a complex of issues. Since German literature had never had a critic comparable to Charles-Augustin Sainte-Beuve, Thomas could claim there was no precedent for the textual analysis he carried out on Kleist's play, and though he'd read it before, he immersed himself in it more deeply, pondering the problem of identity. To write about the merging of human and divine qualities is to suggest, metaphorically or symbolically, that the ego isn't self-contained, that the individual consciousness is connected to external forces and elements. The assumption that each personality is unique can be no more than a convention. (He later wrote disparagingly about Jung, but here he was moving toward a Jungian notion.)

The influence of these ideas on Thomas's novel is apparent at the beginning of the second chapter, which tells the story of Jacob and Esau. Dealing with biblical material, Thomas was handling events that had become inseparable from the narratives that encased them. And these couldn't be taken as accurate. Unlike the history of his own family, or the story of Hanno Buddenbrook's ancestors, the story of Joseph's ancestors was, as recorded in the Book of Genesis, only a "pious abbreviation" of the facts. Centuries must have elapsed between Abraham's death and Jacob's birth. "Many Abrahams, Isaacs and Jacobs had watched the birth of day out of the night without having any excessively precise ideas about time and mortality, without making any clear distinctions between their present and the present of earlier times, or distinguishing their individuality from the individualities of earlier Abrahams, Isaacs, and Jacobs."[36] Passed down from generation to generation, the names were like approximations. The growth of the community was not that of a family tree but of a forest bound together by belief and practice. In dreams Jacob could confuse himself with Abraham, and Joseph with the young Isaac who narrowly escaped being slaughtered as a sacrifice; it was as a spiritual head that Abraham had been the father of his people, and Joseph might not have been his direct descendant. All the identities are blurred.

Nobel Prize

BEFORE THE END OF 1927, Thomas gave a lot of time to readings and lectures. In late October, after traveling to Berlin, where he attended several meetings at the academy,[1] he went on to Stettin and Frankfurt, reading "Disorder and Early Sorrow" and repeating the Kleist lecture. His inclination was to speak out against nationalism and imperialism at every opportunity, and he toured Germany, talking on such subjects as "Freedom and Nobility" ("Freiheit und Vornehmheit") and "Natur und Nation." Answering a questionnaire sent out by *Europäische Gespräche*, he took the view that Britain's imperial greatness was coming to an end, and that Germany shouldn't try to acquire colonies.[2]

Committing himself publicly in this way, Thomas had to reckon with the enmity of the nationalists. His name was being mentioned as a candidate for the Nobel Prize, but it was unlikely that he'd win it without the championship of the German universities, and in Munich the rector was "not only a nationalistic national economist but a narrow-minded Philistine."[3]

Generally, though, Thomas was trying not to assert himself politically. When Zoltán Szántó, who was on the central committee of the illegal Hungarian Communist Party, was about to go on trial in Budapest, Georg Lukács, knowing he'd probably be condemned to death, asked Thomas to send a telegram to the regent of Hungary, Admiral Horthy. When Thomas answered that it wasn't for the writer to intervene in the political arena, Lukács wrote a furious letter, calling him a high-minded liar and condemning him for going to Warsaw as a guest of the PEN Club and talking about humanitarianism, but refusing to take the most elementary humanitarian action. Thomas gave in to this argument and sent a telegram to Horthy.[4]

Inside Germany he was shying away from any kind of political commitment while the tide of nationalism was rising, and by the beginning of 1928 his reticence exposed him to the kind of attack he'd once launched against Heinrich, accusing him of lacking patriotism and taking too much interest in French culture. After an interview he gave the Paris review *Comoedia*, favoring an improvement in Franco-German relations, Thomas was denounced by the *Berliner Nachtausgabe* under the headline "Thomas Mann's kow-tow to Paris." His answer, an open letter to the paper, provoked strong reactions. He was savaged in the *Völkischer Beobachter*, the organ of the Nazi Party, while *Der Tag* carried in its entertainment section an article called "The Disenchanted Mountain." This, he said, was "worth reading as an expression of the mental attitude of certain political or pseudo-political young people. . . . It is pure dynamistic romanticism, pure idealisation of catastrophe for its own sake. . . . These are strange times."[5]

Like other intellectuals, he was pushed toward socialism by the threat of rabid nationalism. In March he wrote an article "Kultur und Sozialismus" for *Preussische Jahrbücher*: "[W]hat would be needed, what could be ultimately German, would be an alliance and pact between the conservative idea of culture and the revolutionary notion of society, between Greece and Moscow, to make the point forcibly."[6] He knew he was still a "beginner" in socialism, "but I am certain that every living creature today must be a socialist and—literally—a social democrat, and I am glad we are in agreement that this implies no rejection of the *so-called* bourgeois, of German culture."[7]

In the Reichstag elections, held on May 20, the Socialist parties gained votes and seats at the expense of the nationalists. The Nazis won only twelve seats, while the Social Democrats increased their poll by over a million votes, but the only real chance of defeating nationalism would have been through a united front—a possibility that was ruled out by the sixth Comintern, which vetoed solidarity between Communists and Social Democrats.

In February and March he had concentrated on the *Joseph* novel, but he'd been intending to interrupt his work after Easter "because I really need to."[8] He and Katia went on a motoring trip through Switzerland and France. It was late June before he settled down again to work on the novel.

At the end of the month he became embroiled in another controversy with the nationalists. The July issue of the *Süddeutsche Monatshefte*, which appeared before the end of June, contained an open letter from its co-editor, Artur Hübscher,[9] who accused Thomas of falsifying *Reflections* by abridging it and of becoming increasingly involved in party politics. Defending himself in a handwritten reply that wasn't intended for publication, Thomas claimed to be "very German" in wanting nothing but those things that are sensible, necessary, favorable to life, and concerned with human dignity, but he admitted to being appalled by the Munich professor who'd welcomed the murder of Rathenau by saying "Bravo, one less!" and by the acclaim being given to "the two flying dunces"—German aviators who'd made the first east-west flight across the Atlantic. Without permission, the *Monatshefte* printed the letter in a pamphlet that was designed to make Thomas look unpatriotic. A copy was sent to the *Münchner Zeitung*, which attacked him.[10]

He and Katia spent the whole of August on the island of Sylt, where Ernst Bertram visited them. But after returning to Munich, Thomas found himself trying to crowd in so much activity alongside the writing that he was unsure whether he was doing justice to his subject matter. "I have to read and reflect and compose beautiful formulations, doing all that on the edge."[11] Ten years earlier it would have been easier to set limits on the time he was willing to give the literary section of the academy, but as the nationalists became increasingly vocal, and politics encroached on literature, it was important to use such influence as the academy could exert. At first Thomas was against inviting only a limited quota of nationalists to join: Members, he thought, should be selected according to their intrinsic merit. But the nationalists quickly formed a dangerous bloc, and when he was invited to speak on Lessing at the academy's celebrations for the bicentenary of his birth, Thomas knew he'd been presented with an opportunity to speak out in favor of moderation and restraint.

At the end of October he left Munich for ten days to give readings from *Joseph* in Austria and Switzerland. Returning during the second week in November, he spent just over a fortnight in Munich before setting out again on the twenty-fourth for three weeks of readings. The tour ended on December 12, and by the fourteenth he had started work on his Lessing lecture.[12]

The feuding between nationalists and republicans in the academy involved constant disagreement about the relative merits of the *Dichter* and the *Schriftsteller*–the "creative writer" and the "author." Even the name *Sektion für Dichtkunst* seemed to favor the nationalists, who championed the *Dichter*, assuming him to have inspirational roots in the soil of the fatherland, while the *Schriftsteller's* values were metropolitan and international–those of the *littérateur*. As part of his campaign against the nationalists, Thomas presented Lessing not only as a *Schriftsteller* but as an opponent of narrow-minded nationalism: He "called patriotism 'a heroic weakness' and declared there was nothing he wanted less than to be acclaimed as a zealous patriot, the kind of patriot who wanted him to forget the duty to be a citizen of the world." Thomas also claims Lessing was aware that nationalism might be no more than a form of provincialism; as he said, "there should be in each state men who stand back from the prejudice of the people and clearly understand the point at which patriotism ceases to be a virtue."[13] At the end of his speech Thomas made a direct appeal: "In the spirit and name of Lessing, we should strive beyond every form of fascism towards a union of intelligence and blood which alone deserves to be called fully human."[14]

The lecture contains evidence of preoccupations he'd developed while working on the *Joseph* novel. Lessing is seen as "the founder of a mythical type—mythical because it is always being incarnated. He is the classical creative writer, the patriarch of all literary intelligence."[15] At times, Thomas says, the concept of the classical can appear in a mythic light. He defines it as

the prototype, the original foundation of a spiritual form of life through the living individual; it is a patriarchal impression of an original type in which later life will recognise itself, in whose tracks it will wander. . . . The classical period is the period of the patriarchs, mythical time, time of the first foundation and shaping of national life.[16]

Several equations are being made on several levels. Without comparing biblical legends with Graeco-Roman myths, he's suggesting they both articulate ideas about the origins of our spiritual life. He was attracted to a pre-historical period in which individual identities seemed to overlap because his own identity could be allowed to overlap freely with the identities he was bringing to life in the fiction. Any guilt he felt about outshining his elder brother could seep into his account of how Jacob tricked Esau out of Isaac's blessing, and how Joseph eclipsed his half-brothers. Thomas later claimed that for a storyteller the attainment of the mythical viewpoint "signifies . . . a new serenity in recognising and shaping." The mythical he said, "represents an early and primitive stage in the life of humanity, but a late and mature one in the life of the individual."[17] But the maturity he'd achieved didn't make him less self-involved; it merely transferred the involvement to a different level. One of the underlying questions is whether Joseph represents the prototype of the spirituality currently incarnated in Thomas Mann.

At the same time, talking polemically to the academy, he could declare, both on Lessing's account and his own, that precision and polemics are both admissible in creative writing. The *Dichter*, he ironically suggests, is "degraded and dishonoured" by any evidence of "sensitivity to the period, the world, what is evil, stupid, demoralising and repellent." The creative writer is expected to "see nothing, notice nothing, have no notion of anything, and feel comfortable in letting his pure ignorance be misused in the service of corruption and private interest."[18]

In April Thomas again suspended work on the novel to prepare for a lecture about Freud at the Auditorium Maximum on May 16. The title was "The Position of Sigmund Freud in Modern Cultural History" ("Die Stellung Sigmund Freuds in der modernen Geistesgeschichte"). Two weeks before delivering this lecture, Thomas described it as "a wide-ranging dissertation on the problem of revolution, with academic intentions and in fact serving the purposes of those who want the psychoanalytical movement to be recognised as the one manifestation of modern anti-rationalism—which offers no kind of handle to reactionary misuse."[19] The lecture, which attracted a lot of antireactionary students, went well.[20]

At the end of May, Thomas went to rest in Gastein, near Salzburg, where he was joined by Heinrich, who was in his fifty-ninth year, "almost an old man," as he said, but his life had entered a new phase.[21] Mimi was refusing to divorce him, but he was passionately involved with the star actress Trude Hesterberg. He'd written a musical for her, *Bibi*, which had opened in Berlin during October, and it was with her in mind that he'd given permission for *Professor Unrat* to be made into a film. Undeterred by the way their own situation was emulating that of Lola-Lola and the schoolmaster, she took the novel to the UFA film studios in Berlin. They hadn't yet made any talkies, and, commissioning Carl Zuckmayer to write a screenplay for their first, they changed the title to *Der blaue Engel*. The director was to be the Austrian Josef Sternberg, who had added the von in Hollywood, where he achieved success in 1927 with *Underworld*, followed in 1928 by *The Last Command*, starring Emil Jannings. Casting Jannings as the schoolmaster, he insisted that the part of Lola-Lola should be played by a twenty-seven-year-old actress who'd been considered for the lead in G. W. Pabst's film of Wedekind's *Die Büchse der Pandora*, Marlene Dietrich. Heinrich threatened to withdraw permission for the film to be made, and though Trude Hesterberg persuaded him not to, the production was almost canceled when the perverse owner of the studios, Alfred Hugenberg, discovered that the novel wasn't, as he'd believed, by Thomas. It was only when he learned how strongly Heinrich disapproved of Zuckmayer's script that he allowed the production to go ahead. This script was used when shooting started in October.

WHEN HUGO VON HOFMANNSTHAL died on July 15 at the age of fifty-five, Thomas felt more upset than he'd have expected. They'd known each other for twenty-two years. "My heart is too full of tears," he wrote in an obituary for the *Neue Freie Presse*, "for words to come out of it, and my thoughts too submerged and dissolved in an infinite feeling of life, death, fate and friendship for me to control myself, or want to."[22] In fact, the two men had become only superficially friendly and had spent little time together. Thomas couldn't attend the funeral because he was committed to making a speech about theater to open the Heidelberg Festival on July 20,[23] but he started by paying tribute to the dead man. "We are mourning a loss that could scarcely have done more damage to the world of culture."[24]

Nine days later, on July 29, Thomas and Katia left with Elisabeth and Michael for a seaside holiday on Danzig Bay. They stayed at the

spa hotel in Rauschen, near Königsberg. Intending, as usual on holiday, to spend the mornings working, but not wanting to pack the bulky
Joseph manuscript, he started a story based on an idea he'd had three
years earlier when at the seaside with Katia and the two younger children in Forte de Marmi.[25]

"Mario and the Magician" ("Mario und der Zauberer") represents his
first serious fictional confrontation with fascism. Neither in 1926, when
observing its effect on the atmosphere in an Italian seaside resort and
on people's behavior, nor in 1929, when reconstructing the events of
three years ago, did Thomas think a German leader would ever attract
so much hero-worship as Mussolini was enjoying in Italy. On the other
hand, if Thomas could no longer describe himself as a nonpolitical
man, it was largely because of what he'd seen in Germany as the cult of
nationalism engulfed liberal values.

RETROSPECTIVELY, the story seems prophetic, but perhaps observations of fanatical patriotism in Germany were filtering into the account
Thomas gives of behavior in Italy, where the whole nation had succumbed to what he'd called "the flatulent influence of the Duce" (see
page 363).

The comments on fascism in "Mario and the Magician" couldn't
have been made in any other form, but, like "Death in Venice," the
story is built almost entirely out of facts. Using his experiences in Forte
de Marmi, Thomas renames it Torre di Venere, which means Tower of
Venus. He uses the nervous aristocratic mother who thought her children might be infected by the sound of Michael's coughing, the incident on the beach with the naked eight-year-old Elisabeth, and the
sadistic hypnotist whose victims included the waiter who'd made
friends with the children. The narrative, which is in the first person, describes the deference of the hotel staff to the Principe X and his family.
Once the Principessa has complained, it's impossible to reassure the obsequious, frock-coated manager that there's no danger of contagion.
His only interest is in kowtowing to the nobility.

Incapable of innocent enjoyment on the beach, people display a new
consciousness of national dignity. Even among the children there are
disputes about flags, quarrels about authority and precedence. The
naked body of the eight-year-old girl provokes hoots from patriotic children, and the bowler-hatted man accuses her parents of abusing his
country's hospitality, insulting its honor.

When the deformed hypnotist, Cipolla, makes his entrance, his top
hat, his cloak with satin collar and velvet lining, his white gloves and
white scarf suggest an eighteenth-century mountebank, but there's no
jocularity in his manner, only arrogance. He wears a striped sash under

his frock coat, while a riding whip with a silver claw handle hangs from his forearm by a leather thong. He lets the whip whistle through the air when he performs his first hypnotic trick, making a defiant-seeming boy stick his tongue out at the audience.

After talking about the physical defect that stopped him from fighting in the war for the greater glory of the Fatherland, Cipolla says the Duce's brother attended one of his performances in Rome. His eloquence impresses the audience, and when a boy, called on stage to chalk figures on a blackboard, says he can't write, Cipolla rebukes him for humiliating the government and the country in front of an international audience. Cipolla keeps up a rhetorical commentary, saying that there's no such thing as freedom of the will, since a will that aims at its own freedom is aiming at the unknown.

Performing card tricks and playing parlor games, he's acting in obedience to a voiceless common will, and he says that commanding and obeying form a single principle. The capacity to command is the reverse side of the capacity for self-abnegation and becoming a tool. While the narrative implies a connection between hypnosis and the political charisma of a dictator, the performer's relationship with the audience is implicitly compared to that of the leader with the people. Writing about willingness to be spellbound, Thomas is writing about eagerness to be dominated. The extent to which the narrator and his wife are themselves under the spell is dramatized by their failure during the intermission to take their tired children away from this unsuitable entertainment.

In the second half of the show Cipolla launches a direct attack on the spectators' willpower. They enjoy themselves without being wholly insensitive to the ignominy inflicted by each of his successes. Put into a deep trance, a young man is made to lie stiffly with his head on one chair and his feet on another. Even when Cipolla sits on him, his body stays in a straight line. Men who resist Cipolla's efforts to make them dance end up by jigging about. People applaud when Mario is tricked into mistaking Cipolla for the girl he loves, and if Thomas is half-hearted in exploring their ambivalence, it may be out of uncertainty about his own attitude to the manipulative skills on display. He brings the story to a melodramatic climax by developing Erika's remark that she wouldn't have been surprised if the waiter had shot the hypnotist: Mario produces a revolver and kills Cipolla. But this is neither convincing nor satisfying. Had he carried the story into the following day, making Mario as willing as the real waiter was to share in the performer's glory by praising him, Thomas could have given himself the time he needed to explore his ambivalence more deeply.

* * *

Thomas and Katia had heard about the beautiful scenery on the peninsula Kurische Nehrung, which almost cuts off the bay Kurisches Haff from the Baltic. When they visited it in the late summer of 1929, they liked it enough to spend a few days in a little fishing village on the dunes, Nidden, on the far side of the bay from Königsberg. Enchanted with the drifting sand dunes and the elks in the forests of pine and birch, they bought the lease of a site on the dunes and commissioned an architect to build them a summer house.

After reading from the *Joseph* novel in Königsberg, Thomas returned at the beginning of September to Munich, where he had over two months of undisturbed work before he received a telegram, on November 12, saying he'd been awarded the Nobel Prize. The man who usually had the decisive voice among the judges was an academic and critic, Martin Fridrik Böök, whom Thomas had offended, five years earlier, by keeping him talking outside the front door of his house in Munich without inviting him in.[26] Since Böök had publicly condemned *The Magic Mountain* as an artistic monstrosity, the news came as a surprise, as did the tribute Heinrich paid later in the day, speaking on the radio and calling Thomas "a master who today speaks for his people."[27] Writing to Maximilian Brantl, he called Heinrich's broadcast a "splendid gesture."[28]

In the next few days messages of congratulation poured in from all over the world, while articles about him appeared in the papers. On November 16 he read part of "Mario and the Magician" at a celebration held by the Bavarian section of the Writers' Schutzverband. On the eighteenth he repeated his Freud lecture to the medical psychology department of the university, and lectured the next day on "Bürgerlichkeit" to Munich's Rotary Club.

Early in December he and Katia left Munich to spend two days in Berlin on their way to Stockholm. After being interviewed in Berlin by international reporters, he gave two readings—from *Felix Krull* at a reception arranged by the International Union of Students, and "Mario and the Magician" at a meeting organized by the League of German Writers.

In the great hall of the Konserthuset on December 10, Thomas was presented to King Gustav V, the crown prince and princess, and members of the Swedish Academy. In his speech of acceptance, he did all he could to identify with Germany. It was the German mind and German prose that were being honored, he said. He was glad to lay the prize "at the feet of my country and people," to which he and those like him felt still more closely bound than at the time of Germany's greatest imperial expansion.

Making a speech in German, Fridrik Böök said it was for *Buddenbrooks* that Thomas was receiving the prize, and the document which the king handed to him was addressed to "Thomas Mann, winner of the literary Nobel Prize of the year 1929, especially for his great novel *Buddenbrooks*, which in the course of the years has won ever increasing recognition as a classical work of the present." But, as Thomas knew, he wouldn't have won the prize without the reputation he'd gained subsequently, mainly through *The Magic Mountain*.[29]

The next day, when he and Katia had dinner with the king in the castle, previous literary prizewinners, including Selma Lagerlöf, were among the guests. On December 20, in an unscripted broadcast, he described the celebrations in Stockholm, and later gave a reading in aid of a Jewish old people's home. When he returned to Munich, two days before Christmas, a banquet was held in the town hall. Spending Christmas quietly at home felt like "being in harbour after a long journey on stormy seas."[30]

TEN YEARS AFTER the end of the war, French troops were still occupying the Rhineland, and reparations payments were still outstanding. In August 1928, Stresemann finally persuaded France to consider early withdrawal and to authorize a new review of reparations. In February 1929 an American banker, Owen Young, headed an international board which in August submitted its assessment to a conference at The Hague. The plan was to give the German economy a chance to expand by allowing reparations to be spread over the next thirty years, and the date settled for the evacuation of the Rhineland was June 30, 1930.

Favorable though these terms were, they didn't satisfy the leaders of the militantly reactionary parties, who collaborated to collect over 4 million signatures supporting a draft law the government was asked to pass, repudiating the war-guilt clause in the Versailles treaty and demanding the immediate withdrawal of French troops. When this so-called Freedom Law was put to a referendum in December, nearly 6 million people voted for it—not enough to carry it, but enough to suggest it might be possible to mobilize the masses against the parliamentary system.

Stresemann died early in October 1929, and at the end of the month the Wall Street crash precipitated an international crisis. During the winter, unemployment in Germany reached the point at which the state's insurance scheme could no longer pay benefits. An iron-and-steel magnate, Emil Kirdorf, attended the Nazis' Nuremberg conference as guest of honor, and, eclipsing both *Buddenbrooks* and *The Magic Mountain*, *Mein Kampf* was selling a steady fifty thousand copies a year. With unemployment rising, morale sinking, extremist demagogues and uniformed thugs active in the streets with truncheons and collecting boxes, membership in the Nazi party rose from 120,000 in 1929 to

800,000 in 1931. Members were contributing 300,000 marks a month, which few of them could afford, to a party that was acting less in their interests than in those of the large-scale capitalists, some of whom were helping to finance it.

In March 1930, Hindenburg unconstitutionally appointed a chancellor without a parliamentary majority, Heinrich Brüning, leader of the Center Party. Believing in fiscal reform and failing to get parliamentary support for his budget, he promulgated it by emergency decree, dissolving the Reichstag, postponing elections until September 14, and enforcing his economic policy by *Diktat*. The gap between republican constitutionalism and Nazi violence seemed to be narrowing.

IN JANUARY 1930, Thomas spent a fortnight in Ettal, mostly working on an autobiographical sketch for the Nobel Prize authorities. He completed it early in February, just before celebrating his silver wedding on the eleventh. The essay pays tribute to the woman who has shared twenty-five years of "this difficult life which demands, above all, patience." He had no idea, he said, how he'd have managed "without the clever, courageous and gently energetic support of this extraordinary spouse."[31] Having been his partner so long, he said, she was entitled to an equal say in how they spent the prize money—200,000 marks.

On February 16 they left for what he called a "tour of inspection" in Egypt and Palestine. He'd almost finished *The Tales of Jacob* (*Die Geschichten Jaakobs*), the first volume of his *Joseph* sequence, but he could revise or rewrite after seeing places where key events had occurred. After leaving Munich, they sailed down the Nile on the steamer *Aswan-Wadi Halfa*. While on board, Thomas read D. H. Lawrence's two psychoanalytical books, *Fantasia of the Unconscious* and *Psychoanalysis and the Unconscious*. He liked Lawrence's "jaunty conservatism" except where it overstepped the borderline of "the unacceptably Fascistic." Lawrence denounces "mental consciousness" as a cul-de-sac. "The mind as author and director of life is anathema." What he advocates is "spontaneous-creative fullness of being." But he cannot justly be accused of cultivating mindlessness or taking refuge in "the sub-human awareness of the solar plexus." Though he has sometimes been called a proto-Fascist, he was too much of an individualist, too reverently committed to the ideal of self-realization. But on the steamer Thomas felt less in tune with Lawrence's nonfiction than he did with the work of Jung, "whose great introduction to *The Secret of the Golden Flower* is for me the book itself."[32] This was a thousand-year-old Taoist alchemical treatise that had been sent to Jung by his friend Richard Wilhelm, translator of the *I-Ching*.

On February 23, Thomas and Katia arrived at the southernmost point of the journey, Aswan, where they stayed at the Cataract Hotel. "You can imagine how I am keeping my eyes open," he wrote to one friend,[33] and to several others he used similar phrases about keeping on the alert.

In March both Katia and he succumbed to dysentery and at the end of the month, in Jerusalem, they were taken into the hospital together.[34] They traveled back through Italy, and when they arrived in Munich on April 16, he'd more or less recovered, but she was still ailing.[35] In spite of the dysentery, Thomas called the journey to Egypt and Palestine "the greatest, the most significant of my life."[36]

In the early summer his main distraction from the *Joseph* novel was the job of writing a new introduction to the collected works of Theodor Storm. Far from having lost the partiality for Storm he displayed in "Tonio Kröger," which alludes reverently to the lyrical love story "Immensee," Thomas lavished the most extravagant praise on his verse. He wrote most of the introduction in June and early July. On July 7, about a week before going on holiday, he had an audience of about a thousand students when he read from the *Joseph* novel at Munich University.[37]

The holiday was the first he and Katia spent in the new house at Nidden, his "little castle of delight," as he called it on a postcard depicting it.[38] It was in the middle of a pine wood, fifteen minutes from the beach. It had brown wooden walls, blue shutters, and a thatched roof.[39] He decided to spend the whole of August there,[40] and on September 2 the Pringsheims joined them to celebrate the professor's eightieth birthday.

Thomas was in Geneva, visiting the League of Nations, on September 15, when the postponed elections were held in Germany. In 1928, 800,000 people had voted for the Nazis, but they now won nearly 6.5 million votes, which made them the second largest party in the Reichstag, with 107 seats. Delegates at the League of Nations were appalled, and on the German stock exchange shares fell by twenty points. But Thomas refused to be depressed. "This so-called National Socialism," he said in a postcard to a friend, "is in my view a colossus with clay feet."[41]

He returned briefly to Munich before leaving again for Ansbach to lecture on Platen in his birthplace. In mid-October he went back to Berlin for a reading from the *Joseph* novel at the academy and to make a speech in the Beethovensaal, where he'd delivered "Die deutsche Republik" as a sixtieth birthday tribute to Hauptmann. Now, under the title "German Address—An Appeal to Reason" ("Deutsche Ansprache—Ein Appell an die Vernunft"), he launched a direct attack on Nazism. In 1914, when he started devoting all his working time to *Reflections*, it was because it would have been frivolous to concentrate on fiction during the war. The crisis signaled by the election result might seem less serious, but another moment had come, he said, when the general distress and the immediate necessities of our existence choke back the writer's thoughts and make art seem idle, ephemeral, superfluous—a mental impossibility. No better off than they'd been during the war, millions of Germans were out of work, hungry, impoverished, hopeless.

But Thomas was no longer an enemy of democracy: "I declare my conviction—and I am sufficiently convinced to commit not only my pen but my person to the issue—that today the political place for the German citizen is in the Social Democratic Party." There were Nazis and S.A. men—members of the party's private army—in the audience. Led by a man in blue glasses, the heckling began when Thomas said the pressures put on Germany by the victorious Allies had been so excessive as to produce a disturbing election result and "a state of feeling which may become a menace to the world." He repeated the phrase he'd used in the postcard: Nazism was a colossus with clay feet. Shouting to interrupt him, the man in blue glasses called him a liar, a traitor, and an enemy of the people, while Hedwig Fischer, who was in the front row, whispered to him (or, according to another version of the story, sent an usher to him with a note) warning him not to go on.

But he did go on, comparing Nazism with orgiastic nature cults and worship of pagan gods. Nationalism was addressing Germany in a "high-flown, wishy-washy cant, full of mystical euphoria with hyphenated prefixes like race- and folk- and fellowship- . . ." The movement was based on a cult of fanaticism and barbarism, more dangerous and more stultifying than the political romanticism that had led Germany into the war. The hecklers became more vociferous and more threatening as Thomas argued that bacchantic frenzy and orgiastic irrationalism were at odds with everything innately German. In reality, he said, the patriotism of the Nazis was hatred, not only for foreigners but for Germans who refused to join the party. The man in blue glasses was Arnolt Bronnen, a writer, formerly a close associate of Bertolt Brecht, and more recently the biographer of Horst Wessel, a dead S.A. leader who'd acquired the status of a martyr, though he'd been killed by a rival for the favors of a prostitute. Bronnen was a prominent party member despite rumors that his father was Jewish and his real name Bronner.

The speech led to heated controversy in the papers, and letters poured in, some hostile, some expressing solidarity. Klaus Pringsheim forwarded a letter from a Hannover schoolboy who said Thomas should be the next president of the Reich.[42] The text of his speech was printed by Fischer as a 50-pfennig pamphlet,[43] and three editions were rapidly sold out. Believing it wasn't yet too late to save Germany from the catastrophe of Nazism, Thomas contemplated direct action in alliance with Heinrich, who drafted a manifesto for the creation of a cultural resistance group. The brothers wanted to enlist the support of Einstein and Hauptmann, together with some well-known intellectuals and industrial magnates. The intention was to campaign with posters, leaflets and other forms of publicity.[44] Not wanting to align himself with the anti-Nazis, Hauptmann refused to sign the manifesto.[45]

There was no question, this time, of putting the novel aside to write nonfictionally about himself, Germany, and politics. In December 1930, Thomas was intending to spend the next summer in Nidden, working on *Joseph and His Brothers* (*Joseph und seine Brüder*), though he felt unsure whether "the reading public has not only caught up with the novel since it was conceived, but overtaken it."[46] He didn't want to abandon it, but with the centenary of Goethe's death approaching, he'd have been glad to put the fiction aside in favor of "a popular Goethe book." In September he had suggested this to Fischer, who was unresponsive, but in December another publisher, Adalbert Droemer of the Knaur-Verlag, offered him an advance of 200,000 marks and a royalty of 20 pfennig a copy for a three-hundred-page book that would be illustrated and sold at 2.85 marks a copy. As Thomas told Fischer, the book belonged absolutely to his "inner programme," and not wanting to exclude him, Thomas invited him to come in on the deal.[47] Averse to co-publishing, he now wanted to go ahead without Droemer, and Thomas said the prospect of writing on Goethe was "enticing and awe-inspiring."[48] He wrote to ask Bertram's advice on whether it was something he could do; he also asked which books he should read by way of preparing himself for the task.[49] But when Droemer threatened to commission another writer, Thomas, doubting whether there would be a market for two popular books on the subject, gave up the idea.[50]

Succumbing to an intestinal infection, he was too ill in January to write the article he'd promised for the first issue of a Berlin-based republican magazine, *Der Staat seid Ihr* (*You Are the State*). On January 18 he wrote to the editor, Gustav Radbruch, asking whether publication could be postponed for a fortnight, and promising to work on the article in Saint-Moritz, where he was going to recuperate.

He missed the "extraordinary general meeting" of the academy's literary section in Berlin on January 27, when Heinrich was elected chairman. Still overestimating the academy's influence, Thomas now felt more hopeful that Germany would "come to its senses."[51]

The next day he left for Saint-Moritz, where he stayed for just over two weeks at the Hotel Chanterella. For *Der Staat seid Ihr* he wrote a piece called "The Rebirth of Decency" ("Die Wiedergeburt der Anständigkeit") and he had several meetings with Jakob Wassermann, who read from his new novel, *Etzel Andergast*, which Thomas found "excellent and rather funny, as always."[52]

Back in Munich, he had six weeks before going to Berlin for Heinrich's sixtieth birthday celebrations on March 27. A few days before leaving, Thomas fell ill again with pains in his stomach and bowels,[53] but he recovered in time to make the journey and attend the banquet given by the academy for the new chairman of its literary section. Thomas's position was now the opposite of what it had been when Heinrich had been his butt as "civilisation's *littérateur*." Asking the same question—Was Heinrich un-German?—Thomas gave it the same answer: Oh yes. But the affirmative no longer had a derogatory ring. His work might be colored by Gallicism. He might have such un-German qualities as clarity, brio, brilliance, psychological instinct, sensual spirituality, artistic *délicatesse*. Should he therefore be accused of literary treason? Shouldn't the Germans feel proud that a German writer could lay as much claim as any Frenchman to these qualities? "It can be said that in the European-German-Latin synthesis you incarnate, the soul is German and only the mind is French."[54] Finding Thomas's speech heartwarming, Heinrich wanted to spend at least a few days with him in the summer.[55]

26

My Task Is to Liquidate

COMPARING GOETHE to Sisyphus, Thomas quoted his summary of his life as "forever rolling a boulder uphill. . . . There were too many claims on my time, from both outside and inside." Thomas could have made the same complaint. Ever since *Reflections*, he'd found it hard to divide his time between fiction and other activities. In different ways the Nobel Prize and the rise of Nazism were exacerbating the problem. By boosting his fame, the prize swelled the flood of invitations to lecture and give readings, while his conscience made him use his prestige and his growing influence in the fight to salvage democracy.

By the beginning of April 1931 he'd written about six hundred pages of narrative about Joseph,[1] and his aim was to complete it by the autumn of 1932. He decided against a Swiss tour, partly because 200 francs an evening weren't enough to tempt him, and partly to economize with time,[2] but if he met his deadline for completing the fiction, he could reward himself by going to the United States at the end of 1932 to give readings at Columbia and other universities.[3]

Meanwhile his French publisher, Fayard, wanted him to be in Paris for the publication of *La Montagne magique*. Staying there from May 6 to May 12, Thomas gave two lectures—one on "Superiority and Freedom" ("Vornehmheit und Freiheit") at the Institut International de Coopération Intellectuelle and the other on Freud at the Sorbonne. Thanks to Félix Bertaux, he met André Gide, whom he liked, and who noted in his diary: "Very good dinner; atmosphere most cordial; conversation relaxed and lively. This was perfect. Thomas Mann and especially his wife speak French perfectly; and in any case their pronunciation, when they speak in German, is always so distinct that I did not miss one word."[4]

In the second week of June, Thomas traveled 120 miles to lecture in Erlangen on Europe as a cultural community, repeating the lecture in Munich the following evening, and in early July he went to Geneva for a conference of the Comité Permanent des Lettres et des Arts. The main question was how new techniques of communication could be used to improve cultural relations. Asked to sum up at the end of the conference, Thomas referred back to the speech that had impressed him most—Paul Valéry's.

Back in Munich, he received a visit from Gide, who was taken on a motoring trip to the Lake of Starnberg. "The two youngest children, gloriously beautiful, accompany us, and Klaus, whom I scarcely knew. All charming, especially Madame Mann."[5]

Glad he again owned a house where he could spend regular summer holidays with the family, Thomas stayed in Nidden from mid-July until early September, working with fewer interruptions than in Munich, and making more headway with the novel. His impulse as a storyteller was always to look back over his shoulder, and then to look back farther into family history. The *Joseph* story involved him with the earliest patriarchs. Nor was it enough to carry the story back beyond Joseph to the three previous generations. Genesis is a narrative attempt to explain the origins of human life, but to a compulsive searcher for origins, any story about a creator poses the problem of who created him. The answer Thomas suggests is that Abraham was God's father in the same way that an author fathers his characters. Asking himself whom or what mankind should serve, the patriarch had answered: "Only the highest," and his quest for the highest led him to God. Afterward, by thinking and teaching, Abraham shaped him further and bodied him forth.[6]

The alternative answer to the question about origins would be that God and the universe had been created by whoever told the first story about them. A main theme in the *Joseph* novels is that all stories and storytellers exist in an echo chamber. There's no such thing as a new story. Jacob is repeating the story of himself and Esau when, favoring Joseph, he cheats his firstborn son, Reuben, of the blessing that is his to pass on. When Joseph tells his young brother Benjamin about the god who is torn into pieces, Tammuz, and sings a song about the sacrificed son, it sounds as if the words are piercing his heart from within. He will be repeating the story of Tammuz and prefiguring that of Jesus when his brothers throw him into a disused well. Its mouth will be sealed with a stone, and after three days the body will have disappeared. The man thought to be dead has come back to life.

Characters are manipulated into emphasizing the repetitiveness of events. Preparing Joseph for the journey that will put him at risk, Jacob remembers how his mother, Rebecca, after contriving that her favorite son should receive the blessing from her blind husband, protected Jacob from Esau's rage by sending him away, although she might never have seen him again. And when Joseph provokes his brothers by going to see them while wearing the coat of many colors, two of them want to kill him with staves, hitting out with all their strength, "as Cain had done." Even in these prehistorical days it was impossible to do anything new: Each initiative echoed one that had already been taken, while storytellers produced nothing but new variations on old stories. This sophisticated account of the *Joseph* story is partly a narrative about the nature of narrative. Playfully, Thomas indulges in anachronisms, working in preechoes of the Crucifixion story and a reference to Orpheus and Eurydice when Jacob, believing Joseph is dead, talks about going down to look for him. The narrative keeps mentioning events and ideas that belong to later periods. The *golem*, for instance—a mythical manmade monster—was dreamed up during the Diaspora, when persecuted Jews needed a story to express their thirst for revenge. But when Abraham talks to Eliezer about making a clay replica and bringing it to life, the shocked servant is anachronistically reminded of the *golem*.

This insistence on the interconnectedness of all stories gives the sequence of *Joseph* novels great resonance. (Thomas didn't yet know how many he was going to write.) The suggestion that Abraham fathered God is developed into a much subtler treatment of the relationship between the divine and the human. The overlap between stories is taken as evidence that earthly objects and events are imperfect replicas of heavenly objects and events, heroes being the counterparts of gods. "It will never be established where a story had its original home—in heaven or on earth. The truth is best served by the statement that they all take place correspondingly and simultaneously here and there, that only to our eyes does it appear as if they came down and went up again. Stories come down in the same way that a god becomes human, becomes earthly and—so to speak—bourgeois." The story about Abram, Eliezer, and their battle against the kings of the east can be told

> as if two gods, master and servant, had fought and defeated a great number of giants or inferior Elohim. This undoubtedly means that, justifiably and in a way which serves the truth, the event is converted back into its heavenly form and reconstituted. But should we therefore deny its earthly reality? On the contrary, it could be said that this is confirmed by its heavenly truth and reality. For that which is above comes down, but without its heavenly model and counterpart, what is below would not know how to happen and would, as it were, be unable to experience itself. In Abram was incarnated what had previously had only a celestial existence. When he battled victoriously with the robbers from beyond the Euphrates, he based himself on the divine, and took support from it.[7]

For Thomas, the nexus between heaven and earth was analogous with the relationships between macrocosm and microcosm, past and present, his own experience and other people's. Five years later, he made the same point in his essay "Freud and the Future" ("Freud und die Zukunft"): "Actually if man's reality lay in the present tense and events happened only once, he would have no idea of how to behave, would be unstable, helpless, embarrassed, confused about himself, would not know which foot to put forward, or what sort of face to make."

Though Thomas was never directly influenced by Jung, the ideas in the *Joseph* novels more often overlap with his than with Freud's. Jung believed that myths and stories which kept recurring in different forms had their source neither in individual experience nor in cultural propagation but in the structure of the human brain and in a part of the psyche that was common to all humanity. While Freud regarded the unconscious as a repository of repressed personal experience, mostly infantile in character, Jung saw it as a medium for putting the individual in touch with the instincts and accumulated wisdom of the race by reflecting the influence of archetypal processes. Archetypes, he believed, weren't inborn ideas but organizing principles, or "typical forms of behaviour which, once they become conscious, naturally present themselves *as ideas and images*, like everything else that becomes a content of consciousness." He came to think of archetypes as existing outside space and time but present in the psyche as an organizing power. Without having read much of his work, Thomas described human behavior as if it conformed to this pattern.

At the same time, he was, as always, writing about himself. Bringing a clay figure to life is analogous to creating a character, and in pondering differences between making a *golem* and begetting a child, he's debating with himself ironically about his own creative powers. The question of whether someone like him should bring children into the world is raised explicitly in his diary, and the question isn't answered by putting quotation marks around the phrase *someone like me* and the word *should*. The *Joseph* story provides opportunities for him to probe his conscience, drawing on both his favoritism for Elisabeth and his homoerotic love for the adolescent Klaus. If these were most apparent in the dialogue after Jacob has caught Joseph exposing himself to the moon, it is a more generalized musing about good-looking boys and young men that we find in a passage about human beauty and its effect on the feelings. Perhaps, we're told, it's nothing but the magic of sex, or sex itself made visible.

> The moment of youth comes into play here, or a magic that the feelings are prone to confuse with beauty, so that youth, unless disfigured by flaws that cause too much discomfort, will most often be perceived as beauty, even by itself, as its smile unmistakably indicates. It has charm—a manifestation of beauty which by its nature oscillates between the masculine and the feminine. A boy of seventeen is not beautiful in the sense of mature masculinity. Nor is he beautiful in the sense of a simply hypothetical femininity—that would be most unappealing. But, undeniably, the charm of youthful beauty always inclines a little towards the feminine in both spirit and form. That lies in its essence, its tender relation towards the world and the

world's to it, based on and expressed in its smile. At seventeen, it is true, one can be lovelier than woman or man, lovely like woman and man, lovely in both ways and all ways, pretty and beautiful, to a degree that turns the heads of both men and women.[8]

In the description of Tadzio's appearance and movements, and in establishing a connection between Pribislaw Hippe and Clavdia Chauchat, Thomas had pointed to the feminine element in youthful male beauty. Again, writing about the divinely well-favored young Joseph, he was writing about the kind of young man that most attracted him. But Joseph remains chaste throughout most of the action.

An account of Jacob's wedding, an excerpt from the first novel, *The Tales of Jacob*, appeared in *Corona* during November 1931, and the second novel, *Young Joseph* (*Der junge Joseph*), was almost certainly completed by the middle of 1932, which means that most of the work must have been done during 1931, for Goethe had died on March 18, 1832, and, wanting to be involved in the celebrations for the centenary, Thomas gave the early part of 1932 mostly to preparing two lectures, "Goethe as a Representative of the Bourgeois Epoch" ("Goethe als Repräsentant des bürgerlichen Zeitalters") and "Goethe's Career as a Writer" ("Goethes Laufbahn als Schriftsteller").

A little over a year earlier, consulting Bertram on whether to write a book about Goethe, Thomas had said he was ill-equipped for the job, adding: "[N]othing will be left for me except to speak from *experience*–on Goethe from experience: a confidence trick of mythical identification with which I could perhaps bridge the gap between Joseph and Goethe."[9] (In bridging the gap between himself and the confidence trickster Felix Krull, he was performing another confidence trick of mythical identification.) Nearly all his literary essays and lectures had been based, like his fiction, on the same empathic trick. His histrionic gifts, which came into play when he was reading from his work, also came into play when he was writing about Schiller, Chamisso, Lessing, or Fontane. He identified with them, almost like an actor playing the part.

He could have done this with Goethe, as he did later when he wrote *The Beloved Returns* (*Lotte in Weimar*), but his preparations for the celebrations of 1932 were complicated by the need to contradict the nationalistic speakers who, predictably, would present Germany's greatest writer as a champion of folkish patriotism. In both lectures, Thomas takes trouble to undermine the position he knew the reactionaries would take. Goethe's cultural epoch, he says, was one of idealistic individualism. He stresses Goethe's affinity with Luther, arguing that the spirit of Protestantism suits nobody better than the German, and that Germany would be nothing without Protestantism. Admitting that audacity is a prerequisite of greatness, he insists that Goethe's audacity was tempered with prosaic bourgeois moderation. Toward nationalism, he declares, Goethe was coldly contemptuous, and his fear of democracy—he detested the French Revolution—was a fear of politicization. Referring indirectly to *Reflections*, Thomas says it had been necessary in 1916–19 to be equally apprehensive about the impending politicization of Germany.

He becomes overtly polemical when he contrasts "the bawling of the patriotic loudmouths" with the cold, critical aloofness of Goethe and Nietzsche. Goethe's conscious desire to educate is directed against the "purely folkish." He talked disparagingly about the *Eddas*, arguing that humanity, needing "lucidity and good cheer," should turn away from barbaric folk-poetry toward periods in which art and literature were more polished.

For Thomas, Goethe's greatness rests on his ability to combine the demonic with the urbane. His need for order, moderation, and form came partly from the need to control his demonically intense temperament.[10] Knowing the nationalists would emphasize the passionate, heroic, and irrational side of Goethe, making him out to be a paragon of qualities possessed only by Germans, Thomas stresses the extent to which his greatness depended on such commonplace bourgeois virtues as diligence and persistence. Even the title "Goethe's Career as a Writer" is provocative, using the word *Schriftsteller* instead of *Dichter* and highlighting the fact of gradual, calculated progression. Thomas is less concerned with genius than with craftsmanship. Goethe's bourgeois orderliness had been instilled by his father, who'd taught him never to abandon a project he'd started. "A tendency to circumspection and slowness, to motherly patience in bearing to maturity is inseparable from his genius. His nature as a creator is really slow rather than stormy or improvisational. . . . He was not a man who constantly made new discoveries and plans; his productivity was essentially a matter of working up and working out conceptions that went back to his youth."[11] He lived for thirty years with the story that was called "Novelle." With *Egmont* twelve years elapsed between conception and first draft, with *Iphigenie* eight, with *Tasso* nine. Goethe worked on the first *Wilhelm Meister* for over sixteen years, and on *Faust* for over forty. Thomas was glad to have such an august precedent for his own habits of working, and equally glad that, like him, Goethe had achieved fame in his early twenties (with *Götz* and *Werther*) before going through a longish period without any comparable success.

Like Thomas's family background, Goethe's was both bourgeois and patrician. In January 1932, writing the lecture on him as representative of the bourgeois period, Thomas took as his starting point the family house in Frankfurt. The stairs, the rooms, the atmosphere all seemed familiar when Thomas paid his first visit to the house, and he recognized that *Buddenbrooks* had taken root in a similar kind of domesticity. He also saw affinities between his own personality and Goethe's, which was described as tolerant without being kindly. Nor did Goethe achieve happiness. He said that if all the good hours of his life were put together, they'd add up to less than a month.

Thomas was suffering intermittently from a toothache, and his bout of flu, which started before Christmas, helped to produce an uneasy atmosphere in the household. The entry in Golo's diary for December 22 runs: "The old man, yesterday taciturn and distant, stayed in bed today out of sheer depression." On Christmas Day Golo wrote: "I cannot say that I feel very comfortable here," and on January 5, 1932, "Here the same miserable situation. Long, drawn-out breakfasts, little work getting done, the old man in a bad mood, mealtimes dreary the minute Erika is not there, boring little walks, even the air, usually a great attraction, hazy à la Heidelberg."[12]

In January, though he hadn't fully recovered from the flu,[13] Thomas did most of his work on "Goethe as a Representative of the Bourgeois Epoch," which he regarded as the more important of the two lectures.[14] Katia and Erika had both been ill,[15] and at the end of the month Thomas took them to Saint-Moritz, where Hermann Hesse was staying with his wife, and the publisher Alfred Knopf introduced them to the Manns.[16]

Thomas delivered the "Career" lecture on February 25 in Bern, where it was well received,[17] and while there, he broadcast a reading from the second *Joseph* novel. On March 18, the day Goethe had died, he was in Berlin, where he delivered his other Goethe lecture to the academy, which had awarded him its Goethe Medal and presented it that evening. He said afterward that he wouldn't have accepted it had he known how much preference was being given to nationalist writers in the academy's other awards; he was appalled by the strident propaganda in some of the speeches made at the Goethe celebrations in Berlin and Weimar.[18]

A nonevent that occurred at the Weimar celebrations was representative of the fatal disunity between the enemies of Nazism. The chancellor, Heinrich Brüning, was present, but though Thomas was both a Nobel Prize–winner and one of the main speakers, the two men didn't meet.[19]

Since 1930, Brüning had been ruling by decree, preserving unity and discipline in his cabinet, but Hitler had been carrying on a spectacularly successful propaganda campaign, blaming inflation, unemployment, and all the other German miseries on the Treaty of Versailles, Weimar republicanism, and the Jews. With no jobs, no prospects, and no money—their parents' savings had been eroded by inflation—former students streamed into the paramilitary groups, the S.A. and the S.S.

(Schutzstaffel, which began as subordinate to the S.A. but grew into an elite), where at least they had a salary and a uniform that boosted their self-importance and their sense of usefulness. They also had hope: Rhetorically and self-confidently, Hitler was promising that Germany would be greater than ever before. *Ein Volk, ein Reich, ein Führer*–one people, one state, one leader.

Observed at close quarters, the man was crude and unimpressive. One afternoon in Munich, finding the Café Luitpold crowded with S.A. men, Klaus Mann decided to drink coffee in the Carlton Tea Room, where Hitler was sitting at a nearby table. Looking "surprisingly ugly, much more vulgar than I had anticipated . . . with a fleshy, nasty nose," he devoured three strawberry tartlets. "He was flabby and foul and without any marks of greatness, a frustrated, hysterical petty bourgeois." In the rosy light of the tearoom, with soft music playing, Hitler was talking to his henchmen about the musical comedy scheduled for performance that evening at the Kammerspiele, starring Therese Giehse. When Hitler said he rather liked her, one of his companions objected that she had Jewish blood–"just a little bit of it if I am not mistaken." Hitler dismissed the calumny with an irritated gesture. "Nasty gossip! After all, I know the difference between a German artist and a Semitic clown." In fact, both her parents were Jewish. But however unlikable Hitler was, Klaus found this close-up view reassuring. Surely this man stood no chance of ruling Germany.[20] Though Thomas never saw Hitler at such close quarters, he arrived at the same conclusion about his vulgarity, saying he precisely mirrored all the most repugnant traits of Wagner, whom Gottfried Keller described as "a hairdresser and a charlatan."[21]

When the eighty-four-year-old Hindenburg, who was approaching the end of his seven years in office, decided to stand for reelection, Hitler, who was being derided by the old man as "that Bavarian corporal," hesitated about whether to oppose him, but his propaganda chief, Joseph Goebbels, talked him into it. When Thomas was asked to make a speech in support of Hindenburg, he refused.[22] The election campaign was ferocious. The Nazis put up posters with captions like "TWO MILLION STOLEN from the state coffers by the Red Prussian ministers!"[23] In the election on March 13, Hitler won 11 million of the 37,650,000 votes cast–30.1 percent. Hindenburg, who won 49.6 percent, would have been beaten without support from the Socialists, while they, even if they'd formed a united front with the Communists, couldn't have defeated Hitler without Hindenburg.

Needing an absolute majority, he was forced into a runoff ballot, to be held four weeks later. With Goebbels, Hitler used funds donated by industrialists to mount a massive campaign. Exploiting his power as a demagogue, he addressed mass meetings at which films and records were given away. He increased his vote by 2 million to 36.8 percent, while Hindenburg won 53 percent. Two days later his government banned the Nazi paramilitary groups, the S.S. and the S.A. But the Nazis took the lead in the four state elections, and in the Prussian parliament, where they'd previously had only 6 seats, they now had 162.

On May 25 the chamber was wrecked when a fight broke out between the Nazis and the Communist deputies. At the end of the month, when Brüning resigned as chancellor, Franz von Papen was invited to form a government. A Catholic cavalry officer, Papen excluded Nazis from the "cabinet of barons" he appointed on June 1, three days before the Reichstag was dissolved in advance of new elections to be held in July. On June 16, two days after Hitler had promised not to oppose him, von Papen rashly lifted the ban on the S.S. and the S.A. Within a month, fifteen people had been killed in clashes between Nazis and Communists, and in the elections on July 31, voters handed the Nazis a decisive victory. Though they still didn't have an absolute majority in the 608-seat Reichstag, they were the biggest party, with 230 seats. In the four years since the 1928 elections, they'd won about 13 million new votes, mostly at the expense of the middle-class center parties. The Social Democrats now had only 133 seats, and the Communists, the third largest party, had 89.

While this was going on in Berlin, Thomas was in Nidden. In spite of the great heat, he resumed work on *Joseph in Egypt (Joseph in Ägypten)*, the third novel in the *Joseph* sequence.[24] Fischer had now read the first two volumes, and so had his wife, Hedwig, who said it had been "a bit like reading 'The History of Humanity,' a new kind of *odyssey*."[25] Fischer wanted to bring the first two volumes out as soon as possible, though Thomas would have preferred to wait till all three volumes—he didn't yet know there'd be four—could be published simultaneously.[26]

Sometimes he felt he should be fighting a harder rearguard campaign for democracy, but for the most part he let himself be carried along by the momentum that had built up, stating his views in articles and lectures but making few overtly political speeches. He didn't want to "take the lead in any political action, call for the creation of a party or seize hold of a flag as leader." It would have been pointless, even if it had been possible, to form a new party representing the interests of the bourgeoisie. As he'd said in "Goethe as a Representative," the bourgeois period was over, and he now claimed, as he had during the war, to be a Socialist.[27] In Vienna at the end of October he addressed a workers' meeting, but couldn't identify with his audience. "It was a pleasure to show these simple souls, who are besieged by triumphant reactionaries, that they have not been abandoned. And how grateful they seemed. I shall never forget it."[28]

In this situation, Erika was being extraordinarily courageous when she launched her anti-Nazi cabaret, *Die Pfeffermühle (The Peppermill)*, in Munich at the beginning of 1933. After traveling around the world with Klaus in 1927–28 and divorcing Gründgens in 1929, she'd worked sporadically as an actress, but whereas Gründgens could thrive in a theater that was becoming more reactionary and nationalistic, she couldn't. Ignoring threats against her life, she persisted in putting on anti-Hitler shows. She and her friend Therese Giehse were the principal performers. Erika wrote most of the material herself, but Klaus was involved as a writer.

His friend and lover Ricki Hallgarten had killed himself in the summer, and in his ensuing depression, Klaus had become dependent on drugs. He'd experimented with them during 1931 and made notes in his diary on the effects produced by different varieties, including hashish, cocaine, and morphia. In February 1933 he was close to suicide. "In the mornings, nothing but the wish to die. When I calculate what I have to lose, it seems negligible. No chance of a really happy relationship. Probably no chance of literary fame in the near future for people like us. If I had any poison, I *certainly* wouldn't hesitate if it weren't for E[rika] and M[other]. Tied through them. But more and more certain that E's death would immediately be followed by mine, that even work wouldn't stop me then."[29]

Thomas underestimated the gravity of the crisis in his son's life, as he did that of the political crisis. Perhaps it was only a temporary imbalance that had made so many people vote for the Nazis. Eager to believe that catastrophe could still be averted, he was as unrealistic as he'd been in August 1914. Things might look bad at the moment, but surely the Germans had a stronger feeling for freedom than the stupid, overconfident Nazis realized.[30] At the academy he defended Heinrich against attacks from rabid nationalists, and when Thomas, after making derogatory remarks about Hitler, received through the post a charred copy of *Buddenbrooks*, he "carefully collected the blackened scraps of paper, because they will one day serve as evidence of the German state of mind in the year 1932."[31]

He'd agreed to give the festival lecture at a Wagner celebration in Amsterdam on February 13, 1933, the fiftieth anniversary of the composer's death, and to repeat the lecture in Brussels and Paris, speaking in French. Postponing work on the novel, he started writing the lecture at the beginning of January, asking Félix Bertaux to take care of the translation into French. His title was "The Suffering and Greatness of Richard Wagner" ("Leiden und Grösse Richard Wagners") and the approach was partly biographical, throwing a lot of emphasis on Wagner's patience and persistence against difficulties and shortcomings that could have made his work negligible. Nietzsche had said that a superficial observer might have judged Wagner to be a born dilettante; Thomas goes further: "Wagner's art *is* dilettantism, monumentalised and raised to the level of genius by his intelligence and tremendous willpower."

The story "Tristan" had illustrated Wagner's relevance to the theme of "sympathy for death" in Thomas's work and to the development that had culminated in *The Magic Mountain*; in the lecture, he describes the "causal nexus" between Wagner's suffering and his music, saying he'd come to "recognise art and disease as one and the same affliction, with the result that he tries to escape—in fact naively—through hydrotherapy."[32] Belief in the therapeutic application of water had been fashionable.

The lecture on Wagner resembles the two lectures on Goethe. Both men are characterized as depriving themselves of the ordinary pleasures. Thomas quotes Wagner as saying: "I live an indescribably worthless life! Of the real joys of life I know nothing at all: for me the joy of life, *love*, is only a thing of fantasy, not experience."[33] In Goethe, Thomas had found a "synthesis of the daemonic and the urbane";[34] in Wagner he finds an "indissoluble combination of the daemonic with the bourgeois."[35]

He finished the lecture on January 29,[36] but he'd decided about nine days earlier against going to Berlin, where he was due to address the Socialist Kulturbund on February 19. He'd written a speech titled "Affirmation of Socialism" ("Bekenntnis zum Sozialismus") and he sent it to be read in his absence, but the meeting was canceled. On January 30, Hitler had become chancellor.

As leader of the largest party since the election of July 31, Hitler had been constitutionally entitled to form a government, but Hindenburg, who gave him an audience on August 13, dismissed him after reprimanding him for the bloodshed caused by his storm troopers in daily clashes with Communists and Social Democrats. In the November elections the Nazis lost thirty-four seats, and the party was close to bankruptcy. At the beginning of December, the grandiosely ambitious commander of the army, Kurt von Schleicher, forced Papen to resign, taking over the chancellorship. He was hoping to split the Nazis and form a coalition by uniting the Center, the unions, and moderate members of the Right. But his social policy antagonized Hindenburg's advisers, and von Papen, aiming to effect a comeback and believing Hitler could be manipulated, even if he were appointed as chancellor, stage-managed an alliance between the Junkers, the industrialists, and the Nazis. "Hadn't those in the know," asks Klaus Mann, "assured us, again and again, that Hitler would hold no real power, but was used by big business and the general staff of the Reichswehr as their puppet and window dressing?" Germany, they explained, "was to be ruled by the I.G. Farben, the United Steel, and Privy Councillor Dr. Hugenberg."[37]

On January 30, when Hitler accepted office as "presidential" chancellor, it was agreed that no appointment could be made in the government without Hindenburg's consent. Papen was made vice chancellor, and there were only two Nazi ministers—Hermann Göring and Wilhelm

Frick. But on the night of January 30, long columns of Nazi storm troopers marched through the streets of Berlin and Munich, carrying torches, singing, and cheering.

Writing to some young people he knew, Thomas warned them against taking part in such processions. The Führer, addressing the crowds from a balcony, had compared the day with August 4, 1914, when war was declared, but, Thomas insisted, without understanding the implications of what he said. There were still grounds for optimism. "Though it may indeed be 'irrational', the German people is basically very intelligent."[38] Three days later he was asking himself whether he could or should try to exert his influence politically. Approaching the age of sixty, he said, he couldn't wage "an upsetting political battle." He should concentrate on tasks that seemed appropriate. "Certainly the moment may come when there is nothing for it but to throw everything aside and put oneself on the barricades. But at the moment one is still praying: 'Take thou this cup from me.' "[39] It's odd that he should compare himself with Jesus when claiming he didn't want to be Germany's savior. After lecturing on Wagner in Munich at the university on February 10, he left for Holland with Katia.

On February 27 the Reichstag went up in flames, and the next day all civil rights were suspended. Though the Communists were blamed, the fire may have been started by the Nazis to give themselves a pretext for "crushing out this murder pest with an iron fist"—as Hitler put it. (Historians still argue about who started the fire.) As commandant of the Prussian police, Göring gave his men carte blanche to shoot, while thousands of young Nazis, enlisted to help them, were free to kill Communists and Socialists. On March 2, Frick instituted imprisonment in concentration camps without trial, and the next day Göring announced: "My measures will not be debilitated by any legal considerations or any bureaucracy. My task here is not to dispense justice; my task is to liquidate and extirpate." In the so-called brown houses—headquarters of the Nazi party—Jews, Communists, and people suspected of opposing the regime were beaten with rubber truncheons.

Thomas, who'd been advised by his doctor to take a holiday, had left with Katia at the end of February for three weeks in Arosa. _Die Pfeffermühle_, which closed when Hitler became chancellor, had made Erika and Klaus so conspicuous as anti-Nazis that they wouldn't have been safe in the streets of Munich. Returning there from the Swiss Alps, where they'd been staying with friends, they were met at the station by their parents' chauffeur, Hans, who warned them not to go out and not to let anyone know they were in Munich. The Nazis were after them, he said. They didn't realize until later that he'd been working for years as a Nazi spy, reporting on the goings-on in the family. He was putting himself in danger by warning them, and they took his advice, staying in hiding till they were ready to leave Munich. When Hans drove Klaus to the station for the last time, he admitted that the car would soon be in the garage at the brown house. A major had his eye on it.[40]

On March 12, Erika and Klaus telephoned Thomas in Arosa, advising him and Katia not to come home. When he pressed for an explanation, they talked vaguely about bad weather and spring cleaning being done in his study. The weather could hardly be worse than the weather in Arosa, he objected, and the spring cleaning couldn't go on indefinitely. Erika and Klaus finally won the argument by promising to escape from the inclement weather, come to Arosa and explain.[41]

Hundreds of people were being arrested as the Nazis rounded up political opponents. On March 9 they occupied the Bavarian state parliament and expelled deputies. Three days later Hindenburg banned the flag of the Republic, ordering the imperial and Nazi flags to fly side by side. On March 15, Hitler proclaimed the Third Reich. Though Göring denied that Germany's Jews were in danger, Jewish people were emigrating. Given the title minister of public enlightenment, Goebbels denounced the "Jewish vampires" who'd accumulated billions of marks by blackmail, trickery, and swindling. Kosher meat was banned on March 14, and two weeks later Hitler ordered a boycott of Jewish shops. All over Germany, uniformed S.A. men stood on guard outside shops owned by Jews, while windows were smashed and posters with anti-Semitic slogans plastered over the windows that survived. Armed with revolvers and broken pieces of piping, storm troopers roamed the streets looking for Jews, who'd be beaten and left lying on the pavement, where no one dared help them. Sometimes Jews were forced to flog one another. Jewish teachers were denied admission to schools and colleges. Jewish lawyers and bankers were barred from their offices, and in Berlin on April 8 all "non-Aryan" officials were ordered to retire.

In Berlin, parliamentary deputies were meeting at the Kroll Opera House, within sight of the burned-out Reichstag, while jackbooted storm troopers stamped up and down the pavement outside, chanting slogans. On March 23, though the Nazis held only 44 percent of the total vote, an "Enabling Bill" gave Hitler the power previously exercised by the president—to rule by decree. Needing a majority of two thirds for the bill to be passed, he had to depend partly on the Social Democrats, but many Communists and Social Democrats were absent from the chamber because they'd been arrested, and once the bill took effect, Hitler could count on the support of the bureaucracy. Previously the Bavarian state attorney's office had conscientiously investigated every murder reported in Dachau, but from now on, anything the government ordered was legal.[42]

Part
Four

Part

Four

The Rule of Silence

IT WAS A DEEP CLEAVAGE and gulf that divided his present from the past—it was the grave. . . . His vital forces collected themselves quickly and easily, which did not prevent him from distinguishing sharply between his present existence and the earlier one, which had led to the grave, or from regarding himself no longer as the old Joseph, but a new one. If to be dead and gone means to be bound irreversibly to a condition that permits no backward signal or greeting, not the slightest resumption of contact with one's former life, if it means to have vanished from that former life and [to] have been silenced without permission to break the rule of silence through any kind of signal and without any conceivable possibility of doing so, then Joseph was dead.[1]

This passage, which comes near the beginning of *Joseph in Egypt*, is strikingly similar to Thomas's diary entry for March 15, 1933, the day after he resigned from the executive committee of the Munich branch of the Schutzverband Deutscher Schriftsteller, the writers' league. He's aware, he says, that he's reached the end of an era in his life; in his fifty-eighth year, he must find a new basis for his existence. What's striking retrospectively is how many of his major achievements—not only literary but also political—belong to the period that started when his exile began.

Ever since the burning of the Reichstag, he'd been oscillating between panic and melancholy. Reluctant though he was to take in what Klaus and Erika had told him over the telephone, he knew he was lucky to be in Switzerland. The telephone call hadn't been the only warning that he'd be in danger if he returned. He'd been denounced in Nazi papers and told he'd been listed as having committed "pacifistic excesses" and "intellectual high treason."[2]

He must resign himself, Erika said, to losing the house and everything in it, but she took the risk of going back in dark glasses. She arrived during a Nazi celebration, when some of the guards were drunk, and found the *Joseph* manuscript. She hid in her room without putting the light on. In the middle of the night she wrapped the manuscript in newspaper and hid it among the tools in her Ford. She put on a Bavarian accent when she spoke to the frontier guards, who were friendly. They could understand why she felt like a trip into the mountains, they said.3 She arrived in Arosa on March 16.

Her account of what she'd seen in Munich pitched Thomas into an ambivalence that was to last for months. He might, he told himself, have to live in exile "for a year or a lifetime,"4 but he also told himself that he might be able to secure a guarantee for his safety if he went back. He wrote to the Munich lawyer Karl Loewenstein for advice; Loewenstein not only advised him to stay in Switzerland but came there himself.5 All those who'd fought for democracy in Germany had been decisively routed. The one consolation for Thomas was that wherever he lived, he was liberated from all the commitments he'd made through a sense of solidarity with other writers and with German society. At one stroke he was released from the obligations he'd taken on without knowing how much of his time they'd consume.6

He was free to concentrate entirely on his fiction, but, uncertain where he was going to live, he was in no state to work. For the first time in his adult life he broke with the routine of shutting himself up in a workroom for at least three hours after breakfast.7 He could have stayed with Hans Reisiger in Austria, while Katia went briefly back to Munich, or they could both stay in Venice with Franz Werfel and his wife, Alma, Mahler's widow.8 They rejected both invitations in favor of staying in Switzerland, either with the art historian Hanna Kiel in Lenzerheide, or in Zurich, where they'd be near Bruno Frank and his wife. Frank was a writer he'd known since 1910 and had visited in Feldafing, where Frank had a small villa, and since 1925 the Franks had been neighbors in Herzogpark.

On March 17, the day Thomas and Katia left for Lenzerheide with the children, Thomas wrote to Max von Schillings, president of the academy, who'd forced Heinrich to resign on February 15 and had circulated members with a questionnaire drafted by Gottfried Benn. Did they wish to go on being identified with the academy in the light of the changed historical situation? They were required to answer either "yes" or "no," and "yes" would entail not only loyal collaboration in "national cultural tasks" but an undertaking not to participate in any public activity against the government. Without giving a categorical "yes," Thomas said he didn't intend to work against the government and did intend to go on serving the cause of German culture. But he wanted to disengage himself from official duties and pursue his private concerns in complete retirement. He therefore wished to resign from the academy.9

At an altitude of 4,785 feet, on the edge of a half-frozen lake, Lenzerheide was surrounded by beautiful alpine scenery. Thomas and Katia were made to feel welcome in Hanna Kiel's small house, but, worrying about diaries and papers he'd left in Munich, he was so unsettled that he couldn't sleep without sedatives. Katia did her best to comfort him, but he was on the point of nervous collapse, with twitching muscles and fits of trembling. His malaise was exacerbated by broadcasts from Germany. They decided to stay for a week before going on to Lugano.

There, staying at the Hotel Villa Castagnola, they saw a good deal of Hermann Hesse and his wife, who lived nearby, in Montagnola. In Lugano, Thomas and Katia went to see the German consul about their passports, which were on the point of expiring, but he'd been ordered not to renew them: the Nazi authorities were hoping to force the Manns back into Germany. Thomas thought of sending Katia back to Munich, but a letter from her parents warned them that a woman whose husband was wanted by the Nazis was liable to have her passport confiscated if she reappeared. Thomas also found himself mentioned in the Basel *National Zeitung*, which said that if he were in Germany he'd be sent to the concentration camp in Dachau.[10]

Elisabeth and Michael had both been at boarding school in Neubeuern, about twenty miles southeast of Munich. She was keen to go back, and was allowed to, but immediately found inexplicable changes not only in the teachers but also in the children. Suddenly they were anti-Semitic, and a teacher who'd previously been popular was denounced by his pupils at the local Nazi headquarters because he refused to start his classes with "Heil Hitler!" and the Nazi salute. After three weeks Elisabeth wanted to leave, and Golo smuggled her back into Switzerland across Lake Constance.[11]

The Hotel Villa Castagnola was expensive, and by early April Thomas and Katia were planning to rent a house near Zurich. On March 22 he'd resumed work on *Joseph in Egypt*,[12] and though it was hard to make headway under these conditions,[13] he was already planning to start a novella about Faust as soon as he finished the *Joseph* novel. Part of the idea's appeal rested on a hunch that the Faust story could be made to symbolize the fate and character of Europe. Perhaps he could somehow incorporate this "arduous holiday experience" of moving from place to place.[14]

Heinrich was already making public statements about the Nazis: He'd launched the first of his passionate attacks on the regime in a French newspaper, the *Dépêche de Toulouse*.[15] Thomas didn't follow suit, although he was soon under pressure to do so, when a Jewish-American admirer, Ludwig Lewisohn, asked him for a statement that could be printed in New York. "If I told you what you wish to hear, my capital and property in Germany would be taken away from me tomorrow, my son would be arrested as a hostage, I do not know what would happen to my old parents-in-law, who are Jewish, no more of my books could be sold in Germany, and I do not know what the other consequences would be."[16] He was still half-expecting the regime to be overturned either by an economic crisis or by intervention from outside, but what would happen to Hitler, "this idolized scarecrow," if the conservatives or the army took control? So many millions of people still worshiped him that he'd have to be installed as a puppet president.[17]

Reluctant to lose his houses and everything in them, Thomas tried to feel less hostile to the Nazis. Perhaps "something deeply significant and revolutionary" was going on in Germany. And after all, he wasn't wholeheartedly unhappy about what was happening to the Jews. It was no disaster that they could no longer dominate the legal system, or that the Nazis had put a stop to Alfred Kerr's "poisonous Jewish-style imitation of Nietzsche." Like many Germans inside and outside Germany, Thomas was half-ashamed of his own *Schadenfreude*: These "secret, disturbing, persistent reflections" could be confided only to his diary, not to his Jewish wife.[18]

But in mid-April he suffered a setback to his hopes of being offered a guarantee of safety if he went home. The *Münchener Neueste Nachrichten* had come out with a favorable review of his Wagner lecture, but in the issue dated April 16–17 it published a letter headed "Protest by Munich, the Richard Wagner City" and signed by forty-five musicians, academics, intellectuals, arts administrators, and municipal officials, including Richard Strauss, Hans Pfitzner, and the conductor Hans Knappertsbusch. Though Thomas had been anything but unsympathetic to Wagner, he was accused of "slander on our great musical genius," and of betraying his commitment to Germany by adopting a democratic and cosmopolitan position.[19] The newspaper had come under the control of Heinrich Himmler and the Bavarian political police, who wanted a pretext to confiscate Thomas's property and, if he returned, take him into "protective custody." Proof of "anti-German attitudes" gave them this right. But to Thomas it looked as though the protest had been spontaneous.[20]

He now had second thoughts about "the rebellion against the Jewish element." He could have understood it, he said, were it not that the Jewish spirit had acted as a restraining force on the Germans. Without it, they were stupid enough to lump people like him together with the Jews, and drive him out with them.[21] But he still wasn't ready to accept expulsion. He even wrote an article in defense of his Wagner lecture, hoping to publish it in the *Frankfurter Allgemeine*. When it was rejected, he offered it to the *Rundschau*, saying: "[I]t would be good, a kind of triumph, if this tone could again be introduced."[22]

Unlike Erika and Klaus, Golo could still show his face in Munich, and in late April Thomas asked him to bring all the *Joseph* material to Switzerland. He arrived with it at the end of the month. But the bulky diaries were still in Munich, and Thomas sometimes woke up in the middle of the night, seized with panic. His fears, he said, were revolving almost exclusively around "this threat to the secrets of my life. . . . The consequences could be dreadful—even fatal." During the day he and Katia spent a lot of time holding hands. She "more or less understands my anxieties about the contents of the suitcase." One evening, at a hotel in Basel, he burst into tears.23

They decided to accept an invitation from the writer René Schickele to stay in a small town near Nice, Sanary-sur-Mer. Schickele had edited the pacifist and Expressionist *Weissen Blätter* from Zurich during the war, and had been living in Sanary since 1932. Heinrich was there, and Schickele offered to help Thomas and Katia find somewhere they could stay for the rest of the spring and summer. Tired of hotels, they needed to rent a house with about six rooms, so that Elisabeth and Michael, now fifteen and fourteen, could live with them, and Erika and Klaus, now twenty-seven and twenty-six, could come to stay.24 Both of them knew, and recommended, Sanary, having often visited Cocteau in Toulon.25 Erika was getting ready to reopen *Die Pfeffermühle* in Zurich.

On their way to Sanary with the two younger children, Thomas and Katia stopped at Basel in another effort to renew their passports. Schickele describes Thomas as looking "unwell . . . very oppressed." Whereas Heinrich had always been "in opposition," as Schickele put it, and always, more or less, in exile, Thomas hadn't come to terms with the fact of losing his fatherland. "If anyone lacks the qualities of a martyr, it is Thomas Mann."26 This was true. Strong though Thomas's principles were, he would have found it hard to obey the Kierkegaardian imperative and "go right to the end of each chosen road at each crossroad." For five weeks he, Katia, and the children stayed at Bandol in the Grand Hotel, and on June 18, after over four months of staying in friends' homes and hotels, they moved into the house they'd rented in Sanary— "La Tranquille," 442, Chemin de la Colline.

AS A JEWISH PUBLISHING HOUSE, Fischer's company was in danger. Now that Samuel Fischer was in his seventies, the business was being run by his thirty-five-year-old son-in-law, Gottfried Bermann, a former surgeon who had become a director of the firm in 1928, calling himself Gottfried Bermann Fischer. Determined to go on publishing in Germany, he claimed to regard Hitler, Göring, and Goebbels as "moderates," and felt encouraged when Thomas's work was excluded from the ceremonial burning of "un-German" books on May 10. Books by Freud, Heinrich Mann, Upton Sinclair, and Erich Maria Remarque were ritually sacrificed in front of Berlin University, and there was a similar bonfire in Munich, watched by thousands of schoolchildren, who were told that the fire burning these un-German books should burn love of the Fatherland into their hearts.

If the Nazis wanted Germany's Nobel Prize–winner to be seen as one of the Reich's cultural assets, Fischer's company stood a chance of surviving as his publisher. Thomas received an offer for *The Tales of Jacob* from the Querido Verlag, which was based in Amsterdam, but Bermann fought hard, arguing, flatteringly, that publication inside Germany would be a triumph for humanity, and, realistically, that publication in Holland would lead to lower sales. Still hoping to go home, Thomas was tempted by Bermann's promise to regularize all his affairs through an intermediary. Asked to give this man power of attorney, Thomas refused, but though he was told at the end of May that all the money he'd deposited in German banks had been confiscated,[27] he agreed to let Bermann bring out *The Tales of Jacob* in the autumn.[28] But he never entirely trusted Bermann. Neither, it seemed to him, did Samuel Fischer.[29]

When he agreed to give Bermann the book, Thomas knew the Nazis would ban it if he spoke out against them or allowed his name to be used in anti-Hitler agitation. But if he was handing over a hostage to his enemies, he wasn't radically changing the situation since they had so many hostages already. Still on sale in Germany, his other books could be banned at any time, as Heinrich's had been, and there was nothing Thomas wanted less than to lose the public that played a key role in giving him not only his income but his sense of identity.

By the end of August, though, he'd begun to have misgivings. The Nazis had confiscated his house in Munich, and Hedwig Fischer had questioned whether the book's central irony would be misunderstood. A non-Jew was retelling an Old Testament story: In the present climate this was enough to provoke an anti-Semitic interpretation, while the press might be unfriendly since he was living outside Germany. Wouldn't Bermann change his mind and let Querido publish the book?[30]

Thomas's situation became still more uncomfortable in September, when Querido launched a monthly, *Die Sammlung*, with Klaus as editor and Heinrich as a member of the advisory board, together with André Gide and Aldous Huxley. Thomas agreed to have his name listed as a future contributor,[31] but the first issue contained a blistering attack on the Nazis by Heinrich, and on October 10, Alfred Rosenberg, director of the Reich's Office for the Furtherance of German Writing, issued a directive forbidding booksellers to handle works by authors who contributed to émigré journals that whipped up hostility to Germany.[32] Bermann was so worried by this development that he came to Sanary and persuaded Thomas to dictate a telegram dissociating himself from *Die Sammlung*. For nearly three years Thomas was going to preserve an awkward balance between Bermann, who was pulling him toward Nazi

Germany, and his two eldest children, who were urging him to identify with the émigré cause. His books were so popular that he could have made Querido Verlag into an important international publisher, had he transferred them to it. Contributions from him would have made both *Die Sammlung* and Klaus more influential. But, wanting his books to go on being sold in German shops and read in German homes, he sided with Bermann.

The telegram provoked the Viennese *Arbeiter Zeitung* to denounce him on October 19, but it published his reply six days later. He'd made the disclaimer because the only alternative was to sacrifice the life of his work and deprive German readers of a book they had awaited for years.[33] But the *Neue Deutsche Blätter*, which was published in Prague, dismissed this explanation, and accused him of rejecting the anti-Fascist cause together with his son's periodical.[34]

Fluent though his French was, he wanted to live where German was spoken. He could have chosen a town of any size, anywhere in Switzerland or Austria, but as he said, he was more of a provincial than a cosmopolitan, and at the end of September he rented a house in Küsnacht, a quiet village on the edge of Lake Zurich, a fifteen-minute drive from the center of the city. In Lübeck he'd been close to canals and boats; in Munich he'd lived for over nineteen years on the banks of the Isar; now he had a view of both the lake and the city, seeing a cluster of ancient buildings with spires, towers, and gables not unlike those of Lübeck. Thomas loved being here, though he was hardly ever seen in the main streets. The lake, which is banana-shaped, stretches southeastward from the city; Küsnacht is on the northeastern bank. Since 1908, Jung had lived in a house by the lake–228 Seestrasse; steep roads lead up to the house Thomas rented in Schiedhaldenstrasse, and he enjoyed being well above the village. The house was spacious but unpretentious, with a magnificent view across the lake. He had reservations about it, calling it "elegant but amateurishly built, ridiculously lacking in soundproofing and inadequately furnished." But it had four bathrooms and six lavatories; he praised "the efficiency of the electric system for heating the water so that one can count on a hot bath every other day."

Here Thomas could settle down once again to write his *Joseph* novel and give frequent readings. "There was the familiar aroma of cigar smoke, leather volumes, and eau de cologne," Klaus wrote. "There was the traditional bric-à-brac pedantically arranged on the desk; and Mielein hastily distributing ashtrays among the audience before the reading begins. And here, evoked by the sonorous voice, appeared Joseph. . . ."[35] The image Monika had of her father was similar: "The desk, laden with ornaments and utensils reflected that elongated, gold-bespectacled dreaming face of Father as characteristically as his yellow Empire chair–cigar smoke and throat clearing, the dog's leash–a shrill musical whistle, the cup of tea—a comfortably measured sipping, the silken housecoat—a disciplined Gemütlichkeit. . . ."[36]

On October 10, while the sonorous voice was peacefully evoking him in Küsnacht, *The Tales of Jacob* was published in Germany, and the first impression of ten thousand copies sold out within a week.[37] It was followed by three more impressions, each of five thousand copies. Reviews, though, were disappointing. Julius Bab was the only critic in Germany to appreciate the comedy[38]; most of the other reviewers gave the impression of being left untouched.[39] This helped to intensify Thomas's sense of having lost contact with German cultural life. His long friendship with Ernst Bertram was over: In mid-November, writing, after long hesitation, to thank him for two books, Thomas said their political differences were too great for their friendship to continue.[40] In fact, though, they went on corresponding, and Bertram even went on sending birthday presents.[41]

Michael, who was studying the violin, was accepted on the highest level in the Konservatorium at Zurich, while Elisabeth, who'd been studying diligently on her own throughout the summer, was taken into the lower sixth form of a Zurich high school.[42] Though a reunion with all the children, Reisiger, and Therese Giehse made his first Christmas in exile a pleasant one,[43] Thomas had the impression that during the nine months of exile, he and Katia had been aging more rapidly than ever before.[44]

JUST AS HE'D BEEN UNDECIDED throughout those nine months about returning to Munich, he was undecided throughout most of 1934 about keeping his German nationality. Writing to Bertram in January, he said he wanted to become Swiss and be buried in Switzerland,[45] but in trying to have him deprived of his citizenship, the political police in Munich were in conflict with the foreign department of the Propaganda Ministry. Thomas negotiated to keep his status as a citizen, though he was no longer in any doubt about wanting to live abroad. In January, despite a rent increase, he renewed his lease on the house in Küsnacht until the end of June.[46]

But he was still verging on neurasthenia. If he drank coffee, it made him tremble with excitement,[47] and he suffered from fits of panic-stricken despair.[48] He'd have enjoyed more peace of mind if his passport had been renewed, his Munich house given back to him, and its contents transported to Switzerland.[49] If his furniture had come, his rent would have been reduced.[50] As it was, when Jakob Wassermann died at the age of sixty-one, Thomas, who was only two years younger, wondered how long his own life would last.[51] Though prone to "empty pomposity and solemn loquacity," Wassermann was "a much greater storyteller than I."[52]

In spite of the tepid reviews, nearly 25,000 copies of *The Tales of Jacob* had been sold by the end of January,[53] and Thomas was forging ahead with *Joseph in Egypt*, letting his feelings about exile overlap into Joseph's. When the Ishmaelite merchants arrive at the frontier fortress of Zel, they're challenged by the officer in charge of the guard: "Above all, how are you going to live? I mean, have you food, and have you ways to survive without being a burden on the state or being driven to steal? But if the former is the case, where is your evidence for it and the written guarantee that you know how to live? Do you have letters to a citizen of this country? Then hand them over. Otherwise you'll have to turn back, and that's all there is to it."[54]

Surrounded by unfamiliar buildings and people in unfamiliar clothes speaking a foreign language, Joseph asks himself how much he has in common with the Egyptians:

> all in all he was not only the child of his mountains but that of a bigger spatial unit, that of the eastern Mediterranean, in which nothing could strike him as entirely strange and unfamiliar. But he was also a child of his time, now vanished, in which he wandered from place to place. . . . And the time, together with the space, created unity and togetherness in the aspect of the world and the form of the spirit. The one really new experience Joseph had on his travels was probably just this: that he and his kind were not alone in the world, not quite incomparable; that many of the thoughts and inspirations of the fathers, the careful view they took of God and their constant speculation had not been extraordinary, distinguishing them from everyone else, but had belonged to the time and the place, to the province of what they had in common with others. . . .[55]

Though it was consoling to recycle some of the discomfort he felt in losing the luxury and stability he'd had, Thomas's anxiety undermined his confidence in the value of what he was writing. There were days when it struck him as a late work—not only in terms of his development but outdated, overelaborate, oversophisticated, and self-conscious—a piece of Alexandrianism.[56] Sometimes he felt like a historical relic, a piece of residue from a past cultural era, and it seemed apt when Eduard Korrodi, writing in the *Neue Zürcher Zeitung*, called *The Tales of Jacob* "the swan song of German literature of individual development."[57]

In early May he settled down to work on *Joseph in Egypt*. Trying to recreate the "hopelessly stricken condition" of Potiphar's wife, Mut-em-enet, when she becomes infatuated with Joseph, he turned up the passionate diary entries he'd made about Paul Ehrenberg. It was saddening to be reminded of his youthfully intense emotion and his frantic oscillation between exultation and despair when he was thirty-four years younger, but even men exclusively interested in the other sex, he wrote, became less passionate as they grew older.[58]

HIS AMERICAN PUBLISHER, Alfred Knopf, had invited him and Katia to cross the Atlantic for the first time, and to spend ten days in New York, where *The Tales of Jacob* was to come out at the beginning of June. They sailed on the *New Amsterdam*, a big liner with shiny white stateroom doors, spacious promenade decks, and luxurious lounges, but the forty passengers were outnumbered by the crew and the five-piece band. Thomas and Katia joined in the deck games—shuffleboard and deck golf on artificial turf. The first-class passengers dressed for dinner and watched movies in the social hall, but they didn't know exactly when they'd arrive. The crossing would take about eleven days, depending on fog, wind, and currents.[59]

After arriving in New York on May 29, Thomas and Katia stayed at the Savoy-Plaza, where they had sumptuous rooms on the twenty-fourth floor. On June 1 he delivered his Goethe lecture at Yale University. Parties were thrown by several clubs—the PEN, the Authors', the Dutch Treat—and to celebrate his fifty-ninth birthday on June 6, Knopf held a banquet for three hundred people at the Plaza Hotel, where the mayor, Fiorello La Guardia, was one of those who saw Thomas blow out fifty-nine candles on a cake and heard him make a speech in English. But wanting to praise Knopf's creativity, Thomas said: "He is not only a publisher—he is a creature too."

Though reporters were eager to question him about the situation in Germany, he knew the Nazi authorities would scrutinize clippings of everything written about his visit. Approached by the Jewish Rescue League, which invited him to give an interview in public, he rejected the invitation, but sent a carefully worded letter expressing approval for what the league was doing, and "joyful sympathy with this noble action." In some European countries, he said, political developments had brought "infinite grief and severe hardship" to countless innocent people.[60]

American newspapers carried reports about the letter, and before the end of the month, German newspapers were denouncing him for this, and for what he'd said in an interview. Having no chance to reply publicly, Thomas found himself making excuses to Bermann. He'd been dealing with a humanitarian enterprise that was trying to help victims of persecution and political refugees from all countries, while in the interview, which had been a short one, he'd restricted himself to repeating remarks he'd already made about anti-Semitism. He couldn't be held responsible for journalistic distortions of what he'd said.[61]

In the next five weeks he came to care less about the reactions of Nazi authorities to what he said. The "Night of the Long Knives" was on June 30. Accused of plotting against Hitler, the leader of the S.A., Ernst Röhm, was dragged from his bed and shot, as were scores of other leading storm troopers. On the same night, Schleicher and his wife were shot at their home on the outskirts of Berlin. Less than four weeks later, the Austrian chancellor, Engelbert Dollfuss, was murdered as the Nazis attempted a coup in Austria, and three hours after Hindenburg's death on August 2, Hitler announced that the presidency was being abolished. He was to be known from now on as Führer and Reichs Chancellor. At the polls, seventeen days later, 38 million people gave him a vote of approval.

Thomas was shocked by the atrocities,

> which doubtless signify a new consolidation of his already tottering power. I cannot say how much they have upset me, how seriously they disturb me and distract me from what I should regard, if only my heart were harder and colder, as the only thing that concerns me. What does the history of the world matter to me, I probably ought to think, if only it lets me go on living and working?[62]

The contradiction between "new consolidation" and "already tottering" points to the contrast between the inference he had to draw and the inference he wanted to draw. But he was objective about the storm troopers, who had shown they consisted of nothing but rabble: They wouldn't otherwise have tolerated the elimination of their leaders.[63] Hauptmann, who'd stayed in Germany and given his loyalty to the Nazis, had been prompted by Hindenburg's death to write a eulogy, which struck Thomas as a stupid piece of mythmaking, feeble and confused. Einstein had been shrewder in calling Hindenburg an old scoundrel. The German appetite for legend and myth could run counter to intellectual honesty, but Jews were "always more acute where truth is concerned."[64] Thomas was still alternating between positive and negative comments on Jews.

In early July, Thomas had been working at the novel, telling the story of Joseph's promotion in Potiphar's household, but he couldn't go on. He felt the same need he'd felt during the war to make a political statement before he resumed "the sublime game of writing."[65] Since the beginning of his exile, he'd kept detailed notes on events in Germany, and he now made extracts from these, adding a commentary. He also wrote to Ida Herz, a Nuremberg bookseller who'd been collecting documents and ephemera relating to him, asking her to send him the text of a speech Hitler had made in Nuremberg about culture.[66] Katia and Erika had been urging him to break his silence. "Perhaps I can deliver a blow that will be felt by the regime."[67] "Men and writers can do only what their fingers itch to do, and it is appropriate that the world crisis is also a crisis in my life and work. I should see it as a sign of being alive. The time seems ripe for the kind of statement I intend to make, and the moment could soon come when I would regret having kept silent for so long."[68]

But his intentions faltered. On a Sunday afternoon at the beginning of August he told "the grown-up children" that "living historically" was not only pointless but contemptible. Afterward he regretted what he'd said,[69] but Heinrich was right when he amiably predicted that Thomas would postpone his political statement. There was no hurry, since everyone knew the truth about the Third Reich. After its demise, an obituary could be written, but it would be superfluous. When Napoleon III was dead, he was called "*cet imbécile de qui personne ne parle plus.*" Wouldn't the same be said of Hitler?[70]

Instead of working on a political statement, Thomas settled down to a lighthearted essay about reading Cervantes on the *New Amsterdam*, "Voyage with Don Quixote" ("Meerfahrt mit Don Quijote"). Writing about the "stage fright" he'd felt when making his maiden journey across the Atlantic, he was also thinking about his fear of speaking out against the Nazis. He'd already let over eighteen months go by since Hitler became chancellor, but Wagner had said that andante was the true German tempo, and there were advantages in doing things slowly. "Space will have its time."

After an early October holiday in Lugano, he resumed work on *Joseph in Egypt* during November. In December, the *Neue Rundschau* published an extract from it, but it was obvious that neither the review nor the publishing house could survive for much longer in Germany. Samuel Fischer died in October: "Another piece of a better period has been lost, and a relationship both professional and personal that had lasted for many years."[71] Thomas wrote an obituary for the *Basler Nachrichten*. A volume of his essays was in preparation, *The Sufferings and Greatness of the Masters*, and though he thought of offering it to a Swiss publisher, he again gave in to Bermann, who was set on keeping the business going till the last minute.[72] Because of Hauptmann's willingness to make peace with the Nazis, Thomas had decided to drop the essay on him, replacing it with "Voyage with Don Quixote."

In January 1935 he took Katia with him on an Eastern European tour of lectures and readings. Giving interviews, he was careful to say nothing that could provoke the Nazis into banning his work, and on returning to Küsnacht, he was worried to find that the Prague paper *Selbstwehr* had reported him as saying more about German anti-Semitism than he'd actually said. He protested in a letter he asked the paper to publish.[73]

Before he and Katia left Küsnacht, 90 percent of the Saarlanders who voted in a plebiscite had opted for integration into Nazi Germany. Depressed by the ineluctable progress Nazism was making, he got the impression that all over the world standards were slipping. He felt like "a survivor from a nobler period." Perhaps this was the main reason he was treated with so much respect on his tour.[74]

He tried to define the debasement of standards in a paper titled "Attention, Europe!" ("Achtung, Europa!"), which he prepared in early March for a congress organized by the Comité Permanent des Lettres et des Arts. It was to be held in Nice at the beginning of April.[75] He complains that the "collectivist age" wants to escape from the forces that make for culture, civilization, and self-discipline, preferring a perpetual holiday from the self, and indulging in Dionysiac primitivism. Referring to Ortega y Gasset's book *The Revolt of the Masses*, Thomas condemns the new barbarism and the indifference of the masses to values that had been fundamental to nineteenth-century idealism. Without sniping directly at Goebbels or Hitler, he attacks the public that consents to have its senses dulled by propaganda instead of making an effort to educate itself.

The congress was due to start on April 1, and until four days before he was due to leave Küsnacht, Thomas intended to go. René Schickele would be there, and so would Heinrich. But in Germany, Thomas's essays were due for publication on March 28, and, nervous that his presence at the congress would upset the Nazi leaders, Bermann tried to dissuade him from going. In March, after letters had been sent to all "non-Aryan" members of the Reich Literary Chamber, banning them from all literary activity, Thomas wrote in his diary that he had a stronger desire than ever to sever all ties with Germany,[76] but he gave in. He sent his paper to Nice, but with instructions that it should neither be read to the congress nor shown to the press. Only members of the committee should be allowed to see it.[77]

In April he almost came out into the open, provoked by newspaper reports of Göring's wedding to Emmy Sonnemann, who was given a piece of jewelry worth about 70,000 marks, while her present to the groom was a luxury yacht. Lufthansa produced a plane for him upholstered in morocco leather and worth 100,000 marks. A gala performance was given of Strauss's opera *Die Ägyptische Helena*, and a young Communist was executed. The show of power would have been incomplete without bloodshed.[78] Thomas thought of writing an open letter to the German people, telling them what the world thought of them and warning them not to become enemies of the human race.[79]

By now he was playing with the idea of writing a story or novel about Goethe. In 1911, at an early stage of preparing "Death in Venice," he'd been intending to center the story on Goethe's elderly amours; but what most attracted him now was the old man's encounter in Weimar with Lotte Buff, the woman who'd once inspired him to write *Die Leiden des jungen Werthers* (*The Sorrows of Young Werther*). Meeting her in 1772, when he was twenty-three and she was nineteen, Goethe fell in love with her, not knowing she was engaged to Johann Kestner. Goethe befriended them before and after their marriage, corresponding with them for two years before he published the novel in 1774. Forty-four years after he'd fallen in love with her, Goethe met Lotte again. In March 1935, Thomas was trying to discover more about this "slightly grotesque encounter late in life," and he found a detailed and rather touching account of it in Felix Theilhaber's 1929 book *Goethe, Sexus und Eros*.[80]

INVITED TO HARVARD together with Einstein to receive an honorary doctorate, he intended to refuse. Though he'd resumed work on *Joseph in Egypt*, he was irritated by the slowness of his progress. But Harvard had rebuffed Hitler's friend Ernst ("Putzi") Hanfstängl when, on being appointed Nazi press chief, he offered the university a scholarship grant. Accepting the invitation, Thomas thought of the effect the news would have in Germany.[81]

His parents-in-law were coming to spend a fortnight in Küsnacht, and he'd have to allow time for celebrations of his sixtieth birthday, which meant he'd have little opportunity to work on the novel between late April and early July. In fact, he did even less work than he'd expected, for he was ill when the Pringsheims arrived, and he was losing faith in the book: "Dejection, exhaustion, listlessness, creative paralysis or semi-paralysis, dissatisfaction with the construction and style of the third volume, which is suffering from chronic swelling and is probably something quite different from—much less than—a novel. The construction should have been lighter and more like a fable. . . . Do I no longer have the energy to carry this work adequately from its beginning to its end?"[82]

In mid-May, after the Pringsheims left, he and Katia went to Nice, where they spent time with Heinrich and René Schickele. Neither Thomas nor Katia liked Heinrich's new woman, Nelly Kröger, whom they found stupid and vulgar. She'd been working as a barmaid when Heinrich met her soon after the unhappy end of his affair with Trude Hesterberg, and many of his friends thought he was reenacting with Nelly the story that could have made Trude into a film star if Sternberg hadn't insisted on using Dietrich.

In celebration of the birthday Heinrich contributed an emotional piece to *Die Sammlung*. "Over German heads, as was said in better days, their classic writers towered like cranes. For exactly this reason, their place and significance, together with yours, are assured, for they move beyond national frontiers. . . . Let us embrace, now, on your sixtieth birthday. Since we are brothers we can do this across celebrations and frontiers as long as we are alive; since we are writers, we can even do it after we are dead."[83]

On May 26, eleven days before the birthday, a celebration was held at the Corso-Theater in Zurich with a performance of a Vivaldi concerto grosso, speeches, the presentation of a gift from the city, a speech of thanks from Thomas, and a staging of excerpts from the third act of *Fiorenza*. On June 6 the whole family gathered in Küsnacht to celebrate, together with Reisiger, Bruno Frank, and other friends. Bermann sent an album with handwritten greetings from nearly all the Fischer authors and other well-wishers, including Einstein, Bernard Shaw, Karl Kerényi, and Knut Hamsun. Thomas received hundreds of letters; what surprised him was that so many of them came from Germany.[84]

28

Speaking Out

ON JUNE 9, 1935, three days after the birthday, Thomas and Katia were in Paris, on their way to the United States. The next day they boarded the SS *Lafayette* in Le Havre, and they were in mid-Atlantic when Erika married the poet W. H. Auden. Klaus had foreseen that the Nazis would expatriate her, and, wanting her to be provided with British citizenship and a valid passport, he asked his friend Christopher Isherwood whether he'd agree to a pro forma marriage. Not liking the idea, Isherwood said his mother would disapprove, but when Klaus approached Auden, who'd never met her, he cabled to say he'd be delighted. Erika flew to England, and they were married on June 15. At the wedding the diminutive Auden was dwarfed by the heavily built Therese Giehse, who was wearing a mannish tweed coat and carrying a large bouquet. Dressed in striped trousers and wearing a carnation, Auden helped Erika, whom he'd only just met, to answer the registrar's questions. Later Auden dedicated a volume of poems to her and, in an autumn letter, described her as "wonderful."[1] Not knowing about the wedding, the Nazis expatriated her the day after she was married.

Thomas and Katia arrived in New York on the nineteenth. The next day, in the presence of six thousand people, he and Einstein received their honorary doctorates from Harvard on a platform under a canopy. Photographs were taken of them in their academic regalia.[2] Stolidly refusing to comment on Hitler's Germany, Thomas was harassed by journalists,[3] and it was a relief to escape into the countryside. Two days after the ceremony, he and Katia went to stay in Riverside, Connecticut, with Hendrik van Loon, a hospitable Dutch-born writer who'd scored a success with *The Story of Mankind*.

It had been partly because of intervention from Franklin Roosevelt that Harvard had awarded the doctorate, and at the end of the month, Thomas and Katia were invited to dinner in the White House. Flying to Washington, they had their first experience of air travel, and he was too nervous to enjoy it. Rattling and shuddering, the plane took off jerkily, and at first he suffered from pressure in his ears and mild nausea. Soon bored by the experience of looking down, he read newspapers.[4] Later, coming to enjoy flying, he said it was like being in a luxurious sanatorium, looked after by lovely stewardesses.[5]

Washington was plunged in a heatwave. The electric fans in the hotel suite had little effect, but Thomas and Katia found the city remarkably beautiful and dignified—more imposing than any other capital city. The next day he bought a white linen suit, and they were driven to view the house of George Washington.

At the White House, one of the butlers showed them into a drawing room, where Eleanor Roosevelt joined them. The only other guests were a few ladies and a young man in a white dinner jacket. They didn't meet Roosevelt till they went into the dining room. Wearing light trousers and a velvet dinner jacket, he struck Thomas as energetic and self-satisfied: "Prime Minister *and* President. They can't get me out." The meal was rather ordinary, and afterward they went upstairs to watch a movie which seemed too long. They were taken into FDR's study, which had marine paintings in it, and Mrs. Roosevelt showed them around the house.[6]

After a few more days in New York, they sailed on a Cunard liner, the SS *Berengaria*, arriving in Cherbourg on July 12 and in Küsnacht on the thirteenth, only two days before the Pringsheims arrived on another visit. They stayed for a fortnight, but this didn't stop Thomas from working on the sequence between Potiphar and his wife before leaving to read in Gastein on August 20. From there he and Katia went on to spend a couple of weeks in Salzburg, where he heard Toscanini conduct.

Clamoring for his expatriation, some of the Nazi papers were quoting comments he'd made, or was alleged to have made, in the United States. In Washington, talking to a reporter from the *Boston Evening Globe*, he'd said that though he wasn't a Communist and wouldn't enjoy living under communism, it might be the only positive ideology that could be used against fascism if freedom was really dead. The interview published in the paper didn't tally with the actual conversation, and Thomas wrote to Bermann, complaining that American journalists had sometimes misquoted him and sometimes quoted statements he'd made before 1933 as if they were new.[7]

For two and a half years he'd been trying, awkwardly, to protect his interests inside Germany. It still wasn't clear whether he'd ever regain possession of his house in Munich or its contents, and while his work was still on sale in German bookstores, it could be banned at any moment, cutting him off from thousands of readers, including hundreds of people who'd written to him on his birthday. Though his books would still be in danger, Thomas was expecting to feel more independent once Bermann moved his business out of Germany.[8]

In mid-September, Thomas found himself thinking about Klaus Heuser again when he had a "very boring evening" with a Zurich publisher, Hans Rascher, who brought his wife and son to dinner. The son, Albert, reminded the children of Klaus, though the consensus was that Klaus had been better-looking. Reflecting on the emotion that had been kindled eight years earlier, Thomas told himself it must have been the final variation on a love he'd never feel again. He envied Goethe, who, less inhibited and less easily exhausted, had sustained his erotic life into his seventies—"always girls."[9]

On Saturday, September 21, after an early morning conference with Bermann about transplanting the company, Thomas was working at his desk when Klaus Heuser arrived at the house. Now twenty-four, he was in Zurich to visit Thomas, but stayed only about ten minutes. He was still slim and boyish. He expected to be kissed, but though Thomas kept looking into his eyes and saying "My God!," no kiss was exchanged. Fortunately Thomas had plenty to distract him through the rest of the day—a walk in the woods with Hans Reisiger, lunch with Ida Herz, a drive with Golo, a meeting with the editor of *Corona*, another drive with Bermann and his wife, dinner with them and Reisiger at a hotel.[10] Bermann still didn't know whether he'd move the business to Austria or Switzerland.

This made it even harder for Thomas to decide who should publish *Joseph in Egypt*, which was giving him more trouble than either of the previous volumes. He took no summer holiday, and in September, wanting to devote the autumn and winter entirely to the novel, he turned down a lecture tour that would have taken him to Vienna, Budapest, and Bucharest.[11] He'd been reading Proust and, astonished by the leisureliness of Proust's narrative, felt sure it was influencing his own pace when he wrote about the psychology of Potiphar's wife.[12] What worried him most was the idea that he should go back to the beginning of the volume, refining and reconstructing.[13]

In November he read the second half of the chapter about husband and wife to Katia, Erika, Therese Giehse, and Elisabeth, who all seemed spellbound. During three years of sporadic work he'd produced 594 manuscript pages, but the novel was still unfinished, and so much of the story remained untold that he'd have to make the trilogy into a tetralogy. He decided that the third volume, ending with the love story, could come out in the spring of 1936 as the first publication of Bermann's new house.[14]

SUMMARIZING AMBITIONS FOR 1936 at the beginning of the year, Thomas set his sights on completing *Joseph in Egypt* and the Goethe novella,[15] but the question still nagging at his conscience was whether to speak out against the Nazis. What he was writing about Joseph in Egypt had little to do with what he was thinking about Hitler's Germany. Occasionally he refers to Egyptian prejudice against Semitic foreigners, and Mut, Potiphar's wife, speaking to a crowd of servants in the courtyard, tries to foment hostility to the Hebrew youth who has come down from his wretched country to this beautiful garden of Osiris. But the story seldom alludes either to Nazism or to what Thomas had in common with his hero as an exile who, by exploiting his talents, could outclass the natives of his adopted country.

Though still gleaning material from pictures and prehistorical reading, and still incorporating some disguised autobiography, he was being more inventive than in any previous fiction. The Bible devotes about five hundred words to the events which occupy over four hundred pages in *Joseph in Egypt*. In the sixth chapter Thomas jokingly claims to be horrified by the scant justice done to circumstantiality in the original version of the story. While accumulating a lot of detail which is vivid and naturalistic, he keeps interrupting the narrative, often stepping back from the story to address the reader directly. Sometimes he shows his hand, taking us into his confidence about the way he's constructing the narrative. He poses questions about everything unstated or underdeveloped in the Bible, which never gives Potiphar's wife a name, merely telling us that she spoke to Joseph day by day, entreating him to lie with her. Does it follow that he gave her occasion? Using the expertise he'd acquired as a storyteller, Thomas fleshes out the sketchy figure of the flirtatious wife and provides a background to her sexual frustration. Emasculated in infancy, her fleshy husband can't make love, and the narrative builds the terse biblical summary of her fixation on Joseph into a subtle progression from indifference to love with a tragic dimension.

Misled by Dudu, an evil dwarf who has no counterpart in the Bible and may have been inspired by Wagner's *Ring*, Mut at first tries to dissuade Potiphar from appointing Joseph as steward, and then refuses to acknowledge the feelings that have been aroused. The development of their relationship spans three years. In the first she tries to conceal her love, in the second she lets it become visible, but it's only in the third that she tries to overcome Joseph's resistance by alternating between inducements and threats. The slowness of this buildup to the climax is essential to Thomas's method.

Joseph's reactions, too, go through distinct phases. In an early phase, the narrative is reminiscent of "Death in Venice" when, fancying himself in the role of educator, he thinks he can lead her thoughts from the physical to the spiritual: After focusing on his eyes, she may come to focus on his preoccupations. Though he's attracted, his resistance is steady, inspired partly by the oath of loyalty he swore to Potiphar when the previous steward was on his deathbed, and partly by piety. His chastity corresponds to his awareness that his God, a onetime demon of the desert, is both possessive and intolerant of passion. Joseph, who sees himself as betrothed to God, is aware of himself as a figure in a story that will be told. He warns Mut not to become a figure of sin, and sin is defined as that which is both commanded and forbidden. God himself has sinned by implanting in humanity strong urges to do what he then forbade us to do. Unlike the animals, we understand sin: At bottom, spirit is nothing but the understanding of sin.

Thomas is at his best when writing about forbidden love and about the overlapping of male and female qualities. Jacob's love for his favorite son is partly a continuation of his love for the beautiful Rachel, who passed on so many of her physical characteristics to her son; later, Potiphar tells Mut that the reason he loves Joseph's company is that the boy reminds him of her. The age at which Klaus had been most attractive to Thomas was the age at which male and female qualities are most piquantly mixed, and like Thomas, Joseph doesn't develop into full sexual maturity until he's well into his twenties. According to the narrative, the advantage of being neither fully male nor fully female is that one stands outside the human pale, and efforts to sustain dignity involve the spiritual, which is, after all, preeminently human, even if spirit comes off badly, in the long run, against animal nature. Mut, though she's a priestess of the god Amun, has to lead a life as hollow and dishonoring to the flesh as the life Joseph leads in his betrothal to God. Thomas would have been unable to empathize so well with them both if he'd been more normal in his sexuality. At his best, though, he can feel, as Joseph does, that the relationship between him and the world is permeated with the spirit of love: He's in love with everything.

But there's something he finds distasteful about the female body and the way it develops in middle age. The intensity of Mut's frustrated love for Joseph changes her physically. Her breasts, which had once been tender and maidenly, grow more voluptuous. Her shoulders and shoulder blades remain fragile, while her thighs develop, reminding him of thighs that could clutch a broomstick. This new body is described as a pathetic accentuation of her femininity, and we're told that she was fully aware of her witchlike state, for witchery is only femininity raised to extravagantly alluring heights. But when the dwarf, Dudu, telling Potiphar that Joseph has tried to force himself on Mut, offers to castrate the beautiful young boy, he gets beaten for his presumptuous suggestion. It's as if Thomas is reprimanding himself for his fantasies about sexuality—if not for his reservations about the female body—and also, perhaps, for the element of escapism in his leisurely preoccupation with a biblical story.

Through the first volume and other books still being sold and read in Germany, he believed himself to be in touch with a public "which by nature and culture is today in opposition to the system now in force, and from which the countermovement can one day emerge."[16] For nearly three years he'd kept silent. Had the moment arrived, he asked himself, when he should encourage resistance to Nazism by making a direct appeal to decent people who could take concerted action?[17] But he'd given little thought to the problem of how they could organize themselves, and he'd probably have gone on procrastinating if it hadn't been for Erika and Klaus.

On January 11, Bermann came under attack when Leopold Schwarz-schild, editor of the Paris-based refugee journal *Neue Tage-Buch*, claimed that contemporary German literature had "transferred abroad." Bermann, the principal publisher still basing himself in Germany, was a Jewish protégé of Goebbels.[18] Thomas riposted with a letter in the *Neue Zürcher Zeitung* which was also signed by Hermann Hesse and the writer Annette Kolb: The attack on Bermann, they said, was "totally unjustified."

Since June 1933, Erika had been trying to persuade her father to break all his ties with Germany and with Bermann; in April 1935, presented with a copy of the essay collection *Sufferings and Greatness of the Masters*, she said she was glad to have it in spite of "the detested publisher's imprint."[19] But after the letter in the *Neue Zürcher Zeitung*, she threatened to have nothing further to do with Thomas. She could see that it was natural for him to do all he could to protect himself from the Nazis, but since Hitler had seized power, she pointed out, his only public protest had been in defense of a publisher still working in Germany, and it had been directed against the editor of an émigré paper. "You are stabbing the whole émigré movement in the back, and all the efforts it's making—I can put it in no other way. . . . Your connection with Dr. Bermann and his firm is indestructible. You seem willing to make any sacrifice for it. If it would be a sacrifice were I to distance myself from you slowly but surely—this is just one more thing to consider. For me it's sad and frightful."[20]

Replying to her from Arosa, where he'd been staying with Katia since the middle of the month, he defended Bermann and defended himself. "People must have patience with me. . . . The day may come, *might* come, when I, uninhibited by raving madness, speak out myself to the world and Germany, saying: 'This is enough. Come on. Away with this rabble.' Perhaps this should not happen too soon." But he admitted to recognizing in her anger an "objectivisation" of his own scruples and doubts.[21]

She replied forcefully, reminding him that he'd done nothing to help her when *Die Pfeffermühle* had been attacked in the *Neue Zürcher Zeitung* and that he'd done Klaus more harm than any of the Nazis had by dissociating himself publicly from *Die Sammlung*.[22] On the day she wrote this letter, Eduard Korrodi published a riposte to Schwarzschild in the *Neue Zürcher Zeitung*. Titling his article "Deutsche Literatur in Emigrantenspiegel," he disparaged the émigré writers as if they were all Jewish and therefore unrepresentative of Germany. The same day Thomas received a telegram from Klaus and from Fritz Landshoff, director of Querido's German division. From Amsterdam they entreated him to answer Korrodi. "This time it is really a matter of life and death for us all."[23]

On January 27, Thomas and Katia returned to Küsnacht and found the seventeen-year-old Elisabeth upset and confused by the row with Erika, "whom she greatly fears and respects." Before leaving Arosa, Thomas had thought of sending an open letter to Korrodi, and Katia had already sketched out a rough draft.[24] He then worked at it over several days. Published in the *Neue Zürcher Zeitung* on February 3, it asked whether some of the writers still inside Germany would prefer to be outside. Besides, no clear separation could be made between the German literature written inside Germany and that written outside, and a concept of Germanism was one of the factors that had made so many writers, not all Jewish, sacrifice their home and possessions, ignoring broad hints that they'd be welcome back. In a previous article Korrodi had attributed the Europeanization of the German novel to the "international quality" of Jews. Thomas pointed out that he and Heinrich had contributed to this Europeanization, and that the international quality of Jews was neither more nor less than their Mediterranean-European quality.

> And this is at the same time *German*; without it Germanism would not be Germanism but an idleness useless to the world. . . . But German anti-Semitism, or that of Germany's rulers, is in the higher sense not at all directed against the Jews or not exclusively against them; it is against Europe and against that higher Germanism itself; it is, as is becoming ever more apparent, against the Christian and classical foundations of Western morality; it is the attempt (symbolised in the withdrawal from the League of Nations) to shake off the ties of civilisation, and this is threatening to create a ruinous alienation between Goethe's country and the rest of the world.[25]

After posting the letter Thomas wrote: "I am finally saving my soul with it and unveiling my deep conviction that nothing good for Germany or the world can come from the present German regime."[26] At last, after living in exile for six years, he'd made a public statement about Hitler and his henchmen.[27] "I had to say something of the sort, and I did it at the moment when someone was tendentiously trying to squeeze me away from the émigrés. . . . It was to some extent a temperamental gesture, a natural reaction to the insulting and infuriating things that occur every day."[28] If it had really been temperamental, it would have been remarkable that he'd managed to keep his temper under control for six years, but it could be seen as a father's belated reaction to impassioned prompting from two grown-up children who were both more temperamental than he was—less lacking in the qualities of a martyr. With his extraordinary mixture of weakness and strength, Thomas was repeating the pattern of 1927, when he'd at first resisted the pressure Lukács had put on him to plead for Zoltán Szántó's life, but had overcome his reluctance to intervene when Lukács called him a high-minded liar (see page 373).

His open letter to Korrodi caused much excitement among Swiss newspaper editors and reporters. Thomas received a mass of grateful letters, some from acquaintances, some from strangers, and one threatening letter, complaining about the vile depths to which people would descend, and saying that only communism could save the world.[29] Klaus wrote to congratulate his father on his beautiful answer to the evil Korrodi,[30] and Hermann Hesse wrote from Montagnola to express regret at the step Thomas had taken. A braver man than Thomas might have come out into the open sooner, but Hesse never came out. His books, too, were being published in Germany, and he assumed that after this, Thomas's would be banned.[31] The reproachful Bermann, who came to see him in Küsnacht, made the same assumption.[32]

More attacks were launched in the party press, where readers were advised not to put his books on their shelves, since Germany was nothing to him but a source of money.[33] Bermann had to be more discreet in advertising his books,[34] but no official action was taken against him, partly, perhaps, because the Nazi leaders were thinking about other things.

Abrogating the treaties of Versailles and Locarno, Hitler ordered a reoccupation of the Rhineland, which had still been a demilitarized zone. Before dawn on March 7, seven hours before Hitler informed the Reichstag of what he was doing, goose-stepping troops marched in. The German High Command was opposed to the venture, and the war minister, General von Blomberg, gave orders that the troops should be withdrawn if the Western powers gave signs of responding firmly. But the Western powers didn't. The British asked the French to do nothing until Hitler's action had been given full consideration, and though the signatories of the Locarno Pact, recalled at the instigation of the French, condemned Hitler's coup, no ultimatum was issued, no action taken.

On the night of March 7, Thomas was so upset by this inaction that he slept badly and had a headache the next day.[35] Hitler proposed a new treaty, guaranteeing peace for twenty-five years, and though the new French premier, Albert Sarraut, found this unacceptable, France could do nothing alone. The British, impressed by Hitler's show of peaceful intentions, pressed for Germany to be readmitted to the

League of Nations. Thomas was appalled by the apathy of the English press and by Anthony Eden's reassuringly moderate statement to the Commons. Thomas even thought of writing to the *Times*.[36]

Bermann was more worried about his problems in moving the business out of Germany. He was allowed to take Thomas's backlist with him, but not Hesse's, which had to be included in what he was selling. He wanted to set the firm up in Switzerland, though it would be necessary to have a Swiss partner, but the Swiss publishers, such as Rascher, who'd been encouraging at first, used their influence to stop him from being granted a residence permit, and Korrodi supported them in their objections.

Until now Heinrich had been the main spokesman for émigré German writers. In September 1935 he'd joined the Presidium of Romain Rolland's World Committee against War and Fascism, and for his sixty-fifth birthday, on March 27, Thomas paid tribute to him in the Paris-based *Neue Weltbühne*.[37] Writing to make plans for a late summer reunion with him on the Riviera, Thomas lavished high praise on his new collection of essays, *Es kommt der Tag*,[38] in spite of strong misgivings about Heinrich's "usual overwrought style."[39]

ON MAY 8, Sigmund Freud was going to be eighty, and Thomas, after being invited to deliver a celebratory lecture in Vienna, started preparing it in April. He called it "Freud and the Future" ("Freud und die Zukunft"). After delivering it to a packed audience in the Konzerthaus on the evening of May 8, he sat between Freud's son and daughter at a banquet in the Hotel Imperial. In the morning Thomas visited Freud in his flat, presenting him with a copy of the address and a portfolio containing manuscript messages of congratulations from Virginia Woolf, H. G. Wells, Stefan Zweig, and others. Afterward Freud told Thomas that the biblical Joseph had been a kind of mythical model for Napoleon, and that the story had been the secret demonic force behind Napoleon's complex career.[40]

At the beginning of June, Thomas and Katia left Küsnacht again for Vienna and Budapest, where he addressed a conference of the Comité International pour la Coopération Intellectuelle, appealing for a defense of Europe's cultural heritage through a "militant humanism," and after a speech by another delegate, Thomas spoke again, impromptu, denouncing the murderers of liberty and advocating militant democracy. At the end of this speech the Czech playwright Karel Capek embraced him, and the applause of the Hungarian audience lasted for a minute. Worried by the press coverage of what he said, the German ambassador telephoned the Home Office to demand that less attention should be paid to Thomas Mann.[41]

He and Katia were staying with Lajos Hatvany, a Hungarian literary nobleman, and Thomas not only repeated his Freud lecture in Budapest on the seventh but read from *Joseph in Egypt* on the ninth. He went on afterward to the opera house, where Bruno Walter was conducting a performance of *Tristan*, but Nazis had been throwing stink bombs, and the smell was vile. The soprano had been sick during the intermission, and making an eloquent gesture of incapacity, she sank back on Tristan's corpse, leaving the orchestra to deal with the *Liebestod*.[42]

In mid-July, when the Spanish Civil War broke out, Thomas was back in Küsnacht, working on the final chapter of *Joseph in Egypt*. A few days later, the commander of the uprising, General Sanjurjo, was killed in a plane crash, leaving the path clear for General Francisco Franco to gain control. The Popular Front government appealed unsuccessfully for help from France, while Mussolini sent 100,000 men to help the Fascist rebels and Germany sent bombers. Thomas was disgusted by the reactionary complacency of the *Neue Zürcher Zeitung* and other newspapers, which condemned the protests made by French Leftists as "dangerous intervention."[43] "It cries out to high heaven. These are supposed to be patriots, these noble generals who with Moroccan moors and foreign bombers massacre their own people, who are fighting for freedom."[44]

At the end of July, Thomas and Katia spent a few days in Sils-Barseglia. Having seen the Engadine only during the winter, they hadn't appreciated the full beauty of the landscape, and Thomas found the atmosphere "remarkably helpful" to him in making the final spurt to finish the novel, which was nearly as long as the first two volumes together.[45]

Undeniably, he could have improved the book by shortening it, but though this was the least autobiographical of his novels, he didn't want to destroy evidence of emotions, experiences, moods.

> One has to go on with such work through various states of being, even through exhaustion; and the strange fact is that afterwards I do not like to disown any of these. Certainly I strike out a good deal that was written yesterday and can be recognised today as misconceived. But in general I am a man of the *scripsi*, and feel a kind of reverence towards what has been produced day by day under specific personal circumstances. In such a book this gives me an inclination—which is probably very inartistic—to see not so much an objective work of art which should be brought to the highest possible pitch of perfection as a record of my life. Retouching it would seem almost deceptive.[46]

Earlier, writing such stories as "Death in Venice" and "Tonio Kröger," he had worked harder at rewriting and revising, cutting and polishing.

At that time he'd been more concerned to produce works of art than to leave a record of his life.

On the morning on Sunday, August 23, after nearly three and a half years of work, he wrote the final words of the novel. The family celebrated by drinking champagne with dinner. Afterward he read out one of the final sections, his audience consisting of Katia, Erika, Golo, Elisabeth, Michael, and Therese Giehse.

They went on drinking punch and eating cake until after midnight.[47] "Oh, the tome has fearfully pedantic *longueurs*, I fear, but I still think it works—a piece of higher frivolity for Germany, which is something Germany needs."[48]

In Berlin, Hitler had opened the Olympic Games, which were bringing international prestige to Nazi Germany, while in Spain the Fascists had closed the frontier with Gibraltar and bombed San Sebastian. The outlook for Europe was gloomy, and Katia thought they should settle in Boston. Thomas didn't want to uproot his life and his work, though "in Germany too she was always the cleverer one."[49]

Four days after he finished the book, they left with the younger children for the motoring holiday they'd planned on the Riviera. After a night in Geneva, they drove down to Saint-Cyr, where they stayed for a few days, spending time with the Schickeles before they drove on to Le Lavandou, where Heinrich joined them, bringing his twenty-year-old daughter, Leonie. But before the holiday was over, Thomas, Katia, Heinrich, and Leonie succumbed to an infection of the skin and chronic soreness of the throat.[50] They left on September 21, taking three days to drive back, and in Küsnacht, Thomas was still unwell, now suffering from erysipelas, as he had in 1916. "The thing is taking its course mildly, without a high temperature, the doctor is satisfied, but the swelling is still on the move. I am being given injections and poultices."[51]

Within four days, he was deep in preparations for a novella, *The Beloved Returns*, "in which I indulge in the fantastic pleasure of putting Goethe back personally on his feet. Bold, isn't it?"[52] Having decided to take a holiday from the *Joseph* tetralogy by writing about Goethe, he'd plunged into the preliminary reading, which was going to be extensive.[53] At the end of the month he told Bermann he was stalking the subject day and night without having decided on the form.[54]

Bermann had made a good start in Vienna, thanks partly to *Joseph in Egypt*, which was harvesting favorable reviews outside Germany, and by early December, the first edition of ten thousand copies had almost sold out. The book wasn't reviewed in the major German papers, but a gratifying critique by Julius Bab appeared in the *Central-Vereins-Zeitung*.[55] Thomas was also pleased with a letter from Hans Reisiger, "who could hardly contain his enthusiasm,"[56] and one from his old friend Paul Amann.[57]

* * *

HEINRICH HAD BEEN STATELESS for three years when he took Czech nationality in 1936, thanks to intervention from Tomáš Masaryk, the former president of the republic, who'd resigned the previous year in favor of Eduard Beneš. It was an initiative taken by an enterprising Czech that enabled Thomas to follow Heinrich's example and become a Czech citizen. Rudolf Fleischmann made linen handkerchiefs out of flax woven and spun by peasants in a village called Proseč on the eastern frontier of Czechoslovakia, near Moravia. After Fleischmann had persuaded the community that Thomas Mann should be invited to become a citizen, he wrote to him in Küsnacht. It was Beneš who advised Fleischmann to visit the Manns there, and on March 8, 1936, Thomas signed a power of attorney for Fleischmann to represent him, and on November 19, 1936, while being formally naturalized as a Czech citizen, Thomas took his oath at the Czech consulate in Zurich. After checking by telephone that Bermann had no objection, he encouraged the Swiss newspapers to publicize his change of nationality.[58] It meant that he could no longer be expatriated, and that the Nazis couldn't confiscate his house in Munich on grounds of expatriation.[59] Fleischmann was sentenced to death when the Nazis discovered what he'd done, and his property was confiscated, but he escaped to Berlin, knowing no one would look for him there.[60]

When his German citizenship was formally taken away with retrospective effect from July 14, 1933, the decree was dated December 2 and headed "Betrayers of the People and Enemies of the Reich." The reasons given were that he'd supported statements made by international organizations manipulated by the Jews, and had made treasonable attacks on the Reich. After the report on December 5 in the *Völkischer Beobachter*, he received telegrams, letters, and other messages of congratulation from all over the world. "It is almost as it was after the Nobel Prize."[61] And in a statement to the *Berner Tagwacht* he explained that he'd already become a Czech citizen and didn't need to comment on the Nazis' action. "In anticipation of it I have already declared on several occasions that I am more deeply rooted in German life and tradition than the vivid but ephemeral apparitions who currently govern Germany."[62] But in a letter to Freud he admitted his days had been "rather darkened" by the loss of his German nationality.[63]

On Christmas Day he was informed that he'd also lost his honorary doctorate at Bonn University.[64] He responded by asking whether a German writer should remain wholly silent when faced with the inexplicable evil being done in his country every day to bodies, souls, and minds, to goodness and truth, to individuals and humanity. The Nazi state had only one purpose: to prepare the people for war by crushing every element of opposition, making the population into a military instrument, incapable of thinking critically.[65] After being quoted in English, French, and Swiss newspapers, the letter was published as a pamphlet in all three countries. In Germany the Nazis couldn't stop the illegal circulation of copies, and on January 26, 1937, Goebbels ordered that Thomas Mann should never be mentioned in German newspapers, since polemical discussion would only make him known in even wider circles, strengthening the inner resistance of those who stayed behind. By mid-February, fifteen thousand copies of the pamphlet had been printed in German by Emil Oprecht, a Zurich bookseller who'd gone into publishing in order to combat Nazism, while Swedish, Dutch, and American editions were ready or nearly ready for distribution.[66]

After this Thomas had little contact with the German writers who'd taken the oath of loyalty to the Nazis. One day, when he was shopping in a large Zurich clothing store, a shop assistant told him that Gerhart Hauptmann was in another department. "Perhaps you'd like to say good day to him?" Thomas replied that he thought it would be better to wait till the end of the Third Reich. "Oh," said the shop assistant, "that's exactly what Herr Hauptmann said."[67]

Hitler Is My Brother

AT THE BEGINNING OF 1937, Thomas would have liked to work steadily at *The Beloved Returns*, but he was distracted by litigation over plagiarism. In March 1936 a Romanian, Sietcu Petru, writing in a Romanian Nazi journal, had alleged that the *Joseph* novels were being based on a verse drama in thirty acts, *Visul Faraonitor* (*Pharaoh's Dream*) by Aurelian Pacurariu. He'd arranged with a Hungarian editor to have his work translated into German by a Jew, who'd sold it through a middleman, Deszö Straussmann, to the Jewish bandit Thomas Mann. Though Thomas wrote to the newspaper *Adeverul* denying that he'd ever read the verse drama or heard of Pacurariu or Straussmann, Pacurariu started proceedings. A lawyer in Timisoara offered to defend Thomas without a fee but warned him that Romanian judges were capable of anything.[1]

He worked on *The Beloved Returns* between January 21 and February 8 while he and Katia were in Arosa. Having hit on the idea of making the elderly Charlotte Kestner revisit Weimar, ostensibly to see her family but really to confront the man who'd made her immortal and had neglected her ever since, Thomas was excited by the idea of introducing Goethe as a character, but, wanting to prepare gradually for his first appearance, he wrote a series of sequences in which Lotte discusses feelings and memories with people who can tell about the man Goethe has become.

The first six chapters are all invested in this buildup to a confrontation between Goethe and Lotte. She has protracted conversations not only with Goethe's assistant, Dr. Riemer, but also with Schopenhauer's sister Adele, a close friend of Ottilie von Pogwisch, the girl about to marry Goethe's son August, and with August himself. The conversations are less like Platonic dialogues than essays, the speakers reiterating facts and ideas that had mostly been put forward in Thomas's lectures on Goethe. In "Goethe's Career as a Writer," he'd accused Goethe (as he might have accused himself) of egoism, pointing out that Goethe could have written a fascinating novel about egoism. Seizing another opportunity to use his technique of identifying with his subject while writing critically about greatness, Thomas confronts Lotte, who has herself been used and abandoned, with some of Goethe's other victims. Riemer has sacrificed his university career to help the great man. August has let his life be shaped by his father's needs: Even his marriage to Ottilie is motivated mainly by Goethe's liking for her and his desire that she should run the household. But without trying to generate narrative momentum, Thomas is content to use his talent for mimicry on the characters, who are made to expound interpretative ideas he has already expounded in his lectures. To punctuate this essayistic exposition, Thomas makes the characters alternate between congratulating each other on their articulacy and apologizing for talking at such length.

It was thirty-two years since, attacked for basing his fiction on living models, Thomas had defended himself by arguing that neither Lotte nor her husband had been so petty-minded as to resent the novel that had given them a more intense, interesting, and durable life than the one they were living.[2] Though Thomas writes less simplistically in his novel about her attitude to the way she was used, he saddles her with feelings that derive more from the outlook of a writer than from empathy with a woman. And having taken pride, when rereading his lecture on the greatness and suffering of Wagner, in thinking it could have been a sequence from *The Magic Mountain*, he now feels entitled to repeat passages from his lecture on Goethe's literary career.

In the early chapters, much of the dialogue is undramatically analytical. Wanting to write, yet again, about the nature of creative genius, Thomas plunges Lotte into a long conversation with Friedrich Wilhelm Riemer, a scholar and literary historian who worked as assistant to Goethe and tutor to his son August. Riemer's style is accurately parodied. Lotte contributes such remarks as "How well you express yourself, Herr Doktor! Listening to you, I can't help feeling grateful for your accurate reasoning!" while the man of letters proceeds with his discourse, comparing literary creativity with the creation of the universe and not only crediting God with the kind of irony that characterized Thomas's work but defending Him from allegations of coldness. How could He be expected to feel enthusiastic about His own work? His attitude must be one of all-embracing irony, which could justly be equated with nihilism. It follows that God and the Devil shouldn't be regarded as opposite principles. If God is everything, he must include the diabolic. Heaven sees you with one eye, while the other is observing you with the iciest negation, the most destructive neutrality. When the two eyes are coordinated in a single vision, the vision is that of absolute art, which combines absolute love with absolute negation. Genius is a horrifying approach to the godlike and the diabolic. Thomas was looking back at what he'd said about irony twenty years earlier in *Reflections* and prefiguring what he was going to write in *Doctor Faustus* about the interdependence of creative genius and diabolic negation.

* * *

AFTER EIGHTEEN DAYS in Arosa he went to Zurich for discussions about the new periodical, a bi-monthly called *Mass und Wert* (*Measure and Worth*). He was invited to be editor in chief with Emil Oprecht as publisher and Ferdinand Lion as managing editor. The idea was to provide a vehicle outside Germany for the best of contemporary German culture. "It should not be polemical but positive, constructive, serving the dignity and authority of the German spirit in a way that is sustaining, befriending the future while retaining what is best from the past." Among potential contributors Thomas approached were Hermann Hesse and the Swiss theologian Karl Barth.[3] The Swiss writer Karl Frey, who used the pseudonym Konrad Falke, accepted an invitation to work with Thomas as co-editor.

He'd been invited to New York by the New School for Social Research, which was offering $2,500 for a series of five readings and lectures. One reason he couldn't refuse was that a donation of $100,000 had been offered to the University in Exile there on condition that he come to rally support. The university had been created by the American Guild for Cultural Freedom, an organization founded in 1935 by Prince Hubertus zu Löwenstein with objectives parallel to those of *Mass und Wert*: to bring together exiled intellectuals who could contribute to the reconstruction of German culture. Thomas, who'd accepted positions on some of the Guild's committees, had joined the university's governing body.

On April 7 he and Katia sailed from Le Havre on the huge SS *Normandie*. Traveling first class, they had a cabin opening onto a private deck, and the dining salon was so big it reminded him of a cathedral. The passage was rough, and Thomas's enjoyment of the luxurious accommodation was spoiled by seasickness, toothache, and, more formidably, pains in his leg due to the onset of sciatica.[4] But needing to improve his English, he worked at it with Katia's help.

After arriving in New York on April 12, he delivered his lecture on Wagner the next day. Two days later, at a banquet to celebrate the fourth birthday of the New School's Graduate Faculty of Political and Social Sciences, he spoke on "The Living Spirit," the spirit being that of German culture, which hadn't been killed by the Nazis.

No longer needing to worry about Nazi reactions to newspaper reports on what he said, he gave interviews freely, and on April 21 he spoke in a synagogue at a memorial service for victims of fascism. There were also dinners, soirees, interviews, visitors, flowers, readings from *The Beloved Returns*, and meetings with Erika, who was making a good impression in New York, where she'd spoken out against Hitler. Thomas met many prominent and influential Americans, including the Meyers. A philanthropic financier in his early sixties, Eugene Meyer owned and published *The Washington Post*; twelve years his junior, his wife, Agnes, was the daughter of German émigrés and fluent in the language. She wrote for her husband's paper, for *The New York Times Book Review*, and for the *Atlantic Monthly*. As a student in Paris, she'd been friendly with Claudel, and she gave signs of wanting to help Thomas. When he was invited to give a February lecture tour in the States, she offered to translate the lecture into English. It was going to be on Wagner. Encouraged by Katia, he made up his mind to spend part of each year in America. "Distancing myself from Europe in this way would be infinitely advantageous to my intellectual freedom and morale."[5]

On April 23, 1937, when he and Katia boarded the *Île de France*, his prospects were much better than when they'd arrived in New York eleven days earlier. Most attractive of all was the idea of working in Hollywood and earning $3,000 a week. Bruno Frank was there, and it seemed possible that both *The Magic Mountain* and *Royal Highness* would be filmed. The eleven days had been so eventful that Thomas had almost constantly been distracted from the sciatica in his leg. But on the boat, pleasant though it was, he was less active and the pain, which became more insistent, was at its worst in the morning. Codeine gave him little relief.[6]

After docking in Le Havre on the afternoon of April 30, they had a two-and-a-half-hour train ride in a Pullman carriage to Paris. He was exhausted and in pain when they arrived. The next day they had a champagne brunch with Annette Kolb at her home on the rue Casimir-Périer, and after a night on the train in a sleeping car, they arrived in Zurich on May 2. The sciatica was almost unbearable, and the next day he consulted Dr. Erich Katzenstein, a neurologist at the Psychiatric Clinic, who prescribed a drug and a tonic, also giving him an electric heating pad to relieve the pain. But it awakened him early the following morning. With his energy sapped, he felt incapable of coping with the demands *Mass und Wert* was going to make, and he thought of tossing the editorial job aside.[7] He worked at the novel, but couldn't average more than a page a day, mainly because he was getting so little sleep, even with pills. After taking a sedative toward midnight, he could usually sleep for three hours before the pain woke him. After taking two sleeping pills dissolved in camomile tea, he could sleep for another two hours. "Then it is over and I cannot find any position that is bearable even for a few minutes." He went on experimenting with different brands of sleeping tablet.[8] He'd been recommended to take the cure at Ragaz, a town with thermal baths on the Rhine in the canton of Saint Gall, and he was intending to go there with Katia after Erika, who was on a visit from New York, had come to stay with them in Küsnacht.[9] Her marriage to Auden hadn't affected her relationship with Klaus, who was still her constant companion; now a drug addict, he was in a Hungarian sanatorium.[10]

Before leaving for Ragaz on June 10, Thomas wrote the foreword to the first issue of *Mass und Wert*. The word *Mass*, he explained, wasn't to be equated with mediocrity or the average. Art always went to extremes, and he associated *measure* with order, light, the music of creation. Art bore within itself a measure which became more than a test in matters of taste and suggested values beyond the aesthetic ones. "We want to be artists and anti-barbarians," he declared, "to observe moderation, to defend values, to love that which is free and daring, and to despise philistinism and ideological rubbish." Without accepting the tenets of Marxism, he wanted to align the new periodical with socialism, which was only a determination not to look for a metaphysical escape from the urgent material demands of the collective social life. Socialists were those who wanted to give life a human meaning.[11] The first issue also contained the opening chapter of *The Beloved Returns*.

In Ragaz, he had to take baths in painful "radium waters."[12] After ten days he still found the cure so strenuous that he couldn't work on *The Beloved Returns*. He read proofs of *Felix Krull*, which was to be published by Querido Verlag, with the second part still in fragmentary form.[13] Believing he was getting gradually better, he stayed in Ragaz for four weeks, and when he left on July 7, he told himself there might be beneficial aftereffects.[14] But he was still suffering pain and still subject to fits of pessimism in which the sciatica seemed like a warning that his life wasn't going to last much longer. Irrationally, this feeling was intensified by the death of Otto Grautoff, who'd been his closest friend for so many years. Grautoff was his junior by a year, and Thomas didn't even know what had killed him.[15]

Needing to stop for a rest every seven or eight minutes when he went out walking, Thomas took a campstool with him. He also had regular vitamin injections. By early August he was suffering less and working on *The Beloved Returns*.[16] The doctor advised him against going to Arosa, but he was planning to spend two weeks or so in Locarno with Hans Reisiger.

He was expecting *The Beloved Returns* to consist of between 300 and 350 pages. The first half was finished before he and Katia left for Locarno on September 15, but while he felt impatient to resume work on the *Joseph* novels, he didn't give all his working time in Locarno to *Beloved*. Instead, though he wasn't going to the States until February, he made a start on preparing the Wagner lecture for his tour, and he'd have to make a speech at the opening of a Thomas Mann archive at Yale University.[17]

While writing the new lecture, Thomas wanted to see Wagner's home, Tribschen, on Lake Lucerne. Nietzsche often went to the house, where Wagner lived from 1866 to 1872. It stands on a promontory in the center of a big park that slopes down to the lake. On October 13, Thomas drove there and toured the rooms with Katia, Golo, Elisabeth, and Reisiger. "Frightful oil paintings, rather Hitler. An absolutely obnoxious Siegfried like a male prostitute. . . . Poem to Cosima to accompany the Idyll—only 'Hm' to be said. Elements of frightfulness and Hitlerishness clearly visible, if only latent and anticipatory, from the pathetic kitsch to the German love of boys."[18] There was a bust of Houston Stuart Chamberlain, who had married Wagner's daughter Eva, nine years after writing *Foundations of the Nineteenth Century*, which was influential in the development of Nazi racist ideology. But in the evening Thomas listened admiringly to records of *Die Walküre*.[19]

Thirteen days later, while he was sketching out a lecture on "The Coming Victory of Democracy" for the American tour, Oprecht telephoned with an invitation from the Stadttheater in Zurich for him to deliver a lecture on Wagner for their new production of the entire *Ring* in mid-November. Though he'd have much less time than he liked for preparation, Thomas was tempted to accept, and he reread what Wagner had written about the *Ring*. "What is personal is repellent. Demands to be 'loved' as a human being."[20]

Though he no longer had anything to lose by lecturing about politics in America, he wasn't sure whether he wanted to. On November 13, discussing the worldwide trend toward fascism over dinner with Katia and Golo, he felt almost uncommitted. Why should he poison his blood and go on sacrificing so much of his time in the effort to resist the inevitable? Who was he trying to save? "No more offers of assistance. No statements and answers. Why provoke hatred? Freedom and frivolity. One should finally stake one's claim to them."[21]

Before he finished the Wagner lecture, he was having serious trouble with his upper jaw.[22] Reluctantly submitting to the dentist's advice, he had some of his teeth extracted and a denture fitted. He still hadn't got used to it by the middle of November. He hated having to wear it and loathed the stale, salty taste produced in his mouth by saliva trapped under the denture.[23] On November 16, when he was delivering his Wagner lecture to the packed Aula of Zurich University, the denture started to hurt at a crucial moment, but he somehow managed to adjust it.[24]

With "The Coming Victory of Democracy" as his subject for the American lecture, he had little hope of finding anything to say that he hadn't already said in denouncing fascism. But since he was going to deliver the lecture in fifteen states, where it would be well covered by newspaper reporters, he could canvass support for Roosevelt's foreign policy, warning the Americans how dangerous it was to compromise with the Fascist leaders—men who couldn't be won over by forbearance, friendliness, amicable concessions.[25] "Democracy and Fascism live, so to speak, on different planets. . . . The Fascist interpretation of the world and of history is one of absolute force, wholly free of morality and reason. . . ."[26] Without explicitly predicting that the world could soon be plunged into a new war, he emphasized that war was helpful to Fascist dictators in distracting attention from domestic issues. There was no longer any such thing as world peace. "An unofficial and unde-clared war is being waged, as an experiment, in remote places with lim-ited means, while the big war apparatus is being carefully saved up—an equivocal, or, at least, not a very explicit situation which Fascism has in-vented and in which it feels very much at home."[27] He was thinking mainly of Abyssinia, which had been annexed by Fascist Italy in May 1936.

Reluctant to be polemical, he felt as if he were writing a kind of po-litical Sunday-school sermon. His aim as a writer was to approximate as closely as he could to telling the whole truth about himself and every-thing else he discussed, but to involve himself in politics was to step back from this ambition. He believed most of what he was going to say in the lecture, but not everything. "Between ourselves, it is a role with which I am identifying in the same way as an actor does with his. And why am I playing it? Out of hatred for Fascism and Hitler."[28] It wasn't until after Christmas that he went back to *The Beloved Returns*, and even then, working on the sequence with Goethe's son, Thomas felt as if he were stealing time.[29]

When he and Katia returned to Arosa on January 10, 1938, it was only a year since they'd been there, but they were glad to resume their normal pattern after the doctor's veto on the Alps during the summer of sciatica. At the railway station they had their luggage loaded onto a sleigh and walked through the town to the hotel, where they were shown up to their usual suite, and Thomas lined his books up on the chest of drawers. The table they were given for dinner was next to the table they'd had the previous year. Disturbed during the night by noisy guests returning from a fancy dress ball, Thomas needed half a Phan-odorm tablet to sleep, and at breakfast his denture made it difficult to eat the rolls that were served with honey. He still needed his stick when he and Katia walked into the village, but it felt as though they'd come home.[30]

He was still deeply depressed by what he saw as a widespread drift toward evil. The only consolation, he said, was the sense of belonging to an elite of better informed, better disposed people. "In the end, the power of this elite to make decisions will probably shape the future."[31] His fear was that German culture would never again be the same. After reading a discerning review of the incomplete *Felix Krull* by an émigré writer, Hermann Kesten, Thomas wrote to him: "Without you Jews there would be no real recognition of German literary works."[32]

This implied that German Jews were somehow separate from German culture.

On February 12, the day they boarded the *Queen Mary*, a conference was held at Berchtesgaden, where Hitler bullied the Austrian chancellor, Kurt von Schuschnigg, into including Nazis in his cabinet, releasing imprisoned Austrian Nazis, and giving them greater freedom of activity. Four days later a pro-Nazi, Arthur Seyss-Inquart, was appointed minister of the interior. Thomas read about this in the ship's newspaper. "Frightful," he wrote in his diary. "Schuschnigg forced to welcome men who murdered Dollfuss and will throw bombs and try to assassinate him. Göring expected in Vienna. Dejection of the Austrian patriots, panic of the Catholics and Jews. Prohibition of everything 'anti-German' naturally, and of periodicals (*Mass und Wert!*). Cowardly and frigid speech by Eden in the House of Commons. Ghastly. The consequences for Prague? The effect on Switzerland?"

In fact, Anthony Eden resigned as foreign secretary only four days later. Neville Chamberlain, who was being conciliatory to both Hitler and Mussolini, was ready to recognize Italy's annexation of Abyssinia, and had provoked the resignation by insisting on meeting the Italian ambassador himself, instead of leaving it to the Foreign Office.

Had they been in the habit of celebrating their wedding anniversary, which was February 11, Thomas and Katia would have realized before they left Europe that they'd been married for thirty-three years. As it was, this didn't dawn on them until they'd been on board ship for a week. They were both unwell. She was having trouble with her eye, he with his stomach. More depressed and less diplomatic than he might otherwise have been, he said he wouldn't like to relive a life in which he'd had so much more pain than pleasure.[33]

They arrived in New York on February 21, and four days later he made a speech at Yale University for the opening of the Thomas Mann Collection. On the tour, which opened at Northwestern University in Chicago a week later, he read his lecture "The Coming Victory of Democracy" without changing the substance of what he'd written, though the tone was influenced by developments in Austria. The tour had been arranged by an agent, Harold Peat, who was pocketing 50 percent of the fees, mostly in the region of $1,000 a lecture. Thomas went on to the University of Michigan at Ann Arbor, the Institute of Arts and Sciences in Brooklyn, and Constitution Hall in Washington.

He was halfway through the tour when Hitler annexed Austria. On February 19, Schuschnigg had told Austrian Jews they had nothing to fear, and on the twenty-fourth promised to defend Austria's independence. It had been guaranteed by the League of Nations, while Germany and Great Britain had signed treaties by which Austrian independence was inalienable, unless the Council of the League decided otherwise. But on March 11, two days after calling for a plebiscite on independence, Schuschnigg was forced to resign. He was succeeded by Seyss-Inquart, who promptly invited Germany to send in troops. On March 13 a Reunification Act was decreed, acknowledging Germany's annexation of Austria. On March 14, with church bells pealing, crowds cheering, and young girls in national dress throwing flowers, Hitler drove into Vienna. Wearing the brown uniform of his storm troopers, he stood in an open car giving the Nazi salute. Headed by tanks and followed by field guns, the procession passed slowly through the exultant crowd toward the Imperial Hotel, where he made a speech from the balcony, promising that Germany would never again be divided. He'd just added 6 million people to the 68 million he already ruled.

Thomas's anger was partly political and partly personal. With Bermann based in Vienna, his books had still been on sale to a large German-speaking public, but now they'd be banned in Austria. Apart from exiles and Swiss Germans, no one would be able to buy the books except in translation. He could do nothing except carry on lecturing about the coming victory of democracy. Within a week, as newspapers reported a warlike buildup of German troops in Austria, it looked as if Czechoslovakia would be invaded. The only question was when. In his diary on March 20, Thomas was already grumbling about the "idiots who did not see that once Austria was surrendered there would be no stopping the process." But his anxiety about the future of Europe was inseparable from anxiety about the future of his work—would anyone still want to read it?[34]

The most urgent problem was whether he and Katia should go on living in Switzerland. What they were witnessing was ominously like a European reprise of what had happened inside Germany during 1933, when Hitler had demonstrated that legality and goodwill were impotent against his brand of terrorism. By murdering rivals and building up an unofficial army of hooligans, he'd overcome all resistance. His army was now official, and he knew how weak the Western powers were. They'd objected to his rearmament of Germany, and inside his own government, these objections had been supported by Hjalmar Schacht, the minister of economics, who, until Hitler removed him at the end of 1937, argued against the strain placed on economic recovery. After the Austrian coup, Britain and France made formal protests but did nothing to stop Hitler from making his war machine even bigger.

Once again Thomas was glad to be away from home at the crucial moment, for there was nothing to stop the Nazis from marching into Switzerland if they wanted to. From the idea of spending a part of each year in the States it was an easy step to the idea of living there, and the influential Agnes Meyer made it easier. As a friend of Cordell Hull, the secretary of state, she could help Thomas to become an American citizen, and in the meantime, she could give indirect financial help by persuading a university to provide a position that would virtually be a sinecure. He could be offered a chair or appointed as a lecturer, and without delivering more than an occasional lecture he'd receive a handsome salary. The university wouldn't even have to find the money, which would come from the Rockefeller Foundation, whose trustees, she later told Thomas, were all friends of his.[35]

With her energy, her wealth, her contacts, her unbounded admiration for him, and the freedom of initiative her husband gave her, Agnes Meyer could be extremely helpful in a country where he was less well known than he'd been in Germany. On the other hand there might be certain dangers in accepting everything she seemed so glad to offer. What did she want in return? Was she attracted to him sexually? He'd have to preserve a delicate balance, graciously and gratefully accepting some favors, but not too many. He could invest time in corresponding with her, he could let her translate lectures and speeches into English, he could help her when she wanted to review his books or write articles about his work, but he must not arouse any expectations he wouldn't be able to disappoint without antagonizing her.

Princeton University offered to employ him as Lecturer in the Humanities at a salary of $6,000 a year. Before accepting, he asked whether she could make the same arrangement for him at Harvard.[36] Hearing that she couldn't, he said yes to Princeton. But this wasn't until the end of May, and his decision to settle in the States had been taken by March 21. "Now that Hitler has been able to launch his criminal assault on Austria with impunity, and will probably meet equally little resistance in the near future when he takes a similar step against Czechoslovakia, Europe is really no longer a place where men of my kind can live."[37]

He wasn't intending to revisit Switzerland even briefly. "Plan that Erika travels to Europe alone, dissolves the household, makes arrangements for the children and for transporting our luggage."[38] Now in his sixty-third year, he'd have to acclimatize himself to life in a country where German wasn't spoken, and he'd found this difficult when living for four months in Sanary. He'd also have to distance himself from his German readers, but sales in Germany had fallen off since he'd written his letter to the dean of Bonn University. It was some consolation that over sixteen thousand copies of *Joseph in Egypt* had been sold in America. There was also a possibility that Alfred Knopf would start publishing books in German, and Thomas rebuffed Bermann when he wrote a letter about the possibility of moving the company to New York.[39]

Most of Thomas's lectures were sold out, and at the last, in Los Angeles on April 1, he spoke at an auditorium that accommodated six thousand people. Altogether, on the lecture tour, his audiences totaled about sixty thousand people.[40] At their hotel in Beverly Hills, the Manns received a visit from Bruno Frank and his wife before going on to a $100-a-plate benefit dinner for the refugees at the spectacular home of the film producer Jack L. Warner. There were many stars among the guests, and in the morning Harold Peat offered to set up another American lecture tour the following year, but Thomas wasn't too bedazzled to read parts of the Schopenhauer essay he'd finished in February—fifty-five pages of manuscript—and to think of how he was going to end *The Beloved Returns*.[41]

American hospitality was generous and deferential. His mood alternated between euphoric appreciation of the luxury on offer in Hollywood and depression about the feebleness of Western Europe's reaction to Fascist aggression. In the Spanish Civil War the rebels were using tanks, field guns, planes, and bombs supplied by Hitler and Mussolini, while Britain and France were giving no help to the beleaguered government. To Thomas it looked as if Chamberlain had made a secret deal with Hitler, sacrificing Czechoslovakia in exchange for Germany's abandonment of colonies it no longer needed, while Poland and Lithuania were to stop Russia from helping the Czechs.[42] The Western democracies seemed to have decided that National Socialism and fascism were an acceptable alternative to communism, which couldn't have been kept in check without these "brutal quack medicines."[43]

Unable to concentrate on *The Beloved Returns*, but feeling more tense when he wasn't writing, Thomas accepted a commission from the monthly *Cosmopolitan* to write a diary-style piece about himself and Germany.[44] It turned into a piece about Hitler. Why was this good-for-nothing moving from one triumph to the next? Again and again he had shown himself to be lazy and incapable of steady work. Unable to ride a horse, drive a car, or beget a child, he had developed a gift for oratory of an inferior kind but magnetic in its effect. Vengeful and full of resentment at his own failure, Hitler was fascinating to a great nation that had been humiliated by defeat. Having taught himself to be a political animal, the former melancholic might succeed in subjugating Europe—perhaps the whole world. But if the artist was often a kind of confidence trickster, wasn't this con man par excellence a kind of artist? During his indolent existence in a moral and mental bohemia, he'd acquired the arrogant conviction that he was destined for a better existence. What about his bad conscience, his sense of guilt, his touchiness, his storing up of compensatory wishes, his need to justify himself, his urge to dominate and subdue, his dream of having the world at his feet, writhing in fear and love? Thomas had to recognize him as a brother— "a rather unpleasant and mortifying brother. He makes me nervous, the relationship is painful to a degree. But I will not disclaim it . . . better, more productive, more honest, more constructive than hatred is recognition, the readiness to make oneself one with what is deserving of our hate."[45] Having used identification as his main tool in writing about great writers, Thomas was now using it on Hitler; having treated his brother like his worst enemy during World War I, he was now thinking of Hitler as a brother.

Heil Chamberlain!

I<small>N</small> <small>EARLY</small> M<small>AY</small> 1938, Thomas and Katia drove from Illinois into Canada so that when they drove back into the United States they could go through immigration procedures. They stayed in New York until May 22. Leaving from Grand Central Station, they had a four-hour trip in Pullman and dining carriages to Kingston, where they were met by Caroline Newton, a psychoanalyst who had offered to let them use her large Rhode Island summer house while they looked for a permanent home. After two days in which she and a girl from Munich shared the house with them, the Manns were left in sole possession. The weather was mild, foggy, and windy. The sixty-two-year-old Thomas found, as he had found before, that island air had an aphrodisiac effect, especially in wet weather.[1]

By June 1, when he was awarded an honorary doctorate at Columbia University, he and Katia had decided that instead of leaving Erika to arrange for their furniture and possessions to be shipped from Switzerland, they'd return to Küsnacht briefly before settling in the States. To have space for the children, they'd need a house with six bedrooms and three bathrooms[2]; looking for it, they made several excursions from Jamestown to Princeton before finding a house on Stockton Street, which they rented for a year at $250 a month.[3] To arrange the lease they had to postpone their departure till June 29, when they sailed from New York on the *Washington.*

After a four-month absence, they arrived in Küsnacht on July 11 and enjoyed their last two months in the little town that had been their home for nearly five years. "Flower-decked breakfast table on the terrace. Happiness and well-being."[4] It was pleasant to walk along the shore of the lake and in the woods that had become so familiar. Thomas was glad to find that anti-Nazi feeling in Switzerland had hardened since the annexation of Austria.[5] In the same way that he'd decided, not so long ago, to spend a part of each year in the States, he now decided that unless war broke out, he'd spend several months each year in France or Switzerland.[6] In mid-August they stayed for eight days in Sils-Barseglia with Erika, who'd been doing journalistic work in Spain with Klaus.

Thomas worked at a lecture which wasn't going to be delivered until four months later—on Goethe's *Faust*. Without knowing he was going to write *Doctor Faustus*, he'd effectively started working on it. Goethe was attracted to Faust, he says, mainly because of his double desire for self-abasement and self-glorification through the pursuit of knowledge, while there was a tension in him between enthusiasm and irony. The urge toward the Absolute, he believed, constituted the divine part of human nature, while irony was the urge toward the diabolical. Combining foulness with grandeur, and ironically counterbalancing Goethe's youthful titanism, Mephistopheles provides a mouthpiece for his critical bitterness, his rebelliousness, his negativism; but sometimes he exchanges roles with Faust, defending life when the human being launches a negativistic attack on it. By making the Devil into a man of the world, Goethe succeeds in exploring the combination of urbanity and demonism in human nature, but fails to explore either the depths of sexuality or the scope of the active life. Wanting a bold sensual excursion, Faust is taken only to Auerbach's tavern, as he is in the old chapbook version of the story. Goethe had left not only a space but a need for *Doctor Faustus*, and Thomas discovered this by committing himself to lecturing at Princeton.

Faust will forfeit his soul if he ever wants to arrest time by telling the passing moment: "Stop for a while. You are so beautiful!" Thomas had these words in mind on September 1, when the moving van arrived to collect the furniture from Küsnacht. "Hold on to time!" he wrote in his diary. "Use it! Pay attention to each day, each hour! They slip away unnoticed much too easily and quickly!" After breakfast he could still use his desk to work at his *Faust* lecture, but after lunch he sat on the stone ledge of the garden terrace while furniture and crates were taken out of the house. Katia and Erika joined him as he watched the moving men carrying the Empire armchair in which he'd written his letter to Bonn University. After tea he worked at the table he'd used five years previously, before the furniture arrived from Munich. Without the cabinets and the radiogram, the living room looked stark.[7]

September 17, the day he and Katia sailed for New York on the *New Amsterdam*, was the day after Chamberlain met Hitler in Berchtesgaden. Konrad Henlein, the leader of the German minority in Czechoslovakia, who had been on the German payroll since 1935, had been instructed to make provocative demands and then precipitate a crisis by organizing a series of riots. In May the Czechs had been frightened into partial mobilization, backed by diplomatic protests from Britain and France. Both were nervous of upsetting Hitler, though he wasn't ready for war, and could have been forced to back down if they'd shown they weren't going to shrug off their commitments to Czechoslovakia. But in March, Chamberlain had said Britain couldn't promise to intervene in the event of an attack, and Thomas couldn't understand why Britain and France both fought shy of challenging Hitler, unless their fear of bolshevism was making him look like the lesser evil. When the *Times* urged the Czechs to surrender the Sudeten territories, Thomas wrote: "England's treachery becomes increasingly clear. The country is to be sacrificed in cold blood."[8] "Never has there been a greater or more stupid calamity."[9]

On board ship he was having trouble with a new denture, and on September 20 his thoughts kept flickering between the soreness of his upper jaw and the betrayal that had made the Czechs capitulate without having their case heard by an international court. Russia had announced that unless the French marched in, it would offer nothing but planes and matériel. Isolated, the Czechs accepted an "international guarantee," agreeing to partition and a plebiscite, but the citizens of Prague were so outraged that neither Englishmen nor Frenchmen could show themselves in the streets. "It is indubitably one of the worst disgraces in history. . . . It is the utter defeat of democracy and all justice." Writers could almost feel justified in turning their back on history. "Limiting oneself to personal and intellectual matters. I need serenity and consciousness of my own priorities. I must not give myself up to impotent hatred."[10]

On September 25, the day after the boat docked in New York, Thomas spoke in English to an audience of eighteen thousand in an auditorium at Madison Square Garden, with another crowd of ten thousand outside. "It is too late," he said, "for the British government to save the peace. They have lost too many opportunities. Now it is the peoples' turn. Hitler must fall! That alone can preserve the peace."[11] This was greeted with a huge ovation, and a Czech spoke as if his country would fight Germany single-handed.

On September 27, Thomas and Katia heard Neville Chamberlain on the radio—"a humane voice, moved, serious, giving not much hope for peace. Better to fight than live in a world where only force rules."[12] But when Hitler called a four-power conference in Munich to discuss the crisis, Édouard Daladier and Chamberlain agreed to meet him and Mussolini without insisting on Czech representation. Hitler revealed that 462,000 men were working on fortifications in the Rhineland, thirty miles deep. "The great new fortresses in the West will be ready by the winter. Behind them stands armed Germany." It was agreed that the Sudeten region of Czechoslovakia should be ceded immediately; the only guarantee to the Czechs was that the rest of their country would be protected against aggression. Czech districts where more than half the people spoke German would be surrendered, along with German-speaking democrats, Socialists, and Jews. When Chamberlain landed in England, he was greeted by a huge cheering throng at the airport, and on October 5, when Hitler led his army into Czechoslovakia, Henlein was appointed commissioner for the Sudeten area.

After arriving in Princeton on September 28, Thomas spoke to Einstein on the telephone. "Never shall I forget how broken Albert Einstein's voice sounded. . . . 'I have never in my life been so unhappy,' he said."[13] Moving into a new house should have been exciting, but Thomas felt disgusted by the weakness of the leaders. "The course history has taken is so dirty, such a filthy road of lying and squalour, that no one should be ashamed of refusing to go along it."[14] In "This Peace" he complained that the collective will of Europe had employed as its instrument

> the classic hypocrisy of English statesmanship . . . What else could it be but hypocrisy, to behave as though one believed those pulings about "our brothers in Sudetenland," when everybody knows that it was not a question of the brothers, but of the Skoda works, Czech industry, Romanian oil, Hungarian grain, Germany's economic penetration eastwards, the liquidation of Czechoslovakia as a military and diplomatic factor, the break-up of the French and Russian alliance, the isolation of France?[15]

Czechoslovakia had been created in 1918 by the Treaty of Versailles, which had now been fully dismantled, while Germany was at least as strong as she would have been had she won the war. Writing to Hermann Hesse, Thomas said: "One has suffered like a dog. Did these English statesmen know what they were doing? I fear they did."[16]

The Stockton Street house belonged to an Englishman. Monika, still unmarried at twenty-eight, was reminded of a haunted castle with creaking stairs, dimly lit rooms, high-backed chairs covered with red damask, weathered walls, and an overgrown garden.[17] But Thomas found it more comfortable than any other home he'd had. "The surroundings are full of parks suitable for walking in, with astonishingly beautiful trees, which are now, in this Indian summer, gleaming in the most splendid colours."[18] But he sometimes felt a strong nostalgia for his rooms in Küsnacht,[19] and at the age of sixty-three, for the first time in his life, he was settling in a country where German was a foreign language. "I am a German writer, and where is my native language to be heard?"[20]

It was gratifying when Alfred Knopf said he was Hitler's most dangerous enemy,[21] but, exiled farther than ever from Germany, and watching the continuing erosion of European culture, he couldn't help being reminded of Roman decadence in the last days of the empire. "Main phenomenon: the gradual absorption of the cultured classes into the masses. 'Simplification' of all functions in political, social, economic and *intellectual* life: barbarisation."[22]

* * *

ARRANGED JUST AS THEY'D BEEN in Küsnacht and, before that, in Munich, the objects on Thomas's writing table declared his determination to go on working in the same way he always had. His method of writing was unchanged. He'd abandoned steel nibs in favor of a fountain pen, but he still wrote by hand, using the morning (from nine till twelve or twelve-thirty) as the main period for creative work. Believing that style had a "symbolic content," and not knowing, at the moment of penning them, which phrases would function as *leitmotivs*, he worked slowly and deliberately, never trying to achieve a higher daily output than a page and a half.

He disliked dictating and resorted to it only for correspondence and passages in lectures and speeches he didn't regard as vital. His handwriting had changed over the years, becoming increasingly difficult to read. Both *Buddenbrooks* and *The Magic Mountain* had been sent to the printer in manuscript, but in Princeton he used to say that Katia was the only person in America who could read his writing. If it had deteriorated, this must be due to the hardening of personal idiosyncracies.

Usually he was working just as hard when he went out for walks, with or without a dog, as when sitting at his table. He'd go on thinking about the current chapter, and when his energy flagged, the best means of reviving it was to move about in the open air. He scribbled a lot of notes, mostly psychological formulations and observations of detail that seemed likely to add color, and he kept these bits of paper at hand when writing his longer works, but he did little redrafting. He made corrections, but seldom rewrote a complete page. Remembering the Goethean precept "Poets should make verse dance to their tune,"[23] he often thought of music as a model that could be rendered in verbal terms. This may have helped him toward keeping his prose free from the influence of moods and weather.[24]

Though he enjoyed the luxuries and advantages brought by success, fame, and help from influential friends, he regarded himself as a victim—an exile who'd lost not only his home and most of his possessions but his public. In Germany, booksellers could no longer display his work; in America, most people could read him only in translation. But he was aware of being exceptionally lucky, and having finally been pushed into speaking out against Hitler, his conscience wouldn't let him go on enjoying his life without helping other writers and intellectuals, Jewish and non-Jewish—both those who were trying to escape from Austria or Czechoslovakia, and those who'd escaped but couldn't finance their improvised refugee existence. Thomas was so well known that he was approached by friends, acquaintances, and strangers. By the end of 1938 he was receiving so many letters that Katia, who'd been helping him with his correspondence, needed two assistants—Molly Shenstone, wife of Allen Shenstone, a professor of physics at Princeton, and Hans Meisel, a novelist who'd won the Kleist Prize in 1927 and emigrated first to Italy, then to Austria, then to America.[25]

Believing that the British government could accommodate refugees in southern Rhodesia, Thomas wrote to the secretary of state for colonies, Malcolm MacDonald.[26] Trying to help a friend of Erika's, a young Austrian poet, Theodor Kramer, who wanted to join his wife in England, Thomas wrote to the home secretary.[27] The Nazis were granting exit visas to Jews, but only on payment of a $2,000 fee, and since Julius Bab's son, who was working as a page in a hotel, couldn't afford to help his father, Thomas tried to interest an American library in buying Bab's collection of ten thousand books about German theater and in employing him as curator.[28] Max Brod, who'd inherited all of Kafka's books and manuscripts, would gladly have donated them to any American or English institution that would rescue him from Czechoslovakia and employ him at a modest salary, but Thomas collected several refusals before an offer was made by the Hebrew Union College in Cincinnati. By then, Brod had escaped to Palestine.[29] Thomas also asked Walt Disney to help Felix Salten, the Austrian Jew who'd written *Bambi*, the book that provided the idea for the film. He was now living penuriously in Switzerland.[30]

At the end of January 1939, Barcelona fell to the Fascists, and at the end of February, though Madrid hadn't yet been taken, Britain recognized the Fascist rebels as the government. There were shouts in Parliament of "Heil Chamberlain!" Seeing that both Britain and France wanted to avoid confrontation with Germany, Thomas assumed that a counterrevolutionary tendency was generally in the ascendant, and war was unlikely.[31] Artists were being put into an impossible position because Nazism was intrinsically so paltry that condemnation of it merely sounded feeble. "Has it ever happened that reality and art have both been so completely inadequate?"[32]

In Goethe's Footsteps

IN AUGUST 1936, completing *Joseph in Egypt*, Thomas had decided to take a brief holiday from the sequence by writing *The Beloved Returns*. Now, nearly three years later, *Beloved* was still unfinished. He worked on it in Princeton at the beginning of 1939, before leaving on March 8 for a five-week lecture tour, and in February, writing the seventh chapter, he regained impetus, as he so often did, by reading aloud to friends.[1] The writer Alfred Neumann, who'd heard him reading in Munich and Küsnacht before they both settled in America, has described these private performances. Thomas would light a cigar before putting on his spectacles and selecting the sheets of manuscript from his desk. But while he was reading the first page, the cigar usually went out, to be abandoned with a sidelong glance of regret. Only one lamp would be lit—a standard lamp next to the armchair where he was sitting. With the dog lying at his feet, he'd lean back, crossing his legs but keeping his back straight, seigneurially relaxed. "Tja," he'd say, before making a few introductory comments. His voice was sonorous, his delivery steady and distinct, the timbre constantly undulating, and he gave each syllable a precise value. If the lucidity of the reading was magisterial, there was nothing magisterial about the movements of the free hand or about the ironic smile, kindly and tolerant, more audible than visible.[2]

Erika, too, has described these readings. After a while, he'd stop. "Well," he'd say without lowering his voice, "that's enough," and when a chorus of voices contradicted him, he'd leaf through his pages of manuscript, looking for a passage that led to the end of a chapter.[3] When there was laughter, he'd join in heartily, sometimes finding it quite hard to steady himself and go on.[4]

After the first two thirds of *Beloved* had built up to Goethe's appearance, the narrative jumps into a stream of consciousness which turns out to be that of the great man. Talking about the prologue to *Faust*, Thomas had commented on Goethe's audacity in making God into a character and putting his own thoughts into the divine mind; now Thomas puts his own thoughts into Goethe's. Most of his conversation is taken from what he wrote, the main exception being his description of the Germans as a people gullible enough to run after any fanatical scoundrel.[5] But it's

Thomas who originates most of these unspoken thoughts; Goethe is even made to articulate ideas—some of them variations on Goethean themes—that Thomas had formulated in his diary. One of these is about the value of time and the importance of not letting even a minute slip past unnoticed. But Thomas makes no connection between this reflection and Faust's pact with Mephistopheles, and generally the novel is lacking not only in comedy and sophistication but in irony.

The best passages are those in which Thomas can legitimately identify with the greatest of his predecessors, as in the chapter when Goethe poses the question Thomas had put on realizing he'd been married for thirty-three years: Does he wish he could be young again? Heroism, he reflects, lies in making the effort to stay alive, while greatness comes only with age. Though a young man can be a genius, greatness consists of the mental strength and power that develop from endurance. Even youthful love is pale in comparison with the tribute a great man pays to lovely adolescence—his powerful emotions exalting her tender loveliness. If we translate *her* into *his*, this applies to the mature Thomas's unconsummated infatuations with young men, but it says little about the mature flirtations of the man who'd written about magical rejuvenation in *Faust*.

When we come to the passage about the return of the beloved, we're forced to question whether the novel derived some of its impetus from the experience of seeing the aging Klaus Heuser when he paid a surprise visit to Küsnacht. In the narrative, moments with girls remind Goethe of previous moments with previous girls. When Marianne sang, she reminded him of Lotte, whose lips had never been more charming than when they opened thirstily for the next word in a song. Each love affair is a celebration and imitation of previous love affairs. But the thought that former lovers are still alive—and aging—is less gratifying than the thought that youthful works, such as *Werther*, are still being read alongside his maturer works.

When Goethe is made to reflect unapologetically on his egotism, Thomas is entering another area where it was almost too easy to empathize. Other people don't realize how serious and fruitful self-absorption can be. By probing secrets in the dark laboratory of his moral being, a great writer comes more intimately to grips with the creative process, just as a thinker such as Nietzsche can understand consciousness by thinking about the way he thinks.

This line of argument circles back to *Buddenbrooks*, though what was then seen as decadence is now viewed optimistically. Like Hanno, Goethe is a latecomer in the family—a late-born child of elderly parents. Nature has taught him that before it dies out, an ancient stock can produce an individual who combines all his ancestors' best qualities, giving them full expression for the first time. A man is entitled to be egocentric if he knows himself to be the last and best result of nature's capacity for taking pains. In Goethe the most dangerous natural tendencies have been refined. His genius is a balancing act between difficulty and love of facility. Art produced like this can't be popular. His Germany is separate from that of the Germans, and Thomas is commenting obliquely on the gullible voters who supported the Nazis when Goethe tells himself that *he* is Germany. Full of philistine spite, the other Germans believe *they* are Germany. But if the devil flies away with them—if they all perish or vanish—Germany will survive: in him.

At the same time Thomas is returning to his preoccupation, less obsessive now than it had been, with accusations of coldness. The problem has become multilayered, because he had not only identified with so many subjects—writers and characters, some real, some fictional, some great, some mythical—but made identification into a theme. Goethe's reputation had given his life a mythical dimension, and Thomas couldn't have written *The Beloved Returns* without the experience of reworking biblical material. "It is a Joseph game, this novel. The imitation of God in which Rachel's son indulges corresponds to my imitation of Goethe: an identification and *unio mystica* with the *father*."[6] In the eighth chapter Goethe is presented as "a great man and at the same time not a man any longer: it is for that reason that people often find him cold and heartless, yes, even Mephistophelian and nihilistic. Their love for him is not free from hatred: through him they feel no less oppressed than blessed."[7]

Once again Thomas is writing about himself, no longer apologizing for the impression he gave of detachment and indifference, but trying to analyze other people's reactions to it. The dinner party his Goethe gives for Lotte is described from her viewpoint, and she's annoyed by the obsequious laughter that welcomes his patriarchal table talk. The other guests' reverence for his intellectual powers is indistinguishable from their respect for his position in society, though his genius has nothing to do with the imperial star on his chest or the title of "Excellency" that makes him unapproachable. It seems all too easy for people to prostrate themselves before spiritual and intellectual qualities when they're packaged in an elegant, elderly man with sparkling eyes and fine hair. She's glad to see that in one of the guests, Riemer, the admiration is tempered with peevish resistance and dislike. It's uncharacteristic of Lotte to wonder what goes on in Goethe's consciousness about the relationship between his talent and his importance, but it's characteristic of Thomas to saddle her with one of the questions that preoccupied him. Visible behind the veneer of fiction is Thomas's ambivalence toward the respect being accorded to him by admirers all over the world.

Another autobiographical strand appears in a point he makes about Goethe in both the *Faust* lecture and the novel: that his tragic sense of guilt was rooted in his early infidelity to Friederike Brion, daughter of an Alsatian pastor. Goethe reprises this in Faust's seduction of Gretchen. Beauty is punished for surrendering to a superior mind, while the superior mind is punished for surrendering to beauty. In *The Beloved Returns*, Goethe's son, August, argues that nothing is more fundamental to creativity than painful renunciation, or what the writer remembers as disloyalty and betrayal. This becomes the pattern and principal theme of his life: All the later renunciations are variations on it. But in trying to understand Goethe's erotic life, Thomas may have been misled by his own pattern. Without ever taking the step from homoeroticism into homosexuality, he'd let himself be diverted into respectability, marriage, and family life.

ON MARCH 13, 1939, Hitler, who'd promised to leave the residue of Czechoslovakia intact, delivered an ultimatum. He wanted complete independence for Slovakia and Ruthenia, payments of gold, and a new government in Prague with a different premier and defense minister. The next day his army marched into Prague, and the German flag was raised on the Hradzin, the castle that had been the Bohemian kings' stronghold. Thomas could only grit his teeth at "Hitler's total success in the East. Occupation of Prague, the steel-manufacturing district. Romania and Hungary will be next. On the Black Sea. Oil and grain. Monstrous gain in strength. No reaction from England or France."[8]

But this time there was a reaction. Hitler's expansionism, as Chamberlain pointed out in the House of Commons, was taking him into territory with no German inhabitants. At the end of the month, after arranging to double the size of the territorial army, Chamberlain was cheered when he pledged to defend Poland against attack. Six days later, Britain, France, and Poland signed a mutual assistance pact, while diplomacy indicated that the Soviet Union would support any military action the Allies took.

Thomas was touring the United States in March, lecturing on "The Problem of Freedom."[9] Both Katia and Erika were traveling with him, taking so many things with them that they used fourteen suitcases, which meant they needed two taxis for each journey between a railway station and a hotel.[10] Though he could lecture in English from a script that had been translated for him, he couldn't cope confidently with questions. Erika sat on the platform with him, translated questions, and gave the audience a free translation of what he told her to say in reply.

In early April he addressed meetings in Beverly Hills and Chicago of the American Committee for Christian German Refugees, which threw a dinner party for him at the Astor Hotel in New York on April 15. Back in Princeton, five days later, he held a seminar on *Faust*, and on May 10 he lectured on *The Magic Mountain*. His relationship with the university deepened on May 18, when he was awarded an honorary doctorate, and his standing in the United States was enhanced when he became the first foreigner to be elected as president by the American League of Writers. He was inaugurated at the congress on June 2, when he spoke about "Writers in Exile." Two days later he was offered an extension of his appointment at Princeton covering the second half of the academic year 1939–40.

Reading in the papers about European events, he felt shamed and agonized by seeing his own mistake repeated in world politics. Just as he'd kept silent about Hitler for too long, England and France were staying passive for too long. "Disconcerting effect of predictable events, their impact always worse than expected." "Thought about the bogus loyalty of England and her connivance in encouraging the redistribution of the economic zones of Central Europe."[11] In May, though Chamberlain had threatened war if Danzig was invaded, and Stalin seemed willing to sign a nonaggression pact with Britain and France, Thomas was expecting "a new Munich."[12]

Though glad he was no longer living in Europe, he still believed he could encourage resistance to Nazism inside Germany. In its campaign against émigré literature, the *Schwarze Korps*, the weekly newspaper of the S.S., had complained that if it were left to the booksellers, nothing would be on sale in Germany except books by writers living abroad. Encouraged by this, Thomas agreed to edit a series of twenty-four pamphlets for distribution inside Germany, published by a committee under the chairmanship of Frank Kingdon, president of Newark University and chairman of the International Rescue and Relief Committee. Among the writers and nonwriters Thomas wanted to commission were Heinrich, Franz Werfel, Stefan Zweig, Bruno Frank, René Schickele, the singer Lotte Lehmann, who was refusing to appear in Nazi Germany, the theater director Max Reinhardt, the film director Wilhelm Dieterle, and the theologian Paul Tillich, who'd all emigrated from Germany at about the same time.[13]

While approaching potential contributors, Thomas was planning a summer holiday in Europe with Katia and Erika. They'd have gone to Switzerland if they hadn't received a cable from the Pringsheims, who, wanting to settle there, were waiting for their emigration visa, which might be refused if the Nazis heard the Manns were in Switzerland. They decided to stay in a Dutch seaside resort, Noordwijk, until the Pringsheims were safely out of Germany.[14] Thomas, Katia, and Erika arrived in Noordwijk on the seventeenth, prepared to make a quick return to the States if "the clouds in the political heaven" began to look stormy.[15]

It was stressful to be so close to a fatherland in which cultural life had been taken over by the Nazis. In Vienna, Hitler had attended the gala opening of Richard Strauss's latest opera, *Friedenstag* (*Day of Peace*), and it was being said that the seventy-five-year-old composer had lunch with the Führer the next day, though probably he only breakfasted with Goebbels. After Thomas's first day in Noordwijk, he was so upset that he started weeping, and could sleep only if he took pills.[16]

The Pringsheims were kept in suspense about their visa, which still hadn't been issued at the beginning of August. Staying in Noordwijk for seven weeks, and enjoying the respite from the problems, correspondence, and distractions that occupied so much of his time in Princeton, Thomas worked every morning in a bathing hut on the beach. Like Aschenbach, he loved writing by the sea, but couldn't work without some kind of roof over his head.[17] On the Noordwijk beach he wrote the introduction that had been commissioned by Random House for a new translation of Tolstoy's *Anna Karenina*, and pressed ahead with *The Beloved Returns*.[18]

He finally left for Zurich with Katia and Erika on August 7 and drove with Katia to Küsnacht:

> the familiar stretch of the even more familiar landscape. . . . Then in the Schiedhaldenstrasse. We drove the car into the open garage, climbed the overgrown steps. The stone wall where I sat while the furniture was carried down to the van. The terrace in front of the dining-room, robbed of the hedge. A glimpse into the living-room with some of the familiar furniture. Upward glance at my study, where the third volume of Joseph, the letter to the Dean, the greater part of *Lotte* came into existence. Deep emotion, convulsed with thoughts about life, sadness and pain . . .[19]

In July, Hitler's territorial ambitions were focused mainly on Danzig and Poland. Arms and military instructors were being smuggled into the Free City, while Britain was finally provoked into threatening intervention if the Poles couldn't maintain the status quo without using force. All over the world conversations kept circling back to the question of whether war could be averted. On August 19, Germany sent out fourteen U-boats to patrol the North Atlantic.

In Sweden, staying in Saltsjöbaden, they met Bermann, who was preparing a new collection of Thomas's work to be published in Switzerland. On August 23, before the news broke that Hitler had signed a nonaggression pact with Stalin, Thomas still doubted whether war would break out; privately he hoped it would, "*because* the outcome would be unpredictable and it would provide a way out of the present situation, probably in Germany too. Above all, to see Hitler marching into another country without a battle would be so repellent that anything would be preferable."[20]

At 5:45 on the morning of September 1, German troops marched into Poland. On the same day, Danzig was bombarded, and its annexation proclaimed. On September 3, Britain and France declared war. Flying from Malmö to London, the Manns had to pass over German territory, where new regulations forced the plane to fly low. When Katia asked why, she was told that on the previous day the passengers' faces had been inspected from a German plane. Thomas was sitting by the window, and she insisted on changing places with him. They arrived safely in London, but on the same flight the next day, the plane was shadowed by a German plane, and a passenger, possibly mistaken for Thomas, was shot dead in his seat.

They sailed from Southampton on September 9 on the SS *Washington*, but the boat that had been so comfortable the previous year was loaded with about two thousand passengers, "who sleep at night on improvised bunks, making the lounges into concentration camps."[21]

While everyone else was hoping the war would soon be over, Thomas could see that a short war would leave everything essentially unchanged. At the risk of brutalization and protracted misery, the fighting should go on long enough to produce fundamental changes everywhere, or at least ripeness for change.[22] Wanting *Mass und Wert* to continue, with Golo replacing Ferdinand Lion as managing editor, Thomas tried to reassess the prospects of drumming up subversion inside Germany. Could people be expected to rebel against Hitler before he'd shown himself to be incapable of leading them to victory?[23] In his foreword to the November–December issue, Thomas wrote: "In this war there can be only one aim: to win for Europe a peace that deserves its name . . . a peace that doesn't serve through the renown of heroic deeds as a protective bulwark for atavistic historical greatness."[24] Privately, in moments of pessimism, he thought the war might last for ten years, bringing civilization to an end. He was sixty-four: Perhaps he'd be dead before peace came.[25]

Bermann, who already had the first seven chapters set up in print, wanted to publish *The Beloved Returns* before Christmas, and, spurring himself on, Thomas finished it in October. At the end of September he hadn't intended to make any public political statement: He needed time to find his way through the confusion.[26] But by early December he was at work on "This War," a polemical sequel to "This Peace." He described it as "energetically pro-British—something written from the heart and from conviction."[27]

War had been inevitable, he argued, since 1933, when the highest tribunal in Germany had presided over the travesty of a trial that followed the burning of the Reichstag. The Germans must have shuddered in shame and horror at the methods their overlords were using to "solve" the Jewish "problem." A great nation had been reduced to barbarity; decent living had become impossible, and the rest of Europe was being threatened with the terrorism that had prevailed in Germany—"perpetual menace, merciless and gloating cruelty, harsh and bloody oppression, warlike tension unrelaxed." A gang of perverted and violent men had led the Germans into disavowing and destroying everything they valued in favor of everything they found "hard and bitter and unnatural—isolation, the hostility of the whole world, deprivation of your civil and intellectual rights, and the loss of many other things. . . . If the German people cannot muster the strength to revolt, if they prefer to look on and wait, to see whether success may not justify their rulers, guilt and disaster will be heaped upon their heads."[28]

Private life had never seemed more irrelevant to public issues, but changes were taking place in the Mann family. After living with Nelly Kröger for ten years, Heinrich decided to marry her, which made less difference to Thomas than the acquisition of a black poodle, Nico, a present from Caroline Newton at the end of October. Taken out for walks in the woods outside Munich, Bauschan had been free to chase rabbits, but in the streets of Princeton, Thomas had to keep Nico on a lead. Inside the house he was mostly at Thomas's feet under the desk in the library, and he was allowed to sleep there until he chewed up a book by Ernest Cassirer.[29]

Thomas had mixed feelings about the decision of his twenty-one-year-old daughter Elisabeth to marry fifty-seven-year-old Giuseppe Antonio Borgese, a lecturer in Italian literature at Chicago University. Borgese had met Thomas and Katia in Chicago; he met Elisabeth when he came to the house in Princeton, hoping to involve Thomas in an association of philosophers and poets pledged to campaign for democracy and global peace. When they were married, a year later, in the university chapel at Princeton, a friend gave them a joint picture of Hitler and Mussolini, the men who'd brought them together, set in tinsel.[30] "With his fifty-seven years," wrote Thomas, who was seven years older, "he must have given up hope of acquiring so much youth. But the child wanted it, and has gone through with it. He is a witty, kind and very well preserved man, that has to be admitted, and the bitterest enemy of his Duce."[31] Thomas may, or may not, have asked himself whether the exceptionally close relationship with him had predisposed the girl to fall in love with a much older man; she has no doubt that her husband was a replacement for her father.[32]

WITHIN TWO MONTHS of finishing *The Beloved Returns*, Thomas heard good news about sales. Bermann, who printed ten thousand copies, had five thousand prepublication orders, and eight thousand copies had been sold by Christmas. Though he claimed that a novel like this one would have had a hundred thousand readers "if Germany still existed,"

Thomas was gratified that with no help from booksellers in either Germany or Austria, so many copies had been bought.[33] Of all his novels, he said, this was the one he loved most, because there was more in it about love and erotic union than in any of the others, notwithstanding the mockery and irony.[34]

Though he'd often felt impatient to resume work on the *Joseph* tetralogy, he deliberately missed the opportunity he now had. Three and a half years had passed since he completed *Joseph in Egypt*, and since he still wanted the four novels to parallel the four parts of the *Ring*, he now had to write a cheerful Götterdämmerung. If he procrastinated about making a start, it was, he claimed, "not because the clay had become dry in the many turbulent years." The old task was still alive inside him, but he was nervous that without a female character as interesting as Rachel or Mut, he wouldn't surpass or even match the level he'd achieved in the third volume.[35]

He decided to indulge in what he called a divertissement and intermezzo,[36] insisting that it wasn't very serious, "at most a curiosity." After starting *The Transposed Heads* (*Die vertauschten Köpfe*) at the beginning of January, he wasn't sure whether he'd finish it.[37] In the seventh chapter of *The Beloved Returns*, Goethe remembers a German translation of *The Journey to East India and China*, which gave him an idea for a poem about a Brahman's wife who became a pariah goddess. He pictured holy women walking every day to the river for water they could carry without a pitcher: In their pious hands the water rounded itself into a crystal ball. In the hands of the poet, even when he isn't sinless, poetry shapes itself in the same way. But the wife was punished after gazing lustfully at the reflection of a youth in the river. Her husband, whose suspicions were aroused when the water refused to form a ball in her hands, dragged her to the sacrificial mound, where he struck off her head. When their son intervened, threatening to kill himself, the father agreed to let the head be put back on the body with a blessing that would revive the dead woman. In his haste, the son stuck his mother's head on a headless body belonging to a woman of the pariah caste. This prefigures the new "divertissement" in which two personalities are mingled when two decapitated bodies are resurrected with transposed heads.

The clever and refined Shridaman has a noble head, while his devoted friend Nanda has a commonplace mind and a well-developed body. The beautiful Sita marries Shridaman but becomes pregnant by Nanda. Both men commit suicide in the shrine of the dark mother, Kali, who gives Sita permission to bring them back to life. Perhaps it's not entirely by accident that she creates what ought to be the ideal husband by putting Shridaman's head on Nanda's body, and the other head on the other body. But things work out badly. Harmony is achieved only when, instead of killing themselves, the men agree to kill each other, and the widow is burned alive on their pyre. Thomas had conceived the story on November 12, 1939, when reading an essay "Die indische Weltmutter" ("The Indian World-Mother") by Heinrich Zimmer in the *Eranos-Jahrbuch* for 1938. His diary for December 9 shows that he'd gone on planning the story, but he didn't start working on it seriously till after Christmas.[38]

As in his work on the *Joseph* novels, he was playing with ancient material—refining, transforming, elaborating, and reconstructing. In a letter to Agnes Meyer at the beginning of 1940, he said he was working on a grotesque Maya tale that belonged to the cult of the Great Mother in whose honor people decapitate themselves—a story about disunity and identity.[39] In its probing of identity it might have struck him as having affinities with Kleist's treatment of the Amphitryon story.

Thomas gave himself yet another pretext for delaying work on the last *Joseph* novel when he committed himself to two lecture tours in January and February, one in Canada, the other in the Midwest and the South. By March he and Katia were tired of living in Princeton. The house was too big for them, and they didn't want to go on paying rent through the summer, when they were going away to avoid the weather that made Princeton almost unbearable. They wanted to spend the summer in California, and possibly stay there for about twelve months. It would be a good place to write the *Joseph* novel. Bruno Frank was still living there, and Thomas liked the idea of spending days in the open air, never far from a swimming pool, settling down to the book and "sustaining for a while the illusion of detachment."[40]

In early May, during a seminar on nineteenth- and twentieth-century German literature, he delivered two lectures "On Myself." Though it was Homecoming Day, which had emptied most of the lecture rooms and filled the streets of Princeton with students escorting girls in summer frocks, his second lecture was even better attended than his first, "so that one can speak of a triumph over the fair sex."[41] But he'd decided to do no more teaching: "For the fourth *Joseph*, if it is to be ready by my 70th birthday (if possible a few years earlier) I must be completely free."[42]

On May 10, the day Winston Churchill took over from Chamberlain as prime minister, German troops marched into Holland and Belgium, and within ten days virtually the whole of Holland had been overrun, most of Belgium, and a slice of northern France. The Allied forces that had been advancing into Belgium were trapped between the sea and two German armies. "All this is only the culmination of seven years' sufferings, which were full of portents and despair over other people's ignorance of the facts and their wish to remain ignorant."[43]

It took over a month to evacuate the survivors by sea from Dunkirk, and on June 22, 1940, France accepted defeat. In newspaper photographs the triumphant Hitler seemed to be dancing with glee. France's rapid surrender would have been humiliating even if the head of the French delegation, General Charles Huntziger, hadn't been made to sign the armistice in the railway coach used in 1918 when the defeated Germans had to sign the Treaty of Versailles. Hitler now took the chair used then by the victorious General Foch. Once again Thomas had both political and personal reasons for being distressed. Heinrich was still in France, and so was Golo, who'd joined the Red Cross as a volunteer ambulance driver. "I am the last to condemn his decision, which I find understandable and decent. But to lose him would be all the more painful in view of the uselessness of his sacrifice."[44] Many émigré German writers were also in danger: The cream of anti-Fascist literature, Thomas said, had settled in France.[45]

Britain couldn't be expected to hold out for long against the combined strength of Germany, Russia, and Italy.[46] Unless the United States joined the war, democracy was heading for defeat. By the beginning of May, Thomas was making private declarations of hostility to the American policy of neutrality, which struck him as myopic and selfish.[47] But he had to be wary of what he said in public: People would be upset if a foreigner criticized American foreign policy. As in his first years of exile, he maintained a discreet but uncomfortable silence.

Edge of Los Angeles

EUGENE AND AGNES MEYER had a town house in Washington, D.C., at 1624 Crescent Place, and a country house north of New York in Mount Kisco. Thomas, who stayed at both, told his hostess she ran the best hotels on two continents.[1] On July 5, 1940, after staying for a few days in Mount Kisco and with the Borgeses for a night in Chicago, Thomas and Katia arrived in Brentwood, on the edge of Los Angeles, and moved into the sumptuous house they were going to occupy for three months. It was "set in a hilly landscape which is strikingly similar to that of Tuscany. I have what I wanted—the light, the dry, constantly refreshing warmth, the advantage of greater spaciousness than we had in Princeton, the trees including holm oaks, eucalyptus, cedars and palms, walks by the sea, which can be reached by car in a few minutes."[2] In twenty-five minutes they could drive into Hollywood; the inconvenience was that most of Thomas's books and papers were being stored, together with their pictures, in Princeton.[3]

It was an ideal place for a summer holiday. Klaus and Erika were there, while Bruno Frank and Bruno Walter were living nearby with their families. "Life could be enjoyable except that our spirits are too oppressed for pleasure or for work, as I found after a few abortive attempts. . . . The hour of decision will come soon, and there is little hope that those mindless fanatics will fail to achieve all their objectives. . . . The position is gruesome—a mental and emotional torture. Everything depends on England's powers of resistance, which are incalculable."[4]

Winston Churchill was using his talent for rhetoric to stiffen Britain's aggressive sinews, but the Germans, apparently preparing to invade England, were shooting down RAF planes and launching aerial attacks on the Royal Navy in the Channel. According to British calculations, the Germans would need at least 250 boats to transport about 100,000 soldiers. The most likely landing places were on the Kentish coast between Dover and Hastings. If Hitler won, Europe would be permanently lost to democracy, and to Thomas. "We must be ready for complete defencelessness and homelessness, with no refuge except eternity. I have always believed in maintaining personal serenity as a means of surviving the most unfavourable circumstances, and I have trusted my ability to adapt. But now I often feel trapped hopelessly."[5]

At the end of July, while he and Katia were worrying about Heinrich and Golo, who were somewhere in France, and about her brother Peter, who was somewhere in Belgium, they became grandparents. Of their six children, none of the four eldest would have children of their own, but Michael's wife, Gret, gave birth in Carmel, California, to a boy, who was named Fridolin. "Grandfatherhood has come late," wrote the sixty-five-year-old Thomas, "and makes little impression on me. The first grandchild, American by birth, has German, Brazilian, Jewish and Swiss blood."[6]

Thomas was feeling permanently exhausted, partly because of the California climate,[7] but he finished *The Transposed Heads* in early August and worked energetically to help German intellectuals in occupied France. An Emergency Rescue Committee was formed in New York by Frank Kingdon, an English-born ex-clergyman who had been the first president of Newark University and had given up his job to study anti-democratic activity in the United States. To raise funds for the committee Thomas and Katia threw a big tea party in their rented house at the end of July. "Our house has become a rescue office for people in danger, people who are crying out for help and people who are going under."[8] As Klaus noted on July 12, "The news from 'our people' in France pours in—only too much of it. Desperate cries for help: that is to say for visas to the United States. They cable from everywhere—from Nice, Marseilles, Vichy, Perpignan, Casablanca. Others are already in comparative safety, in Portugal. Others, in the absolute security of death. New wave of suicides."[9] The international refugee situation became even more complicated when Switzerland threatened to expel many of the German émigrés who wanted to settle there. Hearing that Golo was in an internment camp at Nîmes, Thomas exerted influence, mainly through Agnes Meyer, to save him from extradition and bring Heinrich to America.

Knopf wanted to call the English-language edition of *Lotte in Weimar* *The Beloved Returns*. Thomas found this title "horrible,"[10] but gave in when Knopf explained that American readers wouldn't want to ask for the book in a store if they weren't sure how to pronounce either of the two main words in the title. *The Beloved Returns* did surprisingly well: 18,000 copies had been ordered prior to publication,[11] and 25,000 sold by mid-October.[12] Thomas was glad to be free of the academic work he'd done at Princeton, and though it was hard to pick up the narrative threads of the *Joseph* fiction after neglecting them for four years, he started making notes for the fourth novel, *Joseph the Provider (Joseph der Ernährer)* as soon as he finished *The Transposed Heads*. Refusing invitations to give lectures and readings, he'd written about sixty pages by the end of the year.[13]

As a code of ethical precepts dovetailed into a didactic narrative, the Pentateuch is necessarily humorless, but Thomas's series of novels becomes increasingly comic as it develops. The treatment of God is never more irreverent than in the opening section of *Joseph the Provider*, a prelude modeled with affectionate irony on Goethe's prologue to *Faust* and set in Heaven. In 1941, churchmen were saying world events corresponded to God's intentions, and there was no protest from the Vatican at Hitler's methods of solving "the Jewish problem." But finding the current situation incompatible with the doctrine that God was omnipotent, infallible, and benevolent, Thomas postulates a Heaven in which angels are alert to the dangers of unlimited power.

The notion of humanity is devised by the mighty Shemmael. Wanting evil to enter the world, he persuades God to create an image of Himself which, unlike Himself, is fertile. The angels can only guess at the discussion that went on, but Shemmael may have convinced God that his existence would be more fun if he had to hand out rewards and punishments after making judgments. Besides, he'd had to leave goodness in the limbo of the merely possible until its opposite materialized through humanity. Taking Shemmael's advice, God creates an unflattering image of Himself, and Abraham is brought into existence as His means of achieving self-knowledge. Humanity is the result of His curiosity about Himself. From satire on Goethe, Thomas has proceeded to a Goethean satire on God.

In this antitheology, faith can be no panacea. Joseph's faith in God overlaps with self-confidence based on belief that God is giving him preferential treatment, but the reader is free to infer that what floats him to the top of Egyptian society is only self-confidence. When a messenger predicts that after appearing before Pharaoh, Joseph will soon be back in prison, his answer is that he won't, since he believes he won't. Before being ushered into Pharaoh's presence, he feels certain that his fortunes are about to change, and his optimism is presented as pious. Convinced that God intends him to prosper, he tries to be helpful in the realization of those intentions. This is expedient, but it's also virtuous. As the prison governor reflects, goodness and wisdom lie so close together that they make a man revere the divine. A nimbus of the divine floats around Joseph, and it's easy to confuse a quality with its source. Whether Joseph is a god in disguise or a breathing image of a god, he must be treated with respect, and the respect he commands helps him on his upward path.

BY MID-SEPTEMBER Hitler still hadn't invaded England, but it looked as though he would: He had 3 million soldiers ready for the attack.[14] In the States, men between the ages of twenty-one and thirty-five had to register for military service, but it was unlikely that war would be declared before the presidential elections in November. In London, the Blitz started on September 7, when 300 bombers attacked the East End. By the end of the month, 7,500 people had been killed and over 10,000 injured. On September 15, 185 German planes were shot down in one day.

Thomas and Katia were going back to spend the winter in Princeton, but by the end of September, deciding to settle in California, they had bought a site for a house. There were seven palm trees and a lot of lemon trees on the land. "Here one has Egypt and Palestine at the same time, which must be good for *Joseph*."[15]

On October 3, three days before leaving Brentwood, Thomas addressed an audience of four hundred at a dinner held by the Friends of the Colleges of Claremont, California. His subject was "War and Democracy." If freedom and justice perished, he said, if mankind were reduced to slavery, America would have to bear its share of the guilt. The speech couldn't have been more pro-British, but it was well received, and aware though he was that young Americans were mostly pacifistic, he felt hopeful that within three months, whether the next president was Roosevelt or Wendell Willkie, America would no longer be neutral.[16] Of the two candidates, Roosevelt was more likely to want war, and during the run-up to the election Thomas started a series of monthly broadcasts in German to be relayed by the BBC to listeners inside Germany. He recorded them in Hollywood at the NBC studios.

> German listeners! This is the voice of a German writer whose work and person are outlawed by your rulers and whose works, even when they are about the most German subjects, such as Goethe, can speak only to foreign, free, people in their language, remaining silent and unknown to you. . . . In war there is no longer any opportunity for the written word to penetrate through the wall that tyranny has erected around you. That is why I am glad to seize the opportunity offered to me by the British authorities, to report to you from time to time on what I am seeing here in America, the great and free country in which I have found a homestead.[17]

Though he would get no feedback and have no means of estimating how many people in Germany were listening to him, he was doing all he could to exert political influence.

Heinrich and Golo had crossed the border into Spain, and then into Portugal. From Lisbon they sailed on a Greek ship to New York along with other refugee writers, including Alfred Döblin and Franz Werfel. Thomas, Katia, and Klaus went to meet the ship as it docked on October 13. The mood was festive; there was much hugging and handclasping. Over lunch in the Bedford Hotel, the sixty-nine-year-old Heinrich talked about crossing the Franco-Spanish border at night through the

Pyrenees. The steep path, he said, was "really intended for goats, not for a writer of mature age. And in any case, why had it been necessary? We are not, after all, criminals."[18] And making a speech at a celebration organized in New York by the Emergency Rescue Committee, Thomas acclaimed this "civilian Dunkirk."[19]

After Roosevelt won the election on November 5, Thomas said: "Now it will only be a matter of time before Hitler is destroyed."[20] Nine days later Thomas and Katia went back to Chicago, wanting to be with the Borgeses when Elisabeth gave birth to her first child, but the unborn baby kept everyone waiting, and they were still in suspense on November 26 when the *Chicago Daily Press* proclaimed "High tide for intervention in this country now."[21] This struck Thomas as representative of the feeling among the educated classes. By reelecting Roosevelt the Americans had shown their good sense. "But he should *act* now."[22] In Chicago, Thomas resumed work on the *Joseph* novel, but before the end of the month, deciding they could wait no longer, he and Katia left for Princeton. Three days later the baby was born—a girl who was named Angelica.

Thomas and Katia celebrated Christmas in Princeton with four of their children and friends from Germany and Britain. "It never loses its charm—seeing the candles burning on the tree and the presents spread out. After the meal we played new gramophone records and finally, like a proper paterfamilias, I read from the Bible—from my own, about the two courtiers who are cross-examined in prison, and everyone had to laugh."[23]

On December 28, Thomas and Katia traveled back to see their new grandchild in Chicago. "She gives the impression of being very pleased—and no wonder, for she came into the world with the Second papers."[24] He meant she was born as an American citizen.

In the second week of January 1941, he and Katia were staying with the Meyers in Crescent Place when he made a speech at the Washington town hall under the title "The War and the Future." A reworking of the talk he'd been giving since October on "War and Democracy," it produced different reactions from husband and wife—"foolish suffering from Agnes, enthusiasm from Eugene."[25] What upset her was the direct appeal for America to declare war:

> The greatest thing that is going on today . . . is the growing unification of the entire English-speaking world. . . . The kingdom of the world, the city of man, has now been born as an idea; it will not rest until it has achieved actuality. . . . It is scarcely more than stating a fact to say that the world civil war which rages today is a step in the direction of unity and the general awareness of unity; that it is creating an occasion for common responsibility, and that, though only

in antagonism and embitterment, it is slowly but surely bringing the thoughts of men to coalesce. All separatism today, all neutrality and rejection of the common responsibility, must, I feel, constitute a morally indefensible attitude. There is in this country a formula and slogan for the attitude: "America First." . . . To me "America First" sounds too much like "Deutschland über Alles" not to be a little suspect.[26]

The attack on separatism was judiciously worded, but instead of telling Agnes Meyer how foolish he thought she was being, Thomas promised never to repeat the speech in its present form: "I now find the lecture insufferable because it made you suffer." But would any revision of it be acceptable to her when she thought he should be above politics? He disagreed, knowing his work could never take its place in the German literary tradition if Hitler won the war. Besides, political activities during the last eight years hadn't stopped him from writing *Joseph in Egypt* and *The Beloved Returns*.[27] He had a shrewd suspicion, though, that as literature, all his anti-Nazi speeches were inferior to the reactionary prose he'd produced in the First World War.[28]

Together with Erika, he and Katia went on from Mount Kisco to stay for two days with the Roosevelts in the White House, "where we were accorded astonishing privileges. The giddying acme was the cocktail in his workroom while the other dinner guests had to wait about downstairs. And we had already had an early breakfast with 'him.' " Roosevelt again made a strong impression on Thomas, who compared him with Joseph: "I like this wheelchair Caesar more and more," he wrote.[29] "At once sly, good-natured, spoilt, eager to please and full of sincere faith, he is hard to characterise, but there is something like a blessing on him and I am devoted to him as the man who seems to be the born adversary of the one who must be beaten."[30] Inscribing a privately printed text of "War and Democracy," Thomas wrote in it: "To F.D.R. President of the U.S. and of a coming better world."[31]

With the move to California scheduled for mid-March, Thomas and Katia had to uproot themselves yet again. They'd lived in Küsnacht for five years, but spent less than eighteen months in Princeton. On March 10, the day the movers started their work, Thomas's discomfort was compounded by a toothache.[32] "Already everything looks desperately disorganised downstairs, and I retreated to the bedroom, which is still a wildlife sanctuary for the time being. The whole affair distresses me—we are in for weeks of homeless confusion. . . ." He wasn't sure whether they'd been right to opt for California,[33] and he was depressed enough to say he was looking forward to the time when "nothing is left of me except the things through which I have tried to give other people happiness and help them to live."[34]

But he'd generated so much momentum on *Joseph the Provider* that he could keep going while furniture was being loaded onto vans. On March 13, the day the pictures were taken away, and his favorite chair, which came from Zurich, was moved out of the bedroom, he was working busily.35

The night of March 16 was his last night in his Princeton bedroom, and Katia had to get up at five to sort out papers, deciding which ones could be destroyed. "Her exhausted appearance hurts me."36 After packing his briefcase, Thomas wrote till eleven, despite the whimpering of Nico, the poodle, who'd been nervous ever since the moving men had arrived. In the evening, wearing a hat, Thomas lectured in a New York synagogue on "War and Democracy" before he and Katia spent the night in a hotel. In the morning, at the Maxine Elliott Theater on Broadway, he sat in on a rehearsal of *Gabriele*, a three-act comedy with music based mainly on his story "Tristan" and partly on *The Magic Mountain*. The script was by Leonardo Bercovici. The show opened on March 23 and closed after only two performances.

Thomas and Katia slept on the train to Chicago, and after breakfasting in their hotel, he again settled down to work on *Joseph the Provider*.37 Since Exodus doesn't specify which pharaoh is on the throne, Thomas could choose, and he opted for Amenhotep IV, who introduced Aten, the austere, monotheistic cult of the sun-god Aton, a religion which had affinities with Judaism. Both as a reader of his own work and as a writer, Thomas had learned that the impact of a climax depends less on what's happening than on what has led up to it. In building toward Joseph's interpretation of Pharaoh's dream, he makes Pharaoh do a lot of talking, aware that he's postponing the moment of truth: A man, he says, when his greatest desire is about to be fulfilled, deliberately postpones the consummation, knowing he'll never again be able to enjoy the pleasure of anticipating it.

As a storyteller Thomas is equally capable of playing the opposite trick and letting a character predict a climacteric event. While this epileptic pharaoh is unconscious, his mother tells Joseph he's about to be promoted. Instead of detracting from the effectiveness of the climax, this adds ironic depth at the expense of the Pharaoh, who's innocent enough to think his decision will surprise both Joseph and the old queen.

At the Borgeses' house with Katia and Erika, Thomas read from the chapter about Joseph's interpretation of Pharaoh's dream, and he was gratified by the laughter of the "children."38 He and Katia then had two nights on the train to Colorado Springs, where he was to lecture on *The Magic Mountain*; after getting up at seven to find photographers waiting on the platform, and arriving at 8:30 at the Hotel Broadmoor, he worked at *Joseph the Provider*. He didn't have to lecture till the following

day, and the lunch he was given, in a house with a view of the mountains, followed the menu of Goethe's lunch with Lotte in Weimar.[39] It
rained nearly all the time he was in Colorado Springs, as it did at his
next stopping-place, Denver.[40] Going on to Los Angeles involved another thirty-six hours of railway travel, and after the lecture there, he
and Katia went to bed late, though they had to be up at five to catch a
plane for San Francisco.[41]

When offered an honorary doctorate at Berkeley, California, he'd
hesitated, but in spite of the "jolting and shaking of the aircraft over
mountains whose peaks and ravines lay magnificently above the
clouds," he was glad he'd decided to accept.[42] He and Katia were met at
the airport by a police escort which, ignoring all the traffic lights, drove
them to the campus with sirens howling. He found the campus impressive, and the sun shone on the ceremony. A second ceremony, for his
induction into the Phi Beta Kappa society, reminded him of Free-
masonry, and there was a banquet before he lectured on "Thinking and
Life" ("Denken und Leben"). One of the two lecture halls was served
only by a loudspeaker, but both were overcrowded. Talking about the
thinker's responsibility for life, he said that if Nietzsche were still alive,
he'd have settled in America and been invited to join the Phi Beta
Kappa society in spite of his romantic sins.[43]

On April 8, Thomas and Katia moved into a smallish rented house at
740 Amalfi Drive, Pacific Palisades. It was "white, clean, rustically situated and not impractical, but incompletely furnished." Since there was
still no writing table in the study, he started by working in the bedroom.
There was a small garden, and a view of the ocean from the terrace.[44]

But they couldn't escape the bad news relayed over the radio. Rommel's army, which had left for North Africa at the end of 1940, was advancing rapidly, and on April 6, 1941, the Germans invaded Yugoslavia.
On April 16, five hundred planes dropped about a hundred thousand
bombs in an all-night attack on London, and it looked as if American
intervention would come too late if it came at all. It was hard to picture
Hitler as master of the world, and the world didn't deserve that fate—
not quite.[45] By mid-April Thomas was so depressed that after staying up
most of the night arguing with Katia about the new house, he told the
architect they'd decided not to go ahead.

The depression was compounded by a painful dental crisis which affected Thomas's speech. Convinced that he sounded "ridiculous," he
avoided seeing his friends. But did it make sense to spend $30,000 on a
house? It might turn out, in ten years' time, to have been a good in-
vestment, but in ten years' time, if he was still alive, he'd be seventy-six.
Though Hitler had lost the Battle of Britain, he'd won almost everything else, while in the United States the pro-Fascists seemed to be getting the upper hand. The aviator Charles Lindbergh was applauded in

the newspapers when he argued over the radio that since England was too weak to win the war, helping her would only prolong it.[46] To build a house would be an act of arrogance and stubbornness. Besides, Thomas was undecided about whether to live in San Francisco or go back to the East Coast.[47]

In one of his BBC broadcasts he warned the German people that they had more to fear from victory than from defeat.[48] Roosevelt would probably have been willing to fight Hitler, and so would the American people, but they were being held back by Congress—"by the stupid and evil interests of five hundred villains and idiots."[49]

Making good headway with *Joseph the Provider*—he'd written a hundred pages by April 1950[50]—he sometimes wondered why his work was undisturbed by bad news. Was it a matter of having a phlegmatic disposition, an eccentric mixture of confidence and contemptuousness? He had survived so many European disasters that perhaps his muscles had contracted permanently to protect him from the impact. Or perhaps he was distracted from political realities by the easygoing California atmosphere, the climate, the prevalence of bright colors. Shrubs and flowers were blooming in violet and grape tones that made everything look papery except the oleanders. Although he'd preferred late spring and early summer in Küsnacht and even in Princeton, the season made him euphoric even here, and in the middle of May he instructed the architect to go ahead.[51]

By July 21 he'd completed 268 manuscript pages of the novel, which he found easier to write than any of the earlier volumes.[52] He'd gained enough prowess, self-confidence, and sophistication as a storyteller to let his characters share his knowledge that a story is being told and they are integral to it. From the beginning of the first novel, Joseph has been aware that a myth will evolve out of his experiences, but Thomas keeps finding new ways of developing this idea. He also plays audaciously with the notion of an overlap between his own identity and God's: They're co-authors of the events being narrated.

In early August, he shelved the novel in favor of an introduction to a collection of sermons by Martin Niemöller, a Protestant theologian and pastor who, as an opponent of the Nazi Christians, had been dismissed in 1934 from his post in Berlin. Ignoring his superior, the bishop of Prussia, Niemöller went on preaching and carrying out his pastoral duties until he was arrested in 1937 and sent to a concentration camp. Not knowing whether he was still alive, Thomas wrote that anyone with a human heart would inevitably become a political agitator if a country gave absolute power to a man with soft hands and a voice like a snarling dog's, a man who howled that the state and the nation were God, that he was the state and the nation, that he was therefore God.[53]

Thomas and Katia had invariably gone away for a long summer holiday, but in 1941 they stayed in Pacific Palisades. At the end of July the builders started work on their new house on San Remo Drive, but until it was ready, they'd have to stay in the rented house on Amalfi Drive. They often spent the evening in Hollywood, visiting the same German friends who visited them: "Amongst our palms and lemon trees we live our all too familiar waiting-room life in friendly concourse with the Franks, Werfels, Dieterles, Neumanns—always the same faces, and if it is for once something American, it is also such a strangely dull and genial stereotype that one has had quite enough for a long time."[54]

In 1933, when it was easy to believe the Nazis would soon be ousted, Sanary-sur-Mer had seemed like the ideal refuge for émigré German intellectuals—Jews, left-wingers, anti-Fascists. Later, when it seemed dangerous to be so close to Hitler's Germany, refugees gravitated to Los Angeles, the constellation of municipalities that includes Hollywood. Lion Feuchtwanger, who'd been in Sanary at the same time as Thomas, Heinrich, and the Werfels, advised Bertolt Brecht to settle in Hollywood, saying the cost of living was lower than in New York and the chances of earning a living higher.[55] Besides, the climate was warm and dry: winter was like summer. "Driven into paradise" was Arnold Schoenberg's title for a lecture he gave in the late thirties about German intellectuals and actors who'd gathered there. But conditions were paradisal only for the rich. Jewish actors who'd escaped from the Nazis could sometimes earn money by playing Nazis in Hollywood films; it was harder for writers who could write only in German. As the essayist and critic Alfred Polgar put it, they could "live here in decidedly more comfortable sad conditions than elsewhere. Trees blossom around their wretchedness, and the hummingbird hovers gracefully."

It seemed likely that William Dieterle—he stopped calling himself Wilhelm—would make the *Joseph* novels into a film, though there was no prospect of setting it up immediately.[56] It was partly through Dieterle and his wife, Charlotte, partly through Bruno Frank and his wife, Liesl, that Thomas and Katia met actors, directors, and screenwriters. Dining with the English actor Sir Cedric Hardwicke one evening, they met "the fat director Hitschcock [sic] with his blond wife. He snored after the coffee. Also sleeps at night in a chair."[57] Alfred Hitchcock, who was then forty-two, had been working in Hollywood for two years. On another evening, as guests of the Meyers' daughter Elizabeth and her film producer husband, Pare Lorentz, Thomas met "Mr. Renoir and his Portuguese-Brazilian secretary or girlfriend."[58] Son of the painter, the film director Jean Renoir was forty-seven, and the woman was Dido Freire, niece of the Brazilian film director Alberto Cavalcanti. She and Renoir married two years later.

At the beginning of September, Roosevelt promised to do "everything in our power to crush Hitler and his Nazi forces." American ships started to escort British Atlantic convoys, but there was still no declaration of war, even after seventy American sailors were killed at the end of October when a U-boat attacked a battleship off the west coast of Iceland.

HEARING FROM ERIKA that Agnes Meyer had been the mistress of Paul Claudel, who was twenty-one years her senior, Thomas congratulated himself on stabilizing a nonsexual relationship with her, and reminded himself to be careful.[59] His income and his standing in America were both higher than they'd have been without her intervention, but he'd paid for it by professing more admiration and affection than he felt. In his diaries he called her "silly" and referred to her as "die Meyer." He thought her review of *The Transposed Heads* was "boring," but told her it was "magnificent."[60] Energetically fueling their friendship with flattery and long letters, he went on encouraging her to publish criticism of his work, even when she wanted to write an essay titled "Thomas Mann, the Godseeker."

She'd offered to help if he ever needed funding for his refugee work, and in June, when the Emergency Rescue Committee was short of cash, he asked for $1,000. He wanted to send a few hundred to Oprecht, who was helping destitute German writers in Switzerland; about $350 to the playwright Georg Kaiser, who was trying to emigrate from Switzerland to the States; and about the same amount to Walter Landauer, who'd run the German language department of the Allert de Lange Verlag in Amsterdam and had escaped from the Nazis by jumping out of a window.[61] She sent the money immediately,[62] and in July, inviting her to stay in Pacific Palisades, he offered to let Joseph take a holiday while she was in California "and see how he gets on without me."[63]

She didn't come, but in October he felt secure enough to drop a few hints about financial needs. Before going to New York in November he had to survive the Calvary of a lecture tour. "What else can I do? It is *business*. It brings a few thousand dollars into the house, and the father of a family must buck himself up and bestir himself."[64] She replied promptly and sympathetically: What a hard life he'd had. No, he answered, it had been a blessed life. He was himself full of admiration for the way in which a gifted individual could survive danger, anguish, and adversity, turning even misfortune to advantage, at least in his work. After starting the letter on October 7 and giving it prime working time the next morning, he didn't finish it till the afternoon of the ninth. In his diary he called it a "document of state. . . . Am curious to see what effect it will have."[65]

Like Joseph, he told her, he was a "sad-happy man," prepared for suffering, but confident the darkness would never quench the light God had instilled in him. He went on to analyze the financial risk of investing in a new house. His friend Hermann Hesse had been lucky: A house had been built for him by the Swiss philanthropist Hans Bodmer. In the States, seven doctoral capes had been draped around Thomas's shoulders, but these were tributes that cost the donors nothing. People thoughtlessly assumed he had no financial needs. It was true that he'd won the Nobel Prize, but he'd had to leave most of his money in Munich, while his royalty income had been drastically reduced by the Nazification of Germany and Austria. In furnishing the new house, he said, he and Katia had to think carefully about each chair: Could they afford it?[66] In reality, he hadn't thought it extravagant to spend $1,100 on the layout of the garden.[67]

He was still waiting for Agnes Meyer's response when he left with Katia on October 14 for a six-week tour in the South, East, and Midwest. By lecturing on "The War and the Future," he was aiming to make neutrality less popular. They had two nights on the train to San Antonio, Texas, passing through desert landscape with cacti, dwarf palms, and mountains in the background. Writing in pencil, he finished the chapter about the seven years of plenty.

Arriving in San Antonio, they were driven to a hotel in Austin, where the first lecture was followed by a party at the house of a rich engineer, Mr. Brown, who took them on a sightseeing expedition in the morning.[68] After another night on a train they reached New Orleans, where a letter was waiting. Agnes Meyer would try to help him. They could discuss it at the end of the month when he arrived in Washington.[69]

He and Katia went from New Orleans to Birmingham, Alabama, where, in spite of the humidity and the heat, he worked on the novel in the hotel. Though feeling tired when he gave the lecture on October 21 in a packed hall, he let himself be captured afterward by a bookseller called Gottlieb, who drove him to a country house in the woods. "Guests. Stingy hospitality. A lot of beer. Insensitive exploitation with questions till the last minute. Should not have put up with it. Tormented and overtired to bed at 1:00."[70]

They went on to Point Clear on the Gulf of Mexico, and to Mobile, Alabama, where he found a disappointing letter from Agnes Meyer. "It is lacking in any sign of proper understanding or proper willingness to be generous."[71] But when they arrived in Washington, he found she had a plan to secure him an appointment that involved even less work than the job at Princeton. She knew the poet Archibald MacLeish, who earned a high salary as Librarian of Congress and liked the idea of appointing Thomas as consultant in Germanic literatures. The annual salary would be in the region of $5,000. From Chicago, where he arrived on November 2, Thomas happily wrote to tell her: "Your *distin-*

guished resourcefulness has filled me with genuine admiration. A more beautiful solution would have been unthinkable, and I am artist enough to take almost more pleasure in the form you found for giving than in the content." (He uses the word *Gehalt*, which means both *content* and *salary*.)[72] When he went on to address audiences of about two thousand and four thousand people in the universities of Iowa and Indiana, the experience seemed to be setting the seal on his triumph.[73]

He'd also been trying to help his less fortunate brother. Thanks to the European Script Fund, which had been set up by the director Ernst Lubitsch and the ex-actress-screenwriter Salka Viertel, Heinrich's first year in the States had been subsidized by Warner Brothers, which had put him on their payroll together with some other émigré scriptwriters, at an annual salary of $6,000. But he was given almost nothing to do while Alfred Döblin, author of *Berlin-Alexanderplatz*, was set to work on the movies *Mrs. Miniver* and *Random Harvest*.

These contracts weren't renewed. Heinrich, who was making no effort to learn English, couldn't earn a living, and by the end of September 1941 his wife, Nelly, had sold all her jewelry. Thomas, who'd signed an affidavit in March 1941 promising to take responsibility should his brother be unable to finance himself in the United States, decided to appeal on Heinrich's behalf to the Guggenheim Foundation.[74] Thomas even approached the Soviet ambassador in New York, arguing that as "a faithful friend of the Russian Revolution," Heinrich deserved support from the Soviet Union, but by the end of November it was clear that Thomas must come, once again, to his elder brother's rescue. When Heinrich and Nelly came to dinner, it was agreed that Thomas would immediately provide $300, and make regular monthly payments of a hundred.[75]

After taking him to seventeen cities, his six-week tour ended on November 26, but he found it hard to concentrate on work, knowing he'd be at the house for only three months before moving. He was also suffering from not having access to all his papers. He particularly missed a commentary on the Pentateuch with pencil annotations.[76]

At the beginning of November, Fridolin came to stay with his grandparents—"an exhilarating burden."[77] Thomas had been wrong to think grandparenthood would make no difference to him: He hadn't taken so much pleasure in a child's company since Elisabeth had been in her infancy. Frido was "very bright and easy to handle. His presence makes us feel transported back to the time when we were young."[78] "Fed the little boy with milk chocolate. Heartfelt delight at his sweetness, his laughter over pranks, his own and other people's."[79]

The world was taken by surprise on December 7 when 360 Japanese warplanes attacked the American Pacific Fleet in its home base at Pearl Harbor in Hawaii. In two hours eight battleships and eleven smaller ships were sunk or disabled, nearly two hundred aircraft destroyed, and over 2,400 people killed—soldiers, sailors, and civilians. In September 1940, Japan had signed a pact with Germany and had taken control of French Indochina. America had retaliated by breaking off trade with Japan and freezing her assets. Since then relations between the two countries had deteriorated, and the German foreign minister, Joachim von Ribbentrop, had been urging Japan not to lose the opportunity of establishing a new order in East Asia. But, wanting to avoid war, Roosevelt had appealed personally to Emperor Hirohito a day before the attack on Pearl Harbor.

There was no declaration of war from the imperial headquarters in Tokyo until several hours after the attack. The next day, when Roosevelt appeared before a special joint session of Congress, calling for a declaration of war on Japan, the one dissenting vote came from a pacifist. It wasn't yet clear whether the United States would be involved in war with Germany and Italy, but Hitler threw down the gauntlet to Roosevelt on December 11, when war was declared. By then the president had already made his broadcast to the nation. "He has an enormous understanding of the childishness of the average American. Exhorts discipline and readiness for sacrifice. Long and *difficult* war ahead."[80] After failing to invade Britain, Hitler had made another miscalculation. "Now the lion is awake," wrote Thomas, "and I believe the Japanese were making a great mistake in waking him so roughly."[81]

Citadels of Stupidity

THOMAS HAD AN ATTRACTIVE young man named Konrad Katzenellenbogen working as his secretary. This surname was more often a nuisance than a help, though once, when he'd been driving above the speed limit, the policeman who stopped him let him go, daunted by the prospect of having to spell his name. It was after this that he started to call himself Konrad Kellen.[1]

He noticed that during the two years he worked for Thomas, not a single sheet of paper had to be thrown away. Occasionally a few words would be altered, but never the sequence of sentences, paragraphs, chapters. Occasionally, perhaps once in twenty pages, an idea would be transplanted from one place to another, but "ninety-nine per cent of what he fashioned retained its form and appearance—without so much as a comma added or deleted."[2]

Whenever something amused or delighted Thomas, "a sparkle of recognition, delight, just plain light would come into his eyes, arresting for those at whom he directed it." He never deviated from his routine, always writing between two and three pages in the morning, always going for a walk before lunch—though there were rarely any other pedestrians in the streets of Pacific Palisades—and always lying down for a nap afterward. He had no talent for intimacy. Few people called him Tommy, and when he was with Heinrich, who did, the brothers sat at opposite ends of a sofa, chatting "very much like two college professors who have just been introduced."[3]

NOW THAT AMERICA was at war, German immigrants were to be treated as "enemy aliens." Worried, Thomas wrote to Agnes Meyer on December 27 asking whether this was the status he'd have.[4] He later wrote to Francis Biddle, the solicitor general, whom he knew socially, pointing out that after making so many anti-Hitler broadcasts to Germany, he couldn't reasonably be regarded as an enemy.[5]

Both Thomas and Katia enjoyed having Frido in the house, and, jokingly, Thomas called the little boy his "last love."[6] But it was a revealing joke. Though Klaus had been older, the feeling was similar to that of being "in love" with his own son. There was no question of abusing either child, just as there had been no question of trying to seduce the diminutive ten-year-old Wladyslaw Moes in Venice, but Thomas's reaction to the appeal of the young faces and bodies had an erotic dimension. Frido stayed in Pacific Palisades till mid-January 1942, when his grandparents were going to be in San Francisco. Thomas was to lecture on "How to Win the Peace" at the town hall. When Frido was handed back to his mother, she was astonished at how much he'd developed, and Thomas had the impression that the child didn't recognize her.7

With a massive reception and the showing of a movie, one of the parties in San Francisco lasted from six in the evening till one in the morning. "These Americans," he complained, "know how to take advantage of one, not to say bleed one dry; they themselves have no nerves at all and it does not occur to them that other people get tired."8 The hall was full for the lecture, and so was the platform: Thomas had to wait in the wings while the chairman introduced him. He then gave an eighty-minute talk, followed by questions, and more questions were asked over coffee after lunch in a hotel.9 On his last day in San Francisco he was given a packet of matches with his name printed on them.10

Before leaving Pacific Palisades he'd finished the section dealing with Tamar, a humbly born woman determined to squeeze her way into the history of the world. Reading this sequence aloud after dinner on January 24, when he and Katia were at Bruno Frank's house, Thomas began to feel confident that *Joseph the Provider* wouldn't be an anticlimax after *Joseph in Egypt*.11 He pressed ahead with the chapter about famine in Egypt. Though preparations were already being made for the move into the new house, he wasn't deflected from his work on the novel. On Tuesday, February 3, his desk had to be cleared before the furniture was moved out of his workroom and loaded into the van, but he made notes for the next section. He could write anywhere, and on Wednesday, working at the bureau in the bedroom, he started describing the arrival of Joseph's brothers in Egypt.

Thomas and Katia moved the next day, and on the following morning, after going back to the empty house with the poodle and searching for some reference books in "the wilderness of the study," he settled down to write in the new house, though decorators were still at work and Katia was unpacking.12 At first he had to write in the bedroom, because his new study wasn't ready,13 but it was going to be the most beautiful he'd ever had.14 On February 14 he used it for the first time, writing at the desk from Munich. Once again the Siamese warrior stood between the two lamps, and the Chinese ashtray was in place.15 The room was square, and through the windows he had a view of avocado groves and descending hills, with the Pacific in the distance.16

He had moments of anxiety about their new home—were there too many bedrooms?—but he was luxuriously accommodated in a beautiful setting, with a view of Catalina Island. "You ought to see the landscape around our house," he told Hermann Hesse, "with the view of the ocean, the garden with its trees—palm, olive, pepper, lemon and eucalyptus—the luxuriant flowers, the lawns that were ready for mowing a few days after the seeds were sown. Bright sensory impressions are no small matter in times like these, and the sky is bright here almost throughout the year, sending out an incomparable light which makes everything look beautiful."[17] The beach was only ten minutes away by car. Every day Katia drove him to the promenade overlooking the sea, and she went for a swim while he took a solitary walk.[18]

It had been announced at the end of January that enemy aliens were going to be evacuated from coastal areas,[19] but Thomas discovered that, as Czech citizens, he and Katia were unaffected. Not that this stopped him from campaigning for other German and Italian immigrants. On February 9 he sent Roosevelt a telegram he'd drafted for signature by Toscanini, Bruno Walter, Bruno Frank, Borgese, Count Sforza, and himself. Among those being victimized, it said, were the earliest and most farsighted opponents of the regimes now at war with the United States.[20] The refugees had been much worse off since America entered the war. Together with anti-Semitism, prejudice against foreigners—especially Germans—had increased, while immigration was harder to finance, and the Emergency Rescue Committee was short of funds.[21]

On February 15 the British surrendered Singapore, which they'd believed to be an impregnable fortress and naval base. Thomas already knew the British Empire was doomed. "It is antiquated and through arrogance, incompetence and effete irresponsibility, it has become almost impossible to defend."[22] Hitler obviously had designs on it, but the United States seemed more likely to benefit from its disintegration. It was hard to feel optimistic about war as a means of creating a new world order, and Thomas's spirits were lowered still further in mid-February, when a letter arrived from Erika, who was working for the BBC in London. Her impression was that the war leadership was weak-kneed, with no real will for victory.[23] Thomas had consistently admired Churchill, and in January, when Molly Shenstone sent him a print of the photograph by Karsh, he'd written in English to thank her for "that excellent and most vivid picture of our common hero."[24] But, trusting Erika's judgment, he came to believe that neither Churchill nor Roosevelt was going all out to win.[25] Perhaps the war was no more than a disguise for "a Fascistic conspiracy à la Munich of governments against peoples."[26]

If he criticized the Allied war effort in any of his long letters to Agnes

Meyer, she reprimanded him for his lack of faith in the United States. Though their friendship was now in its fifth year, it was hard to keep it on an even keel. When the Meyers came to California, Thomas gave her less time than she'd expected. When she complained that she'd seen him only *en famille*, he replied that her memory was misleading her.[27] This provoked her into saying their relationship was better when they were at a distance, exchanging letters. Like so much of what she said and wrote, this struck him as "stupid." "My desire to kick the tyrannous old bag out of my life is almost uncontrollable."[28] But in his reply, which was long and polite, he offered to visit her in San Francisco if she was too busy to see his new house in California.[29]

Instead of "Thomas Mann: the Godseeker," she was now planning to write a critical book about three Godseekers, the other two being Tolstoy and Dostoyevsky. Gentle attempts to discourage her would have been ineffectual; a veto would have alienated her permanently. Feeling entitled to offer him advice, she said Joseph should grow into a magnificent adult. Usually Thomas was good at concealing his anger, but now he had trouble. "That is not good, either for you or for me." The book, he explained, was primarily a humorous epic. If it had a place in "the intellectual and moral dialectic of our time," this was because it humanized the myth. But until the end, the maturity of the hero would be left as much in doubt as the maturity of the author.[30]

The fifty-four-year-old woman was trying to achieve a new level of intimacy with the sixty-six-year-old man. (He was the same age as her husband.) "Depressing fixation on my person, withdrawing from social activities to write the desperate work about me. Frightful. In all seriousness still wanting to emerge as the woman in my life."[31] But he went on investing time in long letters, diplomatically fending off her "pedagoguic tyranny."[32] In late March, while he and Katia were putting up with the "fearful" behavior of Heinrich's "frightful" wife—they'd come to stay for a fortnight at the new house[33] and Nelly was seldom sober—the Meyers visited California, staying in a bungalow at the nearby Miramar Hotel. Thomas showed them the new house and visited them in the bungalow, where her husband left her alone with him. They talked "about her work, her situation, about 'us.' "[34] The next day, in his new workroom, he had another "painful conversation" with her,[35] and two days later, after visiting her in the bungalow, reading to her from *Joseph the Provider* and lunching with her, he wrote: "This cannot last much longer." But it was comforting to see the new Library of Congress writing paper with his name on it.[36] When they had another tête-à-tête lunch again on April 4, her last full day in California, she said he was cut off from humanity. Since "Tonio Kröger," his writing hadn't been influenced by his emotions, and that was why he didn't want a relationship with her.[37]

On March 7 he had to appear before a committee that questioned him about his application for American citizenship, and this prompted some troubled self-interrogation about identity and the future. Now nearly sixty-seven, he expected to be in his seventies when the war ended,[38] and knew he'd never again want to live in Germany. It was better to admire "the goodness and greatness" of the Germans from a distance. Hitler wasn't the only cause of what had happened: The Bismarck experiment was being pushed toward its absurd conclusion. The actions of the Nazis could never be forgotten,[39] and Thomas never again wanted to live where German was spoken. His intention was to stay in California for the rest of his life, and after the war to see Europe only as a visitor.[40]

At the end of February the Royal Air Force appointed a new head of Bomber Command—Sir Arthur Harris, who became known as "Bomber Harris." On March 26 two hundred planes launched a heavy onslaught on the Ruhr Valley, and two days later, hundreds of tons of incendiaries and high explosives were dropped on Lübeck, where about a quarter of the built-up area was destroyed. The news made Thomas feel "strangely disoriented."[41] At the end of May, after a thousand bombers attacked Cologne, Churchill announced that a different German town would be raided each night. Upset and ambivalent, Thomas could find only conventional phrases for his feelings. "At last expiation has begun."[42] The destruction of Cologne, he said, was "a deeply serious reparation for the moral feeling which has been relentlessly outraged for years. But one must think of Guernica, of Rotterdam, to 'suppress sympathy'. The Germans now have to learn on their own body what war means."[43]

Alongside the news, the two women putting Thomas under strain were his sister-in-law and Agnes Meyer. As an affectionate gift to his younger brother, the seventy-one-year-old Heinrich produced a drawing to illustrate Joseph's first meeting with his brothers in Egypt.[44] Nelly was now forty-four, and they'd been together just over ten years. Regularly throwing drunken tantrums, she was making Heinrich's life almost unbearable. Thomas tried to intervene, but since Heinrich refused to consider separation or divorce, the problem seemed insoluble.[45] When they came to dinner on June 26, Nelly got drunk again and interrupted Heinrich's reading from his play about Frederick the Great. Thomas left the room without saying goodnight, and decided never to invite them again—a resolution he failed to keep.[46]

He went on investing time and energy in correspondence with Agnes Meyer. The long letter he received on April 9 was "painful, partly because of its terrifying openheartedness." He made up his mind to "practise the art of ignoring,"[47] but told her that with its lyrical power of expression, her letter was the most beautiful and best written she'd ever sent him. Perhaps the reason he found it so appealing was that it contained an echo of her visit to Pacific Palisades, which had struck him as the most successful visit either of them had paid to the other.[48]

Her next beautiful letter was about Goethe, showing, he said, that she had a "fresh and lively relationship with this German miracle." And, since she'd be much better than he was at thinking up titles in English, what should he call the American version of his broadcasts to Germany?[49] Expecting her to be pleased, he said he'd read out some of her comments on Goethe to his family. In a long letter "full of stupidities," she then reprimanded him for being indiscreet. She also enclosed a short story she'd written, "Song at Twilight." "That stupid and tyrannical old bag irritates me."[50] But he spent precious morning time on a flattering letter about the story, saying he hoped to see it printed "in an honourable space."[51] Before he'd posted what he'd written, a "penitent letter" arrived from "the decidedly hysterical woman in Washington."[52]

When plans were being made for him to lecture at the Library of Congress, she suggested he should talk about the *Joseph* novels. He'd have preferred a political subject, but Archibald MacLeish supported her proposal, and Thomas gave in.[53] And still "this stupid and dispiriting friendship"[54] went on. He was relieved that her children persuaded her to shelve her book about him, Tolstoy, and Dostoyevsky,[55] and when she complained that none of his sons had joined the army, he politely explained why they couldn't, and congratulated her on her courage in flying to England, where she wanted to study social conditions.[56] Not that it was unusual for him to deviate sharply in his diary from what he said in letters. When Helen Lowe-Porter sent him her translation of the foreword to *Order of the Day*, his reaction was "inadequate of course," but he wrote to thank her for doing such an "excellent translation."[57]

In mid-August he put *Joseph the Provider* aside to work on a lecture titled "The Theme of the *Joseph* Novels."

IN SEPTEMBER, when two hundred planes dropped such high-caliber bombs on Munich that the explosions were audible on the other side of the Swiss frontier, he felt less ambivalent than he had after the raid on Lübeck. "The idiotic place has historically deserved it." He hoped the prettiest parts of the city had been spared, but Munich was a "citadel of stupidity."[58]

The war still occupied much of his time. Through newspapers and radio programs he kept abreast of what was going on; he thought about it, talked about it, and wrote about it in his diary. The war, he believed, had been avoidable. His biggest grudge against humanity was that the civilized countries hadn't merely failed to scotch the growth of Nazism but had encouraged it. "My resentment about this I shall take with me to the grave."[59] Describing the slaughter, destruction, and suffering, he often used such religious words as "atonement,"[60] and, writing in English to a journalist who'd reviewed *Order of the Day*, he said: "Foolish disobedience to the spirit, or, religiously speaking, to God's will, is undoubtedly the true cause for the world explosion which stuns us."[61]

He still thought the democratic governments had been motivated by fear of a world revolution, and these suspicions were exacerbated when Roosevelt was conciliatory toward the French Vichy government, which was collaborating with Nazi Germany. Now, after three years of war, those who wanted to do a deal with Hitler seemed likely to gain the upper hand. A partitioned world in which the Nazis controlled most of Europe would be even worse than a revolution that established worldwide communism, and in making this point Thomas assumed that the Second World War was only a continuation of the first, and that the Western leaders had been confronted in the thirties with a choice between two forms of totalitarianism. "I would be loyal to Communism and willingly–almost joyfully–submit to its dictatorship if it were the alternative to Nazism."[62] Although he knew more about contemporary history than when he wrote *Reflections*, much of his political naiveté had remained intact.

He was to lecture at the Library of Congress on November 17, and before staying with the Meyers, Thomas and Katia wanted to spend a few days in Chicago with Elisabeth and Giuseppe, who was about to celebrate his sixtieth birthday. On November 9, the day they left Pacific Palisades, Thomas worked on the novel in the morning, and resumed writing when they were on the train. He also started to read Stravinsky's memoirs and made a lot of pencil underlinings. He was making pencil annotations in two other books he was reading, both on Nietzsche–Lou Andreas Salomé's memoir and *Nietzsches Zusammenbruch* (*Nietzsche's Breakdown*) by Ernst Podach. Thomas knew he was close to the end of the *Joseph* series but didn't know what he was going to write next. He'd written or lectured more than once about the three other great Germans who had influenced him most–Goethe, Schopenhauer, and Wagner–but never about Nietzsche. A new diary entry was: "Fateful mysticism, unforgivable, often provoking pity. The 'unfortunate man.' "[63]

After two nights on the train, Thomas and Katia arrived in Chicago, where they found their son-in-law had visions of himself as governor of Sicily once Hitler was defeated.[64] By the time they left, on the fifteenth, Thomas had caught a cold, but, though it was getting worse, it didn't stop him from writing while on the train to Washington. The city looked different from when he'd seen it in the spring of 1940. Now that the United States was at war, barracks and government office buildings were conspicuous in the area around the Lincoln Memorial, and trains loaded with war matériel rolled into the city. After dinner the radio was turned on, and they heard news of an American naval victory off the Solomon Islands.

Before Thomas delivered his speech, Agnes Meyer checked through the script for mistakes.[65] In the Library's Coolidge Auditorium he had an audience of about a thousand people, and he was introduced by Henry A. Wallace, vice president of the United States. The evening ended in a reception at the Meyers' house. Francis Biddle was there, and his wife told Thomas his talk had been like music. He answered: "I always feel a little like a conductor."[66]

Before they left for New York, Agnes Meyer came to say goodbye in his room: "Ghastly affection. Away, away."[67] With their ten pieces of luggage Thomas and Katia were driven to the station, and in the dining car the French headwaiter told them Rommel had surrendered with the remains of his army—a rumor that turned out to be false.[68]

In Hollywood during the summer, an agent, Armin L. Robinson, a friend of Bruno Frank, had been trying to interest Metro-Goldwyn-Mayer in making a film called *The Ten Commandments*, involving Thomas and nine other writers in treating Hitler's violation of each commandment. When the project fell through, Robinson decided to produce a book based on the idea, and in New York on November 24 he offered Thomas $1,000 to write a short introduction to ten essays by famous writers, including Rebecca West, Franz Werfel, and André Maurois. Thomas signed a contract just after the news broke about the destruction of the French fleet in the harbor at Toulon on November 27, a few hours after German tanks rolled into the city. To save the ships from falling into German hands and swaying the balance of naval power, the French commanders had given orders for the fleet to be scuttled by its crews. Munition dumps were blown up, and some of the warships fired on the Germans to gain time for the ships to be sunk.

While Thomas was swept into a series of parties, meals in restaurants, and visits to Broadway shows, he pictured resolute French captains staying on the bridge of sinking ships. On Thanksgiving Day, he and Katia had a turkey lunch with the German novelist Annette Kolb before leaving by train in time to have dinner at Alfred Knopf's country house in Purchase, New York. When they returned to the city, the Meyers had arrived. "No peace. Conversations with the Meyer. Difficult journey before 5 o'clock to her in the Plaza Hotel. Troubles over tea." Cross-questioned, he had to reassure her, and then to make his way wearily back to his hotel in the rain.[69] The next day, before going to a Toscanini concert, he and Katia ate with the Meyers in their hotel: "the wife dégoutant [sic], the husband finally losing his temper in an ill-bred way. Saying goodbye as joyless as appropriate to the relationship."[70]

Thomas and Katia stayed in New York until December 7, when they left for Chicago, mainly to see Frido. When they took him to Walt Disney's *Bambi*, Thomas was seeing it for the second time.[71] Back in Pacific Palisades, he wrote: "Thought and am thinking a great deal about the charming little grandson."[72] In her next letter, Agnes Meyer reminded him not to miss a talk she was going to give on the radio. Dutifully he tuned in and wrote to compliment her.[73] But she soon wrote again to complain that he'd never thanked her for the birthday present she'd sent him—a pair of jade cuff links. He wrote back saying he couldn't have failed to thank her. Perhaps his letter had got lost in the post. But he punctured her pretense of incredulity that he could treat her so badly when the gift had been valuable enough for a man to live on it for a year. This, he said, he could hardly believe. After all, jade was only a semi-precious stone, and he'd seen long jade necklaces which must have cost a fortune if two stones could be so valuable.[74] But he wrote again on Christmas Eve to say how grateful he was for everything she'd done to help him.[75]

Having returned to Pacific Palisades on December 12, he began work a week later on the final chapter of *Joseph the Provider*. He'd started on the *Joseph* novels in November 1925, when he was a man of fifty, still living in Munich. He was now sixty-seven. The last chapter gave him trouble because he thought he'd already said everything he wanted to say. The action finally centers on the blessing given by the dying Jacob to his twelve sons and to his two grandsons by Joseph, Manasseh and Ephraim. Like Thomas, who preferred Frido to his younger grandson, Toni, born in July 1942, two years after Frido, Jacob likes one grandson more than the other. But while Thomas's favorite was the elder, Jacob's is the younger, Ephraim. Wanting his father to follow tradition by putting his right hand on the older son's head and his left on the younger's, Joseph positions the boys in front of the dying man, who, obstinate to the last, crosses his hands. This situation, in which the younger son receives the blessing due to the elder, neatly echoes the story of Jacob and Esau, but after keeping his autobiographical urge in check through most of the tetralogy, Thomas is indulging it. He had been thinking of himself when he wrote about interpenetration between self-confidence and belief that one is destined for greatness, either by God or the chance that presides over the distribution of talents. Whether he was more gifted than Esau or had merely made better use of his gifts, the final trick of the dying patriarch alludes to Thomas's feeling that Heinrich had been done out of the priority he'd expected.

Before lunch on January 4, 1943, Thomas ended the novel: "Thus ends the beautiful story and God-invention of *Joseph and His Brothers*." Before going to bed he wrote in his diary: "I was excited and sad. But it is done, for better or worse."[76] In a letter to Agnes Meyer he said: "So it is accomplished and may well stand as a monument of persistence and endurance, for that is how I am much more disposed to see it than as a monument of art and thought. The idea that art is only an ethical ful-fillment of my life was already stated in my *Reflections*, and I still see my work mainly from this point of view. It is a way of life."[77]

Part
Five

Twelve-Tone Syphilis

AFTER UNDERTAKING to write a foreword for *The Ten Commandments*, Thomas decided he'd prefer to approach the subject fictionally. No longer having Joseph as his companion, he'd console himself with the man who claimed to have written the commandments at God's dictation. The *Joseph* novels had tended to demythify and demystify biblical material, partly through the dry, skeptical, humorous, anachronistic style. He'd have fun applying this style to Moses, and if he'd been analyzing the first recorded examples of love, sibling rivalry, violence, and so on, he could submit the first categorical imperatives to the same treatment. While Jews were being slaughtered, he could erect a literary defense, presenting them as the originators of civilized morality.

He started by looking at Freud's essays on Moses.[1] Freud, as he confessed to Lou Andreas Salomé, had always been haunted by Moses, believing the story could help him to understand what Jewishness was. Freud thought the "embryonic experience of the people, the impact of Moses and the exodus from Egypt had given Jews their character through the centuries."[2]

On visits to Rome, Freud paid almost daily visits to Michelangelo's massive statue of Moses with horns to represent the radiance on his face after he saw God. He's holding the tablets of the law, which were smashed, according to Exodus, when he saw the Israelites worshiping the Golden Calf; according to Freud, the sculpture shows him keeping his anger under control. Freud started work in 1934 on the essays he published in 1938 under the title *Der Mann Moses und die monotheistische Religion*. His original intention had been to write a historical novel, but he acknowledged to Max Eitingon that historical novels weren't his forte—that Thomas Mann was the one to write them. We don't know whether Freud ever discussed Moses with Thomas, but having created a massive fiction in response to Goethe's comment on the sketchiness of the original Joseph story, Thomas now carried out Freud's unfulfilled project by writing "Das Gesetz" ("The Law," or "The Tables of the Law" as it's called in Helen Lowe-Porter's translation).

If the story has little to say about monotheism, this is mainly because Thomas had already written in *Joseph the Provider* about the monotheistic center that was common to Judaism and Amenhotep's religion, Aten. It had been suggested by scholars that Moses was an Egyptian, and in the early thirties Freud told Arnold Zweig that Moses was both Egyptian and strongly anti-Semitic. Disliking Jahweh, a crudely aggressive volcano god, Moses tried to convert the Jews to a more spiritualized, more Egyptian monotheism. But this was too subtle for them, and following a theory the scholar Ernst Sellin advanced in 1922, Freud maintained that the people Moses led out of Egypt killed him, and that the spiritualized religion was revived about eight centuries later by a reformer who adopted the same name—Moses.

Though Thomas had assumed in *The Tales of Jacob* that the names of the patriarchs covered more than a single identity, he rejects the idea of the double Moses. Making his Moses look like Michelangelo—wasn't the man an artist, a sculptor?[3]—he shares Freud's skepticism about the miracles presented in Exodus. In Thomas's story the Egyptian magicians are just as good as Moses's brother, Aaron, at changing rods into snakes, while the slaughter of the Egyptian firstborn is carried out not by the Angel of Death but by Joshua and his band of trained terrorists.

Moses is a killer, too. He slaughters the Egyptian overseer who smashes his nose when he tries to defend a worker who's being beaten. But his passionate love of order is a reaction to what Thomas calls the disorderliness of his birth. Compromising between Freud and the Bible, "The Tables of the Law" features a half-Egyptian Moses, illegitimate son of a handsome Jewish slave and Pharaoh's daughter. Her serving women hide the baby in a box, and pretend to find it in the bulrushes. After being educated in an elegant Egyptian school and rediscovering the invisible deity in a Midianite godhead, he uses it to impose orderliness on the unruly Jewish slaves, inviting them to be the chosen people of the invisible god. Preaching his own moral ideas, he claims that it's speaking through him.

His success in leading them out of Egypt looks miraculous. Afterward he exploits their willingness to believe in a supernatural force, saying they can please God by giving up such slovenly habits as copulating with animals, with brothers or sisters, with other men's wives. Unless they learn what cleanliness is, they'll be nothing but rabble. They must eat only animals that chew the cud and have cloven hoofs. Nor must they shave their eyebrows or tattoo their faces. God is among them and sees everything. On six successive days they can plow the land or make pots, but the seventh day is holy, and no work must be done. After formulating a lot of moral rules, he climbs to the top of Mount Sinai, where he carves ten commandments into two stone tablets. While carving he feels as if rays like horns are standing out from the front of his head: Thomas was treating the business of lawgiving as if it were "a kind of Michelangelesque sculpting with the body of the tribe as raw material."[4]

Moses smashes the tablets when he finds the people worshiping the Golden Calf. The ringleaders are executed, and the narrative suddenly treats God as if he were real when Moses goes back to the mountaintop. God is so jealous and wrathful that Moses has trouble persuading him to give the Jews another chance.

Reading *Candide* while he wrote the story, Thomas introduced an element of Voltairean comedy that had been missing from the *Joseph* novels.[5] But he benefited from the momentum he'd finally generated. Having started "The Tables of the Law" on January 25, he finished on March 13: "I wrote the story down almost without making any corrections in not quite two months, a short space of time, given my way of working. . . . During my work, or earlier, I'd given it the title 'Das Gesetz', meaning not only the Ten Commandments but also moral law in general, which should characterise human civilization."[6] The story ends with a curse ostensibly directed against idolaters. But Thomas is thinking of the war when Moses threatens that blood will flow in such torrents that redness will vanish from the cheeks of mankind.

A week after he started the story, Field Marshal Friedrich von Paulus, commander of the Sixth Army, surrendered at Stalingrad. Hitler, who'd ordered him to fight till the last man was dead, had promoted him to Field Marshal because no German marshal had ever surrendered. But about 200,000 German soldiers had been killed or frozen to death or died of starvation since being surrounded by the Russians in November. In Rostov, too, the Germans seemed to be on the point of giving up. Previously, Nazi newspapers had characterized Russian soldiers as Bolshevistic submen with no faith in their chances of winning; suddenly they were superior in numbers and equipment, while the poor, frail invader was defending civilization against crafty barbarians. In North Africa, Rommel's advance had seemed unstoppable, but General Bernard Montgomery had forced him to retreat.

This didn't mean Hitler was about to surrender. As Thomas said, rephrasing the first line of a war song, "[I]t will be a very long way to Tipperary." And he was pessimistic about the peace that victory would bring. "It will be a Catholic-Fascistic peace. Maybe Europe no longer deserves anything better. But the Anglo-Saxon armies of occupation will probably serve mainly to hold back the overdue revolutions in Germany, France, Italy and Spain."[7] Earlier Thomas had bought war bonds, but recently his main contribution to the war effort had been through broadcasting and writing articles on Germany's future for the Office of War Information.[8]

On March 14, the day after he finished "The Tables of the Law," he cleared his desk of all the notes, pictures, clippings, and books relevant to Joseph and Moses. Instead of giving himself a few days off, he immediately started looking for the notes he'd made in his diaries for his

Faust story. He also arranged to borrow the first German *Faust* book from a library, and a collection of Hugo Wolf's letters. One of the greatest *Lieder* composers, Wolf suffered at the end of his life from mental illness and paralysis. He died in 1903 at the age of forty-three after spending his last six years in a mental clinic.

On March 17 Thomas found in a notebook he'd started during 1901 two brief notes about an artist's pact with the devil. The notes weren't made until 1904,[9] but the notebook reminded him of how preoccupied he'd been in 1901 with Paul Ehrenberg and the abortive novel about their relationship. "Love cannot be experienced more forcefully. Finally I shall be able to tell myself I have faced everything out. The trick was to make it into material for art. Astonished at many things. What was *basic* was the courage, the willingness to compromise, the cautious explanations, the comparative happiness while suffering. The value of irony, which allowed me to take pleasure in a remarkable number of things and to meet real insults with at most: 'That is very kind.' "[10] This suggests that his capacity for irony encouraged a dichotomy between feelings and outward behavior, as in the friendship with Agnes Meyer.

The first note is about a "syphilitic artist" who gets engaged to an innocent girl but shoots himself before the wedding.[11] The second comes seventeen pages later:

> Figure of the syphilitic artist: as Dr Faust and assigned to the Devil. The poison works as intoxication, stimulus, inspiration: when he is carried away by rapture he can create wonderful works of genius, the Devil is guiding his hand. But finally *the Devil carries him off*: paralysis. This is preceded by the business with the pure young girl, with whom it goes as far as marriage.[12]

In 1904, Thomas had been thinking of either writing a short story about this "syphilitic artist" or introducing him into the novel *Maja*. In 1943 he copied out the old notes, adding:

> Have carried this idea around with me a long time. . . . Thoughts of moral deepening attached themselves. It is a matter of the urge to escape from what is bourgeois, moderate, classical, Apollonian, sober, diligent, trusty, into what is drunkenly liberated, daring, Dionysiac, inspired, super-bourgeois, yes, superhuman—above all subjective as experience and intoxicated intensification of the self, regardless of whether the outside world can participate.[13]

Though Shakespeare's plays move effortlessly between the anatomical and the political, reflecting the analogy—commonplace in his lifetime—between disorder in the state and disease in the body, it wouldn't have occurred to Thomas in 1904 that the virus could infect the body politic. It may be irrelevant that he'd read more of Shakespeare's plays by 1943;

Nazism and the war would have made it impossible not to think of giving the idea a political dimension:

> The bursting of civil restraints which proceeds in a pathologically infectious and disintegrating way at the same time *political*. Intellectual-spiritual Fascism, rejection of the humane, use of violence, blood-lust, irrationalism, cruelty; Dionysiac denial of truth and justice, regression to the instincts and uncontrolled "life", which is really *death* or if it is life is *only the Devil's work, the result of infection*. Fascism as a deviation from the bourgeois life-style, mediated by the Devil, leading through drunkenly intensified adventures of subjectivity and inflation of the self to mental collapse and to spiritual—soon also to physical—death: the bill is presented.[14]

He'd found a way in which he could go on writing fiction but could produce a book that would have as much to do with Germany's current situation as *Reflections* had when he wrote it.

Neither music nor Nietzsche is mentioned in these notes. Nietzsche's first book, *Die Geburt der Tragödie*, which pays tribute to Wagner's music-dramas, had habituated Thomas to thinking in terms of a polarity between Dionysus and Apollo, but this habit was so deeply ingrained that it no longer reminded him of Nietzsche. It was probably the idea of syphilis that sparked the connection. Nietzsche's madness had first been attributed to syphilis by a doctor, P. J. Möbius, in 1902, and Thomas, who'd been reading Podach's book on Nietzsche's breakdown, owned a 1909 reprint of Möbius's *Über das Pathologische bei Nietzsche*.

Thomas had been hesitating about whether to finish the confidence trickster novel before immersing himself in the Faust story.[15] He reread the *Felix Krull* material, and Katia wanted him to work on it, but what may have fired his impatience to develop the Faust idea was the realization that he could establish a quadrilateral connection between Nietzsche, the syphilitic artist, Nazi Germany, and the plight of the avant-garde composer. Discussing this, he could write about contemporary creativity in general and his own problems in particular. The syphilitic artist could be a German composer; both his career and his disease could be modeled on those of Nietzsche, who would never be mentioned by name. Instead of offering to renew the composer's youth, the Devil would propose, perhaps in a hallucination, to reinvigorate his creativity, and their pact would somehow be linked to Germany's pact with Nazism.

Not wanting to write a variation on Goethe's *Faust*, Thomas drew on the earliest literary version of the story—the chapbook published in 1587 by the Frankfurt printer Johann Spiess. This was Marlowe's source for the play *Doctor Faustus*, which he wrote two years later. Thomas, who associated sixteenth-century German with Luther, liked the language of the chapbook, and it encouraged him to equate Luther's devil with Mephistopheles. Wanting to connect the twentieth century with the sixteenth, he studied Luther's letters and reproductions of Dürer. He was glad to have a subject that took him back to Germany and back to the past. He didn't want to write about his immediate environment. Friendly though the Americans were, their country struck him as "unfriendly to humanity"–"it offers few arresting impressions. Somehow one must create from the past, from memories, pictures, intuitions."[16]

KNOWING HOW MUCH he'd benefited, ever since planning to settle in the States, from Agnes Meyer's patronage, he went on cultivating her friendship. In January 1943 he lavished high praise on *Britain's Home Front Compared with Ours,* the report she'd written after her transatlantic visit. Her essay, he said, must be counted among "the most informative and appealing writing available on the new England, shaped by the harsh hand of war."[17] In April, when she came to Pacific Palisades, he invited her to tea, took her out for a walk on the promenade, and had dinner with her.[18] But in early May she forwarded a vindictive letter written to her by a woman who lectured at Smith College. Attacking Klaus's treatment of Claudel in a book he'd written on Gide, it irrelevantly denounced Thomas's *Reflections* and his "sinecure" at the Library of Congress.

Irritated that she'd passed on this letter, he wrote to her in a sharper tone than usual.[19] On May 19 he received an "infuriatingly stupid letter from the Meyer, to which I do not propose to write a hasty reply."[20] The next day he was still so angry that he had to release the tension by drafting an answer, but he did so much redrafting that he didn't post it till May 26. He called it a "letter of separation," and before posting it he consulted Katia, who wholeheartedly approved.[21] The letter defended Erika, who'd braved the Blitz in London and hadn't been making a nuisance of herself. "I have suffered a great deal and for a long time at your showing nothing but unconcealed disapproval and rejection towards my children."

As an exile from Germany he'd preserved an awkward silence for three years before speaking out against the Nazis; his friendship with Agnes Meyer had lasted for six years before he gave her any intentional sign of his misgivings:

At my writing table for years I have dedicated more thought, nervous energy and work to it than to any other relationship in the world. I have done my best to let you participate in my inner and outer life, spent hours, when you were there, reading to you from new work unknown to anyone else, shown the most sincere admiration for your patriotic and social activities. Nothing I did was right, nothing was enough. In my letters there was "no trace"–I no longer know of what, probably humanity. You always wanted me to be different from what I am. You did not have the humour or respect or discretion to take me as I am. You wanted to educate, dominate, improve, convert me. In vain have I warned you in all kindness and delicacy that this was an attempt at the impossible, that after almost seventy years, my life was too firmly formed and established.22

She sent a conciliatory reply, "full of misunderstanding and stupidities. Danger that everything will again be as it was. But I do not want to have written my letter in vain, and must take care to achieve more relaxation and distance."23 "Politeness that says nothing is the only possibility."24 But the friendship continued, and he went on devoting a lot of time to their correspondence.

AT THE BEGINNING of May, after their mother, Gret, started doing war work in San Francisco, Frido and Toni came to stay with their grandparents. This was a strain for the sixty-year-old Katia, but Thomas, constantly delighted by Frido's presence, looked for a way of putting him into the *Faust* novel.25 He mentioned this to Bruno Walter, who said the Frido episode should be allegro moderato.26

Thomas's intention was to write a novel of between 250 and 300 pages.27 Before he started drafting it on May 23, just over two months after completing "The Tables of the Law," he'd accumulated over two hundred pages of jottings, and discussed the project with Bruno Frank, who liked the idea of dealing with the cultural crisis in terms of a pact with the Devil. As Thomas explained, the central character, the composer, Adrian Leverkühn, would be so desperate to find his way out of a creative block that he'd pay any price, and the nationalistic frenzy of Nazism would be paralleled by a euphoria that ended in collapse. The main story would be starkly serious, but Thomas, who'd developed a penchant for comedy,28 thought of using a narrator who was innocent, innocuous, and unsophisticated—perhaps a teacher.

Making the narrator start writing on the day he started writing himself—May 23, 1943—Thomas situates Professor Serenus Zeitblom inside Hitler's Germany. This has obvious advantages but involves such problems as finding the right level for his anti-Nazi feelings. He's made to say what Thomas had said in a broadcast to Germany—that the consequences of defeat would be less dangerous there than the consequences of victory. Zeitblom is also made to reflect sadly on public ceremonies, such as burning books, that fly in the face of modernity, harking back to superstitious medieval intolerance. Another problem is that Zeitblom's mind isn't sharp or ironic enough for some of the observations Thomas needs to channel through him. Even on matters of individual characterization, Thomas is naturally more satirical than his narrator, who would, for instance, have been more merciful and less amusing when dealing with the stammer of Kretzschmar, the organist who gives lectures on such subjects as why Beethoven never wrote a third movement for his Piano Sonata Opus 111. (This spelling of the name Kretzschmar will seem unfamiliar to readers of the translation by Helen Lowe-Porter, who drops the z, making the name less Nietzschean.)

Thomas used the word *montage* for his technique of blending fact with fiction and incorporating passages from a variety of literary sources, including the 1587 Faustbook. He introduces real people—some living, some dead—into the action, and, as usual, he models characters recognizably on people he knew. His victims included Hans Reisiger, Paul Ehrenberg, and Annette Kolb. The name Leverkühn is taken from Paul Leverkühn, one of Thomas's guardians after his father's death in 1891. In German the word has connotations with the idea of living boldly.

Adrian takes over some of Nietzsche's experiences in a Cologne brothel, and suffers from the same syphilitic disease (though Thomas was probably wrong to assume Nietzsche contracted it there). He borrows details of a diet from Nietzsche's letters, and borrows from them verbatim when describing symptoms of the disease. He appropriates Schoenberg's twelve-tone system, making Adrian into its inventor, and reproduces events from the life of Tchaikovsky, whose friend Madam von Meck appears as Madame de Tolna. If there was something shameless and predatory about the borrowing, he told himself it was part of a calculated effort to be diabolically outrageous.

While he'd concerned himself in *Buddenbrooks* with the decay of a family, the focus on decadence had progressively widened to take in the whole cultural and political ethos. If he'd always been fascinated by disease, using it partly as a metaphor, he was more ambitious than ever before in suggesting an equation between venereal disease and the fascism that seemed to be infecting the world. When he started the novel, he still believed the war would end in a Catholic-Fascist peace.

His use of music grows out of his lifelong passion for Wagner and out of the way he'd already used music. In *The Magic Mountain,* "Der Lindenbaum" from Schubert's *Die Winterreisse* is given a close relationship with death, but mostly he uses Wagnerian music. In *Buddenbrooks,* Hanno, as if playing a prelude for his own death, improvises in a frantic Tristanesque way. In the story "Tristan," Gabriele approximates even more closely to a musical suicide. Positive and negative feelings toward Wagner had battled in Thomas's mind for a long time. Visiting Bayreuth in October 1937, he'd found "elements of frightfulness and Hitlerishness clearly visible, if only latent and anticipatory"[29] (see page 436).

This association of Wagner with Hitler could have provided a starting point for a novel about music as the Dionysian catalyst in a political subversion of middle-class values. It would have been easy to connect Hitler with the diabolism integral to the Faustian quest for forbidden knowledge, and the central idea for the story was that ill-gotten inspiration should be carried ecstatically beyond itself. Thomas wanted the story to illuminate the desperate plight of modern art, and one question was whether a kind of private spiritual fascism was involved in throwing off the restraints inculcated by conventional education. The idea was so exciting that Thomas found himself soaring into a Faustian quest for musical knowledge that was out of his reach. Though he spent a lot of time listening to music, he didn't feel at home with contemporary works. When he went to concerts or played gramophone records, what he most enjoyed was Wagner, Beethoven, Schubert, Schumann, Mendelssohn, César Franck, Bizet, and other nineteenth-century Romantics. His enthusiasm for Pfitzner's music had been short-lived, and he derived relatively little pleasure from the work of Mahler, Debussy, Ravel, Stravinsky, and Bartók. He found Schoenberg, Webern, and Berg unappealing. In 1947, when he heard Schubert's Trio in B-flat Major, he thought about the fate of music since then—"a lost paradise,"[30] and in 1951 he wrote: "I am at home with the New Music only theoretically. I certainly do *know* something about it, but I cannot really enjoy it or love it. Indeed I have often declared that the triad world of the *Ring* is basically my musical home."[31]

Knowing little about atonalism, he could have settled on Richard Strauss as a composer who continued the Wagnerian tradition and came to terms with the Nazis, but Thomas had always wanted to extend his own education since he wrote novels that were partly about the process by which the hero was educated, and just as he'd gained knowledge while writing *The Magic Mountain* and the *Joseph* tetralogy by researching into unfamiliar areas, he now started informing himself about atonal music.

His mentor was the forty-year-old German musicologist Theodor Adorno, who'd been lecturing on philosophy at Frankfurt until the Nazis expelled him. His father was Jewish, and Adorno was the name of his mother, a singer, daughter of a French army officer. Theodor Adorno, who'd studied composition and piano in Vienna with Alban Berg, had been torn throughout his life between music and philosophy, performance and theory. On July 6 he lent Thomas a book by Julius Bahle, *Eingebung und Tat im musikalischen Schaffen. Ein Beitrag zur Psychologie der Entwicklungs und Schaffungsgesetze schöpferischer Menschen (Inspiration and Activity in Musical Composition: A Contribution to the Psychology of the Laws of Development and Composition in Creative Men)*. This interested Thomas less than the typescript of an unpublished book by

Adorno, *Zur Philosophie der modernen Musik*.[32] This made him feel as if he were coming up against his own ideas clothed in an unfamiliar musical terminology. Writing mainly about Schoenberg, Adorno attacked the consequences of constructivism. Even if rigorously rational analysis was illuminating to the composer, the effect on his music was devastating. Despite enlightened intentions, his compositions were thrown back into a quasi-mythological darkness. This idea seemed so relevant to a novel about cultural decadence that Thomas decided to make his hero compose Schoenbergian music. And, later on in July, he invited Adorno to be his "helper, adviser and participating instructor."

Adorno often called on Thomas, sometimes bringing his wife and his "ape-like dog."[33] Thomas warned him that some of the material he provided would reappear unaltered in the novel. "What belongs in my book must go into it, and will be absorbed."[34] Some of Adorno's ideas and ambivalences were eminently suitable for Kretzschmar, who had been similarly pinioned between music and theory.[35] Expropriating passages from Adorno's musical criticism produces few problems when they're being attributed to Leverkühn but they also influence Kretzschmar's discourses which are filtered through Zeitblom's narrative.

Schoenberg and Stravinsky were both living in California. Spending an evening with Schoenberg in May, Thomas questioned him about his work, and at the end of August spent two successive evenings with Schoenberg and Stravinsky. The Schoenbergs, who lived in Brentwood, were hospitable and provided good Viennese coffee, but their children were badly brought up; with Stravinsky, Thomas discussed Schoenberg.[36] Talking about his memories of the conversation, Stravinsky said that Thomas's "favourite theme was that music is the art most remote from life, the art that needs no *experience*." He remembered Thomas as "a professorial figure, with an erect, almost stiff-necked posture, characteristically, and with his left hand often in its coat pocket. . . . Mann was virtuous—i.e., courageous, patient, kind, sincere; I think he may have been a profound pessimist, too."[37]

Though Thomas was still collecting material when he started the draft on May 23, he had a much clearer idea of how to develop the novel than when he started *The Magic Mountain* or the *Joseph* tetralogy. The work on these had spanned eleven years and eighteen years, respectively. When he began *Doctor Faustus* he was hoping to finish it by the end of the war. (He didn't, but wrote the end within four years of writing the beginning.) He soon found he couldn't work as rapidly as he had with "The Tables of the Law." After about seventy pages he lost impetus,[38] and at the end of July started preparing a lecture for the tour that was to begin in mid-October. In July he claimed that with his right hand he was writing "a very strange novel—the German misery comes into it, too," while "with my left I indefatigably throw stones at Hitler's window."[39]

The lecture, he said, could hardly be called a lecture. "It's more like a high-minded chat about Germany, Wagner, Europe, the coming humanism, about the similarity between our fear of social change and the constant resistance of the ear to progress in music—and a lot else besides."[40] While it would be presumptuous, he said, for German refugees to advise the Allies on how to treat their defeated enemy, it was to be hoped that the mistakes of 1918 would be avoided. The ensuing disasters had been due partly to the weight of the burden inflicted on Germany, and now it wasn't the German people who should be punished but the combination of Junkers, army officers, and industrialists who had contributed so much to causing two world wars. Describing his lecture to Konrad Kellen, who'd left to join the army, Thomas conceded: "I often say frighteningly 'leftish' things, but hope to stop them from having any scandalous effect by covering them over with a lot of rather conservative and traditionalistic icing sugar."[41] Using a title he'd already used in 1940, he called the talk "The War and the Future."

Certainly the future would be different from what had been expected in 1940, when Hitler's armies seemed irresistible. In July 1943 the Germans were routed in the biggest tank battle of the war, in the cornfields around Kursk, south of Moscow. Since February the RAF had systematically bombed the European railway system, industrial plants on the Ruhr, and Berlin. In eight days of daylight raids on Hamburg at the end of July, ten thousand tons of bombs were dropped, and seven square miles of the city devastated. On July 21 a manifesto was published in *Pravda*, printed in German and Russian, calling on German soldiers and workers to choose between Germany and Hitler: They should mutiny and sabotage the war effort. The signatories included politicians, trade unionists, and writers.

In Hollywood, Bertolt Brecht took the initiative, convening a meeting on August 1 at the home of Austrian theatrical director Berthold Viertel and his socialite wife, Salka. Both Thomas and Heinrich attended, together with Lion Feuchtwanger, Bruno Frank, and Ludwig Marcuse, all bringing their wives. The women had coffee downstairs while the men worked in an upstairs bedroom, drafting a statement for the press. Thomas wanted to make no reference to *Pravda*, but he was outvoted. He then collaborated on a text that welcomed the manifesto and called on the German people to "force its oppressors to unconditional surrender and to fight for a vigorously democratic Germany." Thomas signed, but telephoned in the morning to withdraw his support. "The stubborn absurdity of these 'cultural ambassadors,' " fumed Brecht, "momentarily paralysed even me. . . . They agree with Goebbels's equation between Hitler and Germany."[42]

Thomas didn't equate Hitler with Germany but mistrusted the sudden patriotism in the "party-liners" who wanted to set up a Free Germany Committee, including prisoners of war and émigré German writers, and wanted him to preside over it. In his view it wasn't for the Germans to offer the Americans unsolicited advice on what to do with Germany when the war was over, and he suspected that the underlying desire of the Left-wingers was to Sovietize Germany.[43] If a politically neutral committee could be set up with the approval of the American authorities, he'd be willing to get involved, and before setting out on a two-month lecture tour that would take him to Washington, D.C., Massachusetts, New Hampshire, and Canada, he wrote to the undersecretary of state, Adolf Berle, suggesting that they should meet for a discussion in Washington at the end of November.[44]

When Agnes Meyer offered to translate the lecture he was to give in Washington, Thomas rashly agreed.[45] The "icing sugar" wasn't thick enough to stop her from finding some of his "leftish" points dangerously subversive, and she sent an "impudent and extremely annoying" letter.[46] In his conciliatory reply he said he had doubts himself about whether certain passages in the lecture were suitable for public statement.[47] When her translation arrived, it confirmed "how right I am not to take her seriously. A cross which should be carried on the left shoulder—when possible."[48] But he told her he'd been full of admiration and gratitude when reading her translation.[49]

After finishing the lecture, he resumed work on the novel, and by September 22, 109 pages of manuscript were in existence. As usual he read chapters to friends, and Bruno Frank was overwhelmingly enthusiastic, but Thomas found it hard to say anything positive when Frank read from his own work-in-progress. His narrative style was rather like Zeitblom's, but without the irony. "In matters of style," Thomas wrote, "I really admit nothing but parody now. Resemble Joyce in this."[50]

When he and Katia left Pacific Palisades, he carried the *Doctor Faustus* manuscript together with the lecture material in a briefcase he never entrusted to porters.[51] In Washington, he and Katia stayed with the Meyers, and he delivered the lecture at the Library of Congress on October 13. When he met Berle, the official reaction to proposals for the Free Germany Committee was so negative that Thomas decided to withdraw, though he knew this would alienate the activists, including Brecht and the theologian Paul Tillich.[52]

Thomas and Katia went on to New York, where he delivered the same lecture at Hunter College, and then to Boston, where he gave his talk on the *Joseph* novels. In Manchester, New Hampshire, he spoke on "The New Humanism." He then had to cross the Canadian border, and though he'd applied several weeks earlier for a reentry permit, it might not have arrived in time if Agnes Meyer hadn't exerted her influence. "The impression grows," he told her, "that you are running the country."[53]

He was delighted at the evidence of his popularity:

The excited inrush of audiences, the overcrowded halls, the sound-less attentiveness, the gratitude—it is all confusing and incomprehensible. In Montreal the police had to be called out because the crowd, which was too big, refused to give in and was threatening to break the doors in. In Boston about a thousand people had to be turned away. Each time I ask myself: "What do these people expect? I am certainly not Caruso! Will they not be utterly disappointed?" But they never are. They insist that it is the greatest thing they have ever heard. And they tell Katia: "You are a lucky woman." So it must probably all be true.[54]

Returning to Pacific Palisades after an absence of two months, he was captivated all over again by the blueness of the sky and the freshness of the ocean breeze. During the hour of traveling from the railway station to his house, he felt the same suspense as if he were about to arrive at a holiday resort. Among the mass of letters waiting was one from Brecht, who accused him of not believing in German democracy.[55] "If the Russians put Brecht in power in Germany, he would do everything he could to harm me," while Tillich had accused him of "passing the death sentence on Germany."[56] In reply to Brecht he argued that individuals all bear some responsibility for what their nation does, and that it would be premature to form a committee which might "be seen as nothing but a patriotic effort to shield Germany from the consequences of her misdeeds. . . . Let the military defeat of Germany be completed, let the time ripen when the Germans can settle accounts with the destroyers more thoroughly and more ruthlessly than the world would dare to expect from our unrevolutionary people."[57]

35

Incurable Fatherland

AT THE BEGINNING OF 1944, after living in the States for over five years, Thomas and Katia appeared before a tribunal in Los Angeles to answer questions about their application for U.S. citizenship. Knowing they'd need to seem well informed about the Constitution, Katia had done her homework, but Thomas was caught off guard when the lady in charge asked why there was both a House of Representatives and a Senate. When they were standing in front of the judge, she slipped him a copy of *Buddenbrooks* so that he could inscribe it for her, and the judge led them into an office where he asked for Thomas's autograph on a piece of paper.[1] They'd still have to wait at least another three months before they could take their oath as U.S. citizens.[2]

Their financial position improved when *Joseph the Provider* was chosen by the Book-of-the-Month Club. This would guarantee a large sale and at least an extra $25,000. Thomas, who'd been hesitating about whether he could afford a grand piano, decided to buy one.[3] He enjoyed having it, and sometimes when Wagner's music was played over the radio, he joined in on the piano.[4] But his stamina was beginning to flag. The turnover of correspondence was still enormous, and instead of writing in the mornings and dictating letters after lunch, he began to think of sacrificing a morning or two each week to letter-writing.[5] Much as he enjoyed living in Pacific Palisades, he was suffering from low blood pressure, and attributing this to the climate,[6] he thought he'd have been more prolific elsewhere. "One certainly has peace, but the climate is exhausting and soporific. A change of air at least once a year is quite indispensable."[7]

Another worry was that Agnes Meyer wanted to translate *Doctor Faustus*. He procrastinated, saying no decision needed to be taken yet, and that he'd instructed Knopf to make no premature arrangements with anyone else.[8] Luckily, after reading *Joseph the Provider*, she said she didn't feel competent to translate his work.[9] He wrote back agreeing that since she was doing so much war work, the novel was probably something that couldn't be translated "with the left hand."[10] When she met Golo in Washington, she told him his father despised her: It was obvious from his letters. Thomas was amused: "Since these letters are full of devotion, admiration, gratitude, concern, even gallantry, that is a very intelligent observation."[11]

But she was still eager to be useful. When Bruno Frank was too ill to write about *Joseph the Provider* in the bulletin circulated to Book-of-the-Month Club members, she took over the job, and sent Thomas a draft of what she'd written. Quite pleased with it, he briefed her in the way he'd once briefed Otto Grautoff, asking for more emphasis on his "sense of humour and for comicality," and on his gregariousness. "I *greatly* enjoy receiving visitors . . . am exceptionally partial to celebrations, birthdays, champagne, Christmas with children and grandchildren, evenings of reading to a circle of friends, love animals, am generally not without *warmth*."[12]

Always self-conscious, he'd found out from reading *Das Glasperlenspiel* (*The Glass Bead Game*)[13] what impression he'd made on Hermann Hesse. This 1943 novel is set during the remote future in a state that devotes itself to literature and the arts. It's governed by a quasi-monastic elite. The game symbolizes intellectual harmony, and one of its greatest players is Master Thomas von der Trave, who has a complete grasp of its subtlest problems. (The Trave is the river that runs through Lübeck to reach the sea at Travemünde.) A famous, widely traveled, cosmopolitan man, gracious and obliging toward everyone who approaches him, he does everything possible to stop the game from being debased. He's reputed to be a cold rationalist whose relation to the arts is one of remote civility, but he's never solemn, and never allows the game to be used for philosophizing. He has an ironic smile, a rather high-pitched, courteous voice, and his speech is carefully enunciated.

After a long period of assuming, nervously, that Hesse was involved in writing a novel similar to his own, Thomas was pleased to be unimpressed. "Much of it is broad and weak, undramatic, containing nothing of the man that is new."[14] He didn't write to Hesse until nearly a year later, when he pretended to love its "solemn playfulness" and to feel disconcerted by the depth of the affinity between him and Hesse. He signed himself "Thomas von der Trave."[15]

In January 1944 he'd been glad to read about himself in a book called *Stepping Stones to Peace* by Felix Langner, a Berlin writer who was living in England. "Idealists dream of Thomas Mann as the President of the second German Republic, a post which he himself would probably most decidedly refuse."[16] And it was even more gratifying when Franz Werfel, who'd had a severe heart attack and had read *Buddenbrooks* in bed, pronounced it "an immortal masterpiece, indestructible." It seemed strange, he said, to see the author really standing there, at the foot of his bed. He responded positively when Thomas read to him from *Doctor Faustus*, and he was particularly struck by Adrian's tendency to laugh at everything.[17] Thomas, who intended the laughter to indicate the Devil's presence, was pleased, but thought *Buddenbrooks* might be his only work destined for survival.[18]

If *Buddenbrooks* had been thoroughly German, *The Magic Mountain* had been European, and the *Joseph* novels had been "a mythical and humorous poem about humanity."[19] *Doctor Faustus* was distinctively German, but could he bring it off? Sometimes it seemed to be slipping out of his grasp. Perhaps he shouldn't have let it assume the same form and dimensions as *The Magic Mountain*.[20] Not that he was expecting it to be so long. With the chapter about Adrian's dismissal of the prostitute's warning that she could infect him, Thomas had completed 250 pages of manuscript, and thought this was half the novel. In fact it was less than a third.

In April the manifesto of the Council for a Democratic Germany was being sent to potential signatories and to American sympathizers. It recommended that Germany shouldn't be divided into sectors after the war, and that her productivity should be maintained on a high level. After wondering whether he shouldn't, after all, sign,[21] Thomas decided not to.[22] But when asked to make a public statement condemning the council and its manifesto, he refused, pointing out that the signatories included his brother Heinrich and many other liberal intellectuals he respected.[23]

A week later, on June 6, 1944, he celebrated his sixty-ninth birthday, which coincided with the long-awaited invasion of Europe, launched under the command of General Dwight Eisenhower. All through the night, German batteries along the Normandy coast were attacked from the air, as were railways, bridges, and radar stations. In the morning, British and American troops landed at twelve points along a hundred miles of coastline. While Thomas was inspecting his presents from Katia—an armchair for the bedroom, a nightshirt, gramophone records, soap, sweets—Agnes Meyer rang up to pass on some news she'd had from the War Department about coordinated action by the Russians.[24] But neither the news nor visitors bringing flowers, books, cigars, and champagne stopped Thomas from doing a stint of work on the novel.

Seventeen days later, he and Katia had another cause for celebration: On June 23, after more than twelve years of living in exile, they became U.S. citizens. They had an early breakfast and drove to Los Angeles, where they were ushered into a crowded hall. The judge who appeared on the platform sat down to make a patriotic speech. Thomas and Katia took the oath jointly and signed their citizenship papers separately.[25]

Within six days of the invasion, the Allies had linked up their beachheads to form a continuous front. In response, the Germans launched a new Blitz on London, attacking the city in mid-June with flying bombs—pilotless jet-propelled planes that could fly at four hundred miles an hour, carrying almost a ton of high explosives. Antiaircraft guns were ineffectual against them, and Londoners in crowded streets were terrorized by the whine of the rocket engines, followed by a fifteen-second silence that meant the "doodlebug" was about to hit the ground. In Germany the new weapon was called the V-1, which implied that more unpleasant surprises were in store.

In France, to avenge the killing of an S.S. officer, German troops destroyed an entire village, Oradour-sur-Glane, sixteen miles from Limoges. Seven of the seven hundred inhabitants survived the shooting and the fires that were started after the church and houses had been drenched in kerosene and gasoline. By July, Thomas was less conciliatory toward Germany than when he wrote "What Is German?" in May.[26] What should be done to a people that had gassed 1.7 million Jews since 1942? "It should be rendered powerless. It should live, and its inherent goodness and greatness be allowed to develop. But it was not born for power, and should have no more."[27] It should also be reduced in size, he thought.[28]

Some of his opinions could be expressed through Zeitblom, but Thomas wasn't focusing on current events: His intention was to counterpoint the nemesis overtaking Germany with the encroachment of disease in Adrian. Chapter 21, which was written in July 1944, features landings in Sicily during August 1943. Zeitblom is proud of the new torpedoes constructed by German engineers, and the sinking of two big passenger ships by submarines. But he knows Germany can't win the war.

> Our increasingly tragic and heroic disposition seems no longer to let us give up a lost cause before the unthinkable becomes a reality. . . . The war is lost, but that means more than a lost campaign, it really means that we are lost—lost are our possessions and our soul, our faith and our history. It is all up with Germany, it will be all up with her, there are signs of an unmentionable collapse, economic, political, moral and spiritual, in short all embracing. I would not like to have wished for it—what is impending—for it is despair, madness.[29]

Thomas had heard the rumor that Göring was suffering from a kind of dementia that made him want to live like Nero, dressed in a toga, dishing out sweetmeats and distributing jewels to guests at his parties.[30]

In Chapter 17, Zeitblom speculates about Adrian's sexual abstinence. Like Joseph, and like Thomas himself, Adrian is a "late developer" or at least goes through a protracted period of youthful chastity. Not long after his sixty-ninth birthday, expecting to die at the same age as his mother, seventy-one, Thomas began to destroy his earlier diaries.[31] It's understandable that he wouldn't have liked anyone else to read diary jottings about masturbation and involvements with young men, but he was destroying material he might have found useful while he was writing about Adrian's early life. It's possible that the novel embarrassed him by making him recall sacrifices he'd made for the sake of art or success.

In a January letter he had scoffed at the French notion that a night of love was the ideal preliminary for a work of art. "It's better in Turgenev's *A Nest of Noblemen*, where a poor German musician composes his beautiful melody as a substitute for the night of love granted to someone else."[32] Thomas, who never spent a night with any of the men who attracted him, questioned himself compulsively and repeatedly—even in the diaries he allowed to survive—about whether the sacrifice had been worthwhile. Had he lived life to the full? Had he been happy? He tries to reassure himself with memories of kissing this or that young man on the lips. It's possible that what he wanted to destroy was not the evidence of the kisses but the uncertainty about whether they added up to anything significant.

"Erotic nights" and "sexual onsets," as he called them, were less likely to interfere with the routine of hard work when no partner was involved in them, but Thomas was in an artificial situation, producing literature for a culture that had no visible future. Zeitblom is characterized as a liberal humanist, but whereas the humanist in *Reflections* was condemned for feeling better disposed toward European civilization than German culture, Zeitblom can no longer believe culture will survive, and Thomas shared his lack of faith in its future. He was also writing German in an English-speaking country. But awkward though it was to have no direct contact with his readers, it would have been worse in 1944 to be in Germany.

Though he had only limited faith in the talents of Helen Lowe-Porter—when Alfred Knopf commissioned her to translate *Doctor Faustus*, he said: "She wants the pocket-money, Tommy"—Thomas was grateful to have such a wide circulation for his books. Thanks mainly to the Book-of-the-Month Club, twenty thousand copies of *Joseph the Provider* were sold by mid-July,[33] and thirty thousand by the end of November.[34] But he claimed to take more pleasure in a few hundred sales of the German edition, published by Bermann Fischer in Sweden. "Only in the original is the book what it is."[35]

With *Doctor Faustus* he spurred himself on in his usual way, collecting feedback from family and friends by giving readings. His viola-playing son, Michael, was impressed by the reality of the music in the novel,[36] and Heinrich was reduced to tears when Thomas read the sequence about Beethoven's Piano Sonata Opus 111.[37] Sometimes ideas he took from Adorno were hard to integrate,[38] but he made good headway, relentlessly ignoring rheumatic pains during the last week of October. At first the pains seemed to be centering around his liver, and by the last week in October they'd spread into his back. He was also suf-

fering from a cold, and his cough kept him awake at night. In spite of
a painkiller, Empirin, the teeth on the right-hand side of his mouth began to ache, but on Sunday, October 29, he kept the promise he'd
made to the local Democratic party organization. He went to a garden
party in Bel Air, where he made an election speech for Roosevelt, who
was running for a fourth term of office.

Though it was cold and foggy, hundreds of chairs had been set out
on the lawn, but when Thomas arrived with Katia and Elisabeth, only
about two hundred people had shown up. The other performers included a conjurer who made the implausible claim that he was Spanish
and had learned his art from a Chinese sage called Rosenthal. Finding
he had to follow a sixteen-year-old ventriloquist who chatted with a
popeyed doll on her lap, Thomas thought his speech was going to be
too serious, but it went down well, and a great deal of money was collected.[39]

He felt exhausted the next day, and on Tuesday evening, when he
was at a party, a severe headache came on. In the morning, too weak to
get up, he found he had a high temperature. All the symptoms of the
previous week had culminated in a flu that attacked his stomach and intestines. He had to stay in bed for a week, attended by his doctor and
feeling too poorly to eat solid food or write his diary. He got up in time
to vote on November 7, when Roosevelt was reelected, but his weight
had gone down by fourteen pounds and he still had neuralgic facial
pains, centering in his mouth. Neither Empirin nor codeine relieved
them. He'd been given small heating pads of flaxseed to put in his
mouth, and these were helpful at first, but he applied them so desperately that he burned the inside of his mouth.[40]

He was committed to another lecture tour on the East Coast, including an appearance at the Library of Congress. The title was still unsettled, but his intention was to talk about Germany and the Germans. He
started reading sixteenth-century German history and making notes,
but felt so weak he didn't want to go on the tour and didn't think he
could finish the novel. On the morning of November 16 he was still
suffering from neuralgic toothache and still making notes for the lecture; after consultations with his dentist and with Katia, he decided to
cancel the tour and resume work on the novel. "Uneasiness about this
work, which must be finished somehow or other, is another reason for
not letting it be postponed by protracted work on the lecture and the
tour." Though he felt as if he were playing truant from school, he'd
have been playing truant from *Doctor Faustus*, he told himself, if he'd
gone on the tour.[41] By November 19, no longer in pain, he could use
his teeth and work on the novel.[42]

*   *   *

ONE OF ZEITBLOM'S FUNCTIONS in the story is to act as a positive foil for Adrian's negativism. The professor feels uneasy at his friend's love of laughter, which, he decides, has something unhealthy and orgiastic about it. Zeitblom remembers the story Adrian cites from St. Augustine's *De civitate Dei*—that the only man who laughed when he was born was Ham, son of Noah and father of Zoroaster. Adrian later admits he was trying to escape from "this exaggerated feeling for comedy" when he committed himself to theology—only "to find a host of frightful absurdities in it. Why must almost everything strike me as its own parody? Why must I take the view that almost all, no, all the methods and conventions of today's art are fit only for parody?"[43] This was what Thomas had asked himself when comparing his work with that of Bruno Frank, and it was convenient to have Adrian's music as a stalking-horse for investigating his addiction to parody. The problem of needing it was inseparable from the problem of whether art had reached a terminal phase. Reading Harry Levin's book on James Joyce, Thomas had been struck by the two sentences: "As his subject matter reveals the decomposition of the middle class, Joyce's technique passes beyond the limits of English realistic fiction. Neither *A Portrait of the Artist* nor *Finnegans Wake* is a novel, strictly speaking, and *Ulysses* is a novel to end all novels." Joyce, Levin argued, had enormously increased the difficulties of being a novelist. Asking whether the novel hadn't outlived its function since Flaubert and James, T. S. Eliot had suggested that *Ulysses* was an epic, and Levin said: "The best writing of our contemporaries is not an act of creation, but an act of evocation, peculiarly saturated with memories."[44] *Doctor Faustus* could be described as an act of self-criticism peculiarly saturated with memories.

Thomas still hadn't shaken himself free of the self-doubt left over from accusations of emotional coldness. In a confessional letter to Kretzschmar, Adrian calls himself a lost soul, a black sheep. He lacks emotional warmth. He subjugated himself to theology out of contrition, wanting to overcome his cold contumacy. He's unsociable because he's incapable of loving, and this will prevent him from becoming a good artist.[45] The need to laugh comes from the inability to love, and the need to parody from the incapacity for commitment. In Palestrina, unable to share Zeitblom's enthusiasm for the landscape, just as Thomas had been unable to share Heinrich's, Adrian smiles ironically at his friend's raptures,[46] and he dislikes physical contact. "He was in the real sense of the word a man of 'disinclination', of evasion, of reserve, of distance. Physical cordialities seemed quite incompatible with his nature; even his handshake was rare and performed with a certain haste." Yet Thomas loved Adrian more than any other character he'd created. "I have never loved an imagination so much—not Goethe's, not

Castorp's, not Thomas Buddenbrook's, not Joseph's or Aschenbach's. I am filled with an admiring and passionate tenderness for him."[47]

EIGHT DAYS BEFORE CHRISTMAS the prospects of a peaceful end to the year were shattered when Heinrich rang up to say Nelly had killed herself with sleeping tablets. She had made four previous suicide attempts. For years she'd been drinking heavily, and her behavior had become increasingly outrageous. Invited to a dinner party by Heinrich, Ludwig Marcuse was disconcerted when she opened the front door stark naked, and during the meal she kept repeating: "Oh, I've got such an old husband," until Heinrich went up to his room and the guests left.[48] Heinrich, who was seventy-three, had spent two years on a memoir he couldn't sell, and to earn money, Nelly had worked as a nurse in a hospital. "It overtaxes her," Heinrich wrote two days before her death, "and shames me. What can I do?"[49]

Thomas and Katia weren't unhappy at the news of her death, which, according to Golo, they called "a blessing."[50] They gave Heinrich a check for the funeral expenses, and invited him to stay with them as soon as the Borgeses left.[51] At the funeral on December 20 he was in tears. Thomas brought him home, gave him lunch, made him rest on the sofa in the living room, and, after they'd had tea with the Borgeses, gave him wine, groceries, money to redeem the furniture he'd pawned, and a copy of "The Tables of the Law" as a Christmas present.[52] A couple of weeks later, writing to Agnes Meyer, Thomas said: "My brother, who has (fortunately) lost his wife, will now be coming to us for a few weeks. It was high time that this union was dissolved through death. It was ruinous, and we shall have a lot of rebuilding to do."[53]

FOR MONTHS THE PHRASE "retreat to more favorable positions" had been recurring in German news bulletins, but in December, when Eisenhower left the central sector of his Belgian front weakly defended, German troops under Marshal von Rundstedt advanced through the Ardennes forest as they had in 1940. Taking advantage of fog and cloud that made them invulnerable to attack from the air, they advanced about sixty miles before the weather cleared. With Strasbourg and even Paris threatened, it suddenly looked as if the war could go on for a long time. "The Germans," Thomas wrote, "seem to have imitated the Russians, who also knew how to feign impotence."[54] But he was glad to hear from Erika, who'd been in Aachen as an interpreter for the advancing Allied forces, that she'd found a copy of *Buddenbrooks* in almost every household she'd visited.[55]

Asked to resume the broadcasts, which had stopped in May, before the invasion, Thomas spoke to the Germans again on New Year's Day 1945. By then their offensive in the Ardennes had been broken: Heavy bombers had gone into action against von Rundstedt's troops, cutting off their supply lines.

Though neither good news nor bad could deflect Thomas from his literary task, the dialogue between Adrian and the Devil would have been different if he'd written it when he wasn't listening to German newsreaders and their rhetoric about "the holy struggle for freedom against the soulless hordes." Mephistophelian propaganda doesn't become innocuous when Adrian sees it for what it is: The danger lies in affinities it has with what he wants to believe. In November, Goebbels had said the Germans didn't believe themselves to have been elevated above other peoples, but if they could survive when the whole world was attacking them, there must be something special about them. "We firmly believe the German nation has been designated for a great future, for itself but also for other peoples, and that it must prove itself in this war." After reading the reprint of this speech in *Reich*, Thomas noticed the similarity to the arguments in his *Reflections*: "Roughly how I was writing 30 years ago."[56]

Zeitblom, we're told, is merely transcribing Adrian's transcript of his conversation with the Devil. This leaves us free to assume that the Devil exists only in Adrian's diseased imagination, and while previous versions of the story had made the Devil materialize when Faust was at a turning point in his life, Adrian is merely taken farther along a route he has already chosen—or which was chosen for him by a combination of talent and temperament. This is the only way out of the impasse. Goethe's Faust is frustrated because he needs knowledge that has nothing to do with scholarship; Adrian's frustration centers on artistic creativity, and the novel fuses the problems of his personality with the general predicament of the mid-twentieth-century artist.

Thomas is partly writing about his own limitations, his dryness, his compulsive irony, his self-consciousness, his lack of spontaneity, but these limitations are presented as the essential qualities of the artist who can make revolutionary progress during the current crisis of the arts. Thomas is thinking partly of Eliot and Levin, partly of Adorno and his other musical mentors, when he makes the Devil say creativity is drying up.

> All the serious undertakings that are put down on paper show strain and distaste. External, social grounds? Lack of demand? . . . Composition itself has become too difficult, desperately difficult. When work no longer accommodates authenticity, how can one work? But that's how it is, my friend. The masterpiece, the self-sufficient form belongs to traditional art; liberated art rejects it. . . . All the better

composers carry within themselves a canon of what is forbidden, the self-forbidding, which gradually comes to include the possibilities of tonality, and therefore all traditional music. The canon determines what is false, what has become a worn-out cliché. . . . Art becomes criticism—something very honourable, who denies it? . . . The historical movement of the musical material has turned against the self-contained work. It shrinks in time, it disdains extension in time, which constitutes the space of the musical work, letting it stand empty. Work, time and illusion, they are the same, and together they are undercut by criticism. It no longer tolerates illusion and play, fiction, the autocracy of form, which imposes censorship on passions and human suffering, distributes roles, translates into pictures. Now only the nonfictional is admissible, the undramatised, undisguised and untransformed expression of current suffering.

Adrian's response is that the man who knows all this can find freedom beyond criticism by playing with forms that are no longer valid. "I know, I know," says the Devil. "Parody. It could be amusing if it weren't so melancholy in its aristocratic nihilism."[57] The conversation taking place is partly a parody of arguments between good and evil figures in moral allegories and partly a pastiche: Peppered with archaisms, it slips in and out of a style that evokes sixteenth-century German.

What Adrian wants is to escape from intellectual detachment into adventurously committed passion. In his masterpiece, written with the help of disease and the Devil, he will achieve a strictness of form that can be called totalitarian. Not a single note is free. At last he has been cured of his addiction to parody. Zeitblom interprets the achievement in religious terms, but the perspective that has been created is political. What was intended to be the scene of crucial negotiation with the Devil—Thomas thought he was two thirds of the way through the narrative[58]—was written when it looked as if Nazi totalitarianism might not, after all, have been defeated. Was Hitler on the point of using poison gas?[59]

When the concentration camp at Auschwitz was captured at the end of January 1945 by the Red Army, only about five thousand prisoners were still alive, among mounds of emaciated corpses. There are no direct references to the camps in the chapter, but the Devil promises Adrian that he will strike up the march of the future, will break through the paralyzing difficulties of the period, will dare to be barbaric, superseding the humane and all bourgeois refinement.

When Thomas read the beginning of this conversation with the Devil and the account of Hell to Franz Werfel, he was told he'd never written anything better.[60] He knew these were good, but felt unable to raise the middle stretches of the dialogue to the same level: He was too exhausted by all the other work he had to do—carrying on his massive correspondence, preparing broadcasts and after-dinner speeches.[61] The account of Hell would have been inconceivable, he said, without the psychological experience of Gestapo cellars.[62] Reluctant to discuss Hell, the Devil says it can't be described

> because there are no words to cover the real thing, one can use and make up many words, but they are only representative, standing for names that do not exist, cannot claim to describe what can never be described or denounced in words. That is the secret luxury and security of hells, that they are not denouncable, that they are hidden from speech, that they merely are, but do not appear in newspapers, do not become public, cannot be brought by words to critical knowledge, so that even such words as "underground", "cellar", "thick walls", "soundproof", "oblivion", "impregnable" are feeble symbols. One must be satisfied with symbols, my good man, when speaking of hells for there everything comes to an end—not just the descriptive word but absolutely everything—that is their main characteristic and that is what has to be said first, what strikes the newcomer, and what he cannot grasp and does not want to comprehend with his so-to-speak sound senses, because intelligence or some limitation of understanding prevents him, in short, because it is unbelievable, so unbelievable that one's face goes white, unbelievable, although it is immediately apparent on arrival that here everything comes to an end—mercy, grace, consideration, every last trace of regard for the reproachful, incredulous objection: "This can simply not be done to a soul." It is done, it happens, and without any words of reckoning, in inaccessible cellars, a long way outside God's earshot, and to all eternity.[63]

Thomas says that no one who'd understood the nature of Fascist totalitarianism could be surprised or incredulous at the horrors revealed when the war ended. This may have helped him to give the Devil a matter-of-fact tone in speaking about the unspeakable.

Finishing the chapter on February 20, he put the novel aside to start working—three months in advance—on the lecture for the Library of Congress titled "Germany and the Germans." Drafting it between February 27 and March 18, he knew the war would either be over by the end of May, or nearly over. But how much of Germany would be left? "The Nazis have ensured that the body of the Reich will not be rescued alive; it can only fall apart, piece by piece."[64] The Allies were insisting on unconditional surrender, but promising that Germany wouldn't be destroyed.[65]

She would, inevitably, be disarmed and humiliated, but many options would be open to the victorious Allies, and some émigrés had made themselves into apologists for their nation, talking as if Nazism had been imposed from outside. Thomas believed, on the contrary, it had deep roots in German history and the German character. "There are not two Germanies, a bad one and a good one, but only one, in which the best qualities had been corrupted with diabolical cunning into evil. . . . The evil Germany is the good one in misfortune and guilt, the good Germany perverted and overthrown." The people couldn't shrug off responsibility for what had happened since 1933. From the outset, opponents of Nazism had been pitting themselves "against the sum total of German inventiveness, courage, intelligence, obedience, military efficiency—in short against the whole strength of the German people, which stood, as such, behind the regime and fought its battles." The war hadn't been "against Hitler and Himmler, who would have been nothing at all unless German manpower and blind loyalty had been fighting until this very day with leonine courage for these villains."[66]

Thomas was only stating the obvious, but to state it unequivocally was to invite the hostility of all the Germans who'd stayed in Germany and many who hadn't. "The German people, the German character, German psychology should have nothing whatever to do with Nazism. Anyone who knows this to be untrue is treacherous and disloyal. Everybody falls on him with screams of rage because he is endangering the emergence of a strong, centralistic, democratic Reich which could within a short period have Europe in its pocket."[67]

Formulating a statement that would be quoted all over the world, Thomas was putting himself under strain, and he was in poor physical condition. Nearly seventy, he claimed to look fifty-five, while his doctor told him that since biological age was different from chronological age, he shouldn't give way to imaginary weaknesses.[68] But he hadn't regained the weight he'd lost in November, and he often felt unsteady on his feet. Sometimes he thought of himself as a nervous old man, and he knew he needed a long rest, which he couldn't take.[69]

The only solution to his protracted dental problems was to have all his teeth out, and in January he overcame his reluctance. He knew he'd have to live for some time on liquid food, and suffer discomfort, inconvenience, and embarrassment, in between painful, time-taking visits to the dentist, but he needed to accustom himself to the prosthesis by May, when he was leaving for the East Coast.[70] Before the extractions on February 12, he felt nervous all day, but while he was in the dentist's chair, he "withstood everything with a certain cheerfulness, tolerating the horror, if not overcoming it."[71] While his gums were healing, his doctor started him on a course of hormone injections, which lowered his blood pressure and heightened his sexual drive. He discussed this with the doctor, who asked whether he gave way to it and recommended that he should. "Has his sense of humour."[72]

On March 20, Thomas settled down to the novel again, drawing up a chronology for the rest of the action. This caused him a lot of trouble, which he playfully parallels in the narrative: Adrian has trouble with a composition after neglecting for extended stretches to put in the time markings. Though Adrian is to die before 1939, Zeitblom comments on the progress of the war, and this chapter is set in April 1944, when the Allies haven't yet landed in Normandy. The Russians have recaptured Odessa but failed, he says, to "disorganise our retreat." Meanwhile, thousands of British and American aircraft are "darkening the skies" above "Fortress Europa," and it isn't just Germany but the world that is sustaining a heavy loss in the destruction of "educational and literary property" during raids on such cities as Leipzig. The prominence of public events in the novel corresponds to Thomas's change of attitude. When he wrote *Buddenbrooks*, he was still an unpolitical man, but now he maintained: "[N]othing that is living can sidestep politics. Even a rejection of politics is political: it merely connives at the politics of evil."[73]

Thomas had only just started drafting the new chapter when Roosevelt died on April 12, two months after he met Churchill and Stalin at Yalta to discuss the division of Germany into zones and the future of Central and Eastern Europe. He was sixty-three. On April 13, Thomas couldn't work, and couldn't write more than two lines in his diary. He felt moved when Eleanor Roosevelt said: "I am sadder for our people and for humanity than for ourselves."[74] An epoch had just ended, or so it seemed to Thomas: "Humanity has lost a powerful friend, and so have I. The America to which I came will no longer be there. He lifted his country above its level, and there is a certain impatience for the day when it can sink back to where it was. How his absence will be felt as a mediator between Stalin and Churchill, between revolution and Toryism. He was a born mediator. . . . We shall never see his like again."[75] Two weeks later, Thomas still hadn't recovered from the shock: "One feels orphaned and abandoned."[76] In fact, Roosevelt had given the impression at Yalta of being more concerned about defeating Japan than about the European settlement, and this had helped Stalin, who was already in a strong bargaining position, to prepare the ground for establishing Soviet supremacy over Eastern Europe.

Hitler spent the last days of April in a subterranean fortress under the Chancellery, ranting about the incompetence of his generals and the cowardice of those who'd been fighting for him. In his suicide note, which accused both Germans and Jews of failing to help him in his struggle against Bolshevism, he appointed Admiral Karl Dönitz as his successor. On May 1, when Thomas received a telegram from a New York paper asking whether he thought Hitler was really dead, he cabled back: "Who cares?"[77]

Six days later, when Germany surrendered unconditionally, he attributed the Allies' victory mainly to Roosevelt.[78] "It is not exactly elation that I feel," Thomas wrote. Satisfaction was undermined by the ambivalence that was inescapable for the German refugee, and by the "envious hatred" of people attacking him for his insistence on the guilt of the German people.[79] In his first broadcast, Dönitz said that justice must once again reign, and that the objective must be to overcome the hatred that surrounded Germany. She must rejoin the European family of nations. But he neither repudiated Nazism nor admitted any guilt.[80] Thomas shed tears over the destruction of Dresden but "over nothing else," though "this catastrophe affects *everything* German, German history, the German mind."[81]

For fifteen years he'd been waiting for the defeat of Nazism, but now it had come, he could take little pleasure in it. Klaus, who was in Munich as a correspondent for the American army paper *Stars and Stripes*, reported that though the house in the Poschingerstrasse was still standing, it had been gutted. Furniture, books, pictures, and ornaments had all been auctioned. The house had been used for a time as a home for "Hitler brides"—unmarried girls impregnated to produce healthy Aryan children who'd be dedicated to the Führer—and Himmler had lived in it for a time.[82] It was now occupied by refugees and people who'd been bombed out. The other house, in Nidden, had been used by Göring, who transformed it beyond recognition. It was elaborately decorated and furnished, surrounded by paved walks, stables, and servants' quarters.[83]

During May, Thomas's doctor prescribed vitamins and arsenates that failed to make him feel better, yet a series of medical check-ups and X-rays produced no explanation of why he was so listless and exhausted. Taking his daily walk, he'd often need to sit down by the side of the road and wait for the car to pick him up.[84] "I am worried about the condition of my head and my nerves. Everybody tells me I have got thinner. If only I could put on weight, I would not feel so unsteady on my feet."[85] This was written on May 18, three weeks before his seventieth birthday and a week before he had to leave for the East Coast.

After two nights on the train, he and Katia spent a day in Chicago, where Erika met them, and they all stayed with the Borgeses. When Thomas rehearsed his lecture, the audience of four expressed approval, but it was too long, and on the train to Washington, Erika helped him cut it.[86] When he delivered it in the Library of Congress on May 29, the hall was packed and, as usual, the overflow audience listened over loudspeakers without seeing him.

The Manns were staying with the Meyers, who threw a party after the lecture for about fifty people, including the Biddles and Walter Lippmann, who later because editor of the *New York Herald Tribune*. He agreed enthusiastically with Thomas's line of argument, and the evening went well, in spite of the tantrum thrown by Borgese, who was furious that *Die Neue Rundschau*, which had been resurrected in time to honor Thomas's seventieth birthday, had appeared without an article he'd written. It contained tributes by Heinrich, Klaus, Erika, W. H. Auden, Hedwig Fischer, Erich von Kahler, Bruno Walter, Agnes Meyer, and Alfred Neumann.[87] Borgese's typescript had arrived in Stockholm too late.

In Heinrich's tribute, "Mein Bruder," bitterness and envy were thinly disguised, but there was enough affection, "honourable naivety and pride in the family" for Thomas to say he'd been moved to tears.[88] He was pleased with the "love-letter" from Erika in *Aufbau*, which was published in New York.[89] For her, she said, his face had never changed—"the light, attentive eyes under the dark, jagged brows, one of which you like to raise, thoughtful or surprised; the straight, prominent nose, inherited by all your sons and a boon to your caricaturists; the long upper lip with the correctly styled moustache and the long oval chin." Nor had his voice changed. "You only need to read aloud, sitting under the lamp near the desk in the darkened study . . . you only need to read like that, dearest, to make time and place fade into reverie."[90]

On June 3, he and Katia left for New York, where he was to deliver the lecture at Hunter College. The city was sweltering under a heat wave. They again stayed at the Hotel St. Regis, and on his birthday the living room in their suite looked like a flower show. There were heaps of letters and telegrams from all over the world. Alfred Knopf threw a birthday lunch for him and presented him with a large golden cigarette box; Katia gave him a gold fountain pen and mechanical pencil. In the evening, after dinner at Bruno Walter's house, their host accompanied Bronislaw Huberman in a private performance of violin sonatas by Mozart. Handling Huberman's bow, Thomas found it surprisingly heavy. Bruno Walter laughed. "The lightness is in him, not the bow."[91]

"Brouhaha" was the word Thomas used in more than one letter to describe the celebrations laid on for his birthday, but, as he had to admit, this was what he'd wanted, even if he sometimes made out that he didn't.[92] On June 14 he and Katia set out from Grand Central Station on a train overcrowded with soldiers and sailors. The Manns were going to stay by Lake Mohawk in the foothills of the Catskill Mountains. At the Quaker hotel there was no room service and no alcohol, while no cars were allowed inside the grounds, which were quaintly sprinkled with turrets and little bridges. But the surrounding landscape was beautiful, and Thomas enjoyed the spring water, the chamber music in the lounge, the movies shown on the spacious terrace (including *Casanova Brown*, with Gary Cooper), and the walks he and Katia took in galoshes on the shores of the lake.

Over thirty years after staring lovingly at the ten-year-old Wladislaw Moes in the hotel on the Lido, Thomas stared lovingly at a sixteen-year-old American girl, Cynthia, who was walking around with a copy of *The Magic Mountain*. She was visibly excited when, at a musical evening, her mother accosted the author to ask whether she could introduce her daughter. Cynthia had no idea how much he was enjoying the talks they had in the lounge and on the decklike balcony that ran around the building. Before he left on June 24, he told her: "It was always so pleasant to look at you." "Oh," she answered, "really?" She hid when they were going, but watched to see whether he was looking for her.[93]

The next day, over lunch with Agnes Meyer in the uncomfortable heat of New York, he said nothing about the "incomparably preferable little Cynthia."[94] A dinner for about six hundred people was given in his honor at the Waldorf-Astoria by the *Nation* associates. The after-dinner speakers included the secretary of state for the interior and a Supreme Court judge. Thomas had to drink cocktails with the guests of honor before the meal, pose for photographs, make a speech, and then go by taxi to Columbia Broadcasting, where he repeated the speech in a shortened form. But all through the evening, as he said, quoting *Hamlet*, the thought of Cynthia "sat smiling to my heart."[95]

Four weeks later he dreamed he was engaged to a young woman who gave him a red-and-white-striped deck chair, which he took as an allusion to his age. He attributed the dream partly to the hormone treatment, partly to "the Cynthia experience," partly to a meeting the previous day with a charming young male student, and partly to a film he'd seen in the evening with an attractive actress and a leading actor who was neither young nor good-looking.[96]

Come Like a Good Doctor

IT'S IMPOSSIBLE, Thomas said, to joke about either Dostoyevsky or Nietzsche, but that doesn't explain why he'd written about neither, except insofar as he was writing about Nietzsche in *Doctor Faustus*. After agreeing to introduce an American edition of six stories by Dostoyevsky,[1] he found he was simultaneously discussing Nietzsche and a theme that was central to *Doctor Faustus*, as it had been to much of his previous work—the relationship between disease and creativity.

Like some of his characters—Prince Myshkin in *The Idiot* and Kirilov in *The Demons*—Dostoyevsky suffered from epilepsy, which Freud described as the "uncanny disease with its apparently unprovoked convulsive attacks, its changing of the character into irritability and aggressiveness, and its progressive lowering of all the mental faculties."[2] The earliest physicians characterized the sexual climax as a minor epilepsy, which means, as Freud says, that they "recognised in the sexual act a mitigation and adaptation of the epileptic method of discharging stimuli."[3] He viewed Dostoyevsky's epilepsy as a symptom of his neurosis. The boyhood onset of the disturbance came in the form of severe melancholy, as if he were about to die on the spot. A precondition of the neurosis was his innate bisexual disposition, and Freud associates the epilepsy with the guilt that ensued on "defending himself with great intensity against dependence on an exceptionally strong father." Dostoyevsky told his friend Strakhov that irritability and depression after an epileptic attack were bound up with his sense of being a criminal. He couldn't rid himself of the conviction that he'd committed some great misdeed.

He had what Thomas called the face of a criminal saint. Nietzsche, who'd used the phrase "On the Pale Criminal" as a title for one of the sections in *Zarathustra*, regarded Dostoyevsky as the most profound psychologist in world literature. Clearly, his ability to plumb the Satanic depths and to suggest secret guilt was rooted in his disease. Without disease, madness, intellectual curiosity that verges on criminality, certain spiritual and mental achievements would have been out of reach, and in Dostoyevsky, as in Nietzsche, who said he never felt happier with himself than in the periods of the greatest pain,[4] disease had been instrumental in producing something of tremendous value for the future. The great madmen can be called saviors of humanity. "A whole horde and generation of receptive, perfectly healthy lads rushes on the work of the sick genius—a genius because of his sickness—admires, glorifies, exalts it, carries it off, conjugates it, makes it over to culture, which cannot live by home-made bread alone." This sentence appears in Thomas's introduction to the Dostoyevsky stories and in Adrian's conversation with the Devil.[5]

For Dostoyevsky and Nietzsche, disease and crime represented an alternative to middle-class conformism. Nietzsche, says Thomas, was striving above all to escape from his German-ness: He helped to subvert bourgeois morality and sanctioned the rights of willpower to criminal curiosity and psychological effrontery.[6] In Dostoyevsky, too, we encounter our own secret thoughts, which stops us from disowning them. Quoting Edgar Degas, who said an artist should go about his work in the same way that a felon commits a crime, Thomas maintains that creative originality always involves alienation from the received ideas and accepted middle-class values.[7]

Just as Thomas's Devil could hardly fail to repeat some of the ideas expressed by Dostoyevsky's in Ivan Karamazov's legend of the Grand Inquisitor, the direct critical confrontation with Dostoyevsky and Nietzsche was bound to cover some of the same ground as *Doctor Faustus*, which, like *The Magic Mountain,* fully explicates its themes in arguments and conversations. But while Thomas keeps coming back to ideas he's already developed, the vantage point keeps changing as he spirals upward. The relationship between disease and creativity is given one of its most thorough airings in the introduction, and he writes interestingly about Nietzsche's ideas of the Superman and eternal recurrence, pointing out that Dostoyevsky had anticipated both. Kirilov argues that the history of humanity can be divided into two parts: from the gorilla to the annihilation of God, and from that to the transformation of the world and humanity. The Superman appears when man becomes God. And the Devil tells the Grand Inquisitor to remember that the world has already repeated itself billions of times. "What Dostoyevsky, through the mouth of the Devil, calls 'insufferable boredom' is what Nietzsche blesses with Dionysiac affirmation when he cries out: 'For I love you, O Eternity!' " Thomas thinks Nietzsche may have been stirred by an unconscious memory of Dostoyevsky,[8] but it's unlikely that he ever read *The Brothers Karamazov*.[9]

Thomas can't be blamed for being misled by books he read about Nietzsche, but one mistake has serious consequences for the construction of *Doctor Faustus*. Writing about Nietzsche's pathology in 1902, Paul J. Möbius connected the syphilis with an 1865 visit to a brothel described by Paul Deussen in his memoirs of Nietzsche, which had been published in 1901.[10] Nietzsche was twenty when, visiting Cologne to see the sights, he told a street-porter to find a restaurant for him. Instead, the man led him to a brothel, and, as he afterward told Deussen, "I found myself suddenly surrounded by half a dozen apparitions in tinsel and gauze, looking at me expectantly. For a short space of time I was speechless. Then I made instinctively for the piano as being the only soulful thing present. I struck a few chords, which freed me from my paralysis, and I escaped."

As a schoolboy he'd told Deussen he was going to need at least three women, but his friend was left with the impression that Nietzsche remained a virgin throughout his life. Though in 1889, answering questions in the asylum after his breakdown, he said he'd infected himself twice in 1866, it's possible that he misunderstood what he was being asked, and that Deussen was right. There's no other evidence that he ever made love to a woman. Thomas thought Nietzsche must have gone back to the brothel,[11] and in giving Adrian the experience Nietzsche described to Deussen, Thomas makes a snub-nosed gypsy girl brush his cheek with her arm. Afterward he keeps thinking about her until he goes back to find her and, disregarding her warning that she could infect him, makes love to her.

The etiology of Nietzsche's madness is problematic. His father suffered from epileptic attacks, but they may not have been syphilitic; Nietzsche's childhood illnesses, though severe, may not have been hereditary, and if it had been congenital syphilis that sent him mad, the breakdown, which occurred in 1888, when he was forty-four, would probably have been earlier. The stroke he had in 1898 could have been caused by cerebral syphilis, but not the delusions of grandeur he suffered before the breakdown or the ensuing madness. Freud and Jung both helped to propagate a rumor that he contracted syphilis in a Genoese male brothel, but there is no evidence to support this. Nor is it easy to reconcile the hypothesis of *dementia paralytica* with the condition he was in between the breakdown and the stroke. He suffered neither from incontinence nor from serious bodily paralysis, and he retained at least partial control over his memory. The problem may remain unsolved, but it seems unlikely that he ever infected himself with syphilis.

If Thomas was wrong, his mistakes are important only because they led him to write *Doctor Faustus* in the way he did. He assumed that while Nietzsche probably didn't know what he was suffering from, he knew where the long history of pain started. "It is characteristic of paralysis that, presumably through hyperaemia, it sends poisonous feelings of happiness and strength to the affected parts of the brain, and brings with it a subjective heightening of vitality and a real, if, medically speaking, pathological increase of productive capacity."[12] Hyperaemia is an excessive accumulation of blood.

Thomas finished the Dostoyevsky essay on July 17, and on July 21 resumed work on the novel, ten days before the new British prime minister, Clement Attlee, and the new American president, Harry Truman, met Stalin at Potsdam. It had already been announced in Moscow papers that Russia would control about half of Germany, and that Berlin would be divided into four zones. At Potsdam it was easy for Stalin to brush aside the argument in favor of free elections in East European countries, and not only to keep all the territory occupied by the Red Army but to take over parts of Germany occupied by the Americans. According to Thomas's calculations, about 40 million Germans would be expelled,[13] and large tracts of Germany handed over to Poland. It was this that caused the death of the eighty-four-year-old Gerhart Hauptmann, who was turned out of his home in the Silesian mountains when it was requisitioned by Poles. With all his possessions packed, the old man lay down and died.[14]

Not that Poland benefited from the peace settlement: Territorial gains were no compensation for loss of sovereignty. After six years of subjugation to Nazi tyranny, the whole of Eastern Europe was left defenseless against Soviet imperialism. An iron curtain, said Churchill, was being slammed down against the West.

On August 6 the first atom bomb was dropped on Hiroshima; three days later the second exploded on Nagasaki. Japan surrendered unconditionally on August 14, but it was close to defeat anyway, and Thomas suspected that the motive for the slaughter was the Americans' wish to demonstrate that it was they and not the Russians who'd won the war. He tried to persuade himself that the new weapon and the new danger would force humanity to develop its instincts for self-preservation.[15]

What stopped him from concentrating on the novel was an article in the form of an open letter published on August 4 in the *Hessische Post*. It said his duty was to settle in Germany. Extracts from the open letter appeared in other papers, German and American. "Come like a good doctor," it said, as if he could get the country back on its feet. The writer was Walter von Molo, Heinrich's predecessor as president of the Writers' Section in the Prussian Academy. He'd remained a member of the academy throughout the Nazi period, and had gone on writing, publishing a book on Kleist in 1938. "What is grotesque," said Thomas, "is that there they have a firm belief in my enormous influence on the Allies' decisions, at least the Americans', about German affairs."[16] There was no question of accepting the invitation to go back. Planning a holiday in Europe the following summer, he hadn't decided whether he'd even visit Germany.[17] On the other hand, he felt deeply disturbed by the letter, and he couldn't ignore it. He spent a week drafting and redrafting a reply; he even tried it out in the way he sometimes tried out lectures—reading it to a friend, Alfred Neumann.[18]

Describing himself as "an already old man, whose heart muscle has had to meet the demands of these adventurous times," he asked how he could help to raise the German people out of its "deep degradation." The intellectuals and professional people who'd sworn loyalty to the regime had all escaped "the angina of exile, the uprooting, the nervous fright of homelessness." Had they resisted collectively, they could have changed the course of German history. As a citizen of the United States with two sons in the American army and with English-speaking grand-children, Thomas owed both the advantages and disadvantages of his situation to "the character and destiny of the German people," but years of exile had alienated him from Germany. "It is, you must con-cede, a frightening country. I confess that I am scared of German ruins—not only rubble but people."

Though the Witches' Sabbath was over, he had no desire to make contact with those who'd joined in the dance, and he hadn't wanted to read any of the books printed in Germany between 1933 and 1945. "A smell of blood and disgrace clings to them; they should all be pulped." Like the artists and musicians who'd been active in Germany, the writ-ers had condoned and supported the Nazis' infamous activities. Not that Thomas could deny his German roots, though the period hadn't allowed his work to be "anything other than a morbid and already half parodistic echo of German greatness." Even when his books could sur-vive only in English, he'd always written in German and thought of himself as a German writer. But if he could do anything to help the German people, it could be done equally well in California.[19]

He wouldn't have devoted so much time to the letter if he hadn't in-tended it for the press. He still believed that people who'd helped Hitler into the saddle should be punished, and that the moral cleansing of the Germans could have come—and should have come—from inside.[20] In telling the truth about Germany's failure to do what he'd advocated in his broadcasts—to rise up against Hitler—he was hoping for the same kind of support he'd enjoyed in 1936 when, after being expatriated and stripped of his honorary doctorate at Bonn University, he wrote an open letter to the dean. But it was a strategic mistake to make the new letter so long: Newspapers would pluck the most striking sentences out of their context, and some of them would provoke fierce resentment.

Only eight days after von Molo's open letter had been forwarded to Thomas, the *Münchener Zeitung* published an article titled "Die innere Emigration" by novelist Frank Thiess, who argued that some of those who'd "suffered" the regime and "kept faith" with Germany had been, inwardly, just as hostile to Nazism as those who'd left the German peo-ple in the lurch and watched their sufferings "from comfortable box seats abroad." After reading Thomas's reply to von Molo, Thiess wrote a second article, saying Thomas was no longer entitled to consider himself a German writer. His hatred for Nazism was really hatred for Germany. This line of argument appealed to those who wanted to go on thinking well of themselves for "sharing honestly" in Germany's sufferings. As Thomas could see, they'd gladly have shared in the fruits of victory if Hitler had won,[21] but he found himself under attack not only in German newspapers but in the German-language paper the *Neue Deutsche Volkszeitung*, which was published in New York.[22]

If he was being denounced as a coward for leaving Germany, he could say Nazi habits were still alive in those denouncing him, but he was surprised by the ferocity of the German press after his letter to von Molo. His brother Viktor wrote from Munich, advising him neither to put himself at the head of a new intellectual movement in Germany nor to become involved with "denazification." Unnerved, Thomas asked himself whether there were genuine grounds for regarding him as a renegade. There weren't, he decided: "There is too much undenied German-ness in my spirit, language and work."[23] And his conversations with Katia were all carried on in German.

But what did "German-ness" mean? What, for that matter, did "Germany" mean? He was still confronting the same questions he'd asked in *Reflections*, and if his answers were different, so was Germany. Believing, as he did, that Nazism hadn't been imposed from outside but had deep roots in German history, he'd told von Molo that Germany could be equated with neither the Bismarckian Reich nor with the two centuries that could be called the era of Frederick the Great. Thomas wanted a new Germany, democratic and humanistic, to evolve in a future devoid of aggressive nationalism, but he wasn't forgetting that in 1914 he had defended both Frederick the Great's imperialism and the kaiser's.

Writing Chapter 30 of *Doctor Faustus* between September and October 1945, he imputes the views he held in 1914 to Zeitblom, who's writing about 1914 in 1944. The war, he says, was welcome because it offered release from a stagnation that had become unbearable. The moment had come to make sacrifices. Germany had a mission, which allowed the superior individual to feel solidarity with the whole nation. The pro-British Rüdiger Schildknapp, a character based on Hans Reisiger, condemns Hitler's invasions of Belgium, France, and Russia, and sees nothing in the war but "filth, vile smells, amputated limbs, sexual licence and lice." He jeers at the "ideological journalism that presents foul play as historical achievement."[24] Frederick the Great and the meaning of "Germany" come into the argument when Zeitblom talks emotionally about "the mythical emergence of national character that occurs at such historical moments." He finds the invasion of Belgium reminiscent of Frederick's attack on neutral Saxony; and he praises "the speech of our philosophical Reichs Chancellor with its calculated admission of guilt, with the unparaphrasable folk-wisdom of the words

'Necessity knows no law' and its appeal to God that pressures of contemporary life should be given priority over ancient legal documents."[25]

Thomas can now explore the absurdity of defending the Third Reich in the terms he'd used to defend the Second, and to parody what he'd argued thirty years earlier, he reread not only old political writings but old diaries. The technique he called montage allowed him to borrow without acknowledgment from his own work just as he could from anyone else's. For the sequence in which the violinist Rudi Schwerdtfeger pays court to Adrian, Thomas drew heavily on old jottings about fragments of conversation and significant details during his relationship with Paul Ehrenberg. Modeled on him, Rudi is neatly built, with a shock of flaxen hair; he's good-natured, and eager to please. He loves flirting with women, but neglects them when he begins to pursue Adrian, consulting his judgment, asking to be accompanied, opening conversations, and refusing to be discouraged by reticence or rebuffs. When he made the notes, Thomas had been in an agony of uncertainty about how much Paul liked him; forty-five years later he could enjoy his emotional detachment and his total control over what happened in the fiction. But in early August he found himself thinking about Paul as if the passage of time hadn't changed him.[26]

To some extent, of course, every novelist engages in montage, incorporating facts, memories, personal experiences, direct and vicarious, into the narrative, but Thomas was exceptionally eclectic and ruthless. Artists, he claimed, are entitled to appropriate any material that comes to hand. He resurrects his two dead sisters as Clarissa and Ines Rodde, making their mother the widow of a senator. Ines's marriage is based on that of the Löhrs, and when Clarissa commits suicide, Thomas uses his mother's memory of hearing her dying daughter gargling at the washbasin to cool her burning throat. He was equally shameless in appropriating not only Adorno's ideas but the words in which they'd been formulated, just as he'd once copied out passages from medical textbooks. This could lead to embarrassment, as it did when he read the sequence about the Opus 111 Piano Sonata to Bruno Walter, who said nothing better had ever been written about Beethoven—Thomas had a profound understanding of his music. But as Thomas noted, "A great deal from Adorno is taken over in this as mine. Je prends mon bien où je le trouve."[27]

BEFORE THE TRIAL of war criminals began at Nuremberg in November, Erika, now accredited as a journalist, was the only woman reporter allowed inside the Mondorf Hotel, where fifty-two of the Nazi leaders, including Göring, Papen, Alfred Rosenberg, and Julius Streicher, were being held. She wasn't allowed to see them, but she sent in a message saying who she was. Rosenberg's reaction was: "Pfui Deubel!" Streicher grumbled: "Good God! And this woman has been in my room!" Göring was the most excited. If only she'd introduced herself to him, he said, he could have explained everything, and if he'd been in charge of the Mann case, he'd have handled it differently. A German of Thomas Mann's stature could have been fitted into the Third Reich. Erika cabled her report to the *Evening Standard*, which published it on August 11.[28]

Thomas was in favor of the trials, which began on November 20, though it was impossible to arraign all the people who'd committed war crimes. Göring, the liveliest and most unbroken of the accused, expressed regret at the "excesses" of the regime.[29]

Thomas's ability to shut himself off from distractions and overcome malaise had never been tested more severely than during the last two months of the year, when he stoically completed two difficult chapters—thirty-two and thirty-three. Ignoring symptoms and living on the frontier of a fatigue that made it almost impossible to go on working, he refused to give in. He was coughing, suffering from incessant catarrh, and still losing weight: At the end of November he was two pounds lighter than in March.[30] The compulsion to switch from one doctor to another was itself symptomatic. His blood pressure was low, and his bronchia were obstructed with mucus. He swallowed fat red vitamin capsules three times a day, but felt no better. He'd reached the age at which his mother had died and though he wasn't going to follow suit, he thought his life had reached its lowest ebb.[31]

Writing about his mother and sisters in Chapter 32, he might have been more charitable had he been feeling better. The philandering of the widowed Frau Rodde is described unsympathetically, and Ines is sometimes so embarrassed by her mother's behavior that she leaves the drawing room with red cheeks. Clarissa Rodde's theatrical career parallels Carla's: Her letters to Ines show that her success is less artistic than personal and erotic, while Ines marries the boring Helmut Institoris without loving him. What she loves is the facade of bourgeois respectability their marriage will bring. The Frau Senator has helped to implant this need in her daughter by entertaining on a grand scale, and Thomas, thinking of the way his parents and the Pringsheims had entertained, had to ask whether some of the same needs had been implanted in him and Katia. He was thinking of her when he described Ines's habit of loading herself with "mountains of luggage . . . on even the smallest journey away from her well-kept nest." They must "symbolise her need for protection and her nervousness of life."[32] He was alluding not only to Julia but also to the Pringsheims and the paintings they'd bought when he described how Ines and Institoris commission a fashionable portraitist to paint them with their children. Feeling no real love, Ines makes her children into "an ideal bourgeois brood."[33]

Giving her an unhappy liaison with Rudi Schwerdtfeger alongside her unhappy marriage, Thomas is looking back at the friendship he'd broken off to marry Katia. Here his emotional detachment seems incomplete. When Zeitblom condemns Rudi's compulsive need to be liked, his greed for intimacy, and his excessive pliability, Thomas seems vindictive, but he also seems uncertain whether he was paying a higher price than he could afford when he broke with Paul. "What is suffering," asks Ines,

> what are fear and humiliating danger in comparison with the one sweet, unmissable triumph without which one wouldn't want to live: to hold the frivolous, the evasive, the mundane, the soul that tortures with unreliable neatness, but still has real human value and bring it into contact with its better self, to force its foppishness into seriousness, to possess the volatile, but finally, finally, not once but for confirmation and reassurance never often enough, to see it in the state appropriate to its value, the state of devotion, of deep sighing passion?[34]

Zeitblom comments on her "strange equation of value and sensual passion," but as she keeps trying it out in different words,[35] Thomas is approximating a formulation of the question he kept repeating in his diaries: Had he lived life to the full? Here, as there, he could neither pose nor answer the question without thinking about Paul.

He punished himself by ignoring symptoms. Exhausted, enervated, depressed, and ill, he not only wrote the two chapters but developed the Dostoyevsky essay into a lecture, and on December 7, when the catarrh was particularly troublesome, delivered it at the University of California's Royce Hall in Westwood. The conductor Otto Klemperer, who was in the audience, found it impressive.[36]

Though Thomas wasn't suffering any shortage of gratification and encouragement, it's remarkable that he could write such a youthfully virile account of his literary ambitions as he did when Adrian analyzes his musical ambitions. He wants to use mockery as an antidote to romantic pathos, remaining on a high intellectual plane while making his innovations accessible to a wide public. He wants to make tradition felt, but to restructure it, achieving a new simplicity that involves no simplification.[37] This corresponds to Thomas's conviction that art was on its way to extinction unless it could be made to reach a mass audience. "The opposite of the culture we knew," he told Pierre-Paul Sagave, a professor at Strasbourg, "is not barbarism but *collectivism*." In the bourgeois world, art had been a substitute for religion, and the elite called "the public" no longer existed. If art was to survive into the postbourgeois world, it must become more modest, more innocent, more innocuous.[38]

But in *Doctor Faustus* it wasn't enough to generalize about Adrian's intentions. Steering him toward the composition of a masterpiece, Thomas needed a collaborator if the music was to be described, as it would need to be, in detail. To help Adorno to help him, he sketched out what the music was to be: a distinctively German oratorio with orchestra, soloists, choruses, and a narrator. Called *Apocalipsis cum Figuris*, it was to be based either on the fifteen Dürer woodcuts or directly on the Book of Revelations.

> What I need are a few characterising details which will help to make it seem real (one can manage with a few) giving the reader a plausible and convincing picture. . . . I am thinking of something Satanically religious, demonically pious, at the same time tightly structured and criminally indisciplined, often derisive towards art, also something that harks back to the primitive and elemental . . . abandoning divisions into bars and tonal divisions (trombone glissandi) and it should be almost unplayable.[39]

On the day he wrote to Adorno, the BBC transmitted his New Year's greeting to Germany. He'd been asked to recapitulate his reasons for not going there. Just over an hour later on North West German radio, Frank Thiess was again saying that Thomas's hatred for Nazism was really hatred for Germany. He was speaking, Thiess said, with an arrogance and bitterness that were no longer hurtful "because they are dishonourable, and the heart of a poet no longer beats behind them."[40] Soon afterward it was revealed that Thiess and von Molo had both been involved with the Nazis, but this didn't repair the damage they'd inflicted.

Thomas knew that if he wanted to revisit Germany, he should go soon, "or otherwise, I can see this already, the gulf will be unbridgeable."[41] But in 1933, Annette Kolb had said: "To Germany I shall never go back," and this became a catchphrase between him and Katia,[42] though it would have been provocative to exclude Germany when a Brussels agent, Arthur Hohenberg, who'd been recommended by Bronislaw Huberman, offered to arrange a European lecture tour. Thomas's first inclination was to accept, provided the fee was high enough.[43]

But so many of his friends urged him not to set foot in Germany—Erich von Kahler said his life might be in danger[44]—that he changed his mind, suspecting that people were still the same there. He wrote to Hermann Hesse: "Nothing good can come to us from that country. . . . I have come to the conclusion that I should feel no happier there today—even from the political viewpoint—than I did in 1930."[45] In February, generalizing about the Germans, he said: "They have a tendency to be malicious, are self-centred, self-pitying, provincial and arrogant, brutal, in every way unfit for power and with a deep, innate tendency to meanness."[46]

Undeniably, Germany had produced great men—Luther, Goethe, Wagner, Nietzsche—but Thomas felt sure he wasn't one of them. "Oh, all the personalities! I shall no more be remembered than Proust. How much *Doctor Faustus* contains of my temperament. From the outset, that was the most exciting part of the book. Basically a radical confession."[47] He was too depressed to see any merit in it. "Its greatest drawback is that it offers no opportunity for anything really epic or humorous. It is joylessly earnest, not artistically happy."[48]

But in January 1946 he enjoyed working with Adorno, who'd been present at many of his readings from the book and had been given a typescript. They agreed that Adrian's greatest achievement, his oratorio *Apocalypsis cum Figuris*, must proclaim the end of culture and bourgeois civilization by drawing on the whole tradition of apocalyptic art. Adorno didn't like the idea of basing the oratorio on the series of Dürer engravings that had the same title, but instead of being discouraged, Thomas (composing a literary account of music inspired by art inspired by apocalyptic literature) was spurred into drawing on a wider range of sources—not only the Revelations of St. John but the lamentations of Ezekiel, who prophesied the Babylonian exile. Adrian also uses the prophecies of Jeremiah and Dante's account of Hell, which is to say that Thomas, developing his musical ideas in collaboration with Adorno, profited from working in an echo chamber where literature and religion had, for centuries, been voicing ideas about destruction and the Last Judgment that sends souls to eternal perdition.

Thomas divided this chapter into three parts, wanting the description of the oratorio to frame an account of conversations after the end of the First World War at the house of Sextus Kridwiss, where Munich intellectuals and minor royalty discuss cultural trends. Modeled recognizably on Emil Preetorius, who'd been one of Thomas's closest friends in Munich, Kridwiss is described as "a small ageless gentleman with a strong Rhenish-Hessian accent and unusual intellectual animation. Out of pure curiosity he listened to talk about current trends without any discernible involvement in them, describing this and that—whatever he heard about—as 'certainly most significant.'" Believing nothing had changed, Thomas was implicitly discussing trends after the end of the Second World War, but above all—or underneath all—he was answering those who thought he was being harsh in his judgment on Germany.

He suggests that instead of trying to influence the course of events before 1933, the Germans took a perverse and modish pleasure in suspending their moral judgment. The Fascist literary historian who treats writers as blood-and-soil products of specific German districts, the princes of Hesse-Nassau who are studying at the university, the snobbish Jew who cultivates paradox, the visionary poet Daniel zur Höhe, recalled after making an earlier appearance in the story "Zum Propheten," and Helmut Institoris are unanimous in refusing to take the Weimar Republic seriously. They sometimes refer to a 1908 book, *Réflexions sur la violence*, by the revolutionary syndicalist Georges Sorel, who suggested that Europe could be united only by war, and that parliamentary discussion would be impotent to produce political decisions. The energies of the masses could be released only if they were provided with mythical fictions devised like battle cries. The truth was irrelevant; what they needed was a fable, an insane vision, a chimera. So worried by all this that he begins, like Thomas, to lose weight, Zeitblom sees that the war has only helped to articulate a process which had already been under way, and which still underpins new feelings about life. The humane softness of the bourgeois epoch has been swept aside.

In its brilliantly brutal combination of old and new musical forms, Adrian's music expresses the new spirit. Its ironic treatment of tradition condones the rejection of the old values. Adrian makes the same point Thomas had made to the professor at Strasbourg: The antithesis of the culture we knew is not barbarism but collectivism. The oratorio breaks down conventional musical frontiers. On its way to singing polyphonically, the chorus whispers, speaks, hums. Retuned during a drumroll, the tympani achieve glissandi. The chorus is treated like an orchestra, while voices are instrumentalized. The flute performs like a coloratura soprano, while muted trumpets and saxophones suggest grotesque human voices. Loudspeaker effects are introduced, and the tenor sings almost as high as a castrato. Part One ends in a pandemonium of diabolical laughter, which is musically reprised in the heavenly chorus of children that opens the second part. The first and only performance is conducted by Otto Klemperer, and generally Thomas vindicated his idea of montage, integrating Adorno's ideas into his own, fusing fantasy and reality. Adrian's avant-gardism is described with such keen relish that it seems odd Thomas should soon afterward have wanted to hear Mendelssohn's violin concerto twice within three weeks.[49]

Throughout February and March 1946, while he was writing this long chapter, Thomas's diary is full of references to headaches, exhaustion, enervation, high temperatures, and fits of coughing that interrupted his sleep. An X-ray taken a month earlier had revealed a shadow on his lung, but in recommending that he should have his nose and throat treated by a specialist, his doctor was concentrating on secondary symptoms. In the pictures taken in late February by the Canadian photographer Yousuf Karsh, Thomas looks ill,[50] and at the beginning of March an attack of flu kept him in bed for nearly two weeks. His temperature regularly rose to about 102 degrees in the afternoon, although he was taking penicillin every three hours, day and night. The doctor who was treating him, Hans Schiff, then prescribed a mixture of codeine and Empirin, which made him feel better, but even in the second half of March, when he was getting more sleep at night, he had to spend part of the day in bed. His temperature was still unsteady, and on March 20, when the film rights of *The Magic Mountain* were sold to Sir Alexander Korda for $10,000, the news failed to bring Thomas any relief from his headaches and enervation.

Heinrich's seventy-fifth birthday was celebrated with a small party on March 21, and Thomas had written a tribute, "Report on My Brother" ("Bericht über mein Bruder"), which was published in *Freies Deutschland*. Heinrich persuaded him to replace Dr. Schiff with Frederick Rosenthal, who gave him injections of his own blood mixed with novocaine. This didn't help. He felt sure his illness was due partly to the "frightful novel" and partly to the tide of hostile feeling in Germany.[51]

Studying the latest X-ray photographs of Thomas's lungs, and believing the lower right lobe had been infiltrated, Dr. Rosenthal called in a specialist, who agreed. To establish whether an abscess had formed, he said, and whether an operation was necessary, Thomas should have a bronchoscopic examination. An apparatus equipped with a tiny electric light would be introduced through the trachea into the lung, which the doctor would inspect through a kind of periscope. This would irritate the entire respiratory tract, but the specialist thought Thomas would recover within a week. Dr. Rosenthal was in favor of neither the bronchoscopy nor the operation, but Katia got in touch with Elisabeth in Chicago, where an eminent lung surgeon, Elias Adams, was working at the university's Billings Hospital. Content to let other people make the decisions, Thomas found himself being taken to the hospital by means of stretchers, ambulances, and a train with a private bedroom.

The bronchoscopy revealed that he had cancer of the lung; had he taken Rosenthal's advice, he'd have died. Preparations for the operation took eight days. He was subjected to a treatment he had described in *The Magic Mountain*: The activity of the diseased lung was suspended by introducing nitrogen into the thoracic cavity. He was given, in other words, a pneumothorax. Katia, who was staying with the Borgeses, came to spend most of every day at his bedside, and Erika flew to Chicago from Nuremberg to be with him. Two days before the operation he was given a blood transfusion, and Katia spent the whole of the preceding night in an armchair by his bed.

His seventh rib had to be removed and the upper diaphragm displaced; the incision was so long that it would leave a scar from his chest to his back. Afterward, he had three private nurses relieving each other in eight-hour shifts, giving him penicillin injections and helping him when he wanted to move in the bed. Both doctors and nurses encouraged him to go on believing he was exceptionally fit for a man of seventy-one, and in every way a model patient. He suffered from shortness of breath if he moved too fast, but after a few weeks the stitches were removed, and he could soon sit in his dressing gown, looking out of the window, reading Nietzsche and making annotations in preparation for a lecture on him at the Library of Congress in the autumn.

His visitors included Caroline Newton, who brought presents of porcelain; Bermann; and Bruno Walter, who was giving a concert in Chicago. Alfred Knopf sent caviar from New York. Erika stayed on in Chicago and bought new flowers if ever the supply in his room ran low. Surrounded by so much evidence of goodwill, he asked himself whether he deserved it. In *Doctor Faustus* he'd been thinking of himself when he described Adrian's enslavement to the task of composition. Fragile though his health is, he works at least ten hours a day, taking only a brief walk around the pond or up the hill. Even when he's with friends, he's liable to look distracted. His cheeks redden, and his lips part, as if he's listening to an invisible presence that dictates musical phrases he must either remember or jot down. Knowing he'd always given priority to his work, Thomas was faintly puzzled by the attentiveness of Katia, Erika, Elisabeth, and friends who visited him. He'd brought a typescript of the unfinished novel to the hospital, and one day, when Erika started talking in detail about certain incidents, he was quickly reduced to tears. When she apologized for her lack of consideration, he explained they were tears of gratitude.[52]

The penicillin took his appetite away, and he developed a strong partiality to Coca-Cola, which he'd never liked. But after a period of finding it hard to walk as far as the "social room" at the end of the corridor, even when he was holding Katia's arm, he soon recovered his mobility. The first time he put his clothes on, he was taken out to breathe the spring air from a wheelchair with a blanket over his knees, but instead of staying in the hospital for the usual six weeks after the operation, he spent the last few days in a hotel. On his last day in the hospital he autographed copies of his books and, leaning on Erika's arm, answered questions put by local journalists who'd discovered he was being discharged.

Elisabeth drove him to the hotel; after a few days there, he made his way back to Pacific Palisades with Katia and Erika, arriving on May 28. The garden and the view seemed paradisal.[53] He didn't risk smoking even half a cigar till three days later, but it was too soon, and it spoiled his afternoon. The next day he was working at the novel again, going back to incorporate ideas he'd had in the hospital.[54] By mid-June, though he was still short of breath, still in pain, and still had difficulty in walking, he was putting on weight at the rate of two pounds a week.

He could look back on the operation as "a late, unexpected endurance test for my constitution, which passed *cum laude*."[55] But since his back soon started to hurt if he worked at his desk, he had to take up a new working position, sitting in the corner of a sofa and writing on paper clipped to a board. He couldn't go on for long at a stretch, and if he tried to dictate, he became breathless.[56] But he described himself as "the patched up old miracle man."[57]

By the middle of June he was working on the new chapter, but having divided the previous one into three parts to connect the disasters of German history with the apocalyptic music, he now moved to Clarissa Rodde's suicide, which is meant to epitomize the end of the bourgeois period. Though associating it with Julia's suicide, he relies on the events of Carla's, which had seemed to impinge less on him than on Heinrich. Unsuccessful in her theatrical career, but theatrical in her style of dressing and making up, Clarissa is shy and vulnerable. She's seduced by a womanizer who takes his revenge, when she refuses to go on sleeping with him, by wrecking her chances of marriage to a young man from Strasbourg. Like Carla, Clarissa has poison in her possession, and she uses it, just as Carla had, in her mother's house in the country. Like Carla, Clarissa is found dead on a chaise longue with dark blue spots of congealed blood on her face and hands. The suicide note she has left for Henri is worded just like the note Carla had left for Arthur Gibo: "Je t'aime. Une fois je t'ai trompé, mais je t'aime."[58]

37

Staring into Grayness

AT NUREMBERG, where twenty-two Nazi leaders were being tried, the only two who spoke up in defense of Hitler were Göring and Rudolf Hess.[1] The trial was in its final stages: Judgment was to be passed at the end of September. In his final speech, the British chief prosecutor, the attorney general, Sir Hartley Shawcross, said Goethe had predicted fate would strike at the Germans. They had betrayed themselves, and didn't want to be what they were.

> It is sad that they do not know the charm of truth, detestable that mist, smoke, and berserk immoderation are so dear to them, pathetic that they ingenuously submit to any mad scoundrel who appeals to their lowest instincts, who confirms them in their vices and teaches them to conceive nationalism as isolation and brutality.

An article in the *Times Literary Supplement* pointed out Sir Hartley's mistake: He'd been citing a monologue from Chapter 7 of *The Beloved Returns*. Throughout the novel Thomas had judiciously mixed quotation with new material; here, to interpolate an allusion to Hitler, he'd taken the risk of sounding anachronistic. During the war, copies of the novel had been smuggled into Germany, and an anti-Nazi pamphlet, published under the title *Goethes Gespräche mit Riemer*, had included material from the novel in the statements it collected about the German character. The pamphlet had been Sir Hartley's source, and in mid-August, after his mistake was exposed, the British ambassador in Washington, Lord Inverchapel, wrote to ask Thomas for an explanation. He replied that although Goethe had never written these words, he might well have done.[2]

While Thomas was convalescing, Erika stayed on in Pacific Palisades, and the novel benefited from her presence. She'd often helped her father by suggesting cuts in his lectures, and he had enough faith in her editorial skill to let her assist on the novel in the same way. The translator, Helen Lowe-Porter, was already working on it in Oxford, but he recalled the typescript to make cuts. He knew his fiction sometimes contained too much essayistic exegesis, as characters elaborated conversationally on intellectual points: Erika encountered less resistance than she was expecting. They shortened Kretzschmar's lecture, scrapped some of the musical theory, and pared down the conversations between the students. Altogether about forty pages were eliminated.3

By October 6, when Thomas started Chapter 41, he'd written ninety pages since the operation.4 He forged ahead rapidly, though he was again suffering from erysipelas. The itching and inflammation were painful enough to play havoc with his sleep in spite of the ointments, painkillers, and sleeping pills prescribed by the doctor, Rex Stout, who'd taken over from Dr. Rosenthal. Sometimes Thomas tried to sleep in the armchair by his bed, but in late September and early October, rarely sleeping uninterruptedly for more than a few hours, he was exhausted and enervated, but he stoically refused to be deflected from work on the novel. "Even without sleep I will work."5

During wakeful nights he read several Shakespeare plays, including *Much Ado about Nothing*, in which the subplot centers on Benedick's friend Claudio and Beatrice's cousin, Hero—daughter of Lorenzo, Duke of Messina. Jealous of Claudio, the Duke's villainous brother, Don John, tries to discredit Hero: Claudio is made to watch while his friend Borachio woos a woman on her balcony. It's the maidservant, Margaret, disguised as her mistress, but Claudio is taken in and denounces Hero on what should have been their wedding day. While plotting Chapters 41 and 42, Thomas was influenced by this operatic story: Adrian decides to marry a designer, Marie Godeau, and persuades Rudi Schwerdtfeger to act as his intermediary in wooing her. At the same time, Thomas was using material taken from notes for the novel about his relationship with Paul Ehrenberg.6

This relationship was to be crucial in the novel, rather as if Thomas had decided to continue in fiction what he'd aborted in reality. He'd been thinking about Paul as if his looks were immune to the passage of time; now, resurrecting the young Paul in Rudi, he was carrying on a vicarious relationship with him through Adrian and contriving a crisis in which the disintegration of the friendship ensues on Adrian's decision to marry. At work, apparently, were two processes Freud had called the repetition compulsion and abreaction. Over forty-two years had passed, and Thomas's marriage was still intact, but he needed to reproduce the old conflict in a disguised form, trying to liberate himself from the lingering discomfort. In fiction, as in psychoanalysis, words serve as a substitute for action.

He again uses the name Rudolf (or Rudi) as he had in *The Loved Ones* for the young violinist based on Paul. Adrian takes over Adelaide's role, but now, as before, it's Rudi who mostly takes the initiative, making physical contact whenever he can. He's impatient for them to address each other in the second person singular. Though he had cast himself, at the time, in the role of Adelaide, Thomas may by now have forgotten whether he or Paul usually took the initiative, and Adrian is soon so confused that he thinks he did. Zeitblom is quite sure he didn't, but this doesn't resolve the ambiguity, since we've been taught not to trust his judgment.

Adrian never uses the word *love* to characterize the friendship, but talking to Zeitblom, he defines love as an astonishing and rather unnatural change in the relationship between the self and the external world. There is sometimes an "ironic eroticism" in his reactions to Rudi, who says Adrian's friendship is indispensable: It raises him to a higher level.

A turning point comes when Adrian agrees to write a violin concerto for Rudi, but the narrative is vague about what led to this. Zeitblom uses words with erotic connotations—"suitor," "seduction," "bewitched," "conquest"—but refuses to disclose the contents of a letter Rudi kept as a trophy, though he should have destroyed it. It's like the baring of a wound, we're told, and in writing it Adrian was taking a risk. After receiving it, Rudi immediately went to Adrian's country retreat, where he agreed to write the concerto, and they both started using the second person singular. In Zurich, where they lodged at the same private house, they appeared on the platform hand-in-hand to acknowledge the applause at the end of the performance.[7]

Adrian's pact with the Devil has made love taboo, and his decision to marry is presented unemotionally. He meets Marie and her widowed aunt at a dinner party in Zurich. When the ladies visit Munich, they stay at the Pension Gisela, which Adrian recommends. Thomas had been living there in 1902, when he knew Paul. One of his favorite holiday spots had been Ettal, and when Adrian, Rudi, Zeitblom, and the two ladies make an expedition there, he describes the mountain scenery, relying either on memory or possibly on notes for *The Loved Ones*. Adrian wants marriage partly because it will end his relationship with Rudi, and Zeitblom thinks he's not so much in love with Marie as convinced that his life will be better if she shares it. Rudi is informed of the decision before she is, and the formulation is remarkably unemotional:

> Look at the human side. I'm getting on—I'm already forty. Would you as my friend want to see me spend the rest of my life in this hole? I'm telling you, look at me as a human being who's suddenly realised how much time has gone by and how much he wants more domestic warmth and a female companion who is agreeable in every sense of the word, in short a more congenial, more human atmosphere—not just for the sake of taking things easy and being more comfortable in bed but above all because it would give him more motivation and energy for his work—for the human content of his future work.[8]

This is reminiscent of Thomas's letter to Heinrich about not wanting or expecting to be happy with Katia (see page 195). Adrian has used the word *human* four times, and of all the points Rudi could have made in reply, the one he chooses is that Adrian's music owes its greatness to its inhumanity. If he wrote humanly inspired work, it would be inferior. Adrian retorts that this is cruel, coming from the man "who showed astonishing persistence in winning me over to the human and converting me to saying *Du.*" What's again being addressed, though more obliquely than before, is the question of emotional coldness in Thomas. It's only later that the two men discuss Marie and their feelings for her.[9] Rudi claims to be attracted, and when Adrian still expects him to woo her on his behalf, the uppermost consideration seems to be the relationship between the two men. When Marie finally gives herself to Rudi, Adrian feels betrayed, but the possibility is left open that he expected or even wanted to be betrayed. The novel doesn't analyze this. Unlike Shakespeare, Thomas makes the confusion culminate in violence, which comes as a melodramatic anticlimax. Rudi's discarded mistress, Ines, has become addicted to morphine, and she shoots him on a tram. This sequence was written—or put together from notes for *The Loved Ones*—quite quickly: It's easy, said Thomas, to deal with disasters.[10]

While working on these two chapters, he was recovering from his erysipelas. His consultations with Dr. Stout were interrupted at the beginning of October, when, arriving at the Medical Building in Beverly Hills after a night of interrupted sleep, he found that the doctor's office no longer existed. A fire had reduced the building to a ruin with charred, water-stained walls and blackened rubble on the ground. He was reminded of the Leipzig incident in which Adrian was trying to get treatment for his syphilis but the doctors either died or disappeared.[11] Thomas was more fortunate: The writer Wilhelm Speyer, an old friend of Bruno Frank's, recommended a female Jewish dermatologist, Rachelle Seletz. Her office was in downtown Los Angeles, and after the long journey, Thomas had a long wait. She was Russian, with mousy eyes, and her professional life seemed chaotic, but she inspired confidence, and two days later, when he paid her a second visit, his skin was already healing.[12]

The next time he wrote to Dr. Rosenthal, it wasn't to consult him—at least not about himself. Carrying out the long-term intention of introducing a character modeled on Frido, he decided that the boy, Adrian's nephew, would die of meningitis while his uncle was looking after him. In loving the child, Adrian is making a second attempt to defy the Mephistophelian veto, but this time the love becomes more tangible for the reader. Growing bigger, Frido had already lost some of the sweetness he'd had as a young child, but recapturing much of the elflike charm the boy had lost, Thomas passes it on to the five-year-old Nepo-muk, who calls himself "Echo" or, missing the first syllable, "Cho." He has slender, shapely legs, a comely head, and long-lashed blue eyes sparkling with mischief. His voice is silvery, and the explanatory ges-tures that accompany his words are unconnected with what he's saying. Some of his dialogue comes straight from diary entries about Frido. "You are glad I did come, yes?" But Echo is also modeled partly on the Borgeses' solemn daughter Domenica, who hated to be laughed at. Un-derstanding Echo's sensitivity, Adrian silences the other adults when they laugh at him. Graceful, good tempered, and well behaved, the lit-tle boy talks consolingly to the grown-ups when he's most in need of consolation himself, and, as the philosophical Zeitblom puts it, he gives to impermanent becoming the quality of being.

Just as he'd previously seemed at ease with knowledge picked up from medical textbooks, Thomas writes about meningitis as if familiar with it from years of clinical experience. Children are susceptible to it when recovering from measles or whooping cough, and Thomas has prepared the ground by having the boy's parents send him to conva-lesce in the Bavarian countryside after a severe attack of measles. For two months he delights the grown-ups, but then catches a chill that robs his eyes of brightness. Losing his appetite, he becomes fretful, and seems drowsy most of the time. Plaintively calling out "Echo's head!" he reaches out to people around him. When the local doctor eases his headache by drawing off fluid from the spinal canal, he expects the re-lief to last only a few hours. Paralysis of the muscles gives the beautiful blue eyes a distressing squint, and when a specialist is called in, he can do no more than perform a second spinal tap. Soon the little boy is shrieking and gnashing his teeth. Furious spasms send the blue eyeballs rolling in the frail head until coma sets in. Having stimulated himself to write both "Death in Venice" and *The Magic Mountain* by picturing him-self in life-threatening situations, Thomas now gains impetus from pic-turing the death of his beloved grandson.

Adrian blames the disease on the Devil. After abusing him and chal-lenging him to take the child quickly, he announces that it should not be. What should not be? asks Zeitblom. "The good and noble. What is called the human, although it's good and noble. What men fought for, stormed castles for, what prophets joyously announced—it should not be. It'll be taken back. I'll take it back." And when Zeitblom asks what he'll take back, his answer is the Ninth Symphony.[13]

Though he found it painful to inflict even an imaginary death on his winsome grandson, Thomas worked eagerly at the chapter, and finished it on December 11. Michael and Gret would have to be kept in igno-rance as long as possible, but on December 12 he read the two chapters to members of the family, and seemed to be making more impact than with any previous reading. Helen Lowe-Porter, who rarely commented on work she was given to translate, asked: "How could you do it?"[14]

On January 7, 1947, when he saw the novel advertised in Oprecht's new catalogue at 15 Swiss francs in hardback, Thomas felt alarmed.[15] He'd been stricter than ever before in refusing to give lectures, write for newspapers, or accept other commitments, and he'd been neglecting his correspondence. But the book was still unfinished, and it was the final climaxes that would test whether he'd succeeded in fusing the story of Adrian's life with the story of Nazi Germany. In the penultimate chapter, which was written at the end of 1946, Zeitblom describes the events of April 1945 as if they were current. "Our crushed and shattered cities are falling like ripe plums. . . . The dreadful man who last year escaped with his life, which can only be a madly sputtering, flickering life, from the conspiracy of despairing patriots who were trying to save the last remnants and the future of the Reich, ordered his soldiers to sink the attack on Berlin in a sea of blood and to shoot any officer who speaks of surrender."[16]

Formerly loyal to the regime, Zeitblom has been shifted by the experience of war—or by the author—to the opposite position. The underlying question in this section is whether the Germans are guilty. Only a handful of leaders could be tried at Nuremberg, but after the discovery of the death camps, crowds of German civilians were taken on forced visits to view the gas chambers, the unburned bones, the hair shorn from women who'd been gassed. An American general had accused the people of complicity in the slaughter, and Zeitblom agrees: "It is Germans, tens of thousands of them, hundreds of thousands of them who have done what makes humanity shudder." They are "people who will have to live like the ghetto Jews, shut up with each other, because the frightful hatred that has grown up all round them will not allow them to cross the borders. . . . Was this regime in word and deed anything more than the distorted, overblown, degraded realisation of an attitude that must be recognised as authentically characteristic?"[17]

Thomas links this denunciation of Germany to Adrian by saying that the last two years before his breakdown—1929 and 1930—belonged to the spread of what was now being extinguished in blood and flames. In the final paragraph of the epilogue, Faustian imagery will be used to set the seal on the connection between public and private issues. Germany, "with her cheeks hectically reddened," had been devastatingly triumphant—on the point, it seemed, of conquering the world, because of the one pact she intended to keep, the one she had signed with her blood. "Today she is lurching downwards from despair to despair, surrounded by demons, one eye covered by a hand, the other staring into grayness."[18]

The last sections of the novel substantiate Adrian's threat to take back the Ninth Symphony. The Nazi regime, says Zeitblom, had made its victims dream of a new Ode to Joy celebrating their success in liberating themselves. But Adrian's final cantata prophesies only destruction and gloom. Like his apocalyptic oratorio, which almost equated the angelic with the diabolic, his Faust cantata identifies the blessed with the damned. From the old chapbook he takes the scene in which Faust entertains friends in the village of Rimlich, near Wittenberg, where he tells them that the time of settlement is at hand: "I die as a bad and as a good Christian." After setting these words, Adrian writes a set of variations on the theme, and the work is prophetic, looking forward to carnage and destruction. In January 1947, Thomas read this chapter to Adorno, who liked the account of the music but took issue with the ending, which struck him as too upbeat. Recognizing that this objection was valid, Thomas reworked the final section, making it end: "Then nothing more. Silence and night. But the note resonating in the silence without being there, overheard only by the soul, is no longer lamentation fading away. Its meaning has changed. It lingers as a light in the darkness."[19]

The final chapter represents a variation both on the last phase of Nietzsche's life and on the theme of inviting friends to watch the Devil's arrival to collect what is due. Like Nietzsche, Adrian breaks down at the age of forty-four. Like the chapbook Faust, he invites friends to a village, Pfeiffering, where he'll talk about the cantata with a piano at hand for playing extracts. His initial inarticulacy, his non sequiturs, his insistence on speaking in archaic German, his weeping, his inability to play more than a dissonant chord lead up to his collapse, and afterward, like the mad Nietzsche, he has a period in a mental hospital before he's handed over to his old mother, who looks after him. Zeitblom's account of his last visit to his friend echoes accounts by Nietzsche's friends of visiting him before his death.

Thomas finished the novel at 11:30 on the morning of January 29.[20] It was three years and eight months since he'd started. On February 6 the Neumanns entertained him and Katia with champagne to celebrate. He read the Echo episode, and their reaction encouraged him to believe this was the best part of the book. He was told the next day that Kitty Neumann had been awake all night, thinking about the child.[21] Thomas had been revising what he'd written, but from February 9 he devoted his mornings to the lecture on Nietzsche he was to deliver in April at the Library of Congress.

He'd been reinstated on January 25 as an honorary doctor at Bonn University, and he was intending to visit Germany during the European tour he'd planned for May and June, delivering the Nietzsche lecture in England and Switzerland. Dictating a letter to his brother Viktor at the end of January—in English because the secretary spoke no German—he spoke of visiting Munich in May or June,[22] but he wasn't expecting to enjoy the experience after an absence of fourteen years. He didn't have the impression, he said, that the Germans had either learned anything from the war or forgotten anything. He was expecting to find plentiful evidence of nationalism, anti-Semitism, fascism, and nihilism.[23]

Back from a trip to Europe, the Dieterles said that S.S. men, though they were imprisoned in camps, were being issued the same rations as American troops. They could sometimes be seen sunbathing.[24] *Aufbau* reprinted an interview given to a Stockholm paper by the writer Ernst Wiechert, formerly, as Thomas put it, a "prominent member of the Inner Emigration." When he talked about Germany's guilt, he was accused of treachery. Stones were thrown at his windows, and he received so many threats that he asked for American protection. A guard was posted outside his house until he fled to Switzerland. In the interview he said that if Hitler reappeared in Germany tomorrow, between 60 and 80 percent of the people would welcome him with open arms.[25]

Thomas tried to analyze his ambivalence in a letter to Klaus, who'd declared himself to be "anti-German in the good old Uncle Heinrich style." When he thought of all the damage inflicted on him by "the accursed German rabble," Thomas answered, "I still see red and approve of all the punishment inflicted on the race God has smitten." But the term *anti-German* sounded odd. Though it was indisputable that Germanness was "quite a mess," it was good when Nietzsche said it, but when *Time* magazine said the same thing, it merely sounded ignorant. He'd been impressed by the proposals of the French premier, Georges Bidault, for the controlled depopulation of Germany: "Such a strange people should not be so numerous."[26]

In the United States, as Thomas had predicted, Roosevelt's death had been followed by a shift away from liberalism. Truman didn't share his predecessor's contempt for the House Un-American Activities Committee (HUAC), which had existed since 1938. In 1946 it started to operate on the assumption that Hollywood had been infiltrated by Communists. A friend of the Manns, the composer Hanns Eisler, was questioned in September 1946, and ordered not to leave the country; in October, Charlie Chaplin and the playwright Clifford Odets were summoned to appear. The committee divided the men under subpoena into two categories. The cooperative or "friendly" witnesses included Ronald Reagan, Walt Disney, and Gary Cooper; the "unfriendly" witnesses included Bertolt Brecht and the screenwriters Dalton Trumbo and Ring Lardner, Jr. If ex-Communists admitted that they'd been members of the Party, they had to choose between answering questions about other alleged Communists and being cited for contempt of Congress. Protesting in March, Thomas said the restriction of Eisler's freedom was "intended as the initial phase of a sweeping attack on the entire labour and progressive movement in the United States." If the attack continued unchecked, the consequences might be "as disastrous as those which overtook the German people."[27] Nine days after he wrote this, Erika, who'd applied for American citizenship, cabled him to say the decision had been postponed because of her liberal views on marriage and politics.[28] Her lesbianism was no secret to the FBI.

Working on the Nietzsche lecture and preparing himself for his first visit to postwar Europe, the seventy-one-year-old Thomas had to decide how much time and energy he should devote to political campaigning. His name was mentioned when Wilhelm Furtwängler, who'd been conducting the Berlin Philharmonic Orchestra during the war, made a speech to the commission for denazification: "Does Thomas Mann really think one shouldn't play Beethoven in Himmler's Germany?"[29] In March, Thomas wrote three pages of a letter to *Aufbau*, welcoming the fact that "this superb musician" was free to conduct in all four zones of Germany and admitting that he must have suffered "endless difficulties" under the Nazis,[30] but after a conversation with Katia, he decided to abandon the letter as "completely pointless and unseemly."[31]

To write about wartime events in Germany from Zeitblom's viewpoint, he'd assumed he could empathize with the people who'd stayed there. After reading Furtwängler's apologia, he conceded that he couldn't. He finally understood "what a dichotomy there is between our experience and that of those who stayed in Germany. Making contact across this gulf is quite impossible, and though I was incredulous at first, I have become more and more convinced that even my messages during the war and afterwards were regarded in Germany only as ignorant chatter that had no bearing on the experience of the Germans and had a consoling and invigorating effect only outside Germany."[32]

After working on it for six weeks, Thomas finished the lecture on March 17. It emphasizes the importance of an early essay in which Nietzsche challenged the view that historical objectivity was feasible. What we require from the historian, he said, is an artist's ability to recreate past reality.[33] Then, as later, Nietzsche's orientation was toward the aesthetic. It is only as an aesthetic phenomenon, he maintained, that existence and the world are permanently justified. This, argued Thomas, gives him a lot in common with Oscar Wilde. Many of his aphorisms could easily be mistaken for Wilde's. "It is only shallow people who do not judge by appearances," for instance. In fact the resemblance is only superficial, but Thomas made an important point in denying that Nietzsche had provided a philosophical substructure for Nazism. Hostile to democracy, he dreamed of a barbarism that would engender a renaissance of culture, but he belonged more deeply than he realized to the bourgeoisie, while his scorn for happiness was personal, not political. He also detested nationalism, imperialism, racism, and anti-Semitism.

Though Thomas didn't want to lecture on Nietzsche in Germany, he kept thinking, uneasily, about going there: While he was in Europe, he "could hardly avoid paying a short visit to Germany, at least to Munich, the city where I spent 40 years of my life, and where my younger brother still lives."[34] But five days later, when Erika arrived, she convinced him that it would be too dangerous.[35] He'd need a visa from the military government, which would have to take responsibility for his safety, though naturalized Americans weren't legally entitled to protection in their native country. It would be embarrassing to go around Munich with a bodyguard of military policemen, and have precautions against riot taken at every speech he made—a police cordon and checks on the public as it came in. Besides, what could he say? How could he talk about Germany without causing offense? "The Germans basically want to hear nothing said against their Third Reich. . . . Any speech I made would be hot air, evasion, lies, wishy-washy consolation." On Thursday, the day he entertained Heinrich with champagne to celebrate his seventy-sixth birthday, Thomas wrote to tell Viktor he'd decided against coming to Germany. They could meet in Zurich. Erika could probably arrange a visa for Viktor to come there.[36]

The lecture was much too long, but she helped him cut it, and made arrangements for the transatlantic journey. After a lot of hesitation they booked cabins on the *Queen Elizabeth*, which was due to sail on May 11.[37] But first he had to lecture at the Library of Congress and in New York. He and Katia left Pacific Palisades on April 22 to stay with the Borgeses in Chicago on their way to Washington, where they stayed, as usual, with the Meyers. At the Library on April 29 there were capacity audiences, as usual, in both auditoriums, and though Thomas felt nervous at first, the lecture went well.[38]

Together with Katia and Erika, he left the next day for New York, where he gave the lecture to an audience of two thousand at Hunter College.[39] They stayed on in New York till the eleventh, when, with two thousand other people, they embarked on the liner. On board he gave an interview to a Reuters correspondent, who reported him as saying that the Germans "appear full of self-pity, unable to see the chaos in neighbouring countries."[40]

They spent a week in London, staying at the Savoy. Giving a press conference, he said Germany was "already misusing her liberty and democracy," and again accused the Germans of self-pity. "Germany refuses to acknowledge that misery and tragedy are not hers alone, though she herself caused them."[41] Widely reported by the press in Germany, this increased his unpopularity there. His English publisher, Fredric Warburg, organized a reception for him at the hotel, with Harold

Nicolson as one of the guests. Before Thomas delivered the lecture at King's College, London University, on May 20, he said it was appropriate England should be the first European country he'd visited since the war. "It was Great Britain who in 1940, when all seemed lost, saved mankind by her steadfastness from the most horrible slavery. It is very doubtful whether any other nation would have had the spiritual forces of resistance to withstand the terrible trials that were imposed on her."[42]

The next day he recorded an interview in English for the BBC on "Germany: Her Character and Destiny," and another interview in German to be broadcast to Germany. But he was in no state to enjoy any of this. More debilitating than the exhaustion or the enervation was an intestinal disorder that seemed to have started in the chaos at Southampton when two thousand people were struggling to get their luggage off the ship.[43]

Before leaving London, Thomas sent another "message to Germany." Without spelling out reasons for not going there, he wanted to take the edge off any offense he might give, but what he said was non-committal, schoolmasterish, and vague.

> I am fully aware of the extraordinary difficulties and sufferings Germany has to face today, and as a German I participate in them with all my heart. But it must be said that it was not to be expected that a mere two years would be enough for Germany to recover from such a frightful crisis as Germany underwent. But I hope and believe that after two, three or five years, the horizon will be brighter again and that thanks to her congenital efficiency and vitality, Germany does not need to despair of her future.[44]

On May 24, the Saturday of the Whitsun weekend, he, Katia, and Erika flew in a private plane to Zurich, where they were going to stay for over a fortnight. Oprecht, Gret, and the two boys were waiting at the airport. They went to the theater in the evening, and during the next few days met old friends and revisited the Schiedhaldenstrasse, where shopkeepers greeted them warmly.

This was the day hostile articles started to appear in German papers, provoked partly by an ambiguity in the Reuters reports of the interview he'd given: "On the other hand I would not like to pay a visit to Munich and Bonn, where the university recently renewed my award of honorary Doctor of Philosophy, under the Allied bayonets." What he meant was that he'd have preferred to visit these cities without an armed escort, but the sentence was translated into German as if he didn't want to visit either city and thought it was pressure from the Allies that had made the university reinstate him.

The most vicious attack appeared in a Bremen paper, the *Weserkurier*. The writer, Manfred Hausmann, claimed to have seen a letter Thomas had written in 1933 to Hitler's minister of the interior, Wilhelm Frick, begging to come back to the Reich. Thomas hadn't declared his hostility to the regime until 1936, and had still been hesitating in 1934 about whether to go back, as Bermann wanted him to. There had been a good deal of correspondence, some of it with lawyers. Thirteen years later he wasn't sure whether he'd written to Frick, and the allegation was made when he was already becoming unpopular. The Germans were bound to dislike what he was saying in interviews, and to resent the exclusion of Germany from his European tour. All over Germany, newspapers denounced him, but he received a lot of invitations—some private, some from organizations—to visit Germany while he was in Europe. He made courteous excuses, but told Hermann Hesse the Furtwängler affair would have been enough to keep him outside the frontiers. "When I think of Germany at night, I go back to sleep as quickly as I can."45 This inverts the first two lines of a poem in which Heine said that when he thought of Germany at night, sleep evaded him.46

In Zurich, despite humidity and heat, Thomas immediately felt at home again, and had such a good time that he decided to go back every year.47 He ate in elegant restaurants with old friends, and went on shopping expeditions with Katia and Erika. He bought cigars, shoes, stationery, a straw hat. He saw several plays at the Schauspielhaus, including Strindberg's *Traumspiel* (*Dreamplay*) and a performance of *Götterdämmerung* conducted by Hans Knappertsbusch, who'd signed the 1933 complaint about his essay on Wagner.

What he enjoyed most was reading from *Doctor Faustus* at the Schauspielhaus, where, nine years earlier, he'd bade a reluctant farewell to Zurich by reading from *The Beloved Returns*. He was given the same table and the same chair. His first words to the audience were: "This is a reunion, a moving reunion . . ." He was interrupted by thunderous stamping and applause. In the *Neue Zürcher Zeitung*, Edward Korrodi, one of the journalists who'd attacked German émigré writers in 1936, helping to provoke Thomas into speaking out against the Nazis, wrote a warm appreciation of the reading. "What a phenomenon! The evil spirits could not damage the spiritual strength of this man, and the gods sanctioned the exception, granting a long life to their darling—the supple figure, the unfaded hair, the mischief at the corners of his lips, and the absolute charm of the spirit, the voice and the posture."48 After he'd read two sequences from *Doctor Faustus*, the stamping and applause were even more tumultuous.

Finding he could command high fees for lectures and readings, he read from the novel to Zurich students.49 He delivered the Nietzsche lecture at an International PEN conference in Zurich, where he also tried to win back some of the popularity he'd lost in Germany. On the second day of the conference he took an active part in discussions about forming a German PEN Club. He proposed the novelist and historian Ricarda Huch as president and declared his wholehearted support for three German writers who were present—Johannes Becher, Erich Kästner, and Ernst Wiechert. In effect he was recanting what he'd said in his letter to von Molo—that everything published in Germany between 1933 and 1945 should be pulped. And he went to Saint Gall—a drive of two and a half hours—to give a reading from *Doctor Faustus* in aid of a Munich orphanage.[50]

After four weeks in Zurich, he and Katia withdrew for a month's holiday in the Alps. "It is now very beautiful here, and it does one good after all the hustle and bustle. Splendid silent forests of pine trees with rocky scenery and gorges as in a Doré, and the view of the ledges, pinnacles and lofty meadows of the surrounding mountains is also something quite different from the everlasting Pacific."[51] In the hotel he felt attracted to both the flirtatious elevator boy, Louis Marti, and a young waiter, Delvai, who had "an extremely pleasant face and a gentle manner."[52] Later on, Thomas gave him a large tip, not wanting any expensive complications after he got back to the States: His home address had appeared with his letter in the *Neue Zeitung*.[53]

Exhausted by all the traveling, lectures, readings, and parties in his honor, Thomas had wanted a peaceful month in the Alps, but he had to correct galley proofs of *Doctor Faustus*, which were arriving in installments, and to defend himself against the attack by Manfred Hausmann. "Letters into the night" had been René Schickele's phrase for the desperate letters refugees and exiles wrote to the homeland, and Thomas admitted to having written many of them. But he had no copy of any letter to Frick. "If among these appeals sent to a Germany that was rapidly drifting downstream there is a letter to Frick, and if Manfred Hausmann has managed to get possession of it, he ought to publish it in full instead of peddling what is obviously a falsified summary of its contents. I am certain that such a document from the year 1933 will not be discreditable to me."[54]

Hausmann's response was that he'd possessed a copy of the letter till 1942, when he was in danger of having his house searched. He could remember its contents exactly, because he'd read it so many times and read it out to other people. It had been given to him by friends who'd persuaded him to stay in Germany by proving that Thomas Mann wanted to come back. Six weeks later Thomas was vindicated when the letter was found among the Ministry of the Interior's papers. Written to Frick in April 1933, it was about the passport that had expired and the property that had been confiscated.[55]

Reading galley proofs of *Doctor Faustus*, Thomas had mixed feelings.

"Together with some really remarkable features, it has plenty of longueurs, weaknesses and flaws."[56] He was still worrying, and talking to Katia, about the risk of putting in so many undisguised portraits of friends and acquaintances. He thought of these as "murders," but said he'd done penance for them by having the operation on his lung,[57] and claimed to have let everyone else off more lightly than himself, the book being "a sort of radical and diabolical self-portrait."[58] But Annette Kolb was almost certain to recognize herself in Jeannette Scheurl, who's described as having the face of an elegant sheep in which aristocratic and peasant qualities are mingled, in the same way that Bavarian dialect is somehow combined in her speech with a French accent. Though extraordinarily intelligent, she's caught in the naively questioning ignorance of an aging virgin.

On July 20, the day Thomas and Katia left the hotel, Delvai waited on him for the last time, and, bringing the last cup of coffee, made sure his admirer didn't leave without saying goodbye. At the last minute, seeing the waiter in the entrance hall as he was about to step into the car loaded with luggage, Thomas waved.[59]

At the invitation of his Italian publisher, Arnoldo Mondadori, Thomas and Katia spent four days on Lake Maggiore, staying in the "luxuriously uncomfortable country house of this patriarchal family," and they were taken on an excursion to Isola Bella.[60]

They so enjoyed being in Zurich that they spent another fortnight there before leaving in the middle of August for a week in Amsterdam, followed by ten days in Noordwijk, where they returned, after an eight-year absence, to the Huis ter Duin, which Thomas still called "the most beautiful seaside hotel in the world." But prices had shot up, and they were disappointed not only with their bedroom but with the food and the service. It was so hot that he wore short trousers for breakfast on the balcony, and had his first swim in the sea for many years. What he enjoyed most, though, was sitting in a wicker beach chair and writing.[61]

They finally sailed back to the States on the *Westerdam*, a Dutch steamer which had been attacked twice by the Germans and bombed once by the English.[62] Among their fellow passengers was the German painter Max Beckmann and his wife, who was more attractive, Thomas noted, than her husband. Though the Beckmanns joined in such games as Lotto, the Manns spent a good deal of time with them, chatting. After more than three months in Europe, Thomas felt disoriented. "Had the feeling of going back 'once again', as if Europe, after all, has again become home for me and my work. But it is still too uncertain, and one must first see what happens to Germany, Russia and the small countries."[63]

After arriving in New York on Monday, September 8, they stayed for two nights in the St. Regis before going on to Chicago, not just to see the Borgeses but to call in at Billings Hospital, where Thomas was weighed, X-rayed, and had samples of his blood checked. "A very pretty young doctor was in charge." He also saw Dr. Adams, who seemed highly satisfied with him.[64]

When they finally got back to their home in Pacific Palisades on September 14, they'd been away for almost five months.

Suicidal Son

WITH A LOT OF ACCUMULATED correspondence and no more work to do on *Doctor Faustus*, Thomas felt depressed, and on October 7, 1947, he listed four reasons. The trip to Europe had unsettled him. He was impatient to know how the novel would be received when the German edition came out in Stockholm on October 17. He was worried about the witch-hunt for Communists and the change in the American political climate. He was waiting for news from Dial Press about the Goethe anthology he'd agreed to edit in collaboration with Klaus.

He was also worrying about Germany. When Alexander Frey sent him a list of eighty-eight writers who'd taken the oath of allegiance to Hitler, he noticed that one was the director of Munich's municipal library, Hans Ludwig Held.[1] What Thomas felt toward Germany was "a mixture of sympathy and fear or distrust."[2] Sometimes contempt was prevalent, as when he said three quarters of the German people were meschuga—the Yiddish word for crazy.[3] But, more seriously, "the people as a whole never found any other fault with the monster Hitler than that he lost the war."[4] If Germany was rearmed, he thought, it would "have non-Russian Europe in its pocket within fifty years at most."[5] When the writer Hanns Johst said in an interview that Nazism was the only suitable form of government for Germany, Thomas commented: "I think he is right about that."[6]

But if the United States had once seemed a haven of liberty, it was now more like the Weimar Republic in its last days. On October 2, Hanns Eisler was arrested and threatened with deportation. "Nervous dreams of protest, agitation and self-sacrifice, which would no doubt be stupid and would not earn me any thanks."[7] Thomas thought of writing a pamphlet modeled on Zola's "J'accuse," but Adorno dissuaded him.[8] When Eisler came to dinner a week later, he seemed harassed, but Erika helped him to draft an application for Czech citizenship, while Einstein, Chaplin, Heinrich, and Thomas were going to petition that he should be allowed to leave voluntarily.[9] After seeing reports on hearings of the House Committee and realizing that as "witnesses" the accused had no rights,[10] Thomas contributed to a radio program called "Hollywood Fights Back." He'd seen a lot of Hollywood films, he said, and "If

Communist propaganda had been smuggled into any of them, it must have been most thoroughly hidden." Germany had familiarized him with "spiritual intolerance, political inquisition and declining legal security, and all this in the name of an alleged 'state of emergency.' . . . What followed was fascism, and what followed fascism was war."[11]

After waiting in suspense for reactions to *Doctor Faustus*, he was glad to find a long, enthusiastic review by Max Rychner in the Zurich paper *Die Tat*: "The world has never before had a book like this one."[12] Writing to Rychner, Thomas admitted that tears came to his eyes whenever he heard any serious discussion of the book. He'd been both upset and comforted by this, its first formal public assessment.[13] He believed in *Doctor Faustus* as "the best that I have to give and probably the best that I ever had to give, for it is the synthesis of my capacities, my abilities and my knowledge, the most direct, most personal and most passionate of my books, the one in which I have invested more and which has gnawed more deeply into me than any earlier book."[14] By early December the German-language edition had sold ten thousand copies outside Germany.[15]

While compiling the Goethe anthology for Dial Press, choosing material, commissioning new translations, and writing an introduction, Thomas was trying to make up his mind what to do next. He thought of going back to an old idea of translating Cocteau's 1934 play *La Machine infernale*, but Cocteau, who knew Klaus, had been hinting at the possibility of translating one of his plays into French. Though Thomas wrote to Cocteau, trying to encourage this and saying he was still interested in the 1934 play, he knew it would look as if he were trying disingenuously to help his son.[16] But *La Machine infernale* is a reworking of the Oedipus tragedy, and, after *Doctor Faustus*, Thomas wanted to tackle a comic subject. "What would you feel," he asked Hermann Hesse in November, "if I were to entertain myself in my old age by developing the Felix Krull fragment into a full-length picaresque novel?"[17]

It might have seemed a good idea for him to edit an English-language Goethe anthology, but as a collaborator Klaus was less helpful than he might have been if they were living in the same city. Thomas, who read little poetry in English, was ill qualified to make decisions about which of the existing translations he should use—Percy Bysshe Shelley and Sir Walter Scott were among the poets who'd translated Goethe—and (since Auden was too busy on other projects) which English and American poets should be commissioned to make new translations. Thomas's introduction would probably have been better if he hadn't already written about Goethe so many times, both fictionally and critically. The lackadaisically biographical "Fantasia on Goethe" compares the ennoblement of the thirty-three-year-old writer to Pharaoh's promotion of Joseph, and contains variations on so many of the Goethean themes Thomas had already developed that Erika called the introduction a compilation of his earlier essays.[18] Two weeks later he noted that he'd written more of the "Goethe compilation."[19] But after finishing it the next day, he felt glad to have completed something.[20] It was his first serious piece of writing since he'd finished *Doctor Faustus* in January.

In December he wrote a new introduction for the school chapter of *Buddenbrooks*, which was published in a Dial Press anthology called *The World's Best*, and on December 21 he started work on a novel based on a story he'd found when searching in the *Gesta Romanorum* for a plot that Adrian could use for a puppet opera. The story that most appealed to Thomas was about Pope Gregory, who'd been born from a liaison between brother and sister, and had committed incest with his mother. For this he atoned by spending seventeen years on an isolated rock before he was chosen by God to become pope. The story had been told in a medieval poem by Hartmann von Aue. But Thomas, who hadn't read this, had thought of "stealing" the subject from Adrian and using it himself.[21]

It was hard to get started. He was so averse to the idea of writing another book that he wondered whether he'd ever again feel fully involved in work.[22] Wanting him to work on the Cocteau play, Katia began to sketch out a rough translation,[23] but the project came to nothing. He was in no mood to start traveling again, either on holiday or for lectures and readings, but a tempting invitation to Germany came when the liberal mayor of Frankfurt, Walter Kolb, was organizing a centenary celebration for the start of constitutional government. On May 18, 1848, the National Assembly had held its first meeting at the Pauluskirche in Frankfurt, and Kolb wanted to celebrate the centenary by having Thomas speak at a reception on May 18, 1948, in the Palmengarten, the greenhouse used for such events. Believing the Germans were trying to ignore the whole of their past,[24] Thomas would have liked to help Kolb, but after some hesitation, he demurred, describing himself as an old man wearied by hard work and the shocks inflicted by contemporary history.[25]

He'd never be able to make a more definitive statement about contemporary history than he had in *Doctor Faustus*. The German edition wouldn't appear until the autumn, but reactions from German readers were gratifying. Ludwig Marcuse reviewed it in *Aufbau*, calling it the most un-Goethean of all Faust stories,[26] and Hanns Eisler wrote an encomiastic letter: "What particularly impresses me is not only the insight into the theory of composition technique and into the social situation of music, with its contradictions, but also the way in which you have dreamed up musical passages. . . . There are also political formulations with a boldness and an insight into the historical weaknesses of the Germans that is otherwise to be found only in Marx."27 In Sweden the reviewer for *Svenska Dagbladet* was no less impressed, calling *Doctor Faustus* the Divine Comedy of the twentieth century.28

But Thomas still had to face trouble over the musical passages. Both Schoenberg and Adorno felt cheated: He'd taken a lot from them with no acknowledgment. Hoping to pacify Schoenberg, Thomas sent him a copy inscribed: "To the real one,"29 but Alma Mahler stirred up trouble by convincing the composer that his posthumous reputation was in danger. After a long silence, he wrote an angry letter, enclosing what seemed to be an extract from an imaginary article. It purported to be taken from the *Encyclopedia Americana* of 1988. It said that Thomas Mann, originally a musician, had invented the twelve-tone system. After becoming a writer, he at first raised no objection when it was appropriated by a thievish composer, Arnold Schoenberg, but in *Doctor Faustus* he claimed it as his own intellectual property. The article was signed with the name Hugo Triebsamen.

Replying to Schoenberg on February 17, Thomas applauded "the pious zeal with which your disciples guard the glory and honour of the master," but argued that everyone knew who'd invented the twelve-tone system. In identifying music with Schoenbergian music and in attributing the innovations to a fictional composer, the novel hadn't been undercutting Schoenberg's historical importance, but affirming it.30 Four days later Thomas found out from Alma Mahler that Hugo Triebsamen didn't exist—Schoenberg had written the text himself. If the word *Triebsamen* existed, it would mean something like "sprouting seed." Acting as an intermediary, Alma Mahler told Thomas that Schoenberg insisted on an acknowledgment.31 Reluctantly Thomas added a note to appear at the end of the book—not too close to the text, he specified—explaining that the twelve-tone system was the intellectual property of a contemporary composer and theoretician, Arnold Schoenberg. Listening to the song of the Rhinemaidens on an old recording of *Die Walküre* while in the middle of this contretemps, Thomas decided that this one passage was worth as much as the combined output of Schoenberg, Berg, Ernst Krenek, and Adrian Leverkühn.32 He was increasingly inclined to think of Adrian as a real composer.

It was no easier to appease Adorno, who began to tell people what a substantial contribution he'd made.33 Willing to acknowledge help, but unsure how this should be done, Thomas discussed the problem with Adorno, who was pleased when Thomas offered to write an autobiographical book explaining how he'd written the novel. As so often before, he also had to contend with the resentment of friends who found unflattering portraits of themselves. It was easy enough to placate Hans Reisiger and Emil Preetorius, but Annette Kolb was so angry that she never spoke to Thomas again, and neither did her daughter.

Anxiety, exhaustion, and uncertainty about his next book were combining to make him accident-prone, and on the evening of February 26, at a dinner party in the house of the sociologist Max Horkheimer, he fell off a step between the living room and the hallway. The pain was worse than the shock. His left arm was hurting from the shoulder down, and he couldn't move it. His host telephoned Dr. Wolf, an orthopedist, who came along and said there was a slight fracture of the shoulder bone. He treated it, and gave Thomas a painkiller, which didn't eliminate all the pain. In the morning he needed Katia's help to wash, but the pain didn't stop him from working on the new novel. Later on in the morning he consulted his own doctor—yet another new one, Dr. Mendelssohn—who went with him to the X-ray office, where the diagnosis was confirmed. The seventy-two-year-old writer came away with his arm in a sling.[34]

Despite painkillers and sleeping tablets, he went on feeling a lot of discomfort and sleeping only interruptedly, sometimes in the armchair, where he was less in danger of putting weight on his injured arm. An X-ray on March 26 showed that the fracture had almost healed, and by the end of the month he could take a bath without help.[35] Looking back on the accident a few months later, he attributed it to restlessness while making the awkward transition from *Doctor Faustus* to *The Holy Sinner* (*Der Erwählte*).

In old age it's all too easy, when convalescing, to relish the passage of time as if it were identical with amelioration of the condition, but Thomas, anxious about how much longer he could survive, watched the calendar. "The middle of the month already," he noted on March 15. "But at least I am now pressing forwards with a piece of work that promises novelties, and things are better for me than they have been for weeks." He'd made contact with the medievalist Samuel Singer, professor of German literature at the University of Bern. Unable to find a copy of Hartmann von Aue's *Gregorius auf dem Steine* in the United States, even in the Library of Congress, Thomas had approached him in January,[36] and Singer not only lent him a copy but translated the Middle High German, which Thomas understood only imperfectly, and answered such questions as whether the rock on which Gregory stood was in the sea or in a lake.[37]

Singer approved wholeheartedly of the way Thomas had divided his life between literature and politics. "You have intervened powerfully in world events. We were all so grateful to you for that, and we now confront new developments helplessly and despairingly." "Confuses me with Roosevelt," Thomas commented. "And forgets how much better so many things are than they would be if Hitler had won."[38]

In *The Holy Sinner* much depends on the balance Thomas struck between colloquial German and archaism. Calling it "pure experiment, vaguely medieval, linguistically inclining towards the international,"[39] he thought he'd found the language he was using by graduating through the Lutheran German he'd used in *Doctor Faustus* and the curious Swiss German he'd given Echo.[40] At last he felt seriously involved in writing again,[41] and by the end of June he'd completed eight chapters. As in the *Joseph* novels, he was fleshing out a story that had been told only sketchily, and he was again dealing with characters oriented toward the divine, but he was introducing a lot of comedy, partly through mixing the archaic with the colloquial. Since the action was set in the mythical duchy of Flanders-Artois, he was adding a bit of old French to the mixture,[42] and he was enjoying himself.

As in his 1905 story "The Blood of the Walsungs," his instinct when treating incest between brother and sister was to write casually about circumstantial details. Before he makes love to Sibylla, Wiligis slits the throat of a dog that wouldn't stop howling. When he read this chapter to the Neumanns, Anna Jacobson, Monika, Elisabeth, Michael, and Gret, Thomas couldn't help joining in their laughter,[43] but he had no deep commitment to this "legend-novel," as he called it. He thought of it as a postlude to *Doctor Faustus*, a way of passing the time.[44] "But the thing has little meaning," he said.[45]

Certainly it had little relevance to current events, but events themselves seemed pitifully anticlimactic. In June, the eighty-three-year-old Richard Strauss was acquitted by a denazification court in Frankfurt, while Thomas's former friend Hans Pfitzner had been found innocent, in spite of having worked under the Nazis as a cultural senator. In 1946, before the execution of Hans Frank, governor of Poland from 1939, Pfitzner had sent him a telegram: "Dear friend, with you with all my thoughts." "I must say," Thomas wrote with perverse irony, "that is so stupid and Don Quixotic, it goes so far beyond all reasonable bounds that it reconciles one with his acquittal."[46]

ON THE NIGHT OF Saturday, July 10, Klaus tried to kill himself. He'd been living in Santa Monica since the end of May in a rented apartment. He was taken to the hospital, and the police told his parents what had happened. He'd cut his wrist, swallowed sleeping tablets, and then tried to gas himself. Katia, who seldom botched anything she attempted, couldn't stop herself from saying: "If he wanted to kill himself, why didn't he do it properly?"[47] But it was she who went to the hospital at about one in the morning. Thomas didn't want to see Klaus.

In the morning, Erika, who was staying with the Walters, came to see her parents before she went to Klaus, and it was arranged that he, too, should move in with the Walters.[48] On Wednesday afternoon, she came to the house with Klaus's friend Harold to collect her brother's things. Thomas describes Harold as "a good-natured and silent young workman who is supposed to have wept." Thomas wrote "a letter of condolence to Klaus, with Erika partly acting as secretary."[49]

The first time Klaus saw his father, he was told off for wanting to hurt his mother.[50] Thomas seems to have had no idea how deeply he could upset Klaus by suggesting that he would have been less affected than Katia by the suicide. Writing to Adorno, Thomas complained that Klaus was "spoilt by her understandingness about everything—and by mine. . . . The impulse is present in him and all the circumstances favour it—the one exception being that he has a parental home on which he can always rely, though naturally he does not want to. One good sign is that he hates the publicity over his failed attempt because 'it makes it so hard for one to try again.' " This is reminiscent of Thomas's reaction to Carla's suicide in 1910, when he seemed less sorry for her than angry with her for what she'd done to the family. To other friends he blamed Klaus's suicide attempt on the international situation.[51]

At the age of eleven Klaus had written a play about a suicidal schoolboy, and in his autobiographical *Kind dieser Zeit* (*Child of This Time*), published when he was twenty-six, he'd said he was attracted by every form of self-destruction, and had often toyed with the "sweet and terrible idea" of suicide. Two years earlier, in 1930, he'd written an article "Selbstmörder," about friends who thought it better to end their lives than continue the struggle, and in 1932, when Ricki Hallgarten killed himself, Klaus wrote: "Death, which used to seem so alien, has become more familiar since such an intimate friend of my earthly life voluntarily entrusted himself to it. Before going there oneself, one feels rather at home in a place where a friend is living." In July 1941 he wrote: "If I were my own master I would kill myself, as sure as I'm alive. I've never understood why anyone should be afraid of death—when it's only life that's so terrible."

When he volunteered for the U.S. Army in February 1942, he said it wasn't for honorable reasons but from surfeit and masochism. According to Golo, he was close to suicide then, but he made no attempt to kill himself till 1948. He was in financial difficulties, but this was nothing new. What was new was gonorrhea,[52] but this was curable. There was no cure, though, for the lack of love in his relationship with his father. It wasn't just that he'd always felt overshadowed by Thomas, or that they'd never been able to discuss homosexuality. Klaus was at an advantage in knowing he'd opened himself up to impulses his father had rigorously suppressed, but at a disadvantage in needing attention his father had always denied him. The pattern was being repeated when Katia and Erika visited him in a hospital, but Thomas spared only enough time to write a letter. Nor was he willing to admit that Klaus's suicidal impulses had anything to do with lack of love within the family.

Klaus had once believed that his own death would immediately be followed by Erika's, and this had acted as a deterrent against suicide (see page 396). It was obvious now that she'd no longer react by killing herself. Since the end of the war, she'd been spending less time with her brother and more time with Thomas, staying in Pacific Palisades and accompanying him on lecture tours. By the end of 1947 she wanted to write a book about him, while he missed her whenever she wasn't with him. He was keen for her to live at home as "secretary, biographer, nurse, daughter-adjutant."[53] He couldn't have been unaware how unhappy Klaus was at seeing so little of his sister, but it was typical of Thomas not to visit his son in the hospital.

He'd often written about incest, and in the third chapter of *The Holy Sinner* the Duke is jealous when his daughter's only desire is to be with her brother. Sibylla tells Wiligis she enjoys it more when he kisses her than when their father scratches her neck and cheeks with his rust-colored mustaches. But on coming home, Duke Grimald insists that he's still man enough to entertain his daughter. If Wiligis flatters himself that Sibylla is closer to him than to their sound and sturdy father, he can expect to be disabused with a couple of blows. The younger man promptly retreats.

The suicide attempt didn't deflect Thomas from his working routine, but on July 20 he put the fiction aside to start *The Genesis of a Novel* (*Die Entstehung eines Romans*), going through old diaries and underlining passages in red ink. Describing the way he had used fifty-year-old diaries when writing about Rudi Schwerdtfeger, Thomas had yet another opportunity to think about amorous adventures that had made him almost happy.[54]

But if, like Aschenbach, he'd gone through most of his life sacrificing chances of Dionysian passion on the altar of Apollonian restraint, at least he'd been rewarded, like his character, with fame. He was told that because the Book-of-the-Month Club had selected *Doctor Faustus*, Knopf was going to print 250,000 copies.[55]

Even success on this scale didn't make him less compulsive about working. In early August, Thomas had another attack of gastric flu that lasted over ten days. He had a high temperature, felt weak, and sweated with exhaustion, but forced himself to go on writing, though he knew he'd have recovered faster if he'd rested.[56] On Wednesday, August 11, he was so impatient to start working that he didn't take his morning bath, and on Thursday his eagerness made him forget to shave.[57] He was ill again during the first week of September but had recovered sufficiently by the middle of the month to find that sexual desire was giving him no peace.[58]

During this illness he had to decide whether to intercede on behalf of the man who'd once been his friend and collaborator—Ernst Bertram. In 1945, when Thomas had tried to find out what had happened to him, it was impossible to get any news, but on July 23 a letter arrived from one of Bertram's former students asking whether Thomas would testify for him, as Hermann Hesse had. Bertram, who'd lost his professorship in 1946, had been classified by the denazification court as a "lesser offender." Replying to Schmitz, Thomas conceded that Bertram was good, pure, and exceptionally intelligent, but rejected the assertion that he was "never a National Socialist." Without being a card-carrying party member, he'd accepted the racist ideology and had gone on publishing, acting as a spokesman for the official culture. Thomas's view was that Bertram shouldn't be allowed to go on teaching but shouldn't be deprived of his pension.[59]

When Katia read what he was writing about *Doctor Faustus*, she was disturbed by the amount of emphasis he was placing on Adorno's contributions, and Erika agreed with her mother.[60] Thomas could afford to be generous: The book's future in the United States was guaranteed, but, like Knopf, Thomas was highly irritated by critics who attacked it.[61] In *The New York Times Book Review*, writing under the title "Dr. Mann versus a Teutonic Mephisto," Harry Levin suggested that the Devil was "not in such good form as when he interviewed Ivan Karamazov," while "Leverkühn remains a symbolic shadowy figure, whose reserve is accentuated by long tirades in the manner of Luther's table-talk." In Levin's opinion, Romain Rolland's novel *Jean-Christophe* "however dated, is somewhat more convincing in its presentation of musical life," and far from being moved to tears, like so many of Thomas's friends, by Nepomuk's fatal illness, Levin said Adrian had "a blighting effect on the personalities around him, notably upon the little nephew whose death repeats *da capo* the ending of *Buddenbrooks*."[62]

The New Yorker published an article called "A New Deal with the Old Nick" by Hamilton Basso, who called the novel "a thick, heavy pudding" and compared it unfavorably with Goethe's *Faust*. Thomas's "philosophical digressions," he said, "slow down the movement of his book to a pace less lively than a crawl," and in his view, the central character "never really comes to life."[63] Writing in English, Thomas said: "The *New Yorker* should really be ashamed of its Hamilton Basso who is stupid like a tenor and had obviously no inclining of what he was talking about."[64]

It would have taken more than a set of bad reviews to make Thomas wish he were living and working in Germany. On November 2, he was going to vote for the first time in an American election, and while there was no question of supporting the Republican, Thomas Dewey, Thomas hesitated for a long time about whether to vote for Truman or Henry Wallace, who had been Roosevelt's vice president from 1941 to 1945 and had founded a new liberal party called the Third Party. Thomas had become so disenchanted with American politics that he now called the whole Roosevelt era "just one great un-American activity." He hated the House Committee, led by J. Parnell Thomas and John E. Rankin, as much, he said, as he hated Hitler.[65] It seemed that a new kind of president was needed for the new situation. Katia voted for Truman, but, believing Dewey was going to win, Thomas gave his vote to Wallace, as did many other former supporters of Roosevelt, wanting to strengthen Democratic opposition to Republican government. Truman was elected. Would he now have the courage, Thomas wondered, "to get rid of the Fascistic monsters around him? Will the power of the bankers and generals vanish, and the will of the people act as a force towards peace?"[66]

In 1948 it was hard to believe there wouldn't be a third world war. In February, Soviet-backed Communists had seized power in Czechoslovakia, and the ensuing purge had made the country into a satellite. The Soviet military authorities in Berlin had designs on the whole city, and in April they stopped the trains and trucks supplying food to the Allied sectors. For more than twelve months, provisions and fuel had to be delivered by air. At the end of June, Marshal Tito and the other leaders of the Yugoslav Communist Party had been denounced for activities incompatible with Marxism-Leninism, and for favoring the Western powers. But by keeping the confidence of the party, Tito survived and expelled all Comintern supporters.

In November, Erika and Klaus were both denounced in a Munich paper as "leading agents of Stalin in the USA"[67]—another example of the hysteria engendered by the cold war. While Thomas was planning a European lecture tour for the bicentenary of Goethe's birth, one of his reasons for excluding Germany was that it would be difficult to visit both zones. He didn't want to give one precedence over the other; a stay in Germany would involve "pain, confusion and an ill-timed strain on my nerves."[68] He'd been invited to speak at the Goethe celebrations in Frankfurt, but, as he wrote to Hermann Hesse, "I often see it reported in German papers that I am going there next summer, but I do not believe a word of it."[69]

"In Germany," he said, "there are two, three or perhaps four people I would like to see again. The others all make me shudder."[70] The Germans he wanted to see again were probably his brother Viktor and other members of the family. At the end of 1945, when the Nuremberg trials started, Thomas had been in favor of them, but, as he told the United Press Association, he'd since become disillusioned:

> Why did Himmler and Göring have to swallow their cyanide? Why did Ribbentrop and the other Nazi halfwits have to hang on the gallows when today 40% of the higher German functionaries are ex-Nazis, when in Bavaria 60% of the judges and 76% of the public prosecutors are former party members? When the sadistic murderess Ilse Koch is released, and Papen, the guiltiest of the guilty, is permitted to be absolved by the Germans, and when the big industrialists who financed Hitler and helped the Nazi regime into the saddle do not only go scot-free thanks to their international friendships, but are also returned to their posts as industrial leaders and, as deputies of the victors, carry out the German rearmament? Everybody knows that the de-nazification of Germany has failed completely–if there can be talk of failure where no earnest desire for success ever existed.[71]

The winter in California was unusually severe, with snow falling for the first time in seventeen years. Frido and Toni, who were staying with their grandparents, played excitedly in the snow, but Thomas was depressed and irked by the ice on his balcony, the storms, the hail, the constant dripping when the snow began to thaw. One day, when he was out walking with Frido, they found a brightly colored butterfly frozen rigid.[72] Frido wasn't yet nine, but partly because of the way her father treated him, Erika was convinced he'd grow into a homosexual.[73]

Thomas was becoming more inclined to depend on his daughter's judgment. He was having hormone injections, and he was still sexually potent, but acutely aware of how rapidly time was passing, and he was finding it harder to make decisions without consultation within the family.[74] When he finished writing his Goethe lecture, he asked Erika to make cuts,[75] and before sending his statement to the United Press Association, he consulted Katia, Klaus, and Golo. The question of whether to visit Germany was incessantly discussed with both family and friends. The Neumanns, who were still advising him not to go, doubted whether Jews would be safe after the Allied troops withdrew.[76] Erika and Klaus were both against a visit to Germany. When the Bavarian Academy of the Arts was reconstituted, Thomas decided not to join it, but on February 24 he learned that it had elected him president of the literary section, and in March he decided to accept this position, although it would make it harder for him to visit Europe without visiting Germany. He was also being wooed in the Soviet Zone: Awarded the Weimar Goethe Prize, he accepted this, too.

At the beginning of March, though still undecided, he was planning to deliver the Goethe lecture in Munich without visiting any other city:

The Americans would be outraged if he went into the Soviet zone.[77] He had no desire to see what remained of Lübeck after the Allied raids, and he had neither the time nor the energy to travel around Germany.[78] On Friday, March 4, when Heinrich came to dinner, Erika left the table in a rage. "Her irrational grief over the possibility of my visit to Munich. Desultory conversation with sons over the question. Irritating and troublesome on account of Erika." When she came down to breakfast, her eyes were red.[79]

Heinrich was another source of worry: It was hard to see how he'd cope while Thomas, Katia, and Erika were in Europe. Heinrich was seventy-eight and frail. In October, Katia had found him a new apartment within walking distance of Pacific Palisades, and had helped him to settle in, even arranging for a live-in nurse. But there was no telephone, and Heinrich kept turning up at the house for meals, putting a "serious strain" on Katia, who was now nearly sixty-five.[80] When he came to dinner on March 14, he seemed weaker than ever. He had little appetite, and could barely remain good-tempered. There were awkward pauses in the conversation. Before leaving, he had a severe asthma attack and had to recover on the sofa.[81] He had resisted the idea of going into the hospital and turned a deaf ear on conversations about the cost of the nurse. Thomas and Katia both thought him ungrateful for the help they were giving him.[82]

In April, Heinrich was awarded the German National Prize for Art and Literature and invited to become president of the German Academy of the Arts in East Berlin. It was hard for him to decide. In Santa Monica he'd been living in obscurity and penury, depending on charity from his younger brother; the East German appointment would solve his financial problems by putting him in the power of a regime controlled by Moscow and nominally led by men he despised—Walter Ulbricht and Otto Grotewohl.

Klaus left California on March 20, bound for New York and then Amsterdam, where he was to do some work for Querido, before going on to work in the South of France. But he rang up at the end of the month to reiterate his warnings against a visit to Germany.[83] Thomas was still hesitating, but the pressure was mounting.[84] Peter Suhrkamp, Erich von Kahler, and Emil Preetorius were all urging him to make peace with Germany by going there.[85] He was still being attacked in German newspapers,[86] and his lecture on Goethe and democracy was too anti-German to be delivered in Germany. Perhaps he could prepare another lecture while he was in Switzerland, but it would be hard to find the right tone for Munich.[87] In mid-April he was still undecided about whether to go: "I would feel too uncertain of the ground I was standing on,"[88] and in a letter written on April 17 he said he wasn't going.[89]

He was looking forward to being in Zurich again. Two years previously, returning to the United States, he'd been greeted by a passport control official with the words "Welcome home," but he now felt Switzerland to be his favorite country.[90] In America, the anticommunist hysteria made him uncomfortable. On April 2, *Life* published a report on a dinner held at the Waldorf-Astoria by the Council of Arts, Sciences and Professions, which had organized an International Cultural and Scientific Conference for Peace. Photographs of fifty prominent people, including Thomas, were collected under the caption "Dupes and Fellow Travelers Dress Up Communist Fronts."[91] In fact, Thomas hadn't attended the dinner but had sent a long telegram to the chairman, Dr. Harlow Shapley, saying the authorities had been trying to discredit the delegates by issuing visas to delegates from Soviet-controlled countries and refusing them to representatives of Western countries so that the peace conference would look like a communistic venture.[92] Thomas also sent a telegram to Secretary of State Dean Acheson complaining about the refusal of visas to the French, Italian, and Brazilian delegates.[93]

He was already planning the lecture tour that would keep him away from home for four months—there would be fourteen pieces of luggage. Ten days before leaving, he received a letter asking why he'd attended a meeting that had apparently been dominated by Communists and "used chiefly as a sounding board for Communist propaganda."[94] He took time to write a lengthy answer, explaining the facts and adding: "No economist will be able to tell you how we can ever withdraw from the cold war without an economic crisis, and the solution to the latter, of course, would be actual warfare."[95]

At the end of March he heard an unconfirmed report that he'd been awarded Germany's most prestigious literary award, the Goethe Prize, in Frankfurt. Tentatively he began to think of changing his plans to go there,[96] but when he left for Chicago on April 26 with Katia and Erika, he was still uncertain whether to draft a lecture for Germany while in Switzerland. If the only speech he had to make was in acceptance of the prize, it could be short and improvised.[97]

The trip to the East Coast followed the usual pattern, though this time, besides seeing the Borgeses in Chicago, Thomas gave his lecture on "Goethe and Democracy" at the university there, which was also putting on a Goethe exhibition.[98] He had a check-up, with X-rays, in the Billings Hospital before going on with Katia and Erika to Washington, where they stayed with the Meyers. Thomas was not only to deliver the lecture at the Library of Congress on May 2 but to receive the quinquennial award of the American Academy of Arts and Letters. He also had to meet Professor Walter Hallstein, who was about to become the leader of the UNESCO commission when the Federal Republic of Ger-

many was founded on May 23. Now, on behalf of Frankfurt's Oberbürgermeister, Walter Kolb, Professor Hallstein confirmed that Thomas
had been awarded the Goethe Prize and upset Erika by persuading him
to accept it personally on August 28 at Frankfurt's Goethe celebrations.[99] Thomas had finally decided to visit Germany after an absence
of sixteen years.

Both Germanies

AFTER HAVING DINNER in Washington with the Meyers and reading Conrad's *The Secret Agent* on the night train, Thomas arrived in New York with Katia and Erika on May 4, 1949. They got up at 6:15 and breakfasted at the St. Regis, where they stayed for six nights. Thomas lectured on Goethe at Mount Holyoke and Hunter colleges before the three of them made their first transatlantic flight on May 10. In London, staying at the Savoy, they noticed how much more prosperous the city looked than two years previously.[1]

On May 13 he was solemnly dressed in a red gown to become a doctor of letters at Oxford University. Held in a beautiful fourteenth-century hall, the ceremony struck him as "amusing and moving at the same time."[2] He delivered his Goethe lecture in German at the Taylorian Institute. Back in London he met T. S. Eliot at a PEN Club reception but found him "impolite and incidentally unforthcoming." He also saw Fredric Warburg and met Ernest Newman, the *Sunday Times* music critic who had praised *Doctor Faustus*.[3]

On Thursday, May 19, he flew with Katia and Erika to Stockholm. Edgar Baron Uexküll, who'd befriended Thomas in the twenties, met them at the airport. He'd been involved in the plot of July 20, 1944, against Hitler, and had settled in Sweden after being released from a concentration camp. The Swedes seemed well disposed toward Thomas, but a Frankfurt paper, *Tägliche Rundschau*, had invited readers to express views on the award of the Goethe Prize to him. The majority of the published statements were critical of his attitude to Germany. "If there is much more of this sort of thing," he said, "I shall not go."[4]

On Sunday, Uexküll took them to a seventeenth-century castle, where they had dinner with another baron, but they heard that night that Klaus was in a Cannes hospital. He'd made another suicide attempt. Later, a telephone call told them he was dead.

He'd written to Katia and Erika, on May 20, giving no indication of any intention to kill himself. His letter reports on the bad weather in Cannes, on friends and plans for the summer. He suggested meeting Erika in Switzerland during June.[5] She'd written to him on the fifteenth, but the letters crossed in the post, and hers reached him a few hours before he killed himself.[6] She addressed him as "my very dear one," urging him in what was intended as a breezy style to stop taking drugs. "Let's get together really soon and be together and have some healthy fun, so that you get better."[7] According to Golo, it wasn't uncharacteristic or coincidental that Klaus took his life while she was traveling with their parents on one of Thomas's lecture tours.[8]

As before, Thomas ignored the suffering that had led to the suicide, thinking of the survivors: "My inward sympathy with the mother's heart and with E. He should not have done it to them." Staying in Paris, Klaus had been taking morphia, and had killed himself in Cannes with sleeping tablets bought from a New York pharmacy. Thomas, Katia, and Erika went to bed without deciding what they should do. In the morning they agreed he shouldn't cancel his lectures, but shouldn't attend any receptions.[9]

On Tuesday, wearing a dark suit and a black tie, he lectured at the university in Uppsala, where he was given a standing ovation. Golo was in favor of the decision to continue the lecture tour; Erika made up her mind that when they arrived in Copenhagen, she'd fly to meet Klaus's friend Fritz Landshoff in Amsterdam before rejoining her parents in Zurich,[10] but she didn't attend the funeral in Cannes. The only member of the family who did was Michael, who was on tour with the San Francisco Symphony Orchestra. He took his viola, and after the coffin had been lowered into the grave, played a largo.[11]

On the night of Friday, May 27, together with Uexküll, Thomas, Katia, and Erika traveled by sleeping car to Copenhagen, where he lectured at the university to an audience that rose to its feet when he appeared.[12] He drove back to Lund, Sweden, where he lectured on Monday and on Tuesday had his head measured for the laurel wreath with which he'd be crowned by the bishop who awarded his honorary doctorate at the university. For the ceremony, which was in the cathedral, he had to wear a high doctoral hat. The students were carrying flags, and children were dressed in white. After the processional entry, the ceremony, which included a thirty-minute lecture by the physicist Niels Bohr, lasted for three hours.[13]

On Wednesday, June 1, Thomas and Katia were driven to Malmö and flew to Zurich, changing in Copenhagen. The Oprechts and Therese Giehse were among the friends waiting at the airport, and in the evening they went to a performance of *Faust* at the Schauspielhaus. On Thursday the arrival of Klaus's suitcase, typewriter, and overcoat reduced Erika to tears. Thomas had a long talk with her, reminding her that Klaus had suffered several recent disappointments, including a publisher's decision not to reprint his 1936 novel *Mephisto* because Gustaf Gründgens was so popular in Germany.[14] But she knew the suicide had been partly a protest against her increasing closeness with their father. There was some guilt in Thomas's reaction to her grief, while she, aware of his increasing frailty, became more protective, more anxious about the strain produced by public appearances, at the same time admiring his intensity during lectures and readings.[15]

On Saturday he was given a warm reception at the Schauspielhaus, where the president of the Republic attended his lecture. But the Manns didn't attend the party afterward. They stayed in Zurich nearly four weeks, seeing old friends and revisiting old haunts. Driven by Gret to see the house in Küsnacht, Thomas drank coffee in his old workroom.

On Wednesday, June 15, Walter Kolb, the Frankfurt Oberbürgermeister, arrived in Zurich to discuss arrangements for Thomas's visit. Corpulent and friendly, Kolb did his best to dissuade Thomas from going into the Russian zone.[16] Weimar was the other city where Goethe had lived, and to entice Thomas there, the East Germans had offered not only their Goethe Prize of 20,000 marks but the freedom of the city. When a Weimar newspaper announced that he'd agreed to go, it looked like an unsubtle attempt to put pressure on him[17]; he wanted to go, even if the West Germans and the Americans took offense.[18]

On June 27 he left Zurich with Katia and Erika. Expecting the German trip to be exhausting, he wanted to relax for three weeks in the Engadine, going for walks in the woods with Katia. But he devoted a lot of time to preparing a speech for Frankfurt,[19] and the strain of the last few weeks took its toll. On Monday, July 11, his nose started bleeding violently, and the doctor couldn't stanch it. Thomas tried to sleep with a tampon in his nose. The bleeding was intermittent, and after the third violent attack, on Tuesday evening, the doctor worked on him for an hour and a half, trying to cauterize the bleeding, and finally giving him an injection. On Wednesday, when his blood pressure was checked, he was told the loss of blood had done him no harm, but the specialist recommended the removal of a vein that had grown too big. Sedated with cocaine, he had to undergo several sessions of treatment with an electric needle.

On Sunday, after he'd had an almost sleepless night, the bleeding started again.[20] Thomas enjoyed the drive to Zurich on Monday—until the bleeding started again. The specialist he consulted, Professor Bruno Mäder, inspired little confidence, and Thomas had a bad night, troubled by sneezing, mucus, and the failure of the tampon to soak up all the blood.

He was reluctant to part with Erika, who refused to accompany him and Katia on the German trip, and didn't even want to be in Europe while he was in Germany.[21] When he said Klaus wouldn't have been so uncompromising, her answer was: "That's why he killed himself, which is what I now *won't* do. That's some consolation, but not much."[22]

In his "Message for the German People" ("Botschaft für das Deutsche

Volk"), which was published in the July issue of the Munich monthly *Heute (Today)*, he said he'd proved in *Doctor Faustus* that "my heart remained with Germany and that Germany's fate has caused me as much suffering as anyone. . . . As an American citizen I have also remained a German writer, faithful to the German language, which I regard as my true home."23

As he was driven through Frankfurt, he was appalled by the damage and devastation. On Monday there was a press reception in the Kronberg, the Swedish state castle, before the ceremony in the crowded Paulskirche, where Thomas gave the speech he was going to give in Weimar. He had come, he said, neither as a prophet nor to preach a penitential homily. He didn't believe himself to be in privileged possession of the truth. "I come to you as a poor, suffering man who wrestles with the problems of the period like any one of you."

He talked about the damage left by the "national catastrophe" and, in the same sentence, about the division of Germany into zones. He could understand resentment at being under "foreign rule," but it was less objectionable than the "rule of barbarism" which had lasted for twelve years, and for him, he said, the period of foreign rule was already over. "I know no zones. My visit is for Germany itself, Germany as a whole, and not an occupied territory. Who ought to guarantee and represent the unity of Germany if not an independent writer whose true home, as I have said, is the language, which is free and untouched by occupation?" In the audience Katia could hear people asking whether he was a Communist. Afterward the U.S. consul said that as American citizens they couldn't be stopped from going into the eastern zone, but the authorities would disapprove.

Thomas knew little about what was happening in Central and Eastern Europe: His antipathy to American anticommunism predisposed him to look charitably on Soviet expansionism. The Gesellschaft zur Bekämpfung der Unmenschlichleit (Association for Resistance to Inhumanity) urged him to visit Buchenwald, which was only five miles from Weimar, but he decided not to. The camp was being used by the Russians to imprison twelve thousand dissidents. His decision was reported in the *Frankfurter Rundschau*: "My visit is for the old fatherland as a whole, and it seemed wrong to hold myself aloof from the population of the Eastern Zone, to leave them lying, as it were, to the left. Within the framework of this visit it is obviously impossible to make demands that could not be fulfilled by the German authorities that invited me, and the association that is putting the question understands that as well as I do."24

This didn't satisfy Eugen Kogon, a survivor of the camp, whose book, *Der S.S. Staat*, Thomas had read. In an open letter to him, Kogon warned him that what he said in Weimar would win him either the friendship or the hatred of the twelve thousand political prisoners.[25] More aggressively, Rainer Hildebrandt, leader of the Kampfgruppe gegen Unmenschlichkeit (Fighting Group against Inhumanity), declared that neutrality was impossible in a confrontation with inhumanity, and, reminding him of everything he'd said against the inhumanity of Nazism, asked whether he was using a different gauge to measure that of Soviet communism.[26] He found out later that in Buchenwald prisoners were dying of starvation.[27]

Though he'd been at least half serious when saying he'd need protection if he came to Germany, he felt embarrassed when police escorts were provided by municipal authorities that wanted to avoid trouble in the streets. "It is really curious that a life of playing games and dreaming can—if only you go on with it for long enough—lead to your being treated like royalty."[28] At one meeting, a man who'd taken part in the July 20 conspiracy against Hitler, Fabian von Schlabrendorff, called out: "Your soul is different from ours."[29]

Before going on to Munich, Thomas stopped in Stuttgart and Kassel. After his visit to England, he was surprised by the quantity and quality of the food in Germany, but, judging from dozens of letters and countless personal reports, most people thought they were worse off than they'd been under Hitler. Disabled veterans couldn't live on their pensions, and neither could elderly people whose savings had been devalued. Though he hadn't expected to be popular, he was given a friendly reception. His audiences consisted mainly of well-wishers, but he was also cheered and acclaimed in the streets.[30] It looked as if all the paternally liberal municipal officials would be "swept away soon enough, and my visit was probably made at the last possible moment. Development in the direction of renazification is running full speed ahead with our protective help."[31] Since the relaxation of restrictions on publishing, he said, a hundred new Nazi papers had appeared, and predicted that West Germany would be Fascist within two years.[32]

It was harrowing to see how much of Munich had been destroyed. "There was something ghostly about finding this whole chunk of an outlived past in a smashed and tattered state, and seeing human faces emerging that had aged, and I often found myself looking the other way."[33] He talked to the bürgermeister and a lawyer about his house in Herzogpark, but refused to go there.[34] He was guest of honor at a reception given by the Bavarian Academy of Fine Arts in the Prinz Karl Palace. In the morning a press reception was held for him in the debating chamber of the town hall, followed by an official banquet for members of the Bavarian state government, representatives of the American occupying authority, and political parties in the new Federal Republic, together with a few old friends. Thomas gave his lecture on Goethe and democracy in the large auditorium at the Ministry of Economics.

The next day he was collected from Bayreuth in a Soviet military car by the East German minister of culture, Johannes Becher. They drove across the border to Weimar, stopping for lunch in Plauen, where a street had been named the Thomas-Mann-Strasse. In Weimar on Monday, August 1, he breakfasted with General Tulpanov, the Soviet military commandant of Berlin. Thomas then gave his speech in the Nationaltheater, where he was presented with the prize. He handed the 20,000 marks over to the fund for the rebuilding of Weimar's Herder Church. In the hotel he was always surrounded by a throng of officials, policemen, and people who wanted a conversation with him, while letters, telegrams, flowers, and books were always arriving. In the streets he was followed by crowds, photographers, journalists with microphones, and schoolchildren with flags. Generally, poverty was more in evidence than in the Western Zone, but when he spoke to university teachers, he learned that the new generation of students was being recruited exclusively from working-class families.[35]

He didn't entirely ignore the points that had been made to him by Kogon, Hildebrandt, and others. Giving an improvised talk, he said that in Russia, where autocracy and revolution had waged a cruel struggle against each other, they had finally joined hands to form an autocratic revolution, which used the same sinister methods as the tsar's police state but for different purposes. This speech was denounced in the Soviet press.[36]

Thomas and Katia spent only three nights in the Eastern Zone, returning to the West on August 2. Traveling to Amsterdam on a noisy old train, they met young German ex-soldiers who'd fought in Russia and told horrifying stories of starvation and cannibalism.[37] On August 5, Thomas and Katia embarked in Le Havre on the *New Amsterdam*. Before sailing for New York he received a letter from Erika, who'd been listening to radio reports on his visit to the two Germanies. She found it remarkable that two hostile states had both showered him with "godlike honours."[38]

While on board he answered the letter he'd had from Ernst Bertram. Thomas's letter to his ex-student had been helpful, and Bertram's work could once again appear in print. Thomas now said their friendship could be resumed. "I believe you know me as someone who never lets anything go out of his life."[39] He and Katia arrived in New York on August 13, and after spending a few days there and in Chicago, they were back in Pacific Palisades on the nineteenth.

Now that he'd seen something of East Germany, it was even harder for him to advise the seventy-eight-year-old Heinrich whether to settle in East Berlin. In California he was still being ignored; in Berlin he'd be given a villa, an office at the academy, a car, and a chauffeur. When he was sent $3,000 in fees plus $2,000 to cover his traveling expenses, he no longer came to share so many meals with Thomas and Katia: He could now eat equally well at home. But he was becoming senile, and said he wouldn't travel to Berlin unless he could take his American nurse. He'd grown increasingly anti-American, and during the last week of September he was sure he wanted to go, but he gave Thomas the impression of having too little vitality.[40]

In May, when the invitation had been issued, the Soviet authorities had been hoping to get sole possession of Berlin and to have their academy accepted all over Germany. At the beginning of October, the German Democratic Republic was created under a Soviet control commission without any elections. Wilhelm Pieck was made president and Otto Grotewohl prime minister of a mostly Communist cabinet. On October 17, when Heinrich said he was postponing his decision till the spring, Thomas knew he'd never go.[41]

Thomas was seventy-four, and Heinrich's senility was a painful reminder of the aging process. Thomas was getting less sleep at night, and less work done before lunch. Throughout the last three weeks of the year he was weakened by an infection of the middle ear. For some of the time he was partially deaf. He was subjected to several kinds of painful treatment, including irrigation of the aural passages with strong alcohol, which produced inflammation as well as discharges, but the relief was only temporary.[42] As he said in mid-December: "[T]he itching at night is terrible. I have to keep shaking my head and scratching my ear, and I still have some swelling and discharge."[43]

As usual, he refused to let physical discomfort stop him from writing, and having shelved *The Holy Sinner* while in Europe, he wrote eight chapters between August and December. Golo, who was in California, was taking over most of his nonliterary tasks, but Thomas resented the dwindling of his capacity for work. "Should have nothing at all to do, so that I could still do a bit of creative writing in freedom and unhurried leisure, to finish the Gregorius, which is perhaps a worthless experiment, and think about developing the Felix Krull."[44]

Still having trouble with his hearing, he felt ill with anxiety on October 9, when he went by overnight train to lecture on Goethe at the University of California at Berkeley. At a press conference he answered questions about his trip to Germany and the creation of the German Democratic Republic. He then had to speak in a huge hall to an audience of about 4,700, mostly students. They were gratifyingly attentive, and the applause was generous. When a delegation of students asked for his views on the anti-Communists' proposal that all university teachers should be obliged to swear an oath of loyalty, he said the proposal was undemocratic and ought to be resisted.[45]

After enjoying his visit to Berkeley, he was annoyed by the report in the *Los Angeles Times* about his comments on Germany. "Novelist

Thomas Mann said today establishment of a Soviet-sponsored republic in the East German zone has made civil war 'a certainty' the moment occupation troops are withdrawn." He was quoted as saying that the Germans not only tolerated the old Nazi elements "but even prefer them to the Social Democrats because they regard them as possible storm troops in a future war against the east."[46] Reprinted in German newspapers, such comments provoked what he called "hate letters." One of these had the postscript: "I especially hate you because I am a *decent* Jew."[47]

He was refusing most invitations to make public appearances, but, depressed though he was by the persistent ear trouble, he took Katia with him in their new Buick to San Diego, where he was to repeat the lecture Monday, October 24. In San Diego he had an audience of about 2,500, and afterward he and Katia visited the zoo, where they saw a baby gorilla.[48]

Afterward he had only five nights at home before leaving on an afternoon flight to San Francisco, where he'd agreed to meet Jawaharlal Nehru. Prime minister of India since 1947, the sixty-year-old Nehru was with his sister, Vidaya Lakshmi Pandit, the Indian ambassador to Washington, and his forty-two-year-old daughter, Indira Gandhi, the future prime minister. Nehru, who reminded Thomas of Roosevelt, was "very elegant, with clever, pleasant features." They talked about politics and morality.[49] Thomas afterward described him as "a fine, endearing, clever man, certainly cleverer than those who are running this country."[50] Less than two weeks later, though, Thomas found out why Nehru had wanted to meet him: He was asked to write an article in support of the Indian constitution.[51]

Paul Ehrenberg's death took Thomas by surprise. Carl broke the news in a late-November letter. Paul had been staying with friends in Plauen, where he seemed perfectly well until he collapsed. He was taken to the hospital, where his stomach was found to be perforated. The surgeons operated, but an embolism followed eight days later. He was seventy-one.[52]

Upset by the news, Thomas felt more vulnerable to the continuing hostility of Schoenberg, who'd been publishing a series of attacks in various periodicals and had asked Alma Mahler to have nothing further to do with the Manns. Instead, she left flowers to greet them on their return from Europe.[53] The autumn issue of the London quarterly *Music Survey* contained another Schoenbergian assault, exposing musical errors in *Doctor Faustus*; denouncing Thomas as ignorant, unfair, ungrateful, and unteachable; and complaining that he'd never returned the copy of Schoenberg's book on harmony that he'd borrowed. Sending it back, Thomas apologized, saying he'd come to think it had been given to him, and asking whether Schoenberg would object to the publication of a letter he'd written in October 1948 to say he was fully satisfied with the acknowledgment printed at the end of the novel.[54] This had the desired effect: When Schoenberg wrote back at the beginning of the new year, it was to make peace.

The effort involved in corresponding, even in dictating letters, reminded Thomas of his advancing age. Sometimes he felt unsteady on his legs. Another decade was nearly over, and in 1950 he'd complete his seventy-fifth year. Not long after his seventy-fourth birthday he'd been asking himself whether he still wanted to be in California when he celebrated his seventy-fifth. As the year progressed, the idea of settling in Switzerland became more attractive.[55]

THOMAS BEGAN the new decade in a positive mood. Drinking coffee together on New Year's Day, he, Katia, and Elisabeth discussed how much better things were in California than they'd been ten years ago in Europe. It was fifty years since *Buddenbrooks* had appeared, followed, twenty-five years later, by *The Magic Mountain*. In less than six months from now Thomas would be celebrating his seventy-fifth birthday.[56] He was annoyed at having to pay a tax bill of $16,000, which meant he was subsidizing the cold war, but the political climate hadn't deteriorated sufficiently to be intolerable, though he sometimes felt that "in this foreign country which has become so much like home, we are really living in the wrong place."[57]

When Niko, the poodle who'd been Thomas's faithful companion for eleven years, went missing, never to reappear, he was replaced by another poodle, who was named Alger. Alger Hiss had been a State Department official, formerly one of Roosevelt's advisers at the 1945 Yalta conference, and later president of the Carnegie Endowment for International Peace. He was accused in 1948 by a former Soviet agent, Whittaker Chambers, of having passed information to the U.S.S.R. between 1926 and 1937. Under the statute of limitations, he couldn't be convicted of spying, but on January 21 he was sentenced to five years' imprisonment for perjuring himself in front of the House Committee. Congressman Richard Nixon was active in the prosecution, which helped to inflame the anti-Communist fever. At the beginning of February, Klaus Fuchs, a nuclear scientist, was charged with passing atomic secrets to the Russians, and later in the month a junior senator from Wisconsin, Joseph McCarthy, said he had the names of fifty-seven card-carrying members of the Communist Party in the State Department, and that 205 people employed there were Communist sympathizers. He substantiated neither allegation, but the atmosphere was so panicky that he didn't need to.

Thomas's position was clear: "The idea of a world order that is nothing but anti-Communist is no better than one that is Communist; in fact it is worse because it is entirely negative. But both are only escapes into a violent power structure, and can be developed only into Fascistic and imperialistic forms."[58] Again and again, in speeches, interviews, and articles, he tried to prove there was nothing Communistic about wanting the cold war to end in a peaceful settlement between East and West, but while McCarthyism was flourishing, it was hard to adopt a liberal stance without being branded a Communist sympathizer. When the Beverly Wilshire Hotel refused to let the Council of the Arts, Sciences and Professions book a private dining room for a reception, the reason given by the management was that "a communist like Dr. Mann" was to be one of the speakers. This provoked such a furor of protest that the hotel finally accepted the booking.[59]

To Thomas it seemed as if the air was full of malevolent spooks who didn't want him to recover his health. All through January he slept badly because of the itching in his ears, and the discharge from them made him feel unclean. In the second half of the month he was often feverish, coughed a lot, and suffered from headaches. His tongue was almost black, and he thought about giving up smoking, but couldn't bring himself to make the decision. He often tried to sleep in the armchair because it was painful to lie on his ears, and he kept them swathed in dressings covered in ointment. When Bruno Walter called, Thomas refused to see him: He hadn't shaved for a week, and with swollen, bandaged ears felt unfit for company.[60] But at the end of the month he bought an electric shaver, got rid of the beard, and started taking vitamin E.[61]

For Heinrich, who'd decided to accept the invitation to East Berlin, things seemed to be improving. He'd be a rich man there, and a film contract had been offered for the rights to *Der Untertan*, the novel he'd written between 1906 and 1914.[62] But according to the nurse, he was incontinent now and often fell asleep while sitting up in bed.[63] The opening of the academy had been postponed because of him, and Thomas booked a cabin for him on a Polish ship sailing in mid-April.[64]

Heinrich had never stopped thinking about the rivalry between him and Thomas. In *Der Atem* (*Breathing*), his last novel, written in 1946–47, a dying French baroness thinks obsessively about her more highly accoladed sister: "Marie-Louise, my beloved sister, you have beaten me, and beaten me thoroughly, is that a reason for hating me? . . . We should love each other again. It started at home, with everything that happened, that we loved as well as hated each other. . . . How good it is that your heart now knows humility, after so much fulfilled ambition; disappointed people always pay a higher price. . . . I can see you. I should no longer see you. My sister, farewell!"[65]

On the morning of Saturday, March 11, it was impossible to wake

Heinrich. His heart was still beating, but he was in a coma. He had stayed up late the previous evening, listening to music, and had gone to bed reluctantly. At eleven-thirty on Saturday evening, his heart stopped beating. It was a fortnight before his seventy-ninth birthday.

Thomas, who wasn't told until seven on Sunday morning, decided that Heinrich's death hadn't come too early. It was "the most graceful solution." In the evening Thomas listened to the Jack Benny show on the radio, but for the wreath he sent to Heinrich's funeral on Tuesday he wrote a card saying "For my great brother, with love." A collection of obscene drawings was found in Heinrich's desk. The nurse knew he drew fat naked women every day.[66] When the painter Eva Hermann was consulted, she said the drawings were worthless. Golo was instructed to burn them for the sake of the family's honor, but some of them found their way to East Berlin.[67]

The publisher Albin Michel was intent on luring Thomas to Paris for the publication of *Docteur Faustus*. Thomas had been hesitant at first, but had decided before Heinrich died that he wanted to go.[68] He was preparing a new lecture, "The Years of My Life," which he would deliver at the Library of Congress, in Chicago, and in New York, before going to Paris and Zurich, where he was planning to celebrate his birthday. He finished writing the lecture on March 21. "It was produced under a series of headaches that indicated the shattering of my central nervous system through the experience of death. Always knew how much it would cost me. Held in the Library of Congress, this lecture is perhaps a historic act, in greater style than the 1932 speech in the Beethovensaal."

Though it ended with a reasoned repudiation of communism, the lecture would have created a sensation had it been delivered in the Library of Congress. It attacked the "mindless hysteria" of American efforts to buy out the non-Communist world, and insisted that Americans had a lot in common with Russians—openness, lack of inhibition, and "cheerful primitiveness." But the Library had come under attack when the House Committee declared it to be "infested with Communists," and at the end of March, Thomas was told his lecture had been canceled for political reasons.[69]

He accepted the decision of the Librarian, Luther Evans, without arguing, and in his view it only confirmed what had already been apparent. Two days earlier he'd been explaining why he'd signed a protest against the arrest of the lawyers defending the Communist Party leaders. They'd done nothing illegal, and lawyers should obviously have been entitled to immunity, but they were released only when pressure was applied. "Things are happening and things are being prepared which would previously have been unthinkable in a country where Fascism had not yet broken out fully and openly. The 'cold war' is ruining America physically and morally."[70]

Thomas and Katia arrived in Chicago on April 21, and the next day, after Erika helped him make last-minute cuts in his lecture, he went to the university, where the hall, which seated a thousand people, had been sold out within the first half hour of booking, and the lecture was transferred to a large chapel, which was packed. Four days later he gave it in German at the overcrowded Kaufmann Auditorium on Lexington Avenue, New York—an event arranged by *Aufbau*.[71]

On Monday, May 1, Thomas flew with Katia and Erika to Stockholm, where Uexküll met them at the airport. On Tuesday they lunched in a restaurant as guests of Prinz Wilhelm, who introduced Thomas that evening when he gave his lecture to the PEN Club in the Börsensaal of the Swedish Academy. He didn't want to revisit Germany, though the great Albert Bassermann was appearing at Heidelberg as Goethe in the premiere of a dramatization by Hans Feist of *The Beloved Returns*. Overcoming her resistance to going there, Erika agreed to go in his place, and Thomas sent a message that appeared in local newspapers: "In the middle of my eighth decade I send my heartiest greeting to the old homeland. What does it matter whether I am present or not in the flesh? In any case, as fate has willed, the contact is closer than is believed, and my concern, hopes and good wishes are always with you."[72]

Erika flew from Stockholm to Amsterdam, while Uexküull escorted Thomas and Katia to Lund, where he lectured at the university. He and Katia spent the second week of May in Paris, where Albin Michel threw a starry dinner party for him at the Ritz. An autographing session was arranged at a bookshop, and such a long queue formed outside that Thomas had to spend three hours signing copies. In the evening he gave the lecture at the Sorbonne, where over two thousand people turned up, and a bigger auditorium had to be found at the last minute. Of the three speakers introducing him, one was Jules Romains, who took it in good part when Thomas referred to him as Romain Rolland.[73] Thomas spoke in French for fifteen minutes before giving an abridged version of the lecture in German.[74]

Arriving in Zurich on May 16, he and Katia stayed at the Hotel Baur au Lac, where they'd honeymooned in 1905. After six days they went on to Lugano, and paid several visits to the Hesses in Montagnola. Thomas felt he was back in the same situation as in 1933—that they'd come to a place of safety. Revisiting Castiglione after seventeen years, Thomas couldn't help reflecting on "what has happened and altered in the flow of time since then. How many deaths, how much has been spoilt. All my happiness and suffering: world fame, weariness, pain. . . . My youthfulness and capacity for achievement are admired. How deep, often, the weariness."[75] On May 28, Erika arrived, bringing a program from Heidelberg and reviews that were "rather annihilating for the author of the play."[76]

On Wednesday, May 31, they returned to Zurich, where the same room was waiting for them at the hotel, and on Thursday they saw Frido, who excitedly kissed his grandfather, asking which day was his birthday. On Saturday they drove to Küsnacht and walked in the woods, talking about old times. At tea, Frido ate a lot of cakes, and Thomas made him rinse his mouth afterward. On Monday, the day of the lecture at the Schauspielhaus, letters, telegrams, and flowers kept arriving. The audience was exuberantly friendly, and television cameras were recording the event. The next day, Thomas's seventy-fifth birthday, the flow of letters, telegrams, and flowers became torrential, and Frido recited a congratulatory poem by Erika. Elisabeth arrived in time for the dinner party at the Zunfthaus zu Saffran on the Limmat, and so did a delegation from Lübeck, bringing a large marzipan tart.[77] Several friends proposed toasts, and Thomas finally made a grateful speech, "during which I ought to have thought of poor Klaus."[78]

The rest of the family knew the sixty-six-year-old Katia was going to spend three weeks in a nursing home for a hysterectomy, but the news wasn't broken to Thomas till the day after his birthday. On Thursday evening he took her to see Maria Becker in George Bernard Shaw's *Too True to Be Good* at the Schauspielhaus, and on Friday Erika took her into the Klinik Hirslanden. The gynecologist, Professor Traugott, made her take an eight-day course of injections before the operation to reduce the danger of embolism by thinning the blood and lowering the blood pressure. Thomas spent a good deal of time with her in the clinic. "Strange life: nervous tension and the constant feeling of disorder, even when health is good."[79]

On the day of the operation, Tuesday, June 20, Erika spent the whole day in the clinic. Afterward Katia suffered a great deal of pain and was in danger for three days, with problems involving bladder, intestines, and circulation, but on Friday she was giving clear signs of recovery.[80]

Winsome Waiter

ON JUNE 18, 1950, two days before the operation, Thomas and Katia had decided to move away from the lake and the center of the city to the Grand Hotel Dolder, which is on the hills, not far from the Bircher-Benner sanatorium, and Thomas made the move alone on June 23, before Katia had been discharged. One of the waiters, who asked for his autograph, was a little ex-Nazi from Tegernsee, near Munich. He spoke with a Bavarian accent and regularly greeted Thomas with a friendly grin and a comment on the weather. About twenty-five, with brown, wavy hair, he had "the excessively thick head of the Upper Bavarian race." He could see Thomas liked him, but didn't know how much. "What pretty eyes and teeth! What a charming voice! . . . Here is something for the heart."

Franzl claimed to have known the writer Ludwig Thoma and the opera singer Leo Slezak. Thomas, who rarely used the second person singular, would have found it easy with Franzl when they chatted about the young man's plans. He wanted to live in South America, but first he'd like to get a job at a hotel in Geneva and learn French. One day, talking to Franzl in the foyer and staring into his face, Thomas felt Erika tugging at his sleeve. People had been looking at him.[1]

He thought obsessively about the waiter, and tried to contrive meetings that would seem accidental. "His eyes are just too pretty, his voice just too ingratiating, and although my desire does not go far, my happiness, tenderness and love are keen and concealed all day." He wanted to help Franzl find a job in Geneva, and when he went to visit Katia in the clinic, he talked jokingly about his weakness for the waiter, as he did to Erika. He'd wake up thinking about the young man and shave quickly, impatient to have breakfast in the garden, with Franzl waiting on him. At the hotel in Flims four years earlier, the infatuation for the waiter had been more superficial: Franz Westermeier aroused an excitement that had been dormant for twenty-three years, ever since the encounter with Klaus Heuser, an excitement he'd expected never to feel again. Franzl's neck was plump, and, seen in profile, his face was unexceptional, but from in front it was charming, and Thomas loved the graceful way he moved as he served food.

As in Venice, nearly forty years earlier, when he was staying at the same hotel as the ten-year-old Wladyslaw Moes, what Thomas mainly wanted was to look—to have recurrent visual stimulation for fantasies of contact. But whereas the boy had been inaccessible, Franzl might not be. Like any other grand hotel, the Dolder was bustling with waiters, porters, page boys, elevator attendants, and barmen who could all make more money from tips than from salaries, and the attractive ones knew an infallible way of securing a generous tip. At the moment of taking an order, a waiter's eyes were quite close to those of the diner, male or female, and a brief glance could signal an interest that had nothing to do with food. But there was no question, for Thomas, of translating feeling into action. When he read Gore Vidal's novel *The City and the Pillar*, he commented: "Affairs with the different men incomprehensible. How can one sleep with a man?"[2] For him, the frustration was integral to the pleasure, and a hotel was a good setting for the kind of nonevent that could push him into paroxysms of exhilaration and melancholy. There was always the chance of a brief meeting in an elevator or corridor, always the possibility a door would open and Franzl appear, carrying a tray.

He wasn't always friendly. One day, going down in the elevator, he ignored Thomas, who felt wounded. "World fame means a great deal to me, but it is nothing in comparison with a smile from him, the look in his eyes." In the midst of this mental turbulence he dreamed about the boy he'd previously named as his "last love": In the dream Frido was really a girl, which disappointed Thomas.[3]

When Katia was discharged, and Franzl served their lunch, Thomas pointed him out. Asked to bring another salad, he served it gracefully, and, asked about Geneva, he responded: "No job yet." When Thomas took out a cigarette, Franzl lit it, and they exchanged smiles. When he'd gone, Katia said he had flirtatious eyes. Seeing him later, Thomas said "Hello," and Franzl replied with a bow, which made him reproach himself for not having had more presence of mind. Deciding to give the young man 5 francs for "serving so nicely," Thomas wished there were other ways of giving him pleasure. "Indescribable, the charm of the smile in his eyes as he thanked me."

In a few days he'd be taking the convalescent Katia into the mountains, where the air might do her good. "Perhaps it is already over, and it will probably be a relief—the return to work as substitute for happiness. That is how it must be. It is the condition (and the origin?) of all genius."

On July 16, before they left, Franzl said: "Perhaps we shall meet once again, Herr Mann." Thomas, who didn't know how to reply, had plenty of time on the journey to work out what he could have said. Perhaps something like: "I hope so. I've always been glad to see you." The best he could do was write to Franzl from Sils Maria, which they used as a base, looking for a hotel in the Engadine. Thomas said he'd be glad to write a recommendation, should it ever be of any use.[4]

They settled on the Suvretta Haus in Saint-Moritz, and one of the books forwarded to them was a new volume of poems by Michelangelo, translated into German by the Swiss writer Hans Mühlestein.[5] What Thomas enjoyed most was the sense of being authorized to feel love at an advanced age. In his seventies, Michelangelo was still writing love poetry. He wasn't expecting his love to be requited, but his ugliness made him prize the beauty of the young beloved. "His whole erotic seems to be based on the polarity between aging lover and young beloved," but he loved the people he loved less than he loved love itself.[6] Thomas had still been young when he thought of writing about the octogenarian Goethe's desire for the seventeen-year-old Ulrike von Levetzow; at seventy-five, Thomas had something in common with Goethe and the "melancholy sculptor." He was waiting impatiently for a letter. "If the boy in the white jacket knew how eager I am to have a few words from him in my hand, he would be in more of a hurry!"[7]

He decided to write a review article on the book of translations. "I cannot escape from this sensual-suprasensual lovesickness, this Platonic excitement, which can always convert prostration before loveliness into love of God and the spiritual, this crassness in the description of one's own ugliness, of one's own sufferings in love." He was writing about himself when he commented on Michelangelo's "constant receptivity to the power of a beautiful face. For him this is the only pleasure, and, though constantly complaining about the cruelty of the god of love, he calls this a grace," and the experience of loving made him set a higher value on himself.[8]

Thomas could neither relax nor concentrate on finishing the novel. He had no appetite, had headaches, felt dyspeptic, nervous. The other nagging uncertainty was about whether to stay in Switzerland or go back to Pacific Palisades. "The question of nationality and papers in any case very difficult. But almost certain that in the event of going back now we would never be able to get out, and the country would be a great trap for us."[9] His diary keeps making comparisons with their situation in 1933.

On June 25, Communist North Korea invaded the independent South. At the end of the war the country had been occupied by Russian and American troops; it had been divided in 1947, with the 38th parallel as frontier. Refusing to admit a United Nations commission, the Russians set up a Communist republic in the north, while elections were held in the American zone, where the republic that was set up had the support of the United Nations Security Council. But the Soviet Union was boycotting meetings of the council because Mao Tse-tung's China was excluded, while Chiang Kai-shek's Nationalist China was represented in spite of having no territory on the Chinese mainland, its only base being Formosa. The Korean confrontation could have flared into full-scale war, especially when the bellicose Douglas MacArthur was put in command of the American air and naval forces sent under the banner of the United Nations to help the South Koreans and to forestall any attack on Formosa. Each time he opened a newspaper, Thomas felt tense and scared. The United States seemed to want the annihilation of the Soviet Union. Though he'd never expected to leave America as a refugee, friends were advising him to settle in Switzerland.[10]

Nine days after he'd written to Franzl, a reply arrived, saying he'd been really pleased to hear from Herr Mann. He'd got the job in Geneva but had to go on working at the Dolder till the end of the season. He had reactivated a susceptibility in Thomas, who was suddenly more responsive to youthful good looks. "My God how attractive young people are: their faces—even if they are only half-way pretty—their arms, their legs."[11] In Saint-Moritz he watched a young Argentinian tennis player practicing with his coach. Thomas's room overlooked the tennis court, and, interrupting his work, he stood up to watch, admiring the dark-haired boy's body and his athletic, dancelike movements. "Springy restlessness of the body during inactivity on the bench, alternate crossing of the legs, leg-swinging, banging his feet together in their white shoes. . . . White clothes, short trousers, sweater over his shoulders after the practice. . . . The knees. He rubs his leg, as anyone might." Keen air, beautiful mountain scenery, and painful thoughts about Franzl seemed to have sharpened Thomas's awareness of the frustration that had jaundiced his whole life. Nothing in the world was comparable to the charm of youthful masculinity, and as a passive admirer, he'd been condemned to a combination of happiness and deprivation that felt sterile, even if it had been creative. "Close to a desire for death because I can no longer endure the longing for the 'divine boy' (by which I do not mean this particular one)."[12]

He wasn't expecting to recognize the boy in the dining room, and when Erika pointed him out, he no longer looked attractive. Wearing a blue sweater, he was eating with bare legs and hunched shoulders, but when he went back into action on the tennis court, Thomas started admiring him again. In the dining room, Thomas felt envious of men who liked women—even the eighty-one-year-old Siegfried Trebitsch, Shaw's translator, who'd fallen for Erika. Before leaving Saint-Moritz, he read her a love poem he'd written. "Character, spirit, personality, wit, talent, apart from the beautiful eyes have earned him passionate love of the most legitimate and chivalrous kind." Pitying himself for having to be content with images that seemed to linger in his heart,[13]

Thomas felt envious of an octogenarian who was chasing a forty-five-year-old lesbian.

After three weeks in Saint-Moritz, Thomas and Katia went back to Zurich. They stayed at the Baur au Lac but went to lunch with Trebitsch at the Dolder, where Erika, saying she had to make a telephone call, went to look for Franzl, who came to the table and shook hands warmly. The offer of a job in Geneva had fallen through. Thomas gripped his arm. "Saw his face so precisely, the rather slanting brown eyes, the strong teeth, the fawning expression. Toughness of the head and body with a certain childish softness of the character and the speech. . . . Strong, friendly pressure of the hand when we said good-bye." Thinking about it afterward, he decided he had nothing against intimate physical contact, though it wasn't indispensable to passion, which "can manage in the negative mode, in the suspension of the fleshly I-you relationship, can remain tenderness, or in short what is called 'romance.' "[14]

Gradually he slipped back into phlegmatic resignation as ideas about eroticism and thoughts about the novel faded into the practical problem of where to settle. His popularity had waned in both Germany and the United States, reducing his earning power. In France a second impression of *Docteur Faustus* had already come out, but income was no longer keeping pace with outgoings in California. On August 20, after a few days in London, he and Katia flew back to the States, but they felt unsettled, with a growing desire to uproot themselves again. In mid-September he wrote: "I am more and more disgusted with this country."[15]

After doing well during the first ten weeks of the fighting, the North Koreans were taken by surprise in mid-September, when MacArthur launched an armada of 260 ships from Japan. Within ten days his troops had recaptured the South Korean capital, Seoul, and they'd reached the 38th parallel by the end of the month, but instead of stopping there, they pushed on to occupy most of North Korea, though the Chinese prime minister, Chou En-lai, had threatened to intervene if North Korea was invaded. In mid-October, Truman flew out for talks with MacArthur. But on October 26 an army of over 200,000 Chinese soldiers began to surge across the Yalu River, which formed the border between Korea and Manchuria, and continued the advance into North Korea. Wanting to bomb Chinese bases in Manchuria, MacArthur was prepared to risk a full-scale war, and in a press conference on November 30, Truman said that if necessary the atom bomb would be used against the Chinese. "Never," wrote Thomas, "will a country have put itself more in the wrong than this one through its belief that it would be better for the world to end than for it to become Communist. Have we done the right thing to come back here? How can we get away now?"[16]

Speaking in the House of Commons, Clement Attlee promised to meet Truman, who shouldn't have issued the threat without consulting the other signatories of the Atlantic Pact. Early in December, Attlee arrived in Washington with a delegation, and five days later a member of it said: "If they ever meant it, they don't now." Still expecting war with China, and still wanting to get away, Thomas would have liked to sell the house before committing himself to the move, but Erika, advising her parents to leave as soon as possible, offered to arrange the sale.[17]

In spite of the war scare, Thomas managed to finish *The Holy Sinner* on October 26, and though it was a relief to have his desk clear again, it left him with the problem of what to write. He could do what he'd done in 1943 before starting on *Doctor Faustus* and take out *Felix Krull*, but could he go on with it? A lot of the action was going to be set in grand hotels and foreign cities: Did he have enough material? After discussing the idea with Erika, who was encouraging, he considered the Faustian aspect. Schiller had thought Goethe should take Faust out into the world. Could Thomas take Felix out into the world? Rereading what he'd written, he had misgivings. Perhaps it was out of date, or too insubstantial. But there was nothing else he felt like doing, and it would be unbearable, especially in these circumstances, not to be working.[18]

EARLY IN 1951, when peace seemed precarious, it was natural for him to become involved, as Einstein did, in campaigning against the rearmament of Germany, the continuation of the war in Korea, and the exclusion of Communist China from the United Nations. Early in January, Thomas added his signature to a letter from the Committee for Peaceful Alternatives and expressed support for a demonstration it was planning in Chicago. Excusing himself from attending, he said he was an old man whose health would suffer if he left California for the East Coast during the winter.[19] He also supported the American Peace Crusade, which had the scientist Linus Pauling and the nuclear physicist Philip Morrison on its "initiating committee." In January it issued a statement of principles calling for an end to the war in Korea and for negotiation with the two great Communist powers.

Late in January a nuclear explosion in the Nevada desert was followed by another within two days as bombs were tested. White and orange flashes were visible in Pacific Palisades, the ground trembled, and the windows shook.[20] On January 30 the United Nations named China as the aggressor in Korea, and by February 5 the Communists had retreated to within five miles of Seoul. Thomas was plunged into a pessimism reminiscent of his feeling in 1914 that European civilization didn't deserve to survive. While agreeing with an article on foreign policy by Erich von Kahler in the *Bulletin of the Atomic Scientists*,[21] he couldn't help feeling that "everything is in vain. The good books, the warning commentaries, which, rarely enough, get broadcast—none of it has the slightest influence. Obstinately and unstoppably, following the basest laws, destiny takes its course, and I often think it is just as well. If this is what they want, let it happen. Human wickedness deserves a visitation such as the earth has not yet seen, and this civilisation of gluttons, fools and gangsters deserves to go under."[22]

On February 1 a headline in *The New York Times* coupled Thomas's name with that of the black Communist singer Paul Robeson: "Robeson, Mann join new Peace Crusade." The organization, it said, was planning a pilgrimage to Washington, and the other sponsors it named included the novelist Howard Fast and several trade unionists. Alfred Knopf promptly wrote: "I should think that you would keep away from anything which involves even the *name* of Paul Robeson as you would from the Bubonic Plague. I cannot imagine any kind of publicity for you which could be more damaging in every single respect, personal and professional, than this—particularly in this time."[23] Knopf wasn't the only one to be alarmed: Thomas received a lot of letters from friends and acquaintances appalled by the danger that he'd lose his passport, and perhaps his citizenship.[24]

He wrote to the *Times,* saying he'd known nothing about the pilgrimage and that the article put him in a political "neighbourhood and comradeship" he'd publicly rejected. He'd been approached by Philip Morrison, who as a nuclear physicist at Cornell University couldn't be a Communist, and whose statement of principles corresponded to Thomas's convictions.[25] After asking Knopf to use his influence on the *Times* to have the letter printed promptly, Thomas was puzzled when it failed to appear. It wasn't until February 12 that Knopf explained he'd asked the *Times* not to print it, and on the fourteenth Thomas heard that Knopf had discussed the problem with Agnes Meyer, who agreed that since they wanted the article to be forgotten as quickly as possible, the letter would be counterproductive. Thomas was furious to have been kept in the dark about what was going on. "Never before, to my mind, had I been so miserably treated as I seemed to be during that week."[26]

By then he'd withdrawn from the Peace Crusade, and Erika had helped him to draft a statement for the United Press. He hadn't known his name would be linked with those of Paul Robeson and Howard Fast. "I am convinced that any peace movement generally believed to be communist inspired or controlled is bound to hurt rather than help the cause of peace in this country." Since it was hard to discover the true character of an openly political or apparently cultural pressure group, he'd decided never again to take part in any collective action. "Unless I were the sole signer, my signature appearing under any 'protest', 'appeal', 'petition' etc. must henceforth be considered a forgery."[27] In a letter to Philip Morrison he said that instead of wanting to feature prominently on every list of fighters for peace, Communists should realize that their names would only damage the cause they were championing.[28]

Once again political involvement was distracting Thomas from literary activity. Even in a period of calm it would have been hard to go on with a narrative that had been shelved for forty years, especially after characterizing Joseph as a kind of confidence trickster and using some of the ideas evolved for Felix.[29] Resuming work on the novel in early January, and writing on the old squared paper he'd bought in Munich, Thomas was pleasantly surprised to find he could use the old material, making only minor changes. He divided the narrative into short chapters, but kept both structure and substance, transplanting a lot of original pages into the new text. What he presents is a comic and socially downgraded variation on the *Buddenbrooks* theme, but this time the decay of the family and the death of the father force the artist-trickster to make a living by exercising his imagination while exploiting his attractiveness. From what he'd already written, Thomas kept all the narrative about the family background and the education Felix gives himself in the arts of disguise, physical self-control, simulation, and deception. During childhood it's a matter of playing games, as when, using two sticks (as Thomas had) he mimics the movements of a violinist. From this he learns (as Thomas had) that he can win admiration and get what he wants by putting on a performance.

In the 1910 fragment the first-person narrative moves rapidly forward with little dialogue, no long speeches, and no lingering over any single incident. In 1951, Thomas didn't lengthen any of the old incidents, but, continuing the story, he introduces long speeches and longer sequences. The 1910 fragment had ended with the death of the father, which now comes at the end of Part One, but before this Thomas interpolates a long scene in which Felix steals chocolates from a delicatessen. The first time he does this, the theft is unpremeditated, but he goes back to repeat his success. As in so many stories, Thomas couples actions he'd never have taken with ideas that had run through his mind. Felix knows that to spend himself on "loose sociability" would be to dissipate vital energy and reduce the tension of his existence. To get what he wants, he must tread a lonely path. This involves a combination of self-sufficiency and civility. Rudeness debases, while courtesy maintains separateness.

Starting Part Two, Thomas makes Felix do what he himself is doing—returning to a story after a long period of neglecting it. (This is reminiscent of the way he began *Doctor Faustus* on May 27, 1943, by making

Zeitblom sit down to write on May 27, 1943.) Thomas then spurs himself on as he had at the beginning of the 1910 fragment, reminding himself, and the reader, that the story will have thrillerlike elements involving crime and imprisonment.

The first long monologue comes from the godfather (whose name has been changed from Maggotsen to Schimmelpreester). He advises Felix's mother and sister to earn money by running a boardinghouse; Felix should work as a hotel waiter. Thomas was thinking both of Julius Bab's son, who'd done this, and of Franzl. It may also have been the hotel in Düsseldorf that had given him ideas for *Royal Highness*. At the Hotel Saint James and Albany, where Schimmelpreester has secured the promise of a job for Felix, he'll wear livery.

Trying to parody the bildungsroman in *The Magic Mountain*, Thomas had produced little comedy, mainly because he was so serious about educating his hero, but here he writes amusingly about the training Felix needs to be successful as a con man. Education, we're told, comes not from laborious study but from freedom and apparent idleness. A secret machinery is at work, a hidden effort of the senses and the mind. If the subject is made of educable stuff, he can learn in his sleep, but no one can develop talents he didn't have at birth. Thomas is writing about his own education, which had so little to do with his schooling: Once again he has found a mask through which he can talk confessionally without appearing to give away anything about himself.

The first incident to be dramatized at length is the medical examination. Before starting his career as a waiter, Felix has to get himself exempted from military service. Thomas draws on memories of having to appear nude in front of an army medical board, and he had already described the early stages of Felix's self-education in the art of simulating symptoms. In the medical sequence the climax comes in a facial and physical spasm which makes the doctor think he's having an epileptic fit.

The writing was more improvisational than in any of Thomas's recent fiction. He'd start sequences without knowing how he was going to finish them—or whether he'd be able to finish the book. He wasn't even sure how much point there was in trying. Was it anything more than an indirect portrait of his own life?[30] Wouldn't he do better to abandon it in favor of a novel about Luther, Erasmus, and the humanist Ulrich von Hutten?[31]

Though he'd always claimed to be primarily a comic writer, he had never written a full-scale novel that was primarily comic, and the comedy gave him some relief in a period of panic, though the panic was anything but conducive to the "creative buoyancy" he needed to write comedy.[32] With encouragement from aggressive reactionaries, MacArthur was arguing that the military collapse of "Red China" would ensue on invasion of the mainland. In mid-April it looked to Thomas as though Truman was helpless between "the rage of the China lobby and pressure from the outside world, which would like to see the general disciplined or dismissed."33

Panic about war coincided with panic about potency. Three months before his seventy-sixth birthday Thomas thought his sex life was over. He'd rarely allowed himself to masturbate without starting from a full erection, and ever since the trip to Europe, his sexual powers had been waning. Only half-asleep, he pictured himself kissing Franzl goodbye after gazing into brown eyes which looked as if they were melting. "Whether reality *ever* found me able-bodied is another question." Three days later Thomas found he hadn't lost his potency. Writing about Felix's amorous adventures generated sexual tension.34 Part Two culminates in a sexual romp involving Felix, who's now working as an elevator boy, and the rich Frenchwoman whose jewel case he stole when they were going through customs together. She has been shopping, and after taking her up to the second floor, he carries her parcels to her bedroom, ignores the rings that mean other visitors are trying to summon the elevator, helps her off with her mink jacket, and, responding to her obvious interest in him, arranges to come back at eleven in the evening. Then, after arousing him by taking his hand and guiding it inside her décolletage, she undresses him greedily and, complaining about her husband's incompetence as a lover, praises Felix's skill.

Wanting to be degraded and abused, she tells him to call her a whore, and claiming to be extremely intelligent, an authoress, she knocks their heads together, saying the intellect longs for the delights of that which is alive and beautiful in its stupidity. As in *The Magic Mountain*, the amorous dialogue is mostly in French, and she addresses him as *bien aimé*. All beauty is stupid, she says, because it exists for glorification by the spirit, and female beauty is surpassed by the masterpiece of creation—very young men with the legs of Hermes, the god of thieves. Nothing in the world is more enchanting than the young male. (Much of what she says in her long speeches tallies with what Thomas might have said or thought, had he been making love to Franzl.)

She never feels desire for mature intellectual men, she says, and at twenty Felix is almost too old for her. In him she loves the son she has never had, while he illicitly loves his mother in her. Love is nothing but perversion, she explains, kissing the little golden hairs on the dark skin of his armpits. Adamantly refusing to beat her, he confesses that he took her jewel case. He's expecting her to be pleased, and, delighted at the humiliation of being in bed with a thief, she invites him to prowl about the bedroom and steal some of the things hidden under the lingerie in the bureau. She tells him where to find the key and turns off the lamp on the night table. He takes the rings and the pearl necklace she hasn't put away, as well as some pendants, bracelets, brooches, and banknotes.

BY MID-MARCH people seemed to have forgotten about Thomas's involvement in the Peace Crusade, but a new attack was published by a freelance journalist, Eugene Tillinger. He'd contributed to such extremist right-wing papers as *Plain Talk*. Titled "Thomas Mann's Left Hand," the article appeared in the issue published on March 26. "With amazing consistency," it said, "he continues to back every Stalinist organization that carries the word 'peace' in it." It accused him of delivering a series of lectures "in his native German" as if the intention were to prevent Americans from understanding. Though he'd denied signing the Stockholm Peace Declaration in the spring of 1950, Tillinger offered evidence that he'd signed it—a photograph of the text apparently bearing his signature. But this was a forgery. Thomas had already seen it together with a photomontage in which he appeared to be signing the declaration. But he was wearing a suit he hadn't had with him in 1950, and the black tie he'd worn after Klaus's suicide in 1949.

The Freeman had only a small circulation, and the article would have done no damage if it hadn't been taken up by the United Press on March 29, when the head of its Washington bureau, Lyle C. Wilson, denounced Thomas's "Communist-front activities," summarizing what had been said in *The Freeman*. "Without making use of the ugly word itself, the magazine states Mann lied on at least two occasions in denying specific communist activity."[35] The truth, said Tillinger, was that he'd attended both the conference in Stockholm and the second Congress for World Peace.

Thomas considered a libel suit, but this would have been time consuming.[36] On April 5 the *Los Angeles Times* reported he was one of the "notables" who'd been "listed" by the House Committee as "affiliated with various peace organizations or Communist fronts."[37] Six days later *The New York Times* carried an article titled "Mann Again Denies He Is a Communist" with the subtitle: "Says Article by an Accuser Appeared After He Quit Peace Crusade Group." He wrote to *The Freeman*, which published only 600 words from the 1,420 he wrote.

On April 22, listening to a record of the prelude to *Lohengrin*, he started weeping, "as a reaction to all this meanness. Have people ever had to breathe such a poisonous atmosphere, one so oversaturated with stupid vilification?"[38] He felt sure there was less "barbaric infantilism" in Europe.[39] But Erich von Kahler, trying to dissuade him from leaving for Switzerland, told him the story of two friends who caught sight of each other from ships traveling in opposite directions, one toward New

York and the other toward Europe. Each man yells at his friend: "Have you gone crazy?"

Finding it impossible to control MacArthur, Truman dismissed him on April 11, but it seemed possible that both the president and his secretary of state, Dean Acheson, would be impeached.[40] MacArthur, who was popular, launched well-publicized attacks on Truman's "blindness to reality," and the Senate held an inquiry into why the general had been sacked. But the chairman of the Joint Chiefs of Staff, General Omar Bradley, and Secretary of Defense George C. Marshall sided with Truman. MacArthur's strategy, said Bradley, would have led to "the wrong war at the wrong place at the wrong time with the wrong enemy."

Truman had been reprieved, but the peace seemed unstable, and though it was hard to concentrate on comedy, Thomas was glad to have emancipated himself from the political involvements that had drained so much energy all through the thirties and forties. "No one is ever going to get another political word out of me," he announced at the end of May.[41] As he said when refusing to campaign for peace in *Deutsche Woche*, "The world urgently needs it—but I need it too."[42]

By June 2 he'd written 150 pages of new material for *Felix Krull*. Part of the fun he had was that of picturing himself as the "divine boy" he'd worshiped throughout his life. If he'd longed for death during the previous summer, when the syndrome of passive desire seemed unbearable,[43] he could overcome the passivity by twisting the desire backward into imaginative and literary activity. Now, over halfway through his seventies, he was writing in the first person about a young charmer. In his youth he'd assumed the persona of a hunchback; now he was writing from the viewpoint of a beautiful young man.

Last summer, full of desire for Franzl, he'd done nothing except watch, suffer, and unburden himself in a diary no one would read until twenty years after his death; in the summer of 1951, drawing on memories of past suffering, he was playfully identifying with a man so handsome that he couldn't help hurting both men and women. When Felix starts working as a waiter in the hotel restaurant, ladies, young and old, ask for English mustard or Worcester sauce as a pretext for calling him to their table and looking up into his eyes. His superior, an elderly waiter with a sleepy expression, can see that he's in danger of losing his station to Felix. "You'll go a long way, my dear—my best wishes, my blessing!"

Felix is soon given the job Franzl had—serving coffee in the lounge—and the hotel is modeled on the Dolder Grand. In the dining room, fluted columns support the stucco ceiling. The wall lights have red shades, draperies billow at the windows, and the white damask tablecloths are decorated with orchids, napkins folded like fans or pyramids, shining silver, delicate glasses and bottles in gleaming coolers. Like Franzl, Felix makes guests feel welcome, pulls out chairs for them, proffers menus, fills glasses as if nothing gives him more pleasure than attending to their needs.

Instead of making an elderly German writer succumb to his charms, Thomas chooses as his principal victims a pretty eighteen-year-old blonde from Birmingham and a distinguished fifty-year-old Scottish lord—Eleanor Twentyman and Nectan Kilmarnock. (Finding that the name Kilmarnock belonged to a real lord, Thomas changed it to Strathbogie in the English translation.) Ignoring her parents, who reprimand her for staring at the young man, Eleanor wants him to elope with her and father the child which will, she believes, induce them to forgive her and make her rich; Kilmarnock offers him a job as valet together with the prospect of eventual adoption as his son and heir. Trusting fate to have something better in store for him, Felix gently rebuffs both suitors.

Daringly, Thomas gives the Scottish aristocrat his own features, just as he'd given Hauptmann's to Peeperkorn. Kilmarnock is described as a man of medium height, slender, elegantly dressed. His iron-gray hair is still thick and carefully brushed, while his clipped mustache doesn't conceal the almost feminine delicacy of his lips. The large nose juts out to form a ridge between slanting brows that beetle above gray-green eyes, which seem to require an effort of self-discipline to meet anyone else's. Cheeks and chin are clean-shaven, smooth, and well massaged.

THOMAS'S CRITICS weren't going to leave him in peace. After he'd contributed to a *Festschrift* published to celebrate Johannes Becher's sixtieth birthday, Tillinger wrote again in the *New Leader*, accusing Thomas of "extolling the notorious Stalinist agent."[44] And in Congress on June 20, a California representative, Donald Jackson, denounced "one of the world's foremost apologists for Stalin and company. Politically, Mr. Mann indicates a preference for those on the far left, and he rarely misses an occasion to eulogize the mental strait-jacket performances of fellow-apologists."[45] After this he was expecting a summons to appear in front of the House Committee,[46] and, calling him "one of the century's authentic literary giants," *Time* said he often "uses his famous name for causes that have nothing to do with literature." The article was titled "The Company He Keeps."[47]

As the pressure built up, the desire to emigrate became more urgent, but he needed more money than he had. He could barely afford a summer trip to Europe, though his rheumatism was troubling him, and he would have liked to take another cure in Gastein.[48] Even when the Book-of-the-Month Club chose *The Holy Sinner* for September—a decision that would make him at least $25,000 richer—he still hadn't surmounted the financial hurdles in the way of emigration. On May 31, when he sat down with Erika to calculate how much they needed to achieve complete freedom, they arrived at the figure of $140,000. He could aim at making a total of $50,000 from *The Holy Sinner*, $50,000 from selling the house, $30,000 from selling all his manuscripts, and $10,000 from the land he owned.[49]

Ridiculous Satisfaction

SINCE MAKING THEIR FIRST postwar journey to Europe in 1947, Thomas and Katia had gone there in 1949 and 1950, but in 1951 he thought he'd never again want to travel so far.[1] They sailed from New York on July 10, arriving nine days later in Le Havre, where Erika met them. They bought a small English car, a Hillman Minx, and she drove them to Zurich via Paris.

Having briefly revisited Munich two years earlier, Thomas had felt no desire to return, but Frido, who was eleven at the end of July, was near Salzburg, in Strobl on the Wolfgangsee with his parents. At the beginning of August, on their way to stay at the Grand Hotel there for ten days, Thomas and Katia spent a day in Munich, which seemed dreamlike and foreign. They drove through the town to the Herzogpark, where their old house had been partially destroyed and disfigured. In the morning, when they saw Frido, he was hoping they'd buy him a bicycle. Thomas enjoyed holding hands with him when they went out for walks, but, invited to join him for a swim in the lake, Thomas said he was too old and out of practice.[2]

He wanted to spend a couple of weeks in Gastein to take a cure for his arthritis at the "fountain of youth," and Erika looked for a house they could rent. She found one with its own thermal baths, but it wasn't available until August 19, which meant they'd have to spend the first few days in a hotel. In Strobl, Thomas was feeling exhausted, enervated, and able neither to appreciate the beauty of the scenery nor to work.[3] The baths were exhausting, but they seemed to be doing Thomas some good, and he soon felt able to resume work on *Felix Krull*. He was still intending to write an Erasmus story as an interlude,[4] and at the beginning of September he started reading a book on the fifteenth-century humanist Ulrich von Hutten by David Strauss. For the moment, though, he was fully immersed in *Felix Krull*. Intending to spend at least another fortnight in Zurich before flying back to New York, he thought of revisiting the Dolder to rewrite the waiter chapter.[5]

At the end of the first week in September, he and Katia moved to Lugano, and paid several visits to Castagnola, where Hermann Hesse talked about the falsity of American idealism. Both Thomas and Katia were becoming keen to settle in Switzerland, and, hearing of a house that was about to come onto the market outside Ascona, near Locarno, she was in favor of buying it; but he wanted to be in a German-speaking area.[6]

On September 13, Erika drove them back to Zurich. They stayed at the Waldhaus Dolder, which is on the same street as the Grand Hotel but smaller and less luxurious. The assistant manager claimed to have read "Death in Venice" ten times.[7] In Gastein, Thomas had begun to feel some stirrings of erotic rejuvenation, and at the Waldhaus, when he twice woke up with an erection, he didn't know whether he was benefiting from the thermal baths or from his own fiction. He was rewriting the waiter chapter. Masturbating, he felt absurd: "Ridiculous, the satisfaction." But he didn't return to the Grand for another eight days. "Looking around and remembering."[8]

Invited, as he was on every visit, to give a reading at the theater, he chose two chapters from *Felix Krull*. The audience's enthusiasm reinforced his desire to settle in Switzerland[9] and encouraged him to forge ahead with the narrative. Felix's combination of good looks with charm, eloquence, and a histrionic talent had been intended from the outset to give him the chance of moving almost effortlessly into the upper reaches of society. Reading Shaw in order to write about him, Thomas may have started thinking in terms of a male equivalent to Eliza Doolittle, though he'd already had the idea, when he started making notes in 1906, that Felix should impersonate an aristocrat. A great deal of plotting has to be done before Thomas can flesh out this idea, which he'd jotted down in 1906, borrowing it from J. J. Davids's story about Poldi Kirchnegger. Wanting to separate the Marquis de Venosta from his beautiful but socially unacceptable girlfried, Zaza, his parents arrange to send him on a tour around the world. Unwilling to deceive them by taking her with him, the marquis is glad to deceive them by spending their money on sending Felix around the world. This proposal serves as a premise for an episodic series of adventures. To make it more or less plausible, Thomas gets Felix into the habit of squandering some of his money on occasional meals in expensive restaurants, for which he wears evening dress. When the two young men see each other dining alone, the marquis, who has always enjoyed chatting with Felix, joins him, and the plot is hatched.

Ever since Aristophanes, one of comedy's stock themes has been role swapping between master and servant; since writing about Kleist's reworking of the Amphytrion story, Thomas had been especially alert to problems of identity. When Felix starts working as a waiter, the narrative benefits from the pleasure Thomas took in empathizing with Franzl. But to make the most of this comic idea, the narrative needs to put Felix in situations that will test his ability to sustain the impersonation, and there will be little dramatic edge to these sequences unless he seems to be in danger. If Thomas was halfhearted about writing sequences of this kind, it was partly because of doubts about whether it was proper for a man of his age to write this kind of comedy. "Pan-eroticism and jewel-thieving–are these jokes to which a man should devote the last years of his life?"[10]

After flying to New York by Swiss Air–he felt complete confidence in everything Swiss[11]–he and Katia had two meals with their daughter Monika before leaving to see Elisabeth in Chicago. They were both tired, and at the station, when Katia panicked, thinking the railway tickets were lost, Thomas ran in pursuit of the taxi they'd just used, only to find they had the tickets.

Though they spent only three days in Chicago, he worked at the novel and paid two visits to the Field Museum of Natural History. One of his instincts in the *Joseph* novels had been to question how things began; here he was excited by the variety of evidence about the origins of life–sponges that could have survived for 50 million years, a display of equally ancient shells, relics of the earliest organic life on the bed of the ocean. He saw lifelike reconstructions of animals and men that had lived in earlier geological periods–dinosaurs and reptiles, egg-bearing mammals with pouches, apes, caves with Neanderthal men, an ungainly primitive man with bloody knees, his woman carrying a baby on her arm just like a modern woman. The models were all based on skeletal remains. Thomas felt "something akin to biological inebriation. The feeling that all this is at the root of my writing and loving and living– my humanity."

Small, with fluffy hair, the "first Europeans" were depicted as crouching on the ground 10 million years ago. Artists were at work, squatting to paint animal figures on the rock walls of their cave, probably for magical purposes. Between two stone pillars that formed a kind of alfresco temple, the raised arms of a priest held up flowers as an offering to the rising sun. In the aquarium Thomas was struck by the variety of animal and vegetable life. Moved in a way he didn't altogether understand, he knew he wouldn't have found an art gallery so absorbing.[12]

Early in October they made the long journey back to Pacific Palisades. Two weeks later, Erika drove them to Santa Monica, where Yalta Menuhin was playing with Michael in a school hall. The thirty-year-old pianist sister of Yehudi Menuhin, Yalta had boosted Michael's career by becoming his regular accompanist, and they were touring together in a series of recitals. The whole family, including Yehudi, had a high regard for Michael. When Thomas, Katia, and Erika went backstage, it was evident that his relationship with Yalta wasn't merely professional, and drinking coffee together the next morning, Thomas and Katia speculated gloomily on how Gret and Yalta's husband were likely to react.

But Thomas was taken by surprise on November 4, when the husband rang up to say Michael had become violent during a quarrel the previous evening when he and Yalta were on their way to a recital: Wounded above the eye, she was in bed, under doctor's orders. The performance had been canceled, and the husband, who thought Michael was insane, insisted they must never play together again. Their European tour would have to be canceled. By losing his self-control, Michael had done himself irreparable damage. He tried to behave as though nothing serious had happened, but, acting through a lawyer, the husband insisted that he should leave the country, threatening to have him arrested as insane if he ever came back. Yalta confirmed that she never wanted to hear from him again. It was agreed that he should settle in Zurich, where Katia arranged for him to see the neurologist Erich Katzenstein. "I must confess," Thomas wrote, "that I shall be glad when he has gone. I do not like his nature, or his laugh. But I gave him a good talking-to at the meal-table, and said he did not need the association with Yalta."13

Both Katia and Erika reacted to the crisis with physical symptoms: Katia had been suffering from cystitis, which now returned, while Erika's insomnia got worse, and she had pains in her stomach,14 but Thomas went back to his novel. Possibly he damaged it by working at it in the wrong mood; certainly it changes tack when Felix becomes a vehicle for pursuing the intellectual adventure that had started in the Field Museum of Natural History. Four days after the husband's first telephone call, Thomas was greedily devouring a book on biology, and five days later he started work on the chapter in which Felix has a long conversation on a train with a fragile-looking middle-aged man whose eyes are described as starry. (Thomas owed this idea to the Lukácses: Georg had said his father's eyes sent out gleams like stars, and in *The Magic Mountain* Naphta describes his father as "starry-eyed."15 Impersonating the marquis, Felix is on his way to Lisbon, where the man tells him to visit the botanical gardens, which contain tree ferns from the Carboniferous period.

The man introduces himself as Professor Kuckuck, paleontologist and director of Lisbon's Natural History Museum. He has been in Paris to secure skeletal fragments of a long-extinct species of tapir, from which, through many evolutionary stages, the horse is descended. Organic life on earth, he says, has lasted about 550 million years, and man was a latecomer. Life is only an episode, and on the scale of the eons, only a fleeting one; less than 50 million years had passed before the first vertebrates came onto the land from the water. But evolution could then move fast, thanks to a simple idea—creating flesh and blood through the cohabitation of cells.

Suddenly the novel is back in the world of *The Magic Mountain*: The nature of organic life is being explained derogatorily, and here, as there, Thomas enjoys deconstructing the appurtenances of female beauty. However shapely an arm is, we're told, we should never forget that it's merely the hooked wing of the primordial bird and the pectoral fin of the fish. And if naked human beings remind us of pigs, we mustn't forget that the pig has more human qualities than any chimpanzee, while in structural development, the human brain is closest to that of the rat. The conversation, which is like a long essay disguised by interruptions, culminates in a statement about Being and Nothingness. Nothingness had given rise to Being, and Being to life, which consisted of the same raw particles as inanimate nature. Narrative momentum is jettisoned in this long sequence of generalization, but Thomas convinced himself that Felix had to be put in touch with the idea of Being.[16]

This essayistic overloading of a lightweight comic vehicle resulted from Thomas's compulsion to demonstrate there was value in what he was doing: He kept worrying that the story was too insipid and absurd.[17] He also doubted whether he'd be able to finish it, but this was partly because of uncertainty about moving. Sometimes he thought he and Katia were too old to uproot themselves, that if they settled in Switzerland, it would be mainly for Erika's sake. In America her health was breaking up under the strain of successive humiliations and disappointments. In October she was questioned by rude FBI officials: Was she a member of the Communist Party or a paid Stalinist agent?[18] Eighteen years ago, performing her own sketches in the *Pfeffermühle*, she'd been brilliantly successful; now no one would publish the books she wanted to write, and a doctor failed to cure her insomnia.[19]

Thomas made a decision in early December: After a conversation with Katia over breakfast, he instructed agents to find a buyer for their house. "I have less desire to live than to die and rest in Switzerland." He was pessimistic about whether he could "find the mood" to finish *Felix Krull*, and though his body was young for that of a seventy-six-year-old man, his feelings were predominantly negative. "I eat to keep myself nourished and be able to smoke. I have little faith in my future capacity to do things. I am furious over demands, nuisances, tremble with exhaustion on the rare occasions when I have to carry on a telephone conversation. The accumulation of letters and manuscripts fills me with disgust and despair. . . . Almost all my memories are painful, and the future seems to have only failure in store. If I am going to Switzerland it is not to live there, but to die there."[20]

At least half-aware that *Felix Krull* was drifting in the wrong direction, he worked at it joylessly. He'd never been to Lisbon, but relied on pictures, while, writing a tennis sequence, he relied partly on memories of the attractive young Argentinian and partly on photographs of Lew Hoad in action.[21] In mid-January, when he finished the chapter about

Felix's first meeting with Professor Kuckuck, he couldn't feel proud as he usually did on completing a chapter.[22] He realized he was subject to "a damnable inclination to work out every single thing—even something so foolish—in Faustian terms" and to make it into "a peregrination from heaven through the world to hell."[23] But he wrote a chapter about Felix's first meeting with the wife and daughter of Professor Kuckuck before putting the novel aside to write a talk on "The Artist and Society" for the BBC Third Programme, and a foreword to a new collection of his essays. After finishing the foreword on March 20, he didn't relish further work on *Felix Krull*. Perhaps he'd finish the Lisbon episode and another one, set in Argentina, but leave the novel unfinished. Certainly, he wouldn't devote the rest of his life to it. He wanted a more serious task. But what? "If I give up—and I must, I believe—what will take its place?"[24]

Two days later, over early morning coffee, Katia was talking about a Munich woman who'd passed her menopause, started a passionate love affair with her son's tutor, and been excited to think that the power of love had revived her womanhood. But the blood she took to be menstrual was symptomatic of uterine cancer. One of the questions that interested Thomas was whether the disease had intensified her passion. Forty years earlier, writing *The Magic Mountain*, he'd made disease play a part in Hans's love for Clavdia. He wants to see her X-ray, wants to think of corrosion inside the beautiful body. By the beginning of May, Thomas was trying to find a form for the story about the postmenopausal woman. He wrote to Frederick Rosenthal, the doctor who'd supplied medical information for *Doctor Faustus*, summing up the plot and saying that the woman takes the bleeding to be "a sort of love-miracle, a revival of her physical womanliness through the psychic," only to find she's been cruelly deceived by nature. At what stage in the development of the disease would the bleeding start? Would the cancer cause any noticeable physical deterioration, and would it be operable? If so, would the entire uterus be removed?[25]

The doctor asked for more details, and in a second letter Thomas explained that the action would be set in the Rhineland during the twenties, perhaps in Düsseldorf. (This was where Klaus Heuser had lived.) Could the cancer have started as ovarian? Could the ecstatic feeling of love be due partly to irritation in the diseased organ?[26] Within a few days, Thomas was trying to get hold of a Düsseldorf street map,[27] and by the beginning of June he'd succeeded.[28]

His work would be interrupted when he and Katia left for Europe at the end of the month, but he forged rapidly ahead. In *Felix Krull* he'd found it easy to empathize with the lovely Frenchwoman, the Scottish lord, and the girl from Birmingham who fell in love with the handsome waiter; in the story he could again draw on his feelings about attractive waiters and tennis players when writing about an aging widow's excited reactions to the appealing young American who is coaching her son, Eduard, in English. Rosalie von Tümmler becomes aware of her passion during a meal on a warm summery evening when Eduard asks her permission to take off his jacket, and the tutor, Ken Keaton, who has fallen into the pattern of staying for dinner after the lesson, follows suit. Ken is modeled mainly on Ed Klotz, an American history teacher who visited the Manns' house.[29] Eduard is wearing a long-sleeved shirt, but Ken's sleeveless white jersey reveals white, muscular arms, while the shape of his chest is clearly visible. Affected, Rosalie leaves the room. What comes next is a long silent monologue in which Thomas writes variations on the theme of appetites whetted in old people by youngsters. Youth is feminine, Rosalie says, and age masculine. During marital lovemaking it had always been her husband who took the initiative, but now she's the one who wants to do the wooing, and she thinks jealously about local women who are taking lessons from him and possibly flirting with him. She also compares herself with the aging matriarch Sarah, who laughed when she heard God was going to restore her fertility. This prepares the ground for the possibility that something miraculous will happen to Rosalie.

By bringing an American to Germany, Thomas gives himself a chance to generalize about differences in national outlook. An untypical American, knowledgeable about European folklore, Ken attacks his fellow countrymen for their pursuit of the dollar and their insensate churchgoing, their cult of mediocrity, their worship of success, and their indifference to history. Though there are magnificent landscapes in the United States, he says, there's nothing behind them. American cities look as if they were put up yesterday and might be taken away tomorrow, while in museums the cultural treasures all come from Europe. He loves French cathedrals, Italian palazzi, Swiss villages, oak tables in German inns, ancient cities in the Rhineland. Without cataloguing everything Thomas had missed during fourteen years of voluntary exile from Europe, Ken's comments point to some of his reasons for returning.

He'd been trying to keep this plan to himself, but after a newspaper leaked it at the end of March,[30] he had to face questions from reporters and press agencies.[31] When a Munich paper, *Echo der Woche*, suggested that his decision had been triggered by the activities of the House Committee and by the spinelessness of friends who failed to rally in his support, he denied any anti-American feelings. Apart from a few journalistic attacks, he'd encountered nothing but friendliness and had recently accepted an invitation to join the American Academy of Arts and Letters. He was intending to work in Europe for a year or two, he said, but this didn't indicate any breach with the United States.[32] In reality he now found it embarrassing to travel with an American passport,[33] while Erika grew increasingly bitter and irritable whenever the conversation came back to the United States.[34] By early June he was afraid she might kill herself.[35]

Thomas and Katia were planning to leave for Europe at the end of June, but without having decided whether they'd come back to America. If the house in Pacific Palisades was still unsold when they left, they'd have to, and if a buyer suddenly appeared during June, it would have been hard for them to empty the house before they left.[36] Perhaps it would be better not to leave till the house was sold,[37] but Thomas, who was losing weight and taking little pleasure in eating, felt in urgent need of another cure at Gastein.[38]

He'd been unhappy that his work was unavailable in the Soviet Zone of Germany, and had tried to make Bermann negotiate a deal with Aufbau Verlag, but when the East German press illegally brought out editions of *Buddenbrooks* and *The Beloved Returns*, Thomas had no strong feelings. It was gratifying that 30,000 copies of *Buddenbrooks* were sold, and orders placed in bookstores for another 70,000 copies, but he supported neither Aufbau Verlag nor Bermann, who wanted to take legal action. Thomas wrote to the East German publishers, and to Johannes Becher, condemning the illegality of what had been done, but, as he said in his diary, it was really a matter of indifference to him.[39]

In June, when he was awarded the Antonio Feltrinelli Prize by the Accademia Nazionale dei Lincei in Rome, he was glad to be $8,000 richer, but he'd received so many honors and awards that they were no longer exciting. Not that he was indifferent to its value as a boost to his prestige. When the academy failed to publicize the award in the United States, he wrote to Agnes Meyer, asking her to inform the press. "If only because of my honourable enemies it would be a pity if the event passed unnoticed." The citation paid tribute to the achievement of "a living humanism that spiritually transcends the barriers of our age and thus provides guidance for all intellectual activity."[40]

Uncertain whether they'd ever see their California house again, he and Katia left on June 24 to spend two nights in Chicago, flying on to New York, and, three days later, to Zurich. The heat there was overbearing, and they'd planned to stay in the mountains. Thomas wanted to work on the novel, but he was suffering from persistent pain and dryness in his throat. He consulted Professor Mäder, who made a more favorable impression on him than previously, and he paid several visits to the office.[41]

On Tuesday, July 8, they went on to Kandersteg, where the hotel room they'd reserved turned out to be small and primitive. They gave notice that they'd stay only a week and, on July 15, moved into another hotel.[42] Here, too, the room was disappointing, and, working on the story, Thomas had to use the washstand as a writing table. The food was mediocre, but it was good to be on higher ground, away from the heat of Zurich, and he enjoyed watching the tennis players, especially a young man in red, "with bare legs and pretty movements."[43]

Thursday, July 24, was Katia's sixty-ninth birthday, and, breakfasting on the balcony, they talked about the years which "certainly hadn't scurried away. . . . It is a long, slow period that has passed since we married, rich in experience and also achievement." In the evening they had a champagne dinner with Erika at a table laden with flowers. Katia was in favor of going back to California if they couldn't sell the house, but Thomas wanted to leave the question open until November, when they'd know who was going to be the next president.[44]

On August 10 Thomas was due to lecture in Salzburg, where Michael was playing the viola part in Mozart's concertante K. 364. He seemed nervous, possibly because of his parents' presence, and his performance was lacking in breadth of tone. Afterward, when Thomas and Katia went on to St. Wolfgang, Gret seemed unwell and withdrawn. "She does not have an easy time," Thomas noted, "with the nervous and tyrannous father of her children, who is obsessed with egocentric ambition." As before, when Michael had assaulted Yalta Menuhin, Thomas assumed the stance of a detached observer, especially when commenting on weaknesses that resembled his own. It was still only his grandson's company that Thomas enjoyed: "Frido in his swimming trunks, taller, full of joy and tenderness. His pretty blue eyes." But Thomas could no longer see him without thinking about the Echo episode.[45]

Thomas was becoming increasingly dependent on Erika, who'd become more available as her career disintegrated. She was better than anyone else at suggesting cuts when a lecture or article needed to be shortened, and she could mediate between him and Katia when they disagreed. She could side with his superego when he was in danger of making too many compromises; she could act as translator, secretary, interpreter, driver, and personal assistant. When the house in California was eventually sold, she'd be able to go there and arrange for furniture and possessions to be packed and shipped. But ill health and a quarrelsome disposition made her touchy with other people. When Golo's friend Melvin Lasky, editor of *Der Monat*, which had published some of Thomas's work, came to St. Wolfgang, Erika said he was an American agent and a spy. She quarreled with Golo, who then absented himself from dinner. Often bitter and aggressive, she was also liable to have rows with Katia.[46]

Back in Gastein on August 20, Thomas could concentrate on his own health. The doctor said it was important to keep his weight stable, but with his poor appetite, and the difficulties he was having in chewing and swallowing, this wouldn't be easy. They'd invited Hans Reisiger to stay with them in Gastein, and when he arrived, he seemed "just the same, just like Schildknapp. We laughed a lot." Reisi still had a healthy appetite, but at dinner on their first day together, Thomas wanted only soup, ice cream, and coffee. He usually felt exhausted and depressed, but by the end of the month he'd written forty-eight manuscript pages of the story. He was expecting to finish it in another twenty.[47]

It was a strain to be working and taking the baths at the same time. On Saturday, August 30, when he started out on a walk, he had to give up after ten minutes, scarcely able to stay awake. He was becoming reluctant to make any effort of any kind, and he was scared of the dryness in his throat that made him careful about chewing and nervous about swallowing. But he was cheered by the audience's enthusiasm when he read the Professor Kuckuck chapter from *Felix Krull* at the Schauspielhaus on September 17, though he attributed his success more to his bravura performance than to the quality of the chapter, "which is not so good."[48] The tonic effect of the evening still hadn't worn off when, a week later, he ordered a new suit at London House, bought new goatskin gloves, an umbrella, and a malacca cane with a ring on it for his initials.[49]

He'd been planning to make an appearance in Rome during the spring to express his thanks for the prize, but so many of his autumn commitments involved travel that he canceled the Italian trip. But in early October, he thought about having a new house built, although the Pacific Palisades house was still unsold, and if they were staying in Switzerland, they weren't yet in agreement about where they should live. He liked Zurich, but Katia preferred the idea of an Alpine home near the Italian border. Thomas, after living for so long in California, wasn't relishing the prospect of cold winters. In bed at night, he couldn't get his feet warm even with a hot-water bottle.[50]

The autumn brought a series of deaths. Alfred Neumann died on October 3, and six days later, Emil Oprecht. "Nature seems to be having fun and showing that after so many ordeals one still survives these shocks quite well."[51] Erika went with him and Katia to Munich, where they spent four nights at the Hotel Vier Jahreszeiten, and on their first evening saw Therese Giehse in the German premiere of Eduardo de Filippo's *Philumena Marturano*. On October 19, Thomas was greeted with a big ovation when he appeared in the Schauspielhaus to read the Kuckuck chapter from *Felix Krull*, and at the end, the cheers and shouts of "Stay here!" and "Come back!" went on so long that the safety curtain had to be lowered, and the audience swarmed out into the street in pursuit of him. On Tuesday he had a long chat with Hans Ludwig Held, who was still director of the civic library in spite of having sworn loyalty to the Nazis. When Held said the authorities might provide a house if Thomas was willing to settle in Munich, he felt half-inclined to accept.[52]

On returning to Zurich he found that if he and Katia rented a house, a furniture company, Möbel-Pfister, would lend them furniture, free, until their own arrived from California. Within a few days they had decided to go ahead with this plan. On October 29, nearly twenty years after they had left Germany, they went with Erika to Erlenbach, close to Küsnacht. They viewed a house where they could rent the two upper stories. The house was attractive and almost new, with an extensive view of the lake. The ground floor and basement were occupied by a young doctor and his wife. The Manns immediately knew this was where they wanted to live. They could move in before Christmas,[53] but as soon as it was announced that Dwight Eisenhower had been elected president, Katia was in favor of renewing their American passports in case he thought Thomas should be expatriated because of his visit to East Germany.[54]

On Saturday, November 8, after arriving in Frankfurt, he was applauded when he took his seat at a performance of Hauptmann's *Iphigenie in Delphi*. In the morning he was in the Schauspielhaus again to read his lecture on Hauptmann, which he'd based mainly on material provided by the endlessly obliging Reisiger. It was greeted with a huge ovation and a kiss from the widow. On Monday evening he read the Kuckuck chapter to a packed and appreciative audience at the university. Afterward he had to push his way through the admirers thronging around him, asking him to sign copies of his books, and at the Swiss frontier, a customs official asked for his autograph.[55]

In Vienna, with his energy sapped by severe bronchial catarrh and his performances interrupted by fits of coughing, he had to read from *Felix Krull* in the Mozartsaal, lecture on the artist and society in the Konzerthaus, and autograph books in a bookshop. In the small hours of Friday morning he was coughing so much that Katia summoned a doctor, and in the morning a nurse arrived with apparatus for him to inhale penicillin and Emser salts, which made him feel better. Austria was still occupied by the Allies, and the Communist press tried to exploit his presence. He used his illness as an excuse for turning down an invitation to a Soviet gala concert, but at night, wheezing, coughing, struggling for breath, and remembering how his grandmother had died, asphyxiated by emphysema, he felt envious of Heinrich's painless death.

Though he'd kept to his resolution about making no more political statements in public, he agreed to give a press conference in Vienna when the PEN Club wanted to arrange one. A journalist asked for his views about restrictions on freedom in the United States. Knowing he had to be careful, he said American democracy felt threatened and, in the struggle, considered that there had to be a certain limitation on freedom, a certain disciplining of individual thought, a certain conformism. This was understandable, he said, and it did honor to the country that after wartime regimentation, so much opposition was stirring, especially in intellectual circles. According to some of the newspapers, it was during this conference that he refused to answer a question about the advantages of American democracy as compared with that of the "People's Republics." According to him, it wasn't until after the conference was over that an Associated Press journalist put this question to him.[56] In December, feeling obliged to give an explicit answer, he wrote: "All my actions and efforts, all my books and writings, and my whole being show me to be incessantly concerned with the great cultural heritage of the West, contributing to it according to my strength."[57]

On December 4, while Thomas was eating dinner with Katia and Erika, Elisabeth rang up to say that Borgese was comatose with a cerebral thrombosis. He died at midnight, but neither Thomas nor Erika wanted to go with Katia when she left in the middle of the day to be with Elisabeth and the children. Thomas and Erika had dinner together, making plans for the move into the new house, and in the morning Thomas was delighted to receive a telegram from Martin Flinker, a Swiss bookseller and publisher who lived in Paris, telling him to expect a letter from the foreign minister, Robert Schuman, saying he'd been chosen as an officer of the Légion d'honneur. This was an honor Thomas had longed for. "Happy because of America, also because of Germany and Switzerland." Not feeling well enough to make the journey to Paris before the spring, he asked Flinker whether the award could be postponed until then, and wrote to tell Agnes Meyer about it, asking her to spread the news in America.[58]

But he couldn't count on it to protect him against being cited by the House Committee, and he decided to give up his American citizenship if he was. Erika, who still felt bitter toward the United States, would have preferred him to take Swiss nationality and asked the Oprechts' son, Hans, to find out whether it would be available for him. American citizenship would matter to him less once the house was sold. He had reduced the asking price to $55,000, with a down payment of $40,000. He rejected a much lower offer, but six days before Christmas, when it was raised to $50,000, with a down payment of $35,000, the balance to be settled in monthly installments, he decided to accept. It had been empty for almost six months, and still afraid he might be banned from reentering the United States, he was glad to have the matter settled.[59]

They'd been told they could move into the new house before Christmas, but on December 19 it was still dirty, with no oven in the kitchen, no electricity, no running water, and no telephone. Thomas was feeling so ill, so tired of life, so lethargic, so uninterested in eating or smoking that he wondered whether it was worth making the effort to move.

Even his interest in Frido was giving him no pleasure. When he rang up on December 23, the day before he and his brother arrived in Zurich to spend Christmas with their grandparents, Thomas thought he sounded cold and uncommunicative. "At the boarding school they do not think highly of his character, and there, as here, he goes around with unimpressive friends. Possible that the affectionately cherished Echo will develop into nothing special."[60]

Prodding the builders into a final flurry of activity, the architect had the house ready for them on Christmas Eve. Möbel-Pfister had provided not only furniture but a Christmas tree, and Thomas was glad to have such good views of the lake and the mountains, but he felt ill overnight, breathing with great difficulty. There was something wrong with the caviar Katia had bought, and though it was good to know he again had a proper study with a proper writing table, he was worried about the smallness of the living room; the old bookcases were too tall for it. Worst of all, he felt like an old man, no longer capable of much activity.[61]

Love and Mischief

THOMAS HAD BEEN WRONG to think he had too little energy for the move into the new house, but it came at an unfortunate time. He hadn't entirely recovered from his bronchitis, and ill health made it harder for him to cope with having his books in disarray and his correspondence in arrears while the builders were still working noisily. Sometimes he escaped to write letters in the quiet of the Waldhaus Dolder,[1] and he cheered himself up by going around with the red rosette of the Légion d'honneur permanently in his buttonhole, and by flying a Swiss flag from the new car, a Fiat he'd bought in December.

He was glad to have left the "air-conditioned nightmare" behind him. He used Heinrich's phrase for the United States in a January letter,[2] and he hesitated when Paul Hoffmann, Geneva correspondent for *The New York Times*, asked for an interview or an article "on the realities and dangers in the current trend of American policy toward restriction of entry and investigation (and castigation) of non-conformist opinion in all walks of life—everything in short that will be suggested to you by the names McCarthy and McCarran."[3] Chairman of the Senate Internal Security Subcommittee, Patrick McCarran was responsible for the act that obliged all aliens to register, and made it harder for political suspects to obtain entry visas.

Finally rejecting the invitation, Thomas took the risk of explaining his reasons. Even if a new world war were avoided, he said, the future belonged to a totalitarianism that would admit neither democracy nor freedom, and at the age of seventy-seven, he didn't want to provoke a repetition of experiences he'd had in the thirties—expatriation and being dispossessed of his property. Erika, who translated the letter into English for him, urged him not to send it. How could he be sure Hoffmann would keep the contents to himself?[4]

In February, Thomas tried to resume work on the story, but he succumbed to flu and didn't recover fully till mid-March.[5] He'd had a bad winter, and, blaming it on the Swiss climate and the stress of moving, he was unsure whether he'd been right to sell the California house.[6] The story was still unfinished, but he read the first part on February 13 to the PEN Club and finished it on the eighteenth—ninety-one pages of manuscript. He was pleased with the beginning and the ending, less satisfied with the middle.[7]

Certainly, the middle section is weak. Had Chekhov, D. H. Lawrence, or Guy de Maupassant been handling the idea, the bleeding might have started as an apparent climax in the developing relationship between Rosalie and Ken. But in none of his work since *Buddenbrooks* had Thomas dealt realistically with a developing sexual relationship. In *Doctor Faustus* experiments in pastiche and parody had succeeded, partly because style was serving as commentary on substance, while the artistic problems that drove Adrian into the arms of the Devil were problems Thomas had been confronting. In the story, Nature seems to be playing a diabolical trick on the woman, but in assuming that the narrative must take the form of a classical novel,[8] Thomas was sidestepping difficulties he needed to resolve. He'd always found it easy to dramatize infatuation inspired by good looks, and in his best love story, "Death in Venice," the man and the boy never talk to each other. Even when his lovers get as far as making love, as Hans Castorp and Clavdia Chauchat do, they're immediately separated. The lovers in "The Black Swan" ("Die Betrogene") never become lovers, and the narrative is damaged by Thomas's partiality for long speeches. The central conversation, which goes on for eighteen pages, is between Rosalie and her clubfooted daughter, Anna, who tries to discourage her mother from embarking on an affair, and the sequence reads rather like an exchange of letters in an epistolary novel.

At the end of the story Thomas is uncharacteristically heavy-handed in using medical information he'd collected. Rosalie has promised she'll go to Ken's room, but she collapses, bleeding, and when she's in a "gynaecological hospital," two doctors discuss what is revealed first by manual examination and then by incision. Narrative and dialogue bristle with such terms as *carcinoma, lymphatic tissue, metastatis, uremia*, and *hormonal hyperplasia*. In her last words—and this was an irony Thomas relished—Rosalie praises the loving gentleness of Nature, which made her death "borrow the semblance of resurrection."

At last, completing the sixty-page story almost twelve months after giving it priority over *Felix Krull*, he could go back to the novel, and on April 11 he did, but without believing he could finish it, or seriously wanting to.[9]

He broke off to spend the last ten days of April in Rome, a city he hadn't visited since 1897. Though he was impressed with "these piazzas, churches, fountains, obelisks, patterned columns, this melange of centuries, of classical, early Christian and Gothic, this abundance of artistic creations of sensual and mystical piety and genius,"[10] he'd been content to stay away for nearly sixty years. With help from the academy and from a journalist on the *Osservatore Romano*, he succeeded in arranging a private audience with seventy-seven-year-old Pope Pius XII, who spoke fluent German. He, too, had been suffering from a viral infection. "The illness," he said, "all very well. But the treatment! That is what lasts." Thomas had been told that when the pope was a nuncio in Germany, he'd stood outside the Wartburg, the castle associated with Luther, and said: "That is a blessed building." Thomas reminded him of this comment, which he interpreted as a declaration of faith in the unity of all religious belief, and when the pope, by presenting him with a small silver medallion, indicated that the conversation was over, Thomas had no hesitation in genuflecting. His last impression was that the pope, who held his hand for some time, was reluctant to let go of it.[11]

In early June, after spending May in the new house, Thomas and Katia flew to London and drove to Cambridge, where he was awarded an honorary doctorate. He was glad to have a second encounter with Jawaharlal Nehru, who'd come to England for the coronation of Elizabeth II on June 2. After two more days in London, Thomas and Katia flew to Hamburg, where he gave two readings from *Felix Krull*, one to university students and one, at the invitation of the local Goethegesellschaft, in the Konzerthalle, where he had an audience of 2,300 people. Wearing a dinner jacket, sitting at a table, and reading through rimless spectacles from large sheets of manuscript, he delighted the audience, which called him back again and again. He bowed, accepted flowers and finally lifted his arms sideways, as if in a helpless effort to parry the applause.[12] "In life I am a conventional and boring man," he wrote afterward, "but on the podium something like a magnetic personality."[13]

He hadn't been invited to revisit Lübeck, and hadn't been there since 1931, but a quick-witted press photographer, Hans Kripgans, offered to drive him and Katia there in his little Volkswagen. At first Thomas demurred, but seeing he really wanted to make the forty-mile journey, she persuaded him. Bermann's wife, Tutti, and his colleague Dr. Hirsch followed in a second car. In the Volkswagen, Thomas said very little. Kripgans drove him and Katia to the house in Mengstrasse and persuaded them to pose in front of it for a photograph. A bomb had destroyed the house, leaving only the facade intact, and now, eighteen years after the end of the war, the windows on the two upper floors were still bricked or boarded up and the facade was supported on one side by scaffolding.

They went on to Travemünde, which had changed a lot since his childhood, becoming more like an international resort. The lighthouse and the Swiss chalets were the same, but an asphalt promenade had been built where he remembered only wooden boards, and there was a new casino where the bandstand used to be. He and Katia walked along the promenade and stared out at the choppy sea. They would have liked to stay for a few days, but it was too cold.[14] They had lunch in the pump room as guests of the newspaper, the *Lübecker Nachrichten*, and they posed for photographs. Thomas stood outside the pump room, holding his hat in one hand and his cigar in the other. He had the feeling that he was seeing Travemünde for the last time. On the promenade he looked through a telescope fixed to a pedestal and focused on the Russian zone. Afterward they drove back to Lübeck, stopping to look at the Holstentor and the Katharineum. Seeing the playground, he thought once again of borrowing Willri Timpe's pencil.[15]

To celebrate Katia's seventieth birthday on July 24, the children and grandchildren gathered in the house—every room was occupied—and Thomas couldn't help brooding about their forty-eight years together and the prospect of being separated soon by death.[16] The birthday presents included fur coats, handbags, and paintings from Elisabeth's children. After breakfast, he and Katia heard music being played outside the windows of the dining room. Members of the symphony orchestra were playing a birthday serenade. In the evening, two Swiss friends threw a champagne party for her in a private room at the Eden au Lac. Speeches were made and Thomas, in his, mentioned "Kinderkarneval," the oil painting of the five dark-haired Pringsheim children in Pierrot costume. He also recalled the time when they'd had no car, and, cycling over ice on a tramline, she'd fallen off her bike and broken her ankle. He acknowledged the myriad ways in which she had helped him, typing letters, checking royalty statements, welcoming visitors but indicating when it was time for them to leave, and consoling him, when he needed consolation, by saying: "That's all right, you've done quite well—done all you could." The afterworld, he predicted, if it had a good word for him, would also have one in praise of "her vitality, her active loyalty, her endless patience and courage."[17] While he was making the speech, his voice faltered. Looking back, later, on a life in which he'd regularly read from his work and rehearsed lectures and speeches in front of the family, Erika could remember only two other occasions on which this had happened. One was when he read the Echo episode from *Doctor Faustus*, and the other when he read his final speech about Schiller.[18]

Katia was going to be under strain during the move. Since leaving Germany in 1933, they'd had two homes in Switzerland, two in the United States, and another one in Switzerland, but, disappointingly, the new house in Erlenbach was turning out to be too small. There was no space in Thomas's study for the sofa he badly needed, no longer being able to sit stooped at his desk for hours at a stretch. He'd written much of *Doctor Faustus* and *The Holy Sinner* while sitting in a corner of the sofa.[19] He missed the house in Pacific Palisades, and especially the sofa.[20] He also decided, rather tardily, that the new house had a quality he couldn't bear—mediocrity. They agreed to move out no later than April 1954, and hearing that some imposing houses were for sale at reasonable prices between Vevey and Lausanne, they arranged to spend a few days by Lake Geneva during the second week of September so they could start another search for a new home.21 But he found the area rather dreary, while land turned out to be more expensive than they'd been led to believe, and landowners were in no hurry to sell, expecting prices to rise still higher. To find something within their means, Thomas and Katia would have had to move farther away from Zurich than he wanted to.22 What he wanted most of all was a bigger living room, a study with space in it for a sofa, and a bathroom of his own adjoining his bedroom.23

By the middle of 1953, he often felt it was a mistake to go on living. His last substantial work had been *Doctor Faustus*, and he was afraid of surviving without being able to produce anything at all. Eating had become a burden and a torture; the only pleasures left were smoking and coffee, which were both damaging, as was hunching over his desk.24 Ten years previously he'd maintained an output of two or three pages a day; by October he could average only twenty lines.25 He wept while he worked on Felix's discourse about love, which he believed to be original.26 But it's a generalizing monologue not strong enough to fulfill its dramatic function. Kuckuck's pretty young daughter, Zouzou, has been resistant to the idea of love and to the advances of the young man she believes to be the Marquis de Venusta. Her change of heart is prompted by a long argument about kissing as a beautiful deviation from Nature's basic design in which we feel complete inside our own skin and glad not to have other bodies intruding on ours. Love miraculously overcomes this separation when two pairs of eyes become blind to everything except each other, and the two privileged people feel equally impatient to toss all evasions aside, together with their clothes, as they declare their love for each other.

Shrugging off encouragement from Erika and Katia, Thomas couldn't help thinking the material was inappropriate for his age: He felt ashamed to be lavishing so much time on "this rubbish,"27 and his energy level was low. When he went to Dr. Mäder's surgery in Bahnhofstrasse to complain about his ailments, the doctor would often answer by reminding him that he was in his seventy-ninth year.28 He was planning to spend two months in Madeira with Katia at the beginning of the new year, but he wasn't expecting to see California again, or to visit Tokyo, where Michael was performing and seemed likely to settle. Frido and Toni, who were at boarding school in Bern, could spend the holidays with their grandparents.29

Part One—the only part—of *Felix Krull* ends rather abruptly, partly because Thomas was impatient to have done with it, and partly because it was hard for him to read or write at the turn of the year, when he was suffering from a painful furuncle, a kind of boil, on the lower lid of the right eye.[30] It was extremely cold in Zurich, and though he and Katia were leaving—not for Madeira but for Sicily—at the beginning of February, he was puzzling about what to write next. As Alfred Knopf told him: "Tommy, you're a Dichter and you must dicht."[31] Uncertain what to do, he thought of treating Achilles rather in the way he'd treated Joseph, making him the central character in a novel and using Goethe's *Achilleis* as his basic text. "The adviser I would need," he suggested to Karl Kerényi, "would be at hand," and Kerényi wrote back enthusiastically, offering to collaborate. But nothing came of the idea.[32]

At the end of January Thomas bought a house in Alte Landstrasse, Kilchberg, four miles from the center of Zurich. Again he'd chosen a position high above a small town, with a splendid view of the lake. He thought it the prettiest house they'd ever had.[33]

Eight days later he and Katia left to spend two days in Rome on the way to Sicily. They were traveling by train, and between Milan and Rome they spent a night in an unheated sleeping carriage, which was like being in the open air. In Rome they saw Monika, but now that he was taking more interest in Michael because of Frido, Thomas found her the least interesting of all his children. In the summer of 1948 he'd written that Monika seemed to have a "physical disease of the brain,"[34] and at the end of the year he complained about her "hysterical behavior." "Dim-witted love affair too. Disinclination to concern myself with all that."[35]

In Taormina, he and Katia stayed at the San Domenico Palace Hotel, a fifteenth-century monastery, luxuriously converted, but it seldom stopped raining, and, suffering from bronchitis again, Thomas recovered slowly, though dosed heavily with penicillin by the Sicilian doctor.[36]

On the way home they stayed in Rome, Florence, and Fiesole, where they saw Elisabeth. He enjoyed the "reunion with beloved works of art" in the Bargello at Fiesole.[37] He was especially fond of the Donatellos, Cellini's St. John, and Verrocchio's David. Was anything in the world more delightful than the tireless celebration of young male beauty in classical and Renaissance art? He got the impression that there was nothing feminine in the whole gallery, apart from a few bas-reliefs of the Madonna.[38]

They made the move on April 15. He was especially pleased with his new study. It was next to the library, which had a glass door opening onto the small garden terrace.[39] The new house was more spacious than the one in Erlenbach, and less like a fort. (He now called the old house the Fortress of Zel, after the Egyptian fort in the *Joseph* novels.)

On June 6, when Thomas celebrated his seventy-ninth birthday, he received about 120 letters and telegrams, together with a lot of flowers.[40] In the afternoon, Michael, who'd come back from Tokyo, and Frido played a difficult Mozart violin sonata, and at the party in the evening the guests included Gret, Golo, and Bruno Walter's daughter, Lotte. But Thomas could eat only a little, and, feeling exhausted, he wanted to quote Prospero's "And my ending is despair."[41] He felt certain he'd live longer if he gave up smoking, but would it be worth the sacrifice?[42]. Looking back on the past he felt proud of having written *Buddenbrooks, The Magic Mountain,* the *Joseph* novels, and *Doctor Faustus,* but he knew it was wasteful to spend time congratulating himself on past achievements.[43]

Undecided about what to write next, he still felt drawn to Erasmus, Luther, and Ulrich von Hutten. He was considering a kind of Reformation portrait gallery with sketches of them, Charles V, Zwingli, the Anabaptist theologian Thomas Münzer, and the sculptor Tilman Riemenschneider—the idea being to show that their viewpoints and destinies contrasted "in an almost comical way."[44] Instead, he made notes for a play called *Luthers Hochzeit* (*Luther's Wedding*).

Erika had been ailing for some time with mysterious gastric and intestinal troubles. In early July, while she was in a sanatorium outside Lucerne, her parents decided to take her with them on holiday to Saint-Moritz.[45] After a couple of days there in the large and luxurious Suvreta Haus, they went on to Sils Maria. Hermann Hesse, two years younger than Thomas, was no longer trying to work seriously, and was living there with his wife. They spent time together, but ate at separate tables, and when Thomas went out for walks with Katia, Erika would write on his balcony, "where at other times I wasn't allowed to disturb him. Below, as they went out and came back, I heard them in conversation, cheerful and animated like two close friends with a lot to tell each other after a long separation."[46]

After returning to Kilchberg in the middle of the month, they left again for a few days in Cologne and Düsseldorf, where Thomas gave readings and met Ernst Bertram for the first time since the war. His face had aged but his manner was still the same—talkative, friendly, old-fashioned.[47] It was a touching experience, Thomas said, that bridged over the decades. "Between him and me, so far as I am concerned, nothing is painfully unresolved. All these things take care of themselves only too well."[48]

Perhaps he ought to follow Hesse's example, but it was out of the question for him to stop working, however irritable he became about lack of energy and dwindling productivity. Irrationally, he felt guilty about accepting praise for earlier achievements, and though he went on agreeing to new commitments, he was ambivalent about whether he should. The one he took most seriously was the lecture he was to give at

Stuttgart for the celebrations in May 1955 to commemorate the 150th anniversary of Schiller's death. The president of the Republic, Theodor Heuss, who was going to lecture on Schiller, wanted Thomas to be the other principal speaker. "Since I am alive, I had to declare myself willing. Now the task stands ahead of me, and I must carry it before I can think of doing anything else. . . . Perhaps it will do me good and restore my energy to talk about a life that was energetic in the extreme."[49] This was more or less what he'd felt, over fifty years ago, about compulsory military service: Perhaps it would do him good. But Katia and Erika could see that he felt overwhelmed by the responsibility he'd accepted. "Work is such an anxiety," he complained. When they reminded him how successful his lectures had always been, he said this one was exceptionally difficult, and admitted, with a smile, that work was his only real pleasure.[50]

Preparing the lecture, he was impressed by Schiller's unfailing magnanimity. Goethe had often treated him shabbily, not even intervening after his death to save his remains from being lost. Twenty years later, when a skull, which may not have been the right one, was buried in the Grand Ducal library beneath a bust of Schiller, Goethe sent his son, August, to represent him at the ceremony. "He was always unavailable when something was happening that could have moved him too deeply."[51]

Schiller had died in Weimar, and, as in 1949, when he went there with the Goethe speech he'd made in Frankfurt, Thomas was determined not to stay away from East Germany. His books were now on sale there and were in demand. A new impression of *Doctor Faustus* had just been printed—ten thousand copies—and even more of his books would have been sold but for the paper shortage.[52] He believed he could exert influence by refusing to recognize the division of Germany into two halves, and when there was a chance that *Buddenbrooks* would be filmed, he refused to sign away the rights unless a co-production could be set up involving both halves of Germany.[53] In early July, before he'd been invited to speak in Weimar, he'd decided to accept the invitation if it came. He offered to give up the idea of going there if it would force Heuss into canceling the invitation to Stuttgart, but the president left him free to accept both invitations.[54]

At the end of September, when *Felix Krull* was published, Thomas had a big success. Reviewers were full of enthusiasm, and it pleased him that Friedrich Sieburg, writing in a Frankfurt paper, called the book a bildungsroman.[55] Of the twenty thousand copies Bermann had printed, half were sold before publication and the rest by the end of October, weeks before the next impression of twenty thousand was ready. A third impression of twenty thousand copies came out in January 1955, and by the end of March, eighty thousand copies were in existence. As soon as Alfred Knopf had read one, he cabled: "The old master still puts the young ones to shame. Krull is absolutely magnificent."[56] People were clamoring for Thomas to write a second volume. If he had, it would have focused on the strain of living as a confidence-trickster. Felix would have married, and there would have been a prison episode.[57]

In 1954, as he worked on his lecture, Thomas's feeling of affinity with Schiller became deeper and more uncomfortable than it had been fifty years earlier, when, on the centenary of the death, he'd written "Hour of Gravity" for *Simplicissimus*. Schiller, he said, was never an observer of external reality; he had wanted to create everything from within himself. "For me too the world of the eye is not really my world, and fundamentally, like him, *I do not want to see anything*."[58] This was almost exactly what Kurt Martens had said about him as a young man, and it's true that his fiction contains little description. The lecture in Stuttgart was to last for an hour, but, working on it from September till the end of the year, putting everything else aside and neglecting his correspondence, Thomas wrote 120 pages, when all he needed was about twenty-two.

He'd always been vulnerable to illness when he relaxed after completing a long piece of work, and the Zurich weather, which was cold and misty, added to the strain.[59] Feeling in need of sunshine and hoping to find some in Arosa, he planned to recuperate there with Katia and Erika. There was too much snow on the mountain roads for them to drive, and they left by train on January 16, 1955. Hoping to catch up with his correspondence, Thomas took about 250 unanswered letters, but for the first five days the altitude seemed to be doing him no good. On the sixth day, January 22, he felt better: "My eyes are opening to the wintry natural grandeur of the valley, these mountains with comfort laid on by civilisation, though for me they always look as if they should not be trifled with, and I feel towards them as Hans Castorp did—respectful and slightly intimidated, almost pious, I might say. I am always rather irritated by the bourgeois sporting rabble that romps about so irresponsibly, with no feeling for their quiet menace."[60]

On the same day he was attacked by a virus. He had shivering fits and bouts of nausea. His temperature was 102.9 when the doctor started treating him with antibiotics, which reduced it sharply but sent his blood pressure down ominously from 180 to 90. "I feel disquietingly quiet," he said.[61] After spending a week in bed, he was no better. Katia and Erika insisted on calling in the chief physician from the cantonal hospital in Chur. Saying the mountain air was harming Thomas, the doctor had him taken by ambulance to the hospital, where he felt weak, with no desire to eat. Though he was submitted not only to X-rays and blood tests but, under anesthesia, to extraction of marrow from his breastbone, the doctors couldn't explain why his blood pressure was still so low. Discharged on February 7, four days before his and Katia's golden wedding anniversary, he convalesced in Kilchberg with vitamins and heart-strengthening drugs. He was allowed to spend a large part of the day out of bed but was told not to work.[62]

The golden wedding had to be celebrated quietly. Of the five surviving children, Monika was the only one who didn't come, and those who did gave their parents a pretty two-year-old black poodle. He was named Nico, like his predecessor.[63] February 11 was also the anniversary of the day Thomas and Katia had left Munich in 1933, not knowing they'd never go back. Thinking about his past, Thomas again decided, as he had in 1937 on their thirty-third wedding anniversary, that he'd have said no if he'd been offered the chance to relive his life.[64]

Though he'd lost weight, he resumed a normal working routine during the second half of February. Spring and summer were going to be strenuous, with celebrations for his eightieth birthday coming less than a month after the trips to Stuttgart and Weimar. Life would have been easier if he could have rejected more of the honors being conferred on him. The Bürgermeister of Lübeck was offering the freedom of the city. Queen Juliana of the Netherlands wanted to award him the cross of the Order of Orange-Nassau. The East German government wanted him to accept the Stalin Peace Prize and the National Prize, both of which, as an American citizen, he had to refuse, but he resented having to do so. "I will have thrown half a million francs out of the window just out of nervous love for the 'free world', which in any case is a sheer swindle."[65] Accepting awards and honors necessitated journeys, personal appearances, and speeches, but this was a price he willingly paid.

In April, when he heard about the Lübeck bürgermeister's decision, Erika tried to discourage him from going there, because he'd have no time to recuperate after the expeditions to Stuttgart and Weimar. But to be given the freedom of Lübeck would feel like a vindication of everything he'd achieved by severing himself from the family tradition. He'd never been at ease with his memories of paternal disapproval, and *Buddenbrooks* had been partly an attempt to justify himself, but his harsh criticism of the city and its values had alienated his fellow citizens. The freedom of the city would symbolize reconciliation, but a letter from an old classmate, Hermann Lange, reminded him of the breach that could never be healed. It was still galling that his father had written him and Heinrich off as prodigal sons incapable of making a good life for themselves. "It specially struck me that you are constantly aware of the way my father was honoured in Lübeck. I am too, and in the past decades have often thought of him and wished he could have followed my progress a little further, or somehow formed an impression of it. An irrational wish, of course, for this progression, begun with *Budden-*

brooks, in which he was himself a character, and which could have been accomplished only in his absence."66

If Thomas couldn't look happily at his links with the family's past, he could at least enjoy writing to Frido about his latest triumphs. "Now fourteen and a half, he has shot up. He's tall and pretty, with an appealing personality." Having created and destroyed an image of him, Thomas felt not only slightly incredulous that Frido had survived, but also permanently indebted to him. Though Frido still knew nothing about his alter ego, Thomas felt Echo had made the bond between them into something special.67

Before leaving with Katia and Erika for Stuttgart on Sunday, May 7, he couldn't conceal his nervousness. Erika had done most of the work on cutting his one hundred and twenty pages to twenty-two, but he did his best to reassure her that he accepted full responsibility for any deficiencies in the resultant lecture. "God knows," he said, "you've done all you could, and anyway in fifty-five minutes it would be impossible to say very much more." When the day came, he was standing in the hall in his cap and coat, umbrella and walking stick in his hand, rug over his arm, before she and Katia had begun loading luggage into the car. But his nervousness disappeared once the car was in motion. He traveled most of the way with his eyes closed.

At the Hotel Stuttgarter Hof, after tea, he met Theodor Heuss for the first time, and they got on well. The Manns spent the evening with Reisiger (who was living in Stuttgart with his woman friend), the Bermann Fischers, and Trebitsch, who came for the occasion. On Monday, the day Heuss and Thomas were both lecturing on Schiller, they were photographed together and with other dignitaries. Inside the Landestheater the lectures were preceded by a performance of Bach's Overture in D minor. Thomas was the first of the two speakers, and Erika, who was in the wings, thought he'd never spoken better. The audience stood up to applaud, and afterward, sitting motionless as he listened to Heuss, he exuded the quiet satisfaction of a man who knew he'd given his best.68

They broke the journey to Weimar in Kissingen, which is about halfway, and relaxed there for three days. Crossing the border at Wartha on May 13, they were greeted by Becher, his wife, and several carloads of government officials. Thomas described the rest of the journey as comically triumphal. Police in white uniforms held up traffic for the slow-moving convoy of cars. Flags were flying and crowds gathered. People pointed out Thomas to one another. "That's him. That's him." In the streets and in the classrooms he was taken to visit, schoolchildren presented him with flowers. On May 14, when he lectured in the theater, the square outside was black with people listening to the relay over loudspeakers, and when he emerged, applause broke out all over again.

From the windows of all the houses, people were watching, some with opera glasses or old-fashioned field glasses. The next day, while Erika packed, Thomas was inaugurated as an honorary doctor at the University of Jena. Becher, who drove with them to the border, had tears in his eyes as they said goodbye.[69]

Though Erika didn't go with her parents to Lübeck, she realized she'd been wrong in trying to dissuade them from going. In the town hall, where his father had performed his duties as senator, Thomas was presented with the freedom of the city and expressed his gratitude in an emotional speech. He felt tired while he was speaking. In the Stadttheater, where, as a boy of fourteen, he'd heard *Lohengrin* for the first time, the prelude was played in his honor, and he read "Tonio Kröger," together with extracts from the *Joseph* novels and *Felix Krull*. The performance lasted an hour and a half. The audience had paid for admission, but he donated the proceeds–4,000 marks–to an old people's home.[70] He was taken to visit his old school, the Katharineum, and in the playground he thought about Otto Grautoff and Willri Timpe. He felt relieved when he was finally alone with Katia in the railway compartment.[71]

They returned to Zurich less than a fortnight before his eightieth birthday on June 6. He tried to relax, but he was worrying about his application for Swiss citizenship and about the attitude of the German government. The president, Heuss, had seemed better disposed than the chancellor, Konrad Adenauer, but in spite of the accolades from France and Holland, he still hadn't been awarded the highest German order, Pour le Mérite, though it had been rumored that he could expect it either during the Schiller celebrations or on his eightieth birthday. He felt mortified that other men had received it, while he hadn't even been offered a Verdienstkreuz (order of merit). If it was offered to him now, he'd refuse it. He'd accept the Pour le Mérite, but if the government had wanted him to have it for his eightieth birthday, news would have reached him by now.[72] He couldn't have been forgiven for either his statements about German guilt or his visits to the East.

Spread over several days, the celebrations started at midday on June 4 with a ceremony arranged by the city council. The president, Dr. Emil Landolt, made a congratulatory speech, and in the afternoon, at a ceremony arranged by the community of Kilchberg in the Conrad Ferdinand Meyer House, the president of the Swiss Confederation, Dr. Max Petitpierre, spoke in German with a French accent. Thomas was then made an honorary doctor in natural science–a title that especially appealed to him–in the Eidgenössische Technische Hochschule (Swiss Federal Polytechnic Institute). Dr. Petitpierre attended the birthday dinner given in a Kilchberg restaurant. Thomas, who wanted to become a Swiss citizen, took Petitpierre's presence to mean that he'd be exempted from some of the usual formalities and delays.[73]

Alfred Knopf flew across the Atlantic to join in the celebrations, and so, to everyone's surprise, did Bruno Walter, who conducted Mozart's *Eine Kleine Nachtmusik* in the Schauspielhaus. Maria Becker and Therese Giehse were among the actors who took part in dramatized excerpts from Thomas's work. When it was Thomas's turn to make a speech, he momentarily muddled two cities in which he'd lived and said he'd always valued the intelligent receptivity of the Munich audience. Afterward there were about a hundred guests at the party thrown by Gottfried Bermann Fischer.

Over a thousand letters, telegrams, and presents arrived at the house in Kilchberg, together with so many flowers that not enough vases could be found. A birthday party was held there on the morning of June 7. The Standing Conference of West German Ministers of Culture had created a Thomas Mann Fund to support writers who couldn't support themselves, and a Bremen senator arrived with a check for 50,000 marks. Bermann presented Thomas with drawings that had been done for a deluxe leather-bound edition of "Master and Dog," and he was delighted to receive a Festschrift titled "Hommage de la France à Thomas Mann," which had been edited and published by Martin Flinker. Among those who paid tribute in it were Pablo Picasso, Albert Schweitzer, Albert Camus, André Malraux, François Mauriac, Jules Romains, Marguerite Yourcenar, President of the French Republic Vincent Auriol, and several other politicians, including Édouard Herriot, Robert Schuman, and Pierre Mendès-France. Romains said Thomas had given German prose something it had never previously had, and Mauriac praised him for keeping the glory of German genius intact during a period of eclipse. "His life illustrates his work. His greatness does not belong exclusively to literature. He was able to remain a free spirit during a time of slavery. He has preserved Germany's honour."

Another encomium came from Hermann Hesse. In the *Neue Zürcher Zeitung*, he said how much pleasure he'd been getting from the essays in *Altes und Neues*. One of these ended with a passage that could have been equaled by no one else currently writing in German. "I am thinking not of the syntax but the tone, and especially the carefully calculated mixture of love and mischief."

Not only was there no news about the Pour le Mérite, there was no greeting from either Theodor Heuss or Konrad Adenauer. The government's silence was broken only by a telegram from the minister of the interior, Gerhard Schröder. But Thomas was careful to give no sign of disappointment either during lunch, which was hosted by Alfred Knopf at the Eden au Lac, or during dinner, which he and Katia ate with friends in the Baur au Lac. In a letter to Hesse, he said Schröder must have had a hard time getting Adenauer's permission to send the telegram.[74]

At the end of the month Thomas and Katia left for Amsterdam, and stayed at their usual hotel, the Amstel, where he held a press conference. As a contribution to the Festival of Holland he delivered the Schiller lecture in Amsterdam and The Hague before going on to stay at the Huis ter Duin in Noordwijk from July 5. They refused to make a seventy-five-mile journey to have tea with the Queen Mother,[75] but on the eleventh they were received by Queen Juliana at her summer residence outside Amsterdam, Soestdijk Castle. Katia was told not to curtsy, and Thomas often found himself saying "you" instead of "Your Majesty,"[76] just as he'd once said "Katia" instead of "Fräulein Katia." The queen talked about her daughters, Thomas about his grandchildren. After about fifty minutes Thomas and Katia offered to leave, but the queen said she was in no hurry to be rid of them, and they went on chatting for another twenty-five minutes.[77]

Their intention was to stay in Noordwijk. It was often misty, but Thomas loved this stretch of coast, and he worked at the Luther play in a hut on the beach. He wrote forty-six pages of notes for it. It was on July 18 that he first complained about a dragging pain in his left leg, but, taking it to be rheumatic, he paid little attention to it, and tried to stop Katia from telephoning the nearby clinic for gout and arthritis. She called in a doctor who examined the swollen leg and said the pain had nothing to do with rheumatism. Thomas should go straight to bed and stay there until the doctor had discussed the symptoms with a specialist in Leyden, Professor Mulder.

The professor telephoned Katia and told her it was a thrombosis. Hiding her alarm, she told Thomas the doctor had said his veins might be inflamed, and he'd have to stay in bed in case they were. What upset him was that he couldn't see the sea from where he was lying, and the bed couldn't be moved because jolting might have been dangerous.[78]

On the morning of July 21, when the professor arrived to see the symptoms for himself, Katia asked him to say it was inflammation of the veins. He complied, but insisted the patient should stay in bed, not using his leg, and should be taken in an ambulance to either his clinic in Leyden or a hospital in Zurich. Alone with Katia, he warned her the thrombosis might be symptomatic of something that couldn't be diagnosed yet. He'd prescribe medication that would thin Thomas's blood to reduced the danger of clotting, and it would be possible, after two days of this treatment, for him to be flown to Zurich on a stretcher. But on no account must he stand up or move about.

They arranged for him to be flown on July 23 to the cantonal hospital, where the medical director, Professor Wilhelm Löffler, took charge of the case. He was rather a prima donna, Thomas decided, but likable. He'd read *Buddenbrooks*, and praised Hanno's death sequence.[79] Erika, who was suffering from digestive troubles and chronic insomnia, was in a Lucerne sanatorium, but on the morning of July 24, she got up and drove the thirty-five miles to Zurich. There seemed to be no cause for alarm. Thomas had a healthy-looking tan and wasn't in pain. The swelling was going down, and, wrapped in a bandage drenched with alcohol, the leg was protected from the weight of the blankets by a cage. After starting every day by speaking to him over the telephone, Katia spent nine hours with him in the hospital. She took a borrowed gramophone, but Thomas couldn't concentrate on music for more than twenty minutes or so at a stretch.

After two weeks the doctor was pleased with his progress, but Erika, who went back to bed in the sanatorium before visiting him again on August 8, saw he'd lost weight and the sunburn had faded to pallor. It seemed to her that he looked blue: Even his gray-green eyes gave out a blue look. From now on she visited him every day, but only once succeeded in making him laugh, and failed to involve him in planning ahead. Though he was allowed out of bed for an hour every afternoon to sit in an armchair, he'd become impatient with the restrictions on his mobility. Itching eczemas had formed, especially on his feet, which had to be painted regularly with a blue menthol mixture that produced chills. He was eating little, but his stomach felt heavy, and his head, he complained, empty.[80]

On August 10 a telegram arrived: The decision had been taken for the Pour le Mérite to be conferred on him, but the news gave him less apparent pleasure than a visit on the same day from Martin Flinker, who'd compiled "Hommage de la France à Thomas Mann."

Thomas had a bad night and felt too weak in the morning to telephone Katia. Instead, a nurse telephoned her, and she went straight to the hospital. He lost consciousness before she arrived, and his blood pressure was too low to measure. He wouldn't have recovered consciousness if the doctors hadn't revived him with two blood transfusions, drip insertions, and injections. Katia found two doctors and several nurses working on him. Without opening his eyes, he asked what was going on. She said that because he'd eaten nothing for so long, and because his stomach was a little weak at the moment, a new preparation was being dripped into his blood. He said it wasn't unpleasant.

Erika, who arrived at midday, didn't want to alarm him by staying longer than usual. He didn't open his eyes when she touched his arm and told him who she was. Wearily he said he was too weak for a visit. She pleaded with the doctors not to torment him by keeping him alive, but they had no option, they said, because they didn't understand what was happening. His condition had deteriorated so abruptly since yesterday afternoon.

By four in the afternoon he could breathe only with difficulty. From the corridor Erika and Golo saw oxygen equipment being pushed into his room and, half an hour later, pushed out again. He was breathing with less effort, but between 5:30 and 6:30 he was given morphia several times. Talking in French and English, he joked with the doctor, and asked for his glasses, but went to sleep when they were brought to him. When Katia left the room, she didn't let Erika and Golo go in, for fear of waking him. It was pointless for them to spend the night in the corridor, she said. If his condition changed, she'd ring them.

Arriving at the house, they hadn't yet taken off their wet raincoats when the telephone rang. He was dead. It was ten to eight.

The autopsy showed that his thrombophlebitis had been cured, but Professor Mulder had been right to warn Katia that it might be symptomatic of something else. It had been caused by arteriosclerosis in the leg. In one place, where the wall of the artery had become brittle and worn, there was a small tear, no bigger than a grain of rice. Blood had leaked into the surrounding tissue, compressing the nerves and sympathetic fibers until they stopped functioning. The death had been painless.[81]

Tasks

THOMAS MANN'S CAREER corresponded closely to the succession of tasks he set himself. The first was to achieve fame, and he succeeded, not effortlessly but remarkably quickly. By the time he wrote "Tonio Kröger" he could afford to poke fun at the good-looking lieutenant who writes a poem and carries it around in his back pocket, thinking he had plucked a leaf from the tree of art without paying for it with his life. Tonio knows this cannot be done. His artistry has developed as his health deteriorated. He works not in order to earn a living but because he can live in no other way. Assuming that good work is produced only under the pressure of a bad life, and setting no value on himself as a man, he has alternated between lustful self-indulgence and saintly austerity. He has no identity except as a writer.

He seems unlikely to marry: He'll remain an outsider, permanently frustrated in his longing for the bliss of the commonplace. One of Thomas's reasons for marrying Katia Pringsheim was that she seemed as dissimilar as he was to the fair-haired, blue-eyed mediocrities who took no interest in *Don Carlos* or *Immensee*. Writing about Adrian Leverkühn's decision to marry, Thomas was thinking about his own. Unlike Adrian, he didn't suffer from a venereal disease and hadn't made a pact that put love out of bounds; but he wasn't expecting marriage to bring either sexual fulfillment or happiness. Like Adrian, he aimed to improve the quality of his life, and therefore his work. What had changed since he wrote "Tonio Kröger" was that he'd fallen in love with the idea of living a representative life, like a prince.

The analogy between the prince and the writer had roots in his childhood fantasy about being the young kaiser. He drew on memories of this both when wooing the princesslike Katia and when writing *Royal Highness*. From identifying with bizarre outsiders like the hunchbacked Herr Friedemann, Lobgott Piepsam, and Tobias Mindernickel, he was fleshing out his conceit about the writer's representative role. Like the prince, he lives a symbolic life and encourages his public to applaud itself when applauding him.

But the glory entails moral obligations. When Karl Heinrich tells Imma they must both give the nation's needs priority over their personal happiness, he's paralleling Thomas's determination to give his work priority over everything else. Katia would have to share whatever hardships he suffered in the process of producing good art. He wasn't going to indulge, as Tonio had, in dissolute adventures, but he hadn't quite discarded the assumption that a proper healthy normal man doesn't need to write, paint, or compose. Tonio felt sick to death of portraying humanity while having no share in human experience; Thomas wanted to snatch a share of it while continuing his activities as a portraitist. After getting married, he was uncertain whether he'd done the right thing, but his qualms had nothing to do with misleading Katia about the future they were going to share. He was nervous that his art might suffer because of the compromise he'd made with "life."

Aschenbach is put into a more critical perspective than Tonio, and their assumptions about the literary life aren't identical, though many of their premises are the same. Aschenbach is afraid his time will run out before he has completed his task. He wants to express everything that's within him, but feels impatient to grow older, knowing that a writer can achieve greatness only by producing good work at each stage of his development. A perfectionist, he uses his formidable willpower to keep weariness at bay, and, valuing precision, consistently restrains his passions: If he indulged them he'd find himself settling for high-spirited approximations. He's lacking in stamina but compensates with relentless self-discipline: He starts each day by splashing cold water over his chest and back. He believes in dignity as a goal to which every great talent is drawn, but when he finds his creativity blocked, he thinks he's being punished for reining his emotions in too rigorously. Having achieved fame early, he keeps energetically in touch with correspondents all over the world, cultivating goodwill by saying something generous in each letter he sends.

Writing in his mid-thirties about an alter ego in his fifties, Thomas was warning himself about tendencies he must restrain, pitfalls he must avoid. It might be easier to assess how much notice he took of his own caveat if world war hadn't broken out in 1914. As it was, new tasks were set by the international situation. Neither Tonio nor Aschenbach had thought about exerting political influence, but in 1914, when Thomas found he could help soldiers in trenches by writing about Frederick the Great and nationalism, it gave a political dimension to his notion of leading a representative life. He was farther than ever before from being an outsider. As a local politician, his father had worked to raise his fellow citizens' standard of living; as an influential writer, Thomas could contribute to the German war effort.

He saw this as his duty, but it would be simplistic to suggest that this was the main task he set himself. The essays "Wartime Thoughts" and "Frederick and the Great Coalition of 1756" were propagandistic, but

Reflections of a Nonpolitical Man wasn't designed to boost the morale of infantrymen, and wasn't published till the month before the armistice was signed. In it he kept shifting between such private questions as "What made me into the man I am?" and such public ones as "What is Germany?" "What is characteristically German?" In retrospect the book seems important mainly as a bridge between the part of *The Magic Mountain* he wrote before the war and the part he wrote after it. It can also be seen as a step toward *Doctor Faustus*, the novel he intended as a comprehensive statement about Germany.

Critics have written about him as if he moved progressively from reactionary nationalism to radicalism. He was a patriot during World War I; he was hostile to American anticommunism and tolerant of the Stalinist regime in East Germany. He annoyed both the Americans and the West Germans by accepting two invitations to lecture in East Germany. He supported the idea of world government. But his instincts were always conservative: He wanted to preserve what was best in the existing culture. The main difference between German burgherdom and the German bourgeoisie during his lifetime was that the burghers had moral values, cultural traditions, and a pride that was incompatible with Nazism, while the bourgeoisie allowed itself to be infiltrated. None of Thomas Mann's emotions was stronger than his loathing for Hitler, and though Hitler profited from other people's patriotism and their fear of communism, there was nothing conservative about National Socialism. What Thomas inherited from his ancestors and from Lübeck's Hanseatic traditions predisposed him to identify with Goethe and the Germany Goethe had represented. But the values of the patrician merchant, the churchgoing shopkeeper, the conscientious craftsman couldn't survive in Nazi Germany. Thomas became the chief spokesman for the German culture that had nothing to do with Nazism. He was also its leading practitioner.

When *Buddenbrooks* and "Tonio Kröger" were published, it was unpredictable that Germany would ever have a leader like Hitler, or that Thomas would ever become the unofficial leader of the opposition to him. In a 1914 letter he said that as a writer he could never take sides: He'd feel that to do so would rob him of his liberty. But if he had stayed in Germany after 1933 he'd have had to choose between siding with the Nazis and losing his liberty, and though he tried for his first three years of exile not to side against them publicly, he couldn't keep silent any longer. The *Joseph* tetralogy, which he started in 1926 and finished in 1943, rarely has any direct bearing on Hitler and the war, but without having undergone a kind of conversion, he wouldn't have addressed himself as he did to questions that seem relevant to the whole of humanity. In his *Reflections* he was polemicizing against the liberal humanism of his elder brother, and in *The Magic Mountain* he was ridiculing Settembrini's humanist progressivism. But the novel is essentially a European book, unlike *Reflections*, which had emphasized Germany's affinity with Russia in order to minimize her interdependence with Western Europe, and unlike *Joseph and His Brothers*, which is essentially humanist in outlook. Marguerite Yourcenar called the tetralogy one of the great humanistic interpretations of the past. "For the first time a literary work which is intended neither as a defense of the Jewish point of view nor as a Christian exegesis shows us both what unites the Jewish race with, and separates it from, the vast world of pagan religion and myth, and makes us witness that monstrous birth, as it were, of the monotheistic conception of God."[1] Thomas's concerns couldn't have been more broadly based, but his mature novels wouldn't have become what they are if he hadn't been involved in campaigning, polemicizing, agitating, exerting his influence to help the causes and the individuals he believed in.

It might seem odd that a man who did so much to help strangers—refugee writers, exiles, victims of Nazi persecution—did so much harm to his own family. It's easy to forget that he grew up in an ethos that denied children the rights they have today. Many fathers of his generation had too many children and paid too little attention to them. It's also easy to understand that the self-discipline and the grueling schedule Thomas imposed on himself excluded his children from his consciousness throughout most of the working day. After Klaus's death Thomas claimed that he'd been the most talented writer of his generation, but during his lifetime the father took little interest in his son, except when feeling physically attracted to him, and he took most interest in Erika when she was helping him with his work. Of his six children, the only one who's still alive, his youngest daughter Elisabeth, is the only one who had a consistently satisfactory relationship with him. She and Michael were the only two to have children of their own, and Michael, like Klaus, committed suicide, though not until after his father was dead. In 1957, Michael gave up his musical career to study German literature at Harvard. He lectured and wrote about his father, devoting a great deal of working time to the diaries and producing an abridged edition, which was never published. When he killed himself at the age of forty-seven, the family tried, unsuccessfully, to keep the news from the ninety-three-year-old Katia, who lived to the age of ninety-seven.

Frido, too, seems to have been damaged by his intense relationship with his grandfather. He lived for several years in the house at Kilchberg with his grandmother. At the age of twenty-six he married Christine Heisenberg, daughter of the scientist responsible for the uncertainty principle, and wrote an autobiographical novel with the Wagnerian title *Professor Parsifal*. It tells the story of his childhood, describing his grandfather's affection for him as *Affenliebe*, which literally means "ape-love" and, figuratively, doting fondness. He describes the old man's "tendency to misuse his darling a little for his own purposes."[2]

On the other hand, Thomas couldn't have achieved so much without damaging other people's chances of happiness, along with his own. Temperamentally ill-suited to be either a martyr or a hero, he came close to playing a heroic role in keeping German culture alive after Germany had surrendered to the dark forces of Nazism and France had surrendered to Germany. "Thomas Mann is Europe," said Albert Guerard.

Of the other twentieth-century writers torn between literature and politics, the most important were Jean-Paul Sartre and Bertolt Brecht, who were both iconoclastic, antiliterary, and fanatical in their hatred of the bourgeoisie. Neither of them could possibly be equated with Europe. Brecht thought a play was good in proportion to the influence it exerted; Sartre stopped writing novels and declared war on literature in *Qu'est-ce que la littérature*? But after starting his biography of Gustave Flaubert, *L'Idiot de la famille*, in 1954, he was still working on it in 1973. His ambition was to forge a new alliance between Marx and Freud and to say everything that could be said about Flaubert both as an individual and as "an expression of his period." If he still had any lingering regrets about his undeveloped talent as a novelist, he would fight them by representing Flaubert as an idiot propelled into a creativity that was no more than an alibi for passivity, for failing to face the challenges of reality.

Insofar as this argument was intended as an explanation of what fiction is, Thomas Mann's work could serve as a refutation. He faced the formidable challenges of his period, and though his political and semipolitical activities slowed down his literary work, they didn't deflect him. On the contrary, it was his respect for cultural tradition in literary work that fortified him to fight as effectively as he did against Nazism and against those who wanted to counter it with its own weapons. Thomas kept the spirit of Goethe alive.

Never again will it be possible to produce such a corpus of great novels and reach such a wide audience. Unlike other masters of modernism—Proust, Kafka, Joyce, Eliot, Pound—he was never obscure, never demanded too much of the reader for his books to be bestsellers. Writing autobiographically, he also treated issues of general interest, because he was dealing with contemporary history, social and political. Today, the only way to reach such a big audience (without producing pulp fiction) is to use the visual media. But there can be no visual coefficient to the sophisticated self-consciousness of Thomas's heroes, and it's through this that he analyzes their links with society and the pressures on their psychic integrity. He was right to regard himself as a latecomer. He was the last great European man of letters.

Notes

PROLOGUE

1. "Tonio Kröger."
2. Ibid.
3. Letter to Otto Grautoff, July 21, 1897.
4. Letter to Otto Grautoff, November 8, 1896.
5. *On Myself (Über mich selbst)*.
6. "The Clown."
7. "A Sketch of My Life" ("Lebensabriss").
8. Friedrich Nietzsche, preface to *Menschliches, Allzumenschliches*, part 2.
9. Letter to Heinrich, March 27, 1901.
10. Letter to Otto Grautoff, November 26, 1901.
11. *Münchner Neueste Nachrichten,* November 1901.
12. Letter to Heinrich, February 13, 1901.
13. Postcard to Heinrich, February 28, 1901.
14. Letter to Heinrich, April 1, 1901.
15. *Buddenbrooks*.
16. Ibid.
17. Friedrich Nietzsche, *Zur Genealogie der Moral,* sec. 2.
18. "Death in Venice."
19. Ibid.
20. Letter to C. M. Weber, July 4, 1902.

CHAPTER 1

1. W. H. Dawson, *The Evolution of Modern Germany* (London, 1908).
2. Friedrich Nietzsche, *Beyond Good and Evil (Jenseits von Gut und Böse)*.
3. Ibid.
4. Heinrich Mann, "My Brother," in Charles Neider, *The Stature of Thomas Mann*.
5. Heinrich Mann, *Gesammelte Werke,* vol. 18, pp. 420–22.
6. "Lübeck als geistige Lebensform."
7. Letter to Felix Neumann, August 21, 1846.
8. Family archives.
9. "Der Maskenball," in Heinrich Mann, *Das Kind*.
10. Heinrich Mann, *Gesammelte Werke,* vol. 18, pp. 420–21.

11. "Kinderspiele" (1904).
12. Julia Mann, *Aus Dodos Kindheit*.
13. "Kinderspiele."
14. "Portrait of the Mother" ("Das Bild der Mutter").
15. "Kinderspiele."
16. Ibid.
17. Ibid.
18. Letter to Otto Grautoff, March 28, 1895.

CHAPTER 2

1. "Lebenslauf," 1936.
2. "Lübeck als geistige Lebensform."
3. Sigrid Anger, ed., *Heinrich Mann* (1977), p. 21.
4. Letter from Heinrich Mann to Ludwig Ewers, September 16, 1891.
5. "The Clown" and "Portrait of the Mother."
6. "Meiner Zeit" in *Gesammelte Werke,* vol. 11, pp. 307–308.
7. Ibid., p. 9.
8. Letter to Hermann Lange, March 19, 1955.
9. Letter to Frieda Hartenstein, October 14, 1889.
10. Heinrich Mann, "L. Fantasien über mein Vaterstadt."
11. Letter from Senator Mann to Heinrich, February 22, 1890.
12. "Hundert Jahre Reclam."
13. *Lübeckische Blätter,* May 25, 1890.
14. Family papers in Heinz Ludwig Arnold, *Sinn und Form Sonderheft Thomas Mann*.
15. Viktor Mann, *Wir waren Fünf,* p. 13.
16. "Fragment über das Religiöse," *Dichterglaube* (Berlin, 1931).
17. Viktor Mann, *Wir waren Fünf*.
18. "A Sketch of My Life" ("Lebensabriss").
19. Golo Mann, *Mein Vater Thomas Mann*.
20. Letter to Otto Grautoff, February 22, 1901.
21. Letter to Otto Grautoff, September 2, 1900.

22. "A Sketch of My Life."
23. *Buddenbrooks.*
24. Second notebook for *Buddenbrooks.*
25. "Tonio Kröger."

CHAPTER 3

1. "Gladius Dei," *Stories of Three Decades.*
2. Viktor Mann, *Wir waren Fünf,* pp. 27–29.
3. "A Sketch of My Life" ("Lebensabriss").
4. Letter to Otto Grautoff, September 1894.
5. Letter to Otto Grautoff, December 1894.
6. "Vom Beruf des Deutschen Schritftstellers in unserer Zeit: Ansprache an den Bruder."
7. Peter R. Franke, *Der Tod des Hans Hansen,* p. 8
8. Paul Bourget, *Cosmopolis* (Paris, 1893).
9. *Notizbuch* 1, p. 24.
10. Ibid., pp. 55–56.
11. Letter to Otto Grautoff, March 5, 1895.
12. Letter to Ludwig Ewers, December 3, 1894.
13. Letter to Otto Grautoff, November 13–14, 1894.
14. "A Sketch of My Life."
15. Letter to Otto Grautoff, January 20, 1895.
16. Letter to Otto Grautoff, March 3, 1895.
17. Letter to Otto Grautoff, March 5, 1895.
18. Letter to Otto Grautoff, March 28, 1895.
19. Letter to Otto Grautoff, May 16, 1895.
20. Letter to Otto Grautoff, end of May 1895.
21. Letter to Otto Grautoff, May 16–17, 1895.
22. Ibid.
23. Letter to Otto Grautoff, May 16, 1895.
24. Letter to Otto Grautoff, ca. June 28, 1895.
25. Letter to Otto Grautoff, June 18, 1895.
26. Letter to Otto Grautoff, end June 1895.
27. Letter to Otto Grautoff, undated, late May 1895.
28. Letter to Otto Grautoff, November 1894.
29. Letter to Otto Grautoff, February 2, 1896.
30. Letter to Otto Grautoff, n.d., August 1895.
31. "A Sketch of My Life"; letter to Otto Grautoff, July 6, 1895.

CHAPTER 4

1. Gustav Dahms, *Berliner Presse-Handbuch* (Berlin, 1895).
2. Heinrich Mann, "Jüdischen Glaubens," in *Das Zwanzigste Jahrhundert,* August 1895.
3. Letter to Otto Grautoff, n.d., August 1895.
4. Letter to Julia Mann, October 10, 1895.
5. Letter to Otto Grautoff, October 5, 1895.
6. "A Sketch of My Life" ("Lebensabriss").
7. Peter R. Franke, *Der Tod des Hans Hansen,* p. 8.
8. Letter to Otto Grautoff, February 2, 1896.
9. Letter to Otto Grautoff, May 23, 1896.
10. Letter to Otto Grautoff, February 17, 1896.
11. Howard Nemerov, "Themes and Methods in Stories by Thomas Mann," in *Poetry and Fiction* (New Brunswick, N.J., 1963).
12. Letter to Otto Grautoff, April 6, 1897.
13. Letter to Otto Grautoff, March 19, 1896.
14. R. A. Nicholls, "Nietzsche in the Early Work of Thomas Mann," *Modern Philology* 45, 1955.
15. Letter to Otto Grautoff, November 8, 1896.
16. Radio interview with TM, September 15, 1953.
17. Letter to Otto Grautoff, September 29, 1896.
18. Letter to Korfiz Holm, November 6, 1896.
19. Letter to Otto Grautoff, November 8, 1896.

CHAPTER 5

1. "A Sketch of My Life" ("Lebensabriss").

2. Letter to Otto Grautoff, January 13, 1897.
3. Letter to Otto Grautoff, January 4, 1897.
4. Letter to Otto Grautoff, January 13, 1897.
5. Letter fragment to Otto Grautoff, undated, ca. January 1897.
6. Letter to Otto Grautoff, February 17, 1896.
7. Letter to Otto Grautoff, May 16, 1895.
8. Letter to Otto Grautoff, April 23, 1897.
9. Letter to Otto Grautoff, July 21, 1897.
10. Ibid.
11. Letter to Otto Grautoff, August 20, 1897.
12. "Lübeck als geistige Lebensform."
13. Ibid.
14. Ibid.
15. Peter R. Franke, *Der Tod des Hans Hansen,* p. 15.
16. Letter to Julius Bab, June 28, 1948.
17. Letter from Johann Marty.
18. Letter from Heinrich to Karl Lemke, January 29, 1947.
19. *Buddenbrooks.*
20. *Notizbücher* 7, p. 119.
21. *Buddenbrooks.*
22. Ibid.
23. Ibid.

CHAPTER 6

1. Volker Hage, *Eine Liebe fürs Leben: Thomas Mann und Travemünde* (Hamburg, 1993).
2. Letter to Otto Grautoff, December 11, 1897.
3. Letter to Otto Grautoff, December 29, 1897.
4. Peter R. Franke, *Der Tod des Hans Hansen,* p. 4.
5. "Lübeck als geistige Lebensform."
6. *Notizbuch* 3, 1899.
7. Ibid., pp. 2–5.
8. Postcard to Korfiz Holm, May 12, 1898.
9. Letter to Otto Grautoff, May 9, 1898.
10. Letter to Otto Grautoff, May 14, 1898.
11. Letter to Otto Grautoff, October 25, 1898.
12. Ibid.

13. "A Sketch of My Life" ("Lebensabriss").
14. Arthur Holitscher, *Lebensgeschichte eines Rebellen* (Berlin, 1924).
15. *Notizbuch* 3, p. 31.
16. Letter to Kurt Martens, July 8, 1899.
17. *Autobiographisches,* p. 22.
18. Klaus Schröter, *Thomas Mann in Selbstzeugnissen,* p. 16.
19. Kurt Martens in Klaus Schröter, *Dokumente,* p. 14.
20. Schröter, *Thomas Mann in Selbstzeugnissen,* p. 16.
21. Ibid., pp. 16–17.
22. Ibid., p. 15.
23. "Tonio Kröger."
24. Carl Ehrenberg autobiographical sketch quoted in Mendelssohn, pp. 382–83.
25. Letter to Paul Ehrenberg, June 29, 1900.
26. Ehrenberg autobiographical sketch.
27. "A Sketch of My Life."
28. "A Sketch of My Life."
29. Letter from Wagner to August Röckel, August 23, 1856.
30. Letter from Wagner to Franz Liszt, autumn 1854.
31. *Reflections of a Nonpolitical Man (Betrachtungen eines Unpolitischen).*

CHAPTER 7

1. Friedrich Nietzsche, *Götzendämmerung,* sec. 20.
2. *Buddenbrooks.*
3. Ibid.
4. Ibid.
5. *Die Gesellschaft,* November 15, 1899.
6. Letter to Kurt Martens, August 4, 1899.
7. Viktor Mann, *Wir waren Fünf.*
8. Letter to Paul Ehrenberg, June 29, 1900.
9. Ibid.
10. Letter to Otto Grautoff, July 18, 1900.
11. Letter to Otto Grautoff, August 30, 1900.
12. "In Memoriam S. Fischer."
13. Letter to Otto Grautoff, September 2, 1900.
14. Peter R. Franke, *Der Tod des Hans Hansen,* p. 11.
15. Viktor Mann, *Wir waren Fünf,* p. 111.

16. Letter to Paul Ehrenberg, June 29, 1900.
17. Letter to Heinrich, April 27, 1912.
18. Letter to Heinrich, November 25, 1900.
19. Letter to Heinrich, October 24, 1900.
20. Letter from Samuel Fischer, October 26, 1900.
21. Letter to Heinrich, November 2, 1900.
22. Letter to Otto Grautoff, November 3, 1900.
23. Letter to Kurt Martens, November 1900.
24. Letter to Heinrich, November 25, 1900.
25. Letter to Heinrich, April 27, 1912.
26. Letter to Heinrich, November 25, 1900.
27. Letter to Heinrich, April 27, 1912.
28. "A Sketch of My Life" ("Lebensabriss").
29. Letter to Heinrich, January 8, 1901.
30. Letter to Heinrich, January 21, 1901.
31. Letter to Agnes Meyer, December 15, 1942.
32. Letter to Heinrich, January 8, 1901.
33. Letter to Heinrich, February 13, 1901.
34. Letter to Otto Grautoff, February 22, 1901.
35. Letter to Heinrich, March 7, 1901.
36. Letter to Heinrich, April 1, 1901.
37. Letter to Heinrich, March 27, 1901.

Chapter 8

1. Letter to Paul Ehrenberg, May 26, 1901.
2. Ibid.
3. Letter to Heinrich, May 7, 1901.
4. *Notizbuch* 4.
5. Ibid.
6. Hans Wysling, *Bild und Text bei Thomas Mann* (Bern, 1975).
7. "Gladius Dei," p. 198.
8. Ibid., p. 201.
9. Ibid., p. 213.
10. Letter to Paul Ehrenberg, July 18, 1901.
11. Ibid.

12. Letter to Heinrich, February 13, 1901.
13. "Über die Kunst Richard Wagners."
14. "Tristan."
15. Letter to Otto Grautoff, November 6, 1901.
16. *Berliner Tageblatt,* quoted in "A Sketch of My Life" ("Lebensabriss").
17. Letter to Paul Ehrenberg, January 28, 1902.
18. *Notizbuch* 7, p. 62.
19. Ibid., p. 67.
20. Ibid., p. 52.
21. "The Loved Ones" ("Die Geliebten").
22. Ibid.
23. *Notizbuch* 7.
24. "Die Hungernden."
25. Letter to Paul Rache, Mendelssohn, pp. 504–505.
26. Letter to Kurt Martens, October 16, 1902.
27. "Tonio Kröger."
28. Letter to Paul and Carl Ehrenberg, Mendelssohn, p. 511.
29. "Portrait of the Mother" ("Das Bild der Mutter").
30. Ibid.
31. "Tonio Kröger."
32. Ibid.
33. Ibid.
34. Ibid.
35. Max Brod, *Über Franz Kafka* (Frankfurt, 1974), p. 46; Arthur Schnitzler, *Tagebuch 1913–16* (Vienna, 1983), p. 159.
36. Georg Lukács, *Thomas Mann,* p. 10.
37. Interview with Nathalie Sarraute, in *Süddeutscher Zeitung,* February 26, 1986.
38. Charles Neider, *The Stature of Thomas Mann,* p. 437.

Chapter 9

1. Klaus Schröter, *Thomas Mann in Selbstzeugnissen,* p. 24.
2. "A Sketch of My Life" ("Lebensabriss").
3. Quoted by TM in "Goethes Laufbahn als Schriftsteller."
4. *Neue Zürcher Zeitung,* December 5, 1903.
5. Charles Neider, *The Stature of Thomas Mann,* p. 38.
6. *Rheinisch-Westfälische Zeitung,* August 9, 1903.

7. Arthur Holitscher autobiography. Mendelssohn, p. 503
8. "Das Ewig Weiblich," in *Freistatt*, March 21, 1903.
9. *Notizbuch* 7, p. 117.
10. Letter from Julia Mann to Heinrich, March 10, 1904.
11. *Notizbuch* 7.
12. Viktor Mann, *Wir waren Fünf,* p. 27.
13. Letter from Carla Mann to Heinrich, November 21, 1903.
14. *Notizbuch* 7, pp. 83–95.
15. Ibid., p. 145.
16. Ibid., pp. 99–101.
17. Mendelssohn, p. 510
18. *Notizbuch* 7; draft of letter to Otto Grautoff, dated August 29, 1903.
19. *Notizbuch* 7, p. 121.
20. Ibid., pp. 121–23.
21. *Der Tag,* February 14 and 17, 1904.
22. Letter to Heinrich, December 5, 1903.
23. Letter to Samuel Fischer, October 29, 1903.
24. *Notizbuch* 7, p. 128.
25. Letter to Heinrich, December 5, 1903.
26. Letter to Walter Opitz, December 5, 1903.
27. Letter to Samuel Fischer, December 14.
28. Letter to Heinrich, December 23, 1903.
29. Letter to Heinrich, January 8, 1904.
30. Letter to Ida Boy-Ed, December 14, 1903.
31. Letter to Heinrich, February 27, 1904.
32. Ibid.
33. Friedrich Nietzsche, *Jenseits von Gut und Böse,* sec. 242.
34. Ibid., sec. 202.
35. Letter to Erwin Rohde, October 8, 1868.
36. "Der französische Einfluss," in *Die Zeit,* January 1904.

CHAPTER 10

1. Katia Mann, *Unwritten Memories,* p. 15.
2. Letter to Heinrich, February 27, 1904.
3. Ibid.
4. Ibid.
5. Ibid.
6. Katia Mann, *Unwritten Memories,* pp. 4–20.
7. Letter to Heinrich, March 27, 1904.
8. Hans Wysling, *Bild und Text bei Thomas Mann* (Bern, 1975).
9. Thomas Mann Archive (Zürich), Folder x, 13b Mat, sheet headed Savonarola.
10. "At the Prophet's" ("Beim Propheten").
11. Ibid.
12. Ibid.
13. Letter to Katia, early April 1904.
14. *Notizbuch* 7, p. 129.
15. Letter to Katia, end of April 1904.
16. Ibid.
17. Letter to Katia, mid-May 1904.
18. Letter to Katia, early June 1904.
19. Letter to Katia, beginning of June 1904.
20. Letter to Katia, June 6, 1904.
21. Letter to Katia, June 1904.
22. Letter to Kurt Martens, June 9, 1904.
23. Quoted in letter to Katia, June 1904.
24. Letter to Kurt Martens, June 13, 1904.
25. Letter to Katia, June 1904.
26. Letter to Katia, late June 1904.
27. Letter to Kurt Martens, July 14, 1904.
28. Ibid.
29. Ibid.
30. Ibid.
31. Letter to Katia, mid-July 1904.
32. Letter to Ida Boy-Ed, August 19, 1904.
33. *Notizbuch* 7, p. 147.
34. Langen's catalogue, summer 1904.
35. Mendelssohn, p. 619.
36. Letter to Katia, mid-August 1904.
37. Letter to Katia, late August 1904.
38. Letter to Katia, end of August 1904.
39. Katia Mann, *Unwritten Memories,* p. 19.
40. Letter to Katia, early September 1904.
41. Letter to Katia, late August 1904.
42. Letter to Katia, mid-September 1904.
43. Letter to Katia, late September 1904.
44. Letter to Ida Boy-Ed, October 7, 1904.

45. Letter to Philipp Witkop, October 30, 1904.

CHAPTER 11

1. Letter to Hilde Distel, ca. November 5, 1904.
2. Katia Mann, *Unwritten Memories,* p. 21.
3. *Lübecker General Anzeiger,* December 3, 1904.
4. Katia Mann, p. 24.
5. Letter from Julia Mann to Heinrich, January 4, 1905.
6. Letter to Heinrich, December 23, 1904.
7. *Notizbuch* 7, p. 153.
8. Letter to Heinrich, February 18, 1905.
9. Letter to Philipp Witkop, May 14, 1905.
10. *Notizbuch* 7, final pages.
11. Letter to Kurt Martens, March 14, 1905.
12. Ernst Müller, *Schiller: Intimes aus seinem Leben,* Berlin, 1905
13. Katia Mann, p. 22.
14. "Little Grandma."
15. *Notizbuch* 7, passim; letter to Heinrich, December 5, 1905.
16. Letter to Heinrich, December 5, 1905.
17. Ibid.
18. Letter to Heinrich, March 13, 1906.
19. Letter to Ida Boy-Ed, September 3, 1905.
20. "The Blood of the Walsungs" ("Wälsungenblut).
21. Ibid.
22. Letter to Heinrich, October 22, 1905.
23. "The Blood of the Walsungs."
24. Letter to Ida Boy-Ed, November 11, 1905.
25. Ibid.
26. Ibid. and letter to Heinrich, November 20, 1905.
27. Ibid.
28. Letter to Samuel Fischer, February 6, 1906.
29. *Lübecker General-Anzeiger,* November 7, 1905.
30. *Münchener Neueste Nachrichten,* February 15 and 16, 1906.
31. Letter to Heinrich, March 13, 1906.
32. Letter to Heinrich, March 21, 1906.

CHAPTER 12

1. Letter to Kurt Martens, March 28, 1906.
2. *Notizbuch* 9.
3. Ibid.
4. Letter to Kurt Martens, April 16, 1906.
5. Letter to Heinrich, January 17, 1906.
6. Ibid.
7. *Notizbuch* 7 at the end, copied into *Notizbuch* 9, at the beginning.
8. Vienna and Leipzig, 1906.
9. *Notizbuch* 9.
10. Hans Wysling, *Bild und Text bei Thomas Mann* (Bern, 1975).
11. Letter to Heinrich, June 11, 1906.
12. Katia Mann, *Unwritten Memories,* p. 29.
13. Letter to Heinrich, June 22, 1906.
14. Letter to Heinrich, June 7, 1906.
15. Letter to Heinrich, June 11, 1906.
16. Letter to Samuel Fischer, July 15, 1906.
17. Mendelssohn, p. 704.
18. *Unwritten Memories,* p. 22.
19. Letter to Hugo von Hofmannsthal, July 25, 1909.
20. Letter from Hedwig Pringsheim to Dagny Bjornson, March 8, 1908; Hans-Rudolf Wiedemann, *Thomas Manns Schwiegermutter erzählt: Lebendige Briefe aus grossbürgerlichem Häuse* (Lübeck, 1985), p. 26.
21. Letter to Heinrich, May 27, 1907.
22. Ibid.
23. Letter to Heinrich, July 5, 1907.
24. Mendelssohn, p. 741
25. Letter to Heinrich, January 15, 1908.
26. Letter to Heinrich, February 6, 1908.
27. Letter from Julia Mann to Ludwig Ewers, April 20, 1908.
28. Letter to Ludwig Ewers, May 16, 1908.
29. Letter to Heinrich, June 10, 1908.
30. Ibid.
31. Letter to Ida Boy-Ed, September 11, 1908.
32. "Zur Lösung der Judenfrage," in *Die Lösung der Judenfrage,* Julius Moses, ed. (Berlin, 1907), cited by Marcus.
33. Conversation with Klaus and

Erika at the end of the German edition of her *Ungeschriebene Memoiren (Unwritten Memories)*.

34. Letter to Ludwig Ewers, January 13, 1908.
35. Letter to Samuel Lublinski, December 6, 1908.
36. Letter to Ludwig Ewers, January 13, 1909.
37. Letter to Heinrich, December, 7, 1908.
38. "The Railway Accident" ("Das Eisenbahnunglück").

CHAPTER 13

1. Letter to Heinrich, December 27, 1908.
2. Letter to Korfiz Holm, quoted by Mendelssohn, p. 760.
3. Letter to Samuel Fischer, April 20, 1909.
4. Letter to Heinrich, April 1, 1909.
5. Postcard to Walter Opitz, after May 11, 1908.
6. Letter to Walter Opitz, June 11, 1909.
7. Letter to Ludwig Ewers, July 5, 1909.
8. Ibid.
9. Letter to Ludwig Ewers, August 23, 1909.
10. Letter to Heinrich, March 25, 1909.
11. Letter to Heinrich, June 3, 1909.
12. Letter to Samuel Fischer, April 20, 1909.
13. *Notizbuch* 9, p. 62.
14. Ibid., p. 53.
15. Letter to Walter Opitz, August 26, 1909.
16. Letter to Ida Boy-Ed, September 25, 1909.
17. Letter to Samuel Fischer, October 26, 1909.
18. Letter to Heinrich, January 10, 1910.
19. Letter to Hermann Hesse, April 1, 1910.
20. *Neue Rundschau*, December 1909.
21. Letter to Kurt Martens, January 11, 1910.
22. Letter to Heinrich, September 30, 1909.
23. Letter to Kurt Martens, January 11, 1910.
24. Letter to Maximilian Brantl, January 11, 1910.
25. Letter to Heinrich, December 18, 1909.
26. Letter to Heinrich, June 16, 1910.
27. Letter to Heinrich, March 20, 1910.
28. "Samuel zieht die Bilanz oder der kleine Prophete" ("Samuel Draws Up the Balance, or the Little Prophet"), *Die Schaubühne*, January 20, 1910.
29. "Der Doktor Lessing," in *Literarische Echo*, March 1, 1910.
30. "Justifications" ("Berechtigungen"), in *Literarische Echo*, April 1, 1910.
31. Letter to Walter Opitz, April 18, 1910.
32. Letter to Ida Boy-Ed, June 28, 1910.
33. Letter to Samuel Lublinski, June 13, 1910.
34. Letter to Maximilian Harden, June 29, 1910.
35. Letter to Paul Ehrenberg, July 12, 1910.
36. Ibid.
37. Letter to Heinrich, August 4, 1910.
38. Sigrid Anger et al., eds., *Heinrich Mann: Werk und Leben in Dokumenten und Bildern 1871–1950* (Berlin, 1971), pp. 461–64.

CHAPTER 14

1. Mendelssohn, pp. 967–68.
2. "Tristan."
3. Letter to Maximilian Harden, August 21, 1910.
4. Letter to Maximilian Harden, August 30, 1910.
5. Katia Mann, *Unwritten Memories*.
6. Letter to Gustav Mahler, September 1910.
7. "How Jappe and Do Escobar Fought" ("Wie Jappe und Do Escobar sich prügelten").
8. Ibid.
9. Letter to Heinrich, March 24, 1911.
10. "Death in Venice" ("Der Tod in Venedig").
11. Ibid.
12. Ibid.
13. Letter to Carl Maria von Weber, July 4, 1920.
14. Gilbert Adair, "The Real Story of Death in Venice," magazine section of *Sunday Correspondent*, April 8, 1990.

15. Mendelssohn, p. 873.
16. Quoted by T. J. Reed, *Thomas Mann: The Uses of Tradition,* p. 154.
17. Monika Mann, p. 80.
18. "Death in Venice," p. 614
19. Hermann Weigand on Dr. Faustus, *Thomas Mann in Context,* Papers of the Clark University Centennial Symposium, Ken Hughes, ed. (Worcester, Mass., 1978).
20. Letter to Ernst Bertram, January 28, 1910.
21. Golo Mann, *Reminiscences and Reflections,* p. 26
22. "Death in Venice."
23. Letter to Ernst Bertram, August 11, 1911.

CHAPTER 15

1. Monika Mann, pp. 6–7.
2. Klaus Mann, *The Turning Point,* p. 8.
3. Ibid., p. 5.
4. Georg Lukács, *Die Seele und die Formen* (Berlin, 1911).
5. T. J. Reed, *Thomas Mann: The Uses of Tradition,* pp. 164–66.
6. Ibid., p. 638.
7. Ibid., p. 608.
8. Golo Mann, *Reminiscences and Reflections,* pp. 10–11.
9. Letters to Josef Ruederer, March 29 and September 20, 1911.
10. Letter to Kurt Martens, February 14, 1912.
11. Golo Mann, pp. 10–11.
12. "Death in Venice" ("Der Tod in Venedig").
13. Ibid.
14. Letter to Josef Ponten, June 6, 1919.
15. Letter to Carl Maria Weber, July 4, 1920.
16. Letter to Heinrich, April 2, 1912.
17. Letter to Heinrich, April 27, 1912.
18. *On Myself (Über mich selbst).*
19. "Tristan."
20. *The Magic Mountain (Der Zauberberg).*
21. Ibid.
22. Letter to Hans von Hulsen. Burgin and Meyer, *Thomas Mann: Ein Chronik seines Lebens,* p. 36.
23. "On Myself."
24. Friedrich Schlegel, *Lucinde* (Insel edition), p. 81.
25. "Death in Venice."

26. Frank Wedekind, *Schauspielkunst* (Munich and Leipzig, 1910), p. 35.
27. Letter to Maximilian Harden, December 29, 1912.
28. *Der Tag,* December 4, 1912.
29. "On Myself."
30. Letter to Jakob Wassermann, November 25, 1912.
31. Letter to Ida Boy-Ed, March 24, 1913.
32. *Neue Rundschau,* June 1913.

CHAPTER 16

1. Mendelssohn, p. 928.
2. Ibid., p. 929.
3. Letter to Kurt Martens, May 26, 1913.
4. Letter to Ernst Bertram, July 24, 1913.
5. Letter to Hans von Hülsen, September 9, 1913.
6. Letter to Ludwig Ewers, September 9, 1913.
7. *Notizbuch* 10, 1913 entries, p. 1.
8. Ibid., p. 5.
9. "A Sketch of My Life" ("Lebensabriss").
10. Letter to Julius Bab, August 31, 1913.
11. Letter to Heinrich, November 8, 1913.
12. Letter to Heinrich, November 11, 1913.
13. Letter from Franz Kafka to Milena Jesenska, undated, 1920.
14. Letter to Jakob Wassermann, December 11, 1913.
15. "Master and Dog" ("Herr und Hund").
16. Heinrich Breloer, *Treffpunkt im Unendlichen: Die Lebensreise des Klaus Mann,* NDR Television documentary, 1984.
17. Charles Neider, *The Stature of Thomas Mann,* p. 10.
18. Letter to Bruno Walter on his seventieth birthday.
19. Klaus Mann, *The Turning Point,* p. 31.
20. Letter to Heinrich, January 7, 1914.
21. Letter to Ludwig von Hofmann, January 14, 1914.
22. Letters to Otto Grautoff, April 22, 1914, and Ida Boy-Ed, April 27, 1914.
23. Letter to Philipp Witkop, June 7, 1914.

24. Letter to Hans von Hülsen, June 10, 1914.
25. "A Sketch of My Life."
26. *The Magic Mountain (Der Zauberberg)*.
27. Ibid.
28. Ibid.

CHAPTER 17

1. Golo Mann, *Reminiscences and Reflections*, p. 19.
2. Klaus Mann, *The Turning Point*, pp. 27–28.
3. Letter to Jakob Wassermann, March 13, 1913.
4. Golo Mann, pp. 18–19.
5. Letter to Heinrich, July 30, 1914.
6. "A Sketch of My Life" ("Lebensabriss").
7. Letter to Heinrich, August 7, 1914.
8. Klaus Mann, p. 31.
9. *Das Forum*, April 1914.
10. Erich Mühsam, *Tagebuch*, August 27, 1914, Heinrich Mann Archive.
11. "Heinrich Mann," undated manuscript in the archive of Agnes Speyer-Ulmann.
12. Golo Mann, p. 24.
13. Letter to Heinrich, August 7, 1914.
14. Letter to Samuel Fischer, August 22, 1914.
15. "A Sketch of My Life."
16. *Mind and Art (Geist und Kunst)*, Note 124.
17. Letter to Philipp Witkop, November 11, 1914.
18. Letter to Ernst Bertram.
19. *Der Zauberberg (The Magic Mountain)*.
20. Letter to *Svenska Dagbladet*, May 11, 1915.
21. Klaus Mann, p. 34.
22. Letter to Samuel Fischer, June 7, 1915.
23. Letter to Hedwig Fischer, June 24, 1915.
24. Letter to Ernst Bertram, July 5, 1915.
25. Klaus Mann, p. 35.
26. *Notizbuch* 10.
27. Letter to Walter Opitz, September 23, 1915.
28. Letter to Paul Amann, August 3, 1915.
29. Ibid.
30. Letter to Paul Amann, October 1, 1915.

31. Golo Mann, p. 31.
32. *Notizbuch* 12.
33. Letter to Philipp Witkop, December 16, 1915.
34. Letter to Ernst Bertram, June 8, 1916.
35. Letter to Ernst Bertram, January 5, 1916.
36. Letter to Ludwig Ewers, April 6, 1921.
37. Letter to Maximilian Brantl, June 18, 1916.
38. Letter to Ernst Bertram, January 15, 1916.
39. *Pan*, January 1911.
40. *Die Weissen Blätter*, November 1915.
41. Draft of letter from Heinrich, January 5, 1918.
42. Klaus Mann, pp. 38–39.
43. Golo Mann, p. 25.
44. Letter from Ernst Bertram to Ernst Glöckner, January 29, 1916.
45. Marianne Krüll, *Im Netz der Zauberer*, p. 239.
46. Ibid., chap. 5.
47. Ibid., chap. 4.

CHAPTER 18

1. Letter to Jacob Wassermann, March 29, 1916.
2. Klaus Mann, *The Turning Point*, p. 37.
3. Golo Mann, *Reminiscences and Reflections*, pp. 32–33.
4. Interview with Golo Mann, in *Die Welt*, March 11, 1987.
5. Letter to Maximilian Harden, January 12, 1916.
6. Letter to Jakob Wassermann, March 29, 1916.
7. Letter to Samuel Fischer, April 12, 1916.
8. Letter to Paul Eltzbacher, December 1, 1916.
9. "Master and Dog" ("Herr und Hund")–Notes on Bashan's Character.
10. Ibid.
11. Letter to Paul Amann, September 5, 1916.
12. Letter to Ernst Bertram, August 28, 1916.
13. Letter to Paul Amann, December 16, 1916.
14. Letter to Philipp Witkop, November 28, 1916.
15. Letter to Paul Amann, November 25, 1916.

16. Letter to Ernst Bertram, November 25, 1916.
17. *Notizbuch* 11, p. 50.
18. Ibid.
19. *Vossische Zeitung,* November 4, 1916.
20. "Against Justice and Truth" ("Gegen Recht und Wahrheit"), in *Reflections of a Nonpolitical Man (Betrachtungen eines Unpolitischen).*
21. Letter to Heinrich, January 7, 1914.
22. Heinrich Mann, *Ein Zeitalter wird besichtigt.*
23. Letter to Philipp Witkop, February 21, 1917.
24. Letter to Ida Boy-Ed, March 11, 1917.
25. Letter to Hans von Hülsen, March 18, 1917.
26. Letter to Paul Amann, March 25, 1917.
27. Letter to Ernst Bertram, May 28, 1917.
28. Letter to Bruno Walter, June 24, 1917.
29. Golo Mann, pp. 26–27; letter to Bruno Walter, June 24, 1917.
30. Letter to Kurt Martens, June 1, 1917.
31. Golo Mann, pp. 31–32.
32. Letter to Philipp Witkop, October 4, 1917.
33. Heinrich Mann, "Möglichkeiten einer künftigen Weltfrieden," *Berliner Tageblatt,* December 25, 1917.
34. *Berliner Tageblatt,* December 27, 1917.
35. Draft of letter from Heinrich to Thomas, December 30, 1917.
36. Marianne Krüll, *Im Netz der Zauberer,* p. 239.
37. Letter to Heinrich, January 3, 1918.
38. Draft of letter from Heinrich, January 5, 1918.
39. Letter to Heinrich, January 3, 1918.
40. "A Sketch of My Life" ("Lebensabriss").
41. *Notizbuch* 12.
42. Letter to Ernst Bertram, February 6, 1918.
43. Letter to Paul Amann, March 2, 1918.
44. "On Belief" ("Vom Glauben") in *Reflections.*

45. Letter to Ida Boy-Ed, April 27, 1918.
46. Letter to Paul Amann, May 23, 1918.
47. Letter to Ida Boy-Ed, August 13, 1918.
48. Letter to Philipp Witkop.
49. Letter to Ernst Bertram, July 17, 1918.
50. Letter to Kurt Martens, June 27, 1918.
51. Letter to Paul Amann, July 11, 1918.
52. Ibid.
53. *Tagebücher,* September 11, 1918.

CHAPTER 19

1. Letter to Ernst Bertram, July 23, 1918.
2. Letter to Ida Boy-Ed, August 13, 1918.
3. Letter to Philipp Witkop, September 13, 1918.
4. Letters to Karl Martens, September 11, 1918; A. Gerhard, September 11, 1918; and Philipp Witkop, September 13, 1918.
5. *Tagebücher,* September 18, 1918.
6. Letter to Ernst Bertram, September 21, 1918.
7. Ernst Bertram, *Nietzsche* (Berlin, 1918).
8. *Geist und Kunst,* Hans Wysling, ed., p. 211.
9. *Tagebücher,* September 13, 1918.
10. *Tagebücher,* December 29, 1918.
11. *Tagebücher,* September 12, 1918.
12. Christiane von Hofmannsthal, *Tagebücher und Briefe des Vaters an die Töchter,* ed. Maya Ranch and Gerhard Schuste (Frankfurt 1991).
13. *Tagebücher,* September 17, 1918.
14. *Tagebücher,* September 28, 1918.
15. *Tagebücher,* October 14, 1918.
16. *Tagebücher,* September 28, 1918.
17. *Tagebücher,* September 16.
18. *Tagebücher,* September 14, 1915.
19. *Tagebücher,* October 30, 1918.
20. *Tagebücher,* October 4, 1918.
21. *Tagebücher,* December 1, 1918.
22. Munich, 1963.
23. Golo Mann, *Reminiscences and Reflections,* p. 318.
24. *Tagebücher,* November 8, 1918.
25. *Tagebücher,* November 11, 1918.
26. *Tagebücher,* November 7, 1918.
27. *Tagebücher,* November 8, 1918.

28. *Tagebücher,* November 19, 1918.
29. *Tagebücher,* November 10 and 12, 1918.
30. *Tagebücher,* November 29, 1918.
31. *Tagebücher,* November 7, 1918.
32. Klaus Mann, *The Turning Point,* p. 44.
33. *Tagebücher,* January 3, 1919.
34. *Tagebücher,* February 17, 1919.
35. *Tagebücher,* January 10, 1919.
36. *Tagebücher,* February 21 and 22, 1919.
37. *Tagebücher,* February 21 and 24, 1918.
38. *Tagebücher,* February 22, 1919.
39. *Tagebücher,* February 24 and 27, 1919.
40. *Tagebücher,* March 25, 1919.
41. *Tagebücher,* March 17, 1919.
42. *Tagebücher,* March 24, 1919.
43. *Tagebücher,* April 5, 1919.
44. *Tagebücher,* April 7, 1919.
45. *Tagebücher,* April 15, 17, 19, 1919.
46. *Tagebücher,* April 12 and 17, 1919.
47. *Tagebücher,* April 20 and June 7, 1919.
48. *Tagebücher,* April 21 and 22 and May 4 and 8, 1919.
49. *Tagebücher,* April 12, 22, and 30, 1919.
50. *Tagebücher,* April 30, 1919.
51. *Tagebücher,* April 17, 1919.
52. *Tagebücher,* May 1, 1919.
53. *Tagebücher,* May 5, 1919.
54. *Tagebücher,* February 24, 1920.
55. *Tagebücher,* May 1 and 16, 1919.
56. Marianne Krüll, *Im Netz der Zauberer,* pp. 250–51.
57. *Tagebücher,* September 21, 1919.
58. *Tagebücher,* September 13, 1919.
59. *Tagebücher,* July 24, 1919.
60. *Tagebücher,* November 25, 1919.
61. Letter to Gustav Blume, July 5, 1919.
62. *Tagebücher,* July 2, 1919.
63. *Tagebücher,* July 2 and 6, 1919.
64. "Tischrede auf Pfitzner," reprinted in the *Süddeutsche Monatsheft,* October 1919.
65. Postcard to Philipp Witkop, July 19, 1919.
66. Letter to Korfiz Holm, August 10, 1919.
67. *Tagebücher,* November 2, 1919.
68. *Tagebücher,* June 23, 1919.
69. *Tagebücher,* November 14, 1919.
70. Letter to Carl Maria Weber, July 4, 1920.
71. *Tagebücher,* December 4–12, 1919.
72. *Tagebücher,* December 15, 1919.
73. *Tagebücher,* December 22, 1919; Bruno Walter in Charles Neider, *The Stature of Thomas Mann,* p. 104.
74. Letter to "Jack," May 10, 1922.

CHAPTER 20

1. Letter to Hermann Graf Keyserling, January 18, 1920.
2. *Tagebücher,* March 14, 1920.
3. *Tagebücher,* March 13, 1920; letter to Ernst Bertram, March 16, 1920.
4. *Tagebücher,* March 3, 1920.
5. *Tagebücher,* January 8 and July 11, 1920.
6. *Tagebücher,* February 29 and March 12, 1920.
7. *Tagebücher,* April 11 and May 5, 1920.
8. *The Magic Mountain (Der Zauberberg).*
9. *Tagebücher,* May 26 and June 6, 1920.
10. Letter to Carl Maria Weber, July 4, 1920.
11. *The Magic Mountain.*
12. *Tagebücher,* July 14, 1920.
13. *Tagebücher,* October 17, 1920.
14. *Tagebücher,* April 4, 1921.
15. *Tagebücher,* May 5, 1920.
16. Klaus Mann, "Der Vater lacht," in *Abenteuer des Brautpaars* (Munich, 1981).
17. *Tagebücher,* July 25, 1920.
18. *Tagebücher,* October 17, 1920.
19. Marianne Krüll, *Im Netz der Zauberer,* p. 424.
20. *Tagebücher,* March 23 and April 8, 1920.
21. *Tagebücher,* March 26, 1920.
22. *Tagebücher,* May 21, 1920.
23. *Tagebücher,* July 5, 1920.
24. Letter to Philipp Witkop, December 16, 1920.
25. *Tagebücher,* December 29, 1920.
26. *Tagebücher,* December 31, 1920.
27. *Tagebücher,* March 1, 1921.
28. *Tagebücher,* January 2, 1921.
29. Ibid.
30. *Tagebücher,* February 6, 1921.
31. *Tagebücher,* February 23, 1921.
32. Ibid.
33. *Tagebücher,* June 8, 1921.
34. *Tagebücher,* March 1, 1921.
35. Ibid.
36. *Tagebücher,* April 4, 1920.

37. *Tagebücher,* May 24, 1921.
38. "Lübeck als geistige Lebens-
    form."
39. Letter to Philipp Witkop, June 9,
    1921.
40. June 6, 1921; Letters to Philipp
    Witkop, June 9, 1921, and Ernst
    Bertram, June 10, 1921.
41. *Tagebücher,* May 22, 1921.
42. Letter to Ernst Bertram, June 30,
    1921.
43. *Tagebücher,* July 16 and 26, 1921.
44. *Tagebücher,* July 26, 1921.
45. *Tagebücher,* September 17, 1921.
46. *Tagebücher,* September 17, 1921.
47. "Zur jüdischen Frage," in *Autobi-
    ographisches,* p. 96.
48. *Tagebücher,* October 29, 1921.
49. *Tagebücher,* December 1, 1921.
50. *Tagebücher,* November 20, 1921.
51. Judith Marcus, *Georg Lukács and
    Thomas Mann: A Study in the Sociol-
    ogy of Literature* (Amherst, 1987),
    pp. 47, 68, 176–77.
52. Letter to Ernst Bertram, February
    2, 1922.
53. Marcus, pp. 68–69, 143.

CHAPTER 21

1. Cable from the Munich correspondent of the *Leipziger Tageblatt.*
2. Card to Heinrich, January 31,
   1922.
3. Letter to Ernst Bertram, February
   2, 1922.
4. Letter to Arthur Schnitzler, September 4, 1922.
5. "Goethe und Tolstoy," 1922.
6. Letter to Ernst Bertram, June 2,
   1922.
7. Arthur Eloesser, *Thomas Mann,* pp.
   193–94.
8. *Frankfurter Zeitung,* April 16, 1922.
9. Letter to Ernst Bertram, July 8,
   1922.
10. Letter to Ida Boy-Ed, July 16,
    1922.
11. Golo Mann, *Reminiscences and Re-
    flections,* p. 56.
12. Letter to Kurt Martens, October
    10, 1922.
13. Postcard to Heinrich, October 20,
    1922.
14. Letter to Ida Boy-Ed, December 5,
    1922.
15. Letter to Heinrich, February 17,
    1923.

16. Ibid.
17. Letter to Ernst Hanhart, January
    20, 1923.
18. Letter to Heinrich, February 17,
    1923.
19. *Neue Rundschau,* March 1923.
20. Letter to Ernst Bertram, March 1,
    1923.
21. "A Sketch of My Life" ("Lebens-
    abriss").
22. Letter to Ernst Bertram, May 2,
    1923.

CHAPTER 22

1. *The Magic Mountain (Der Zauberberg).*
2. Conversation with Elisabeth
   Borgese Mann, February 28, 1994.
3. Letter to Albert Bonniers Vorlaget,
   May 26, 1923.
4. Letter to Heinrich, October 17,
   1923.
5. Letter to Gerhart Hauptmann,
   April 11, 1925.
6. *Frankfurter Zeitung,* December 25,
   1923.
7. Letter to Julius Bab, April 23, 1925.
8. Letter to Carl Hebling, February
   13, 1924.
9. Letter to Arthur Schnitzler, November 22, 1923.
10. Letter to Ernst Bertram, February
    19, 1924.
11. Georg Lukács, *Die Seele und die For-
    men.*
12. Postcard to Hermann Ebers, April
    11, 1924; letter to Hermann Pongs,
    April 14, 1924.
13. James Gindin, *Galsworthy's Life and
    Art* (London, 1987).
14. Postcard to Ernst Bertram, May 12,
    1924.
15. Letter to Helen Lowe-Porter, May
    20, 1924.
16. Klaus Mann, *The Turning Point,* pp.
    94–97; Marianne Krüll, *Im Netz der
    Zauberer,* pp. 308–309.
17. Letter to Ida Boy-Ed, July 21, 1924.
18. Letter to Josef Ponten, February 5,
    1925.
19. Ibid.
20. Letter to Annette Kolb, January 16,
    1925.

CHAPTER 23

1. Letter to Erich Ebermeyer, September 2, 1924.

2. Letter to Ida Boy-Ed, December 4, 1924.
3. Letter to Herbert Eulenberg, January 6, 1925.
4. Letter to Samuel Fischer, January 8, 1925.
5. *Gesammelte Werke*, vol. 9 (1960), pp. 166–69.
6. Letter to Ernst Bertram, February 4, 1925.
7. Interview with Michael Mann, 1975, quoted in Frederic Tubach and Sally Tubach, *Michael Mann*, pp. 148–51; interview with Golo Mann, in *Die Welt*, March 11, 1987.
8. Interview with Michael Mann, quoted in Tubach and Tubach.
9. Letter to Ernst Bertram, February 4, 1925.
10. Letter to Ernst Bertram, June 14, 1925.
11. "A Sketch of My Life" ("Lebensabriss").
12. "Unterwegs," in *Vossische Zeitung*, April 12, 1925.
13. Postcard to Heinrich, March 18, 1925.
14. Postcard to Ernst Bertram, March 9, 1925.
15. Klaus letter of January 15, 1926.
16. Klaus Mann, "Kindernovelle," in *Abenteuer des Brautpaars*.
17. Letter to Erika, October 17, 1926.
18. Hermann Hesse, *Autobiographical Writings*, trans. by Denver Lindley (London 1973), p. 225.
19. Letter to Julius Bab, April 23, 1925.
20. *Neue Freie Presse*, April 26, 1925.
21. Harry Graf Kessler, *Tagebücher* (Frankfurt, 1961), pp. 441–42.
22. Letter to Gerhart Hauptmann, April 11, 1925.
23. Letter to Erika, May 7, 1925.
24. Letter to Ernst Bertram, June 14, 1925.
25. Letter to Hans Pfitzner, June 23, 1925.
26. Postcard to Ernst Bertram, September 21, 1925.
27. Letter to Lilli Diekmann, September 27, 1925.
28. Letter to Ida Herz, October 31, 1925.
29. Letters to Max Brod, November 4, 1925, and Ida Herz, November 6, 1925.
30. Interview with Golo Mann, *Die Welt*, March 11, 1987.
31. Neider, *The Stature of Thomas Mann*, "The Theme of the Joseph Novels."
32. Letter to Ernst Bertram, December 25, 1925.
33. "Pariser Rechenschaft," in *Über mich selbst*.
34. Ibid.
35. Ibid.
36. Ibid.
37. Letters to Ernst Bertram, February 15, 1926, Philipp Witkop, February 22, 1926, and Margarete Hauptmann, February 27, 1926.
38. Letter to Félix Bertaux, March 16, 1926.
39. Letter to Fritz Endres, April 17, 1926.
40. Letter to Hugo von Hofmannsthal, March 18, 1926.
41. Letter to Josef Ponten, May 24, 1926.
42. Letter to Ernst Fischer, May 25, 1926.
43. "Lübeck als geistige Lebensform."
44. Klaus Mann, *The Turning Point*, p. 116.
45. Letter to Hugo von Hofmannsthal, September 7, 1926.
46. Letter to Félix Bertaux, August 1, 1926.
47. Letter to Hugo von Hofmannsthal, September 7, 1926.
48. Letter to Otto Hoerth, June 12, 1930.

CHAPTER 24

1. T. J. Reed, *Thomas Mann: The Uses of Tradition*, p. 328.
2. Ernst Bertram, *Nietzsche: Versuch einer Mythologie* (Berlin, 1918), p. 6.
3. *Die Geschichten Jaakobs*.
4. Letter to Richard Coudenhove-Kalergi, September 17, 1926.
5. Letter to Hans von Hülsen, October 5, 1929.
6. Letters to Ida Boy-Ed, October 9, 1926, and Ida Herz, October 11, 1926.
7. Letter to Hedwig Fischer, March 4, 1927.
8. Letter to Erika, October 17, 1926.
9. Letter to Hugo von Hofmannsthal, November 14, 1926.

10. "A Sketch of My Life" ("Lebens-abriss").
11. Letter to Ida Boy-Ed, December 1, 1926.
12. Letter to Erika, December 23, 1926.
13. Ibid.
14. Letter to Ernst Bertram, December 28, 1926.
15. Letters to Arthur and Grete Nikisch, January 1, 1927, and Adele Gerhard, January 4, 1927.
16. Postcard to Gerhart Hauptmann, February 9, 1927.
17. Postcard to Josef Ponten, February 7, 1927.
18. Letter to Hans Ludwig Held, February 11, 1927.
19. Letter to Karl Vossler, February 10, 1927.
20. Letter to Jakob Horovitz, June 11, 1927.
21. Letter to Heinrich, March 15–16, 1927.
22. Postcard to Ernst Bertram, May 11, 1927.
23. Golo Mann, *Reminiscences and Reflections*, pp. 131–32.
24. Letters from Klaus, June 2, 1936, and December 26, 1936.
25. Interview with Golo Mann, in *Die Welt*, March 11, 1987.
26. Letter to Ida Herz, August 18, 1927.
27. Postcard to Heinrich and Mimi Mann, August 19, 1927.
28. Letter to Josef Ponten, August 21, 1927.
29. Postcards to Ernst Bertram, September 4 and 24, 1927.
30. *Essays*, vol. I: *Literatur*, p. 258.
31. *Tagebücher*, February 20, 1942.
32. Letter from Heinrich, August 23, 1927.
33. Letter to Heinrich, August 29, 1927.
34. Postcard to Ernst Bertram, September 24, 1927.
35. Letter to Reclams Universum, n.d., late September/early October 1927.
36. *Gesammelte Werke*, vol. 4, p. 189.

CHAPTER 25

1. Letter to Gerhart Hauptmann, November 13, 1928.
2. Letter to *Europäische Gespräche*, n.d., published December 12, 1927.

3. Letter to Philipp Witkop, December 29, 1927.
4. Judith Marcus, *Georg Lukács and Thomas Mann: A Study in the Sociology of Literature* (Amherst, 1987), pp. 40–41.
5. Letter to Willy Haas, March 11, 1928.
6. "Kultur und Sozialismus," *Preussische Jahrbücher*, April 1928.
7. Letter to Will Schaber, n.d., spring 1928.
8. Letter to Paul Nikolaus Cossmann, April 4, 1928.
9. Letter to Artur Hübscher, April 18, 1928.
10. Letter to Stefan Grossmann, August 5, 1928.
11. Letter to Oskar Loerke, October 28, 1928.
12. Letter to Max Rychner, December 14, 1928.
13. *Essays*, vol. I: *Literatur*, p. 246.
14. Ibid., p. 257.
15. Ibid., p. 247.
16. Ibid., pp. 244–45.
17. Address at the Library of Congress, 1942, in Charles Neider, *The Stature of Thomas Mann*, p. 221.
18. *Essays*, vol. I: *Literatur*, p. 252.
19. Letter to Charles du Bos, May 3, 1929.
20. Letter to Ernst Bertram, May 19, 1929.
21. Letter from Heinrich to Félix Bertaux, December 31, 1928.
22. *Essays*, vol. I: *Literatur*, p. 354.
23. Letter to Gerty von Hofmannsthal, July 20, 1929.
24. *Essays*, vol. I: *Literatur*, pp. 354–55.
25. "A Sketch of My Life" ("Lebens-abriss").
26. Letter to Martin Fridrik Böök, December 21, 1929.
27. Heinrich Mann, *Das Öffentliche Leben* (1932).
28. Letter to Maximilian Brantl, January 7, 1930.
29. Letter to André Gide, January 20, 1930.
30. Letter to Ernst Bertram, December 27, 1929.
31. *On Myself (Über mich selbst)*, pp. 145–46.
32. Letter to Hans Ludwig Held, March 1, 1930.
33. Letter to Ida Herz, February 27, 1930.

34. Letter to Ernst Bertram, April 8, 1930.
35. Letter to Arthur Eloesser, April 18, 1930.
36. Letter to Ernst Bertram, April 1, 1930.
37. Letter to Ida Herz, July 8, 1930.
38. Postcard to Ida Herz, July 27, 1930.
39. Monika Mann, p. 77.
40. Letter to Helen Lowe-Porter, July 27, 1930.
41. Postcard to Ida Herz, September 21, 1930.
42. Letter to Klaus Pringsheim, November 3, 1930.
43. Letter to Ida Herz, October 24, 1930.
44. Letter to Gerhart Hauptmann, October 23, 1930.
45. Letter to Gerhart Hauptmann, October 28, 1930.
46. Letter to Hans Blunck, December 2, 1930.
47. Letter to Hedwig Fischer, December 9, 1930.
48. Letter to Ivan Schmeliov, January 4, 1931.
49. Letter to Ernst Bertram, December 29, 1930.
50. Letter to Hedwig Fischer, January 15, 1931.
51. Letter to Félix Bertaux, February 8, 1931.
52. Letter to Erika, March 1931.
53. Letter to Karl Vossler, March 22, 1931.
54. "Ansprache an den Bruder," *Briefwechsel,* Hans Wysling, ed., p. 134.
55. Letter from Heinrich, June 15, 1931.

CHAPTER 26

1. Letter to Félix Bertaux, April 8, 1931.
2. Letter to Hans Bodmer, June 13, 1931.
3. Letter to George Sylvester Viereck, June 21, 1931.
4. André Gide, *Journal,* May 13, 1931.
5. Ibid., first Saturday in July 1931.
6. *Gesammelte Werke,* vol. 4, pp. 425–27.
7. Ibid., p. 423.
8. Ibid., pp. 394–95.
9. Letter to Ernst Bertram, December 29, 1930.

10. Letter to B. Fucik, April 15, 1932.
11. *Essays,* vol. I: *Literatur,* p. 223.
12. Golo Mann, *Reminiscences and Reflections,* pp. 212–13.
13. Letters to Ida Herz, January 11, 1932; J. Chapiro, January 14, 1932; and Martin Platzer, February 7, 1932.
14. Letter to Ida Herz, February 5, 1932.
15. Letter to Helen Lowe-Porter, January 27, 1932.
16. Letter to Hans Reisiger, February 21, 1932.
17. Letter to Hans Reisiger, March 4, 1932.
18. Letters to O. Loerke, March 28, 1932, and Fritz Strich, March 30, 1932.
19. Klaus Mann, *The Turning Point,* p. 243.
20. Ibid., pp. 236–37.
21. *Tagebücher,* March 20, 1934.
22. Letter to Walter Goetz, March 26, 1932.
23. Golo Mann, p. 260.
24. Letter to Hedwig Fischer, n.d.
25. Letter from Hedwig Fischer, June 21, 1932.
26. Letters to Ernst Bertram, July 23, 1932, and Martin Platzer, July 26, 1932.
27. Letters to H. G. Erdmannsdörfer, September 8, 1932, and Ida Herz, November 15, 1932.
28. Letter to Hans Reisiger, October 30, 1932.
29. *Tagebücher,* February 19, 1933.
30. Letter to Paul Schiemann, November 26, 1932.
31. Letter to Hermann Hesse, December 22, 1932.
32. "The Suffering and Greatness of Richard Wagner" ("Leiden und Grösse Richard Wagners").
33. Ibid.
34. Ibid.
35. Ibid.
36. Letter to Ida Herz, January 29, 1933.
37. Klaus Mann, p. 262.
38. Letter to Erich Ziebarth and friends, February 1, 1933.
39. Letter to Kurt Schlesinger, February 4, 1933.
40. Klaus Mann, pp. 263–65.
41. Erika Mann, *Escape to Life* (Boston, 1939), p. 6.

42. *Bayern unter dem Nationalsozialismus,* cited in Golo Mann, p. 294.

CHAPTER 27

1. *Gesammelte Werke,* vol. 4, p. 668.
2. Letter to Lavinia Mazzucchetti, March 13, 1933.
3. Erika Mann, *Escape to Life,* p. 7.
4. Letter to Lavinia Mazzucchetti, March 13, 1933.
5. Letters to Karl Loewenstein, March 7, 11, 29, 1933.
6. *Tagebücher,* March 15, 1933.
7. Erika and Klaus in Charles Neider, *The Stature of Thomas Mann.*
8. *Tagebücher,* March 15, 1933.
9. *Tagebücher,* March 19, 1933.
10. *Tagebücher,* March 27–29, 1933.
11. Conversation with Elisabeth Mann Borgese, February 28, 1994.
12. Letter to Ida Herz, March 22, 1933.
13. Letter to Ida Herz, May 19, 1933.
14. *Tagebücher,* April 3 and 6, 1933.
15. *Dépêche de Toulouse,* February 25, 1933.
16. Letter to Ludwig Lewisohn, April 12, 1933.
17. *Tagebücher,* April 5, 1933.
18. *Tagebücher,* April 10, 1933.
19. *Münchener Neueste Nachrichten,* April 16–17, 1933.
20. Golo Mann, *Reminiscences and Reflections,* pp. 299–300.
21. *Tagebücher,* April 20, 1933.
22. Letter to Gottfried Bermann Fischer, July 18, 1933.
23. *Tagebücher,* April 30 and May 3, 1933.
24. Letter to René Schickele, April 21, 1933.
25. Sybille Bedford, *Aldous Huxley,* vol. 1 (London, 1973), p. 276.
26. René Schickele; *Tagebücher,* May 8 and 15, 1933, in *Werke in Drei Bände* (Cologne, 1959).
27. Letter to Klaus, May 31, 1933.
28. *Tagebücher,* June 8, 1933, and July 20, 1933.
29. *Tagebücher,* May 2, 1934.
30. Letter to Gottfried Bermann Fischer, n.d., ca. August 24, 1933.
31. Letter to Klaus, August 24, 1933.
32. *Börsenblatt für den Deutschen Buchhandel* (Nazi pamphlet), October 10, 1933.
33. *Arbeiter Zeitung,* October 25, 1933.

34. *Neue Deutsche Blätter,* November 1933.
35. Klaus Mann, *The Turning Point,* p. 277.
36. Monika Mann, in *The Saturday Review,* June 4, 1955.
37. Letter to Carl Hebling, October 25, 1933.
38. Letter to Ida Herz, November 5, 1933.
39. Letter to Alex Frey, December 30, 1933.
40. Letter to Ernst Bertram, November 19, 1933.
41. Letter to Ernst Bertram, June 24, 1934.
42. Letter to Julius Meier-Graefe, December 23, 1933.
43. Letter to Viktor Wittkowski, December 25, 1933.
44. *Tagebücher,* February 11, 1934.
45. Letter to Ernst Bertram, January 9, 1934.
46. *Tagebücher,* January 1, 1934.
47. *Tagebücher,* February 21, 1934.
48. *Tagebücher,* March 14, 1934.
49. *Tagebücher,* February 28, 1934.
50. Letter to René Schickele, April 2, 1934.
51. *Tagebücher,* January 2, 1934.
52. Letter to Ernst Bertram, January 9, 1934.
53. Letter to Alfred Knopf, January 20, 1934.
54. *Gesammelte Werke,* vol. 4, pp. 716–17.
55. *Joseph in Egypt (Joseph in Ägypten),* pp. 730–31.
56. *Tagebücher,* March 20, 1934.
57. Letter to René Schickele, April 2, 1934.
58. *Tagebücher,* May 6, 1934.
59. "Meerfahrt mit Don Quijote" ("Voyage with Don Quixote"), *Essays of Three Decades.*
60. Letter to Jewish Rescue League, n.d., before June 9, 1934.
61. Letter to Gottfried Bermann Fischer, June 29, 1934.
62. Letter to Karl Kerényi, August 4, 1934.
63. *Tagebücher,* August 4, 1934.
64. *Tagebücher,* August 5, 1934.
65. Letter to Karl Kerényi, August 4, 1934.
66. Letter to Ida Herz, August 25, 1934.

67. Letter to René Schickele, August 10, 1934.
68. Letter to Karl Kerényi, August 4, 1934.
69. *Tagebücher,* August 5, 1934.
70. Letter from Heinrich, September 20, 1934.
71. Letter to Ida Herz, October 22, 1934.
72. Letters to Gottfried Bermann Fischer, November 1 and 11, 1934.
73. Letter to the editor of *Selbstwehr,* February 3, 1935.
74. *Tagebücher,* January 31, 1935.
75. Letter to Ida Herz, March 14, 1935.
76. *Tagebücher,* March 23, 1935.
77. Letter to Massimo Pilotty, March 30, 1935.
78. *Tagebücher,* April 10, 1935.
79. *Tagebücher,* April 19, 1935.
80. *Tagebücher,* March 23, 1935.
81. *Tagebücher,* March 16, 1935.
82. Letter to Ferdinand Lion, April 29, 1935.
83. *Die Sammlung,* June 1935.
84. Letter to René Schickele, June 7, 1935.

CHAPTER 28

1. Humphrey Carpenter, *W. H. Auden: A Biography* (London, 1981), pp. 186–97.
2. *Tagebücher,* June 21, 1935.
3. Letter to Gottfried Bermann Fischer, September 5, 1935.
4. *Tagebücher,* June 28, 1935.
5. Monika Mann, in *The Saturday Review,* June 4, 1955.
6. *Tagebücher,* June 29, 1935.
7. Letters to Fischer Verlag, n.d., and Gottfried Bermann Fischer, September 5, 1935.
8. *Tagebücher,* September 5, 1935.
9. *Tagebücher,* September 14, 1935.
10. *Tagebücher,* September 21, 1935.
11. Letter to Ida Herz, September 12, 1935.
12. Letter to René Schickele, November 24, 1935.
13. Letter to René Schickele, July 25, 1935.
14. *Tagebücher,* November 3, 1935; letter to Alfred Knopf, November 8, 1935.
15. *Tagebücher,* January 1, 1936.
16. Letter to Harry Slochower, September 1, 1935.
17. *Tagebücher,* January 7, 1936.
18. Leopold Schwarzschild, in *Neue Tage-Buch,* January 11, 1936.
19. Letter from Erika, April 20, 1935.
20. Letter from Erika, January 1, 1936.
21. Letter to Erika, January 23, 1936.
22. Letter from Erika, January 26, 1936.
23. Telegram from Klaus Mann and Fritz Landshoff, January 26, 1936.
24. *Tagebücher,* January 27, 1936.
25. Open letter to Eduard Korrodi, February 3, 1936.
26. Letter to Annette Kolb, February 2, 1936.
27. *Tagebücher,* February 3, 1936.
28. Letter to René Schickele, February 19, 1936.
29. *Tagebücher,* February 7, 1936.
30. Letter from Klaus, February 5, 1936.
31. Letter from Hermann Hesse, February 9, 1936.
32. Letter to René Schickele, February 19, 1936.
33. Letter to Hermann Hesse, March 7, 1936.
34. *Tagebücher,* May 1, 1936.
35. *Tagebücher,* March 8, 1936.
36. *Tagebücher,* March 9 and 14, 1936.
37. *Neue Weltbühne,* March 26, 1936.
38. Letter to Heinrich, July 20, 1936.
39. *Tagebücher,* August 14, 1936.
40. *Tagebücher,* May 13, 1936. Freud repeated his ideas about Joseph and Napoleon in his letter to Thomas, November 29, 1936.
41. Letter to Heinrich, July 2, 1936.
42. Ibid.
43. *Tagebücher,* July 21 and August 13, 1936.
44. Letter to Ida Herz, August 14, 1936.
45. Letter to Ida Herz, July 25, 1936.
46. Letter to Alexander Frey, November 10, 1936.
47. *Tagebücher,* August 23, 1936.
48. Letter to Bruno Walter, October 18, 1936.
49. Letter to Max Mohr, August 26, 1936.
50. Letter to unknown person, September 19, 1936.
51. Letter to Heinrich, September 27, 1936.
52. Letter to Anna Jacobson, November 13, 1936.

53. Letter to Frida Uhl-Strindberg, October 3, 1936.
54. Letter to Gottfried Bermann Fischer, October 31, 1936.
55. *Central-Vereins-Zeitung,* November 5, 1936; letter to Julius Bab, November 9, 1936.
56. Letter to Gottfried Bermann Fischer, October 24, 1936.
57. Letter to Paul Amann, November 25, 1936.
58. *Tagebücher,* December 3, 1936.
59. Letter to Jan Kozak, November 30, 1936.
60. Imre Bekessy, *How Rudolf Fleischmann from Proseč met Thomas Mann.* Translation of an article that appeared during 1937 in a Hungarian newspaper, privately printed and sent out as a Christmas card by Rudolf and Dr. S. Fleischmann from an address in Preston, Lancs, 1957.
61. Letter to Gottfried Bermann Fischer, December 5, 1936.
62. Letter to the editor of Deutsche Information in the *Berner Tagwacht* and the *Pariser Zeitung,* n.d.
63. Letter to Sigmund Freud, December 13, 1936.
64. *Tagebücher,* December 25, 1936.
65. Letter to the dean of Bonn University, New Year's 1937.
66. Letter to Lavinia Mazzucchetti, February 20, 1937.
67. Golo Mann, *Erinnerungen an meinem Vater,* p. 16.

CHAPTER 29

1. *Tagebücher,* January 1, 1937.
2. "Ein Nachwort," *Lübecker General Anzeiger,* November 7, 1905.
3. Letters to Karl Barth, February 22, 1937, and Hermann Hesse, February 23, 1937.
4. *Tagebücher,* April 7, 9, 10, 1937.
5. Letter to Karl Kerényi, May 4, 1937.
6. *Tagebücher,* April 28, 1937.
7. *Tagebücher,* May 4, 1937.
8. *Tagebücher,* June 2, 1937.
9. Letter to René Schickele, May 31, 1937.
10. Letters to Klaus, June 4, 1937, and Lajos Hatvany, June 16, 1937.
11. Foreword to first issue of *Mass und Wert,* September-October 1937.

12. Letter to Hermann Hesse, June 16, 1937.
13. Letter to Otto Basler, June 21, 1937.
14. Letters to Karl Löwenstein, June 26, 1937; Helen Lowe-Porter, July 6, 1937; and Herman Hesse, July 10, 1937.
15. *Tagebücher,* July 17, 1937.
16. Letter to Kuno Fiedler, July 20, 1937; *Tagebücher,* August 2, 1937.
17. Letters to W. Isaakow, September 20, 1937, and Ida Herz, October 9, 1937.
18. *Tagebücher,* October 13, 1937.
19. Ibid.
20. *Tagebücher,* October 26, 1937.
21. Ibid.
22. Letter to Kuno Fiedler, October 27, 1937.
23. *Tagebücher,* December 24, 1937.
24. *Tagebücher,* November 16, 1937.
25. Letter to René Schickele, January 27, 1938.
26. *Order of the Day,* p. 143.
27. Ibid., p. 144.
28. Letter to René Schickele, November 27, 1937.
29. Letter to Alfred Neumann, December 28, 1937.
30. *Tagebücher,* January 11, 1938.
31. Letter to Félix Bertaux, January 4, 1938.
32. Letter to Hermann Kesten, January 30, 1938.
33. *Tagebücher,* February 19, 1938.
34. *Tagebücher,* March 20, 1938.
35. *Tagebücher,* June 27, 1938.
36. Letter to Agnes Meyer, n.d., dictated May 24, 1938.
37. Letter to Agnes Meyer, March 21, 1938.
38. *Tagebücher,* March 20, 1938.
39. Letters to Gottfried Bermann Fischer, April 8 and 15, 1938.
40. Letter to René Schickele, July 15, 1938.
41. Letter to Ferdinand Lion, February 13, 1938; *Tagebücher,* April 1, 1938.
42. *Tagebücher,* March 22, 1938.
43. Letter to unknown female correspondent, May 21, 1938.
44. Letter to Agnes Meyer, April 13, 1938.
45. "A Brother," in *Order of the Day.*

CHAPTER 30

1. *Tagebücher,* May 24 and June 11, 1938.

2. Letter to Christian Gauss, June 6, 1938.
3. Letter to Gottfried Bermann Fischer, June 24, 1938; *Tagebücher,* June 27, 1938.
4. *Tagebücher,* July 7, 1938.
5. Letters to Agnes Meyer, July 18, 1938, and Heinrich, August 6, 1938.
6. Letter to Fritz von Unruh, July 19, 1938.
7. *Tagebücher,* September 1, 1938.
8. *Tagebücher,* September 8, 1938.
9. *Tagebücher,* September 19, 1938.
10. *Tagebücher,* September 20 and 21, 1938.
11. *Order of the Day,* p. 180.
12. *Tagebücher,* September 27, 1938.
13. *Order of the Day,* p. xiv.
14. Letter to Erich von Kahler, October 19, 1938.
15. *Order of the Day,* pp. 167–77.
16. Letter to Hermann Hesse, December 6, 1938.
17. Monika Mann, p. 91.
18. Letter to Erich von Kahler, October 19, 1938.
19. *Tagebücher,* December 20, 1938.
20. Letter to Agnes Meyer, October 6, 1938.
21. *Tagebücher,* September 26, 1938.
22. *Tagebücher,* December 20, 1938.
23. Prelude to *Faust.*
24. Letter to Viktor Polzer, March 23, 1940.
25. Letter to Gottfried Bermann Fischer, December 6, 1938.
26. Letter to Malcolm MacDonald, January 10, 1939.
27. Letter to home secretary, April 27, 1939.
28. Letters to Frank Altschul, January 18 and 27, 1939.
29. *Tagebücher,* February 27, 1939; letters to Hendrik van Loon, February 15, 1939, William H. Bragg, February 20, 1939, and H. M. Lydenberg, April 17, 1939.
30. Letter to Walt Disney, February 9, 1939.
31. *Tagebücher,* February 20, 1939.
32. *Tagebücher,* February 14, 1939.

CHAPTER 31

1. *Tagebücher,* February 20, 1939.
2. Charles Neider, *The Stature of Thomas Mann,* pp. 98–100.

3. *Aufbau,* June 8, 1945.
4. Conversation with Elisabeth Mann Borgese, February 28, 1994.
5. Letter to John B. Cunningham, August 22, 1941.
6. *On Myself (Über mich selbst),* p. 92.
7. Ibid.
8. *Tagebücher,* March 14, 1939.
9. *Tagebücher,* March 29, 1939.
10. *Tagebücher,* March 12, 1939.
11. *Tagebücher,* March 16 and 28, 1939.
12. Letter to Agnes Meyer, May 20, 1939.
13. Letters to Heinrich, May 14, 1939, and Franz Werfel, May 26, 1939.
14. *Tagebücher,* June 5 and 6, 1939.
15. Letter to Ida Herz, June 16, 1939.
16. *Tagebücher,* June 18, 1939.
17. Letter to Viktor Polzer, March 25, 1940.
18. Letter to L. Servicen, August 13, 1939.
19. *Tagebücher,* August 9, 1939.
20. *Tagebücher,* August 23 and 25, 1939.
21. Letter to Heinrich, November 26, 1939.
22. Letter to Golo, September 26, 1939.
23. Ibid.
24. Foreword to *Mass und Wert,* November–December 1939.
25. *Tagebücher,* September 19, 1939.
26. Letter to Golo, September 26, 1939.
27. Letter to Stefan Zweig, January 4, 1940.
28. *Order of the Day,* pp. 190–225.
29. Letter to Caroline Newton, November 5, 1939.
30. Neider, p. 35.
31. Letter to Heinrich, November 26, 1939.
32. Conversation with Elisabeth Mann Borgese, February 28, 1994.
33. Letters to Stefan Zweig, January 4, 1940, and Kuno Fiedler, February 22, 1940.
34. Letter to Heinrich, March 3, 1940.
35. Foreword to *Joseph and His Brothers (Joseph und seine Brüder).*
36. Letter to Agnes Meyer, July 27, 1940.
37. Letter to Agnes Meyer, January 5, 1940.
38. *Tagebücher,* December 9 and 26, 1939.

39. Letter to Agnes Meyer, January 5, 1940.
40. Letters to Caroline Newton, April 8, 1940, and Kuno Fiedler, June 26, 1940.
41. Letter to Agnes Meyer, May 4, 1940.
42. Letter to Agnes Meyer, March 22, 1940.
43. Letter to Agnes Meyer, May 25, 1940.
44. Letter to Emil Oprecht, June 15, 1940.
45. Letter to Bert Berg, June 26, 1940.
46. Letter to Kuno Fiedler, June 26, 1940.
47. Letter to Martin Beheim-Schwarzbach, May 3, 1940.

CHAPTER 32

1. Agnes Meyer, *Out of These Roots: The Autobiography of an American Woman.*
2. Letter to Erich von Kahler, July 8, 1940.
3. Letter to Charles Jordan, September 26, 1941.
4. Ibid.
5. Ibid.
6. *Tagebücher,* July 31, 1940.
7. Letter to Agnes Meyer, August 8, 1940.
8. Letter to Alexander Frey, August 10, 1940.
9. Klaus Mann, *The Turning Point,* p. 331.
10. Letter to Carl Helbling, September 13, 1940.
11. Letter to Alfred Knopf, August 29, 1940.
12. *Tagebücher,* October 24, 1940.
13. *Tagebücher,* August 26, October 26, November 20, December 20 and 31, 1940.
14. *Tagebücher,* September 14, 1940.
15. Letter to Ida Herz, October 4, 1940.
16. Letter to Ida Herz, October 4, 1940; *Tagebücher,* November 7, 1940.
17. "Deutsche Hörer!," BBC radio broadcast.
18. Klaus Wendepunkt augmented German edition of *The Turning Point.*
19. Thomas Mann Archive, Zurich
20. Letter to Kuno Fiedler, November 15, 1940.
21. "The Lotus Eaters," by Herbert Agar, *Chicago Daily Press,* November 26, 1940.
22. Letter to Hendrik van Loon, November 29, 1940.
23. Letter to Agnes Meyer, December 25, 1931.
24. Letter to Hendrik van Loon, December 30, 1940.
25. *Tagebücher,* January 13, 1941.
26. "The War and Future," in *Order of the Day.*
27. Letter to Agnes Meyer, January 24, 1941.
28. Letter to Caroline Newton, September 1, 1940.
29. Letter to Bruno Frank, February 4, 1941.
30. Letter to Agnes Meyer, January 24, 1941.
31. *Tagebücher,* January 14, 1941.
32. *Tagebücher,* March 10, 1941.
33. Letter to Agnes Meyer, March 12, 1941.
34. Ibid.
35. *Tagebücher,* March 13, 1941.
36. *Tagebücher,* March 17, 1941.
37. *Tagebücher,* March 18 and 19, 1941.
38. Letter to Erich von Kahler, March 30, 1941.
39. *Tagebücher,* March 23, 1941.
40. Letter to Erich von Kahler, March 30, 1941.
41. Ibid.
42. *Tagebücher,* March 26, 1941.
43. Letter to Erich von Kahler, March 30, 1941.
44. *Tagebücher,* April 8, 1941.
45. *Tagebücher,* April 9, 1941.
46. *Tagebücher,* May 20, 1940, and May 10, 1941.
47. Letter to Hermann Kesten, n.d., postmarked April 13, 1941; letters to Agnes Meyer, April 18, 1941, and Kurt Wolff, April 21, 1941.
48. *Tagebücher,* April 23, 1941.
49. *Tagebücher,* May 9, 1941.
50. Letter to Gottfried Bermann Fischer, April 19, 1941.
51. Letters to Erich von Kahler, May 25 and June 1, 1941.
52. Letter to Ida Herz, September 23, 1941; *Tagebücher,* July 21, 1941.
53. "Niemöller," in *Order of the Day.*
54. Letter to Bruno Walter, May 6, 1943.
55. Ronald Hayman, *Bertolt Brecht*

(London and New York, 1983), p. 255.

56. *Tagebücher,* September 13, 1941.
57. *Tagebücher,* August 20, 1941.
58. *Tagebücher,* September 29, 1941.
59. *Tagebücher,* May 19, 1941.
60. *Washington Post* and *New York Times Book Review,* June 8, 1941; letter to Agnes Meyer, June 11, 1941; *Tagebücher,* May 24, 1941.
61. Letter to Agnes Meyer, June 11, 1941.
62. Letter to Agnes Meyer, June 18, 1941.
63. Letter to Agnes Meyer, July 26, 1941.
64. Letter to Agnes Meyer, October 3, 1941.
65. *Tagebücher,* October 8 and 9, 1941.
66. Letter to Agnes Meyer, October 7, 1941.
67. *Tagebücher,* September 19, 1941.
68. *Tagebücher,* October 15–17, 1941.
69. *Tagebücher,* October 18, 1941.
70. *Tagebücher,* October 21, 1941.
71. *Tagebücher,* October 25, 1941.
72. Letter to Agnes Meyer, November 3, 1942.
73. *Tagebücher,* November 7, 1941.
74. Letter to Oscar Maria Graf, October 1, 1941.
75. *Tagebücher,* October 29 and 30, 1941.
76. *Tagebücher,* November 26, 1941.
77. Letter to Agnes Meyer, November 28, 1941.
78. Letter to Georg Martin Richter, December 6, 1941.
79. *Tagebücher,* December 2, 1941.
80. *Tagebücher,* December 9, 1941.
81. Letter to Agnes Meyer, December 27, 1941.

CHAPTER 33

1. Conversation with Elisabeth Borgese Mann, February 28, 1994.
2. Konrad Kellen, *Yale Review,* March 1965.
3. Ibid.
4. Letter to Agnes Meyer, December 27, 1941.
5. Letter to Francis Biddle, December 31, 1941.
6. Letter to Antoinette von Kahler, n.d., about June 14, 1942.
7. *Tagebücher,* January 17, 1942.
8. Letter to Agnes Meyer, January 22, 1942.

9. Ibid.
10. *Tagebücher,* January 20, 1942.
11. *Tagebücher,* January 24, 1942.
12. *Tagebücher,* January 6, 1942.
13. *Tagebücher,* January 7, 1942.
14. Letter to Herman Hesse, March 15, 1942.
15. *Tagebücher,* February 14, 1942.
16. Konrad Kellen, *Yale Review,* March 1965.
17. Letter to Hermann Hesse, March 15, 1942.
18. Katia Mann, *Unwritten Memories,* p. 120.
19. *Tagebücher,* January 29, 1942.
20. Telegram to Franklin D. Roosevelt, February 9, 1942.
21. Letter to Kurt Klaber, February 15, 1942.
22. *Tagebücher,* February 13, 1942.
23. *Tagebücher,* February 18, 1942.
24. Letter to Molly Shenstone, January 29, 1942.
25. *Tagebücher,* March 22, 1942.
26. *Tagebücher,* March 25, 1942.
27. Letter to Agnes Meyer, February 18, 1942.
28. *Tagebücher,* February 21, 1942.
29. Letter to Agnes Meyer, February 21, 1942.
30. Letter to Agnes Meyer, March 8, 1942.
31. *Tagebücher,* March 2, 1942.
32. *Tagebücher,* March 9, 1942.
33. *Tagebücher,* March 3 and 18, 1942.
34. *Tagebücher,* March 30, 1942.
35. *Tagebücher,* March 31, 1942.
36. *Tagebücher,* April 2, 1942.
37. *Tagebücher,* April 4, 1942.
38. *Tagebücher,* January 28, 1942.
39. Letter to Kurt Hiller, March 30, 1942.
40. Letter to Hermann Hesse, March 15, 1942, and Kuno Fiedler, May 10, 1942.
41. Letter to Agnes Meyer, May 5, 1942.
42. Letter to Ida Herz, June 5, 1942.
43. Letter to Kuno Fiedler, June 4, 1942.
44. *Tagebücher,* May 1, 1942.
45. *Tagebücher,* April 21 and 29, 1942.
46. *Tagebücher,* June 26, 1942.
47. *Tagebücher,* April 9, 1942.
48. Letter to Agnes Meyer, April 11, 1942.
49. Letter to Agnes Meyer, April 27–28, 1942.

50. *Tagebücher*, May 22–23, 1942.
51. Letter to Agnes Meyer, May 26–27, 1942.
52. *Tagebücher*, May 27, 1942.
53. Letters to Verner Clapp, July 6, 1942, and Agnes Meyer, July 23, 1942.
54. *Tagebücher*, August 19, 1942.
55. Letter to Agnes Meyer, July 25, 1942.
56. *Tagebücher*, August 19 and 27, 1942; letter to Agnes Meyer, August 20, 1942.
57. *Tagebücher*, July 13, 1942; letter to Helen Lowe-Porter, July 16, 1942.
58. *Tagebücher*, September 20, 1942; letter to Rudolf Humm, September 24, 1942.
59. Letter to Agnes Meyer, June 27, 1942.
60. *Tagebücher*, July 5, 1942.
61. Letter to John T. Frederick, November 2, 1942.
62. *Tagebücher*, July 5, 1942.
63. *Tagebücher*, November 13, 1942.
64. *Tagebücher*, November 11, 1942.
65. *Tagebücher*, November 18, 1942.
66. Ibid.
67. *Tagebücher*, November 22, 1942.
68. Ibid.
69. *Tagebücher*, November 29, 1942.
70. *Tagebücher*, November 30, 1942.
71. *Tagebücher*, December 11, 1942.
72. *Tagebücher*, December 13, 1942.
73. Letter to Agnes Meyer, December 15, 1942.
74. Letter to Agnes Meyer, December 19, 1942.
75. Letter to Agnes Meyer, December 24, 1942.
76. *Tagebücher*, January 4, 1943.
77. Letter to Agnes Meyer, January 5, 1943.

CHAPTER 34

1. *Genesis of a Novel*.
2. Letter from Sigmund Freud to Hans Ehrenwald, December 14, 1937.
3. Letter to Richard Weil, August 9, 1945.
4. Letter to Agnes Meyer, February 17, 1943.
5. Letter to Schalom Ben-Chorin, August 10, 1945.
6. *Genesis of a Novel*.
7. Letter to Agnes Meyer, January 28, 1943.
8. Letter to Klaus, March 9, 1943.
9. *Notizbuch* 7, pp. 138 and 155, Thomas Mann Archive.
10. *Tagebücher*, March 17, 1943.
11. Ibid., p. 138.
12. Ibid., p. 155.
13. Thomas Mann Archive, Manuscript 33, folio 8.
14. Ibid., folio 9.
15. *Tagebücher*, March 21, 1943.
16. *Tagebücher*, April 11, 1943.
17. Letter to Agnes Meyer, January 5, 1943.
18. *Tagebücher*, April 2, 1943.
19. Letter to Agnes Meyer, May 8, 1943.
20. *Tagebücher*, May 19, 1943.
21. *Tagebücher*, May 25–26, 1943.
22. Letter to Agnes Meyer, May 26, 1943.
23. *Tagebücher*, May 31, 1943.
24. *Tagebücher*, June 1, 1943.
25. *Tagebücher*, May 4, 1943; letter to Bruno Walter, May 6, 1943.
26. *Genesis of a Novel*, pp. 25–26.
27. Letter to Agnes Meyer, July 6, 1943.
28. *Tagebücher*, June 2, 1943.
29. *Tagebücher*, October 13, 1937.
30. *Genesis of a Novel*, p. 181.
31. Letter to H. H. Stückenschmidt, October 19, 1951.
32. *Tagebücher*, July 17, 1943.
33. *Tagebücher*, September 30, 1943.
34. Letter to Theodor Adorno, October 5, 1943.
35. Ibid.
36. *Tagebücher*, August 27–28, 1943.
37. Igor Stravinsky and Robert Craft, *Expositions and Developments* (London, 1962).
38. *Genesis of a Novel*, p. 43.
39. Letter to Felix Braun, July 31, 1943.
40. Letter to Agnes Meyer, August 27, 1943.
41. Letter to Konrad Kellen, August 19, 1943.
42. Letter to Paul Hagen, August 6, 1943; Bertolt Brecht, *Arbeitsjournal*, August 1, 1943; James K. Lyon, *Brecht in America* (Princeton, N. J., 1980), p. 261.
43. Letter to Agnes Meyer, August 9, 1943.

44. Letter to Adolf Berle, November 18, 1932.
45. Telegram to Agnes Meyer, August 28, 1943.
46. *Tagebücher,* September 12, 1943.
47. Letter to Agnes Meyer, September 13, 1943.
48. *Tagebücher,* September 17, 1943.
49. Letter to Agnes Meyer, September 18, 1943.
50. *Tagebücher,* September 19, 1943.
51. *Genesis of a Novel.*
52. Letter to Agnes Meyer, December 5, 1943.
53. Letter to Agnes Meyer, October 27, 1943.
54. Ibid.
55. *Tagebücher,* December 8, 1943.
56. Letter to Agnes Meyer, December 5, 1943.
57. Letter to Bertolt Brecht, December 10, 1943.

CHAPTER 35

1. *Tagebücher,* January 5, 1944; letter to Agnes Meyer, January 7, 1944.
2. Letter to Agnes Meyer, January 22, 1944.
3. *Tagebücher,* January 17, 1944.
4. *Tagebücher,* June 18, 1944.
5. Letter to Erich von Kahler, January 16, 1944.
6. *Genesis of a Novel,* p. 69.
7. Letter to Kurt Wolff, May 20, 1944.
8. Letter to Agnes Meyer, February 16, 1944.
9. *Tagebücher,* January 31, 1944.
10. Letter to Agnes Meyer, February 2, 1944.
11. *Tagebücher,* February 14, 1944.
12. Letter to Agnes Meyer, April 28, 1944.
13. Zurich, 1943.
14. *Tagebücher,* May 5, 1944.
15. Letter to Hermann Hesse, April 8, 1945.
16. Felix Langner, *Stepping Stones to Peace* (London, 1943).
17. *Genesis of a Novel,* p. 60.
18. *Tagebücher,* January 11 and 13, 1944; letter to Erich von Kahler, January 16, 1944.
19. Draft for letter to C. B. Boutell, January 21, 1944.
20. *Tagebücher,* February 19, 1944.
21. *Tagebücher,* April 22, 1944.

22. Letter to Reinhold Niebuhr, April 23, 1944.
23. Letter to C. Fadiman, May 29, 1944.
24. *Tagebücher,* June 6, 1944.
25. *Genesis of a Novel,* p. 69.
26. Letter to Thelma Thompson, July 20, 1944.
27. Letter to Agnes Meyer, July 11, 1944.
28. *Tagebücher,* July 11, 1944.
29. *Doctor Faustus.*
30. *Tagebücher,* November 18, 1944.
31. *Tagebücher,* June 20, 1944.
32. Letter to Agnes Meyer, January 22, 1944.
33. Letter to F. Warburg, July 14, 1944.
34. Letter to Alfred Knopf, November 28, 1944.
35. Letter to Kate Hamburger, October 2, 1944.
36. *Tagebücher,* July 21, 1944.
37. *Tagebücher,* July 19, 1944.
38. *Tagebücher,* September 29–30, 1944.
39. *Tagebücher,* October 29, 1944; *Genesis of a Novel,* pp. 81–82.
40. *Tagebücher,* November 1–8, 1944; *Genesis of a Novel,* pp. 82–83.
41. *Tagebücher,* November 16–17, 1944; letter to Agnes Meyer, November 17, 1944; *Genesis of a Novel,* pp. 83–84.
42. *Tagebücher,* November 19, 1944.
43. *Doctor Faustus.*
44. *Genesis of a Novel,* p. 76.
45. *Doctor Faustus.*
46. Ibid.
47. *Tagebücher,* July 22, 1944.
48. Interview with Golo Mann, in *Die Zeit,* February 23, 1973.
49. Letter from Heinrich to Eva Lips, quoted in her book *Zwischen Lehrstuhl und Indianerzeit* (Berlin, 1965).
50. Nigel Hamilton, *The Brothers Mann,* p. 329.
51. *Tagebücher,* December 17, 1744.
52. *Tagebücher,* December 20, 1944.
53. Letter to Agnes Meyer, January 7, 1945.
54. Letter to Alfred Knopf, January 5, 1945.
55. Letter to Alfred Knopf, January 12, 1945.
56. *Reich,* November 26, 1944; *Tagebücher,* January 16, 1945.
57. *Doctor Faustus.*

58. Letter to Agnes Meyer, January 7, 1945.
59. *Tagebücher*, February 14, 1945.
60. *Tagebücher*, May 3, 1945.
61. Letter to Agnes Meyer, April 24, 1945.
62. *Tagebücher*, February 20, 1945; *Genesis of a Novel*, p. 89.
63. *Doctor Faustus*.
64. *Tagebücher*, February 4, 1945.
65. *Tagebücher*, February 12, 1945.
66. *Gesammelte Werke*, vol. 12, p. 946.
67. Letter to Agnes Meyer, March 29, 1945.
68. Letter to Heinrich, April 8, 1945.
69. Letter to Bruno Walter, March 1, 1945.
70. *Tagebücher*, January 15, 1945.
71. *Tagebücher*, February 3, 11, 12, 1945.
72. *Tagebücher*, March 9, 1945.
73. Letter to Hermann Hesse, April 8, 1945.
74. *Genesis of a Novel*, p. 93.
75. Letter to A. W. Heinitz, April 19, 1945.
76. Letter to Erich von Kahler, May 1, 1945.
77. Ibid.
78. *Tagebücher*, May 7, 1945.
79. Ibid.
80. Ibid.
81. *Tagebücher*, May 15, 1945; letter to Anna Jacobson, April 25, 1945.
82. *Tagebücher*, September 29, 1945.
83. Erika Mann, "Brief an meinem Vater," *Aufbau*, June 8, 1945.
84. *Genesis of a Novel*, p. 97.
85. *Tagebücher*, May 18, 1945.
86. *Tagebücher*, May 28, 1945.
87. *Die Neue Rundschau*, June 6, 1945.
88. Letters to Golo, June 22, 1945, and Heinrich, June 9, 1945.
89. *Tagebücher*, June 13, 1945; *Aufbau*, June 8, 1945.
90. *Die Neue Rundschau*, June 6, 1945.
91. *Tagebücher*, June 13, 1945; *Genesis of a Novel*, pp. 100–101.
92. Letter to Alfred Neumann, postmarked June 11, 1945.
93. *Tagebücher*, June 15–24, 1945; *Genesis of a Novel*, p. 105.
94. *Tagebücher*, June 25, 1945.
95. Ibid.; letter to Kuno Fiedler, August 20, 1945.
96. *Tagebücher*, August 19 and 20, 1945.

CHAPTER 36

1. "Dostoyevsky—in Moderation," introduction to *The Short Novels of Dostoyevsky* (New York, 1945).
2. Sigmund Freud, "Dostoyevsky and Parricide," *Complete Psychological Works*, vol. 21.
3. Ibid.
4. Friedrich Nietzsche, *Ecce Homo* and *Menschliches, Allzumenschliches*.
5. *Doctor Faustus*.
6. *Essays*, vol. I: *Literatur*, p. 169.
7. Ibid., p. 173.
8. Ibid., p. 175.
9. Hayman, *Nietzsche*, p. 304.
10. Paul Deussen, *Erinnerungen an Friedrich Nietzsche* (Dresden, 1901).
11. "Nietzsches Philosophie," in *Neue Studien*.
12. *Essays*, pp. 173–74.
13. *Tagebücher*, August 3, 1945.
14. *Genesis of a Novel*, p. 155.
15. Letter to Agnes Meyer, August 25, 1945.
16. Ibid.
17. Letter to Gerard Speyer, September 3, 1945.
18. *Tagebücher*, September 4, 1945.
19. Letter to Walter von Molo, September 7, 1945.
20. Letter to Joseph Publitzer, August 8, 1945.
21. *Genesis of a Novel*, p. 114.
22. Max Barth, in *Neue Deutsche Volkszeitung*, September 15, 1945.
23. Letter to K. Tucholsky, October 28, 1945.
24. *Doctor Faustus*.
25. Ibid., p. 407.
26. *Tagebücher*, August 7, 1945.
27. *Tagebücher*, July 23, 1945; letter to Theodor Adorno, December 30, 1945.
28. Erika Mann, *Briefe und Antworten*, pp. 207–208.
29. *Tagebücher*, December 2, 1945.
30. *Tagebücher*, November 29, 1945.
31. Letter to Agnes Meyer, December 14, 1945; *Genesis of a Novel*, p. 119.
32. *Doctor Faustus*.
33. Ibid.
34. Ibid.
35. Ibid.
36. *Tagebücher*, December 7, 1945.

37. *Doctor Faustus.*
38. Letter to Pierre-Paul Sagave, postmarked January 28, 1946.
39. Letter to Theodor Adorno, December 30, 1945.
40. Broadcast by Frank Thiess on December 30, 1946, reprinted in the *Ruhr-Zeitung,* January 5, 1946.
41. Letter to Bruno Walter, February 9, 1946.
42. Letter to Anna Jacobson, June 9, 1946.
43. Letter to Agnes Meyer, February 6, 1946.
44. *Tagebücher,* February 13, 1946.
45. Letter to Hermann Hesse, November 25, 1945.
46. Letter to Rudolf Humm, February 3, 1946.
47. *Tagebücher,* January 1, 1946.
48. *Tagebücher,* January 13, 1946.
49. *Tagebücher,* June 7 and 30, 1946.
50. *Tagebücher,* February 20, 1946; *Genesis of a Novel,* p. 130.
51. *Tagebücher,* May 28–April 1, 1946.
52. *Genesis of a Novel,* pp. 139–45.
53. *Genesis of a Novel,* pp. 145–48; *Tagebücher,* May 28, 1946.
54. *Tagebücher,* May 31 and June 1, 1946; *Genesis of a Novel,* p. 151.
55. Letter to Viktor, June 15, 1946; *Tagebücher,* June 17 and 18, 1946.
56. Letter to Ida Herz, June 14, 1946.
57. Konrad Kellen, *Yale Review,* March 1965.
58. *Doctor Faustus.*

CHAPTER 37

1. *Tagebücher,* September 1, 1946.
2. Letter to Lord Inverchapel, August 17, 1946.
3. *Genesis of a Novel,* pp. 162–63.
4. *Tagebücher,* October 6, 1946.
5. *Tagebücher,* September 23, 1946; *Genesis of a Novel,* p. 167.
6. *Tagebücher,* October 26, 1946.
7. *Doctor Faustus.*
8. Ibid.
9. Ibid., pp. 577–83.
10. *Genesis of a Novel,* p. 167.
11. *Tagebücher,* October 1, 1946; *Genesis of a Novel,* p. 166.
12. *Tagebücher,* October 9 and 11, 1946; *Genesis of a Novel,* pp. 166–67.
13. *Doctor Faustus.*

14. *Genesis of a Novel,* p. 174; *Tagebücher,* December 12, 1946.
15. *Tagebücher,* January 8, 1947.
16. *Doctor Faustus.*
17. Ibid.
18. Ibid.
19. Ibid.
20. *Tagebücher,* January 29, 1947.
21. *Tagebücher,* February 6 and 7, 1947.
22. Letter to Viktor, January 27, 1947.
23. Letter to Félix Bertaux, January 12, 1947.
24. *Tagebücher,* December 22, 1946.
25. *Aufbau,* January 3, 1947; *Tagebücher,* January 7, 1947; *Genesis of a Novel,* p. 182; letter to Viktor, March 27, 1947.
26. Letter to Klaus, March 19, 1947.
27. *The German American,* March 7, 1947.
28. *Tagebücher,* March 16, 1947.
29. Speech to Berliner Spruchkammer, December 17, 1946.
30. Draft of letter to *Aufbau,* March 10, 1947.
31. *Tagebücher,* March 11, 1947.
32. Letter to Manfred George, March 11, 1947.
33. "Untimely Reflections on the Uses and Disadvantages of History in Life" ("Unzeitgemässe Betrachtungen vom Nützen und Nachteil der Historie im Leben").
34. Letter to Alice Dorbecker, March 21, 1947.
35. *Tagebücher,* March 26, 1947.
36. Letter to Viktor, March 27, 1947.
37. *Tagebücher,* April 24, 1947.
38. *Tagebücher,* April 20, 1947.
39. *Tagebücher,* May 3, 1947.
40. *Chronik,* p. 208.
41. *New York Times,* May 18, 1947.
42. Reprinted in *Tagebücher,* 1946–48.
43. *Tagebücher,* May 21, 1947.
44. *Frankfürter Neue Presse,* May 24, 1947.
45. Letter to Hermann Hesse, June 14, 1947.
46. Heinrich Heine, "Nachtgedanken," 1843.
47. Letter to Ernst Benedikt, June 28, 1947.
48. Edward Korrodi, in *Neue Zürcher Zeitung,* June 10, 1947.
49. *Zürcher Student,* no. 3, 1947.
50. *Tagebücher,* July 13, 1947.

51. Letter to Alfred and Kitty Neumann, July 14, 1947.
52. *Tagebücher,* July 2 and 7, 1947.
53. *Tagebücher,* July 17, 1947.
54. Letter to *Neue Zeitung,* June 25, 1947, published in the paper on July 7, 1947.
55. *Tagebücher,* 1946–48, pp. 580–81.
56. Letter to Alfred and Kitty Neumann, July 14, 1947.
57. *Tagebücher,* July 18, 1947.
58. Letter to Jacques Mercanton, July 19, 1947.
59. *Tagebücher,* July 21, 1947.
60. *Tagebücher,* July 27–31, 1947.
61. Letters to Agnes Meyer, September 3, 1947, and Hermann Hesse, November 27, 1947; *Tagebücher,* August 17–18, 1947.
62. *Tagebücher,* September 4, 1947.
63. *Tagebücher,* August 31, 1947.
64. *Tagebücher,* September 12, 1947.

CHAPTER 38

1. Letter to Alexander Frey, September 17, 1947.
2. Letter to Ernst Penzoldt, September 17, 1947.
3. Letter to Hedda Eulenberg, July 6, 1947.
4. Letter to Howard Nelson, October 3, 1947.
5. Letter to Herbert Eulenberg, July 26, 1947.
6. Letter to Constance Hallgarten, October 18, 1947.
7. *Tagebücher,* October 3, 1947.
8. *Tagebücher,* October 4, 1947.
9. *Tagebücher,* October 11, 1947.
10. *Tagebücher,* October 20, 1947.
11. Reprinted in *Tagebücher,* 1946–48, p. 909.
12. *Die Tat,* October 18, 1947.
13. Letter to Max Rychner, October 26, 1947.
14. Letter to Agnes Meyer, December 3, 1947.
15. Ibid.
16. Letter to Jean Cocteau, October 8, 1947; *Tagebücher,* October 1 and December 16, 1947.
17. Letter to Hermann Hesse, November 27, 1947.
18. *Tagebücher,* November 8, 1947.
19. *Tagebücher,* November 22, 1947.
20. *Tagebücher,* November 23 and December 18, 1947.

21. *Genesis of a Novel,* p. 119.
22. *Tagebücher,* June 8, 1948.
23. *Tagebücher,* January 14, 1948
24. *Tagebücher,* January 3, 1948.
25. Letter to Walter Kolb, January 4, 1948.
26. *Aufbau,* January 16, 1948.
27. Letter from Hanns Eisler, January 18, 1948.
28. *Tagebücher,* April 22, 1948.
29. Letter to Michael, January 31, 1948.
30. Letter to Schoenberg, February 17, 1948.
31. *Tagebücher,* February 21 and 24, 1948.
32. *Tagebücher,* February 22, 1948.
33. *Tagebücher,* February 8, 1948.
34. *Tagebücher,* February 26–27, 1948.
35. *Tagebücher,* March 6, 8, 26, 28, 30, 1948.
36. Letter to Samuel Singer, January 20, 1948.
37. Letter to Samuel Singer, March 8, 1948.
38. *Tagebücher,* April 15, 1948.
39. Letter to Samuel Singer, April 13, 1948.
40. Letter to Agnes Meyer, May 22, 1948.
41. *Tagebücher,* May 3, 1948.
42. Letter to Hermann Hesse, June 1, 1948.
43. *Tagebücher,* July 16, 1948.
44. Letter to Karl Kerényi, July 17, 1948.
45. *Tagebücher,* December 6, 1948.
46. Letter to Hermann Hesse, June 1, 1948.
47. Conversation with Elisabeth Mann Borgese, February 28, 1994.
48. *Tagebücher,* July 11–12, 1948.
49. *Tagebücher,* July 14, 1948.
50. Letter to A. Adorno, July 12, 1948.
51. Letter to Otto Basler, July 20, 1948.
52. *Tagebücher,* August 8, 1948.
53. *Tagebücher,* February 1, 1948.
54. *Tagebücher,* July 20, 1948.
55. *Tagebücher,* August 13, 1948.
56. *Tagebücher,* August 2–5, 1948; letter to Agnes Meyer, August 11, 1948.
57. *Tagebücher,* August 11–12, 1948.
58. *Tagebücher,* September 6–7 and 17–18, 1948.
59. Letter to Werner Schmitz, July 30, 1948.
60. *Tagebücher,* September 12 and October 22 and 27, 1948.

61. *Tagebücher,* November 10, 1948.
62. *New York Times Book Review,* October 31, 1948.
63. *New Yorker,* October 30, 1948.
64. Letter to Joseph Angell, November 8, 1948.
65. Letter to Agnes Meyer, September 7, 1948.
66. *Tagebücher,* November 3, 1948.
67. *Echo der Woche,* October 22, 1948.
68. Letter to Johannes Becher, January 2, 1949.
69. Letter to Hermann Hesse, January 4, 1949.
70. Letter to Karl Silomon, February 4, 1949.
71. Letter to Benjamin H. Cook, February 12, 1949.
72. *Tagebücher,* January 10–11, 1949.
73. *Tagebücher,* January 4, 1949.
74. *Tagebücher,* January 2 and 31 and February 15, 1949.
75. Letter to Erika, February 8, 1949.
76. *Tagebücher,* February 6, 1949.
77. Letter to Emil Preetorius, March 9, 1949.
78. Letters to Alfred Meyer, January 20, 1949, and Agnes Meyer, March 3, 1949.
79. *Tagebücher,* March 4–5, 1949.
80. *Tagebücher,* November 14, 1948.
81. *Tagebücher,* March 14, 1949.
82. *Tagebücher,* October 22, 1948, and March 21, 1949.
83. *Tagebücher,* March 20 and 30, 1949.
84. Letter to Oskar Maria Graf, March 8, 1949.
85. Letter to Gottfried Bermann Fischer, April 10, 1949.
86. Letter to Otto Basler, March 13, 1949.
87. Letter to Hans Reisiger, March 13, 1949; *Tagebücher,* April 26, 1949.
88. Letter to Rudolf Goldschmidt-Jentner, April 14, 1949.
89. Letter to Hermann Stresau, April 17, 1949.
90. Letters to Viktor, March 16, 1949, and Ellen Fischer, March 16, 1949.
91. *Life,* April 4, 1949.
92. Telegram to Harlow Shapley, March 17, 1949.
93. Telegram to Dean Acheson, March 21, 1949.
94. Letter from Francis Biddle, early April 1949.
95. Letter to Francis Biddle, April 14, 1949.
96. *Tagebücher,* March 30, 1947.
97. *Tagebücher,* March 30 and April 26, 1948.
98. *Tagebücher,* April 28, 1949.
99. *Tagebücher,* May 3, 1949.

CHAPTER 39

1. *Tagebücher,* May 19, 1949.
2. Letter to Alfred Knopf, June 20, 1949.
3. *Tagebücher,* May 19, 1949.
4. *Tagebücher,* May 21, 1949.
5. Letter from Klaus to Katia and Erika, May 20, 1949.
6. Marianne Krüll, *Im Netz der Zauberer,* p. 20.
7. Letter from Erika to Klaus, May 15, 1949.
8. Golo Mann, "Erinnerungen an meinem Bruder Klaus," in Klaus Mann, *Briefe und Antworten,* vol. 2, pp. 319–51.
9. *Tagebücher,* May 22, 1949.
10. *Tagebücher,* May 24, 1949.
11. Letter from Heinrich to Karl Lemke, June 15, 1949.
12. *Tagebücher,* May 29, 1949.
13. *Tagebücher,* May 31, 1949.
14. *Tagebücher,* June 2, 1949; letter to Friedrich Grosshut, June 5, 1949.
15. *Tagebücher,* June 14, 1949.
16. *Tagebücher,* June 15, 1949.
17. *Tagebücher,* June 18, 1949.
18. Letter to Hans Reisiger, June 28, 1949.
19. *Tagebücher,* July 12, 1949.
20. *Tagebücher,* July 12–17, 1949
21. *Tagebücher,* July 21–23, 1949.
22. Letter to Hans Reisiger, June 28, 1949.
23. *Heute,* July 1949.
24. *Frankfurter Rundschau,* July 28, 1949.
25. *Schwäbische Landeszeitung,* August 1, 1949.
26. Ibid.
27. Letter to Heinrich Walter, September 8, 1949.
28. Letter to Erich von Kahler, September 10, 1949.
29. *Neue Zürcher Zeitung,* July 25, 1949.
30. *New York Times Magazine,* September 25, 1949.
31. Letter to Erich von Kahler, September 10, 1949.

32. Letters to Agnes Meyer, September 8, 1949, and Hans Reisiger, September 8, 1949.
33. Letter to Emil Preetorius, October 20, 1949.
34. *Tagebücher,* August 4, 1949.
35. *Tagebücher,* August 4, 1949; *New York Times Magazine,* September 25, 1949.
36. Letter to Paul Olberg, August 27, 1949.
37. *Tagebücher,* August 4, 1949.
38. *Tagebücher,* August 6, 1949.
39. Letter to Ernst Bertram, August 9, 1949.
40. *Tagebücher,* September 2, 9, 11, 20, 1949.
41. *Tagebücher,* October 17, 1949.
42. *Tagebücher,* November 2, 1949.
43. Letter to Hans Reisiger, December 13, 1949.
44. *Tagebücher,* November 22, 1949.
45. *Tagebücher,* 1949–50, pp. 688–89.
46. *Tagebücher,* October 11, 1949; *Los Angeles Times,* October 11, 1949.
47. *Tagebücher,* October 18, 1949.
48. *Tagebücher,* October 26, 1949.
49. *Tagebücher,* November 2, 1949.
50. Letter to Hermann Hesse, November 2, 1949.
51. *Tagebücher,* November 15, 1949.
52. Letter from and letter to Carl Ehrenberg, November 22, 1949; *Tagebücher,* January 1, 1950.
53. *Tagebücher,* August 19 and 30 and September 14, 1949.
54. Letter to Schoenberg, December 19, 1949.
55. *Tagebücher,* August 13 and December 21, 1949.
56. *Tagebücher,* January 1, 1950.
57. Letter to Theodor Adorno, January 9, 1950.
58. Draft for message to be read at a meeting of the Southern California chapter of the Council of the Arts, Sciences and Professions on January 14, 1950, in *Tagebücher,* 1949–50, pp. 684–85.
59. Letter to Theodor Adorno, January 9, 1950.
60. Letter to Bruno Walter, January 27, 1950.
61. *Tagebücher,* January 30 and 31, 1950.
62. *Tagebücher,* January 31, 1950.
63. *Tagebücher,* January 19, 1950.
64. *Tagebücher,* February 8, 1950.
65. Heinrich Mann, *Der Atem* (Amsterdam, 1949).
66. *Tagebücher,* March 11, 12, 14, 1950.
67. Conversation with Elisabeth Mann Borgese, February 28, 1994.
68. Letter to Emil Oprecht, March 8, 1950.
69. *Tagebücher,* March 28, 1950.
70. Letter to Walter Perl, March 25, 1950.
71. *Tagebücher,* April 23 and 30, 1950.
72. *Rhein-Neckar Zeitung,* June 3–4, 1950.
73. Letter to Jules Romains, ca. May 20, 1950.
74. *Tagebücher,* May 13, 1950.
75. *Tagebücher,* May 23–24, 1950.
76. *Tagebücher,* May 28, 1950.
77. Letter to Paul Amann, November 7, 1950.
78. *Tagebücher,* May 31 and June 1, 2, 3, 5, 6, 1950.
79. *Tagebücher,* June 16, 1950.
80. Letter to Lion Feuchtwanger, June 25, 1950; *Tagebücher,* June 20, 21, 22, 23, 1950.

CHAPTER 40

1. *Tagebücher,* June 25 and July 3 and 7, 1950, and March 6, 1951.
2. *Tagebücher,* July 8, 9, 10 and November 24, 1950.
3. *Tagebücher,* July 8, 1950.
4. *Tagebücher,* July 11, 12, 13, 14, 16, 17, 1950.
5. Hans Mühlestein, *Michelangelo-Übersetzungen* (Celerina, 1950).
6. "Die Erotik Michelangelos."
7. *Tagebücher,* July 20, 1950.
8. "Die Erotik Michelangelos."
9. *Tagebücher,* July 18, 1950.
10. *Tagebücher,* August 1 and 4, 1950.
11. *Tagebücher,* July 19, 1950.
12. *Tagebücher,* August 6, 1950.
13. *Tagebücher,* August 6, 7, 8, 1950.
14. *Tagebücher,* August 15–16, 1950.
15. *Tagebücher,* September 15, 1950.
16. *Tagebücher,* November 29, 1950.
17. *Tagebücher,* November 21 and December 2, 1950.
18. *Tagebücher,* November 25 and 28, 1950.
19. Letter to Robert Havighurst, January 11, 1951.
20. *Tagebücher,* January 29, 1951.

21. "Foreign Policy Today," in *Bulletin of the Atomic Scientists*, December 1950.
22. Letter to Erich von Kahler, February 1, 1951.
23. Letter from Alfred Knopf, February 2, 1951.
24. Letter to Philip Morrison, February 18, 1951.
25. Draft of letter to *New York Times*, February 3, 1951.
26. *Tagebücher*, February 12 and 14, 1951; letter to Alfred Knopf, February 14, 1951.
27. Statement to United Press, February 12, 1951.
28. Letter to Philip Morrison, February 18, 1951.
29. Letter to Otto Basler, January 8, 1951.
30. *Tagebücher*, April 25, 1951.
31. *Tagebücher*, March 22, 1951.
32. Letter to Kurt Klaber, April 9, 1951.
33. *Tagebücher*, April 9, 1951.
34. *Tagebücher*, March 6 and 9, 1951.
35. Letter to *Aufbau*, April 3, 1951.
36. *Tagebücher*, April 3, 1951.
37. *Los Angeles Times*, April 5, 1951.
38. Letter to Erich von Kahler, April 23, 1951.
39. Ibid.
40. *Tagebücher*, April 13–14, 1951.
41. Letter to Hanns Fischer, May 28, 1951.
42. Letter to Karl Jakob Hirsch, September 29, 1951.
43. *Tagebücher*, August 6, 1950.
44. *New Leader*, June 18, 1951.
45. *Congressional Record*, June 18, 1951.
46. *Tagebücher*, June 20, 1951.
47. *Time*, June 25, 1951.
48. Letter to Dora Jacob, May 6, 1951.
49. *Tagebücher*, June 1, 1951.

CHAPTER 41

1. *Tagebücher*, July 11, 1951.
2. *Tagebücher*, August 2, 1951.
3. *Tagebücher*, August 6 and September 19, 1951.
4. Letter to J. Lesser August 20, 1951.
5. *Tagebücher*, September 2, 1951.
6. *Tagebücher*, September 12, 1951.
7. *Tagebücher*, September 14, 1951.
8. *Tagebücher*, September 5, 18, 20, 28, 1951.

9. *Tagebücher*, September 24 and 28, 1951.
10. Letter to Ferdinand Lion, April 28, 1952.
11. *Tagebücher*, October 1, 1951.
12. *Tagebücher*, October 2, 3, 4, 5, 6, 1951; letter to Hermann Hesse, October 14, 1951.
13. *Tagebücher*, October 21–22 and November 4–5, 7, 26–27, 1951.
14. *Tagebücher*, November 5, 1951.
15. Judith Marcus, Georg Lukács and *Thomas Mann: A Study in the Sociology of Literature* (Amherst, 1987), pp. 70 and 81.
16. Letter to Paul Amann, December 23, 1951.
17. *Tagebücher*, December 12, 1951.
18. *Tagebücher*, October 24, 1951.
19. *Tagebücher*, November 24 and December 12, 1951.
20. *Tagebücher*, December 5, 12, 15, 1951
21. Hans Wysling, *Bild und Text bei Thomas Mann* (Frankfurt, 1989).
22. *Tagebücher*, January 18, 1952.
23. Letters to Theodor Adorno, January 9, 1952, and Ria Drevermann, January 20, 1952.
24. *Tagebücher*, April 3 and 4, 1952.
25. Letter to Dr. Frederick Rosenthal, May 5, 1952.
26. Letter to Dr. Frederick Rosenthal, May 13, 1952.
27. Letter to Grete Nikisch, May 17, 1952.
28. Letter to R. Oberloskamp, June 5, 1952.
29. Wysling, *Bild und Text*.
30. *Tagebücher*, March 31, 1952.
31. *Tagebücher*, April 25, 1952.
32. Letter to *Echo der Woche*, May 17, 1952.
33. *Tagebücher*, March 16, 1952.
34. *Tagebücher*, February 22, 1952.
35. *Tagebücher*, June 6, 1952.
36. *Tagebücher*, June 21, 1952.
37. *Tagebücher*, May 27, 1952.
38. *Tagebücher*, June 4, 1952.
39. *Tagebücher*, June 10, 1952.
40. Letter to Agnes Meyer, June 17, 1952.
41. *Tagebücher*, July 2 and 5, 1952; letter to Agnes Meyer, July 5, 1952.
42. *Tagebücher*, July 9, 11, 16, 1952.
43. *Tagebücher*, July 13, 14, 16, 1952.

44. *Tagebücher,* July 24, 1952.
45. *Tagebücher,* August 9, 12, 13, 1952.
46. *Tagebücher,* August 16 and 23, 1952.
47. *Tagebücher,* August 23, 24, 30, 1952; letter to Alexander Frey, August 31, 1952.
48. *Tagebücher,* September 17–18, 1952.
49. *Tagebücher,* September 24, 1952.
50. *Tagebücher,* October 1, 1952; letter to Kuno Fiedler, October 17, 1952.
51. Letter to H. W. Brann, October 25, 1952.
52. *Tagebücher,* October 22, 1952; letter to J. Lesser, October 29, 1952.
53. *Tagebücher,* October 29, 1952; letter to Kuno Fiedler, November 16, 1952.
54. *Tagebücher,* November 5, 1952.
55. *Tagebücher,* November 12, 1952.
56. *Volkstimme,* November 19, 1952; *Tagebücher,* November 28, 1952; letters to Lynn Heizerling, December 29, 1952, and Agnes Meyer, February 8, 1953.
57. *Aufbau,* December 19, 1952.
58. *Tagebücher,* December 5–6, 1952; letters to Martin Flinker, December 11, 1952, and Agnes Meyer, December 24, 1952.
59. *Tagebücher,* December 11, 12, 16, 19, 1952.
60. *Tagebücher,* December 19 and 23, 1952.
61. *Tagebücher,* December 25 and 29, 1952; letter to Anna Schickele, December 28, 1952.

CHAPTER 42

1. Letter to Ida Herz, January 16, 1953.
2. Letter to Julius Bab, January 25, 1953.
3. Letter from Paul Hoffmann, January 1953.
4. Letter to Paul Hoffmann, January 30, 1953; letter from Erika, January 28, 1953.
5. Letter to H. Bremer, March 11, 1953.
6. Letter to Helen Lowe-Porter, April 4, 1953.
7. Letters to Otto Basler, March 18, 1953, J. Lesser, March 18, 1953, Hans Reisiger, March 21, 1953, and Lore Rumelin-Wibel, March 27, 1953.

8. Letter to Theodor Adorno, March 8, 1954.
9. Letters to Albrecht Goes, March 31, 1953, and H. W. Brann, May 12, 1953.
10. Letter to R. Bandinelli, May 3, 1953.
11. *Tagebücher,* May 1, 1953; letter to Rudolf Humm, November 21, 1953.
12. Albrecht Ziessler, *Hansestadt Lübeck* (Lübeck, 1955), pp. 72–75.
13. Letter to Kuno Fiedler, June 16, 1953.
14. Letters to Otto Basler, April 17, 1955; A. and Grete Nikisch, May 31, 1955.
15. Volker Hage, *Eine Liebe fürs Leben,* pp. 9, 54–55.
16. Letter to Kuno Fiedler, July 19, 1953.
17. "Katia Mann zum siebzigsten Geburtstag," in *Autobiographisches.*
18. Erika Mann, "Das letzte Jahr," in *Autobiographisches,* p. 294.
19. Letter to L. Marcuse, April 17, 1954.
20. *Tagebücher,* March 18 and July 6, 1953.
21. Letter to Hans Reisiger, September 8, 1953.
22. Letters to Robert Faesi, November 1, 1953, and Erich von Kahler, January 2, 1954.
23. *Tagebücher,* August 24, 1953.
24. *Tagebücher,* June 20 and July 6, 1953.
25. Letter to E. Hilscher, October 8, 1953.
26. *Tagebücher,* July 18, 1953.
27. *Tagebücher,* October 11, 1953.
28. Letter to Hans Reisiger, September 8, 1953.
29. Letters to Tourist Office, Funchal, December 15, 1953, Claire Goll, December 12, 1953, Hans Reisiger, December 7, 1953, and Erich von Kahler, January 2, 1954.
30. Letters to W. Bredel, December 31, 1953, and Hans Reisiger, January 1, 1954.
31. Letter to W. Emrich, January 18, 1954.
32. Letter to Karl Kerényi, January 19, 1954.
33. Letter to Frido, May 4, 1954.
34. *Tagebücher,* August 28, 1948.

35. *Tagebücher,* December 31, 1948.
36. Postcards to Richard Schweizer, February 8, 1954, and Anna Jacobson, February 14, 1954; letters to Erika, February 15, 1954, and Theodor Adorno, March 8, 1954.
37. Letters to L. Leibrich, March 7, 1954, and K. Mampell, March 10, 1954.
38. *Tagebücher,* March 1, 1954.
39. Letter to Agnes Meyer, June 21, 1954.
40. Letter to unknown woman, June 9, 1954.
41. *Tagebücher,* June 6, 1954; letter to Erika, June 7, 1954.
42. *Tagebücher,* May 25, 1954.
43. *Tagebücher,* June 19, 1954, and August 28, 1953.
44. Ibid.
45. Letter to W. Herzog, July 2, 1954.
46. Erika Mann, "Das letzte Jahr," p. 294.
47. *Tagebücher,* August 29, 1954.
48. Letters to W. Emrich, August 18 and September 1, 1954.
49. Letter to Emil Preetorius, September 6, 1954.
50. Erika, Mann, "Das letzte Jahr," p. 298.
51. Letter to Erich von Kahler, August 12, 1954.
52. Letter to R. Braungart, September 29, 1954.
53. Letter to H. Rodenberg, February 7, 1955.
54. Letters to Gottfried Bermann Fischer, July 5, 1954, W. Hoffman, November 28, 1954, and Kuno Fiedler, April 29, 1955.
55. *Die Gegenwart,* September 25, 1954.
56. Letters to Lavinia Mazzucchetti, January 8, 1955, and Otto Basler, March 26, 1955.
57. Letters to J. Lesser, November 3, 1954, and R. Braungart, November 18, 1954.
58. Letter to Karl Kerényi, December 5, 1954.

59. Letter to Lavinia Mazzucchetti, January 8, 1955.
60. Letter to Hans Reisiger, January 22, 1955.
61. Erika Mann, "Das letzte Jahr", p. 300.
62. Ibid.; letter to Agnes Meyer, February 9, 1955.
63. *Tagebücher,* February 11 and 15, 1955.
64. Letter to Agnes Meyer, February 9, 1955.
65. Letter to Ida Herz, December 19, 1954.
66. Letter to Hermann Lange, March 19, 1955.
67. Letters to Lavinia Mazzucchetti January 8, 1955, and Robert Faesi, May 11, 1955.
68. Erika Mann, pp. 309–15.
69. *Tagebücher,* May 1, 1955; Erika Mann, pp. 317–19; letter to Kuno Fiedler, June 19, 1955.
70. Erika Mann, pp. 320–21; letter to H. Marty, June 20, 1955.
71. *Tagebücher,* May 1955.
72. Ibid.
73. Letter to Hermann Hesse, June 10, 1955.
74. Ibid.
75. *Tagebücher,* July 4, 1955.
76. *Tagebücher,* July 11, 1955.
77. Erika Mann, p. 337.
78. Ibid., pp. 337–39.
79. *Tagebücher,* July 22, 1955.
80. Erika Mann, pp. 336–45; letter to the Michael Mann family, August 9, 1955, and Lavinia Mazzucchetti, August 10, 1955.
81. Erika Mann, pp. 350–56.

Epilogue

1. Marguerite Yourcenar, "The Humanism of Thomas Mann," *Partisan Review,* spring 1956.
2. Frido Mann, *Professor Parsifal,* p. 180.

Selected Bibliography

■

By Thomas Mann

Autobiographisches, edited by Erika Mann. Frankfurt, 1968.
Frage und Antwort. Interviews mit Thomas Mann 1909–1955, edited by Volkmar Hansen and Gert Heine. Hamburg, 1983.
Gesammelte Werke, in 13 vols. Frankfurt, 1960–74.
Gesammelte Werke in Einzelbände. Frankfurter Ausgabe der Werke Thomas Manns, edited by Peter de Mendelssohn. Frankfurt, 1980.
Notizbücher 1–6 and *7–12,* edited by Hans Wysling and Yvonne Schmidlin. Frankfurt, 1991–92.
Tagebücher, 1918–21, 1933–34, 1935–36, 1937–38, 1940–43, edited by Peter de Mendelssohn. Frankfurt, 1979–82.
Tagebücher, 1944–46, 1946–48, 1949–50, 1951–52, edited by Inge Jens. Frankfurt, 1986–93.
Über mich selbst: Autobiographische Schriften, edited by Peter de Mendelssohn. Frankfurt, 1983.
Werke, paperback edition in 12 vols. Frankfurt, 1967; new edition, 1975.

CORRESPONDENCE

Briefe 1889–1955 und Nachlese, 3 vols., edited by Erika Mann. Frankfurt, 1961–65.
Briefe an Otto Grautoff und Ida Boy-Ed, edited by Peter de Mendelssohn. Frankfurt, 1975.
Briefe an Paul Amann, edited by Herbert Wegener. Lübeck, 1959.
Breifwechsel mit Autoren, edited by Hans Wysling. Frankfurt, 1988.
Briefwechsel mit seinen Verleger Gottfried Bermann Fischer 1932–55, edited by Peter de Mendelssohn. Frankfurt, 1973.
Die Briefe Thomas Manns. Regesten und Register, 5 vols., edited by Hans Burgin, Hans-Otto Mayer, Gert Heine, and Yvonne Schmidlin. Frankfurt, 1976–87.
Thomas Mann an Ernst Bertram. Briefe aus den Jahren 1910–1955, edited by Inge Jens. Pfullingen, 1960.
Thomas Mann–Agnes E. Meyer Briefwechsel, edited by Hans Rudolf Vaget. Hamburg, 1986.
Thomas Mann–Alfred Neumann Briefwechsel, edited by Peter de Mendelssohn. Heidelberg, 1977.
Thomas Mann–Heinrich Mann Briefwechsel 1900–1949, edited by Hans Wysling. Frankfurt 1968
Thomas Mann–Heinrich Mann Briefwechsel. Frankfurt, 1975; new edition, 1984.
Thomas Mann–Karl Kerényi Gespräch in Briefen, edited by Karl Kerényi. Zurich, 1960.
Thomas Mann–Robert Faesi Briefwechsel. Zurich, 1962.

IN ENGLISH TRANSLATION

All published in London and, unless otherwise stated, translated by Helen T. Lowe-Porter.
Royal Highness, translated by A. Cecil Curtiss, 1916.
Bashan and I (Herr und Hund), translated by Herman George Schaeffauer, 1923.
Buddenbrooks, 1924.
The Magic Mountain, 1927.
Death in Venice, 1928.
Early Sorrow, 1929.
Mario and the Magician, 1930.
A Sketch of My Life, 1931.
Three Essays, 1932.

Past Masters and Other Papers, 1933.
Joseph and His Brothers
   The Tales of Jacob, 1934.
   Young Joseph, 1935.
   Joseph in Egypt, 1938.
   Joseph the Provider, 1944.
Joseph and His Brothers (in one vol), 1948.
Stories of Three Decades, 1936.
The Coming Victory of Democracy, translated by Agnes E. Meyer, 1938.
This War, translated by Eric Sutton, 1940.
Lotte in Weimar (U.S. version titled *The Beloved Returns*), 1940.
The Transposed Heads: A Legend of India, 1941.
Order of the Day: Political Essays and Speeches of Two Decades, translated by Helen T. Lowe-
   Porter, Agnes E. Meyer, and Eric Sutton, 1943.
The Tables of the Law, 1945.
Essays of Three Decades, 1947.
Doctor Faustus: The Life of the German Composer Adrian Leverkühn as Told by a Friend,
   1948.
The Holy Sinner, 1951.
The Black Swan, translated by Willard R. Trask, 1954.
Confessions of Felix Krull, Confidence Man: The Early Years, translated by Denver Linley,
   1955.
Last Essays, translated by Richard and Clara Winston and Tania and James Stern, 1959.
Stories of a Lifetime, in 2 vols., 1961.
The Genesis of a Novel, translated by Richard and Clara Winston, 1961.
Diaries 1918–39, edited by Hermann Kesten, translated by Richard and Clara Win-
   ston, 1983.
Reflections of a Nonpolitical Man, translated by Walter D. Morris. New York, 1983.
Death in Venice and Other Stories, translated by David Luke, 1990.

TRANSLATED CORRESPONDENCE

The Letters of Thomas Mann 1889–1955, 2 vols. selected and translated by Richard and
   Clara Winston, 1970.
The Hesse–Mann Letters, edited by Anni Carlsson and Volker Michels, translated by
   Ralph Manheim, 1976.
Letters to Paul Amann, 1982.

BY OTHER MEMBERS OF THE MANN FAMILY

Mann, Erika. *Briefe und Antworten*, 2 vols. Munich, 1984.
———. "Das letzte Jahr. Bericht über meinem Vater," in *Autobiographisches*. Frankfurt,
   1968.
Mann, Frido. *Professor Parsifal*. Munich, 1985.
Mann, Golo. *Mein Vater Thomas Mann*. Lübeck, 1970.
Mann, Heinrich. *Ein Zeitalter wird besichtigt*. Stockholm, 1946.
———. *Gesammelte Werke*, 24 vols. Berlin and Weimar, 1965–73.
———. "Zola," in *Die Weissen Blätter*, November 1915.
Mann, Julia. *Aus Dodos Kindheit*. Konstanz, 1903.
Mann, Katia. *Meine ungeschriebene Memoiren*, edited by Elisabeth Plessen and Michael
   Mann. Frankfurt, 1974.
Mann, Klaus. *Abenteuer des Brautpaars: Die Erzählungen*. Munich, 1976.
———. *Briefe und Antworten*, 2 vols. Munich, 1975.
———. *Tagebücher*, 6 vols. Munich, 1989–91.
Mann, Michael. *Michael Mann: Fragmente eines Lebens. Lebensbericht und Auswahl seiner
   Schriften*, edited by Frederic C. and Sally P. Tubach. Munich, 1983
Mann, Viktor. *Wir waren Fünf*. Konstanz, 1949.

IN ENGLISH

Mann, Erika. *School for Barbarians: Education under the Nazis.* New York, 1938.
Mann, Golo. *Reminiscences and Reflections: Growing Up in Germany*, translated by Krishna Winston, 1990.
Mann, Katia. *Unwritten Memories*, edited by Elisabeth Plessen and Michael Mann, translated by Hunter and Hildegarde Hannum, 1975.
Mann, Klaus. *The Turning Point: Thirty-Five Years in This Century.* New York, 1942.
Mann, Monika. *Past and Present,* translated by Frances Reid and Ruth Hein. New York, 1966.

ON THOMAS MANN

Arnold, Heinz Ludwig, ed. *Sinn und Form Sonderheft Thomas Mann.* Berlin, 1965.
Baumgart, Reinhard. *Das Ironische und die Ironie in den Werken Thomas Manns.* Munich, 1964.
Bergsten, Gunilla. *Thomas Manns "Doktor Faustus." Untersuchungen zu den Quellen und zur Struktur des Romans.* Lund, 1963.
Blackmur, Richard. "Parody and Critique: Notes on Thomas Mann's *Doctor Faustus.*" In *The Kenyon Critics: Studies in Modern Literature from The Kenyon Review*, John Crowe Ransom, ed. New York, 1951.
Böhm, Karl Werner. *Zwischen Selbstzucht und Verlangen: Thomas Mann und das Stigma Homosexualität. Untersuchungen zu Frühwerk und Jugend.* Würzburg, 1991.
Brennan, J. G. *Thomas Mann's World.* Columbia, 1942.
Bürgin, Hans, and Mayer, Hans-Otto. *Thomas Mann—Ein Chronik seines Lebens.* Frankfurt, 1965.
Carnegy, Patrick. Faust as Musician: A Study of Thomas Mann's Novel "Doctor Faustus." London, 1973.
Carstensen, Richard. *Thomas Mann—sehr menschlich.* Lübeck, 1975.
Eloesser, Arthur. *Thomas Mann. Sein Leben und Werk.* Berlin, 1925.
Faesi, Robert. *Thomas Mann, Ein Meister der Erzählkunst.* Zurich, 1955.
Fischer, Gottfried Bermann. *"Bedroht—Bewahrt." Weg eines Verlegers.* Frankfurt, 1967.
Flanner, Janet. "Goethe in Hollywood." *The New Yorker*, December 13 and 20, 1941.
Franke, Peter Robert. *Der Tod des Hans Hansen. Unbekannte Dokumente aus der Jugend von Thomas Mann.* Lübeck, 1991.
Hage, Volker. *Eine Liebe fürs Leben. Thomas Mann und Travemünde.* Hamburg, 1993.
Hamburger, Michael. *A Proliferation of Prophets: Essays on German Writers from Nietzsche to Brecht.* Manchester, 1983.
Hamilton, Nigel. *The Brothers Mann.* London, 1978.
Heller, Erich. *The Ironic German.* London, 1957.
Karst, Roman. *Thomas Mann oder Der Deutsche Zwiespalt.* Vienna, 1970.
Koopmann, Helmut. *Thomas Mann, Konstanten seines literarischen Werkes.* Göttingen, 1975.
———, ed. *Thomas Mann.* Darmstadt, 1975.
———, ed. *Thomas-Mann-Handbuch.* Stuttgart, 1990.
Krüll, Marianne. *Im Netz der Zauberer: Eine Andere Geschichte der Familie Mann.* Frankfurt, 1973.
Kurzke, Hermann. *Thomas Mann, Epoche—Werk—Wirkung.* Munich, 1985.
Lesser, Jonas. *Thomas Mann in der Epoche seiner Vollendung.* Munich, 1953.
Lukács, Georg. *Thomas Mann.* Berlin, 1957.
Marcus, Judith. *Georg Lukács and Thomas Mann: A Study in the Sociology of Literature.* Amherst, 1987.
Mayer, Hans. *Thomas Mann.* Frankfurt, 1984.
Mendelssohn, Peter de. *Der Zauberer. Das Leben des deutschen Schriftstellers Thomas Mann,* 2 vols. Frankfurt, 1975 and 1992.
Meyer, Agnes E. *Out of These Roots: The Autobiography of an American Woman.* Boston, 1953.

Moulden, Ken, and Gero von Wilpert. *Buddenbrooks-Handbuch.* Stuttgart, 1988.

Neider, Charles, ed. *The Stature of Thomas Mann.* New York, 1947.

Nicholls, R. A. *Nietzsche in the Early Work of Thomas Mann.* Berkeley, 1955.

Reed, T. J. *Thomas Mann: The Uses of Tradition.* Oxford, 1974.

———, ed. *Der Tod in Venedig.* Oxford, 1971.

Reich-Ranicki, Marcel. *Thomas Mann and His Family,* translated by Ralph Manheim. London, 1989.

Scherrer, Paul, and Hans Wysling. *Quellenkritische Studien zum Werk Thomas Manns (Thomas Mann Studien 1).* Munich, 1967.

Schröter, Klaus. *Thomas Mann in Selbstzeugnissen und Bilddokumente.* Reinbek, 1964.

———, ed. *Thomas Mann im Urteil seiner Zeit. Dokumente 1891–1955.* Hamburg, 1969.

Sprecher, Thomas. *Thomas Mann in Zürich.* Zurich, 1992.

Thomas, R. Hinton. *Thomas Mann: The Mediation of Art.* Oxford, 1956.

Weigand, Hermann. *Thomas Mann's Novel "Der Zauberberg."* New York, 1933.

Winston, Richard. *Thomas Mann: The Making of an Artist 1875–1911.* London, 1982.

Wysling, Hans. *Thomas Mann heute. Sieben Vorträge.* Bern and Munich, 1976.

———. *Dokumente und Untersuchungen. Beiträge zur Thomas-Mann-Forschung (Thomas-Mann-Studien 3).* Bern, 1974.

Yourcenar, Marguerite. "The Humanism of Thomas Mann." *Partisan Review,* spring 1956.

Index

"Abdankung" ("Abdication") (H. Mann), 220–21
abenteuerliche Simplicissimus Teutsch, Der (Grimmelshausen), 119
Acheson, Dean, 558, 584
Adams, Elias, 528, 545
Adenauer, Konrad, 611, 612
Adler, Friedrich, 295
Adorno, Theodor, 495–96, 508, 522, 525, 526, 527, 537, 546, 549, 552, 554
"Affirmation of Socialism" ("Bekenntnis zum Sozialismus") (Mann), 397
"Aischa" (Mann), 97
À la recherche du temps perdu (Proust), 286
Amann, Paul, 262, 286, 294, 309, 428
American Peace Crusade, 578, 579–80, 583
Amphytrion (Kleist), 370, 371–72, 458
Andersen, Hans Christian, 353
Anja and Esther (K. Mann), 358
anti-Semitism, 115, 193, 232, 238–39, 337, 408, 413, 476, 503; "Blood of the Walsungs" and, 213–15; of Nazis, 334, 393, 394, 398, 399, 405, 406, 412, 414, 424, 462
Arosa, 398, 399, 404, 423, 431–33, 437, 608; *see also* Waldsanatorium
Atem, Der (Breathing) (H. Mann), 569
atom bomb, 519, 577, 578
"Attention, Europe!" ("Achtung, Europa!") (Mann), 415
"At the Prophet's" ("Beim Propheten") (Mann), 197–98, 214, 253
Attlee, Clement, 519, 578
Auden, W. H., 418, 434, 547
Aue, Hartmann von, 548, 550
Auer, Erich, 312
Aufbau, 514, 538, 539, 548
Austria, 81, 236, 311, 317, 341; Nazis in, 438–39, 453–54; refugees from, 447–48
Austria-Hungary, 81, 82; in World War I, 279, 280, 286, 310

Bab, Julius, 271–72, 356, 410, 428, 448
Baden, Prince Max von, 309, 310
Bahle, Julius, 495
Bahr, Hermann, 102, 107–8, 236
Barth, Karl, 433

Bassermann, Albert, 571
Basso, Hamilton, 554
Baumeister, Adolf, 209
Becher, Johannes, 543, 565, 585, 594, 610, 611
Becker, Maria, 572, 612
Beckmann, Max, 544
Beloved Returns, The (Lotte in Weimar) (Mann), 391, 415–16, 420, 428, 431–32, 433, 435, 437, 441, 449–52, 454, 455–57, 461, 531, 542, 571, 594
Benn, Gottfried, 179, 404
Bercovici, Leonardo, 466
Berg, Alban, 495
Berle, Adolf, 498
Berlin, 82, 99, 101, 103, 306, 310, 311, 320, 397, 497, 555; Nazis in, 395, 398, 399, 407, 428; TM in, 179, 184–85, 206, 211, 212, 215, 267, 294, 295, 325, 326, 331, 338, 358, 366, 368, 380, 383, 385–86, 393
Berliner Tageblatt, 102, 168, 217, 237, 246, 247, 299
Bermann, Tutti, 602
Bermann Fischer, Gottfried, 407–9, 412, 414, 415, 417, 419, 420, 423, 425, 426, 429, 439, 440, 454, 504, 529, 542, 594, 607, 612; *Beloved Returns* and, 428, 455, 456
Bernstein, Elsa, 193, 194
Bernstein, Max, 193
Bernus, Alexander Freiherr von, 223
Bertaux, Félix, 360, 387, 396
Bertram, Ernst, 268, 275, 287, 290, 294–95, 297, 353, 565; TM's friend-ship with, 252–53, 274–75, 292, 303–8, 310, 329, 331, 332, 335, 336, 352, 359–60, 365, 375, 385, 410, 554, 606
Bible, in TM's works, 69, 75–76, 354, 358–59, 421, 526
Bidault, Georges, 538
Biddle, Francis, 474, 481, 513
Bie, Oscar, 123, 214, 282
Bielschowsky, Albert, 329
Biermann, Alice, 98, 131, 132
Biermann, Guido, 98, 131
Bilse, Fritz Oswald, 215

"Bilse und ich" (Mann), 215, 216, 218, 228, 344
Bircher-Benner clinic, 233, 247, 263
Biryukov, Pavel I., 329
Bismarck, Otto von, 81–84, 89, 96, 222–23, 237, 245
"Black Swan, The" ("Die Betrogene") (Mann), 601
Blake, William, 233
blaue Engel, Der (film), 221, 377
"Blood of the Walsungs, The" ("Wälsungenblut") (Mann), 211–17, 229, 327, 551
Bodmer, Hans, 471
Bohr, Niels, 561
Bonn University, 226, 317, 429, 440, 520, 537
Böök, Martin Fridrik, 380–81
Book-of-the-Month Club, 500, 501, 504, 553, 585–86
Borgese, Angelica, 464
Borgese, Domenica, 535
Borgese, Elisabeth Mann, 303, 318, 329, 358, 363, 377–78, 388, 407, 408, 410, 420, 428, 436, 456, 464, 480, 513, 528, 529, 568, 572, 589, 598, 605; TM's relationship with, 303, 308, 314, 353, 369, 390, 456, 619
Borgese, Giuseppe Antonio, 456, 464, 480, 513, 514, 598
Bourget, Paul, 108, 116, 117
Bousset, Therese, 87
Boy–Ed, Ida, 207, 214, 220, 228, 235, 240, 302, 331, 338, 352
Bradley, Omar, 584
Brahm, Otto, 233
Brandes, Georg, 122, 324
Brantl, Maximilian, 274, 287, 292, 380
Brecht, Bertolt, 119, 384, 469, 497, 499, 538, 620
Brion, Friederike, 452
Brockdorff-Rantzau, Count von, 315
Brod, Max, 448
Bronnen, Arnolt, 384
Bruhns, Julia da Silva, *see* Mann, Julia da Silva Bruhns
Brüning, Heinrich, 382, 393, 395
Budapest, 272, 332–33, 426–27
Buddenbrooks (film), 340, 607
Buddenbrooks (Mann), 68, 70–71, 72, 129–43, 148, 149, 150–52, 154–57, 159–61, 163, 165, 166, 171, 173, 188, 207, 218, 235, 266, 272, 324, 360, 362, 380–81, 393, 450, 494, 500, 501, 502, 507, 548, 594, 618; autobiographical elements in, 85, 87, 89, 93, 94, 96, 103, 129–36, 149, 244, 272; disease in,

133, 151–52, 263, 265; Dose libel case and, 215, 216; *Joseph and His Brothers* compared with, 359, 364; reviews of, 68, 168–69, 178, 179, 217, 239, 271; *Royal Highness* compared with, 211–12, 222, 236; sales of, 168, 171, 177, 178, 179, 184, 188, 194, 223, 298, 317, 381, 594
Buff, Charlotte, 416, 431–32
Burckhardt, Jakob, 158, 197

Caspar Hauser (Wasserman), 231
Cassirer, Paul, 237
Cervantes, Miguel de, 414
Chamberlain, Eva Wagner, 436
Chamberlain, Houston Stuart, 436
Chamberlain, Neville, 438, 441, 444–45, 448, 452, 453
Chambers, Whittaker, 568
Chamisso, Adelbert von, 247, 254
Chaplin, Charlie, 538, 546
Chekhov, Anton P., 77, 136
China, 576, 577, 578, 581–82
Chou En-lai, 577
Churchill, Winston, 458, 460, 476, 478, 512, 519
Claudel, Paul, 470, 492
"Clown, The" ("Der Bajazzo") (Mann), 67, 77, 89, 125–27, 130, 132
Cocteau, Jean, 547, 548
"Coming Victory of Democracy, The" (Mann), 436–37, 438
communism, 311, 313, 314, 320, 374, 419, 546–47, 555, 558, 568–69
Communist Party, German, 311, 312, 357, 394, 395, 397, 398, 399, 415
Communist Party, Hungarian, 332–33, 373
Communist Party, U.S., 570, 591
concentration camps, 398, 399, 405, 468, 509, 563–64
Confessions of Felix Krull, Confidence Trickster (Die Bekenntnisse des Hochstaplers Felix Krull) (Mann), 95, 163, 169, 220, 233, 238, 239–40, 253, 259, 270, 437, 491, 547, 578, 580–85, 587–93, 604–5, 607–8; comedy in, 77–78, 347, 588–89; readings from, 246, 294, 295, 357, 380, 588, 596, 597, 602, 611
Conrad, Joseph, 366
Conrad, Michael George, 109
"Contessina" (H. Mann), 181
Cooper, Gary, 538
Corneille, Pierre, 225
Cosmopolis (Bourget), 108, 116
"Criticism and Creation" ("Kritik und Schaffen") (Mann), 122

Curtius, Ernst Robert, 332
Czechoslovakia, 341, 439, 440, 441, 444–46, 447–48, 452, 555

Daladier, Édouard, 360, 445
Davids, J. J., 220, 588
Davos, 73, 259–60, 262–65, 325–26
"Death" ("Der Tod"), 121, 127, 130, 140
"Death in Venice" ("Der Tod in Venedig") (Mann), 63, 67, 68, 74, 75, 77, 140, 176, 177, 246, 248–54, 257–62, 266–67, 268, 271, 272, 298, 306, 318, 321, 322, 364, 378, 421, 601, 617; Apollonian vs. Dionysian elements in, 74–75, 78, 261, 262, 266; disease in, 76, 265–66, 271; *Magic Mountain* compared with, 270, 271, 275–76, 321, 328, 347
Degas, Edgar, 517
Dehmel, Richard, 110, 112–13, 301
Delbrück, Rudolph von, 82
democracy, 76, 236–37, 290, 294, 299, 300, 330, 436–37, 438, 597–98; in Germany, 308, 309, 311, 334, 336–37, 352, 384, 395, 404, 499
Denmark, 143, 144–45, 561
Derleth, Ludwig, 197–98, 253
Deussen, Paul, 517–18
"deutsche Republik, Die" (Mann), 383
Dewey, Thomas, 555
Dial Press, 546, 547, 548
diaries of TM, 63–64, 69, 72, 251, 315–16, 318, 322–23, 325, 403, 406, 407, 411–12, 415, 438, 444, 450, 458, 470, 482–83, 489–90, 527, 575, 584; destruction of, 63, 69, 118, 503–4
Dieterle, Charlotte, 469, 538
Dieterle, William, 453, 469, 538
Dietrich, Marlene, 221, 377, 416
"Disillusionment" ("Enttäuschung") (Mann), 122, 127
Disney, Walt, 448, 482, 538
"Disorder and Early Sorrow" ("Unordnung und frühes Leid") (Mann), 355–56, 373
Distel, Hilde, 145
Döblin, Alfred, 463, 472
Doctor Faustus (Marlowe), 491
Dohm, Hedwig (daughter), *see* Pringsheim, Hedwig Dohm
Dohm, Hedwig (mother), 211, 268
Doktor Faustus (Mann), 76, 77, 405, 432, 444, 490–96, 498, 500, 501–10, 512, 521–26, 529–37, 542–44, 546, 553, 570, 577, 580–81, 601, 604, 607; disease and, 491, 494, 534, 535; music in, 494–96, 504, 508–9, 525, 535, 537,

549, 567; Nietzsche and, 491, 494, 516–18, 537; reviews of, 547, 548–49, 554
Dollfuss, Engelbert, 413, 438
Dönitz, Karl, 512, 513
Dose, Johannes, 215–16
Dostoyevsky, Fyodor M., 73, 127, 290–91, 297, 477, 479, 516–17, 524
"Double Leavetaking" ("Zweimaliger Abschied") (Mann), 102–3
"Dr. Biebers Versuchung" ("Dr. Bieber's Temptation") (H. Mann), 166–67
Dreyfus, Alfred, 288
Droemer, Adalbert, 385
Dürer, Albrecht, 525, 526

East Germany, 555, 556, 557, 562–67
Ebers, Hermann, 354
Ebert, Friedrich, 310, 311, 320, 338, 344, 357
Eckermann, Johann Peter, 137
Eden, Anthony, 426, 438
Effi Briest (Fontane), 113, 131, 318
Ehrenberg, Carl, 145–46, 159, 171, 182, 195, 199, 206
Ehrenberg, Paul, 145–46, 147, 154, 156, 195, 236, 304, 325, 494, 564; TM's break with, 182, 193, 198, 524; TM's emotional involvement with, 69, 75, 159–62, 167–70, 172, 181–82, 183, 193, 251, 316, 411–12, 490, 532
Eichendorff, Joseph Freiherr von, 146, 294
Einstein, Albert, 358, 384, 413, 416, 417, 418, 546, 578
Eisenhower, Dwight D., 502, 507, 597
Eisler, Hanns, 538–39, 546, 548–49
Eisner, Kurt, 310, 312, 313
Eitingon, Max, 487
Eliot, T. S., 506, 508, 560
Eloesser, Arthur, 336
Emergency Rescue Committee, 461, 464, 470, 476
Endeavors (Bemühungen) (Mann), 353, 358
Erasmus, Desiderius, 354, 587, 606
Erlenbach, 597, 598–99, 603–4
Eschenburg, Theodor, 309
"Essay on the Theatre" (Mann), 225, 226, 234
Eulenberg, Herbert, 352
Eulenburg, Prinz Phillip von, 240
Evans, Luther, 570
Ewers, Ludwig, 94, 95, 110, 270

Falckenberg, Otto, 239
Faltin, Hermann, 308

"Fantasia on Goethe" (Mann), 547–48
fascism, 77, 334, 378–79, 427, 436–37,
  438, 448; *see also* Nazism, Nazi Ger-
  many
Fast, Howard, 579
Faust (Goethe), 359, 392, 444, 449–50,
  452, 462, 491, 508, 554
Fehling, Hermann, 99
Feist, Hans, 571
Feldafing, 312–13, 316, 323, 325
Feuchtwanger, Lion, 469, 497
Fichte, Johann Gottlieb, 291, 333
Fielitz, Alexander von, 91–92, 95, 106,
  117
Fiorenza (Mann), 138–39, 158, 163, 181,
  186, 196–97, 206, 207, 208, 214, 270,
  359; production of, 225, 226, 267,
  302, 318, 357, 358, 362, 417; reviews
  of, 217, 267
Fischer, Ernst, 361–62
Fischer, Hedwig, 179, 384, 395, 408
Fischer, Samuel, 99, 119, 123, 125, 127,
  155, 171, 179, 215, 220, 223, 232,
  235, 247, 254, 259, 269, 271, 281, 298,
  317, 331, 344, 351, 355, 366, 384, 395,
  407, 408, 414; *Reflections* and, 293,
  303, 309; TM's correspondence with,
  153, 154, 156–57, 159, 161, 222, 293,
  300, 303, 338, 385
Flaubert, Gustave, 226, 620
Fleischmann, Rudolf, 429
Flinker, Martin, 598, 612, 614
Florence, 138–39, 158, 162–65, 357, 605
Foerster, Friedrich Wilhelm, 290
Fontane, Theodor, 113, 131, 149, 178,
  240, 244–45, 253, 254, 317–18
France, 66, 253, 288, 311, 335, 339–40,
  343, 427, 452, 453; appeasement and,
  439, 441, 444–45, 448; Germany's re-
  lations with, 338, 339–40, 343,
  373–74, 381, 425, 439; in World War
  I, 280, 283, 286, 293, 306; in World
  War II, 455, 458–59, 461, 480, 481,
  502–3
Franco, Francisco, 427
Frank, Bruno, 274, 292, 311, 404, 417,
  434, 441, 453, 506; in California, 458,
  460, 469, 497, 498, 501
Frank, Hans, 551
Frank, Liesl, 469
Frankfurt, 225, 226, 335, 563, 597;
  Goethe's house in, 392–93
Frankfurter Zeitung, 286, 292, 336–37,
  343, 346
Franz Ferdinand, Archduke of Austria-
  Hungary, 279, 284
Frederick the Great, 211, 212, 219,

224–25, 234, 253, 337, 342, 521; TM's
  essay on, 283–85
Frederick William IV, King of Prussia,
  81
Frederick and the Great Coalition (Mann),
  285
"Frederick and the Great Coalition of
  1756," 283–84, 617
French Revolution, 296, 305, 330, 392
Freud, Sigmund, 147, 252, 276, 389, 390,
  429, 487, 488, 516, 518, 532; TM's
  lectures on, 376–77, 380, 387, 426,
  427
"Freud and the Future" ("Freud und die
  Zukunft") (Mann), 389, 426, 427
Frey, Alexander, 546
Frey, Karl (Konrad Falke), 433
Frick, Wilhelm, 397–98, 542
Frisch, Efraim, 331–32
Frühlingssturm, Der (Spring Storm), 101–3
Fuchs, Klaus, 568
Fudakowski, Jan, 250
"Fulvia" (H. Mann), 188–89
Furtwängler, Wilhelm, 539, 542

Galsworthy, John, 349
Gandhi, Indira, 567
Geburt der Tragödie, Die (Nietzsche), 491
"Gefallen" (Mann), 107–10, 112, 113,
  127, 153
"Geiger John Baring, Der" ("The Fiddler
  John Baring") (Martens), 143
"Geist und Tat" ("Intellect and Action")
  (Mann), 287–88
*Genesis of a Novel, The (Die Entstehung eines
  Romans)* (Mann), 553
George, Stefan, 197–98, 253, 322
"German Address–An Appeal to Reason"
  ("Deutsche Ansprache–Ein Appell an
  die Vernunft") (Mann), 383–84
German culture, 68, 76, 82, 122, 283,
  316, 330, 346, 347, 374, 380, 433,
  437–38
Germany, 253, 308–16; Allied occupation of, 519, 556; army service in,
  103, 124, 154–57; British relations
  with, 237, 279, 280, 425–26, 438, 439;
  elections in, 357, 374, 382, 383–84,
  394–95, 397, 413; French relations
  with, 338, 339–40, 343, 373–74, 381,
  425, 439; nationalism in, 81, 96, 338,
  373–75, 378, 384, 391, 392; postwar,
  519–23, 531, 538–43, 546, 548,
  555–59, 562–67, 609–11; revolution
  in, 309–15, 320; Soviet zone of, 555,
  556, 557, 562–67; suffrage in, 236–37,
  315; TM's return visits to, 556–59,

Germany *(cont.)*
562–65, 587, 596, 602–3; unification
of, 81–82, 84, 96, 237, 282; in World
War I, 279–302, 304–6, 308–11, 315,
316; *see also* Nazism, Nazi Germany
"Germany and the Germans" (Mann),
510–11
Gesellschaft, 103, 109, 110, 139, 143, 152
"Gesetz, Das" ("The Law" or "The Tables
of the Law") (Mann), 487–89, 493
*Gespenst des Golem, Der (The Ghost of the
Golem)* (Held), 368
"gestohlene Dokument, Das" (H. Mann),
127
Gibo, Arthur, 240–42, 530
Gide, André, 332, 387, 388, 408
Giehse, Therese, 394, 396, 410, 418, 420,
428, 561, 596, 612
"Gladius Dei" (Mann), 163–65, 167
Glasperlenspiel, Das (The Glass Bead Game)
(Hesse), 501
Glöckner, Ernst, 253
Goebbels, Joseph, 394, 399, 407, 415,
423, 430, 508
Goethe, August, 431, 432, 452, 607
Goethe, Johann Wolfgang von, 73, 89,
111, 113, 117, 120–21, 137, 178, 210,
216, 220, 251, 318, 327, 329, 350, 385,
387, 420, 457, 462, 467, 479, 508, 531,
546, 547–48, 605, 607, 620; *Joseph and
His Brothers* influenced by, 354, 359,
363, 462; TM's lectures on, 329–31,
335, 337, 353, 361, 391–93, 395, 397,
431, 432, 444, 558, 560, 564; TM's
novel about, *see Beloved Returns, The*;
TM compared with, 392–93, 575, 578,
618
Goethe, Sexus, und Liebe (Theilhaber), 416
"Goethe as a Representative of the Bour-
geois Epoch" ("Goethe als Repräsen-
tant des bürgerlichen Zeitalters")
(Mann), 391–93, 395, 397
"Goethe's Career as a Writer" ("Goethes
Laufbahn als Schriftsteller") (Mann),
391–93, 397, 431, 432
Goethes Gespräche mit Riemer (anti-Nazi
pamphlet), 531
Gogol, Nikolai V., 127
Goncharov, Ivan A., 145
Goncourt, Edmond de, 130, 132
Goncourt, Jules de, 130, 132
Göring, Emmy Sonnemann, 415
Göring, Hermann, 397–98, 399, 407, 415,
438, 503, 513, 522–23, 531
Götterdämmerung (Wagner), 254
Göttinen, Die (The Goddesses) (H. Mann),
165, 179–80

Götzendämmerung (Twilight of the Idols)
(Nietzsche), 150, 265
Götz von Berlichingen (Goethe), 178
Grammann, Alexander, 91
Grautoff, Otto, 78, 92, 101, 154, 156,
435, 611; as book reviewer, 68, 168,
178; TM's correspondence with, 65,
68, 107–13, 118, 119, 123, 125,
126–27, 129, 131, 132, 139, 145, 155,
160, 167–68, 183; TM's marriage and,
207, 208
Great Britain, 82, 311, 339, 360, 373,
448, 452–55, 476; appeasement and,
425–26, 438, 439, 441, 444–46, 448;
Germany's relations with, 237, 279,
280, 425–26, 438, 439; in World War
I, 280, 283, 286, 310; in World War
II, 455, 459, 460, 462–63, 467–68,
476, 478, 489, 492, 502–3
Grieg, Edvard, 117
Grotewohl, Otto, 557, 566
Gründgens, Gustaf, 358, 362, 396, 561
Guerard, Albert, 177
Gustav V, King of Sweden, 380–81

Hallgarten, Ricki, 318, 349, 396, 552
Hallstein, Walter, 558–59
Hamburg, 83, 84, 93, 302, 310, 331, 358,
362, 602
Hamlet (Shakespeare), 109, 245
Hamsun, Knut, 417
Hanfstängl, Ernst (Putzi), 416
Harden, Maximilian, 240, 245, 292
Hardwicke, Sir Cedric, 469
Harrer, Karl, 334
Harris, Sir Arthur, 478
Hartenstein, Frieda, 97
Hartleben, Otto Erich, 117
Hartungen, Christoph Hartung von, 165,
167, 174, 263
Harvard University, 416, 418, 440
Hatvany, Lajos, 427
Hauptmann, Gerhart, 66, 72, 99, 184,
185, 231, 270, 282, 337, 344–45, 350,
357, 366, 383, 519, 597; Nazis and,
384–85, 413, 414, 430; Peeperkorn's
resemblance to, 344–45, 350, 352, 357
Haushofer, Karl, 109
Hausmann, Manfred, 541–42, 543
Hegel, Georg Wilhelm Friedrich, 147
Heimann, Moritz, 156
Heine, Carl, 225
Heine, Heinrich, 97, 102, 117, 542
Heine, Thomas Theodor, 119, 141
Heisenberg, Christine, 619
Held, Hans Ludwig, 367–68, 546, 596

Henlein, Konrad, 444, 446
Hermann, Eva, 570
Hermanns, Leo, 321
Herz, Ida, 413, 420
Herzog, Wilhelm, 281, 311
Hess, Rudolf, 531
Hesse, Hermann, 179, 235–36, 356, 393, 405, 423, 425, 426, 433, 446, 471, 476, 501, 525, 542, 547, 554, 555, 587, 606, 612
Hesterberg, Trude, 377, 416
Heuser, Klaus, 75, 370–71, 420, 422, 450, 573, 592
Heuser, Werner, 75, 370
Heuss, Theodor, 607, 610, 611, 612
Heyck, Eduard, 197
Hildebrandt, Rainer, 564, 565
Himmler, Heinrich, 406, 511, 513
Hindenburg, Paul von, 309, 311, 357, 382, 394–95, 397, 399, 413
Hirohito, Emperor of Japan, 473
Hiss, Alger, 568
Hitchcock, Alfred, 469
Hitler, Adolf, 69, 76, 343–46, 393–99, 406, 407, 413, 414, 415, 423, 428, 438–42, 452–56, 494–95, 520, 538, 564, 618; anti-Semitism of, 334, 393, 394, 399, 462; appeasement and, 425, 438, 439, 441, 444–46; World War II and, 459, 462, 465, 467, 468, 469, 473, 478, 480, 481, 489, 497, 511, 512, 521, 546
Hoad, Lew, 591
Hoffman, Johannes, 312, 313
Hoffmann, E.T.A., 116, 152
Hoffmann, Paul, 600
Hofmann, Ludwig von, 274
Hofmannsthal, Gerty von, 231
Hofmannsthal, Hugo von, 225, 231, 267, 308, 318, 341, 357, 366, 377
Hohenberg, Arthur, 525
Hölderlin, Friedrich, 71, 322
Holitscher, Arthur, 142, 150, 154, 156, 179
Holland, 311, 338, 349, 396, 398, 408, 458, 613
Holm, Korfiz, 139, 141, 159, 232
Holy Sinner, The (Mann), 550–51, 553, 566, 578, 585–86
"Hommage de la France à Thomas Mann," 612
Horkheimer, Max, 550
Horovitz, Jakob, 368
Horthy, Miklós von Nagybanya, 373
"Hour of Gravity" ("Schwere Stunde") (Mann), 209–10, 244, 608
House Un-American Activities Commit-
tee (HUAC), 538–39, 546, 568, 570, 583, 585, 593, 598
"How Jappe and Do Escobar Fought" ("Wie Jappe und Do Escobar sich prügelten") (Mann), 74, 246–47, 249, 284
"How to Win the Peace" (Mann), 475
Hübscher, Artur, 374
Hugenberg, Alfred, 377
Hull, Cordell, 439–40
Humperdinck, Engelbert, 193
Hungary, 313, 332–33, 341
"Hungry Ones, The" ("Die Hungern-den") (Mann), 170–71, 179
Huntziger, Charles, 459
Hutten, Ulrich von, 587, 606
Huxley, Aldous, 408
Huysmans, Joris-Karl, 66

Ibsen, Henrik, 66, 89, 99, 102, 110, 112, 124, 138, 224, 307
"Idea of Education in Goethe and Tolstoy, The" ("Der Idee der Erziehung bei Goethe und Tolstoy") (Mann), 329–31, 335, 337, 353, 361
Impekoven, Niddy, 325
Im Schlaraffenland (In the Land of Cockaigne) (H. Mann), 133, 157–58, 207–8
Independent Socialist Party, German, 310, 311, 322
"indische Weltmutter, Die" ("The Indian World-Mother") (Zimmer), 458
In einer Familie (H. Mann), 103
"Infant Prodigy, The" ("Das Wunderkind") (Mann), 187–88, 207
Infant Prodigy, The (Mann), 284, 298
"innere Emigration, Die" (Thiess), 520
"In the Looking Glass" ("Im Spiegel") (Mann), 227
Isherwood, Christopher, 418
Italy, 459; fascism in, 334, 378–79, 427, 437, 438 TM in, 63, 74, 113–16, 122–23, 124, 127–28, 137–39, 158, 161–65, 216, 225–26, 227, 358, 363, 378, 601–2, 605

Jackson, Donald, 585
Jagd nach Liebe, Die (The Hunt for Love) (H. Mann), 181, 186, 188, 203, 216, 241
Jakobsky, Ludwig, 110
Jaloux, Edmond, 360
Jannings, Emil, 377
Japan, 472–73, 519

Jens, Inge, 64
Jenseits von Gut und Böse (Beyond Good and Evil) (Nietzsche), 82
Jesenska, Milena, 272
Jessen, Friedrich, 260, 265, 326
Jews, Jewishness, 288, 311, 331–32, 381, 445, 448, 469, 556; Austrian, 438, 447; culture and, 194, 214, 437–38; in TM's work, 116, 213–15, 229, 342; *see also* anti-Semitism
Johann Siegmund Mann, Corn Merchants, Commission and Transport Agents, 84–85, 86, 93, 96, 98–99, 101, 131, 134
Johst, Hanns, 546
Joseph and His Brothers (Joseph und seine Brüder) (Mann), 75–76, 163, 307, 354–55, 358–60, 363–69, 371, 372, 385, 388–91, 431, 458, 487, 502, 618, 619; Goethe's influence on, 354, 359, 363, 462; myth in, 359, 364–65, 367; readings from, 375, 380, 383, 409–10, 420, 427–28, 466, 611; research for, 354–55, 367–68; *see also Joseph in Egypt; Joseph the Provider; Tales of Jacob, The; Young Joseph*
Joseph in Egypt (Joseph in Ägypten) (Mann), 158, 395, 403, 405, 411–14, 416, 420–22, 427–28, 440, 449, 457
Joseph the Provider (Joseph der Ernährer) (Mann), 461–62, 466, 468, 475, 477, 479, 482–83, 487–88, 500, 501, 504
Joyce, James, 77, 506
"Jüdischen Glaubens" ("Jewish Faith") (H. Mann), 115
Juliana, Queen of the Netherlands, 609, 613
Jung, Carl Gustav, 372, 382, 390, 409, 518
"Justifications" ("Berechtigungen") (Mann), 239

Kafka, Franz, 159, 177, 272, 448
Kahler, Erich von, 525, 557, 578, 583–84
Kahr, Gustav von, 344, 345–46
Kaiser, Georg, 470
Kanova, Mimi, 281, 335, 377
Kant, Immanuel, 96, 117, 146–47
Kapp, Wolfgang, 320
Karsh, Yousuf, 527
Kassner, Rudolf, 258
Kästner, Erich, 543
Katharineum (TM's school), 95, 96, 97, 101, 103–4, 362, 611
Katzenstein, Erich, 434, 590
Kaulbach, Friedrich, 183

Kellen, Konrad (formerly Konrad Katzenellenbogen), 474, 497
Keller, Gottfried, 195, 394
Kerényi, Karl, 417, 605
Kerr, Alfred, 122, 235, 267, 406
Kerr, Walter, 360
Kessler, Harry Graf, 309, 357
Kesten, Hermann, 437
Kestner, Charlotte Buff, 416, 431–32
Kestner, Georg Christian, 432
Kestner, Johann, 416
Keyserling, Hermann Graf, 320
Kiel, Hanna, 404, 405
Kielland, Alexander Lange, 124
Kierkegaard, Sören, 348–49
Kilian, Magdalena, 280
Kind dieser Zeit (Child of this Time) (K. Mann), 552
"Kinder Karneval" (Kaulbach), 183, 603
"Kindernovelle" (K. Mann), 356, 366
Kingdon, Frank, 453, 461
Kirdorf, Emil, 381
"kleine Professor, Der" (Mann), 110
kleine Stadt, Die (The Little Town) (H. Mann), 237
Kleist, Heinrich von, 89, 370–73, 458, 519
Klemperer, Otto, 524, 527
Knappertsbusch, Hans, 406, 542
Knoll, Rudolf, 97, 174, 246–47
Knopf, Alfred, 393, 412, 440, 446, 461, 481, 500, 504, 514, 553, 554, 579, 605, 608, 612
Kogon, Eugen, 563–64, 565
Kolb, Annette, 423, 434, 481, 494, 525, 544, 549
Kolb, Walter, 548, 559, 562
kommt der Tag, Es (H. Mann), 426
Korda, Sir Alexander, 528
Korean War, 575–78, 584
Korrodi, Eduard, 332, 411, 424, 425, 427, 542
Kramer, Theodor, 448
Kraus, Karl, 300
Kripgans, Hans, 602
Kritik der Moderne (Bahr), 107–8
Kröger, Nelly, *see* Mann, Nelly Kröger
Kubin, Alfred, 143
"Kultur und Sozialismus" (Mann), 374
Kurz, Fräulein, 366
Küsnacht, 409–16, 424, 428–29, 443–44, 446, 454, 562, 572

Lagerlöf, Selma, 381
La Guardia, Fiorello, 412

Lampe, Arno, 366
Landauer, Walter, 470
Landolt, Emil, 611
Landshoff, Fritz, 424, 561
Lange, Hermann, 609
Langen, Albert, 117, 119, 127, 141, 159, 167, 173, 195, 237
Langner, Felix, 501
Lardner, Ring, Jr., 538
Lasker-Schüler, Elsa, 206
Lasky, Melvin, 595
Lawrence, D. H., 382
"Leben–nicht Zerstörung" ("Life–Not Destruction") (Mann), 299–300
Lehmann, Lotte, 453
Leiden des jungen Werthers, Die (The Sorrows of Young Werther) (Goethe), 216, 392, 416
Lenin (Vladimir Ilyich Ulyanov), 296, 309, 320, 337
Leoncavallo, Ruggiero, 125
Leopardi, Giacomo, 71
Lessing, Gotthold Ephraim, 318, 375–76
Lessing, Theodor, 222, 238
Leverkühn, August, 99
Leverkühn, Paul, 494
Levetzow, Ulrike von, 251, 575
Levin, Harry, 506, 508
Lewisohn, Ludwig, 405
Library of Congress, 471, 477, 479, 480, 481, 492, 498, 505, 510, 513, 529, 540, 558, 570
Lie, Jonas, 124, 130
Liebermann, Max, 358, 366
Liebknecht, Karl, 309
Lindbergh, Charles, 467–68
Lion, Ferdinand, 433, 455
Lippmann, Walter, 513–14
Literarische Echo, Das, 168, 180, 227, 239
Little Herr Friedemann (Der kleine Herr Friedemann) (Mann), 137, 139, 153, 298
"Little Herr Friedemann" ("Der kleine Herr Friedemann") (Mann), 66–67, 75, 117–21, 123, 127, 130; "The Clown" compared with, 125, 126, 127
Litzmann, Berthold, 226, 326
Litzmann, Grete, 326
Lloyd George, David, 315
Loewenstein, Karl, 404
Löffler, Wilhelm, 613, 614
Lohengrin (Wagner), 109, 120, 290, 583
Löhr, Eva-Marie, 279, 368
Löhr, Ilse-Marie, 279, 368–69
Löhr, Josef, 155–56, 180, 207, 227, 279, 368
Löhr, Julia Elisabeth Therese Mann, 88,

97, 101, 106, 115, 117, 124, 131–32, 139, 145, 227, 279, 522, 523, 530; marriage of, 155–56, 207; suicide of, 368–69; TM's marriage and, 207, 208
Löhr, Rose-Marie, 279, 368–69
London, 349, 540–41, 560, 602
Lorentz, Elizabeth Meyer, 469
Lorentz, Pare, 469
Loved Ones, The (Die Geliebten) (Mann), 134, 162–63, 169–70, 181, 182, 199, 532–34
Löwenstein, Prince Hubertus zu, 433
Lowe-Porter, Helen, 266–67, 479, 487, 494, 504, 531, 536
Lübeck, 83–93, 95–106, 109, 137, 177, 258, 296, 409, 478, 479, 609; TM's returns to, 143–44, 149, 206–7, 219, 302, 331, 361, 362, 557, 602, 611; in TM's work, 126, 130, 131, 137, 173, 207, 216, 307, 361, 362
"Lübeck als geistiger Lebensform" ("Lübeck as a Spiritual Concept of Life") (Mann), 307, 361, 362
Lübeckische Blätter, 99, 101, 235
Lubitsch, Ernst, 472
Lublinski, Samuel, 168, 203, 238–40
Ludendorff, Erich von, 306, 309, 346
Ludwig I, King of Bavaria, 163
"Luischen" (Mann), 124, 125, 127, 128, 217
Lukács, Georg, 177, 257–58, 267, 306, 332–33, 336, 348, 362, 373, 425, 590
Lukács, Josef von, 257, 332–33, 590
Luke, David, 266–67
Luther, Martin, 391, 491–92, 606
Luxemburg, Rosa, 309

MacArthur, Douglas, 576, 577, 581–82, 584
McCarran, Patrick, 600
McCarthy, Joseph, 568, 600
MacLeish, Archibald, 471, 479
Madame Legros (H. Mann), 295–96
Mäder, Bruno, 562, 594, 604
Magic Mountain, The (Der Zauberberg) (Mann), 166, 229, 269–72, 275–76, 281, 284, 298, 302, 313–14, 317, 320–22, 324–29, 330, 335–36, 340–53, 361–62, 367, 380, 381, 387, 397, 466, 494, 502, 515, 618–19; Davos sanatorium and, 73, 263–65; "Death in Venice" compared with, 270, 271, 275–76, 321, 328, 347; *Felix Krull* compared with, 581, 582, 590–91; World War I and, 281, 282, 286–90, 313–14

Mahler, Alma, 549, 567

Mahler, Gustav, 245–46, 248

Mann, Carla Augusta Olga Maria (sister), 88, 101, 106, 124–25, 139, 186, 225, 281; acting of, 171, 180, 181, 184, 208, 222, 225, 240; in *Doctor Faustus*, 522, 523, 530; suicide of, 240–42, 369, 552

Mann, Christine Heisenberg, 619

Mann, Elisabeth (aunt), 98, 131–32

Mann, Elisabeth Marty (grandmother), 86, 87, 89, 98, 99, 424

Mann, Elisabeth Veronika (Medi), *see* Borgese, Elisabeth Mann

Mann, Emilie Wunderlich (grandfather's first wife), 86

Mann, Erika (daughter), 89, 227, 232, 243, 255, 256, 260, 269, 274, 314, 329, 337, 349, 363, 413, 418, 420, 423–24, 428, 440, 443, 444, 449, 470, 476, 492, 507, 514, 539–42, 548, 551–62, 565, 576–77, 587–91, 594–98, 600, 603, 604, 606–11, 619; acting of, 318, 325, 355, 358, 396; anti-Nazi cabaret of, 395–96, 398, 407, 423; birth of, 214–15; health problems of, 285, 393, 591, 606, 613–14; Joseph manuscript saved by, 403–4; Klaus's suicide attempts and, 551–53, 560–62; lesbianism of, 349, 539, 577; marriages of, 362, 418, 434; Nuremberg trials and, 522–23; in United States, 433, 452, 460, 513, 528, 529, 531–32, 539, 540, 546, 551–59, 571, 586, 591

Mann, Fridolin (grandson), 461, 472, 474–75, 482, 493, 534–35, 541, 556, 572, 587, 595, 599, 604, 606, 610, 619–20

Mann, Friedel (uncle), 93, 95, 98, 134

Mann, Gottfried Angelus (Golo) (son), 2, 235, 253, 255–57, 260, 269–70, 285, 292, 318, 329, 365, 368, 369, 405, 406, 428, 436, 455, 459, 461, 463, 500, 552, 556, 561, 566, 570, 595, 606, 615; birth of, 232; on father, 281, 289, 358, 370, 393; Klaus's relationship with, 314, 323

Mann, Gret (daughter-in-law), 461, 475, 493, 535, 541, 562, 589, 595, 606

Mann, Heinrich (Luiz Heinrich) (brother), 84, 87–89, 91, 92, 95, 97–101, 108, 109, 114–15, 123, 179–81, 218, 220, 225–27, 240–42, 246, 268, 327, 408, 414, 424, 429, 453, 504, 507, 609; anti-Nazi activities of, 384–85, 405, 408, 416–17, 426;

Buddenbrooks and, 129, 131–34; death of, 569–70; father's relationship with, 95, 98, 99, 100, 103; financial problems of, 237, 281, 472; in France, 405, 407, 416, 428, 459, 461; health problems of, 103, 128, 165, 335, 428; Hesterberg's affair with, 377, 416; in Italy, 113–15, 122, 124, 128, 133, 143, 156, 158, 162, 179, 203, 235; literary ambitions of, 85, 95, 97, 100, 103, 106, 107, 111, 112, 127, 186; marriages of, 281, 282, 456; paintings and drawings of, 88, 89, 95, 100, 125, 570; political views and liberalism of, 188–89, 237, 281, 287–88, 313, 324, 344, 368, 502; Prussian Academy and, 368, 371, 385, 386, 396, 404; Schmied's affair with, 221–22, 227; sexuality of, 95, 108, 118, 153, 221; TM's correspondence with, 69–70, 157–61, 162, 188–89, 194, 195, 207, 208, 211, 212, 214, 215, 217, 220, 221–22, 231, 233, 247, 272, 280, 282, 300–302, 335, 340, 355, 534; TM's criticism of, 179–80, 186, 188, 202–3, 373; TM's relationship with, 88–89, 91, 107, 127, 133, 134, 157–58, 179–80, 188, 202, 207–8, 214, 217, 226, 233, 281–82, 287–90, 295–96, 299–302, 325, 355, 357, 380, 426, 472, 474, 507, 569; TM compared with, 130, 173, 202–3, 373; in United States, 463–64, 472, 478, 507, 546, 557, 565–66; World War I and, 281–82, 287–88, 295–96, 300–302

Mann, Heinrich (Thomas Johann Heinrich) (father), 84–88, 91–96, 98–101, 103, 141, 168, 194, 208, 243, 362, 365, 609; *Buddenbrooks* and, 129, 132; business dealings of, 84–85, 88, 92, 93, 111; death of, 100–101, 121, 148–49; TM compared with, 189

Mann, Joachim Siegmund (great-great grandfather), 86

Mann, Johann (great-great-great-great grandfather), 86

Mann, Johann Siegmund (grandfather), 86

Mann, Johann Siegmund (great-grandfather), 86

Mann, Julia da Silva Bruhns (mother), 86–90, 95, 96, 101, 103, 106, 114, 115, 124, 132, 139, 155, 157, 180, 185, 189, 207, 217, 280, 308, 338, 522, 523; Carla's death and, 240, 241; death of, 341; family background of, 86–87; husband's death and, 100–101; husband's estate and, 99–100, 106–7; husband's relationship with, 98, 99; pregnancies and childbirths of, 87, 88, 98; TM's marriage and, 207, 208; TM's relationship with, 89–90, 91, 101, 103, 106, 109, 113

Mann, Julia Elisabeth Therese, *see* Löhr, Julia Elisabeth Therese Mann

Mann, Katia Pringsheim (wife), 70, 142, 155, 182–84, 193–217, 219, 222, 225–28, 230, 234–35, 240, 243–45, 255–57, 269, 271–75, 281, 286, 325, 326, 329, 331–33, 335, 337, 340, 341, 349–50, 355–56, 360–63, 366–68, 370, 374, 375, 377–78, 380–83, 398, 405, 426–28, 433–39, 602, 611, 619; family background of, 70, 71, 182–83, 193, 194; in France, 407, 416, 418, 428, 434; Gide's views on, 387, 388; health problems of, 73, 259–60, 262, 271, 272, 285, 314, 315, 316, 321–22, 332, 361–63, 366, 383, 393, 428, 438, 572–73; Jewish background of, 182, 193, 194, 203, 213, 232; Klaus's suicide attempts and, 551–53, 560–61; marriage of, 63, 69–72, 193, 207–8, 616–17; as model for Sieglinde in "Blood of the Walsungs," 211–14; as model for Imma in *Royal Highness,* 228, 229, 232, 316; as mother, 255, 260, 323; nervous breakdowns of, 285, 317; postwar European visits of, 541–44, 560–63, 565, 571–75, 587–89, 594–99, 602–10, 612–15; pregnancies of, 209–12, 214–15, 223, 232, 240, 259, 302, 303, 304, 308, 314; revolution and, 310–11; Swiss exile of, 404–5, 407, 409, 410, 413, 420, 424; TM's admiration for, 70, 193, 194, 204; TM's betrayal of, 217, 221; TM's correspondence with, 199–204, 210, 260, 316, 323; TM's courtship of, 193–204, 316; TM's death and, 613–15; TM's disagreements with, 288, 308, 311, 322, 343, 467; TM's marital problems with, 316, 317, 323; TM's sexual relationship with, 64, 70, 72, 76, 209, 315, 316, 322–23; TM's tributes to, 382, 603; in United States, 412, 418–19, 433, 434, 438, 443–45, 447–48, 452, 458, 461, 463–69, 471, 474–77, 480–82, 492, 493, 500, 505, 513, 514, 528, 529, 537, 548, 551–58, 565, 567, 568, 571, 589–92; World War I and, 288, 292

Mann, Klaus Heinrich (son), 223, 232, 255–56, 260, 269, 274, 275, 281, 289, 292, 314, 318, 329, 337, 349, 356, 358, 388, 394, 397, 407, 409, 434–35, 443, 513, 546, 547, 555, 556, 557; anti-Nazi activities of, 396, 398–99, 408, 409, 423, 424; drug addiction of, 323, 396, 435; father's love for, 72, 76, 323, 369, 390, 474–75; health problems of, 271, 285; homosexuality of, 323, 349, 396, 552; suicide attempts of, 551–53, 560–62, 619; in United States, 460, 461, 463, 551–53; writing of, 323, 355, 356, 358, 362, 366, 396, 492, 552, 561

Mann, Leonie (niece), 428

Mann, Magdalena Kilian (sister-in-law), 280

Mann, Michael (son), 314, 329, 338, 343, 358, 363, 377–78, 388, 405, 407, 410, 428, 461, 504, 535, 561, 589–90, 595, 605, 606, 619; father's relationship with, 353, 370

Mann, Mimi Kanova (sister-in-law), 281, 335, 377

Mann, Monika (daughter), 240, 251, 255, 256, 259, 260, 269, 365, 446, 589; on father, 409–10; father's relationship with, 273, 605; Golo's relationship with, 256–57; health problems of, 285

Mann, Nelly Kröger (sister-in-law), 416, 456, 472, 477, 478, 507

Mann, Siegmund (great-great-great grandfather), 86

Mann, Thomas (Paul Thomas): American citizenship of, 478, 500, 502, 593–94, 598; awards and honors of, 317, 365, 373, 380–81, 382, 387, 393, 416, 418, 429, 453, 467, 471, 520, 537, 541, 556, 557–59, 560, 562, 565, 594, 602, 609, 611, 614; childhood of, 87–95; daily routine of, 243–44, 255; death of, 613–15; depressions of, 69, 104, 159, 186, 219, 220, 332, 437, 438, 441, 465, 467, 546, 604; diary of, *see* diaries of TM; early writing of, 97, 102–3, 107–10, 114–24; editorial jobs of, 141–42, 143, 150, 158, 167; education of, 91–93, 95, 96, 97, 101, 103–4, 109, 110, 111; family background of, 84–88, 179; as father, 72, 77, 227, 255, 260, 269, 273, 289, 303, 308, 314, 323, 343, 353, 358, 369–70, 551–53, 561–62, 619; financial problems of, 113, 141–42, 158, 160, 274, 281, 317, 338, 586; financial security of, 70, 178, 205; guilt feelings of, 67, 77, 153, 211, 250, 356, 562, 606; health problems of, 156–57, 165, 174, 198–99,

Mann, Thomas *(cont.)*
219, 232, 233, 247, 293, 294, 299, 316,
329, 332, 361, 367, 382, 385, 393, 428,
433, 434, 435, 438, 500, 504–5, 513,
523, 527–30, 532, 541, 550, 553–54,
562, 566, 597, 608–9, 613–15 homoeroticism of, 63, 64, 69, 70, 73–75, 97,
101, 167–70, 200, 246, 250, 251, 275,
276, 316, 322, 323, 328, 329, 331,
369, 370–71, 390–91, 411–12, 420,
422, 452, 474–75, 503, 543, 573–77,
582; literary ambitions of, 63, 67, 68,
71, 97, 103, 152; marriage of, *see*
Mann, Katia Pringsheim; military service of, 154–57, 159, 282, 286, 294;
nervousness and anxiety of, 64,
210–11, 234, 247, 274, 281, 292, 294,
308, 315, 316, 318, 329, 367, 405, 407,
410, 411, 439, 441–42, 476, 566, 607,
610; passion of, 63, 69, 74, 75, 97,
101, 159–62, 167–70, 172, 174,
181–82, 183, 193, 251, 252, 323; poetry of, 68, 97, 102–3, 110, 125, 152,
262, 308, 312, 313, 314; political
commitment of, 76–77, 347, 361, 365,
373, 378, 403, 463, 539, 578–80, 620;
public vs. private image of, 63–64, 67,
68, 70, 71–72, 77–78; self-confidence
of, 110, 130, 142, 204; self-hatred and
self-disgust of, 67, 68, 69, 118, 125,
150–51; self-portraiture of, 63–67,
70–71, 72, 74, 77–78, 125–27, 173,
244, 253; self-promotion of, 68, 152,
168, 199, 501; suicidal feelings of,
159, 160; Swiss exile of, 403–7,
409–17, 420–26, 431–39, 443–44
Thomas Mann Fund, 612
Mann, Toni, 482, 493, 541, 556, 599, 604
Mann, Viktor (Karl Viktor) (brother), 98,
100, 101, 106, 112, 124, 125, 129,
132, 139, 140, 141, 142, 154, 155,
180, 181, 202, 227, 241, 280; in postwar Germany, 521, 537–38, 540, 555;
TM's marriage and, 207, 208
*Mann von vierzig Jahren, Der (The Man of
Forty Years)* (Wassermann), 280
Manolescu, George, 219–20
Marcks, Erich, 318
Marcuse, Ludwig, 497, 507, 548
Margaritis, Loris, 187
"Mario and the Magician" ("Mario und
der Zauberer") (Mann), 378–79, 380
Marshall, George C., 584
Martens, Armin, 117, 145, 155, 183;
TM's love for, 69, 74, 97, 162, 172,
174, 251 "Tonio Kröger" and, 69, 97,
172, 174

Martens, Ilse, 97, 100, 131, 145, 150, 155;
TM's answers to questionnaire of,
117, 194
Martens, Kurt, 142–43, 145, 150, 152,
155, 161, 168, 171, 180, 187, 196,
200–201, 208, 218, 219, 309, 338, 608
Marti, Louis, 543
Marty, Elisabeth, *see* Mann, Elisabeth
Marty
Marty, Emma, 91
Marty, Heinrich, 98
Marty, Johann Heinrich, 86, 144
Marty, Wilhelm, 131, 137
Marx, Karl, 309
Marx, Wilhelm, 357
März, 235–36, 268
Masaryk, Tomáš, 429
Mass und Wert (Measure and Worth), 433,
434, 435, 438, 455
"Master and Dog" ("Herr und Hund")
(Mann), 273, 293, 303–4, 313, 356,
612
Mauriac, Franáois, 361
Medici, Lorenzo de, 163
"Meeting" ("Begegnung") (Mann), 115
Mein Kampf (Hitler), 381
Meisel, Hans, 448
Meistersinger, Die (Wagner), 298
Mendelssohn, Peter de, 63, 64, 299,
527
Menschliches, Allzumenschliches (Nietzsche),
129
Menuhin, Yalta, 589–90
Menuhin, Yehudi, 589
Mephisto (K. Mann), 362, 561
Merezkhovsky, Dmitri, 330
Merian, Hans, 110
"Message for the German People"
("Botschaft für das Deutsche Volk")
(Mann), 562–63
Meyer, Agnes, 434, 439–40, 458, 460,
461, 464–65, 470–72, 474, 476–79,
481–83, 490, 492–93, 498, 502, 507,
515, 579, 594, 598
Meyer, Elizabeth, 469
Meyer, Eugene, 434, 440, 460, 464, 477,
481
Michel, Albin, 570, 571
Michelangelo, 487, 488, 575
"Mimik Bund" (acting club), 318
"Mind and Art" ("Geist und Kunst")
(Mann), 234, 253, 283
Minna von Barnhelm (Lessing), 318
Möbius, P. J., 491, 517
Moes, Wladyslaw, 250, 266, 369, 370,
475, 574
Molo, Walter von, 519–21, 525, 543

Moltke, Count Kuno von, 240
"Moment of Happiness, A" ("Ein Glück") (Mann), 180, 187
Mondadori, Arnoldo, 544
"Monolog" (Mann), 68, 152
Montgomery, Bernard, 489
"Moonlight" ("Das Mondlicht") (Mann), 114
Morgenröthe (Nietzsche), 109
Morrison, Philip, 578, 579, 580
Mozart, Wolfgang Amadeus, 286
Mühlestein, Hans, 575
Mühsam, Erich, 179, 270, 311
Müller, Ernst, 209
Müller, Friedrich, 308
Münchener Neueste Nachrichten, 112, 215, 216, 309, 319, 406
Munich, 103–13, 116–19, 121, 124, 138–43, 145–61, 165, 167–72, 184, 193–202, 204–11, 223, 227, 246, 254–57, 269, 271–74, 326–27, 408, 409, 479, 513, 540; anti-Nazi activities in, 383–85, 395–96, 399; cultural life of, 105–6, 118, 183, 233–34, 295–98, 303, 358; Nazism in, 334, 345–46, 394, 398, 407–8, 445; revolution in, 310–11, 313, 314–15; TM's postwar visits to, 564, 587, 596; in TM's work, 163–64
Munich University, 368, 383, 398
"Murderer Bittenfels Overpowered by Sunset, The" (Mann), 125
"Music in Munich" (Mann), 297
Musil, Robert, 172, 221, 282, 318
Mussolini, Benito, 378, 427, 441, 445, 456
"Mysterium" (H. Mann), 181

Napoleon I, 81, 84, 198, 426
Napoleon III, 414
National Assembly, German, 81, 315, 322
National Socialist German Workers' Party (NS-DAP), 334, 343–46, 381–82, 383, 395; *see also* Nazi Germany; Nazism
"Natural Law and Humanity in World Politics" (Troeltsch), 346–47
Nazism, Nazi Germany, 69, 76, 78, 334–35, 336, 393–99, 403–48, 452–56, 519–23, 525–27, 542, 546, 547, 551, 564, 618; in Austria, 438–39, 453–54; book burnings in, 407–8; in *Doctor Faustus*, 491, 493, 494–95, 521–22, 526–27, 536; in elections, 374, 383–84, 394–95; Nuremberg trials and, 522–23, 531, 536, 555–56;

publication and sale of Mann's books in, 407–11, 414, 415, 419, 422–23, 440, 447; Spanish Civil War and, 427, 441; TM's attacks on, 383–85, 396, 424–25; TM criticized by, 374, 403, 405, 412; in World War II, 455, 458–63, 465, 467–71, 473, 476, 478–81, 489, 491, 497–99, 502–3, 507–13
Nehru, Jawaharlal, 567, 602
Nehru, Vidaya Lakshmi Pandit, 567
Nemerov, Howard, 118
Neue Deutsche Rundschau, 119, 123, 172, 179
Neue Freie Presse, 186, 246, 318, 357, 377
Neue Merkur, 283, 331–32
Neue Rundschau, 186–87, 206, 214, 215, 219, 228, 232, 233, 236, 268, 271, 282–85, 294, 338, 341, 355, 406, 414, 514
Neue Zürcher Zeitung, 332, 411, 423, 424, 427, 542
Neumann, Alfred, 449, 519, 537, 556, 596
Neumann, Kitty, 537, 556
"New Humanism, The" (Mann), 498
Newman, Ernest, 560
Newton, Caroline, 443, 456, 529
New York Times, The, 579, 583, 600
New York Times Book Review, The, 554
Nicholas II, Tsar of Russia, 279–80, 296
Nicolson, Harold, 540–41
Nidden, 383, 385, 388, 395, 513
Niemöller, Martin, 468
Nietzsche, Elisabeth, 326
Nietzsche, Friedrich W., 82, 108, 113, 117, 119, 146, 203, 266, 268, 297, 326, 329, 358, 392, 396, 435, 450, 467, 480; Bertram's book about, 306–8, 364; *Doctor Faustus* and, 491, 494, 516–18, 537; TM's lecture on, 529, 537, 539–40, 542; TM influenced by, 67–68, 71, 72, 108–9, 114, 129, 149, 150, 189, 265, 283, 291, 294, 295, 307, 362, 491
Nietzsche (Bertram), 306–8, 364
Nixon, Richard M., 568
Nobel Prize, 373, 380–81, 382, 387, 471
Noordwijk, 453–54, 544, 613
Novalis (Baron Friedrich von Hardenberg), 266, 324
Nuremberg, 318, 344
Nuremberg trials, 522–23, 531, 536, 555–56

"Occult Experiences" ("Okkulte Erlebnisse") (Mann), 341, 346

Odets, Clifford, 538
"Old Fontane, The" ("Der alte Fontane")
 (Mann), 244–45
Old King, The (Der alte König) (Mann),
 110
"On Myself" (lectures) (Mann), 458
"On the Jewish Question" (Mann),
 331–32
"On the Psychology of Suffering" ("Zur
 Psychologie des Leidenden") (Mann),
 116
Opitz, Walter, 186, 233, 240
Oprecht, Hans, 598
Oprecht Emil, 433, 436, 470, 536, 541,
 561, 596
Ortega y Gasset, José, 415

Pabst, G. W., 377
Pacurariu, Aurelian, 431
Pagels, Hermann, 93
Pagliacci (opera), 67, 125
Painlevé, Paul, 360
Palestine, 382, 383, 448
Palestrina, Italy, 114, 128, 130
Palestrina (Pfitzner), 297–98
Pan, 110, 112–13, 117
Pan-Europa movement, 360–61, 365
Panizza, Oskar, 115
Pannwitz, Rudolf, 315
Papen, Franz von, 395, 397, 522–23
Paris, 359–61, 387, 396, 434, 570, 571
"Pariser Rechenschaft" (Mann), 361
Parsifal (Wagner), 234, 329
Pauling, Linus, 578
Paulus, Friedrich von, 489
Peat, Harold, 438, 441
PEN Club, 349, 361, 368, 373, 542–43,
 560, 597, 600
Petitpierre, Max, 611
Petru, Sietcu, 431
Pfeffermühle, Die (The Peppermill), 47,
 395–96, 398, 423, 591
Pfitzner, Hans, 297–98, 302, 317, 357–58,
 406, 495, 551
Philip II, King of Spain, 341, 354
*Picture Book for Good Children (Bilderbuch
 für artige Kinder)* (Mann and H.
 Mann), 124–25
Pieck, Wilhelm, 566
Pius XII, Pope, 602
Platen, August, 365, 383
Plato, 258
Platzer, Martin, 325, 326
Podach, Ernst, 480
Pogwisch, Ottilie von, 431, 432
Poincaré, Raymond, 339

Poland, 368, 441, 452, 454–55, 519
Polgar, Alfred, 469
Ponten, Joseph, 371
"Position of Sigmund Freud in Modern
 Cultural History, The" ("Die Stellung
 Sigmund Freuds in der modernen
 Geistesgeschichte") (Mann), 376–77
"Postscript, A" ("Ein Nachwort") (Mann),
 215–16
Prague, 414, 445, 452
Preetorius, Emil, 247, 294, 526, 549, 557
Pricken, Liane, 241
Priester, Die (Mann), 97
Princeton, N.J., 443, 446–49, 456, 458,
 460, 464, 465–66
Princeton University, 440, 444, 452–53,
 458
Pringsheim, Alfred, 182–83, 184, 193,
 194, 195, 198, 199, 201, 207, 213–14,
 239, 245, 259, 272, 274, 292, 368, 383,
 405, 416, 453, 523–24; TM's al-
 lowance from, 205, 206, 210, 215, 281
Pringsheim, Hedwig Dohm, 182–83,
 194–98, 201, 202, 206, 207, 212,
 225–26, 230, 259, 272, 274, 292, 383,
 405, 416, 453, 523–24
Pringsheim, Katia, *see* Mann, Katia
 Pringsheim
Pringsheim, Klaus, 183, 194, 196,
 199–202, 210–15, 384
Pringsheim, Peter, 272, 316, 461
Printz, Robert, 223, 232
"Problem der deutsch-französischen
 Beziehungen, Das" ("The Problem of
 Franco-German Relations") (Mann),
 332
"Problem of Freedom, The" (Mann), 452
Professor Parsifal (F. Mann), 619–20
Professor Unrat (H. Mann), 221, 251, 377
Proust, Marcel, 89, 154, 286, 420, 526
Prussia, 81, 283, 337, 338
Prussian Academy of the Arts, 366, 368,
 371, 385, 396, 404, 519

Racine, Jean, 225
Radbruch, Gustav, 385
"Railway Accident, The" ("Das Eisen-
 bahnunglück") (Mann), 231, 265
Ranke, Pastor, 101, 129
Rankin, John E., 555
Rantzau, Count Hans Kaspar von, 93
Rascher, Albert, 420
Rascher, Hans, 420, 426
Rathenau, Walther, 303, 337, 338, 343,
 374
Reagan, Ronald, 538

"Rebirth of Decency, The" ("Die Wiedergeburt der Anständigkeit") (Mann), 385

Reed, T. J., 258, 262, 364

Reflections of a Nonpolitical Man (Betrachtungen eines Unpolitischen) (Mann), 76, 287–91, 293, 294, 295, 297, 298, 302–7, 309, 322, 324, 332, 336, 353, 374, 392, 432, 492, 504, 508, 521, 618, 619

Réflexions sur la violence (Sorel), 527

Reichstag, 237, 309, 334, 374, 382, 383, 395, 398, 403, 425, 455

Reinhardt, Max, 233–34, 267, 355, 453

Reisiger, Hans, 494, 549; TM's friendship with, 269–70, 336, 404, 410, 417, 420, 428, 435, 436, 595–96, 610

Remarque, Erich Maria, 177

Renan, Ernest, 117

Renoir, Jean, 469

"Report on My Brother" ("Bericht über mein Bruder") (Mann), 528

Reuter, Gabriele, 184–85

"Revenged" ("Gerächt") (Mann), 152–53

Revolt of the Masses, The (Ortega y Gasset), 415

Rheinhardt, Emil Alphons, 327

Rhineland, 311, 315, 358, 381, 425, 445

Ribbentrop, Joachim von, 473

Richard, Count Coudenhove-Kalergi, 360–61, 365

Richter, Georg Martin, 312, 316

Richter, Johann Paul Friedrich (Jean Paul), 327

Riemer, Friedrich Wilhelm, 431, 432, 451

Rilke, Rainer Maria, 168–69, 236

Ring, Der (Wagner), 130, 138, 147, 266, 421, 436, 457

Riva, 165, 167, 171–72, 195, 199

Robeson, Paul, 579

Robinson, Armin L., 481

Röhm, Ernst, 413

Roland, Ida, 360

Rolland, Romain, 426, 554

Romains, Jules, 361, 571

romanticism, German, 324, 329, 346, 361–62

Rome, 113–16, 122, 124, 128, 137–38, 143, 358, 487, 601–2, 605

Rommel, Erwin, 467, 481, 489

Röntgen, Wilhelm, 193

Roosevelt, Eleanor, 419, 465, 512

Roosevelt, Franklin D., 418, 419, 465, 505, 512, 538; World War II and, 463, 464, 468, 469, 473, 476, 480, 513

Rosenberg, Alfred, 408, 522–23

Rosenberg, Hermann, 206

Rosenthal, Frederick, 528, 532, 534, 592

Rousseau, Jean Jacques, 329–30, 335

Royal Highness (Königliche Hoheit) (Mann), 195, 196, 211–12, 222–25, 228–33, 235–36, 237, 244, 246, 252, 260, 268, 272, 288, 298, 317, 616–17; notes for, 183–86, 199; serialization of, 228, 232, 233

Ruhr, 338, 339–40, 343, 497

Rundstedt, Gerd von, 507–8

Russia, 253, 313, 360, 441; Germany and, 290–91, 325; in World War I, 279–81, 283, 286, 296; *see also* Soviet Union

Russian Revolution, 296, 297, 330–31

Rychner, Max, 547

S.A., 393–94, 395, 399, 413

Salomé, Lou Andreas, 480, 487

Salten, Felix, 448

Sammlung, Die, 408, 409, 416–17, 423

"Samuel zieht die Bilanz oder der kleine Prophete" ("Samuel Draws Up the Balance, or the Little Prophet") (Lessing), 238–39

"Samuel zieht die Bilanz und Tomi melkt die Moralkuh oder der Sturz zweier Könige" ("Samuel Draws Up the Balance and Tommy Milks the Moral Cow or the Collision of Two Kings") (Lessing), 239

Sarraut, Albert, 425

Sarraute, Nathalie, 177

Sartre, Jean-Paul, 173, 620

"Save Democracy" ("Rettet die Demokratie") (Mann), 357

Savonarola, Girolamo, 138–39, 158, 163, 180, 181, 186, 197

Schacht, Hjalmar, 439

Schäfer, Wilhelm, 371

Schaukal, Richard, 139, 179, 217, 218

Schauspielerin, Die (The Actress) (Mann), 281

Scheidemann, Philipp, 309, 315, 334

Schickele, René, 287, 407, 415, 416, 428, 453, 543

Schiff, Hans, 528

Schiller, Johann Christoph Friedrich von, 73, 96, 97, 103, 125, 184, 209–10, 244, 578, 607–8, 610

Schillings, Max von, 404

Schlabrendorff, Fabian von, 564

Schlegel, Friedrich, 266

Schleicher, Kurt von, 397, 413

Schmidt, Saladin, 302

Schmied, Ines, 221–22, 227, 237

Schnitzler, Arthur, 177, 231, 272, 318, 335, 341, 351
Schoenberg, Arnold, 469, 494, 495, 496, 549, 567–68
Schopenhauer, Adele, 431
Schopenhauer, Arthur, 71, 114, 138, 146–49, 164–65, 167, 266
Schrenck-Notzing, Albert Freiherr von, 338–39
Schubert, Franz, 120, 494, 495
Schubring, Julius, 96
Schuman, Robert, 598, 612
Schuschnigg, Kurt von, 438–39
Schwabe, Toni, 179–80
Schwarzschild, Leopold, 423
Schweigart, Max, 180
Seele und die Formen, Die (The Soul and Forms) (Lukács), 257–58, 362
"Selbstmörder" (K. Mann), 552
Seletz, Rachelle, 534
Sellin, Ernst, 488
Seyss-Inquart, Arthur, 438, 439
Shakespeare, William, 109, 216, 217, 245, 325, 490–91, 532
Shapley, Harlow, 558
Shaw, George Bernard, 349, 417, 572, 588
Shawcross, Sir Hartley, 531
Shenstone, Allen, 448
Shenstone, Molly, 448, 476
Sieburg, Friedrich, 607
Simplicissimus, 117, 119, 121, 123, 127, 140, 152, 209, 220–21, 247; TM's job at, 141–42, 143, 150, 158
Singer, Samuel, 550
"Sketch of My Life" (Mann), 366
Skowronneck, Richard, 122
Smith, Edith, 162
Smith, Mary, 162, 163
Social Democrats, German, 309, 310, 312, 322, 374, 384, 394, 395, 397, 398, 399, 567
Socrates, 72, 258
"Song of the Little Child" ("Gesang vom Kindchen") (Mann), 262, 308, 312, 313, 314, 356
Sonnemann, Emmy, 415
Sorel, Georges, 527
Soviet Union, 452, 453, 454, 472, 519, 555, 575–76; in World War II, 489, 497, 509
Spain, 341, 342, 463–64
Spanish Civil War, 427, 428, 441, 443, 448
Spengler, Oswald, 316, 317
Speyer, Agnes, 281
Speyer, Wilhelm, 534
Spiess, Johann, 491–92

"Spirit and Essence of the German Republic, The" ("Geist und Wesen der deutschen Republik") (Mann), 343
S.S. (Schutzstaffel), 393–94, 395, 538
S.S. Staat, Der (Kogon), 563–64
Stalin, Joseph, 453, 454, 512, 519, 555, 585
Stechlin, Der (Fontane), 149, 178
Sternberg, Josef, 377, 416
Stifter, Adalbert, 299
Stinnes, Hugo, 354
Stollberg, Georg, 158
Stolterfoht, Heinrich, 87
Stories of Three Decades (Mann), 266
Storm, Theodor, 98, 103, 257, 383
Stout, Rex, 532, 534
Strauss, David, 587
Strauss, Richard, 117, 179, 234, 318, 406, 415, 454, 495, 551
Straussmann, Deszö, 431
Stravinsky, Igor F., 480, 496
Streicher, Julius, 522–23
Stresemann, Gustav, 344, 348, 381
Stürmische Morgen (H. Mann), 221
"Suffering and Greatness of Richard Wagner, The" ("Leiden und Grösse Richard Wagners") (Mann), 396, 397, 406, 432, 433
Sufferings and Greatness of the Masters, The (Mann), 414, 423
Suhrkamp, Peter, 557
"Superiority and Freedom" ("Vornehmheit und Freiheit") (Mann), 387
Sweden, 380–81, 454, 504, 546, 560, 571
Symposium (Plato), 258, 267
Szabó, István, 362
Szántó, Zoltán, 373, 425

Tag, Der, 187, 268, 297, 374
Tales of Jacob, The (Die Geschichten Jaakobs) (Mann), 382, 391, 408, 410, 411, 412, 488
Tasso (Goethe), 330, 392
Tchaikovsky, Pyotr Ilich, 494
Ten Commandments, The (Robinson), 481, 487–89
"Tendences spirituelles de l'Allemagne d'aujourd'hui, Les" ("Spiritual Tendencies in Germany Today") (Mann), 360
Ternina, Milka, 183
Tesdorpf, Krafft, 99, 106, 121
Teufel, Lily, 325
Thälmann, Ernst, 357
Theilhaber, Felix, 416
Thiess, Frank, 520–21, 525

"Thinking and Life" ("Denken und Leben") (Mann), 467
"This Peace" (Mann), 446, 455
"This War" (Mann), 455
Thoma, Ludwig, 142
Thomas, J. Parnell, 555
"Thomas Mann" (Walden), 206
Tillich, Paul, 453, 498, 499
Tillinger, Eugene, 583, 585
Timpe, Willri, 145, 183, 251, 603, 611; TM's love for, 69, 74, 101, 160, 172, 174, 251
"Tobias Mindernickel" (Mann), 127, 128–29
Tolstoy, Leo, 73, 138, 140, 218, 299, 325, 349, 454, 477, 479; TM's lecture on, 329–31, 335, 337, 353, 361
Tölz, 227–28, 234–35, 240, 241, 245, 246, 254, 257, 259, 271, 272, 275, 279, 284, 285–86, 293, 298–99, 302, 304
Tonio Kröger (Mann), 179, 298
"Tonio Kröger" (Mann), 64–65, 76–77, 98, 104, 143–45, 168, 169, 171–77, 185, 186, 203–4, 218, 245, 257, 261, 272, 282, 291, 306, 324, 383, 477, 611, 616, 617, 618; Denmark in, 143, 144–45, 174, 175; Martens and, 69, 97, 172, 174
Tornabuoni, Giovanna, 163
Transposed Heads, The (Die vertauschten Köpfe) (Mann), 457–58, 461, 470
Travemünde, 94–95, 100, 137, 211, 602–3
Trebitsch, Siegfried, 576–77
Tristan and Isolde (Wagner), 145, 146, 147, 151, 266, 274, 427
"Tristan" (Mann), 142, 165–67, 173, 179, 180, 244, 263, 271, 298, 397, 466, 494
Troeltsch, Ernst, 346–47
Truman, Harry S, 519, 538, 555, 577–78, 582, 584
Trumbo, Dalton, 538
Turgenev, Ivan, 216, 504

Ulbricht, Walter, 557
Ulmann, Emil, 281
United Press Associations, 556, 579–80, 583
United States, 311–12, 387; anti-Communism of, 538–39, 546, 558, 560, 563, 568–69, 570, 583, 585, 591, 598; elections in, 463, 464, 505, 555, 597; Korean War and, 575–78; TM's move to, 439–48; TM's visits to, 412, 418–19, 433–34, 438–39; in World War I, 296–97, 306; World War II and, 459, 462–65, 467–70, 472–77, 480–81, 502

Untertan, Der (H. Mann), 281, 287, 569
Unwritten Memories (Meine ungeschriebenen Memoiren) (K. Mann), 193, 204, 250

Valéry, Paul, 387
van Loon, Hendrik, 418
Vasari, Giorgio, 158, 197
"Vater lacht, Der" ("The Father Laughs") (K. Mann), 323, 356
Venice, 63, 74, 122, 225–26, 227, 248–52, 257, 261, 262, 354, 357
Versailles, Treaty of, 315, 334, 381, 393, 425, 446, 459
Vidal, Gore, 574
Vienna, 121, 272, 318, 332, 333, 341, 365, 395, 426, 428, 439, 453–54, 597–98
Viertel, Berthold, 497
Viertel, Salka, 472, 497
Villari, Pasquale, 158, 197
Villiers de l'Isle-Adam, Count Philippe Auguste Mathias de, 224
"Vision" (Mann), 102
Visul Faraonitor (Pharaoh's Dream) (Mann), 431
Vitzhun von Eckstadt, Hermann Graf, 246
Voltaire, 283, 489
"Vom deutschen Republic" ("On the German Republic") (Mann), 337–38
Vor dem Leben (K. Mann), 355
Vor Sonnenaufgang (Before Sunrise) (Hauptmann), 66, 72
"Voyage with Don Quixote" ("Meerfahrt mit Don Quijote") (Mann), 414

Wagner, Cosima, 436
Wagner, Eva, 496
Wagner, Richard, 113, 117, 130, 138, 145, 146, 147, 149, 212, 234, 236, 254, 266, 290, 320, 358, 364, 394, 414, 435–36, 491; *Doctor Faustus* and, 491, 494–95; TM's lectures on, 396–97, 406, 432–36; TM's sublimation of sexuality and, 101, 109; in TM's work, 66, 68, 120, 151, 213, 214, 421
Wahlverwandschaften, Die (Elective Affinities) (Goethe), 111, 318
Walden, Herwarth, 206
Waldsanatorium, 260, 262–65, 326, 361–62
Walküre, Die (Wagner), 213, 214
Wallace, Henry A., 481, 555
Walter, Bruno, 274, 297, 318, 460, 493, 514, 522, 529, 569, 612
Walter, Gretel, 274
Walter, Lotte, 274, 606

"Walter Weiler" (Mann), 112–13, 117, 126
"War and Democracy" (Mann), 463–66
"War and the Future, The" (1940) (Mann), 464–65, 471
"War and the Future, The" (1943) (Mann), 497
Warburg, Fredric, 540–41, 560
"Wardrobe, The" ("Der Kleiderschrank") (Mann), 140–41
Warner, Jack L., 441
"Wartime Thoughts" ("Gedanken im Kriege") (Mann), 282–85, 286, 617
Wassermann, Jakob, 121, 179, 231, 280, 385, 410–11
"Way to the Churchyard, The" ("Der Weg zum Friedhof") (Mann), 153–54, 158
Weber, Carl Maria, 262, 322
Wedekind, Frank, 141, 267, 270, 302, 349, 377
Wedekind, Pamela, 349, 358
Weimar, 246, 326, 393, 562–65, 607, 610–11
Weimar Republic, 315, 322, 334–40; unemployment in, 381, 384, 393–94
Wells, H. G., 349
Welt als Wille und Vorstellung, Die (The World as Will and Representation) (Schopenhauer), 146–47, 149
Werfel, Alma, 404
Werfel, Franz, 404, 453, 463, 501, 509
Wessel, Horst, 384
Westermeier, Franzl, 573–77, 581, 582, 584
Wharton, Edith, 369
"What Is German?" (Mann), 503
Whitman, Walt, 336–37
Wiechert, Ernst, 538, 543
Wieland, Christoph Martin, 305
Wild Duck, The (Ibsen), 110, 112
Wilde, Oscar, 66, 539
Wilhelm, Richard, 382
Wilhelm II, Kaiser of Germany, 141, 208, 222–23, 236–37, 310, 311, 344; World War I and, 279, 280, 306
Wilhelm Meisters Wanderjahre (Goethe), 330, 350, 392

Willkie, Wendell, 463
"Will to Happiness, The" ("Der Wille zum Glück") (Mann), 72, 114, 116–17, 119, 121, 127, 140, 213
Will to Power, The (Der Wille zur Macht) (Nietzsche), 114
Wilson, Lyle C., 583
Wilson, Woodrow, 296–97, 312, 315, 320
Winterstein, Eduard von, 267
Wir waren Fünf (K. Mann), 106
Witkop, Philipp, 205, 325, 329
Wittgenstein, Paul, 318
Wolf, Hugo, 490
Wolzogen, Baron Ernst von, 110, 112, 143
World War I, 73, 76, 268, 279–302, 304–6, 308–11, 315, 316, 383, 384
World War II, 455, 458–81, 491, 507–13; bombing in, 478, 479, 492, 497, 502–3, 519
"Wunderbare, Das" (H. Mann), 112
Wunderlich, Emilie, 86
Wysling, Hans, 220

"Yearning and Form" ("Sehnsucht und Form") (Lukács), 258
"Years of My Life, The" (Mann), 570–71
Young, Owen, 381
Young Joseph (Der junge Joseph) (Mann), 391
Yourcenar, Marguerite, 619

Zimmer, Heinrich, 458
Zimmermann, Adolf, 296
Zimpe, Hermann, 146
Zola, Émile, 108, 287–90, 300
Zuckmayer, Carl, 377
Zukunft, 179, 217, 240, 245, 292
Zur Genealogie der Moral (On the Genealogy of Morals) (Nietzsche), 109, 116, 138
Zurich, 208, 332, 407, 410, 417, 420, 430, 433, 437, 454; TM's postwar visits to, 541–44, 561–62, 571–72, 577, 594, 597, 611–12
Zwanzigste Jahrhundert, Das (The Twentieth Century), 114–15, 116, 119, 122, 188, 232
Zweig, Arnold, 488
Zweig, Stefan, 239, 357, 453